Letts study aids

Revise World History

A complete revision course for O level and CSE

Peter Lane

Formerly Head of History, Coloma College of Education

Charles Letts & Co Ltd
London, Edinburgh & New York

First published 1984
by Charles Letts & Co Ltd
Diary House, Borough Road, London SE1 1DW

Reprinted 1986

Editor: Mark Wright

Design: Ben Sands
Illustrations: Liz Dawlings and Peter McClure

Acknowledgements: The author and publishers are
grateful to the following for permission to use their
photographs and cartoons: The Mansell Collection, p 18;
Punch, p 179; Radio Times Hulton Picture Library, p 179

ISBN 0 85097 619 7

Printed and bound by
Charles Letts (Scotland) Ltd

Preface

In a rapidly changing world success in examinations has become even more important as one of the keys to future prospects. This book has been designed as a complete guide for students preparing for GCE O-Level, Scottish CE Ordinary Grade and CSE examinations in Modern World Affairs. Different Examining Boards have different titles and starting dates for the papers they set. Some (at both O Level and CSE Level) take 1870 as the starting point and have syllabuses which are headed, *British, European and World History*. Some entitle their papers *Twentieth-Century World History to 1970* while others head their papers *World Affairs from 1919 to the Present Day*. This book has been planned and written to help all these students.

In writing the book I have considered the standards and demands of various Examination Boards. I was helped by many years experience as a teacher (preparing students for the Oxford and the London Boards) and as an examiner (for the London, Welsh and Oxford and Cambridge Boards). I was fortunate in that I was able to draw on the considerable help and constructive advice of colleagues with long experience in teaching and examining for other Boards.

I have also borne in mind the problems facing students preparing for their examinations. The analysis of the various examination papers, of different types of examination questions and the suggestions on how to answer these questions are designed to be among the more valuable sections of the book.

The core material in Part II consists of a detailed but simplified account of the subject matter. The various headings and sub-headings make it easier for students to learn and remember the essential points which are further developed in each Unit. The cross-references in each Unit help the student to go back over material already studied in depth. Such cross-references help students to understand connections and to learn how to move about in time and space.

The Self-Test Units in Part III have been drawn up to help the student to judge his or her own progress. Many of the questions in these Self-Tests have been taken from examination papers and are the more valuable a guide as a result.

The suggestions on answering questions (Part IV) should help the student to understand clearly what examiners are looking for and to see how different types of questions should be tackled.

In Part V there is a selection of examination questions of various types from all the Examining Boards. This provides the student with the opportunity of tackling the types of questions which will have to be faced in the coming examination.

I am grateful to the various Examining Boards for their permission to use the questions previously set in their examinations. I am grateful to my colleagues Richard Maples (teaching for Cambridge and EAEB), Joan Kennedy (teaching for AEB and examining for London) and Ritchie Greig (teaching and examining for the Scottish Examination Board).

Their helpful advice, careful reading and constructive comments have helped to improve the book. I am equally grateful to many fellow-examiners for London, Oxford and Cambridge and for WJEC who, over the years, have given me the benefit of their advice and guidance.

I have been fortunate in the support and encouragement provided by the editorial team at Charles Letts and Company Limited and by the comments offered by the panels of teachers and readers who were engaged to read the script. It is clear that the aim of the publishers and teacher-readers was to provide a high quality Revision Aid for students.

I am grateful to the teachers and students who have written after using a previous Revision Aid—*Revise History 1750–1980 (British Political and Social)*. I hope that this book will be as useful as that one proves to be.

Peter Lane, 1983

Contents

Part I
Introduction
Preparing for the examination

1 Why revise?

You may know people who do not appear to do much preparation before examinations, yet who still obtain high marks. You may also know people who spend a great deal of time at revision, some even studying up to the day of the examination.

It is impossible to define the best method for all candidates, people are different and what suits one may not do for another. But long experience has shown teachers and examiners that most people learn more, gain in confidence and perform better in examinations after they have made suitable preparation by a sensible programme of revision.

2 Planning your revision

Some people prefer to read a Unit (or Chapter) several times before testing themselves to see whether they have understood the work they have studied. Others prefer to make notes as they read and to use these for revision purposes. In each Unit in Part II you will find that the key points are emphasized. You might make a list of these and use them as headings for essays.

Almost everyone learns best by tackling small portions of work. Study one Unit, test yourself on it and then decide whether you have understood that Unit. By the time you have gone through all the necessary Units, you should have a list of topics which need further revision to help you overcome your weaknesses.

3 A revision timetable

A complete revision requires a good deal of time and needs sensible planning. The following timetable is based on the assumption that the examination takes place in mid-June. If your examination takes place in May, November or January, obviously you will need to change the suggested dates.

1 End of March

(a) Check how well you did in the mock examinations so that you can see which topics you need to study carefully.
(b) Make up a timetable using the Units in this book and any other topics you need to study.
(c) The timetable should cover April and May and you should plan to do extra work during the Easter holidays.
(d) The timetable should be drawn up to allow you to finish your revision by the end of May. This will give you two weeks for further revision of your weaker points and a final revision of the main points in the days before your examination.

2 April and May

Allow yourself about one hour every day for History revision.

3 June

Revise the main points, using the Self-Test section and the examination questions in Part V. Make a list of the main points needed to answer any of the questions in that section.

4 Taking the examination

1 Read the paper carefully Almost every Report made by examiners complains that candidates did not understand the questions asked or failed to use the information supplied in the examination paper. If the examiners ask you to 'Give an account of Mao Tse-Tung's career' they expect less analysis than they expect from answers to 'Account for Mao Tse-Tung's victory over Chiang Kai-shek'. If you are asked to 'Give an account of Mussolini's **domestic** policy' do not waste time by offering accounts of his foreign policy.

2 Tick off the questions you intend to do As you read through the paper, tick off the questions which you think you could answer. Then check the instructions at the head of the paper to see how many questions you have to do, and from which sections, if the paper is sub-divided into sections.

Having ticked off a number of questions, go back through the paper and choose those which you intend to do. As you do this, number the questions – 1, 2 and so on – to remind yourself which questions you intend to tackle first, which next and so on to the end. Always do first the question you think you can answer best; this will give you confidence for the rest of the paper.

3 Plan each answer before you start This refers to questions which require you to write either an essay or a brief note on some item. It does not refer to the fixed-response questions. Guidance on such planning is given in Part IV. 3.9.

4 Time yourself If you only answer half the questions asked for, you cannot expect to get more than 50%, even if you get full marks for each answer. It is important to answer the required number of questions. To help you do this you should:

(a) Before the examination practise doing questions in the time allocated. This is important because you have to find out how much you can write in the 25 or 30 minutes which you can spend on an essay-type question.

(b) In the examination room Make a note of the time which you will allow for each question. If, for example, you have to do four essays in two hours you will have 100 minutes in which to write your answers (if you have spent 20 minutes on planning as suggested in Part IV.3.9.) This means that each answer should take 25 minutes. So if you start writing at 2.00 pm you should finish your answer to the first question at 2.25 pm, your second should be finished at 2.50 pm and so on.

(c) When answering the paper keep an eye on your proposed timing and on the clock. When you get to the end of the time allocated to an answer, stop writing, even if you have not completed the answer. Leave a space and, if you have time, you can complete the answer later. It is better to have answered all five questions (if that is the number required) even if the answers are incomplete, than to answer only three – which you might do if you take five minutes more for this answer and a further five minutes for another.

5 Answering the questions There is more advice on this in Part IV. Here you should remember that the examiners have to mark a large number of papers. They will appreciate it if your work is neat, although they will not object if you have crossed out such things as plans for essays. They will object to a sort of shorthand which some candidates use, such as Jap for Japanese, or A-H for Austria-Hungary. The use of accepted initials (NATO, UNO, OPEC, and so on) is quite in order. Examiners will not give you any credit for the use of 'etc.'; they will think that this means you do not know any more. If you really do know more, then write it down so that the examiners can award the marks you deserve.

Analysis of examination syllabuses

	AEB O (58)	AEB O (146)	AEB O/A (181)	Cambridge O 2110.5 (2)	Cambridge O 2110.6 (2)	JMB O A (1)	JMB O A (1)	JMB O G (1)	JMB O G (1)	London O B 262 (2)	London O C 263 (2)	NIGCE O (1)	Oxford O 2834 (1)	Oxford O 2836 (2)	O&C O 2640.12 (2)	O&C O 2640.12 (1)	O&C O 2640.14 (2)	O&C O 2640.14 (1)	SEB Ord. Tr. (1)	SEB Ord. Alt. (2)	SUJB O 2171.B (1)	SUJB O/A 8066. (1)	WJEC O Oe (1)	WJEC O Og (1)
Course work	35%		50%			40%																		
Teacher assessment	15%																							
Fixed-response questions	●					●		●	●															
Multiple-choice questions								●	●	40%	40%													
Stimulus material	●	●		●	●	●				●	●	●	●	●	●	●	●	●	●	●	●	●	●	
Free-response questions	●	●	●	●	●	●	●	●	●	●	●	●	●	●	●	●	●	●			●	●		●
Prescribed topics	●			33%	33%							●			●	●	●	●		3	opt.	opt.		
British component				●	●	●	●	●	●	●	●	●	●	●					●		●		●	
1 Germany, 1870-1914	●			●		●	●	●	●	●	●	●	●	●	●	●		●			●		●	
2 France, 1870-1914	●			●		●	●	●	●	●	●		●	●	P.T.	P.T.	●	●		P.T.	●		●	
3 Russia, 1855-1914	●			●		●	●	●	●	●	●	●		●		P.T.	●	●			●	●	●	
4 The Eastern Question, 1870-1914	●			●		●	●	●	●	●	●				P.T.	P.T.			●	P.T.	●	●	●	
5 Africa, 1870-1914	●		●	●	●	●	●	●	●	●	●		●	●							●		●	
6 The Far East, 1870-1918	●			●	●	●	●	●	●	●	●				●	●					●		●	
7 The United States of America, 1870-1917	●			●		●	●	●	●	●	●				●	●					●		●	
8 International relations, 1870-1914	●			●	●	●	●	●	●	●	●	●			●	●	●	●			●		●	
9 The First World War, 1914-18	●	P.T.	●	●	P.T.	●	●	●	●	●	●	●	●	●			●	●	●	P.T.	●		●	●
10 Russia, 1914-28	●		●	●		●	●	●	●	●	●		●	●			●	●	●	●	●	●	●	●
11 Russia, 1928-41	●	P.T.	●	●	P.T.	●	●	●	●	●	●		●	●			●	●	●	P.T.	●	●	●	●
12 Peacemaking – Germany and Austria	●		●	●	●	●	●	●	●	●	●	●	●	●			●	●			●		●	●
13 Peacemaking – Turkey	●			●	●	●	●	●	●	●	●		●	●			●	●			●		●	●
14 The League of Nations	●		●	●	●	●	●	●	●	●	●	●	●	●			●	●			●		●	●
15 Germany, 1919-33	●		●	●	●	●	●	●	●	●	●	●	●	●			●	●			●		●	●
16 The United States of America, 1917-33	●	P.T.	●	●	P.T.	●	●	●	●	●	●		●	●			●	●	●	P.T.	●	●	●	●
17 China and Japan, 1914-49	●		●	●		●	●	●	●	●	●			●			●	●			●		●	●
18 International relations, 1919-29	●	P.T.	●	●		●	●	●	●	●	●	●	●	●			●	●	●	P.T.	●		●	●
19 The United States of America, 1932-41	●	P.T.	●	●		●	●	●	●	●	●		●	●			●	●	●	P.T.	●	●	●	●
20 Hitler's Germany, 1933-39	●	P.T.	●	●		●	●	●	●	●	●	●	●	●			●	●	●		●		●	●
21 Italy, 1918-39	●		●	●		●	●	●	●	●	●		●	●			●	●			●		●	●
22 The British Empire, 1918-39	●	P.T.	●	●		●	●	●	●	●	●	●	●	●			●	●			●		●	●
23 International relations, 1930-39	●		●	●		●	●	●	●	●	●	●	●	●			●	●	●		●		●	●
24 Spain, 1919-39	●	P.T.	●	●		●	●	●	●	●	●	●	●	●					●		●		●	●
25 The Second World War, 1939-42	●	P.T.		●		●	●	●	●	●	●		P.T.	P.T.	P.T.		P.T.				●		●	●
26 The Second World War, 1942-45	●	P.T.	●	●		●	●	●	●	●	●		P.T.	P.T.	P.T.		P.T.				●		●	●
27 The United Nations Organisation	●		●	●		●	●	●	●	●	●	●	●	●			●		●		●		●	●
28 International relations, 1945-53	●	P.T.	●	●		●	●	●	●	●	●	●	P.T.	P.T.			●		●	P.T.	●	●	●	●
29 Russia, 1945-83	●		●	●		●	●	●	●	●	●	●	●	●			●		●		●		●	●
30 Eastern Europe, 1945-83	●		●	●		●	●	●	●	●	●	●	●	P.T.			●		●		●		●	●
31 Western Europe integration	●		●	●		●	●	●	●	●	●	●	P.T.	P.T.			●		●		●		●	●
32 The United States of America, 1945-83	●		●	●		●	●	●	●	●	●	●	P.T.	P.T.	P.T.		P.T.		●		●		●	●
33 China, 1949-83	●		●	●	●	●	●	●	●	●	●	●	●	●			●		●		●		●	●
34 The Indian sub-continent, 1939-83	●		●	●		●	●	●	●	●	●	●	●	●			●		●		●		●	●
35 The Far East, 1945-83	●		●	●		●	●	●	●	●	●	●	P.T.	●			●		●		●		●	●
36 Africa, south of the Sahara, 1945-83	●	P.T.	●	●	P.T.	●	●	●	●	●	●	●	●	●			●		●		●	●	●	●
37 North Africa and the Middle East, 1945-83	●		●	●	●	●	●	●	●	●	●	●	●	●	●		●		●		●			●
38 The Third World and some current problems	●		●	●	●	●	●	●	●	●	●	●	●	●		●			●		●		●	●
39 Abbreviations and Glossary	●	●	●	●	●	●	●	●	●	●	●	●	●	●	●		●		●	●	●	●	●	●

Analysis of examination syllabuses

	ALSEB	EAEB			EMREB	LREB			NREB	NICSE	NWREB	SREB		SEREB	SWEB	WJEC	WMEB		YHREB		
Level	CSE	CSE	CSE	CSE	CSE	CSE	CSE	CSE	CSE	CSE	CSE	CSE	CSE	CSE	CSE	CSE	CSE	CSE	CSE	CSE	CSE
Syllabus	B	N/E	N/S	S/B	3	A 140	B 141	C 144	Alt.1	C	C	R/C	R/D	E 22.A	C	A	1	2	A YR	D WYL	E
Number of papers	1	1	1	2	2	1	1	1	1	2	2	2	2	1	2	1	1	2	1	2	2
Course work	30%	30%	30%		20%	20%	20%		25%	30%	30%	20%	20%	20%	opt.						
Teacher assessment														30%							
Fixed-response questions	•				•	•	•	•	•	•	•	•	•						•	•	
Multiple-choice questions		20%	20%	20%	•			•	•	•	•	•		•				•	•	•	•
Stimulus material	•	25%	25%		•	•	•			•	•	•	•				•	•		•	•
Free-response questions	•	25%	25%	60%	•	•	•	•	•	•	•	•	•	•	40%	•	•	•	•	•	•
Prescribed topics				20%					•							•		•	•	•	
British component	•			•					Alt.1					30%		•			•		1/3

#	Syllabus	ALSEB	EAEB N/E	EAEB N/S	EAEB S/B	EMREB	LREB A	LREB B	LREB C	NREB	NICSE	NWREB	SREB R/C	SREB R/D	SEREB	SWEB	WJEC	WMEB 1	WMEB 2	YHREB A	YHREB D	YHREB E
1	Germany, 1870-1914	•	•	•	•	•	•	•	•		•	•	•		•	•	•	•	•		•	•
2	France, 1870-1914	•	•	•		•	•	•	•		•	•	•	•		•		•	•		•	•
3	Russia, 1855-1914	•	•	•	•	•	•	•	•		•	•	•	•	•	•		•	•	•	•	•
4	The Eastern Question, 1870-1914	•	•	•			•	•	•				•			•		•	•		•	•
5	Africa, 1870-1914	•	•	•			•	•	•				•			•		•	•		•	•
6	The Far East, 1870-1918	•	•				•	•	•				•		•	•		•	•	•	•	
7	The United States of America, 1870-1917	•	•	•	•		•	•	•				•	•		•		•	•		•	•
8	International relations, 1870-1914	•	•	•	•	•	•	•	•	•	•	•	•	•	•	•	•	•	•	•	•	•
9	The First World War, 1914-18	•	•	•	•	•	•	•	•	•	•	•	•	•	•	•	•	•	•	•	•	•
10	Russia, 1914-28	•	•	•	•	•	•	•	•	•	•	•	•	•	•	•	•	•	•	•	•	•
11	Russia, 1928-41	•	•	•	•	•	•	•	•	•	•	•	•	•	•	P.T.	•	•	•	•	•	•
12	Peacemaking – Germany and Austria	•	•	•	•	•	•	•	•	•	•	•	•	•	•	P.T.	•	•	•	•	•	•
13	Peacemaking – Turkey	•	•	•			•	•	•		•	•	•	•		•	•	•	•	•	•	•
14	The League of Nations	•	•	•	•	•	•	•	•	•	•	•	•	•	•	•	•	•	•	•	•	•
15	Germany, 1919-33	•	•	•	•	•	•	•	•	•	•	•	•	•	•	P.T.	•	•	•	•	•	•
16	The United States of America, 1917-33	•	•	•	•	•	•	•	•	•	•	•	•	•	•	P.T.	•	•	•	•	•	•
17	China and Japan, 1914-49	•	•	•	P.T.	•	•	•	•	opt.	•	•	•	•	•	P.T.	•	•	•	•	•	•
18	International relations, 1919-29	•	•	•	•	•	•	•	•	•	•	•	•	•	•	•	•	•	•	•	•	•
19	The United States of America, 1932-41	•	•	•	P.T.	•	•	•	•	•	•	•	•	•	•	P.T.	•	•	•	•	•	•
20	Hitler's Germany, 1933-39	•	•	•	•	•	•	•	•	•	•	•	•	•	•	P.T.	•	•	•	•	•	•
21	Italy, 1918-39	•	•	•	•	•	•	•	•	•	•	•	•	•	•	P.T.	•	•	•	•	•	•
22	The British Empire, 1918-39	•	•	•	•	•	•	•	•	•		•	•	•		•	•	•	•	•	•	•
23	International relations, 1930-39	•	•	•	•	•	•	•	•	•	•	•	•	•	•	•	•	•	•	•	•	•
24	Spain, 1919-39	•	•	•	•	•	•	•	•	•		•	•	•	•	•	•	•	•	•	•	•
25	The Second World War, 1939-42	•	•	•	P.T.	•	•	•	•	•		•	•	•	•	•	•	•	•	•	•	•
26	The Second World War, 1942-45	•	•	•	•	•	•	•	•	•		•	•	•	•	•	•	•	•	•	•	•
27	The United Nations Organisation	•	•	•	P.T.	•	•	•	•	•		•	•	•	•	•	•	•	•	•	•	•
28	International relations, 1945-53	•	•	•	P.T.	•	•	•	•	•		•	•	•	•	•	•	•	•	•	•	•
29	Russia, 1945-83	•	•	•	•	•	•	•	•	•	•	•	•	•	•	•	•	•	•	•	•	•
30	Eastern Europe, 1945-83	•	•	•	•	•	•	•	•	•	•	•	•	•	•	•	•	•	•	•	•	•
31	Western Europe integration	•	•	•	•	•	•	•	•	•	•	•	•	•	•	•	•	•	•	•	•	•
32	The United States of America, 1945-83	•	•	•	P.T.	•	•	•	•	opt.	•	•	•	•	•	•	•	•	•	•	•	•
33	China, 1949-83	•	•	•	•	•	•	•	•		•	•	•	•	•	•	•	•	•	•	•	•
34	The Indian sub-continent, 1939-83	•	•	•	•	•	•	•	•		•	•	•	•	•	•	•	•	•	•	•	•
35	The Far East, 1945-83	•	•	•	•	•	•	•	•		•	•	•	•	•	•	•	•	•	•	•	•
36	Africa, south of the Sahara, 1945-83	•	•	•	•	•	•	•	•	opt.		•	•	•	•	•	•	•	•	•	•	•
37	North Africa and the Middle East, 1945-83	•	•	•	•	•	•	•	•	opt.		•	•	•	•	•	•	•	•	•	•	•
38	The Third World and some current problems	•	•	•	•	•	•	•	•			•	•	•	•	•	•	•	•	•	•	•
39	Abbreviations and Glossary	•	•	•	•	•	•	•	•	•	•	•	•	•	•	•	•	•	•	•	•	•

EXAMINING BOARDS: ADDRESSES

General Certificate of Education–Ordinary Level (GCE)

AEB	Associated Examining Board Wellington House, Aldershot, Hampshire GU11 1BQ
Cambridge	University of Cambridge Local Examinations Syndicate Syndicate Buildings, 17 Harvey Road, Cambridge CB1 2EU
JMB	Joint Matriculation Board Manchester M15 6EU
London	University of London, School Examinations Department 66–72 Gower Street, London WC1E 6EE
NIEC	Northern Ireland Schools GCE Examinations Council Beechill House, 42 Beechill Road, Belfast BT8 4RS
Oxford	Oxford Delegacy of Local Examinations Ewert Place, Summertown, Oxford OX2 7BX
O and C	Oxford and Cambridge Schools Examination Board 10 Trumpington Street, Cambridge; *and* Elsfield Way, Oxford OX2 8EP
SUJB	Southern Universities' Joint Board for School Examinations Cotham Road, Bristol BS6 6DD
WJEC	Welsh Joint Education Committee 245 Western Avenue, Cardiff CF5 2YX

Certificate of Secondary Education

ALSEB	Associated Lancashire Schools Examining Board 77 Whitworth Street, Manchester M1 6HA
EAEB	East Anglian Examinations Board The Lindens, Lexden Road, Colchester, Essex CO3 3RL
EMREB	East Midland Regional Examinations Board Robins Wood House, Robins Wood Road, Apsley, Nottingham NG8 3RL
LREB	London Regional Examinations Board (*formerly:* MREB Middlesex Regional Examinations Board) Lyon House, 104 Wandsworth High Street, London SW18 4LF
NIEB	Northern Ireland CSE Examinations Board Beechill House, 42 Beechill Road, Belfast BT8 4RS
NREB	North Regional Examinations Board Wheatfield Road, Westerhope, Newcastle upon Tyne NE5 5JZ
NWREB	North West Regional Examinations Board Orbit House, Albert Street, Eccles, Manchester M30 0WL
SEREB	South East Regional Examinations Board Beloe House, 2–4 Mount Ephraim Road, Royal Tunbridge Wells, Kent TN1 1EU
SREB	Southern Regional Examinations Board 53 London Road, Southampton SO9 4YI
SWEB	South Western Examinations Board 23–29 Marsh Street, Bristol BS1 4BP
WJEC	Welsh Joint Education Committee 245 Western Avenue, Cardiff CF5 2YX
WMEB	West Midland Examination Board Norfolk House, Smallbrook Queensway, Birmingham B5 4NJ
WYLREB*	West Yorkshire and Lindsey Regional Examining Board Scarsdale House, 136 Derbyshire Lane, Sheffield S8 8SE
YREB*	Yorkshire Regional Examinations Board 31–33 Springfield Avenue, Harrogate, North Yorkshire HG1 2HW

*Yorkshire and Humberside Regional Examinations Board, at the *YREB* address, now embraces *WYLREB* and *YREB*

Part II

1 Germany, 1870–1914

1.1 Germany, a new nation-state

After 1871 Germany was one of the most important states in Europe. However, in 1870 Germany did not exist as a unified state. To understand her importance after 1871, we have to see how Germany came into being.

1.2 The German Confederation, 1815 (*see Fig. 1.10A*)

In **1815** when Napoleon was defeated, there were **thirty-nine separate states** in the German Confederation. Each had its own ruler, government and foreign policy. Some states were powerful.

1 **Austria**, largely Catholic, was the most powerful. Under the Hapsburg monarchs Austria had gained an Empire in Europe, containing Poles, Hungarians, Italians, Croats, Slovenes – as well as Germans.

2 **Prussia**, in the north and largely Protestant, had become increasingly powerful. But in 1815 she was unable to stand up to Austria.

3 **Bavaria, Hesse-Cassel, Hanover, Westphalia, Saxony and Wurtemburg** were other large states. These, and the many smaller states, usually followed Austria in domestic and foreign policies.

1.3 The Prussian Zollverein (*see Fig. 1.10A*).

1 **Prussia** had grown from its eastern origins in Brandenberg. By 1815 it included:
 i **agricultural regions** in East Pomerania and East Prussia;
 ii **industrial regions** in Silesia and the Rhine Provinces.

2 In **1816** the Prussian government abolished **customs duties** on goods passing from one region of the state to another. This led to lower prices, a growth in trade and a rise in living standards.

3 In **1819** several smaller states joined this **customs union** which remained under Prussian control. The larger states refused to join on those terms – they wanted a share in its running.

4 In **1826** the Catholic states of Bavaria and Wurtemberg formed their own **customs union**. They could see the benefits of such a union, but were too jealous of Protestant Prussia to join the older Prussian-dominated union.

5 In **1833** Prussia enlarged its customs union – and called it the **Zollverein**. New states were admitted on a basis of equality – tariff policies had to be agreed by all the states and not imposed by Prussia. **Hamburg** and **Hanover** still refused to join.

6 In **1849 Austria** applied to join the Zollverein. The application was rejected by Prussia's friends; they wanted to end Austrian control.

7 In **1853**, the Zollverein signed a commercial treaty with Austria – a sign of its independence of Austrian influence.

8 In **1867**, after the Austrian War (see 1.10) the Zollverein was reorganized to include **all German states, except Austria, Hamburg and Bremen.**

1.4 The importance of the Zollverein

1 The removal of internal tariff barriers was one of the reasons for the **industrial expansion** of Germany.

2 The customs union gave Germany an **economic and industrial unity** long before it had any political unity.

3 It gave **Prussia the leadership**, in economic and industrial affairs. Later this gave her the chance to take the political lead.

1.5 Attempts to form a united Germany, 1848–50

You do not have to know in detail the attempts made in 1848–49 to create a united Germany. You should note the following:

1 In **1848** there were many revolutions throughout Europe, when 'liberal' revolutionaries tried to force their rulers to become constitutional rulers.

2 In **Prussia** and other German states, the Liberal revolutionaries forced rulers to produce democratic constitutions.

3 In **1849–50** most of the rulers withdrew those constitutions. Only in **Prussia** did the King maintain the constitution.

4 In **1848–49** representatives from all the German states met in the **Frankfurt Parliament**. These liberals offered the crown of a united Germany to **Frederick William IV, King of Prussia.** He refused it:
 i he did not think a monarch should accept a crown from 'the gutter' of a democratic Parliament;
 ii he was afraid that Austria might declare war on Prussia if he accepted the crown;
 iii the liberal constitution gave the monarch only a limited power.

1.6 The development of Prussia, 1850–62

1 The **population** continued to increase.

2 Many **factories** were built; steam power was introduced.

3 **A railway system** provided the basis for:
 i **industrial growth**, in iron, steel, coal and engineering;
 ii **increased trade**, as goods travelled more quickly and cheaply;
 iii **a modern postal system**.

4 A modern **education system** was developed.

5 This **industrial revolution** made the Prussian people prosperous and the ruler richer. Other German states admired Prussia's achievement. This helps explain why many joined the Zollverein.

1.7 The challenge to Austria, 1857–62

1 In 1857 Frederick William IV became too ill to rule. His brother, William, became Regent in 1858.

2 In 1861 **William** became King of Prussia.

3 A former soldier, the new king appointed **von Roon** as Minister of War and **von Moltke** as Chief of the General Staff.

4 He decided to increase the **size of the army**.

5 The Prussian Parliament, (the **Landtag**) did not like the new taxes needed to pay for the doubling of the size of the army.

6 In **1861** Parliament approved the new taxes – by only one vote.

7 In 1862 Parliament refused new tax increases. This threatened William's plans for the army. What would he do?

8 He appointed **Otto von Bismarck** as Minister-President.

1.8 Otto von Bismarck

1 He was born in 1815, son of a **Prussian landowner ('Junker')**.

2 In **1847** he was Prussian representative at the Diet (of the Confederation) at Frankfurt.

3 He was opposed to the liberal revolutionaries in 1848.

4 He approved the King's refusal to accept the German Crown.

5 In **1851** he was again Prussian representative at the Diet.

6 In **1859** he was sent as Ambassador to **Russia**. In **1862** he was transferred to **Paris**.

1.9 Bismarck, Minister-President, 1862

1 King William I had to find someone to overcome the opposition of the Prussian Liberals to his army plans (1.7.7).

2 Von Roon suggested that he send for Bismarck.

3 As Minister-President, **Bismarck also failed** to get Parliament to vote for the increased taxes **in 1862**.

4 He simply announced that the **new taxes would be imposed and collected** in spite of Parliament's opposition and anger.

5 The King realized that the people would accept such behaviour only if Prussia benefitted from it. This helps to explain Prussian policy after 1862.

1.10 German unification and the Three Wars. 1862–1871 (*see Fig. 1.10A*)

1 In **1864** Bismarck persuaded Austria to join Prussia in a war against Denmark to get back the Duchies of **Schleswig and Holstein** from the Danes. After defeating Denmark, the two German states ruled the Duchies jointly.

2 Bismarck laid his plans for a future **war with Austria**:

i he won **Russian friendship** by refusing to let foreign troops cross Prussia to go to the help of the Poles who were in revolt against their Russian rulers in 1863 (3.9);

ii **Italy** became an ally when Bismarck promised her **Venetia** (part of the Austrian Empire) on Austria's defeat;

iii **France**, under **Napoleon III,** agreed to remain neutral after Bismarck hinted that France could have **Belgium** or some **Rhineland states** once Austria had been beaten.

3 In **1866** Austria and Prussia quarrelled over the way in which the Duchies were being governed. A war broke out.

4 Within **six weeks** the Prussian army was everywhere victorious. The main reasons for Prussia's unexpected victory were:

i the superiority of the **Prussian army**, organized by von Roon and von Moltke, and supplied with better weapons by **Prussian industry**;

ii **Austrian difficulties** with her subject peoples;

iii Bismarck's success in **isolating Austria** from possible allies.

5 Austria and Prussia signed **The Treaty of Prague, 1866**:

i the **old (1815) German Confederation** was abolished;

ii a **North German Confederation** was set up, under Prussian leadership (Fig. 1.10A);

iii the **Catholic States of the south** were left alone;

iv Prussia took no territory from Austria, except **Venetia** which was given to Italy;

v Prussia annexed Holstein and retained Schleswig.

This was a lenient Treaty. Austria would be less likely to seek 'revenge' on Prussia.

7 It brought the war to a speedy end, before France and other countries had time to interfere as they might have done.

8 The Franco-Prussian War, 1870–71 was almost inevitable:

i **Bismarck** wanted such a war. He built up **a new army**, on the Prussian model, from the North German Confederation;

ii **Russia** agreed to stay neutral in the event of such a war when Bismarck supported her breach of the **Treaty of Paris** (1856) and her building of naval bases on the Black Sea;

iii **Italy** agreed to remain neutral, when France refused to withdraw a French garrison from **Rome** which prevented the Italians from capturing that city for their new unified state;

iv **France** was made to appear an **aggressive country**. When Napoleon III asked Bismarck for his 'promised reward' (1.9.2), he was **outwitted by Bismarck**.

(a) When suggested that he should occupy **Belgium**, the **British** were angered, and remained neutral when Bismarck went to war with France.

(b) When he suggested that he should take some **Rhineland territory**, the **Catholic States of southern Germany** were alarmed, and less opposed to Prussia than before (1.3.4).

(c) When he suggested that he might buy (and take) **Luxemburg**, he only succeeded in driving all the **German states** more firmly into Bismarck's 'camp'

9 We are not concerned about the details of the war. You have to note that;

i the much-fancied **French army** was defeated;

ii the North German army surrounded **Paris** (autumn 1870);

iii **Napoleon III** abdicated;

iv a **Republican government** was set up to continue the war;

v **Paris** was forced to surrender (Jan. 1871) after a **long siege**.

1.11 The creation of the German Empire, 1871

1 At Versailles, once the home of the Kings of France, France and Prussia signed a preliminary peace to end the War.

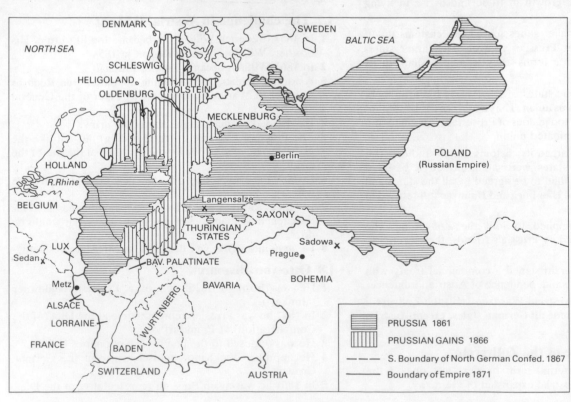

Fig. 1.10A
The Prussianization
of Germany,
1861–1870

2 Here, too, Bismarck announced the creation of a new **German Empire**, made up of the old North German Confederation plus the Catholic states of southern Germany. Only **Austria** was excluded.

1.12 The Treaty of Frankfurt (May 1871)

1 This was signed after negotiations which followed the Treaty of Versailles (1.11.1).

2 In this harsh Treaty:

i **Alsace and Lorraine** were ceded by France to Germany. These lands had many valuable coal and iron deposits;

ii **France** had to pay an **indemnity** (or compensation) of £200 million to Germany;

iii France had to allow a **German army to remain in occupation of France** until this compensation had been paid.

1.13 The constitution of the German Empire, January 1871

1 The Empire consisted of a **confederation of 25 states**.

2 The rulers of the states (kings, dukes, etc.), had great power in the internal affairs of their own states.

3 The King of Prussia became the Emperor of Germany (the **Kaiser**). He had a great deal of power:

i he had **full control of the army,** and, later, **the navy**;

ii he alone **could declare war** and make peace treaties;

iii he **appointed all the Ministers** in the Empire, including the Chief Minister (or **Chancellor**). The Cabinet was responsible to him and not, as in Britain, to Parliament.

4 The German Parliament consisted of **two Houses** or Chambers:

i **the Bundesrath** consisted of 58 delegates appointed by **the state rulers**. The number of delegates from each state varied; **Prussia**, the largest state, sent 17 delegates. Since only 14 votes were needed to get any measure rejected, Prussia in fact controlled the Bundesrath, the more important of the two Houses;

ii **the Reichstag** was elected by universal manhood suffrage in a secret ballot. This was a much more democratic system than Britain had in 1871. There were **382 members** in the Reichstag; half of these came from Prussia which had sixty per cent of the Empire's population—in the industrial Ruhr, the Saar and Upper Silesia;

iii **the powers of the Reichstag** were very limited:

(a) its consent was needed for the levying of **new taxes**, but not for the continuation of old taxes;

(b) it could debate proposals for **new laws** sent to it by the Bundesrath and it could suggest amendments. The consent of both Houses was needed for any new laws. Because Prussia controlled the Bundesrath (1.13.4 (**i**)), the Reichstag had **little chance** of pushing through anything which Prussia might not like;

(c) it could be **dissolved** by the Emperor with the approval of the Bundesrath. The Emperor could then call fresh elections.

5 The Prussian Parliament (or **Landtag**) was not elected by universal manhood suffrage but by a system of three-class voting. This gave control of the Landtag to the **wealthier, landowning class**. Since Prussia controlled the Bundesrath and dominated the Reichstag, it was, in fact, these wealthy landowners who had a great deal of influence throughout the Empire. After the fall of Bismarck (1.28) their influence was to become even stronger.

6 The Chancellor, or Chief Minister, was appointed by the Emperor. He was responsible only to the Emperor. **Bismarck** was the first Chancellor of the German Empire. As long as he could control the Emperor, he could do almost what he wanted. It was only when a new Kaiser decided to exercise his full powers that Bismarck lost control. Between 1871 and 1890 the German Empire and the whole of Europe were dominated by Bismarck.

1.14 Political parties in the Reichstag, 1871

1 The National Liberals were the largest party in the 1871 Reichstag. They represented the interests of German industrialists. These wanted the new Empire to succeed. They wanted a long period of peace during which industry and trade might grow.

2 The Conservatives, with about 100 seats in 1871, represented the interests of the **aristocrats** and the **rulers of the states**. Many of these complained of the 'Prussianization of Germany' (1.16).

3 The Centre Party, with about 60 members, represented the interests of the **Catholic Church**. Most of them came from the northern Rhineland and Bavaria, which had once looked to Austria for leadership. Many of them resented control by **Protestant Prussia**.

4 The Socialists were not a large group in 1871. They were to become very important as we shall see in 1.23–25.

5 There were approximately 100 other members in the 1871 Reichstag. Few of them were fervent supporters of Bismarck and Prussia. But few of them could agree on how best to oppose the new power.

1.15 Bismarck's immediate problems, 1871

1 In Germany, as in most other countries in Europe, there were **racial minorities**. There were a few million non-Germans–French (in Alsace and Lorraine) Danes (in Schleswig) and Poles. In **Austria** such minorities provided major problems. This did not happen in Bismarck's Germany because:

i they were relatively **few** in number;

ii they were **scattered** throughout the country;

iii they had **little in common**; e.g. the French wanted to get back to being ruled by France and were not concerned about Poles or Danes.

2 Local 'nationalism' existed in large states such as Hanover. This might have made them less fervent German nationalists.

3 The Catholics were to become a major problem (1.17).

4 Industrial towns created **social problems**–sanitation, water supply, refuse disposal and housing. It was from these towns that there emerged a **strong working class political party** (1.22–25).

1.16 The Prussianization of Germany

1 Criminal and commercial law A common code of law imposed throughout the Empire ended the inconsistencies found when each state had its own legal system.

2 A code of civil law and a central court of criminal appeal were set up.

3 The Prussian mark became the basis for a single monetary system.

4 Education was organized on the Prussian model. New textbooks were issued; children from all the states had a common education.

1.17 Bismarck and the Catholics

1 Protestant Prussia had defeated Catholic Austria and France, as steps towards unification. Many Catholics resented this.

2 The Centre Party seemed more concerned with Catholic affairs than with German affairs.

3 Bismarck thought that everyone ought to work in the interests of the Empire. This was a **centripetal** (or centralizing) policy. The Catholic Church looked to **Rome and the Papacy** and not to Berlin and the Empire. This was a **centrifugal** (or going away from the centre) policy. Bismarck decided to attack the Church in Germany.

1.18 Bismarck and Papal Infallibility, 1870

1 In 1870 the **Vatican Council** (a meeting of all the Catholic bishops and leaders) announced its decisions about Papal Infallibility. This said that when **the Pope** makes a statement *ex cathedra* (i.e. to the whole Catholic Church) on a question of **faith or morals**, he is guided by God, so that he can never be wrong.

2 Few people noticed that there were very few occasions when the Pope spoke in this way. Many, wrongly, thought the Council was claiming that the Pope could never be wrong on any issue.

3 Most Catholics accepted the new teaching.

4 Some Catholic **professors and teachers** in Germany refused to accept it. The Pope demanded that they be sacked from schools and universities.

5 Bismarck supported these **Old German Catholics** as they were called–the 'new' Catholics having accepted the new teaching.

6 Bismarck argued that **education was a state matter**. He claimed that the Church had no right to sack the old Catholics from their teaching posts. The Church, on the other hand, insisted it was right. Catholic students were forbidden to go to lectures by opponents of Papal Infallibility or to services led by Old German Catholic priests.

1.19 The Kulturkampf–the campaign by the State against the Church

1 The Centre Party took up the struggle on behalf of the Church.

2 The National Liberals supported Bismarck.

3 In 1872 the Jesuits, the leading Catholic teaching order, were expelled from Germany. When the Pope refused to receive the German Ambassador to the Vatican, he was recalled to Germany.

4 In 1873 all German schools were placed under the control of government inspectors; in the past Catholic schools had been inspected only by churchmen.

5 **Marriage** had once been a Church-only ceremony. In 1874 the law was changed; all marriages had to take place before government-appointed officials.

6 **Falk** was the Minister of Church Affairs (Public Worship) in Prussia. In May of 1873, 1874 and 1875 he introduced a series of laws in Prussia (the May Laws):
 i the Church was **forbidden to publicly excommunicate** "old" priests;
 ii **all candidates for the priesthood** had to study at a state university for three years and pass a state examination before starting their priestly studies;
 iii the state had to approve **the appointment of Catholic clergy** to teaching posts, and could refuse that approval if it wished;
 iv **all Catholic schools, colleges and universities** had to be open for inspection by state officials;
 v **all religious orders** were either dissolved or expelled.

1.20 The Church and the Kulturkampf

1 **The Pope** declared the May Laws to be invalid.

2 **The Catholic clergy** defied the Laws; many were sent to prison; others were fined; more were expelled from Prussia and Germany.

3 **Ordinary Catholics** supported their bishops and clergy.

4 **The Centre Party** gained more support and seats.

1.21 Bismarck calls it off

1 **The Socialist Party** had grown in strength because of the continued industrialization of Germany. Bismarck wanted the support of the Catholic Centre Party in his struggle with the Socialists (1.22).

2 **The Liberals** supported Bismarck against the Church. They might not do so if he fought the Socialists. He needed the Centre.

3 In **1878** a new Pope, Leo XIII, let it be known that he was ready to arrive at a compromise with Bismarck and Falk.

4 In **1879** the **Falk Laws** were suspended and in **1879** repealed. Religious orders, other than the Jesuits, returned to Germany.

5 The state kept the power to inspect schools and to hold civil marriages. Otherwise the Church recovered all its old power.

6 The Catholic Centre Party now supported Bismarck's government.

1.22 The Socialist Party

1 The **German Social Democratic Party** (SDP) was set up in 1869 by **Bebel**, a follower of Karl Marx.

2 **Marx** (1818–1883) was a German who lived most of his life in exile in London. Together with a German industrialist (**Engels**) he produced the Communist Manifesto (1848) and *Das Kapital*, the first volume of which appeared in 1867.

3 Marx believed that the workers (or **proletariat**) should rise in a violent revolution against their capitalist-bosses (landowners and employers). After the overthrow of the capitalist system, they would set up a Communist system in which:
 i all the means of production, distribution and exchange would be owned **collectively** (i.e. by all the people);
 ii there would be no private industry, investment or banking;
 iii everyone would be rewarded 'according to his needs' after he had worked 'according to his ability'.

1.23 Bismarck and the Socialists

1 Bismarck hoped that **the democratic constitution** (1.13.4ii) would win the support of the masses for the new Empire.

2 **The industrial revolution** created many social problems (1.15.4). It was these problems which led to the growth of the SDP.

3 Few German socialists thought that a violent revolution would be needed to change things. They hoped that a strong Socialist Party would persuade the government to pass the needed reforms.

4 In **1871** the Party won only three seats in the Reichstag (1.13.4).

5 In **1877** it won 12 seats and had 500 000 votes.

6 Bismarck was alarmed at this growth.

7 In **1878** there were two attempts to assassinate the Kaiser. Bismarck claimed that these had been organized by the Socialists.

1.24 The campaign against the Socialists

1 **The Enabling Law** (1878) allowed the government to declare a state of emergency whenever it wanted to.

2 This Law allowed the police to break up political meetings.

3 Socialist publications were banned.

4 Over 1500 leading socialists were arrested.

5 The Party continued to grow. In **1890** it got one and a half million votes; in 1914 over four and a quarter million.

1.25 Bismarck and a fresh approach

1 Bismarck realized that he could not crush socialism.

2 He introduced a series of reforms, hoping to win popular support:
 i **national insurance against sickness** (1883)) for all workers;
 ii national insurance **against accidents at work** (1884);
 iii a system of **Old Age Pensions** (1889).

3 This 'generous' policy failed to draw support away from the Socialists. In 1896 (after Bismarck's fall) the SDP was the second largest party in the Reichstag.

4 Bismarck's fall in 1890 was due, in part, to a quarrel between the new Kaiser (1.29) over the way to deal with the Socialists

1.26 Bismarck and the Tariff Question

1 The National Liberals were Bismarck's main supporters (1.14.1).

2 They had seen how Prussia gained from the Zollverein (1.3). This led them to demand international Free Trade. They hoped that such a policy would benefit the whole world.

3 By **1879** other European countries had become industrialized. They sent their goods into free-trade Germany. This led German industrialists (Liberal supporters) to form the **National Economic Union** to demand a German tariff on foreign imports.

4 Bismarck's main supporters in Prussia had been the land-owning Conservatives (1.14.2). These **Junkers** became wealthier as industrial workers bought their agricultural output.

5 By **1879** American farmers were selling huge quantities of wheat in free-trade Germany. This harmed the interests of the Junker class. They joined the Liberals in their demand for a German tariff.

6 Bismarck might have rejected these demands from industrialists and farmers, but there was also a **military need** for a tariff.

1.27 The Army and the Tariff Question

1 Since 1866 and the time of the North German Confederation (1.10.5) the central government had got its money from:
i postal and telegraph services;
ii such low import duties as existed;
iii contributions by each of the states to the central government.

2 By 1879 Bismarck realized that this revenue would have to be increased because his **foreign policy** needed:
i a **larger and better-equipped army**;
ii a **network of roads and railways** to carry the army to the frontiers when war broke out.

3 He also needed money to pay for:
i the **larger Civil Service** needed to run the Empire;
ii the **social welfare system** he planned (1.25).

4 He might have got this money from **new taxes** approved by the Reichstag. This would give greater power to that House. Bismarck did not want this to happen.

5 Tariffs would provide the money needed. So, reluctantly, he brought in a system of protective tariffs. (May-July, 1879).

6 The Liberals opposed him, but they ceased to be a problem:
i many joined the SDP to campaign for more social reform;
ii many more, fearing socialism, joined the Conservatives.

1.28 Bismarck and colonies

1 In 1870 Bismarck thought that:
i Germany ought to concentrate on her internal development;
ii attempts to gain colonies would annoy Britain which might become an ally for France and help her regain Alsace and Lorraine.

2 After the introduction of the tariff system he realized:
i colonies could provide **raw materials** for German industry;
ii they would also be **markets** for German goods;
iii they could be '**living space**' for the growing population.

3 In **1882** a **German Colonial Union** was forced to campaign for the acquisition of German colonies.

4 In **1884** Bismarck called an international conference in Berlin. Here the major Powers agreed on **the division of Africa**. Germany gained:

i **1885** South West Africa, Togoland and the Cameroons;
ii **1890** the naval base of Heligoland by agreement with Britain;
iii **1890** Britain recognized German claims to German East Africa (later called Tanganyika) while Germany recognized Britain's claims to Kenya and Zanzibar.

1.29 The fall of Bismarck, 1890 (*see Fig. V.3.1A*)

1 In **1888** William I died. Bismarck had usually been able to rely on his support and had generally got his own way with this Kaiser.

2 The new Kaiser, **Frederick**, was married to a daughter of Queen Victoria. She and Frederick disliked Bismarck; they wanted a more liberal and democratic system of government. But within three months of coming to the throne, the Kaiser died of cancer.

3 **1888** was the year of the Three Emperors: **Kaiser William II** succeeded his father, Frederick.

4 This Kaiser was only 28 years old. He had never got on with his parents, but had always admired his grandfather, William I.

5 He was born with a paralysed left arm which prevented him from being as active as other members of the aristocracy and made him bitter.

6 By **1890** the young Kaiser had quarrelled with Bismarck about:
i **the Socialists** William II opposed Bismarck's attempts to crush Socialism; he wanted to come to terms with the SDP;
ii **the colonies** The Kaiser thought Germany ought to have more;
iii **a navy** The Kaiser wanted to challenge British sea power;
iv **foreign policy** The Kaiser wanted to side openly with Austria-Hungary even if this meant a quarrel with Russia (see 8.4–8.10).

7 In 1890 Bismarck was forced to resign.

1.30 Bismarck's successors

1 Von Caprivi was Chancellor from **1890 to 1894**. He allowed the anti-socialist laws to lapse (1890), hoping the welfare system would lead to a fall in support for the Socialists. In fact the party continued to grow (1.25).

2 Hohenlohe (1894–1900) tried to get the Reichstag to renew the attack on socialism (1895) but failed.

3 Admiral Tirpitz was appointed German Naval Secretary (or Minister) in June 1897. He drew up plans for a large German navy, and helped found **the German Naval League** to popularize the demand for a navy. His appointment and policies were steps along the road to war. Other steps were:
i **1890** the acquisition of Heligoland (1.28.4);
ii **1895** the completion of the Kiel Canal between the North Sea and the Baltic.

4 Colonel-General von Moltke (son of Bismarck's von Moltke–1.7.3) became chief of the German General Staff. He got the support of the Kaiser for a larger German army. This was welcomed in Germany because:
i it created a demand for iron, steel, coal and engineering products so that it helped German industry;
ii the larger army was seen as a sign of German importance.

5 Von Bülow was Chancellor from 1900 to 1909. He had to face opposition in the Reichstag from parties opposed to the increasing power of the militarists such as Tirpitz and von Moltke. But this opposition was unable to restrain the Kaiser and his ministers.

6 Bethmann-Hollweg became Chancellor in 1909. The chief interest of his government lay in foreign affairs (Unit 8).

1.31 Bismarck's foreign policy, 1870–1890

On this important topic see 8.1–8.9

2 France, 1870–1914

2.1 The Franco-Prussian War, 1870–71
(*see Unit 1.10.8*)

1 **Napoleon III**, nephew of Napoleon I, became Emperor of France in December 1852, after a **coup d'état**. By 1870 he was **unpopular**.

2 During the **Austrian-Prussian War** of 1866 (10.10.3) he remained neutral, hoping that Bismarck would reward him with (i) Belgium, (ii) the land on the left bank of the Rhine and/or (iii) some territory in Southern Germany.

3 **Negotiations with Bismarck** brought trouble for Napoleon (1.10.8.iv).

4 **Russia** and **Italy** supported Bismarck (1.10.2).

5 **The Spanish throne** was vacant after a revolution. The Spanish asked Prince Leopold, a relative of the King of Prussia, to accept the throne. This request led to a war:
i **the French** told the Prussian king that they would not agree to his relative becoming King of Spain;
ii **Bismarck** hoped France would declare war;
iii **the Prussian King** let Bismarck down; he persuaded his relative to withdraw his acceptance of the Spanish throne;
iv **the French** demanded that the King make an official renunciation of his relative's claim to the throne;
v **the King** refused, during an interview with the French Ambassador whom he met at the spa town of **Ems**;
vi the King sent Bismarck a telegram about the interview;
vii Bismarck altered the **Ems telegram** to appear as if the king had been rough and abrupt with the French Ambassador;
viii he then published the Ems Telegram. **The angry French public** marched to the Imperial Palace to demand war on Prussia.

2.2 The Fall of Napoleon III

1 **The French** thought that they would win the war, but
i their **army** was badly organized;
ii army **supplies** were lacking; there was not enough **ammunition**; **weapons** were not as modern as those used by the Prussians.

2 **The Prussian army** was well organized:
i **Von Roon** and **Moltke** (1.7) had made their preparations; the army ran like a well-oiled machine;
ii the **railways** took armies to the front quickly;
iii Prussian **industry** produced the munitions.

3 **MacMahon** was defeated at **Worth** in August 1870.

4 **Bazaine** was defeated by a second Germany army and forced to take refuge in the fortress town of **Metz**.

5 **Napoleon** and **MacMahon** marched to relieve Metz. They were defeated at **Sedan** and Napoleon surrendered, 2 September 1870.

2.3 Uncertain Government

1 **The Germans** continued to advance and **besieged Paris**.

2 **Gambetta**, a leading opponent of Napoleon III, proclaimed a **French Republic** in Paris (**September 1870**).

3 **A Provisional Government of National Defence** was set up in Paris to lead France in the struggle against the invaders.

4 Gambetta escaped, in a balloon, from Paris to raise **fresh armies in the south and west**. These untrained and badly-armed men were unable to drive the Germans from Paris.

5 **In January 1871 Paris surrendered** and an armistice (*) was signed.

2.4 Peacemaking

1 The Provisional Government (2.3) had not been elected by the French people. It did not have the power to make a peace treaty.

2 After the armistice a **National Assembly** was elected to decide whether to continue with the war or to make peace.

3 This Assembly met at **Bordeaux, January 1871**.

4 This Assembly agreed to the **Treaty of Frankfurt (1.12)**.

2.5 The Assembly versus the Parisian Republicans

1 **The Republic** of 1870 was created by **Parisians** (2.3.2).

2 **Republicans** wanted to **continue the war**.

3 The majority of the French people were **peasant farmers**. They wanted the war to end.

4 In the elections for the **National Assembly** (January 1871) the peasants chose men who wanted to make peace.

5 The majority of these supported some form of **monarchy** – although they did not agree who should be ruler (2.10).

6 They did not try to bring back a monarch immediately. They realized that such a monarch would have been blamed for the harsh terms of the Treaty of Frankfurt.

7 The Assembly therefore **elected** an old politician, **Thiers**, as Chief of the Executive Power. It did not call him President, nor did it proclaim a Republic.

2.6 The Paris Commune (*Fig. 2.6A*)

1 **The people of Paris** resented the fact that the Assembly on leaving Bordeaux met at **Versailles**, the old monarchical palace, and not, as they demanded, in the capital.

2 They also resented **the monarchist majority**. Parisians wanted the Assembly to proclaim a **Republic**.

3 They had been angered and humiliated when the **German army marched**, in triumph, **through the streets of Paris** – and more angered by Thiers' having allowed this '**march of the victors**'.

4 The **German occupation** of forts to the north of Paris was a constant reminder of the **humiliating Treaty**.

5 The Assembly passed **two Acts** which angered Parisians:
i during the war **all property rents** within Paris had been suspended. The Assembly decided that they should be repaid to landlords – with interest.
ii the people of Paris had raised their own National Guard as part of their defence during the German siege. The Assembly decided to **disarm the National Guard**, to end payment to its members and to remove its cannons from the city.

6 Troops loyal to the Versailles government were sent to get the cannons (**March 1871**).

7 The **Parisians resisted** and fighting broke out.

8 There then took place the formation of **the Commune**:
i as in revolutionary cities in the south (**Lyons** and **Marseilles**), **the red flag** was flown over the Paris Town Hall;
ii a General Council (or Commune) of ninety members was elected **to govern Paris**. Paris was to be self-governing and completely independent of the Assembly.

9 You should note that the members of the Commune were drawn from every social class. **It was not a communist gathering**.

2.7 Thiers and the Commune, March–May 1871

1 **Thiers** was determined to **bring the Commune down**. He could not allow 'the tail (Paris) to wag the dog (France)'.

2 **The Germans** allowed the Assembly's forces to attack Paris, and even handed back prisoners of war to **MacMahon** to help.

3 In May he forced his way **into Paris**. Fierce street fighting continued in the barricaded streets.

4 The supporters of the Commune made a last ditch stand in the **Père Lachaise cemetery**.

5 Many **buildings** were destroyed, many **hostages** shot, including the Archbishop of Paris.

6 The Versailles forces finally won **(May 1871)**. Many supporters of the Commune were executed and others exiled.

2.8 The effects of the Commune

1 Many **Parisians** remained **hostile** to the Thiers government – and, later, to the Republic which succeeded it.

2 The uprising **frightened many European leaders**. Bismarck used this fear in his policy of isolating France (8.2)

3 **Thiers** was **popular** with the rich French who had feared that the Commune might be the beginning of another revolution like that of 1789. They gave generously to the loans floated by the government to pay off the compensation demanded at Frankfurt. The £200 million was paid in less than three years and the German army withdrawn sooner than Bismarck had imagined.

2.9 Thiers, 1871–73

1 Thiers had already played an important part:

i he was **head of the Bordeaux Assembly** which made peace;

ii as **head of the Executive Power** he put down the Commune;

iii he had got the **loans** to pay the German compensation.

2 Once the German army of occupation was withdrawn he reorganized the French army and brought in a **strict law of conscription**.

3 As a reward for his work, the Assembly declared him **President of the Republic**, although the majority of members were monarchists.

4 **Thiers** supported the claims of the **Orléanist candidate** for the throne (2.10). But by 1873 he realized that it would be impossible to bring back a monarch.

5 He suggested in **1873** that the Assembly should write a **Republican constitution**. The Assembly rejected the proposal, and in **May 1873** forced **Thiers to resign**.

2.10 The Monarchists' plot, 1873–75

1 **MacMahon**, a monarchist, was chosen to succeed Thiers.

2 There were **three possible claimants** to the throne:

i the **Bourbons** were the family overthrown in 1791, restored in 1815 and overthrown again in 1830. Their leader in 1873 was the Comte de (or Count of) **Chambord,** grandson of the king deposed in 1830;

ii the **Orléanists** (who had had Louis Philippe as King from 1830 to 1848) were represented by the **Comte de Paris**, Louis Philippe's grandson;

iii the **Bonapartists** put forward the claims of Napoleon III's son, the **Prince Imperial**, aged seventeen.

3 The Royalists agreed that the claims of the Prince Imperial could be dismissed. Napoleon III even more than his uncle, the great Napoleon, was not of the royal 'race'.

4 **The Bourbon and Orléanist factions** finally agreed that;

i the old and childless **Chambord** would be King;

ii the younger **Paris** would be named as his heir.

5 Then they threw it all away. Chambord refused to accept the **tricolour flag** as the national emblem. The flag of his France would be the **white flag** of the Bourbons, with its lilies (or *fleur de lis*).

6 **MacMahon** said 'The guns would have gone off on their own' because there would have been **widespread opposition** to this rejection of the flag which had been the national emblem since 1791.

7 **Royalists hoped** to wait until Chambord died when the Comte de Paris would become King.

8 But **MacMahon** summed up the position when he admitted, **'It is the Republic which divides us least.'**

2.11 The Republican constitution, 1875

1 **Gambetta** rallied the anti-royalist forces in the Assembly which in **January 1875** voted by a majority of one vote in favour of a **Republican constitution**.

2 **A President** was to be head of state. He would be elected every **seven years** by the members of the two Houses of Parliament. The royalists only agreed to allow the constitution through on condition that the President was given very great powers:

i he **chose the ministers** to form the government;

ii he could **introduce laws** himself;

iii if the Parliament passed anything with which he disagreed, he could **demand further debates** in Parliament;

iv on the advice of the Senate (below) he could **dissolve the Chamber (below) and call for fresh elections**.

3 There were two houses in the **French Parliament**:

i the **Senate** or Upper House was to be elected every **nine years** by an electoral college chosen by **each department** throughout France. This is an example of **indirect elections**;

ii the **Chamber of Deputies** was the Lower House. Every **four years** all men over the age of twenty-one were entitled to vote for members of the Chamber. This is an example of **direct elections**.

4 **Ministers**, although chosen by the President, were **responsible to the Senate and the Chamber**, which had the right to reject government proposals. If the government were defeated on a major issue there might be fresh elections. However, it was more usual for there just to be a change of government. There were **many short-lived governments** – fifty by the time war broke out in 1914.

5 The Republic was called the **Third Republic**. There had been a First Republic from 1793 to 1805 and a Second from 1848 to 1852.

2.12 MacMahon's final years, 1875–79

1 **MacMahon** was **President** in succession to Thiers.

2 After **1875** he used his powers to try **to prevent Republicans** from getting too much of their own way.

3 **Fresh elections** were called in **1876**. These resulted in:

i a Republican majority in the **Chamber of Deputies**;

ii **a monarchist majority** in the **Senate**.

4 In **1877** MacMahon used his powers in union with the Senate to **dismiss the Chamber** and call for fresh elections. He hoped for a monarchist majority, but did not get it.

5 He appointed a monarchist, the **Duke de Broglie as Prime Minister**.

6 But MacMahon's hopes were dashed by the French people. In **1878 the Republicans** gained a number of seats in **the Senate** so that they controlled that body as well as **the Chamber**.

7 **MacMahon** acknowledged that he had lost. He **resigned** to make way for **Jules Grévy, a Republican**. In **1879**, the **Republicans** had **the Presidency** and control of **both Houses of Parliament**. It seemed as if the Republic was, at last, safe.

2.13 Why did the monarchists fail and the Republic survive?

1 **The legacy of Napoleon III**. His reforming activity and his aggressive foreign policy made a 'liberal' Republic appear as an attractive alternative.

2 **The royalists** failed to present a realistic alternative. The Republic appeared to MacMahon and other members of the upper classes as the most logical alternative (20.10.8). It was already an attractive alternative as far as the middle classes were concerned.

3 **The extreme left** was not a threat, particularly after the defeat of the Commune (2.6–2.8). There was no danger that a liberal Republic would pave the way for extreme Socialism.

This deprived the right-wing monarchists of a possible argument against the Republic.

4 The economic depression, of the 1870s did not affect France as much as it did Germany and Britain. Thiers had laid a firm basis for economic recovery (2.8–2.9) so that the royalists could not argue that republicanism led to depression.

5 The Republic was in many ways a **constitutional monarchy in disguise** (2.11.2) although it was liberal and democratic in appearance. It was not likely that this republican government would pass any truly radical measures. Indeed, although there were to be many changes of government by 1914, almost all of them were very conservative and similar in outlook. There was too little for royalists to disagree with.

2.14 Jules Grévy, President, 1879–1887

1 Jules Ferry was Prime Minister 1881–83 and 1883–85. His governments were responsible for:
 i **pardoning** exiled and imprisoned supporters of the **Commune**;
 ii allowing **trade unions** freedom–although the government did not repeal the old Laws of Association under which unions and other organizations had been persecuted;
 iii removing **press censorship**;
 iv tackling the question of **education** (see below).

2 The importance of education had been recognized by the Republican, **Gambetta**, who declared that the French had not been beaten by the Prussian army but by the **Prussian schoolmasters**. Prussian education had turned out a more intelligent workforce, more intelligent soldiers and the technicians who produced the munitions:
 i the French educational system–primary, secondary and university–was controlled by the **Catholic Church** which republicans blamed for the failure of the French system. They also accused the **Church of being monarchist** and **anti-Republican**. Gambetta said 'Cléricisme, voilà l'ennemi' ('Clericalism, there is the enemy');
 ii a **national**, government-supported system of **primary education** was set up for children between the ages of six and thirteen;
 iii **priests, monks and nuns were forbidden** to teach in these schools;
 iv **state secondary schools**, (or *lycées*) had been set up by Napoleon I for boys. Ferry established similar schools for **girls**.
 v it was **forbidden** to provide **religious instruction** in these schools which were staffed by laymen and laywomen. Priests and nuns were free to give that instruction outside school hours;
 vi the **Jesuits** were expelled from France. **Other religious orders** were allowed to exist provided that they registered as required by the **Laws of Association;**
 vii these 'authorized orders' could run their own schools, which received no financial help from the government. These private schools (or *écoles*) were supported by richer Catholics.

3 French colonies were set up in **Tunis** which, to Bismarck's delight, angered Italy and Britain which feared French expansion. Colonies were also set up in **Annam** and **Tonkin**–additions to the existing **French Indo-China**. In 1884 France took part in the Conference at **Berlin** (1.27.4) and gained **French West Africa**.

2.15 Republican problems

1 Grévy and Ferry were not always popular with the French Parliament. When Ferry tried to bring in **Factory Acts** to improve conditions for workers, the **Senate** rejected them.

2 As the fear of a monarchist revival died out, divisions appeared among the **Republicans**. They **split into rival groups**.

3 One result of this was **frequent ministerial changes**.

4 This 'in-and-out' series of governments made the Republican form of government **less popular**. Monarchy, after all, provided a stable form of continual government.

5 In **1887** Grévy was succeeded by **Carnot**.

6 The outstanding figure in the government at that time was the Minister of War after 1886, **General Boulanger.**

2.16 General Boulanger

1 In **1886** President Grévy's son-in-law was involved in a **financial scandal** concerning the sale of honours.

2 In **1887** a French frontier official, **Schnaebelé**, was arrested on French soil by a German policeman. This was a reminder of the power of **Germany** and the loss of **Alsace** and **Lorraine**.

3 Grévy and, later, Carnot seemed unable to stand up to the Germans. Many **French people** looked for someone who might take charge of the country. Such a one might:
 i **make France great** again–and stand up to Germany;
 ii bring **strong government**–and fewer ministerial changes;
 iii get rid of **corruption**;
 iv **end the quarrel with the Church** (a wish of **Catholics**);
 v ensure the **continuation of the Republic** (the wish of the **anti-Catholics**).

4 Many people thought that such a saviour existed in the shape of the Minister of War, **General Boulanger. Handsome** (unlike most of the politicians), frequently seen riding on his **black horse** (a reminder of military power) he became **very popular** as he demanded the reforms which many people wanted to see.

5 He demanded that the **Presidency should be strengthened** (which pleased the monarchists). He asked that the **army be strengthened** (and those who hoped to regain Alsace and Lorraine supported this).

6 In **1888 six constituencies** chose him as their Deputy (see 2.11.3).

7 He then demanded the **abolition of the Senate** (which pleased the radical republicans), called for **democracy in the army** (which pleased the left-wing and the anti-clericals).

8 In **1889** it appeared that he might get elected for many more seats in the Chamber.

9 Those who supported him (the Church and army, the anti-clericals and radicals, the fervent republicans and the anti-Germans) hoped that he might lead a **march on the Parliament**, dismiss the two Houses and seize power.

10 The government finally took courage. It accused him of **treason**–plotting the overthrow of the Republic. Instead of standing up to the government **Boulanger ran away to Belgium**.

11 Three years later he **committed suicide**. The Republic had come through one crisis. Another was waiting to threaten it.

2.17 The Panama Scandal, 1889–1892

1 In **1869** the French engineer, **Ferdinand de Lesseps**, completed the **Suez Canal**.

2 In **1879** it was proposed to build a **Panama Canal** and de Lesseps was asked to take charge of the project.

3 A company was formed, money borrowed from the public, hoping that the new canal would be as successful as the Suez Canal.

4 In **1889** the company went **bankrupt**, long before the canal was complete. The reasons for **de Lessep's failure** were many:
 i he had underestimated the **difficulties** involved;
 ii he had made serious **errors in engineering**;
 iii **the climate** made working very difficult.

5 In **1892** an investigation showed that much of the money raised was used to **bribe politicians** so support the scheme.

6 De Lesseps was sentenced to five years in prison, but this did not help investors in the bankrupt company.

7 This **corruption** led many French people to have less confidence than ever in the Republican system.

8 Others blamed the financiers for the bribery and for the company's collapse. Some of the financiers (bankers, stockbrokers and others) were **Jewish**. This led to an outburst of **anti-semitism** in France. It was this anti-semitism which provided the Republic with yet another crisis in 1894.

2.18 The Dreyfus Affair, 1894–1906

1 In **1894** an army Captain, Alfred **Dreyfus**, was charged with having sold military secrets to the Germans.

2 The main evidence against Dreyfus was an unsigned document called the *bordereau*, said to be in his handwriting.

3 An army court martial found him **guilty**. He was degraded (stripped of his rank, all the buttons and decorations torn off his uniform in front of the soldiers of his regiment).

4 The army court then sentenced him to **imprisonment for life on Devil's Island**.

5 The Dreyfus family argued:
i that the **trial had been unfair**; the defence had not seen all the papers involved;
ii that **Dreyfus** had not written the *bordereau*.

6 A Colonel **Picquart** became convinced of Dreyfus's innocence.

7 in **1896** he claimed that **Major Esterhazy** had forged the *bordereau*.

8 This accusation divided French public opinion:
i the **anti-Dreyfusards** supported the army court martial and argued that Dreyfus was guilty. This was the 'party' of
(a) the **wealthier families** which produced most **army officers**;
(b) the **monarchists** who saw a chance to **weaken the Republic**;
(c) the **clergy**, opposed to attacks on the **Catholic Church**;
(d) the **anti-Semites**. Dreyfus was a Jew–one of the few non-Catholics to become an army officer. Most officers had been trained at the Catholic military academy, St. Cyr.
ii **The Dreyfusards** said Dreyfus was innocent and the Catholic officer-class was guilty of anti-Semitism. This 'party' consisted of:
(a) those who wanted a **more democratic army** and were opposed to the Catholic domination of the forces;
(b) the **anti-clericals** who argued that the Dreyfus case showed how right they were to attack the Church;
(c) **the Republicans** The case damaged their form of government and showed that the army was outside government control;
(d) **many literary men** who wrote pamphlets and books supporting Dreyfus's innocence.

9 **1898** an army court found **Esterhazy** (2.18.7) **innocent**.

10 Emile Zola, a leading novelist, then wrote a famous letter headed *'J'accuse'*. This was published in the socialist newspaper *L'Aurore*. Zola accused the army of corruptly mishandling the affair. There was a good deal of public argument over this letter; France became bitterly divided between the **Catholic right** and the **Republican left**.

11 Zola, arrested and found guilty of treason, fled to Britain.

12 The government brought **three documents** before the Chamber of Deputies to show Dreyfus's guilt.

13 Picquart said that two of the **documents** had nothing to do with the case while the third had been forged.

14 A Colonel Henry confessed to having forged the document–and then committed suicide.

15 In **1899 Esterhazy** (see point 7 above) fled to Britain where he confessed to having **forged** the *bordereau*.

16 This led to the calling of a **Court of Cassation** which laid aside the verdict at Dreyfus's first trial and ordered a fresh one.

17 In spite of the admissions of Henry and Esterhazy the army court martial **again found Dreyfus guilty**, but reduced his punishment to one of ten years imprisonment.

18 The government stepped in to give **Dreyfus a pardon**–but said nothing about his guilt.

19 In **1906** the case was re-opened. A **Court of Cassation** laid aside the result of the second trial, **declared Dreyfus innocent** and said Esterhazy was guilty of forging the *bordereau*.

20 Dreyfus was restored to the **army** where he was **promoted** and given the highest award in France; the **Legion of Honour**.

2.19 Another clash with the Catholic Church, 1901–07

1 It is difficult for us to understand the hatred which the **Dreyfus affair** aroused in France. Families were divided; old friends quarrelled; there was even street fighting.

2 It is also difficult to understand the important part played by **religion** in French affairs during this period (1870–1914). We have seen how Ferry and Grévy limited the power of the Catholic Church (2.12). The bitter arguments over the Dreyfus affair led to a more violent attack on the Church.

3 Waldeck-Rousseau became Prime Minister in **1899**. It was his government which was responsible for three attacks:
i a new **Law of Associations** (1901). Older Laws of Association (2.14.1 and 2.14.2) said that **any association or society** with more than twenty members had to **be approved by the government**. These laws had not been rigorously enforced and many religious orders had been formed without government permission.
The new Law of 1901 said that:
(a) **non-religious societies** were legalized;
(b) **religious associations** had to seek permission;
(c) they had to **submit their rules** for government approval;
(d) all unauthorized associations were banned from teaching:
ii **religious orders** which did not apply for or failed to get government sanctions were suppressed;
iii over **1500 religious houses** were closed.

4 In **1904 Waldeck-Rousseau** resigned. His successor, a former Jesuit priest, **Combes**, was violently anti-Catholic.

5 In **1905** the **Law of Separation** was passed:
i this ended the **Concordat** (or agreement) between the French government and the Vatican, reached in 1802;
ii the government stopped the payment of salaries to **Catholic priests**, although it continued to pay pensions to retired priests;
iii **all churches and cathedrals** became state property;
iv associations for public worship (*Associations culturelles*) were to be formed. The government would give permission to such associations to use churches and cathedrals.

6 Jews and **Protestants** formed their own associations.

7 Pope **Pius X** forbade **French Catholics** to do so.

8 In **1907** the government **relaxed the law**. Priests could negotiate for the use of churches–without forming an association.

9 Many people had seen the **Church** as a menace to the Republic. It had supported **MacMahon, Chambord, Boulanger,** the **anti-Dreyfusards** and seemed to be very powerful. It is worth noting that the attacks on the Church after 1875 were supported by the majority of French voters. No minister lost power because of a Catholic revolt at the ballot box. It is possible that the power of the Church had been more apparent than real. Certainly by 1905 it had ceased to be an important issue in French politics. Only a minority of French people remained loyal to the Church.

2.20 Socialism

1 France was slow to become **industrialized**. The majority of the people were **peasant farmers** and lived in small villages.

2 Industrial workers were relatively few in number. **Trade unions** were small and until the 1890s there were few Socialist Deputies in the Chamber. France was very different from

Germany where the Socialist Party was a very large one (1.21–23).

3 In **1884 trade unions** were legalized, although workers employed by the government were not allowed to form or join unions.

4 Trade unions set up their **own Labour Exchanges** in industrial towns where they organized unemployment benefit and other social services for their members.

5 **Alexandre Millerand** was the Socialist leader who helped the party to grow. Many Radicals joined the party when the Republican governments did little for the working class.

6 In **1893** Millerand led **45 Socialist Deputies** in the Chamber and, in the unstable Republican system, had a little influence.

7 In **1899–1902** he was a minister in Waldeck-Rousseau's government which:
i in **1900** reduced the working day to **11 hours**;
ii in **1904** further reduced it to **10 hours**;
iii **failed** to enforce these regulations properly.

8 **Millerand** was a moderate. In **1902** he was expelled from the party which had been re-organized on **Marxist lines**. The next significant leader of the party was **Jean Jaurès** who was assassinated in Paris on 30 July 1914 because of his opposition to French entry into the war.

2.21 Syndicalism

1 The failure of Republican governments to do much for the working class led to demands by workers for more direct action.

2 French trade unions were known as **Syndicats**, and have given their name to an extremist movement called syndicalism.

3 **Syndicalists aimed at:**
i destroying **Parliamentary institutions** by strikes and sabotage;
ii giving the workers in every industry complete **control of their industry**.

4 It was the syndicalists who fixed on **May Day** as a day for working class demonstrations and marches.

5 By **1900** about half a million men belonged to the organization which had nothing in common with the moderate trade unions of Great Britain or the moderate Socialist Party of Germany.

6 In **1909** the syndicalists organized a nation-wide **railway strike**. The minister concerned with the railways, **Aristide Briand** (a moderate Socialist) called all the striking workers up for **military service**. To have continued the strike would have allowed the government to put workers on trial for treason. The strike was broken.

7 In **1912** a European War appeared possible. A **coalition government** was formed to ensure national safety. Syndicalism became less important.

3 Russia 1855–1914

3.1 Tsar Alexander II (1855–81)

1 The ruler of Russia was known as the Tsar–or Emperor.
2 Alexander II became Tsar in 1855 during the **Crimean War**.
3 That war had shown how inefficient Russia was:
i her **industry** was unable to supply enough munitions;
ii her **agriculture** was unable to supply enough food;
iii her **Civil Service** was unable to organize the war.

4 Once he had made peace with Britain and France (1856) the Tsar decided on a policy of reform.

3.2 The Russian peasants

1 Most of Russia's **agricultural land** was owned by:
i **the Tsar** himself;
ii the small number of **nobles**;
iii a larger number of lesser nobles or **gentry**.

2 The majority of the Russian people living on the land were **serfs**, or semi-slaves.
(a) They had to **work three days a week** for their owner.
(b) They **paid most of Russia's taxes** in the poll tax.
(c) **Their masters** could sell them; punish them severely without trial (flogging was common).
(d) They could be **conscripted** for service in the forces.

3 **Each serf family** had about **15 acres** to farm for their own benefit–but they **did not own the land**.

3.3 The effects of serfdom

1 **Agriculture** was **inefficient**. There was no incentive for serfs to work hard; any profit would go the the owners.

2 **Industry** was developing, but there was a **shortage** of **labour**. Serf labour was not free to move to the factories.

3 **Revolutionaries** from Western Europe might persuade the downtrodden serfs to revolt. Alexander II said; 'It is better **to abolish serfdom from above** rather than await the time when it will begin to **abolish itself from below**.'

3.4 The Edict of Emancipation, 3 March 1861

1 **Few nobles agreed** with the Tsar's ideas. Even these **demanded payment** for their loss of slaves and land.
2 **44 million peasants** were set free by the Edict:
i they could now **own land**;
ii they were **free to move** from the estates–but they had **to carry passports** to show the police when asked;
iii they did not have to work on the nobles' land.

3 **Not so free**. The former serfs did not become owners of any land immediately–they had to pay for it:
i **government surveyors** divided the land between the former owners and the former serfs:
ii on average a **former serf family got about 8 acres**–less than when they lived on a master's estate;
iii that land had **to be paid for**. It was valued by a government official. The government paid the owner and the ex-serfs paid **instalments for forty-nine years**.

4 **The mir** (or village **commune**) became, as it were, the new owners:
i each year the 'elders' of **the mir** divided up the 'freed' land according to the numbers in each family;
ii **the mir** collected the debt instalments.

3.5 Discontented peasants

1 **The population increased** from 50 million in 1850 to approximately 82 million in 1900.
2 **The annual division of the land** by the **mir** after 1861 led to every family getting a **smaller and smaller plot**.
3 Most peasants remained **inefficient**. They produced enough to feed their families but few produced enough to sell for profit. This led to **food shortages** in the growing towns.
4 Many gave up farming because they **could not pay the annual instalments**. Some became **workers** for more successful ex-serfs (called **kulaks** in Russian). Some went to work in **industrial towns**. Here they lived in primitive conditions (3.15).

3.6 Local government reform

1 The nobles and the gentry had run the countryside–seeing to the building of bridges, hospitals and schools.

2 After the Emancipation of 1861 it was necessary to find some other way to govern the countryside.

3 The **mir** or commune was the **bottom rung** of the ladder of government. There were **elections in each mir** to choose its leaders.

4 District councils (**zemstvos**) had been controlled by the nobles. **After 1861** these councils were elected by:
i **nobles**;
ii **townspeople**;
iii **peasants**, the former serfs.

5 These **zemstvos** looked after the building and maintenance of **roads** and **bridges** and ran the country's improved **school system**.

6 The district **zemstvos** were a **second rung** on the ladder of government–above the **mir**.

7 A **third rung** on that ladder was the **provincial zemstvos**. Delegates went from various district zemstvos–a case of **indirect election**. They looked after the **public health system** and chose **magistrates** for the new law courts (3.8.2).

3.7 Discontented liberals

1 **Democratic elections** to the mir and the district zemstvos **pleased many liberals**–nobles, gentry and townspeople.

2 This partial democracy also **made them discontented:**
i government-appointed **Provincial Governors** could ban any demand of a zemstvo;
ii while **the Tsar** had created three tiers or rungs of government (mir, District zemstvos and Provincial zemstvos) he was **unwilling to call a national council**–or Parliament;
iii **he went further**. The members of the various zemstvos were **forbidden**, to meet in **national conferences** to discuss common problems. Maybe the Tsar feared that such a gathering might have led to a demand for a constitutional government.

3.8 Other reforms by Alexander II

1 The Press
i **Censorship** was relaxed; writers could criticize the government. Alexander hoped to bring his critics into the open;
ii **newspapers and journals flourished**–the number of national newspapers increased from 6 to 16 by 1881.

2 The legal system
i As in other countries **judges** and **magistrates** were appointed for **life** and could not be dismissed by the government;
ii **equality before the law** of all Russians was proclaimed;
iii **trials** had to be held in **public**;
iv the system of **trial by jury** replaced the system by which a nobleman-judge or magistrate had tried cases.

However there were limits to the legal reforms:
i **political offenders** were not tried by jury;
ii **peasants** had their own special courts;
iii so too did **editors** of critical newspapers. These could not even speak in their own defence during a trial.

3 The Army
i In **1874 all classes** became liable for military service–and not only the peasantry;
ii **length of service** fell from twenty-five to fifteen years;
iii **flogging of soldiers** was forbidden.

4 Education
i **Primary Education** District **zemstvos** built **10 000 schools** as a means of tackling massive illiteracy.
ii **Secondary schools** There were two kinds of schools:
(a) the **old-fashioned schools** taught mainly classics (Latin and Greek) and did not offer science;
(b) **modern schools** offered science.

iii **Universities** admitted only students from the old-fashioned schools. The government thought that science was '**dangerous**'.

3.9 Alexander and Poland, 1863

1 Russia had expanded its territory at various times so that it **included many non-Russian peoples**.

2 The Poles were one such people–their country had been seized by Russia **during the Napoleonic Wars**.

3 In **1863** the **Poles rose in revolt** because:
i **the reforms** created a 'liberal' atmosphere;
ii **the defeat in the Crimean War** (1853–56) suggested that Russia might be too weak to put down a revolt;
iii **the Italians** had risen against Austria (1859–61);
iv the incident which sparked off the rising was the closing down of the Polish Agricultural Society in Warsaw. Anti-Russian demonstrations took place which led to troops firing on the crowd.

4 Napoleon III of France wanted to help his fellow-Catholics in Poland. **Bismarck** refused to allow French troops to go through Prussia–and so gained Russian friendship (1.10.2).

5 The rising was put down with **great cruelty**.

6 Alexander II and his ministers then **encouraged**
i **Russian nationalism**; they blamed the Poles for trying to break up the Russian Empire;
ii **Pan Slavism** and the union of the Slavs of South Eastern Europe under Russian leadership (4.3.1.).

3.10 Revolutionary developments

1 The reforms of Alexander II led to the growth of revolutionary movements;
i **each reform** whetted the appetite for more;
ii **educational development** created a more literate people able to read and understand the arguments of Radicals;
iii **the land reform** left many people dissatisfied (3.5);
iv **industrial towns** created their own problems (3.15).

2 Nihilists (from the Latin word **nihil** meaning **nothing**):
i this group of revolutionaries thought that everything from **the past had to be destroyed**:
ii then **a new society** could be built;
iii using the greater freedom of the press, the movement won a great deal of support; many thousands joined;
iv but the old system did not go away peacefully. So the nihilists began to use **terrorist tactics**. Bombs, guns and knives were used in attacks on government officials and in **1866** on **the Tsar** himself;
v **the government** then turned to **repressive methods**:
(a) thousands were arrested and exiled to Siberia.
(b) since many leading nihilists were students, there was an attempt to restrict entry to universities to those who could be shown to be 'reliable'–i.e. loyal to the Tsar;
(c) editors of newspapers could be dismissed if they did not reveal the names of writers of nihilist articles.

3 The Narodniki (the name given to the many thousands of students) went in the early 1870s to preach revolutionary ideas to the peasants). They were **not very successful** because:
i **most peasants** could not understand the ideas;
ii peasants were **shocked** by the free and easy behaviour of the 'townies';
iii **the local priests** had great influence and persuaded people to attack the students. The movement fizzled out, but it led Alexander to tighten up university entrance.

4 Socialism, as taught by **Marx** (see 1.21) had some influence in the 1870s in Russia:
i **the village commune** attracted some Russian revolutionaries. They saw it as the ideal socialist society–land held by the commune (3.4.4) shared out according to the families' needs;

ii **some socialists**, imitating the Narodniki, tried to preach the need for a **peaceful revolution** by the peasants;

iii **others**, led by **Michael Bakunin**, once a nihilist, wanted a **violent uprising** to sweep the Tsarist system away.

3.11 The death of Alexander II, 1881

1 The Tsar had started out by being 'The Liberator'.

2 He had made many important reforms.

3 But he had **failed** to satisfy all the people. Unable to get more changes by peaceful means they turned to terrorism.

4 In **1866** there was an attempt to assassinate **Alexander II**. In **1879** he survived two further attempts on his life. In one, five shots missed him. In another his **Winter Palace** was dynamited–but the Tsar was away.

In **1880** the dining room in the Winter Palace was mined when, again, the Tsar was away and a mine on a track along which his train was travelling did not explode.

In **1881** the terrorists **killed Alexander** in a bomb attack.

3.12 Alexander III (1881–1894)

1 The new Tsar declared that his father's reforming policies had been wrong–and had failed.,

2 He promised to **'turn back the clock'** and undo the reforms.

3 He gave a free hand to his chief Minister, **Pobedonostev**.

3.13 Pobedonostev

1 He had been **Alexander's tutor** in 1865.

2 Alexander III made him the **Chief Procurator of the Holy Synod** controlling the Russian Church, a powerful organization.

3 He was responsible for the harsh policy:

i **the secret police** (the Okhrana) were given greater powers to hunt down revolutionaries and terrorists;

ii **more people** were imprisoned, executed or exiled;

iii **education** came under stricter control.

(a) **Universities** Entry was restricted to classical students; teachers were spied on and critics of government sacked.

(b) **Secondary schools** No child from the working class or from the peasant class was allowed to go to secondary school.

(c) **Primary schools** These were put under the control of the Church, and obedience to government taught to all children;

iv **the Press** was more closely supervised. Fourteen newspapers critical of the government were shut down;

v **Land Captains**–drawn from the old nobility–were appointed with powers over all other local officials. They also replaced magistrates appointed by Alexander II;

vi **minority races** The Baltic regions of Latvia, Estonia and Lithuania had been allowed to retain their own languages and customs. Now they had to teach the **Russian language** which became the official language for use in courts, press and in dealings with government officials. In **Poland** Russian was made compulsory in all schools:

vii the Lutheran (Protestant) Church was persecuted.

4 **The Jews** Attacks on Russian Jews had often taken place in the past. Under Pobedonostev there were more serious attacks or **pogroms**:

i Jews were not allowed to live in the countryside but **only in towns**;

ii fewer of them were allowed **secondary education**;

iii priests of the Orthodox Church encouraged people to attack Jews and their homes having labelled them **'Christ killers'**;

iv this **anti-semitism** allowed people to take out their anger (at the Tsar and the government) on the Jews.

3.14 Russian industrialization

1 The idealistic **Narodniki** (3.10.3) thought the **Russian peasants** were the important section of Holy Russia.

2 **The Russian Church** was opposed to most of the Narodniki's ideas–attacks on the Tsar, the need for a revolution and socialism. But the Church shared the notion that Holy Russia was a 'better' country than any of the 'pagan' countries of Western Europe.

3 **Pobedonostev** shared this belief and **opposed western ideas**–jury service, free press and science in schools.

4 But **Holy Russia was poor**, inefficient and militarily weak. If Russia were to be stronger, if her people were to have a better standard of living, then **industrialization** would have to take place. And with industrialization would come **western ideas**–on trade unions and demands for political development.

5 Some industrialization had taken place:

i in **1855** there was **only one railway** in Russia. By **1860** over **one thousand miles of line** had been opened and by **1888 13 000 miles**;

ii this gave a boost to the development of the **iron, steel and coal industries**;

iii **a textile industry** had also been started–centred on two or three industrial centres.

6 **Foreigners** played an important part:

i **British textile firms** supplied the machinery for the Russian textile industry–and the skilled workpeople needed to run it;

ii **John Hughes** from South Wales formed the New Russian Company to build factories in the **Donetz Basin**;

iii **Siemens of Prussia** built the Russian telegraphic system and had factories in St. Petersburg;

iv **the Nobel brothers** of Sweden began the Russian oil industry and in the 1880s built the first Russian oil tankers.

7 **France**, now Russia's ally, provided a good deal of the money needed to pay for the machinery and raw material which Russia had to import (8.11.6).

3.15 Paying for the industrialization

1 The Russians had to pay **interest on money borrowed** from France and other foreign lenders. They also had to **repay the money** borrowed over a period of years.

2 Russia **earned the money** for those payments by exporting wheat.

3 To get this wheat the government **increased taxes paid by peasants**–and got the money in the form of grain.

4 The peasants were left **even poorer** than before.

5 **Industrial workers**, too, suffered from this export of wheat. **Prices** were kept high because there was never enough grain available. Sometimes there were **famines**–but exports had to be maintained if possible. The shortage of food and the high prices added to the burdens of **industrial workers** who already suffered because of **poor housing, poor working conditions** and **low pay**–and from not being allowed to have **trade unions**.

6 But there was another price to be paid:

i the number of **town workers increased**–and they were less under Church control than were the peasants;

ii Holy Russia became **'diluted' with westernization**. Foreign industrialists taught people the benefit of working (selfishly) **for a profit**, showed that **science** was essential (and so attacked Pobedonostev's ideas).

3.16 Sergei de Witte

1 De Witte, **Minister of Finance 1892–1903**, was responsible for the attempt to industrialize Russia at that time.

2 **Foreigners** played major roles in this industrialization. It was fitting that the Minister should be a foreigner, of **Dutch ancestry**.

3 **Agriculture** was Russia's main industry. De Witte thought that to be strong Russia had to develop industrially.

4 In **1892** he obtained foreign loans for the building of the **Trans-Siberian railway**–completed in **1902**.

5 By **1900 coal** production had reached **15 million tons** (compared with over **200 million tons in Britain**).

6 Cotton production in Central Asia allowed the textile industry to grow in Poland and the Moscow region.

7 Wool, iron and **steel** and other industries grew. Between **1885 and 1900** the output of industry multiplied by three and the **number of industrial workers** reached **three million**.

8 Tariffs on imports of goods which Russian factories could produce helped the development of new industries.

9 Government income had to be increased to get the money to pay for the foreign loans (see Unit 3.15). De Witte managed this in various ways. One was to give the government the sole right (or **monopoly**) of selling **alcoholic drink**. This gave the government an interest in increasing sales of such drink (which provided one quarter of government revenue). This tended to increase the amount of drunkenness.

3.17 The development of the revolutionary spirit (*3.10*)

1 The Social Revolutionary Party (SRP) was founded in **1901** out of earlier attempts to **rouse the peasants** (3.10.3 and 3.10.4):

i **the peasants' standard of living** fell as a result of industrialization. They had to pay most of the taxes;

ii one sign of **their poverty** was the high death rate, the result of poor living conditions and poor diet;

iii in **1882** a **Peasants' Land Bank** was set up to help peasants to buy land. But **interest rates** were very high while payment of the instalments for land grants made after 1861 (3.4.3) left little money for new purchases;

iv the **SRP** hoped to incite the peasants to a violent revolution. To encourage them the SRP carried out **terrorist acts** against Land Captains (3.13.3) and other government officials.

2 Alexander III was often attacked. In **1887** a plan to assassinate the Tsar failed, and the plotters were arrested and tried. One was **Alexander Ulyanov**. His execution caused his younger brother, **Vladimir**, to become a revolutionary, better known as **Lenin**.

3 The Liberals (known from the Russian initials for their **Constitutional Democratic** party as the **Cadets**), hoped to persuade the Tsar to give Russia a **British-style parliamentary government**. They drew most of their support from the zemstvos (3.6).

4 The Social Democratic Labour Party (SDLP) was formed in **1898**:

i it had its main support among the **industrial workers**;

ii its policies were **Marxist** (see 1.22);

iii **it did not believe that terrorism could succeed**.

3.18 The creation of the Bolshevik Party.

1 The SDLP was often attacked by the secret police.

2 Lenin's carreer is typical of most leaders of the SDLP:

i in **1895** he was arrested;

ii in **1897** he was again imprisoned;

iii he was **exiled to Siberia** from **1897 to 1900** and then forced to live abroad.

3 Lenin and his fellow-exiles published a newspaper, **Iskra** (*The Spark*) which they smuggled into Russia.

4 In **1903** the committee producing **Iskra** had meetings in Brussels and, after being driven from Belgium, in London.

5 During these meetings they argued over the question 'What should a revolutionary party be like?'

6 Some, led by **Trotsky**, wanted the SDLP to become a **mass party** like the SRP.

7 Others, led by **Lenin**, wanted the SDLP to be a **small party**. Every member ought to be a **dedicated revolutionary** who understood fully what the Marxist revolution would be about.

8 The argument ended with a vote:

i the majority (**Bolsheviks** in Russian) agreed with **Lenin**;

ii the minority (**Mensheviks** in Russian) agreed with **Trotsky**.

3.19 Nicholas II (1894–1917)

1 In 1894 Alexander III died–a natural death.

2 Nicholas II said that he would follow the 'principle of **autocracy*** as firmly and unswervingly as my late father.' There would be no Russian parliament.

3 Personally, Nicholas was a kind man and a good father–but had no idea of the problems facing Russia.

4 Alexandra, his wife, was a **German princess**, a reminder of the influence of foreigners on Russian history. She had no sympathy with reform. She had a **great influence** over Nicholas II.

3.20 V.K. Plehve

1 Plehve became **Minister of the Interior** in 1902, when his predecessor was assassinated.

2 He was in charge of the domestic government.

3 His policies were like those of **Pobedonostev** (3.13):

i he organized **anti-Jewish demonstrations** and pogroms*;

ii he pressed on with the **Russianization** of such regions as Finland, Armenia, Poland and the Baltic Provinces.

4 But **his policies were different** in some ways:

i he was frightened at the success of the **SDLP** in winning support among the industrial workers;

ii **government spies** were sent to work in factories. They tried to persuade men to strike–so that possible leaders of industrial workers could be picked out and arrested.

5 He believed in the idea of a **Holy Russia** of peasant people loyal to the Tsar and the Church. This **opposed de Witte's policies**. In 1903 **Plehve** persuaded Nicholas to **sack de Witte**.

6 But the **discontent continued**–with terrorist attacks, workers' strikes and peasant riots.

7 It was **Plehve** who persuaded the Tsar to have **'a short, victorious war' against Japan**. This would win support for the Tsar and help to put an end to the unrest in Russia.

3.21 The Russo-Japanese War, 1904-05

1 The course of the War will be examined in Unit 6.8.

2 Here you have to note the following:

i it began on February 4 1904 and lasted until the signing of the Treaty of Portsmouth, (USA), September, 1905;

ii poor leadership led to **heavy defeats** on land and at sea;

iii **heavy casualties** affected many Russian families;

iv the transport system was unable to cope with the demands to carry military supplies as well as peacetime goods. There was a **shortage of food** in industrial towns.

3.22 Unrest in Russia, 1904–05

1 In **1904 Plehve was assassinated** by Social Revolutionaries.

2 The **Union of the zemstvos** demanded **constitutional reforms**. They wanted free speech, fair trials, the abolition of the secret police, a Russian parliament.

3 The **SDLP** organized a series of **strikes** and demonstrations. They wanted an end to the war and to rule by the Tsar.

4 The **peasants** in various regions rioted. Land Captains and members of the nobility were killed.

3.23 Bloody Sunday, 22 January 1905 (*Fig. 3.23A*)

1 Father Gapon, a Russian priest, was a government spy sent to work among industrial workers.

2 The **SDLP** planned to hold a massive **anti-Tsarist demonstration** in the capital, St. Petersburg in January 1905.

3 To stop the SDLP getting the credit for a demonstration, Gapon and other **government agents planned their own**.

Fig. 3.23A Bloody Sunday, 1905

4 Industrial workers and their families gathered from all parts of the capital to march to the Tsar's Winter Palace.

5 They carried with them **their petitions**:
i they complained about low **wages**, poor **housing**, high **prices**, long **working hours**;
ii they asked for some sort of **Parliament**;
iii they said they were **loyal to the Tsar**.

6 Nicholas, fearing the demonstration, had gone to another palace at **Tsarkoseloe** some miles away.

7 The guards at the **Winter Palace**, frightened that the demonstrators might turn violent, **fired at the mob**.

8 **130** people were killed, over **3000** injured. The rest fled.

3.24 Deep unrest

1 Strikes took place in industrial towns.

2 Sailors on the battleship, *Potemkin,* **mutinied** in June 1905. No other ship in the Black Sea fleet tried to stop the mutineers on the *Potemkin* as they bombarded the port of **Odessa**.

3 In October 1905 a railway strike started in Moscow and became a **national railway strike**. Food did not get to industrial towns.

4 Trotsky created a number of workers' councils (or **soviets**) in factories in St. Petersburg and Moscow.

5 Non-industrial workers–teachers, lawyers and doctors– **supported the soviets** and the demand for the overthrow of the inefficient and cruel system of government.

3.25 The October Manifesto, 1905

1 De Witte who had opposed the declaration of war, was recalled as **Chief Minister (October 1905)** after the signing of the Treaty of Portsmouth which ended the war (3.21.2).

2 The Tsar issued a **Manifesto** in which he promised reforms:
i a Russian Parliament (or **Duma**) would be called;
ii he would make **no new laws** without the Duma's approval.

3 Many people were satisfied with this development.
i **The Liberals** (3.17.3) welcomed the constitutional development which they had been demanding for many years;
ii **many strikers** went back to work hoping that an elected **Duma** would pass the reforms they wanted.

4 The soviets led by the SDLP did not think that the Tsar's promises were enough.

5 Peasants in the countryside did not see how a **Duma** would help them; they continued to riot.

6 The Tsar got **his army** back from the Far East (December 1905) and felt more secure:
i the leaders of the **soviets** were arrested;

ii in **December 1905** Moscow workers began an **armed rising**. This was put down by the **armed forces**.

3.26 The Tsar's trickery

1 **The war** was over—even if it had been lost.
2 **The army** was back at home, its officers loyal to the Tsar.
3 **The Tsar's advisers** knew that the revolutionaries would not be satisfied by the promises of October 1905.
4 **The French** made fresh loans, April 1906.
5 **The Russian People's League** was a **right-wing** organization which carried out terrorist attacks on reformers of all kinds.
6 In **May 1906**, just before the first **Duma** was due to meet, Nicholas issued his **Fundamental Law of the Empire:**
i **autocracy**, God-given, could not be subject to a **Duma**;
ii **control of government spending** and of taxation would not be left to the elected **Duma**;
iii **the Duma** would have **only a very limited power** to introduce new laws.

3.27 Electing a Duma, 1906

1 There was a complicated **system of voting**:
i **most men** were allowed to vote in a **secret ballot**;
ii but **direct elections** only took place in the **large towns**;
iii **most representatives** were elected by an **indirect system** which had been designed to make sure that the **landowners** and the **non-socialist peasants** would get elected.

2 It was hoped that this would produce a **conservative Duma** loyal to the Tsar.

3.28 The first Duma, May 1906

1 The Liberals (or **Cadets**) won the majority of seats.
2 They demanded **full control** of government taxation.
3 They reminded the Tsar of the **October Manifesto** and the promise of constitutional government.

4 The Tsar's answer was to **dismiss the Duma** and call fresh elections. The leading Cadets fled to Viborg in Finland. They issued a Manifesto, inviting the voters not to pay taxes or serve in the army.

3.29 The second Duma, February–June 1907

1 **Peter Stolypin** became Prime Minister in succession to de Witte.
2 We will see more of his policies in 3.31.
3 A conservative, he wanted to 'carry through effective reforms but at the same time face revolution, resist it and stop it.'
4 **For the elections** to the Second **Duma** Stolypin:
i **refused to allow some candidates** to stand for election;
ii **imprisoned** known anti-Tsarist candidates;
iii took many voters' names **off the voting lists**;
iv threatened **Jews** with death if they dared vote.

5 In spite of all this the **second Duma** proved to be **more** radical than the first:
i moderate and constitutional **Liberals lost seats**;
ii the revolutionary-minded **SDLP won 65 seats**.

6 **Stolypin** asked the Duma to condemn **terrorism**. It refused.
7 **The Tsar** demanded the arrest of the SDLP members on the ground of **treason**. The **Duma** refused to agree.
8 **This Duma**, like the first, was **dismissed**.

3.30 Later Dumas, 1907–14

1 **The electoral laws** were further changed in **1907**:
i **Social Democrats could not stand** as candidates;
ii possible **trouble-makers** were arrested and imprisoned.
2 The third and fourth **Dumas** (1907–14) were 'loyal' to the ideas of the Tsar and Stolypin.

3.31 Stolypin's reforms

1 Revolutionaries remembered Stolypin's **repression**:
i after the failure of the 1905 'revolution' some **1500 people** were executed. Stolypin's answer was that 4000 officers had been assassinated or injured by terrorists;
ii **Russianization** was pushed through in Finland and other regions;
iii **the Jews** were harshly treated;
iv **elections** were 'fixed' and the **Dumas** made 'harmless'.
2 **Many peasants remembered only his reforms**:
i **the mir** was abolished (3.4.4);
ii **peasants could now own** or rent their own land without any interference from the commune;
iii **Peasant Banks** helped peasants to buy their own land;
iv many did so. These richer peasants (or **kulaks**) were the more go-ahead. They made their land **profitable;**
v one result of this was that there was **enough food** for the town workers and for the export trade;
vi another result was that the **kulaks** became much **more loyal** to the Tsar—and opposed to the revolutionaries.

3.32 Too little, too late?

1 In spite of his reforms Stolypin was unpopular with many people. In **1911** he was **assassinated in a Kiev theatre** in the Tsar's presence.
2 By that time **Rasputin** had become a strong influence:
i he was a **monk** who had gained the reputation of being 'a holy man'—in spite of his wild style of life;
ii the Tsar's wife, **Alexandra**, was a religious woman who, after 1905, came **under Rasputin's influence**,
iii in 1907 the Tsar's son. **Alexis**, seemed to be dying from haemophilia. Rasputin prayed over him and the boy lived. This confirmed the monk's reputation with the Tsar and his wife;
iv by **1912** there were many **sordid stories** of the way Rasputin lived with many ladies of the Tsar's court.
3 These stories lessened the loyalty towards the Tsar.
4 But in **July 1914**, when Russia went to war against Austria–Hungary, the **Tsar seemed secure on his throne**:
i **industry** was growing; the influence of the **SDLP** failing;
ii the **countryside was at peace**. More **kulaks** enjoyed the ownership of their land, the influence of the **SRP** was failing.
5 It was the **First World War** which was to show how slender was the hold which the Tsar had over his people.

3.33 Russian foreign policy, 1870–1914

1 The Balkans 1875–78 (or the Eastern Question) (see Unit 4. 5–4.10).
2 The Russo-Japanese War, 1904–05 (see Unit 6.8).
3 The Franco-Russian Alliance, 1892–95 (see Unit 8.11).
4 The outbreak of the First World War (see Unit 8.21).

4 The Eastern Question, 1870–1914

4.1 What was the Question about?

Today we might think that the Eastern Question must have been concerned with Asia. However, Asia did not play a major role in world affairs until the end of the nineteenth century (Unit 6). The Eastern Question was about the Turkish Empire.

4.2 How many parts were there in the Question?

There were **three main parts** in the Question.

1 Turkey had, in past times, conquered large parts of South Eastern Europe. By the early part of the nineteenth century it was clear that the Turks were **no longer able to control that large Empire**. There were **many rebellions** and, in Greece, a successful independence movement. (Fig. 4.4A). **So** one part of the Question was, **'Can Turkey survive?'**

2 Greece was the **first of the Christian states** to break away from rule by the Muslim Turks. During the nineteenth century **other Christian peoples** tried to follow that example. The Turkish Empire was crumbling. **The second part of the Eastern Question** was: **'What will happen to that Empire?'**

3 The European Powers each had their own interests in the affairs of Turkey (4.3). So the **third part** of that Question was: **'What would the Powers do as Turkey crumbled?'**

4.3 The interests of the Great Powers

1 Russia was the **largest of the Slav nations. Many Slav peoples** lived inside the Turkish Empire–Serbs and Slovaks in particular. These, and the Bulgars, Rumanians and Albanians, also had a **religious link** with Russia. They were all members of the **Orthodox Church**. So Russia made herself the champion of the Slavs (and developed the **Pan-Slav** movement for that purpose):

 i **if they rebelled** against Turkey, **Russia would help** them gain their independence;

 ii she hoped that **they would be grateful** and allow her to influence their trade and foreign policies;

 iii Russia wanted **an outlet to the Mediterranean Sea**. To achieve this she could do one of two things:

(a) she could help one of the Christian peoples to gain control of **the Aegean Sea coast** where **Salonika** could become the Russian-dominated outlet for Russia's trade;

(b) she could capture **Constantinople**, (Fig. 4.4A) gain control of the **Dardanelles** and develop her **Black Sea ports**.

2 Britain saw Russia as a threat to:

 i **British India**. Russian expansion in Central Asia brought Russia to the borders of Afghanistan–and India;

 ii **British interests in Persia and the Middle East**. Britain did a great deal of trade with the countries of the Middle East. If Russia expanded she would threaten that trade;

 iii **the Suez Canal** had been opened in 1869 (2.17). This 'life line of the Empire' allowed British ships to get quickly to Australia, New Zealand, India, Malaya and Hong Kong. If Russia got her outlet on to the Mediterranean she might threaten this Canal and British trade.

So **Britain's policy** in the Eastern Question was:

 i **to maintain Turkey** as a buffer against Russia;

 ii **to oppose** the creation of a number of **small, independent states**, which would become Russian satellites*;

 iii **to oppose Russian policy** all the time.

3 Austria only became closely involved in the Eastern Question **after 1870**. By then she had **lost her power** in:

 i **Italy** (1.10.2);

 ii **the German Confederation** (1.11).

In Fig 4.3A you will see that the **Austro-Hungarian Empire** included a number of **Slavonic peoples**–Serbs, Croats and Slovenes (the Southern Slavs) as well as the Şlovaks (or Northern Slavs). The Emperor of Austria-Hungary, **Franz Joseph**, and his ministers, decided to try to **extend Austria's power** in a south-easterly direction (see arrow on Fig, 4.3A). This would achieve two objects: It would:

Territory lost by Turkey as a result of the Balkan War of 1913

Dates refer to the year in which independence was gained from Turkey

Fig. 4.4A The Balkans, 1878–1914

i **make up for the losses** in Italy and Germany;

ii **stop** the creation of a Russian-backed Slav nation in **Serbia** which would attract the support of Slavs living inside the Austro-Hungarian Empire. If they succeeded in freeing themselves, Austria would be even less powerful.

4.4 The interests of the Christian subjects of Turkey

1 In Fig. 4.4A you can see that part of **modern Greece** became independent of Turkish rule in **1830**.

2 **Turkish government in the nineteenth century**:

i it was **corrupt**. Its ministers thought only of making money for themselves. Higher taxes paid by the Christian peoples brought no benefit to those peoples;

ii it was **inefficient**. The Turkish rulers became lazier and put Christians into positions of authority.

iii it was **cruel**. This was shown by the frequent massacres of Christian peoples.

3 **Backed by Russia** the peoples of the Turkish Empire began to develop ideas of **self-government**.

4.5 The crisis of 1875–77

1 **1875** The peoples of **Bosnia** and **Herzegovina** rebelled because of:

i ill-treatment of Christians;

ii increasing taxation.

2 **1876 Serbs, Montenegrins** and **Bulgarians** joined in.

3 **The Turks' answer** to the rebellion was **even greater cruelty**. Men, women and children were driven into local churches where they were burned alive. The news of these **Bulgarian atrocities** attracted widespread attention:

i **Gladstone**, leader of the Liberal Opposition, wanted Britain to drive the Turks, **'bag and baggage'** out of Europe;

ii **Austria** saw a chance to take **Bosnia** and **Herzegovina**;

iii **Disraeli**, the British Prime Minister, **feared** a breakup of Turkey and a **Russian advance**;

iv **Russia** claimed that she had to go **to the help of the Christians** suffering under Turkish misrule;

v **Bismarck** said that he had **no interest** in Turkish affairs–he had enough to cope with in Germany (1.14–1.24).

4.6 The Russo-Turkish War, 1877–78

1 **Russia** was the **only Power** which helped the Christians.

2 **Austria-Hungary** remained neutral.

3 **May 1877 Russian troops** crossed the River Danube (Fig. 4.4A).

4 **July 1877** they reached **Plevna** where the Turks held out until December 1877.

5 **The fall of Plevna** allowed the Russians and Bulgarians to sweep on towards **Constantinople** (Fig. 4.4A).

6 **Britain** sent a naval force to the Dardanelles and threatened to declare war on Russia if she continued her advance.

7 **January 1878**, the Turks signed an **armistice** to end the war.

4.7 The Treaty of San Stefano, 1878

1 **Turkey lost** most of her European Empire. **She kept** only outlying areas of **Bosnia, Herzegovina, Albania** and the region of **Thrace** guarding the **roads to Constantinople**.

2 **Bulgaria** became independent. She was given territory which stretched from the **Danube to the Aegean Sea**. This gave her the long coastline and the port of **Salonika**.

3 **Romania, Serbia** and **Montenegro** were given their **independence**. This pleased the Slav peoples. **Serbia**, who thought of herself as the leading Slav nation in the region, **hoped** that she might one day **get Bosnia and Herzegovina**.

4 **Russia** took **Kars** and **Batum** as well as part of **Bessarabia**.

5 **Romania**, which lost part of Bessarabia to Russia, was given the **Dobruja** as compensation.

4.8 The other Powers and the Treaty

1 **Britain threatened to make war on Russia** if this Treaty remained in force. She was **alarmed** at:

i **the break up of Turkey**–the buffer to Russian advance (4.3.2);

ii the creation of **Bulgaria** with its long coast line. Britain believed that through this satellite Russia would threaten **British interests in the Mediterranean** (4.3.2).

2 **Austria-Hungary was alarmed** by Russia's advance and by the growth of **Serb nationalism**. She saw this as a threat to:

i her ambitions in **Bosnia** and **Herzegovina** (4.5.3 and Fig. 4.4A);

ii the safety of the Austro-Hungarian Empire. Serbia might encourage rebellion by Slavs inside that Empire.

3 **Bismarck of Germany feared a war** between **Russia** on one side and **Austria-Hungary, Britain and Turkey** on the other. He did not want to see his **Dreikaiserbund** break up (8.3).

4 So **Russia** gave way and **agreed** to hold an **international conference** to arrange the future of the Balkans.

4.9 The Congress of Berlin, 1878

Before the Congress met in June, the major Powers had made a number of **secret agreements**:

1 **Bulgaria** was divided into **three parts** (Fig. 4.4A):

i **a northern part**, independent under a Bulgarian prince;

ii **a central part**, Eastern Rumelia, under a Christian Governor-General–but **under the rule of the Sultan**;

iii **the southern part**, including Macedonia and the coast **line was given back to the Sultan**.

2 **Britain** gained **Cyprus**. This would be a naval base from which Britain would keep an eye on Russian progress.

3 **Russia** kept **Kars, Batum and part of Bessarabia**.

4 **Serbia, Montenegro**, and **Romania** retained their **independence**.

5 **Austria**, which had played no active part against Turkey was **allowed to administer Bosnia** and **Herzegovina**.

4.10 The diplomatic effects of the Congress of Berlin

1 **Bismarck**, chairman at the Congress, had **supported Austria's demands** to be allowed to occupy Bosnia and Herzegovina.

2 **Russia**, a member of Bismarck's Dreikaiserbund (8.3) was **angered by Bismarck's attitude**. This was to play a part in the future of international relations (8.11).

3 **Austria** was grateful for Bismarck's support. She agreed in **1879** to **a formal Alliance with Germany** (8.5).

4.11 The failure of the Congress settlement, 1878–1908

1 **The Sultan** promised the Congress that he would never again ill-treat his Christian subjects. In fact, **massacres** took place at regular intervals, the worst being the **Armenian Massacres** of **1895–96** when 30 000 were killed in Armenia and another 6000 in Constantinople.

2 **Bulgaria and Eastern Rumelia united in 1885**. The new and larger state did not turn out to be a Russian satellite.

3 **Serbia** and **Montenegro were angered** by Austria's control of Bosnia and Herzegovina. This led to **increasing friction**.

4.12 The revolt by the 'Young Turks', 1908

1 **Patriotic Turks** were angered by the break-up of the Empire.

2 They wanted a **democratic country** run on Western lines.

3 **Army officers** led a successful revolt in **1908**.

4 They forced the Sultan, **Abdul Hamid** ('Abdul the damned') to promise to bring in a system of parliamentary democracy.

5 In **1909** he tried to go back on his promises. He was **deposed** by the revolutionaries.

6 The new government promised **Christians equal rights** with Muslims. This gained support for their revolution.

7 In fact they, like the deposed Sultan, did **not keep their promises**. This was to be a cause of trouble in 1912 (4.14).

4.13 The European Powers and the revolt of 1908

1 Many liberals in Western Europe welcomed the news of the revolution and the coming of 'democracy' to Turkey.

2 Austria's foreign minister, **Aehrenthal**, persuaded the Russian foreign minister, **Isvolsky**, to agree that Austria could annex **Bosnia** and **Herzegovina**. This made these Slav provinces a part of the Austro-Hungarian Empire.

3 Russia agreed to do this because Austria promised to agree to persuade the other Powers to allow Russia to have the right to send her ships through the **Dardanelles** (see Fig. 4.4A).

4 Austria cheated. Having annexed the two Provinces she did not keep her promise to Russia.

5 Russia was angered by this. But, as we shall see in Unit 6.8 she was in no fit state to go to war about it.

6 Serbia was angry. The annexation seemed to mean the end of the Serbian dream of a large Slavonic kingdom. But without Russia's help Serbia could do nothing.

4.14 The Balkan League, 1912

1 Turkey had a counter revolution (**1912**), the democratic system was overthrown and the **old repressive system** brought back.

2 Venizelos, a Greek statesman, realized that the Christians in Turkey would suffer even more harshly than ever.

3 He persuaded Serbia, Montenegro and Bulgaria to join Greece in the **Balkan League**. He hoped that they would persuade the Turks to deal fairly with their Christian subjects.

4.15 The First Balkan League War, 1912–13

1 Italy took advantage of the unrest preceding the revolution to seize **Tripoli**, the last remaining part of the Turkish Empire in North Africa (Fig. 5.1A).

2 War was declared by the Italians in **September 1911**.

3 In 1912 the **Balkan League** declared war on Turkey.

4 Austria and **Germany** thought that Turkey would win.

5 In **six weeks** the forces of the League overran **European Turkey** except for Eastern Thrace around Constantinople.

6 This success alarmed the major Powers:

i **Russia feared** that **Bulgaria** would seize **Constantinople**;

ii **Austria feared** that **Serbia** might gain an outlet on to the Adriatic by taking the region now known as **Albania** (Fig. 4.4A).

7 The major Powers forced the League and Turkey to end the fighting and come to a **Conference** to settle affairs.

4.16 The Treaty of London, 1913

1 Turkey was allowed to retain only **Eastern Thrace**.

2 The League's members then tried to agree on a **division of the rest of the region**.

3 They could not agree, particularly over the division of Macedonia–and **went to war with each other**.

4.17 The Second Balkan League War, 1913

1 Bulgaria claimed that she had supplied most of the army in 1912. She wanted the **largest share of Macedonia**.

2 Bulgaria attacked Serbia when she occupied part of Macedonia.

3 Serbia was joined by **Romania** (which had not fought in the first war of 1912–13), **Montenegro, Greece and Turkey** which saw a chance to get back some of her former territory.

4 Bulgaria was easily defeated and forced to agree to a Treaty.

4.18 The Treaty of Bucharest, August 1913

1 Turkey made small gains, including the city of **Adrianople**.

2 Serbia and Greece kept those parts of Macedonia gained by the Treaty of London.

3 Austria insisted on **Albania** having the Adriatic coast between Greece and Montenegro. This kept **Serbia land-locked**.

4 Romania gained territory on the Black Sea, from Bulgaria.

4.19 The effects of the Balkan League Wars

1 Serbia became a **larger** country. This **alarmed Austria** which was concerned about the effect of this expansion on the 7 million Serbs, Croats and Slovenes living in her Empire.

2 Austria had prevented Serbia gaining the port she wanted on the Adriatic. This **angered Serbia**.

3 Like Serbia, **Austria wanted ports**. She had her eye on **Salonika** which with other parts of Macedonia went to Greece in 1913 (see Fig. 4.4A). This ensured that Austria maintained her ambition to expand to the south–even if it meant war.

4 In 1913 **the Kaiser** told **Austria** that he would support her if she went to war with Serbia. So too, would **Turkey**–anxious to get revenge for earlier defeats, which left her much reduced in size.

5 The Serbs, on the other hand, allowed **terrorist gangs**, such as the **Black Hand**, to train on Serb soil before undertaking terrorist activities inside the Austro-Hungarian Empire.

6 Russia declared that, in the event of a war between Austria and Serbia she would **support Serbia**. So too, presumably, would Russia's ally, France (8.11.9).

4.20 Sarajevo, 28 June 1914

1 The heir to the Austrian throne, the **Archduke Francis (Franz) Ferdinand, supported Slav claims** to greater control by Slavs of their own affairs–but inside the Empire.

2 June 1914 He and his wife made a tour of **Bosnia** and **Herzegovina**.

4 On **28 June** they were in the Bosnian capital, **Sarajevo**.

5 They were **assassinated** by a Bosnian student–**Gavrilo Princip**.

6 Princip, a member of the **Black Hand**, had links with Serbia.

7 Austria used this assassination as an excuse for **declaring war on Serbia**. We will study this in more detail in Unit 8.22.

5 Africa, 1879–1914

5.1 The 'Dark' Continent

1 In the **15th and 16th centuries** Portuguese and Spanish sailors had found a route around the Cape of Good Hope to the Far East.

2 In the **18th century** the British, Spanish and Portuguese had set up trading settlements along the African coast (Fig. 5.1A).

3 For **Britain** in particular Africa was a **valuable trading area**. **Slaves** were collected in ports in **West Africa**, taken to the **Spanish colonies** in South America and to the **British colonies** in southern North America and sold at great profit.

Fig. 5.1A   European possession in Africa, 1875

4 When the **slave trade was abolished (1807)** European powers maintained **trading links** with the coastal regions.
5 But until **1850** little was known about the **African interior**.

5.2 Difficulties facing the development of the interior

Even after explorers had found out more about Africa there were many problems.
1 **The climate** was hostile.
2 **Diseases** such as malaria and sleeping sickness killed many people and animals.
3 Africa's **physical features** presented many obstacles:
 i the north was mainly a **desert**, difficult to cross;
 ii south of the desert was an **almost inpenetrable forest**;
 iii the coast provided few good harbours;
 iv the rivers were obstructed by rapids and waterfalls. Many of these were near the coast and blocked attempts to explore.
4 The native **people were hostile**. This is hardly surprising, given the European record as **slave-traders**.
5 **Transport** was a major problem:
 i many **rivers** were not navigable—or only with difficulty;
 ii camels were needed in the northern desert;
 iii horses were killed by disease-carrying tsetse flies.
The development of the **railway** and, later, the **steamship** were major aids in the work of opening up Africa.

5.3 The work of the explorers

1 **From around 1790 to about 1870** a number of explorers, mainly British, undertook voyages of exploration into Africa.
2 Many of the explorers were helped by the **Royal Geographical Society of Great Britain**. Its members wanted to know more about the geography of the vast land mass of Africa.
3 Because of their work Africa became better known:
 i they wrote **books** and **pamphlets** about their voyages;
 ii they **lectured** to large audiences;

iii they **interested other peoples** in the possibilities that existed in Africa. In particular they gained the attention of **Christian missionaries** and, later, of European traders.
4 But the **explorers** did not go out to Africa to help develop trade. They were **interested only in gaining knowledge**.

5.4 The work of the missionaries

1 Christians in many European countries believed they had a duty to bring **Christianity to the African people**.
2 **Catholics** founded **religious orders** for this work.
3 **Protestants** in Britain founded the **London Missionary Society**.
4 In **1840 David Livingstone** was sent by the London Missionary Society to Africa. His work turned out to be **part exploration** and **part religious**:
 i in the **Cape Province (5.20)** he **quarrelled with the Dutch** because of their ill-treatment of black people;
 ii **Livingstone**, like other Europeans, thought that **white civilization was superior to black**. Europeans had the duty to give the black people the blessings of Christianity, better social conditions and increased trade;
 iii in **1841** Livingstone went to work in the interior—in **Bechuanaland**;
 iv in **1849** he crossed the vast **Kalahari desert**. On this journey he discovered **Lake Ngami**—which has since dried up;
 v in **1851** he discovered the **River Zambezi** along which he **explored to the west (1853–54)** until he reached **Luanda**. This journey proved that the **Zambesi's rapids and gorges** would be **major obstacles** to its use as a trading route;
 vi in **1855** he followed the **Zambesi to the east**. He discovered the falls which he named **Victoria Falls**. He reached the coast at **Mozambique**, the first person to **cross the continent**;
 vii in **1856–57** he lectured throughout Britain. This led to the formation of the **Royal Niger Company (5.7.6)**;
 viii in **1858** as **British consul** for the east coast of Africa he was instructed to **explore east and central Africa**;

ix on his voyage he had the use of a **steamboat** which made travel easier–but still had to face the problems of rapids, waterfalls and gorges. In **1859** he discovered **Lake Nyasa**;

x during these various journeys he was frequently attacked by Portuguese slave-traders. Only in **1873**, the year of Livingstone's death, was the **slave market on the island** of **Zanzibar finally closed**;

xi in **1865** he journeyed to find the **source of the Nile**. Travelling from Portuguese East Africa, he went through the region we now call **Zambia**;

xii for six years he lost contact with the outside world–a reminder of the problems of working in Africa;

xiii during that time he **discovered more lakes**, explored **Lake Tanganyika** and **mapped thousands of square miles**;

xiv **H.M. Stanley**, a Welsh-born reporter, was sent to look for Livingstone. In **1871** he met up with him at a camp near **Lake Tanganyika**. Stanley left after four months but Livingstone stayed behind and died in May 1873.

5.5 The work of the traders before 1870

1 European traders had long been active in the **coastal regions**.

2 With the ending of the **slave trade** some tried to develop trade with African peoples living **further inland**.

3 The difficulties they faced are outlined in 5.2.

4 The world-wide fall in **agricultural prices around 1870** led to a fall in the incomes of many traders and firms. This, too, led to an attempt to develop trade with the interior. It was hoped that this might lead to:

i **new sources** of different **raw materials**;

ii **new untapped markets** for the sale of European goods.

5.6 Governments and Africa before 1870

1 European governments played little part in the development of African trade before 1870.

2 Most statesmen agreed with Disraeli, **'Colonies are a millstone around our necks'**. The reasons for this view were:

i **the expense** involved in gaining colonies, **wars** with local people and/or with some rival European country;

ii this had happened in **India, Canada** and the **West Indies**;

iii the British also had the **American experience** to look back on. They helped to found 13 separate colonies on the eastern seaboard of America. They had spent money to defend those colonies from the American Indians and the French. Then in

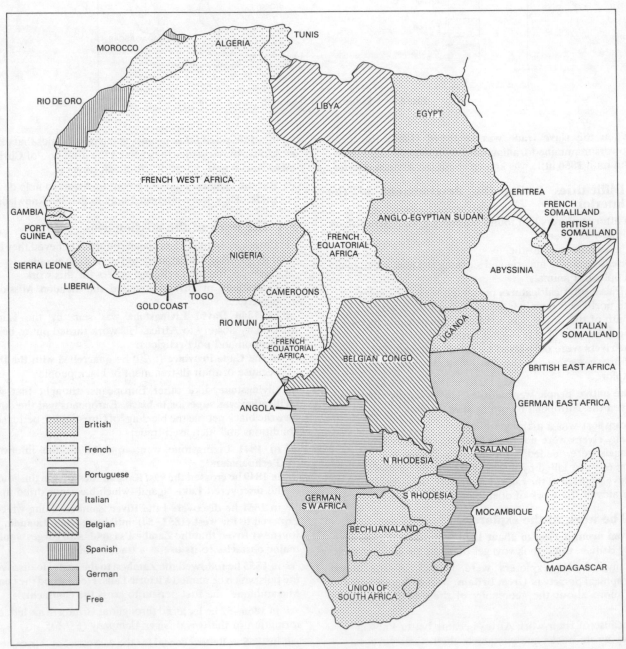

Fig. 5.7A Africa, 1914

the 1770s the colonists had rebelled, won their War of Independence and left the British with nothing save a larger National Debt.

5.7 Governments and Chartered Companies

1 In 5.8–5.10 we will examine the so-called 'Scramble for Africa' which took place in the 1880s and 1890s. In this 'Scramble' almost all Africa was divided out amongst the European powers (Fig. 5.7A).

2 This development was carried out by **trading companies** which governments encouraged **to develop certain territories**.

3 If a territory (e.g. Nigeria) was to be **developed** so that trade could increase, someone had to spend (or **invest**) a large amount of money. This was required for:
 i **building harbours and railways;**
 ii **establishing trading posts;**
 iii **clearing forests** for agricultural development.

4 **Firms** were willing to do this only if they thought they had a good chance of making a **profit**.

5 To help to **guarantee a profit**, governments gave companies the sole right (or **monopoly**) of trade in an area.

6 **Examples** of such companies were:
 i the **Royal Niger Company** (formed **1884**) which advanced British trading interests in what is now called **Nigeria**;
 ii the **British East Africa Company** (formed **1887**) which developed the area now known as **Uganda**;
 iii the **British South Africa Company** formed by Cecil Rhodes in **1889** for the development of the region north of the Cape–now known as **Botswana** and **Zimbabwe**.

7 Having got the government's approval (or Charter) these **companies sent out traders** to develop the area named in their Charter. These would make **agreements with local chiefs**:
 i often the chiefs gave the **whole of an area** (e.g. Nigeria) to the Company in return **for a rent fixed by the Company**;
 ii companies got the **sole right to mine** wherever they wished;
 iii chiefs agreed **not to allow anyone else** to trade or mine in their territory.

8 **The governments** of the European countries **helped** by:
 i founding **schools of tropical medicine**–to discover ways of preventing tropical diseases from spreading;
 ii **agricultural development** in the universities of home countries–where **scientists** developed **new strains of seeds** or **new breeds of animals** better fitted for the tropics;
 iii **trading policies** (including tariffs) meant to help the country's own Companies.

9 There were **frequent clashes** between workers of a Company and
 i **Europeans** working for a rival Company. French and British traders in **Nigeria** often clashed as did German traders in **German East Africa** with British traders in **Uganda**;
 ii **native chiefs and tribes** who resented the way in which the Europeans 'stole' their land. (See 5.25–26 for the effect of Europeanization on the African.)

10 **Companies** provided **private armies** to guard their officials. They also called on **governments to send armies** to defend the territory granted to them in their Charters. There were **frequent wars** with **Ashanti**, **Matabele** and **Zulus** (5.20).

11 Sometimes it appeared likely that a particular Company was going to have to give up trading because its management was not able to make the region profitable. Then **governments stepped in** to declare the region a **colony**. The British government acquired colonies in this way in:
 i **Nigeria**, 'bought' from the Company in **1899–1900**;
 ii **Uganda**, handed over by the Company in **1893**;
 iii **Kenya** which only became a separate colony in **1920**.

12 It is important to note that **the flag followed trade**.

5.8 The 'Scramble for Africa' in the 1880s and 1890s

1 In **1875** European powers held **small coastal strips** (Fig. 5.1A).

2 By **1914 the whole continent** had been colonized. Only Abyssinia in the east and Liberia in the west were independent.

3 This was achieved without a European war.

4 **Colonial rivalry,** the jealousy of one country for another, was one of the causes of war in 1914 (Unit 8.15.1).

5.9 Reasons for the 'Scramble'

1 It was possible, after 1875, because:
 i **transport** became easier with the development of the steamship (for river travel) and the railway;
 ii **knowledge** of the interior was increased by the work of explorers, missionaries and earlier traders.

2 **The decline of Turkey** (4.2) made it easier for Europeans to seize colonies in North Africa.

3 **Naval strategy** explained the seizure of certain coastal regions. **Britain**, for example, extended its control over **southern Africa, Egypt** and **Aden** to safeguard trade routes through the Suez Canal and the Indian Ocean.

4 **The balance of power** helps to explain why, if one country made a gain in Africa, others felt they had to do so.

5 **National pride** in **France** needed some boost after the defeat of 1870–71 (1.11). This helps to explain French interest in gaining African territory (5.12).

6 **New nationhood** in **Italy** and **Germany** explained ambitions in these countries to gain colonies–in Africa and elsewhere.

7 **Economic forces** were, however, the most important (see 5.10).

5.10 The economic reasons for the 'Scramble'

1 **Raw materials** obtained cheaply from an African colony, would boost profits and employment of a domestic industry.

2 **Markets** for some European goods could be created among the African peoples. This had been true before the abolition of the slave trade and of slavery. As the coastal regions became less profitable after these reforms, Europeans pushed further into the interior in search of new markets.

3 **Tariffs** by European countries and by the developing USA (7.9) made it **increasingly difficult** for countries to sell goods abroad. This forced them to look for new markets, or face industrial decline and rising unemployment.

4 **Money** Many rich people in Europe had become used to lending money to firms in their countries. As each country achieved a certain level of industrialization, there were **fewer chances of such lending**. This caused the potential lender (or **investor**) to look for new places in which to invest. **The French** lent money to help **Russian industrialization** (3.14.7).
Africa provided a good prospect to investors:
 i there were **mines**–for gold, diamonds, copper and other metals which could be profitably sold in the industrial world;
 ii there were other **raw materials**–palm oil, cocoa and coffee which could be grown at a profit;
 iii **profits** on an investment would be **higher in Africa** than in Europe because land and labour were cheap and plentiful.

5 **Marxists,** such as **Lenin**, and **economists**, such as the Englishman, **Hobson**, noted this drive for colonies as a desperate attempt by the **capitalist system** to keep going–it could no longer depend on the industrialization of the white man's world.

5.11 The Belgian Congo–the spur to joint action

1 **King Leopold** of the Belgians set up an African International Association in **1876**.

2 This was the **first example of government involvement** on a large scale.

3 He claimed the **Congo** region, explored and mapped by **Stanley** (5.4.4) who was financed by the Belgian king.

4 France (5.9.5) then acted by claiming control of the **Lower Congo** (5.9.5) and **Britain** claimed **Egypt** (5.16).

5 Bismarck realized that there was a danger of war between rival claimants to the same regions.

6 He called a **Colonial Conference** in Berlin, **1884–85**.

7 Representatives of all European powers drew boundary lines across the map of Africa and agreed on each other's claims. The boundaries made little sense. Villages were cut in half; tribes were divided between one country and another.

8 But the division was done **peacefully**.

5.12 French Africa

1 North Africa had already been colonized by France:

i the city of **Algiers** was occupied in 1830; **Algeria** was acquired in **1839**, although it was not developed until after 1870;

ii **Tunisia** was claimed and conquered in **1881**. The French argued that Tunisians were causing trouble on the border with Algeria; **Bismarck encouraged** this expansion because:

(a) it took French attention from **Alsace** and **Lorraine** (1.11);

(b) it brought **France into conflict with Italy** which also wanted to gain a North African Empire. This ensured that Italy would not side with France in the event of a Franco-German war.

iii **Morocco** was on Algeria's western border and France seized it to stop frontier incidents.

2 West Africa. The French had had trading posts on the mouths of the **River Senegal and Congo**. After **1880** explorers pushed inland:

i they pushed north to link up with Algeria–**crossing the huge Sahara desert to do so**;

ii they pushed **east across the Sudanese grasslands** south of the desert. This brought them into **conflict with Britain** (5.19).

3 East Africa. French missionaries and traders had developed **Madagascar** which the French claimed officially in **1885**. **Somaliland** was claimed in **1888**.

5.13 German Africa

1 Bismarck had not been interested in colonial gains.

2 A German African Society was set up in **1878** to interest people in African development. The **Colonial League** (1882) led the demand for a German overseas Empire.

3 Economic reasons (5.10) led Bismarck to agree with the imperialists who wanted a larger Empire.

4 South West Africa German traders settled north of the Orange River, northern frontier of the British Cape Province:

i when attacked by natives they asked Bismarck for help;

ii in **1884**, at the Colonial Conference, he obtained **all the region between the Orange River and Portuguese Angola**. Britain kept the naval base at Wallfish Bay in this region;

iii the British did not easily accept this German expansion in South West Africa. The British argued that this was the 'natural' region for expansion from the Cape. However in **1884 Britain needed German support over the Egyptian question** (see 5.16). In return she conceded South West Africa.

5 Togoland and **the Cameroons** were claimed by a German explorer in **1884**. British and German traders often clashed with each other but their governments took no part in such incidents.

6 East Africa In **1884** Germany claimed a large area of East Africa–today mainland **Tanzania**. To the north were the **British colonies of Uganda and Kenya**; to the south were British colonies in Northern Rhodesia (modern Zambia). **Clashes between the British and German governments** seemed likely because:

i **traders** from the two countries fought for trade;

ii **boundaries** between the various territories were not clear.

7 An Anglo-German agreement, 1890. The danger of a colonial war was averted by this agreement in which:

i **the boundaries** of German and British East Africa were agreed;

ii **Germany** granted **Britain control of Zanzibar**;

iii **Britain** returned the island of **Heligoland**, seized in the Napoleonic Wars. The Germans wanted it as a naval base.

5.14 Italian Africa

1 Italy, like Germany, was **a 'new' nation**, united by a series of wars and agreements between 1859 and 1870.

2 The Italians claimed colonies for **prestige reasons**.

3 Eritrea, a narrow strip of desert was occupied in **1882**.

4 Somaliland, another desert region, was seized in **1889**.

5 Abyssinia was attacked in **1896**. The Italians suffered a major defeat at **Adowa** and the attempted seizure was called off.

6 Tripoli was claimed in **1911** (4.15 and Fig. 5.1A).

5.15 British Africa

1 Zanzibar was acquired in **1890** (5.13.7).

2 The Zambezi was accepted as the boundary between **British** and **Portuguese East Africa** (Mozambique) in 1891.

3 Uganda and **Kenya** were acquired when the East Africa Company faced bankruptcy in **1892**.

4 Nigeria was acquired from the **Royal Niger Company in 1900**.

6 Egypt, the **Sudan** and **South Africa** deserve longer treatment.

5.16 The British and Egypt

1 The Suez Canal had been opened in 1869 (2.17). It was built and owned by a French Suez Canal Company.

2 The Khedive, or ruler of Egypt, owned almost half the shares in the Company. The Canal ran through his territory.

3 1875 the Khedive needed money to pay gambling debts.

4 Disraeli, British Prime Minister in 1875, borrowed **the £4 000 000** needed to buy the shares, from the bankers, the Rothschilds. (Parliament was not in session at the time. To have waited for Parliament to meet might have lost Britain the chance to gain these shares.)

5 After 1875 **Britain and France governed Egypt jointly**. Both countries appointed commissioners and other officials to ensure that Egypt remained peaceful, that the Canal ran properly and that the shareholders got their annual interest.

6 In **1881** there was a nationalist revolt led by a young officer, **Arabi Pasha**, who wanted to drive the foreigners from Egypt.

7 The French withdrew their officials.

8 Gladstone, British Prime Minister in 1881, sent in a naval force and an army led by **Sir Garnet Wolseley**.

9 The naval force bombarded **Alexandria (1881)**. The army defeated the rebels at the battle of **Tel-el-Kabir (1882)**.

10 The British then appointed **Sir Evelyn Baring** (later Lord Cromer) as **Consul-General**. It was Baring who transformed Egypt into a modern state by the time of his retirement in 1907.

5.17 Britain and the Sudan, 1881–85

1 The Sudan had been claimed by the Khedives of Egypt.

2 It was administered by **Egyptian officials** from Khartoum.

3 In **1882** Gladstone sent Baring and other officials to govern Egypt–but **refused to send any to the Sudan**.

4 In **1883** a religious fanatic, **the Mahdi**, led the Sudanese in **a nationalist revolt** against their Egyptian rulers.

5 Gladstone claimed that **this Egyptian affair** had nothing to do with Britain.

6 In **1884** public opinion forced him to send out a British force to bring **Egyptian officials back from the Sudan**.

7 General Gordon was given command of this force.

8 When he got to **Khartoum** he disobeyed orders. He decided to stay in the Sudan and **to defeat the Mahdi**.

9 The Sudanese rebels **besieged Gordon in Khartoum**.

10 **Gladstone** refused to send a relief expedition to help Gordon until, in **1885**, he again gave way to public opinion.

11 The expedition arrived at **Khartoum** two days after **Gordon** was killed when the Sudanese overran the capital.

5.19 Britain and the Sudan, 1896–98

1 **1896 General Kitchener** was sent to avenge Gordon and to reclaim the Sudan for British-controlled Egypt.

2 He built a **railway line up the Nile valley** along which his army approached Khartoum.

3 In **1898** at **Omdurman**, the Sudanese (or **Dervishes**) were mown down by the modern rifles and field guns.

4 **Sudan** came under **Anglo-Egyptian rule**.

5 Three days after the battle Kitchener heard that the French, under **Captain Marchand**, had reached **the Nile at Fashoda**.

6 This was part of the **French drive across the Sahara Grassland** (5.12.2).

7 **The Nile** was important to Egypt. The cotton crop depended on the waters from the Nile. Control of the river would lead to control of the Egyptian economy.

8 For several weeks the rival armies faced each other across the Nile. Newspapers in Britain and France became warlike.

9 In the end **the French agreed to withdraw**. **The Nile was recognized as a British interest**. In return the British recognized **French claims in parts of West Africa**.

10 The fact was that the French had retreated. This led to **ill-feeling in France** against Britain.

5.20 The British and South Africa up to 1879

1 **Dutch settlers** had colonized **the Cape of Good Hope**.

2 **The British** had seized this during **the Napoleonic Wars** and had retained it by peace treaties signed in **1815**.

3 In **1820** British settlers and missionaries arrived.

4 They disagreed with **Dutch treatment of blacks** (5.4.4).

5 After the **abolition of slavery (1833)** the Dutch (or Boer) settlers left the Cape. **On their Great Trek** they crossed the Orange River and founded **two new and independent republics–the Orange Free State** and **the Transvaal**.

6 **The British** extended their holding. In **1843** they occupied **Natal** and built a naval base at **Durban**.

7 In **1867** diamonds were discovered at **Kimberley** in the **Orange Free State**.

8 The British **seized** part of the Orange Free State, **Griqualand**.

9 Another part of the Orange Free State was seized in **1868** and named **Basutoland**.

10 In **1877** the Zulus, led by **Cetawayo**, attacked the Boers in the **Transvaal**. **Disraeli** sent a British army to defend them and announced that Britain had **'temporarily' annexed the Republics**.

11 **The British lost** the battle of **Isandhlwana but defeated the Zulus** at **Ulundi (1879)**.

12 This saved the **Boers** who **demanded an end to British occupation**.

5.21 The British and South Africa, 1879–1899

1 **Disraeli refused** to withdraw from the two Boer Republics.

2 In **1880 Transvaal** announced its independence.

3 **Gladstone**, British Prime Minister in 1880–85, called **a conference** to discuss the future of the Boer Republics.

4 **The Boers attacked** the British army before this conference had finished its work. This was the start of the **First Boer War**.

5 At **Majuba Hill** (1881) the Boers defeated the British.

6 Gladstone's announcements of **British withdrawal** and of British recognition of the independence of the Boer Republics was soon as a result of that defeat.

7 Because of the expansion of German South West Africa, the British declared that **Bechuanaland** was a British protectorate (1885). The Boers were caught in a British pincer movement.

8 In **1885** gold was discovered on **the Rand** in the **Transvaal**.

9 **Cecil Rhodes** founded the **British South Africa Company** (5.7.6).

10 Rhodes made an agreement with the **Matabele**. The Company gained control of the territory to the north of Bechuanaland and the Transvaal (now part of **Zimbabwe**).

11 As **Prime Minister of the Cape Colony**, Rhodes aimed at:
  i enlarging **British interests** in Africa;
  ii building **a Cape-to-Cairo railway** though British-held territory;
  iii an enlarged **British South Africa**.

12 **Paul Kruger** was the Boer **President of the Transvaal**.

13 He and his fellow-Boers did not play any part in the development of the gold and diamond holdings on the Rand.

14 This development was the work of non-Boers, known by the Boers as **'Uitlanders'** or 'Outsiders'.

15 **The Boers refused** these 'foreigners' any civil rights:
  i they could not **vote** in elections;
  ii they could not hold **official positions**;
  iii the **tax system** was organized to hurt the industrialists more than the Boer farmers.

16 **Chamberlain**, the British Colonial Secretary (1895–1903) **encouraged Rhodes** to plan for a British drive to the north.

17 **Rhodes** had appointed a **Dr. Starr Jameson** as administrator of Matabeleland (now part of **Zimbabwe**).

18 **Jameson and Rhodes plotted with the 'Uitlanders'** who were to rise in rebellion against Kruger; Jameson and Rhodes would attack the Republics.

19 At the last minute the **'Uitlanders'** called off their rising. Jameson's raid did take place.

20 The Boers praised Kruger when **the Jameson raid** ended with the capture of its leader and the defeat of his small force.

21 Rhodes was forced **to resign** as Prime Minister of the Cape.

22 **The German Kaiser** sent a **telegram** to congratulate Kruger.

5.22 The Second Boer War, 1899–1902

1 **The Uitlanders** sent a Petition to the British government. In this they outlined their **complaints** against the Kruger government and asked for British help.

2 **Chamberlain** sent an **army** to the Cape which Kruger saw as a threat. When the British refused to withdraw this army, the **Boers invaded the Cape**.

The War (1899–1902) falls almost naturally into three periods:
  i **October 1899–January 1900** The Boers had the larger forces and took the initiative. They besieged British forces in **Ladysmith** (Natal), **Kimberley** (the Cape) and **Mafeking** (Bechuanaland). In **December 1899** there was a **'Black Week'** when British attempts to relieve these towns failed;
  ii **February 1900–August 1900** Lord **Roberts** and Lord **Kitchener** led large armies which **relieved the besieged towns** and **captured Johannesburg** and **Pretoria** (the capital of the Transvaal).

3 **The guerilla war** Many people thought the Boers would now give in. However, they continued a guerilla war. **Kitchener** then enclosed large areas behind lines of barbed wire guarded by **fortified blockhouses**. Behind the wire he destroyed farms where Boers might have helped the guerillas. Women and children were herded into **concentration camps** where poor hygiene and bad administration caused the deaths of thousands.

5.23 Treaty of Vereeniging, 1902

The Boers were forced to ask for peace. This led to the signing of a Treaty. This said that:

1 **the Transvaal and the Orange Free State** were annexed by Britain;

2 **the Boers** were to get **self-rule** inside a **Federal Union**;

3 **£3 million** was to be paid to the Boers as compensation for the damage done to their farms.

The creation of **the Union of South Africa, 1910,** was welcomed by the Boer leaders, Smuts and Botha.

5.24 Africa and European crises

1 There were **clashes of interest** in various parts of Africa:

i **British and French** interests clashed in **West Africa** (5.7.9) and at **Fashoda** (5.19.8);

ii **British and German** interests clashed in **East Africa** (5.7.9) and in **South West Africa** (5.13.4).

2 However, only at **Fashoda in 1898** (5.19.8) did it seem that war might break out.

3 In Unit 8 we will study the development of international relations. We will see how the British and French became more friendly, settling their differences over Egypt. Britain recognized French interests in Morocco–but that led to a protest from Germany. In 1905 and 1911 there was fear that a major war might break out. But on this see Unit 8.16–17 and 8.20.

5.25 The beneficial impact of Europe on Africans

1 **Africans gained some benefits** from European involvement. Europeans waged war on **slave traders**. While some of these were European (mainly Portuguese) after 1833, the majority were **Arabs**. They took slaves from various parts of East Africa, used **Zanzibar** as a slave market until the Europeans closed it down in 1873 (5.4.x). The Portuguese and Arabs could not have got the slaves without the **co-operation of many African chiefs**.

2 **Education** for African children, by Christian missionaries before colonial governments accepted this responsibility, opened up employment opportunities for many Africans.

3 **Medical treatment** was largely provided at mission hospitals.

4 **Medical knowledge** of tropical diseases was increased by European study. This led to the development of cures for various diseases and for campaigns to wipe out the causes of others.

5 **Transport** by road, rail and steamship made travelling easier.

6 **Industrial development** of mines, plantations, local industries as well as **commercial development** of harbours, railways and office centres increased job opportunities for Africans.

7 An **African middle class** of prosperous, educated and town-dwelling Africans was created. This class led campaigns for the end of colonial rule after 1945 (see Units 36 and 37).

5.26 The unfortunate effects of Europe on Africa

1 Even Livingstone thought little of African civilization (5.4.4).

2 He and other Europeans helped **to destroy it**:

i their **religions** were condemned as 'pagan' and they were persuaded to become Christian, or **'Black Europeans'**. Being a Christian brought some benefits (education, job prospects); many Africans became 'mealie Christians'–converted in appearance only;

ii many **religious customs** were condemned without a full understanding of their importance to Africans. One of the main reasons for the later rebellion by the Kikuyu of Kenya was the tribal memory of the way in which Scottish missionaries had tried to wipe out female circumcision (36.7).

3 Attacks on their religion and customs left many **Africans with no firm roots**–in African tradition or in their new-found Europeanized Christianity.

4 Many tribes were driven from **tribal homelands** to allow for European economic development. Settlers took the best land, ignoring the effect this had on the native people.

5 Until the second half of the twentieth century their was little **African involvement in the government of the colonies**. This helps to explain some of the problems faced by Africans since the end of colonial rule (Units 36 and 37).

6 The Far East, 1870–1918

6.1 The condition of China, 1870

1 **Foreign traders and governments** had forced Chinese governments to allow Europeans to trade in China:

i **1793** the first attempt by the **British to trade in China**;

ii **1839–42** the Anglo-Chinese War, or the **Opium War**;
As a result of victory the **British forced China** to:
(a) hand over **Hong Kong** to the British (Fig. 17.11A);
(b) **open up five ports (Treaty Ports)** to foreign trade.

iii **1856 the Arrow War** involved a British-registered ship caught smuggling into China. The **British** government waged another war. **France** became involved because of the murder of a **French missionary**. The **Chinese were defeated** and forced to sign the **Treaty of Tientsin (1858)**;

iv **1858–60** the Chinese government was faced with **a revolution** by a religious-led movement known as the **Taiping Rebellion**. This threatened the government. At first it was **supported by foreign traders and governments** who hoped to get increased privileges as a result of the divisions in China.

v **1860** difficulties with **the Taipings made it impossible** for **the government to carry out the 1858 Treaty. Anglo-French** armies attacked the capital, **Peking**; burned the Summer Palace and forced the Emperor to sign the **Treaty of Peking (1860)**:
(a) **eleven more Treaty ports** were named;
(b) the British and French won **trading rights in the Yangtze Valley**.

iv **1860–64** the **British and French** armies now helped the Chinese government to **put down the Taiping Rebellion**.

2 **The Chinese government, 1870:**

i the **Emperor of China** ruled as an autocrat*;

ii the royal family were known as **the Manchus**. The Manchus (from Manchuria–Fig. 17.11A) invaded China in 1634, defeated the last Ming Emperor and imposed **'foreign' rule** on China;

iii the success of foreigners in the nineteenth century (6.1) showed the Chinese people that **their Manchu government was inefficient**. This was not entirely the fault of the government:
(a) **Chinese industry** was backward and could not produce modern weapons;
(b) **Chinese pride** was responsible for the contempt in which they held westerners ('red-haired devils' or 'barbarians'). Few Chinese thought they could learn from the despised West.

iv the Manchus were still blamed for the way in which western countries won concessions in China;

Fig. 6.3A The Russian octopus

v **the Chinese peasant:** there were many large towns in China where some industry and commerce was carried on. But the majority of the people were peasant-farmers. They had a very poor standard of living because:

(a) their **methods of production** were inefficient;

(b) **landlords** took most of the crops they produced;

(c) **government taxes** took some of what was left.

This inefficient and corrupt system came under increasing pressure during the nineteenth century as the **population grew**. One result of that pressure was a **number of famines** which swept through China killing millions.

6.2 The condition of Japan, 1870

1 **Catholic missionaries** had gone to Japan in the sixteenth and seventeenth centuries. By the middle of the seventeenth century **the Japanese had driven most of these foreigners out**.

2 Japan remained 'closed' to foreigners for two centuries.

3 In **1853** an American naval force, led by **Commodore Perry**, went to the harbour of **Yokohama**. Perry had a letter from the President of the USA asking for:

i **permission to trade** with Japan;

ii **safe harbours** for American ships in bad weather.

4 In **1854** the Japanese opened their country to foreign trade.

5 The **Meji leaders** of Japan then set about making their country **as westernized as possible**–so that they could stand up to the foreigners with their large ships, heavy guns and efficiency.

6 Industry:

i **Japanese** were sent to work in the industries of every country and to learn the reasons for western success;

ii **foreigners** were invited to help Japan. Industries, railways and shipyards were built with foreign help;

iii by **1900 Japan** no longer needed foreign help. She had already become a **major industrial power**.

7 The **Japanese army** was trained by German officers.

8 The **Japanese navy** was trained by British officers.

9 **Western-type schools** were set up, modelled on those of France and Germany.

10 Modern methods of **banking and business** were copied from the United States.

11 **A new constitution** was written (1868). Parliament, the Diet, was elected by the people. It only met for three months a year. **Power remained with the Emperor and his advisors.**

6.3 Russia and the Far East, 1856–90

1 A major factor in Russian foreign policy was the attempt to get **an ice-free port**, to allow importing and exporting of goods all the year round.

2 Russia tried to get such a port in the **Baltic** and on the **Aegean** (4.3.1).

3 This policy made Russia look like an aggressor. The cartoon (Fig. 6.3A) illustrates Japanese fears–but it also illustrates the fears of Britain and other countries.

4 In **1853** Russia had tried to win control of the **Dardanelles** to allow her to use her **Crimean ports** freely. This led to the Crimean War and Russia's defeat.

5 **Russia** then turned to the **Far East and to Central Asia**.

6 **1858** She advanced **from Siberia** eastward into the **Amur Province**. 1860 She set up the **Maritime Province** on the Pacific Coast (Fig. 17.11A).

7 The port of **Vladivostock** (**'Mistress of the Pacific'**) was built and the **Trans-Siberian Railway** built to link it with **Moscow**. The railway was not completed until 1916.

8 This railway had to cross the **Manchurian Plain** and brought Russia into **contact with China** when this section was finished, 1903.

9 Vladivostock was not an ice-free port. Russia now looked for chances to get such a port elsewhere in the Far East.

6.4 The Sino-Japanese War, 1894–95

1 Some of the outlying parts of the Chinese Empire had already been acquired by western powers. **Britain** seized **Burma** and **France** took several Provinces in what became French Indo-China (6.6.4).

2 **Korea** was the part of **China nearest Japan** (Fig. 17.11A).

3 **Japan wanted this region** for her growing population and as a market for Japanese goods.

4 **Russia**, already well established in Manchuria, also **wanted Korea**–and an ice-free port.

5 For some time the **Japanese**, in agreement with the Chinese, had kept a **legation in Seoul**, the capital of Korea.

6 After a Korean revolt they got permission to keep **soldiers in Seoul** to guard the legation.

7 In **1894** there was another Korean revolt. Both **China and Japan sent in troops to put it down**.

8 **The Japanese then refused to withdraw** their forces. The Chinese sank a Japanese warship and war was declared.

9 **Japanese victories** brought the war to a quick end.

10 **The Treaty of Simonoseki, 1895:**

i **Korea was to be independent** of China;

ii **Japan** was given **southern Manchuria**, the **Pescadores, Formosa** and the valuable **Port Arthur** on the **Liao Tung peninsula** (Fig. 17.11A);

iii Japan also got **trading concessions** in China itself.

6.5 The western powers and Japan, 1895

1 **Russia was alarmed** at this Japanese advance.

2 **France and Germany** saw Japan as a threat to their trading position in the Far East.

3 **The three nations** threatened to make war against Japan if she did not re-write the Treaty of 1895.

4 **Japan was forced** to give up her mainland possessions, including Port Arthur.

6.6 The western powers and China, 1895–1898

1 **The western powers** used the Japanese victory to force even **more concessions** out of the weak Manchu government.

2 **Germany** seized and colonized **Kiao-chow** (1897) on the mainland (Fig. 17.11A).

3 **Britain** seized and colonized **Wei-hai-Wei** (1898) just to the north of Kiao-chow (Fig. 17.11A).

4 **France** extended her colonies in **Indo-China** as did the **British** in **Burma**. It seemed that there might be a '**Scramble for China**' as there had been for Africa (5.8).

5 **Russia** seized **Port Arthur** (1898), and had her ice-free port.

6.7 Hostility between Japan and Russia

1 **Port Arthur** Russia helped force Japan to hand back Port Arthur to China (6.5.4). Then she seized it for herself.

2 **Manchuria** Having taken Port Arthur (1898), Russia went on to occupy Manchuria in 1900, taking advantage of the weak position of the Chinese government during the Boxer Rising (6.11). She linked **Port Arthur with Harbin** on the incomplete Trans-Siberian Railway.

3 **Korea** Both countries expanded their trade in Korea. They agreed to the **39th parallel of latitude** as the dividing line between their 'spheres of influence'. But competition was bound to increase the friction between the two countries.

4 **Britain** had been the most important of the countries trading with China. By 1900 she **was alarmed**:

i **Russia** was increasing her activities in China. Britain had always opposed Russian power (4.3.2);

ii **Russia and Germany** were friendly. Until 1890 they had been linked in the Dreikaiserbund (8.3). Britain feared that they might try to dominate the Far East.

5 **Japan** She was **angry at the Russian seizure of Port Arthur**. Britain was the one western country that **had not helped to drive Japan from that port** in 1895 (6.5.4).

6 **Britain and Japan:**

i they **both feared Russia**;

ii **both** of them were **naval powers**;

iii **Britain** feared an attack by **Russia allied with Germany**;

iv **Japan** was **planning a war against Russia**.

7 **The Dual Alliance, 1902:**

i Britain and Japan signed an alliance in **1902**;

ii they agreed that **if either** was at war with only one country (i.e. Russia) **the other would remain neutral**;

iii but if **one ally was at war with two countries** (e.g. Russia and Germany) **the other would join the war**;

iv this was particularly **valuable for Japan**. But it also **gave Britain an anti-Russian ally** in the Far East.

6.8 The Russo-Japanese War, 1904–05

1 **The causes:**

i **long term:** Japan and Russia had been opposed to one another over **Korea** and **Manchuria**. The **Port Arthur** affair (6.5.4 and 6.7.5) increased that hostility;

ii **immediate:** in **1904** Japan put proposals to Russia about the **military and trading policies** of both countries in Korea and Manchuria. These were rejected by Russia;

iii **Plehve:** Plehve, the Tsar's main adviser, wanted a '**short victorious war**' (3.20.7).

2 **The course of the war:**

i **the Japanese** attacked a Russian fleet in **Port Arthur**, February 1904;

ii **Port Arthur** was **beseiged by Japanese forces** and captured in **January 1905**;

iii **the Russian fleet** in the Baltic sailed for the Far East in October 1904. Its **inefficiency** was seen in:

(a) **the time** taken to get ready to sail (eight months);

(b) **its attack** on the British herring fleet on the Dogger Bank–on the assumption that this must be the Japanese fleet;

(c) the **sinking of a Russian ship** by a Russian torpedo during this **Battle of the Dogger Bank**;

(d) its **lack of preparation** for the battle with the Japanese when finally the fleet got to the Far East;

iv at **Tsushima** in **May 1905** the Russian fleet was destroyed by the Japanse, only a few small ships escaping;

v **on land** the Japanese inflicted a heavy defeat on the Russians at Mukden in Manchuria when 90 000 casualties were suffered and 40 000 prisoners captured.

3 **The Treaty of Portsmouth (USA), 1905:**

i President **Theodore Roosevelt** of the USA called both sides to a peace conference. This is an indication of the late arrival of the USA on the international scene (7.23);

ii the terms of the Treaty were:

(a) **Russia** had to take her troops **from Manchuria**;

(b) **Japan** acquired **Port Arthur** and the **southern half of the island of Sakhalin**;

(c) **Korea** was to be a **Japanese 'sphere of influence'**.

6.9 The effects of the War

1 **Japan** emerged as the most important country in the Far East. She planned further attacks on China.

2 **Russia** had a Revolution (3.22–3.25) which though it failed, was a sign of the weakness of the Tsar's position.

3 **China** was shown to be incapable of handling its affairs.

6.10 To reform China, 1900

1 The **Russo-Japanese** war had been fought by two non-Chinese powers **to decide the future of a part of China** (Korea).

2 Even before this War, **the Manchu government** had been seen to be **unpopular** because:

i of the increasing **power of western states** in Chinese affairs. In the **Treaty Ports** (6.1.1.) these countries built warehouses offices, shops and other businesses – and walled their 'estate' to keep out the Chinese. In **French 'estates'** the streets had **French names. German, British and French soldiers paraded the streets**:

ii **the Manchus** were incapable of resisting the west. This was made clear by the **colonization of Wei-hai-Wei by Britain** and of **Kiao-chow by Germany** (6.6);

iii **western influence** was increasing in other ways; Christian **missionaries** were trying to destroy the old religion and convert the people to Christianity.

3 Some Chinese opposed this **westernization** and hated the government for allowing it.

4 Others wanted the government to adopt western methods and ideas. **The Japanese** had done so successfully.

5 In **1898** the Emperor announced a number of reforms (**in the Hundred Days of Reform**):

i naval and agricultural **colleges** were to be founded;

ii western-style **examinations** would be held to allow China's most able children to get on;

iii the **army** would be modernized;

iv a liberal-minded **government** would be set up.

6 The Emperor's aunt, the **Empress Dowager**, united all those who were opposed to such westernization. Army officers **arrested the reformers** and **imprisoned the Emperor**.

6.11 The Boxer Rebellion, 1900

1 Few **peasants** were involved in the arguments between the reformers and the traditionalists.

2 They did, however, share the **anti-foreigner attitudes** of the traditionalists.

3 **A semi-religious organization** which taught the ancient form of self-defence, or **boxing**, became a centre for anti-foreign and anti-reform Chinese.

4 In **May 1900** the activities of the 'Boxers' led to widespread **attacks on Europeans and their industries**:

i **the railway** between Peking and Tientsin was destroyed;

ii **churches** were burnt down;

iii **Christians** – European and Chinese – were slaughtered.

5 **An international army** led by Admiral Seymour was **defeated** trying to get to Peking to relieve the foreign legations.

6 The **Chinese government** supported the Boxers and **declared war** on all foreigners (**June 1900**).

7 **Another international force** was gathered. Troops came from the USA, Britain, France, Germany, Austria, Italy and Japan. The commander-in-chief was a German.

8 The course of the War:

i 14 July **Tientsin** was captured;

ii 14 August **Peking** was captured;

iii October The **last of the Boxers** surrendered;

iv September 1901 The **Boxer Protocol** was signed by twelve major governments. This forced the Chinese government to:

(a) **apologize** for the massacres and damage to western property;

(b) agree to the **execution** of the leading Boxers;

(c) **agree on compensation** to be paid to the foreigners;

(d) accept the presence in the capital, Peking, of **a foreign army** to guard foreign legations.

6.12 China after the Boxers

1 **Hatred of foreigners** increased.

2 It was clear that the **traditionalists** would not be able to drive the foreigners out.

3 Many Chinese accepted the **need for westernization**.

4 This would be **opposed by the Manchus**. They would have to be replaced by a western-style democratic government.

6.13 Sun Yat-Sen

1 Sun emerged as the leader of the anti-Manchu and pro-westernization movement.

2 Born to a poor peasant family he grew to **dislike**:

i **landlords** who took so much from the peasants;

ii **merchants** and **money lenders** who cheated the peasants.

3 A child of a **Christian** family he learned:

i the benefits of **westernization**;

ii a **hatred for the Manchus**.

4 His brother, an emigrant to Honolulu, paid for his education at a **Chinese mission school** and for his medical training in the **English College in Hong Kong**.

5 In **1892** he qualified as a doctor – **one of China's first western-educated doctors**.

6 He gathered around him **other Chinese students** who formed:

i the **Revive China Society (1894)**;

ii **a revolutionary group** who tried to seize Canton (1895);

iii the people who went to **Japan, Hawaii** and the **USA** where Chinese emigrants supported them with **money**.

7 In **1896** Sun was in **London**. The Chinese government planned to kidnap him and return him to China for trial and death.

8 He escaped, helped by the Foreign Office and Scotland Yard.

9 In **1905** he was in Japan where he formed the **Sworn Chinese Brotherhood**. Later this became known as the **Kuo Min Tang**. At its first meeting Sun laid down the outlines for the future of the Chinese nation, the **Three Principles** of the **Kuo Min Tang**:

i the Principle of **Nationalism** . . . the freedom of China from western domination;

ii the Principle of **self-sovereignty** (or democracy) . . . with the rights to elections and parliamentary control of government;

iii the Principle of the **People's Livelihood** . . . involving the question of the ownership of land and industry.

6.14 The 1911 Revolution

1 After 1905 Sun was accepted by all Chinese revolutionaries as the official leader of the revolutionary movement.

2 In 1908 both the hated Empress Dowager and the weak-willed Emperor died. The government of the three-year old Emperor was controlled by a reactionary Prince Ch'un who dismissed many officials. Many of these offered to help Sun.

3 A rising by peasants after a bad harvest in the Yangtze Province was put down by the army (September 1911).

4 On **October 10th ('Double Tenth')** there were a series of risings by Sun's supporters in **southern China**.

5 Many sections of the **army** supported the rebels.

6 By the end of **November** the rebels had control of the country **south of the Yangtze** – including cities such as **Canton** and **Shanghai** where **anti-foreign feeling** was high.

7 **Nanking**, the old capital of China, was taken, **November 1911**.

8 In Nanking the rebels set up a **Provisional Government** for their Republic. Their forces marched north to **attack the Manchu capital of Peking**.

9 Most army generals refused to march against the rebels.

10 In **Peking** the loyal section of the army was commanded by an energetic **General Yuan Shih k'ai**. He **attacked the rebels** and drove them south of the Yangtze.

11 Then he opened negotiations with the rebels. **He wanted to**:
i get rid of the **Manchus**;
ii put off the **reforming movement**;
iii **take power** for himself.

6.15 Sorting out the position, 1911–12

1 On Christmas Eve 1911 **Sun** arrived in China from the USA.
2 He was named the **first President** of the United Provinces of China.
3 **Yuan** forced the Manchu boy-Emperor to sign a declaration of **abdication. The Manchu dynasty came to an end**.
4 **The Nanking Assembly** which supported Sun was afraid of a civil war in which Yuan with his army would defeat the Republican forces.
5 In **1912** Sun resigned his position and **allowed Yuan** to become the President of the Chinese Republic.

6.16 The Republic betrayed

1 **Yuan** lived in **Peking** and not in Nanking–the home of the Assembly.
2 He proved to be an **autocrat**:
i he **expelled Sun's supporters** (the Kuo Min Tang) from the Assembly;
ii in **1914** he **dismissed the Assembly** and declared himself sole ruler of China.
3 In **July 1913** Sun organized a **second revolution**. but this was **put down by Yuan's forces** which captured Nanking.
4 Yuan was accepted by most Chinese as a successful leader.
5 His position was not really that strong. He depended on the loyalty of other army leaders.

6.17 The War Lords

1 Many **army generals** were more powerful than the provincial governor appointed by the government.
2 Their badly-paid, ill-dressed and poorly disciplined soldiers often **attacked the peasants and townspeople**. This was one way of getting the food and money which the government under Yuan did not send them.
3 **Yuan** died in **August 1916** after he had failed to get himself declared Emperor. His successor, **Li Yuan Hun**:
i restored the **Republic constitution** of 1912;
ii recalled the **Parliament** dismissed in 1912.
4 But Li was unable to cope with the **War Lords**.
5 **Some** of these fought with one another to try to gain control of the government.
6 **Others** fought government troops to ensure that they alone controlled a certain region.
7 In all this fighting the **people of China** suffered badly:
i **farms** were ruined; millions died from **famine**;
ii **town life** became difficult–**drains** broke down; **roads** were destroyed, **trade** was interrupted. Millions died from the fevers and diseases following a breakdown in urban life.

6.18 China and the First World War, 1914–16

1 When the war broke out in July–August 1914, **China** declared herself to be **neutral**.
2 **Japan**, Britain's ally (6.7.7) **declared war on Germany**:
i she invaded Germany's **Pacific islands**;
ii she claimed the German colony of **Kiao-chow** on the Chinese mainland–but promised to return it to China.
3 However, when asked to leave, Japan issued the **Twenty-one Demands**. These included:

i Japanese rights to **former German colonies** in China;
ii **extra mining and railway rights** in China which would have the most powerful influence in China;
iii that **only Japan should be given new trading rights** in China;
iv that **Japanse financiers and military experts** be appointed to advise the Chinese government.
4 **Yuan** signed an agreement (**May 1915**) giving the Japanese most of what they wanted.
5 There was an **outbreak of anti-Japanese** activity in China. Japanese goods were **boycotted**; factory workers refused to work in Japanese owned **industries**; Chinese **servants** refused to work for Japanese masters.

6.19 Sun in power, 1917

1 The terrible conditions in China (6.17) led **Sun** to call a meeting of the **National Assembly in Canton**.
2 Most of the **Kuo Min Tang members** who had been expelled by Yuan met and declared themselves the **government of China**.
3 **Sun** was elected **President of China**.
4 His government controlled **only Canton** and part of the province of **Kwangtung**–and even there depended on a **War Lord**.
5 Elsewhere the **War Lords** were in charge. Nationalist feeling was strong (as was seen in the anti-Japanese outbreak in 1915). There was also a spirit of **despair** as trade died down, farming failed and disease killed off millions.
6 **Foreign countries** refused to recognize Sun as the President. They pretended that whoever was in power in Peking was the head of the government.
7 The foreigners preferred the activities of the War Lords to the thought of an anti-western and democratic government.

6.20 The Treaty of Versailles, 1919

1 This ended the war with Germany (Unit 12).
2 It confirmed **Japan's claim** to the former German colony of **Kiao-chow** on the Chinese mainland.
3 This was against the spirit of at least one of **Wilson's Fourteen Points** (Fig. 12.1A).
4 This led to the **outbreak of nation-wide demonstrations against foreigners** in 1910. We will see the results of this in Unit 17.

7 The United States of America, 1870–1917

7.1 A late arrival

European countries dominated the world during this period. They **divided Africa** amongst themselves (5.8). They **dominated Asia**, although the **arrival of Japan** towards the end of the period was a sign of things to come (Unit 6). **The emergence of**

the United States was another sign that European powers would, one day, no longer control the world's affairs.

7.2 The American constitution

1 A Republic In **1783** the original 13 colonies (Fig. 7.5A) of British North America won their **War of Independence**. They decided never to be governed by a king. America is a **Republic**; the head of state is a President (7.3.3).

2 A written constitution Having won their independence in 1783, the leaders of the 13 colonies wrote out their constitution and agreed on it in **1787**. Several of the States (or former colonies) were unwilling to sign the original document. This led to the writing of **Ten Amendments in 1791**. There have been another **fourteen Amendments** since then. We will study some of these in this Unit.

3 Checks and balances The leaders of the revolution against Britain believed that the king, George III, had too much power. When they wrote their constitution they did their best to see that no part of their government (7.3) would be too powerful:

i **the central government** has three parts (7.3.3). The writers of the constitution made sure that these parts were kept **separate**. The powers of each part were carefully defined to make sure that **no one part** could become too powerful;

ii **States' Rights** America is a Union of states which freely entered into **a Federation**; (hence the Federal Bureau of Investigation, or the FBI). **Each state** had to **give up some of the powers** it had enjoyed before the formation of the Union. The **Federal (or Central) government** alone has the **right** to **print money, declare war, make peace**, decide on **import and export duties** and **form an army**. On the other hand, the **Federalists** (those who wanted a strong central government) **had to please states** which were reluctant to join such a Union. For this reason **every state has kept certain powers**. From time to time there have been disputes between the Central government and some State governments over States' Rights. In the **1860s differences** between Central government and States of the South **led to the Civil War** (7.11.2). In more recent times, as we will see in Unit 32, there have been disputes about the treatment of the negroes in various states.

7.3 The government of the USA

1 The three parts The government consists of **Legislature** (7.3.2), **Executive** (7.3.3) and **Judiciary** (7.3.4).

2 The Legislature makes the laws (the Latin word *leges* = laws or rules). In the USA the Legislature is known as **the Congress** and is divided into two bodies:

i **the Senate** this is the **Upper House** and the more important of the two bodies making up Congress:

(a) Senators: the voters of **each state** elect **two senators** to represent the state.

(b) Elections Senators are elected for a term of **six years**. This gives them **more independence** than the members of the House of Representatives who are elected for only two years. It also gives them the appearance of being **more powerful than the President** who is elected for four years.

ii **the House of Representatives** this is a **much larger body** than the Senate:

(a) Congressmen, as the members are called, are **elected on the basis of population**. The more heavily populated states have more Congressmen than the lightly populated States. The House of Representatives is **elected every two years**. This pleases those who believe in **democracy; the electors** have much more **control over a Congressman** than over a Senator.

3 The President:

i **Election** the President is elected for **four years**. In theory he is indirectly elected by an electoral college chosen by the people of the various states. In practice he is directly elected by the votes of the people;

ii **Presidential elections** take place in the November of **each Leap year**. The successful candidate takes office at the beginning of the following year;

iii **presidential powers:**

(a) the Cabinet The President chooses his team of Ministers. Because of the belief in the separation of power (7.3.3) **none of these can have a seat in Congress**;

(b) the President is **Commander-in-Chief of the Armed Forces**;

(c) foreign policy The President is responsible for the country's foreign policy; he can **declare war** and **make peace** treaties. But, in keeping with the belief in 'checks and balances', he has to get the **approval of two-thirds of the Senate** for his actions. We will see that Presidents did not always get that approval (14.6).

(d) Veto The President can veto (or set aside) any Bill which comes from Congress. However, if such a Bill is passed again by a majority of two-thirds in both chambers of Congress it automatically becomes law (16.7.8).

(e) Higher appointments While the President picks his own Cabinet and appoints the judges to the Supreme Court (7.3.4), he has to get the **approval of the Senate** for such 'higher' appointments. This limits his freedom.

(f) The Executive, or the body which has to carry out the laws passed by the Legislature (or lawmakers) is the **President plus his ministers**. In the USA the Executive is often called the **Administration**.

4 The Judiciary

i This is represented by the **Supreme Court** of the USA;

ii this court consists of a **Chief Justice and eight associate judges;**

iii all these judges are **appointed by the President**. But they are appointed **for life** so that they may be independent of political pressure;

iv **their task** is to decide whether laws passed by Congress are in keeping with the spirit and letter of the original Constitution (and its Amendments). The Court has become known as **'the sacred Guardian of the Constitution'**;

v **their decisions** have to be obeyed by President, Congress and State governments.

7.4 The American 'frontier'

1 In Europe the word frontier usually means the **geographical boundary** between countries.

2 In the USA such a boundary (e.g. between the USA and Canada or the USA and Mexico) is known as the **border**.

3 To Americans 'frontier' means **'the limits reached by civilization'**.

4 Their early history is one of constantly **pushing the frontier out to the west** until the Pacific had been reached.

5 The thirteen original states (still remembered in the **stripes on the US flag**) were strung between the eastern-seaboard and The Appalachian mountains (Fig. 7.5A). Some **pioneers** soon pushed through the mountains to the west.

6 By **1800** the frontier had reached the **Mississippi** and the town of **St. Louis** was a frontier town.

7 In **1803** there took place the **Louisiana Purchase** (Fig. 7.5A);

i in the reign of King Louis XIV of France, an explorer, La Salle, had explored the length of the Mississippi and had claimed the river basin for France under the name of Louisiana. This had gone to Spain at the Treaty of Paris (1763), ending the war in which Britain had driven France from Canada;

ii in **1800 Napoleon** forced Spain to hand **Louisiana** as well as Florida to **France**;

iii Napoleon dreamt of a large Empire in North America. However, the war with Britain needed all his attention – and money. He could not afford to fight the Americans as well;

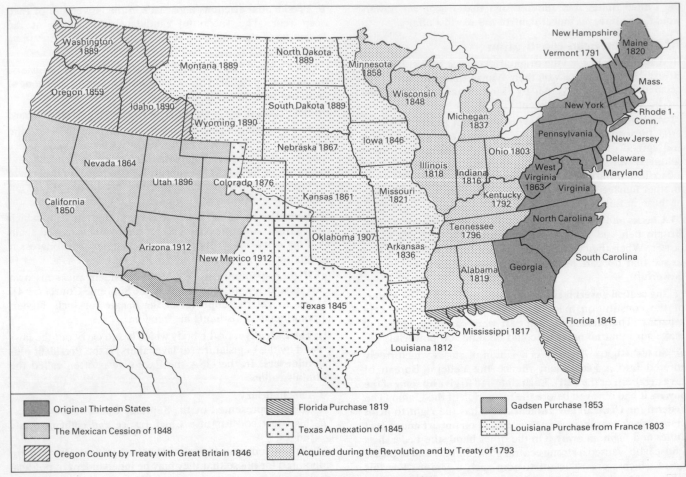

Fig. 7.5A   The expansion of the USA

iv in **1803** Napoleon **sold to the US government the territory** stretching from the Mississippi to the Rocky Mountains (and from the Gulf of Florida to the Canadian border) for **fifteen million dollars**. As the map shows (Fig. 7.5A) the addition of a million square miles of largely unexplored territory doubled the size of the United States.

7.5 'Go West, young man, go west'

1 1804–06 President **Jefferson**, who had arranged the Louisiana Purchase, sent out two explorers, **Lewis** and **Clark**. They followed the **course of the Mississippi** and went on to reach **the Pacific**, proving that the continent could be crossed.

2 1806–36:
i **fur traders and trappers** moved west in search of the beaver whose fur was needed for the hat trade;
ii **pioneers** opened up trails along which families could move into the almost unknown. (Fig. 7.5A);
iii **new states** were formed when enough settlers had made their homes in a particular region.

3 1845 A **war with Mexico** (during which there occurred the Battle of the Alamo) led to the acquisition of **Texas**, and further defeats led the Mexicans to cede the whole of the area from **Texas to the coast in 1848** (Fig. 7.5A).

4 1848 The discovery of gold in **California** led to a gold rush which took thousands of people to the Far West.

5 By the **1860s railways** linked the east and west coasts of the continent. Industrial goods could be carried from the east; agricultural produce could be taken from the far-west and the mid-west to the large towns and cities of the east.

6 So the **'frontier'** was pushed ever westwards by a great westward migration. What would the Americans do once the frontier could no longer be pushed further westwards?

7.6 The American (Red) Indians

1 The original settlers in the thirteen colonies fought several large wars and many battles against Indian tribes which resented the settlers' occupation of their tribelands.

2 The moving of 'the frontier' to the west brought the 'immigrants' into further conflict with the Indians living on the Great Plain between the Mississippi and the Rockies.

3 In **1851** Congress passed a law which forced the **Plain Indians** to live in reservations.

4 Between **1865 and 1876** Indian resistance to the white settlers increased. The Indians resented the mass slaughter of the **buffalo** which was the basis of their economy. There were **300 major battles** between Indians and the US army in this period.

5 Gradually the **Indians lost the power and will** to fight:
i the disappearance of the **buffalo** destroyed their main livelihood and source of meat and clothing;
ii the **better-armed soldiers** of the US army won most of the pitched battles;
iii many **Indians were tempted to side with the white settler** – by bribery or out of fear.

6 In **1890** the last of the **Sioux** tribe were destroyed at the **Battle of Wounded Knee**.

7 By **1900** there were only about **250 000 Indians** in the USA.

7.7 The cattle farmers

1 The clashes with the Indians had largely resulted from the expansion of the cattle ranching business:
i some ranches led to the displacement of some Indians;
ii when ranchers drove their cattle from Texas to markets in Illinois, Colorado and California (Fig. 7.5A) the Indians attacked and destroyed the cattle;
iii ranchers naturally asked for US reprisals.

2 The development of the **railway system** led to the building of **railway cattle terminals** to which cattle could be driven (over a shorter distance) before being transported by rail to the industrial towns.

3 Driving cattle to the terminals **often exhausted the animals**. This led to the development of the **open range**. Graziers would buy young cattle, feed them on the range for three or four years and then sell them in the cattle markets.

4 The **growth of industrial towns** and of a large urban population led to **increasing demand for meat**. This led to an increase in the number of cattle prospectors on the range from **Kansas to Montana** (Fig, 7.5A).

5 During the **1880s** there were so many of these prospectors that the **range became overcrowded** and the price of meat fell.

6 This led to the development of the **homestead**. Each grazier fenced in his holdings and grazed his own herd.

7.8 Arable farming

1 There was a spread of arable farming on the **Great Plains**.

2 In **1862** Congress passed **the Homestead Act**. Settlers were allowed to farm units of **approximately 160 acres**. Many of the governments of the **new states** offered **land cheaply**, or **in some cases free**, to attract settlers. **Railway companies** also bought land and offered it cheaply to prospective settlers in the hope that this would lead to increased use of the railway system.

3 The **railway system** opened up the country and made it **easier for settlers** to move. But more importantly it:

i **increased the market** for agricultural products. Perishable goods such as vegetables and dairy produce could be carried quickly over long distances;

ii **carried goods cheaply.** The cost of transporting the bulky produce, such as wheat, fell sharply once the railways had replaced the horse-drawn wagons.

4 Machinery The early settlers in the new states of the Great Plains had few sources from which to get workmen. This meant that from the beginning US farming had to become more mechanized than European farming:

i **ploughs** able to cope with the soil of the Great Plains led to an increased production of wheat;

ii machines for **reaping, binding and threshing** became increasingly efficient. In the **1880s** the **combine-harvester** enabled a farmer to harvest seventy acres in a single day.

5 Science also helped the farmer. New strains of seed were developed to resist droughts common in the mid-west. **Research** helped to eliminate diseases in cattle and pigs. **Laboratories** in California showed how to grow fruit and vegetables successfully.

6 The agricultural boom led to huge increases in production. **Exports** of wheat and other produce to Europe led to a sharp fall in food prices. This had a bad effect on European farmers (1.26.5), but it led to a rise in living standards for most Europeans.

7 Immigrants from Europe flocked to the 'new country'. Over **five million arrived in the 1890s**. Many of these became farmers; in the 1880s over seventy per cent of the people of Wisconsin (Fig. 7.5A) were of foreign origin.

8 More farming Between 1860 and 1900 the amount of land farmed doubled to over 800 million acres.

7.9 Industry in the USA

1 Most industry was in **the north-east**.

2 Immigrants provided plenty of cheap unskilled labour.

3 Before the Civil War (1861–65) the USA was largely an agricultural country. It was the **Civil War** which led to the first expansion of the northern industry:

i there was a **demand for coal, iron and steel** to provide the munitions needed by the Northern Armies;

ii there was **an expansion of the railway system** to carry the Northern troops. This, too, led to an expansion of the coal, iron and steel and engineering industries.

4 By **1900** the USA was the **world's industrial leader**, producing more coal, iron, steel and railway lines than any other country. It had more and much larger factories than any other country.

7.10 Industrialists and the government

1 After **1865** businessmen and industrialists gained **control of the Congress:**

i they organized the **elections** of Representatives and Senators who were their friends;

ii they **paid special firms** to supervise the passage of **favourable legislation** through Congress;

iii they **bribed** Congressmen and judges to favour industry in their laws and judgements.

2 Congress brought in laws which favoured industry and removed any existing laws which might have hampered industrial development. This was in keeping with the spirit of **self-reliance** to be found on 'the frontier'.

3 The Supreme Court helped industrialists by judgements which **removed almost all barriers** to private enterprise.

4 Industrialists supported this belief in freedom:

i **Vanderbilt,** the railway king, asked 'Can't I do what I want with my own?';

ii **Carnegie,** the steel king, said 'What do I care about the law? Haven't I got the power?';

iii **Morgan,** the financial king, when called to the White House by President Roosevelt, said, 'Mr. President, I'll get my lawyer and you get yours.';

iv talking of the **Supreme Court,** one industrial 'king' told a President: 'You buy your judges and I'll buy mine. We'll see whose stays bought the longest.'

5 It is not surprising that **conditions** in US towns and factories were **worse** than those found in Britain in the early industrial revolution:

i **hours of work, working conditions** and **wages** were fixed by employers. **Trade unions** were small, weak and easily crushed;

ii **towns** grew up around the industrial centres with little care for **sanitation**. **High death rates** were common.

7.11 The problem of the Southern States

1 In **1861** eleven Southern States declared that they were leaving the 'union'. They formed their own **Confederacy**.

2 They were afraid that President **Lincoln** might push through a constitutional Amendment to **abolish slavery**.

3 Lincoln made war on the south, not in the cause of slavery, but **to preserve the union of the States**.

4 The war lasted for four years, 1861–65.

5 Its **effects on the south** were:

i **agricultural devastation**;

ii loss of **600 000 men,** one fifth of the male population;

iii **starvation and the outbreak of disease**;

iv the ruin of the south's **cotton industry**.

6 Slavery was abolished. Lincoln announced (September, 1862) that all slaves would be free from 1st January, 1863. The Thirteenth Amendment, which abolished slavery, was passed by Congress on 18th December, 1865. There were many far reaching effects of this abolition:

i **what were the freed blacks to do?** In Russia, Alexander II gave the freed serfs some land (3.4). Lincoln did not go that far. Congress set up **Freedman's Bureau** which set up **special camps** where blacks were given some assistance. But the death rate in these camps was high;

ii **who would govern the southern states?** States which accepted the law on the Emancipation of Slaves were allowed to form their own governments again. But many of these introduced their own **'Black Codes'** to prevent blacks owning land, working at skilled trades, serving on juries, carrying arms and maybe most importantly, having the right to vote;

iii **what about the relationship between the southern whites and the northern whites?** The victorious North produced Radical politicians who pushed through the Fourteenth Amendment which said: 'No state shall abridge the privileges of citizens of the United States nor shall any state deprive any person of life, liberty or property without due process of law.' If southern politicians refused to accept this amendment they were unable to hold office.

7 Southern opposition:
i some southern politicians won back power and passed **state legislation** to hinder the progress of blacks;
ii other southerners formed **secret societies** such as the **Ku Klux Klan** to terrorize blacks trying to exercise their civil rights and whites who supported them.

8 In **1870** Congress passed the **Amnesty Act** to restore the political rights of all southern politicians:
i there was an increase in **intimidation of blacks**;
ii **southern whites** elected to Congress called themselves **Democrats** because it was Republicans under Lincoln who had abolished slavery;
iii **the Supreme Court** favoured the white racists. It ruled that the Fifteenth Amendment did not give anyone the right to vote (as it seemed to do: 'The right of citizens of the US to vote shall not be denied or abridged by the US or by any State on account of race, color or previous condition of servitude'.) Governments in the Southern States took away the right to vote from blacks.

9 In **1877** the last Federal troops were withdrawn from the south. **Southern whites had an even freer hand.**

10 The south was to remain a problem for the remainder of the twentieth century as we will see in Unit 32.

7.12 The giant trusts

1 John D. **Rockefeller** was the leading industrialist in the USA in the period 1860–1900.

2 He believed that the large firm (or **corporation**) which controlled all (if possible) of an industry was the natural outcome of private enterprise. It would have **certain advantages**:
i it would have **great resources** and be able to afford new **developments** and **inventions**;
ii because it was so big; such a firm would be **less likely to go bankrupt** as many small businesses did.

3 **Rockefeller** made his first fortune in **oil** during the Civil War before setting up the Standard Oil Company.

4 By **1880** he controlled **ninety per cent of US oil production** as well as most of the world's market in oil.

5 **Andrew Carnegie** (7.10.4) was the **steel 'king'**. He controlled most of the steel supply needed by the developing railway system. In **1901** a merger between his firm and other steel firms produced the **United States Steel Corporation**.

6 J. Pierpont Morgan (7.10.4) was a **financial 'king'**. He controlled banks and other sources of investment and helped organize giant corporations. He paid **Carnegie 250 000 000 dollars for his share in the United States Steel Corporation in 1901.**

7 These were the three leading capitalists of the time. Others included **Philip Armour**, the pork packer, **Cornelius Vanderbilt** (7.10.4), the controller of much of the railway system and **Averell Harriman** who controlled most of the rest of the railway system.

7.13 The government and the trusts, 1885–89

1 The giant firms certainly 'delivered the goods'. The United States became the **world's industrial leader**.

2 They made their **owners very wealthy**. Vanderbilt spent 2 million dollars in the building of a house – and 9 million dollars in furnishing it. **Carnegie** gave 400 million dollars to charities before he died. **Rockefeller** created a foundation which spent 530 million dollars on medical research.

3 But **others suffered** in the making of this wealth. **Children** worked 16 hours a day in factories; **miners** trying to form trade unions faced attacks by private armies hired by the trust owners.

4 Smaller industrialists and **farmers** also suffered. Some were forced to pay a very high freight charge on railways while the powerful few were able to get much lower freight charges. Telephone and other companies charged the trusts a lower rate than that paid by the smaller firms.

5 'Muckrakers' was the name given to critics who attacked the 'robber barons'. These included journalists, pamphleteers and novelists such as Upton Sinclair whose book *The Jungle* (1906) exposed the horrors of Chicago's meat-packing industry.

6 President **Cleveland** (1885–89) was the first to try to gain some government control over the industrial giants. He set up the **Interstate Commerce Commission** in **1887**. This could prevent railway companies from raising freight charges.

7 But the **political power of the trusts** was very great (7.10). **The Supreme Court** ruled in favour of the trusts when cases were brought before it (7.10.3). 'The best judges stayed bought' said one trust owner.

8 In **1896** the Republican McKinley became President and the **Interstate Commission** had its powers cut down.

7.14 The American trade union movement

1 American workers were slow to form trade unions:
i American industrialization was a **new development**. There was no history of craft societies as in pre-industrial Britain;
ii most American workers were **immigrants**, grateful for the political freedom they had and for the chance to get work;
iii the constant flow of immigrants (7.8.7) allowed industrialists to recruit **non-unionized labour** if workers formed unions;
iv American workers shared **'the frontier' spirit** and believed in the benefits of **free enterprise**.

2 1869 The National Labour Union was formed, but collapsed a few years later.

3 1869 The Knights of Labour were founded to form separate unions in the different states and to create some form of union co-operation.

4 1886 A bomb outrage in Chicago was blamed on the Knights and **the organization collapsed**.

5 1886 The American Federation of Labour for skilled workers, was formed. While supporting free enterprise it demanded a fair share in the new prosperity.

6 1900 Only half a million of the seventeen million factory workers were organized in trade unions.

7.15 The trusts under fire, 1903

1 There was a **business depression** in **1903** when shareholders lost 600 million dollars. Trusts, it seemed, did not always manage their affairs well.

2 Congress investigated the depression. It found that many **trusts used criminal means to get control**.

3 The investigation showed that **trusts did not make new inventions or use those offered to them**. This was the opposite of the claim made by Rockefeller (7.12).

4 The investigation published reports on **working and social conditions** which showed that the attacks on 'the robber barons' had been justified (7.13.5).

5 **Reforms** A number of reforming organizations were set up. These succeeded in pushing through important reforms:

i by **1914** there were **child-labour laws** in forty-three states (but none in the remaining five states);

ii many states passed laws on **compulsory school attendance** – but others did not;

iii **the electoral laws** were changed. Presidential candidates in the political parties had now to go through a **primary election** in most states. The registered members of the political parties then had a direct vote in the adoption of candidates. **This cut down the power of the 'robber barons'** to influence the choice of candidates. This is still the system by which Presidents are elected.

7.16 Theodore Roosevelt, 1901–09

1 **Roosevelt** became President when McKinley was assassinated in 1901.

2 He was a colourful character having been a boxer, bear hunter (hence the Teddy Bear toy), a friend of cowboys and leader of soldiers in the Spanish-American War (7.21.8).

3 Both at home and abroad he believed that the government should wield **'the big stick'** against its opponents.

4 In **1904** he forced the break up of the **Morgan-Rockefeller Northern Securities Corporation** which controlled a large section of US industry.

5 He made **mine owners** accept arbitration on demands by the United Mineworkers Union for better wages and conditions.

6 He set up the **Bureau of Corporations** to investigate and report publicly on the activities of the great trusts.

7 He set up a **Department of Commerce and Labour** where civil servants could supervise industrial affairs.

8 He set up an **anti-trust division in the Department of Justice** where specially trained lawyers led the drive against the trusts.

9 He increased the powers of the **Inter-State Commerce Commission** over railway freight charges.

10 He called for the development of programmes of **social welfare**. In this, as in much else, the USA lagged behind European countries such as Britain and Germany (1.25).

7.17 Woodrow Wilson, 1912–1920

1 William Howard **Taft**, the Republican President, 1909–12, carried on with Roosevelt's policies of **'trust busting'**.

2 **Wilson**, Democratic President 1912–20:

i he pushed through **the Clayton Anti-Trust Act** (1914) outlawing many business practices of large companies;

ii he **cut import duties** and exposed US industry to foreign competition hoping that this would lead to lower prices and a rise in living standards;

iii he set up **special law enforcement commissions** to see that factory legislation was obeyed. However, the decisions of successive **Supreme Courts** limited their power.

7.18 The expansion of the United States after 1865

1 **1867** The USA bought **Alaska** from Russia for one and a half million pounds.

2 In the 1840s US politicians watched the expansion of the European powers into **Asia** (6.5.6).

3 The US developed the theory that **'the American mission'** was to help backward nations of the Pacific and South America as well as to protect American trading interests in China and Japan.

7.19 Making the Pacific more American

1 In the **1850s fifty small Pacific islands** were brought under US control. These provided the fertilizer **guano**.

2 **Costa Rica** was developed by the building of railways.

3 **Mexico** and other South American countries were helped by the **American development of copper and silver mines**.

4 **Samoa** This was a valuable **staging-post** for American ships on the trans-Pacific routes. In **1899** the USA gained the harbour of **Pago Pago**, leaving Britain and Germany to argue about control of the rest of the island.

5 **Hawaii** In **1877** the US developed the **Pearl Harbour naval base**. The islands proved to be good for sugar growing and became important to the US. Agreements were made with the islands by which no other foreign nation was allowed to get trading rights with Hawaii. Between 1894 and 1898 there was a Hawaiian attempt to reassert its independence but in **1898** the **islands were annexed to the USA**.

6 **The US navy** In **1884** a Naval War College had been set up and its first president was the naval historian **A. T. Mahan**. Under his influence the US navy grew until in **1898 it was the world's third largest navy**.

7.20 Expansionist politicians

1 In **1895** while McKinley was President there was a border dispute between **Venezuela and British Guyana**.

2 **Roosevelt** Assistant Secretary to the Navy, wanted the US to make war and **drive the British** from the American continent.

3 Calmer counsels prevailed. The British Prime Minister, Lord **Salisbury**, submitted the case to international arbitration. The case was settled in Britain's favour in 1899.

7.21 The Spanish-American War, 1899

1 In **1895** there were a series of risings by **Cuban nationalists** against Spanish rule.

2 The Cuban rebels **asked for US help**.

3 Roosevelt wanted the US to help the rebels.

4 In February **1898** the US battleship, *Maine*, was blown up in Cuban waters. There was **no proof** that the Spaniards were responsible for the sinking of the ship.

5 **McKinley** wanted to keep out of the war. But the **war party** forced him into a declaration of war in **April 1898**.

6 **The Spanish fleet** was destroyed by the US navy in Manila Bay, in the Spanish-controlled Philippines.

7 **Troops** landed in July and **captured Manila**.

8 **In Cuba** Roosevelt led a force of troops nicknamed **'the Rough Riders'** who gained the **surrender of Cuba in July 1898**.

9 The USA then announced the **annexation of Cuba, the Philippines, Puerto Rica** and **Guam**.

10 In **1898** there was a **Philippino revolt** against US rule. This was not finally defeated until **1901**.

11 **Cuba** remained under US direct rule until **1902** when it was allowed self-government again.

7.22 The Panama Canal

1 **De Lesseps** failed to build a canal across the Panama isthmus (2.17).

2 In **1880** Britain and the USA agreed that there would **be no attempt** to build a canal except as a **joint British-US venture**.

3 In **1901** Britain surrendered her rights under the 1880 agreement. The USA was free to build a canal.

4 **The French Company** had sold its rights in the Canal to the USA. The agreement said that the **money** due should be **paid to** the **government of Colombia**.

5 To prevent such payments, the **US supported a Panamanian rebellion** which led to the **separation of Panama from Colombia**.

6 The construction of the Canal started in **1904** and the first ship sailed through the completed Canal in **1913**.

7 **The Canal zone** remained under US control, independent of the government of Panama.

7.23 The US emerges as a world power

1 The US prevented European powers from arranging a

division of **China** along the lines of the 'Scramble for Africa'.

2 US forces formed **part of the foreign army** which crushed the Boxer Rising in 1900.

3 In **1905** Roosevelt helped arrange the **Treaty of Portsmouth, New Hampshire**, which ended the Russo-Japanese War (6.8.3).

4 The US took part in the discussions following the **Moroccan crises** (8.17.5).

7.24 The US and the First World War, 1914–17

1 **Wilson** was President when the First World War broke out in 1914.

2 He had to take account of **widespread hostility to Britain**:

i millions of **Irish-Americans** hated Britain because of her ill-treatment of Ireland;

ii millions of **German-Americans** were loyal to the Fatherland;

iii millions of **Russian-Jews** had fled to America and hoped for a German victory over the hated Tsar;

iv many **Americans were opposed to Japanese expansion** in the Pacific. Japan was one of the Allies in 1914.

3 It is not surprising that in August 1914 Wilson argued that the **US had to remain neutral** in Europe's 'Civil War'.

4 However several things tended to make the **US support** the British and French causes:

i there was a long tradition of **friendship with France** which had helped the Americans against Britain in the 1770s;

ii **large sums of money were loaned** to the Allies to help them buy the war goods they needed from American industry. If the Allies lost the war, these loans would not be repaid.

5 **German policy also** turned US opinion in the Allies favour:

i the attack on **neutral Belgium** shocked many Americans;

ii **submarine attacks** on neutral vessels, including passenger shipping, angered Americans. When the British ship, the *Lusitania*, was sunk in May 1915, **124 Americans** were among the 1198 who lost their lives.

6 In **1916** Wilson was re-elected President on the promise that **he would keep the US out of the war**.

7 **German policy** however again helped the Allied cause:

i in **January 1917** the Germans announced their resumption of an **unrestricted submarine campaign**—against all shipping;

ii in **January 1917** the German Foreign Secretary, **Zimmerman**, sent a note to the German Ambassador in Mexico in which he **proposed an alliance between Mexico and Germany** and the declaration of a **joint war against the USA**.

8 In **February and March 1917** Wilson tried to get the Germans to call off their submarine campaign. Their failure to do so led him to declare war on **2 April 1917**. The USA now marched to the front of the world stage for the first time.

8 International Relations, 1870–1914

8.1 The objectives of Bismarck's foreign policy

1 **Peace** Germany was united as the result of three wars (1.10). After 1871 Bismarck wanted peace:

i the **Catholic states** had been reluctant to become part of the Prussianized Empire. They might have left if Germany had been involved in an unsuccessful war after 1871;

ii **Germany industry** needed time to take advantage of the newly acquired **Alsace-Lorraine** coal and iron fields;

iii **other problems** arose after 1871–the Catholics, the Socialists and the demand for colonies. Bismarck wanted time to deal with these **internal problems**.

2 **France** Bismarck realized that France would want a **war of revenge** to try to get back Alsace and Lorraine (1.11):

i he did not fear France on her own;

ii he was afraid of a war on **two fronts**–against France and some French ally;

iii the main object of his foreign policy was to make sure that no one allied with France.

3 **Britain** To ensure Britain's friendship (8.12) Bismarck was careful not to do anything to annoy her:

i **colonies**; he resisted the German demand for a larger Empire (1.27). He was afraid that looking for an Empire would bring Germany into conflict with Britain;

ii **Navy**; he did not try to build a German Navy which Britain would have seen as a threat.

4 **The other major Powers** We will see below how Bismarck dealt with Austria, Russia and Italy.

8.2 The isolation of France

1 **The Republic** Bismarck emphasized that Republican France must be opposed to rule by monarchs. This propaganda* scared off Russia and Austria.

2 **French colonies** Bismarck urged France to look for colonies:

i this would **distract attention** from the losses of 1871;

ii it would also push France into conflict with other countries.
Italy and France quarrelled over Tunisia–Tripoli (5.12.1).
Britain and France quarrelled over Egypt and the Sudan (5.19) and over colonies in Asia (6.6.4).

3 **Austria** and **Russia** were drawn closer to Germany.

8.3 The Dreikaiserbund (or League of Three Emperors) 1873

1 **Austria** was defeated by Prussia in 1866. How did Bismarck persuade the Austrian Emperor to link up with his old enemy?

i **Austrian expansion** into the Balkans could only come about if Germany supported Austria;

ii **Prussia** had treated Austria very leniently in 1866 and Austria was grateful for that;

iii so in **1873** talks were held in Berlin.

2 **Russia** heard about the talks and asked to be invited.

3 **Bismarck** explained the danger from republican France (8.2.1).

4 **The Three Emperors** agreed to be friendly to one another **and** guard against revolutionary activity by France.

5 **France** was now without friends.

8.4 Austria versus Russia

1 Russian and Austrian policies were in conflict in the Balkans (Unit 4.3 and Fig. 4.4A).

2 At the **Congress of Berlin** Bismarck supported Austria (4.10). There were three reasons for choosing Austria:

i if he chose **Russia**, he would anger **Britain** (4.3.2);

ii **Austria** would be **easier to control** than Russia;

iii Austrian expansion into the South East would be **good for German trade**, as it would leave the River Danube open.

8.5 The Dual Alliance, 1879

1 In **1879** Bismarck made a **secret treaty** with Austria.

2 **The terms** of the treaty or alliance favoured Austria:

i if **Germany were attacked** by one country (e.g. **France**) Austria would remain neutral;

ii if **Germany were attacked by two countries**, Austria would come in on Germany's side;

iii **if Austria went to war with Russia,** Germany would come in on Austria's side.

3 The German Emperor, William I, did not like this alliance. He thought it was aimed against his nephew, Tsar Alexander II, but Bismarck overcame his opposition.

8.6 The League of the Three Emperors, 1881 and 1884

1 The League had been a friendly understanding in 1873 (8.3.4).

2 In 1881 it was strengthened. Bismarck persuaded the three Emperors to sign a treaty. They promised that none of them would help a fourth country (obviously **France**) if that country went to war with any of the three nations.

8.7 The Triple Alliance, 1882

1 In 1881 France occupied Tunis (2.14.3.).

2 Italy had ambitions in that area. Later on, in 1912, she took Tripoli (4.15).

3 Italy was annoyed by the French occupation of Tunis.

4 Bismarck got her to join Germany and Austria in a Triple Alliance.

5 Italy insisted that she would never fight Britain. Her long coastline made an easy target for the Royal Navy.

8.8 The Eastern Question again, 1885–87

1 In 1878 the Congress of Berlin had created a 'small' Bulgaria. (4.9.1 and Fig. 4.4A)

2 In 1885 Bulgaria and Eastern Rumelia (Fig. 4.4A) united under a nephew of Tsar Alexander II.

3 In 1886 Serbia declared war on Bulgaria—and was defeated.

4 Russia organized the kidnapping of the Bulgarian ruler hoping to force him to become more pro-Russian.

5 Bulgaria refused to accept him as their leader. He was replaced by **Prince Ferdinand of Saxe-Coburg** in 1887 He followed an anti-Russian and pro-German line.

8.9 The Reinsurance Treaty, 1887

1 Russia was angered by this loss of influence.

2 Austria was encouraged by the anti-Russian movement in Bulgaria and by the defeat of the Serbs.

3 Bismarck was afraid that Austria might declare war on Russia and so drag Germany into a war (8.5.2).

4 In 1887 Bismarck made a secret treaty with Russia. In this **Reinsurance Treaty** he promised:

i German support for Russia's claims to influence in **Bulgaria**;

ii German neutrality in an Austro-Russian war, if Austria was the aggressor.

5 This was contrary to the terms of the Dual Alliance with Austria (8.5.2). Bismarck had been driven to dishonesty.

6 This became clear in **1888** in another row over the choice of the German Prince Ferdinand as ruler of Bulgaria.

7 Bismarck published the terms of the Dual Alliance. Russia would have to fight Germany if she went to war with Austria.

8.10 William II and Bismarck, 1888–1890

1 In Unit 1.29 we saw how the grandson of William I came to the throne in **1888**.

2 He **quarrelled with Bismarck** over the question of *i* the treatment of **socialists**; *ii* Germany and **colonies**; and *iii* the proposals for **a Germany Navy**.

3 He also differed with Bismarck on foreign policy:

i he wanted to come out strongly in **support of Austria**;

ii he wanted Germany, as well as Austria, to get control and **influence in the Balkans**.

4 We have seen that in **1890** Bismarck resigned.

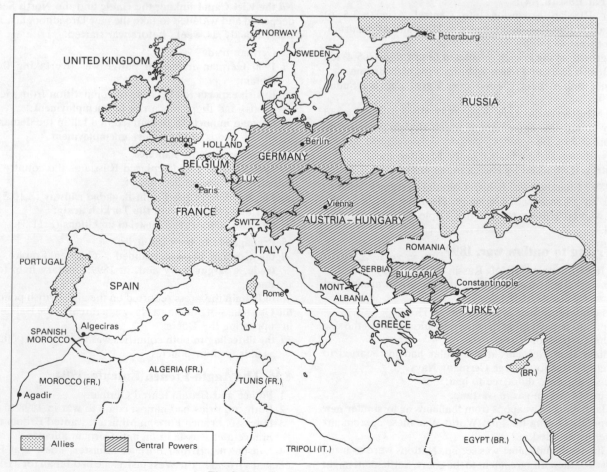

Fig. 8.12A European Camps and Crises

8.11 The Franco-Russian Alliance, 1892–95

1 The Reinsurance Treaty of 1887 was not renewed in **1890**.

2 William II made it clear that he wanted Germany to become an important influence in the Balkans.

3 The Berlin-Baghdad railway:
i this was to go via **Constantinople**, capital of Turkey;
ii it would lead to **increased German trade** in the Middle East;
iii **Austria** supported the scheme. She was promised large **territorial gains** in the Balkans as a reward.

4 Russia now felt as isolated as France was after 1871.

5 But these were **traditional enemies**:
i they had fought each other in the Crimean War, 1853–56;
ii France was a democratic republic, Russia an autocracy;*
iii France had an **anti-clerical policy** (2.14 and 2.19); Russia was dominated by the Orthodox Church (3.13).

6 Economics helped draw the two countries together:
i **France** had recovered from the Franco-Prussian War;
ii **Russia** needed **foreign loans** to pay for the imports needed for her **industrialization**. France could arrange such loans.

7 The navies of the two countries exchanged visits.

8 The press in both countries wrote friendly articles.

9 The Franco-Russian Alliance was signed in **1892**, confirmed in 1894, and strengthened in **1897**. Each nation promised to help the other if attacked by **Germany**.

8.12 Britain and 'splendid isolation'

1 Britain was not a member of either **Armed Camp**.

2 During the nineteenth century Britain had played only a **small role in European affairs**. She had not, for example, interfered in any of **Bismarck's wars** (1.10).

3 The Eastern Question was the one issue which involved British interference. Britain did all she could to **block Russia's power** in the Balkans.

4 Britain's opposition to Russia and France:
i she **feared Russian influence** in the Balkans (4.3.2) and in the Far East (6.7.4);
ii after Russian expansion into Central Asia (6.3.5–6) Britain feared Russian influence in **Tibet** and **Afghanistan**, as a threat to India;
iii the growth of **the French colonies** in **Indo-China** (6.5.4) led to British fears of French ambitions towards **Burma**.
iv France and Britain clashed over **Egypt** and **the Sudan** (5.19).

5 The Mediterranean Agreement, 1887 Britain, Austria and Italy signed this agreement in which **Britain promised to help**:
i **Italy**, if attacked by France in the Mediterranean;
ii **Austria**, if attacked by Russia in the Balkans.

6 In **1897** Chamberlain, British Colonial Secretary, tried to arrange an alliance with Germany. He failed, because the Kaiser wanted Britain to join the Triple Alliance. Britain refused.

8.13 Trying to outlaw war, 1899

1 In 1899 Nicholas II of Russia (Unit 3.19) called a conference to find ways of limiting the growth of armies and navies.

2 This conference met at **the Hague** in Holland.

3 No nation believed that the others would cut down the size of their armies or navies.

4 William II of Germany in particular had just started to develop plans for **a large Germany Navy**.

5 The Conference did agree **to ban**:
i the use of **poison gas** in wartime;
ii the launching of weapons from **'balloons or by similar new weapons'**. During the First World War these agreements were disregarded.

6 An International Court was set up. Nations were to bring the causes of their disagreement to the court. Settlement might then be reached without war.

8.14 Britain and the effects of the Boer War, 1899–1902

1 Britain took **a long time** to conquer the Boers (5.22).

2 What would Britain do in a major war?

3 Kaiser William II sent a telegram congratulating the Boers when the Jameson Raid failed (5.21).

4 What might the Kaiser have done with a large enough Navy to take German troops to help the Boers?

5 The Anglo-Japanese Alliance, 1902 (6.7.6 and 6.7.7). This was Britain's first formal alliance:
i it recognized **Britain's need** of Japanese help against Russia in the Far East;
ii it was a by-product of the Boer War (8.14.2).

8.15 The growth of Anglo-German hostility

1 Kaiser William II
i he was Queen Victoria's grandson and Edward VII's nephew;
ii he was **jealous** of the size of the **British Empire**. His colonial ambitions led to his anti-British attitude;
iii **Britain feared** Germany's search for colonies. She replaced Russia and France as the major threat to Britain's interests

2 The German Navy:
i **1892** Admiral von Tirpitz persuaded William II that Germany needed a large navy;
ii **1897** the Reichstag passed the first Naval Bill;
iii **1900** a Navy Law doubled the size of Germany's fleet;
iv the British feared that a German Navy would be used to fight Britain;
v **Admiral Fisher** led the British demand for an improved British Navy to safeguard Britain against Germany;
vi **1906** a new battleship, the *Dreadnought*, was launched. It was faster and stronger than any battleship in the world;
vii the Germans built nine Dreadnought-class ships between 1909 and 1911. Britain finally built eighteen although the popular cry had been, 'We want eight and we won't wait';
viii **the Kiel Canal** linking the Baltic and the North Sea was deepened and widened to take the new Dreadnoughts. It was ready exactly six weeks before war started.

3 German trade
i **1900** German **industrial power** was overtaking that of Britain;
ii **British exports** fell because of competition from German goods–and there was a **rise in unemployment**;
iii **German imports** to Britain led to a fall in the demand for British goods, and to **more unemployment**.

4 Germany and the Balkans
By **1900** Germany had replaced Russia as the country to be feared in this region because of:
(a) The building of the **Berlin-Baghdad railway** (8.10.3);
(b) German offers to train **the Turkish army**;
(c) German support for **Austrian ambitions** (8.11.3).

5 Propaganda in both countries
i the German press demanded a German **Empire**, more **trade**, a larger **Navy** and, in 1899, military help for **the Boers**;
ii in Britain the press reported on the anti-British policies of the Germans–in building a Navy as a threat in the Balkans and in supporting the Boers;
iii **the ill-feeling** in both countries was used by the politicians as aids to their policies.

8.16 The Anglo-French Entente, 1904

1 France and Britain feared Germany.

2 Both countries had almost come to war in 1898 (5.19).

3 Delcassé, French Foreign Minister, wanted Britain to join France and Russia in an anti-German alliance.

4 Lansdowne, British Foreign Minister, knew that Britain needed a friend in the West just as she had Japan for a friend in the Far East.

5 State visits by **Edward VII** to Paris and **President Loubet** to London created a mood of good will.

6 In **1904** they agreed to settle their past differences:

i France recognized Britain's control of **Egypt**;

ii Britain accepted **Morocco** as a French zone of influence;

iii long-standing disagreements about **Newfoundland fisheries** were settled and would not cause future dispute.

7 The Entente was **not an alliance**; it said nothing about what either country would do if the other went to war.

8 **Military talks** between the army chiefs of staff of both countries were allowed. These led to the discussion of how each country would use its armies in the event of a war–with, or course, Germany. In this way the **Entente changed its nature** without politicians always being aware of the change.

8.17 Germany and the Entente, 1905–06

1 **William II** was annoyed that Germany had not been consulted about the Anglo-French division of North Africa.

2 **1905 The First Moroccan Crisis**. He went to **Tangier** and declared that Germany would help the Sultan of Morocco to **resist French attempts** to control his country.

3 He demanded an international conference to reconsider the affairs of North Africa.

4 **The French** feared war. Delcassé resigned in protest when France agreed to hold an international conference.

5 In **April 1906** the Conference met at **Algeciras** in Spain:

i **Britain and the USA** supported France;

ii **France** was given control of the Moroccan Bank, the customs and excise system, the supply of arms and the maintenance of a police force.

6 **The Entente** was strengthened by this diplomatic 'victory' over Germany.

7 **Britain and Germany** were even more hostile to each other.

8.18 The Anglo-Russian Entente, 1907

1 **Delcassé,** having arranged the Entente in 1904, had also wanted Britain to become friendly with France's ally, Russia.

2 Britain's **fears of Russian power declined**:

i Germany and Austria were the **new threat in the Balkans**;

ii **Russia's defeat** by Japan in 1904–05 (6.8) lessened fears of Russian ability to affect British interests.

3 In **1907** an Entente was signed in which the two countries settled their past differences:

i in **Afghanistan**, Russia kept her trading interests but agreed not to threaten British India;

ii in **Persia** the two countries agreed on their spheres of influence. **Russia** became the dominant influence in the **north** around Teheran. **Britain** had control of the **south**, including the rich oil deposits. There would be a neutral zone between the two–to lessen the danger of conflict.

4 As with the Anglo-French Entente, this one said nothing about what would happen in the event of a war.

8.19 The Eastern Question, 1908

In Unit 4.13 we saw how Austria took advantage of Turkish weakness to annex Bosnia and Herzegovina. Russia was in no condition to oppose her. France would not agree to a declaration of war over this issue.

8.20 1911 The Second Moroccan Crisis

1 **1911** There were a number of risings against the inefficient ruler of Morocco.

2 France sent an **army to Fez**, the capital, to restore order.

3 **The Kaiser**, fearing that France might annex Morocco, sent a gunboat, the *Panther*, to Agadir on the west coast.

4 He claimed that he wanted to **protect German businessmen** in Morocco–but there were none there.

5 He was testing the Anglo-French Entente again.

6 **The British Foreign Minister, Grey**, feared that Germany might be going to build a **naval base at Agadir**.

7 The British Chancellor of the Exchequer, **Lloyd George**, declared that Britain might have to go to war to stop this threat to her naval and trading interests.

8 **The Germans** demanded an **apology** for this warlike speech–but did not get one.

9 **The British navy** was put on a war footing.

10 But, as in 1905, a **Conference** settled the issue:

i it met in **Paris**;

ii France gave Germany a strip of the **French Congo**;

iii Germany agreed to **France** having a free hand in **Morocco**.

11 **The Entente** had once again been shown to work. Indeed, it became stronger. Talks were held between the chiefs of the **Naval Staffs** of both countries. It was agreed that:

(a) the **French fleet** should be concentrated in the Mediterranean to guard British and French interests;

(b) the **British fleet** should be concentrated in the North Sea to guard British interests and the northern coast of France.

12 You will see that this almost made the Entente into an Alliance. Could Britain remain neutral if France were at war? If she did, what would happen to a German naval attack on the French ports on the northern coasts? The French fleet would not be there to guard French interests.

8.21 The Balkans again, 1912–13

1 Balkan countries were involved in two wars (4.13–18).

2 These wars were settled by international conferences.

3 They left Serbia and Austria hostile to each other (4.19).

8.22 And so to War, July–August, 1914

1 The Austrian Archduke was killed at **Sarajevo**, 28 June 1914 (4.20).

2 Statesmen assumed this crisis would be settled by a conference.

3 Austria wanted to use this as a chance to crush Serbia.

4 **5 July William II** told Austria that she could count on **German support** in whatever she did.

5 **23 July Austria** sent a series of **demands (an ultimatum)** to Serbia. If accepted they would have virtually ended Serbian independence.

6 **24 July Serbia** accepted most of the demands and asked for time to consider the rest. She asked that the dispute be sent to **the International Court** (8.13.6).

7 **25 July Austria refused** the Serb request. **Russia** announced that she would have to start mobilizing her forces.

8 **28 July Austria** declared war on **Serbia**.

9 **30 July Russia** ordered **partial mobilization. Germany** demanded that this be called off.

10 **1 August Russia refused** to do as Germany asked. **Germany** then declared war on **Russia**, which was followed by her declaration of war on France on 3 August.

8.23 War by timetable

1 The list of dates in 8.22 indicates the almost inevitable way in which the nations went to war.

2 This was less the fault of the politicians in 1914 than of the system they had allowed to be built up.

3 **Vast armies** had been created in various countries. Plans for their use in event of war had been made out.

4 Success in war depended on **speed of attack**. To achieve this speed, military plans were linked to **railway timetables**:

i **mobilization of forces** meant that men had to travel to military centres–by rail;

ii once mobilized, **armies had to be got to the front** as quickly as possible–by rail.

5 Once mobilization had started, then the politicians were in the hands of their military staffs.

8.24 The Schlieffen Plan and Britain's entry into the War (*Fig. 9.1A*)

1 Count von Schlieffen had been **Chief of the German General Staff** between 1891 and 1906.

2 The alliance between France and Russia forced Germany to plan for a **war on two fronts**.

3 **1905** Schlieffen drew up a plan to knock **France** out of the war in a few weeks before turning to fight **Russia**.

4 **The Plan:**

i German armies would advance into France **through Belgium**, which was largely undefended;

ii they would **swing around Paris** to link up with German armies attacking from the south.

5 **Britain and Belgium:**

i In **1839** Britain and other nations had signed the treaty of London to maintain the **neutrality of Belgium**;

ii Germany invaded Belgium on **3 August**;

iii Britain demanded a **withdrawal**;

iv **Germany refused**. The Kaiser and his Ministers could not believe that Britain would go to war over the 1839 treaty. The German Chancellor, **Bethmann-Hollwegg** dismissed it as '**a scrap of paper**';

v **4 August** Britain declared war.

6 **Britain and France:**

i some Ministers wanted Britain to declare war as soon as France was involved. They argued that the results of the **naval talks** (8.20.11–12) imposed a moral obligation on Britain;

ii other Ministers did not agree. Indeed two resigned after the British declaration of war on 4 August and the invasion of Belgium. Many others might have done so if the government had gone to war in support of her French and Russian friends;

iii the Schlieffen Plan brought a united Britain to war.

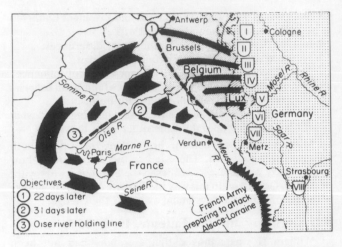

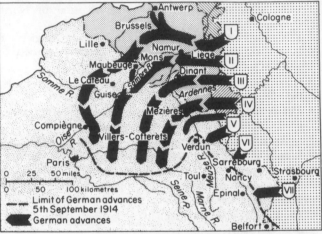

Fig. 9.1A   The Schlieffen Plan

9 The First World War, 1914–1918

9.1 The German plan, 1914 – 'A knock-out blow'

1 **Bismarck** had feared a 'war on two fronts' (8.1.2).

2 **William II's** rejection of Bismarck in 1890 (1.29) led to the Franco-Russian Alliance (8.11).

3 **Schlieffen** had drawn up his famous 'Plan' for the quick defeat of France (8.24). He thought Russia could not become involved in any war for some months after its outbreak because of the time needed for full mobilization of the Russian army. He thought that Russian military administration was highly inefficient.

4 **The Plan** (Fig. 9.1A):

i **the French** would want to take Alsace and Lorraine (1.12);

ii **the French** would expect the main German attack to come from the Metz area of Germany. **Verdun** was made into a strongly fortified city to withstand a German advance;

iii Schlieffen's plan differed from French expectations:

(a) **the main German attack** would come from the north;

(b) **seven German armies** were to drive through Belgium and Northern France, sweep around **Paris** (which would surrender) and link with armies advancing through the central region;

(c) **Verdun** would then be attacked from the front and rear – and would surrender.

iv there was a strict timetable to which each of the armies had to stick. This is illustrated in Fig. 9.1A. The final link up between the various armies was to be completed within 48 days;

v once France was beaten Germany would then switch armies to the Russian front and defeat that Eastern enemy.

5 **Moltke,** chief of the General Staff in July 1914, had to put the Schlieffen Plan into practice.

9.2 The failure of the Plan, July–August 1914

1 **Russia** mobilized more quickly than had been expected. Some German troops had to be transferred to the Eastern Front from the attack through Belgium, where Belgian troops fought bravely and checked the advance.

2 **Britain** entered the war on 4 August. The Schlieffen Plan had not taken that into consideration. Within days the British Expeditionary Force, commanded by Sir John French, was in Belgium. Its task, agreed with the French (8.16.8), was to defend Mons.

3 **Mons** was directly in the path of the German advance and here the British had their first taste of the War:

i **British rifle fire** was so rapid that the Germans thought the troops had machine guns;

ii **British losses** were very high. Some regiments (e.g. the Cheshire) lost almost all their men;

iii but the **German advance was delayed**. British resistance at Mons and the slow retreat after the Battle, gave the French more time to prepare.

4 At **Ypres** another army, commanded by Sir Douglas Haig, made another stand in another bloodbath.

5 Von Kluck, the German commander in France, saw that he could not keep to the Schlieffen Plan. His armies (weakened when Moltke sent troops to Russia) had been too long delayed by the British resistance.

6 Von Kluck changed the plan of attack (Fig. 9.1A):
i instead of going around Paris the Germans turned south **(to the east of Paris)**;
ii this left **the Channel ports** along the coast free from attack–and enabled British reinforcements to get to France.

7 Joffre was the commander of the French troops which rallied on the northern banks of the **River Marne. Sir John French** commanded the British who first held the Germans along the Marne, then drove them back–in some places across the **River Aisne.**

9.3 Trench warfare, the Western Front

1 By December 1914 the opposing armies were dug in and trenches ran from Switzerland to the Channel coast (Fig. V.3.2.2.A).

2 Life in the trenches was very hard. Rain turned the trenches into **muddy pathways** along which troops moved into positions; **men slept where they could** in their uniforms; **cooking facilities** were scarce–armies lived off tinned food; **dead bodies** littered the space between the opposing trenches ('No Man's Land'); packs of **rats** attacked men–dead and alive–and their supplies.

3 Defending the trenches was fairly easy. Massed rolls of **barbed wire** were laid in front of the trenches. This made enemy advance very difficult and slow. **Machine guns** allowed gunners in the defending trench to wipe out large numbers of advancing troops.

4 Attacking the trenches was difficult and costly:
i an **artillery bombardment** was made by large guns in the rear. Thousands of shells were fired on the enemy lines. It was hoped that this would frighten the enemy, smash the barbed wire and make advance easier;
ii such bombardments only **warned the enemy** who were then better prepared when the attacking troops jumped from their trenches and advanced across 'No Man's Land';
iii the **advancing troops** were normally weighed down with their packs, trenching tools, ammunition bandoliers, Mills bombs and other weapons.

5 The generals on both sides wanted to break through the enemy lines. Although their attacks never worked they insisted on yet more.

6 Major battles took place in
1915 at Ypres, Loos and Vimy Ridge;
1916 at Verdun (see below) and the Somme (see below);
1917 Ypres again (in the Battle of Passchendaele), Vimy Ridge, Cambrai (where massed tanks were first used) and Messines;
1918 the Marne (again) and St. Quentin.

7 Verdun was the fortress town built for the defence of the Rhine (Fig. 9.1A). It was of little real value once trench warfare had become the pattern of things. Indeed the French ought to have abandoned it and straightened out their lines of defence:
i the French government refused to allow a withdrawal fearing a panic if such a fortified town were handed over to the Germans;
ii the Germans realized this and made a series of heavy attacks from **21 February 1916 to the end of June**;
iii the Germans lost 281000 men in these attacks;
iv the French lost 315000 men. The commander of Verdun, Pétain, became a national hero. His slogan, **'Ils ne passeront pas'** 'They shall not pass'), became a popular declaration of French determination.

8 The Somme was Britain's most costly battle:
i it started on **1st July 1916**; 60000 men were killed out of a force of 100000 men. Many more were seriously injured; still more drowned in the sea of mud created by the collapse of the drainage system under artillery bombardment;
ii the battle ended in the **middle of November 1916**. Britain has suffered 400000 casualties in this 'graveyard of Kitchener's army'. German and French losses were equally heavy–and almost nothing had been gained.

9.4 New weapons

To try to break the deadlock both sides introduced new weapons.

1 Poison gas was first used by the Germans at the second battle of Ypres (1915).

2 The tank was invented by the British. It was first used on **the Somme** in 1916. Travelling at about 3 miles per hour, most got bogged down in the mud while others were easily destroyed by enemy artillery. Even those which broke through the enemy lines were captured by the Germans because they had got too far ahead of supporting troops. Only in 1917 (at **Cambrai**) were tanks used properly; they proved to be a very effective weapon.

3 Mining of enemy lines by **sappers** (the nickname for **engineers**) was developed as an underground method of attack. Men burrowed beneath 'No Man's Land' and the enemy lines, where they planted loads of explosives. When these were blown up, the enemy trench system and the soldiers in it were destroyed. But such activities were often and easily discovered and the sappers killed before they could complete their work.

4 The aeroplane
i at the outbreak of war this was an **inefficient, slow and unarmed** machine which, at best could only go at about 70 m.p.h.;
ii at first generals used aeroplanes to **spot** enemy movement;
iii at Verdun, planes were used **to support** the German attack;
iv on **the Somme**, they were used **to bomb** enemy positions;
v in **1917** the Germans developed the first **two-engined bomber**. By 1918 both sides had developed aircraft industries to produce stronger engines and by the end of the war there were **four-engined bombers**. One of these, in 1919, made the first Atlantic crossing;
iv the Germans were the first to work out how to **fire a machine-gun through the revolving propeller**. A Fokker EI was fitted with interrupter gear in 1915; by 1916 the British and French had also learned to do this and the aeroplane became slightly more efficient. But in general aircraft played little part in the War.
Five **zeppelins** bombed eastern ports and London.

9.5 The Eastern Front

1 In August 1914 Russian troops invaded **East Prussia** (Fig. 1.10A).
2 Generals Samsonov and Rennenkampf won small victories and planned to march on to Berlin (10.3).
3 German troops were withdrawn from France (9.2.1) and defeated the Russians at the **Battle of Tannenberg** where 90000 Russians were captured.
4 At the Battle of the **Masurian Lakes** the Germans again defeated the Russians and drove them from East Prussia.
5 At **Lemberg** the Russians defeated the Austrians, and many Slavs in the Austrian army surrendered without fighting.
6 1915–16 The Germans drove the Russians back. 2 million Russians died as they retreated. In June 1916 **Brusilov** launched a series of attacks and defeated the Austrians–but lost 1 million men. These losses played a part in the movement against the Tsar (Unit 10).

9.6 Gallipoli

1 The **Allies** (Britain and France) sent munitions to Russia via the northern ports of Murmansk and Archangel.

2 Turkey entered the war on Germany's side (October 1914). This gave the German-Turkish allies control of the **Dardenelles**, linking the Mediterranean and the Black Sea.

3 The Allies wanted to gain control of the Dardanelles so that supplies could more easily be sent to the Russians.

4 The naval attack, March 1915:
i a fleet of old battleships tried to get through the Dardanelles;
ii several were sunk by mines and the plan was abandoned;
iii the Turks defending the Dardanelles had almost run out of munitions and might have given in to another attack.

5 The military attack, April 1915:
i a small force commanded by **Sir Ian Hamilton** tried to capture **Gallipoli** as a step to an attack on Constantinople from the rear;
ii Hamilton **delayed** his attack. The Turks had time to prepare;
iii **Mustapha Kemal** led the Turkish defence;
iv in **April 1915** British, Australian and New Zealand troops (the *ANZAC*s) landed and tried to climb the steep cliffs of the straits;
v for eight months they made a series of costly attacks;
vi in **December 1915** the government called off the venture and the troops were withdrawn from Gallipoli.

9.7 Salonika (*Fig. 4.4A*)

1 The British failure led Bulgaria to enter the war on Germany's side (October 1915). She wanted revenge on Serbia for the defeats of 1913 (4.14–19).

2 Serbia was quickly defeated.

3 The Allies, having withdrawn from the Dardanelles, sent 600 000 men to **Salonika** to show they had not abandoned Serbia.

4 This army suffered from a shortage of food and supplies and many men died of malaria and other diseases.

9.8 Palestine (*13.11*)

1 The Turks threatened to invade British-controlled Egypt.

2 The British attacked the Turks to prevent such an invasion.

3 The British advance into **Mesopotamia** was meant to protect British **oil supplies** on the Persian Gulf.

4 At **Kut-el-Amara** the Turks defeated the British (1916).

5 T.E Lawrence ('Lawrence of Arabia') played a part in bringing the Arab tribes on to Britain's side against their Turkish overlords. While their part in the fighting was useful, the British had to face the problem of paying the price which Lawrence had promised – Arab national independence (13.11).

6 In **1917** the British and their Arab allies defeated the Turks in a series of battles. They captured **Baghdad** and, in **December 1917 General Allenby** captured Jerusalem. His entry into **Damascus** in **September 1918** marked the end of fighting in this region.

9.9 The war at sea

1 The role of the British Navy
i to ensure **free flow** of goods and troops to and from Britain;
ii to **blockade** enemy ports, to keep food and other supplies from reaching the enemy. Food shortages in Germany in 1918 played a part in the demand for an end to the war;
iii to **guard** colonies and other possessions from attack;
iv to capture enemy colonies.

2 The Germany Navy
i it had been built as a challenge to Britain (8.15.2);
ii the widening and deepening of the Kiel Canal (8.15.2) allowed the navy to get from its bases and into the North Sea

and to escape back to its bases whenever it needed to;
iii the Germans won a victory at the **Battle of Coronel** (1914) off the coast of Chile but suffered a major defeat at the **Battle of the Falkland Islands** where Admiral Von Spee's fleet was almost wiped out.

3 The Battle of Jutland, 1916
i there had been small battles in the North Sea. The Battles of **Heligoland Bight** (1914) and of the **Dogger Bank** (1915) were indecisive; neither side could claim victory;
ii the German High Fleet only sailed once into the North Sea. In one day's fighting at **Jutland** in May 1916 a British naval force led by Admiral **Jellicoe** had a running battle with the German fleet led by Admiral **Scheer**. Once again the battle was indecisive. Both sides claimed partial victory:

(a) the British argued that the German retreat to their bases marked a British victory. Certainly the German High Fleet never came to battle again;

(b) the Germans claimed a victory because the British had suffered much heavier losses. Their fleet had better armour to protect their ships, better armaments which inflicted the damage on British ships and better technical and naval awareness.

9.10 Submarine warfare

1 The submarine (or Under-water Boat) was a weapon for attacking British and other Allied shipping.

2 1915 The Germans declared an **all-out submarine campaign**:
i their submarines sank not only **Allied shipping** but **any ship** suspected of trading with the Allies;
ii there were attacks on **passenger-carrying shipping**. Perhaps the most important ship that was sunk was the British Cunard liner, the *Lusitania*, sunk off the coast of Southern Ireland; 1198 people died, including **124 Americans**;
iii the Americans protested and the Germans called off their all-out campaign.

3 Attacks on Allied shipping continued. Various methods were tried to halt the success of the submarine:
i **echo-sounders** were fitted to Royal Naval protection ships. It was hoped that these would then be able to discover the submarines before they could attack merchant shipping;
ii **depth charges**. Ships were fitted with equipment to fire these 'bombs' which exploded underwater and, if well-aimed, damaged or destroyed submarines;
iii **Q-ships**. These were merchant ships manned by Royal Naval crews and carrying hidden guns. These ships might tempt submarines to attack on the surface – when the naval guns could damage or destroy them.

9.11 The second all-out campaign, 1917

1 The **German generals** led by Ludendorff, argued in 1917 that their government had to make a decisive push for victory. The **heavy losses** on the Western Front and the **food shortages** at home could not be allowed to continue for much longer.

2 In **January 1917** the Germans announced the return to the all-out campaign. This was very successful:
i in February 1917 **266 ships** were sunk; in March another **338** and in April another **430**;
ii in **April 1917** Britain had only **six weeks supply of wheat** (for flour) left. Britain might be starved into surrender.

3 The convoy system was forced on a reluctant navy by Prime Minister Lloyd George. Instead of merchant ships sailing alone, they were organized into groups which could be guarded by Royal Naval destroyers. It was hoped that this would make it harder for submarines to attack merchant shipping.

4 This system succeeded. **Fewer British ships were lost.** By March 1918 German **submarines** were suffering very heavy losses; more were being sunk than were being built.

9.12 The USA enters the war, April 1917 (7.24)

1 **President Wilson** had been re-elected in 1916 after a campaign in which he promised to keep America out of the war.

2 It was the resumption of **the all-out submarine campaign** which helped to change American opinion in favour of the Allies.

3 Allied **propaganda** also changed American opinion:
  i the Germans were shown as cruel attackers on small Belgium;
  ii stories appeared in American newspapers of the savage behaviour of German troops;
  iii the cruelty of the submarine campaign was highlighted; women and children passengers drowning as a result of an attack were shown to be victims of German barbarity;
  iv cartoons drawn to show German savagery appeared in popular papers and magazines.

4 **American troops** did not play a large or immediate role in France. But America's entry into the war ensured a continual supply of food and the promise that, if the war went on, there would be a large number of fresh troops on the Allied side.

9.13 The Germans defeated

1 In **March 1918** the war was finely balanced:
  i the **Allies** had gained the support of the **Americans**;
  ii the **Germans** had forced **Russia** out of the war (10.22) and this allowed the transfer of troops from the Eastern Front;
  iii the **submarine campaign** was affecting life in Britain;
  iv the **British blockade** was affecting life in Germany;
  v **heavy losses** on the Western Front affected both sides. French troops mutinied after Verdun; German troops were badly affected by the gloomy news from home.

2 **Ludendorff,** the German commander, decided to make an all-out attack in France to end the war quickly.

3 **The German attack**
21 March 1918 The British at **Arras** and **Amiens** were overrun but managed to regroup. By 31 March they were holding the Germans.
April The attack switched to the north. Again, there were battles in Flanders fields around **Ypres**. Again, the British held the Germans, and the breakthrough did not take place.
May The Germans then attacked the French on the **Aisne**. Again they had initial victories—the French retreated to the **Marne**. The road to Paris was again open. But this attack was halted with the help of the **American troops**, a **British army** with an **Australian corps** led by General Monash and **French determination** to resist.

4 **The Allied counter attack**
July Allied troops came under the control of a Supreme Commander-in-Chief, **Marshal Foch**. He ordered a series of counter-attacks along the front from the Marne to Amiens. For the first time the German army broke.
August At **Amiens** the British defeated the Germans—in what Ludendorff called '**the blackest day in the history of the German army**'.
September Allied attacks continued to succeed. The British won victories in Flanders around **Ypres**; the Americans won victories in the south around **Verdun**. The French won victories in the centre. The Germans were forced to give up their line of defences known as the **Hindenburg line**.

5 **German collapse**
  i From **Salonika** Allied forces advanced into Bulgaria, Serbia and Austria. Bulgaria asked for peace on 29 September 1918, the Austrians on 3 November;
  ii **Allenby** was victorious in the Middle East (9.8.6);
  iii in **Italy** the Austrian forces collapsed;
  iv in **Germany** there were uprisings:
(a) **4 October** Ludendorff asked for a **truce** in the fighting on the Western Front. The Allied reply was Wilson's Fourteen Points (Fig. 12.1A):

(b) fighting continued when Germany rejected these points.
(c) In **Kiel, sailors** of the **High Fleet mutinied**.
(d) In **Berlin** and other cities, **people rose** against the Kaiser's government which had failed to deliver the promised victories, and which, in 1918, could not provide food.

6 **Further Allied victories** led to a major change in Berlin.
(a) A new Chancellor, **Prince Max of Baden**, persuaded the Kaiser to abdicate (9 November 1918) in the hope that this would prevent a Bolshevik revolution in Germany;
(b) German representatives went to meet French representatives at **Compiègnes** to discuss an end to the fighting.

9.14 The Armistice

1 The Germans hoped that the peace would be based on the Fourteen Points which they had earlier rejected.

2 The Allies argued that this rejection allowed them to dictate a different set of terms.

3 The **German fleet** had to be surrendered.

4 The **German army** had to leave all occupied territory.

5 The **Allied blockade** would continue until a Peace Treaty had been signed.

6 The left bank of the **Rhine** had to be evacuated and the right bank of the Rhine had to be demilitarized.

7 A small minority of Germans wanted to fight on. However:
  i **Ludendorff** and other army leaders did not want to see their forces humiliated. They advised acceptance of the harsh terms;
  ii **Prince Max** and other politicians did not want the civilian population to suffer any longer. They feared a Bolshevik revolution. They **advised acceptance** of the harsh terms.

8 The Armistice was signed and at **11.00 a.m. on 11 November 1918** the Great War came to an end.

10 Russia, 1914–1928

10.1 Support for the war, 1914

1 The majority of the **Tsar's ministers** hoped that war would put an end to criticism of the government.

2 Most **radicals** welcomed war. They hoped that the Tsar, to gain the support of the people, would make concessions.

3 The **Russian masses** rallied to the support of 'the Little Father' in a wave of patriotic fervour.

10.2 Opposition to the war, 1914

1 **Agrarian reformers** continuing the work of Stolypin (3.31) wanted a period of peace. They remembered Stolypin's warning: 'Our internal situation does not permit us to pursue an aggressive foreign policy.'

2 **Some ministers** remembered the disastrous consequences of the defeat in the Russo-Japanese War, 1904–05 (3.21–3.25).

3 **Rasputin,** 'the evil monk' (3.32) warned the Tsar: 'With the war will come the end of Russia.'

4 The **Bolsheviks**, led by the exiled Lenin, opposed Russia's entry into the war, condemning it as 'a capitalists' war' which would bring no benefits to the working class.

10.3 Speedy mobilization and immediate success

1 **30 July 1914** The Tsar signed the order for mobilizing troops because Austria had declared war on Serbia.

2 **31 July 1914** Posters appeared calling up Russian reservists.

3 **1 August 1914** Germany declared war on Russia.

4 **Russian troops** were the first **into action**:

i **Cossack regiments** of the regular army invaded **East Prussia**;

ii **victories** were won at **Stalluponen** and **Gumbinnen**;

iii many imagined that, when the millions of reservists were called up in late August–September, the **Russian 'steamroller'** would trundle on to Berlin. Victory seemed certain.

10.4 Defeats

1 **August 26–28** The Germans defeated Samsonov at **Tannenberg**. 90000 Russians were captured. Samsonov committed suicide.

2 **September 9–12** The Germans attacked Rennenkampf at the **Masurian Lakes** and drove the Russians from East Prussia.

10.5 Stalemate

1 **The Austrians** were less successful than the Germans. At **Lemberg** superiority in numbers enabled the Russians to defeat the Austrians.

2 Many **Slavs** in the Austrian-Hungarian armies deserted.

3 **Hindenburg** took command of German forces.

4 **Warsaw** was attacked–but held by the Russians.

6 **Lodz**; three German divisions were lucky to escape.

7 The Germans withdrew some of their best forces from France to help to end the fighting in the east.

10.6 1915–16

1 The Russians fought on a front **800 miles long**.

2 The peasants in the **Russian army** fought bravely against **German artillery and machine gun fire**.

3 In retreating, the Russians lost **two million men**.

4 **Russian industry** managed to produce more war goods. Between 1914 and 1916 production of **rifles** increased by 200 per cent, of artillery by 400 per cent and of **machine guns** by 300 per cent.

10.7 The Brusilov offensive, 1916

1 **June 1916** General Brusilov counter-attacked.

2 **The Austrians** lost many men in this attack.

3 A million Russians **died**; another million **deserted**.

10.8 The growth of criticism, 1916, was caused by:

1 **Russian industry** being less efficient than German industry was unable to produce weapons of the same quality or in the same quantities;

2 **Russian generals** who were incompetent. Younger officers became critical;

3 **the Tsarina** who had too much power:

i when Prime Minister **Kokovstov** criticized Rasputin the Tsarina persuaded the Tsar to sack him (January 1915);

ii his 75-year-old successor lasted only until the middle of 1916. He was replaced by Rasputin's favourite, **Stürmer**, an incompetent and corrupt junior minister.

4 **The Duma** was led by **Rodzianko** whose son was a junior officer under Brusilov:

i he asked the Tsar to form a **ministry based on the Duma**. This, he claimed, might gain wide support from the people;

ii **the Tsarina** persuaded her husband to 'remember the autocracy' and to reject this offer of help from 'a democratic Duma'.

5 **Generals** were dismissed or changed to other posts because 'Rasputin has had a vision'.

10.9 The Russian people, 1916

1 **Food supplies became scarce** because:

i **the Ukraine**, the largest corn producing area was lost;

ii **the railway system** could not cope.

(a) Many miles of line had been **destroyed** at the front.

(b) **The army used it** to transport munitions, soldiers, the wounded and food and other supplies;

(c) **industry used it** to transport raw materials and coal, finished products and munitions;

(d) **farmers used it** to bring in fertilizers, machinery and animal feed and to take away their food products;

(e) **town merchants used it** to bring in corn, meat and other farm produce;

iii **farms were less productive.**

(a) Many **young workers** had gone into the forces. The old and the women left behind could not do all the work.

(b) Many farmers **refused to sell** their corn in the towns. What could they buy for the money they got?

(c) **Corn prices** were fixed by the government. Other prices were free. The farmer resented being asked to pay higher prices for consumer goods.

2 **Food prices rose**

i **the government** was unable to control prices charged by merchants in towns;

ii **skilled workers** received higher wages–and could cope with the higher prices for food;

iii **most workers were unskilled**. They could not cope with the increases in rents and food prices;

iv for many people there was a **fall in living standards** as the cost of living rose more quickly than did wages.

3 **The weather** November–December 1916 was unusually severe. This added to the misery of the millions of workers.

10.10 The beginning of the end, November 1916– February 1917

1 **Shadow Ministries** were set up with the Tsar's approval by members of the Duma. **A Council of National Defence** had Ministers of Industry, Trade, Fuel, Agriculture and Food Supplies, Transport, Navy and Finance. But these 'Ministries' had no member of the government on them. They had no real power.

2 **The All-Russian Union of the Zemstvo** (3.6–3.7) Delegates from various local zemstvos formed committees to try to help the war effort. They were in touch with similar committees set up by trade unions and local government officers. But all these had no real power.

3 **Political criticism** at meetings of these committees and 'Ministries' was aimed at:

i the **Tsarina's** power and policies;

ii **Rasputin's** influence and behaviour;

iii the **incompetence** of the government;

iv the failure of the **generals**.

4 **The Tsar**, foolishly, left the capital for **Mogilev** where he took control of the army. This gave the Tsarina even more power.

5 **Food queues** were commonplace. Occasionally there were **riots** when supplies ran out or prices were very high.

6 **Cossacks** loyal to the Tsar put down these riots.

7 **Rasputin** was murdered in December 1916 by aristocrats who hoped to free the Tsar from 'the evil influence'.

8 **Mutinies** in the army became frequent. Men wanted to get away from the incompetent generals and the constant defeats.

10.11 The background to the February Revolution

In 1751 most countries reformed their calendars to take account of the fact that, until then, there had been no leap years so that the world had, as it were, 'lost eleven days'. The Russians had not made that reform. This explains why the

Russians write about the **February Revolution** and we write about a **March Revolution**.

1 10 February Strike at the large Petilov steel works in Petrograd. Men demand 50 per cent increase in wages.

2 19–21 February Many other workers join the strike.

3 23 February Rioting at bread queues; striking workers join in. Police and troops attack the rioters.

4 24 February Thousands demonstrate in Petrograd. Cossacks begin to show sympathy.

5 24–25 February The election of the first workers' councils (or **soviets**). Strikers joined by middle classes.

6 25 February Workers occupy factories; police do not always come on to the streets; Cossacks attack mounted policeman attacking a flag-carrying demonstrator. Said one man: 'I knew then that the Revolution had started'.

7 25–26 February The Tsarina tells the Tsar (by letter) that all is under control except for a handful of rioters. The Tsar sends an order to army commander, Petrograd, to suppress all disturbances.

8 26 February Troops attack and rioters disperse; Prime Minister orders Duma to dissolve.

9 27 February Duma remained in session. Meeting of Petrograd Soviet consisting of delegates from factories, shops, offices, schools and soldiers' and peasants' delegates. **Duma and Soviet both in Tauride Palace.**

10 27 February Kerensky, leader of the Peasant Party in the Duma, demands the Tsar's removal, by force if necessary. Soldiers join the demonstrators.

10.12 The overthrow of the Tsar

1 27 February Duma still meeting; Army commander, Petrograd, declares martial law–but staff cannot find glue to stick up the notices. Tsar's ministers meet at Admiralty building but go home when electricity fails.

2 28 February The Tsar left **Mogilev** to return to Petrograd. Train diverted to Pskov 100 miles from the capital.

3 Generals and ministers tell Tsar that a revolution is taking place.

4 The Tsar thinks of abdicating and naming his son as successor.

5 On **2 March** he signs a decree of abdication naming his brother Michael as successor. Michael refuses the post.

6 3 March Tsar abdicates. This was the end of the Romanov dynasty.

10.13 And what followed?

1 The Duma chose a set of new Ministers:
i Prince Lvov, of the Union of Zemstvo, was Prime Minister;
ii Miliukov, of the Cadets (3.28), was Foreign Minister;
iii Kerensky was Minister of Justice.

2 The Petrograd Soviet continued to meet. It made no effort to take power, although it issued **Soviet Order No. 1** saying that orders to soldiers had to be approved by the Soviet. Some of the 3000 members of the Soviet were also in the Provisional Government–Kerensky being Deputy Chairman of the Soviet.

10.14 The Provisional Government

1 It announced a programme for **future reform**.

2 It decided to **continue the war** against Germany.

3 Both showed that the Government was **out of touch** with the feelings of the people:
i the majority of **soldiers** did not want to fight;
ii the **town workers** wanted immediate action on food supplies, prices, working conditions and wages;
iii the **peasants** demanded more land.

4 The feelings of the people were shown by:
i the **revolt** of sailors at the naval base at **Kronstadt**;
ii **mutinies** in the army when officers were shot;
iii **attacks** on noblemen's estates;
iv **strikes** for an eight hour day (May 1917);
v an increased number of **local soviets**;
vi **growing hostility** between the Government and the delegates at the Petrograd Soviet.

10.15 Lenin's return, April 1917

1 Lenin was **in exile** in Switzerland when the Tsar fell.

2 The Germans wanted to get Russia out of the war.

3 They paid him to return to Russia in a sealed train.

4 His first speech called for a wider 'socialist' revolution.

5 April 7 In the Bolshevik paper, *Pravda*, Lenin outlined his policies. His **April Theses** urged his followers:
i not to support the Provisional Government;
ii to try to create a Republic of workers' and peasants' Soviets;
iii to work for the nationalization of all land, workers' control of all factories and farms and an end to the war.

10.16 The Bolsheviks versus the Provisional Government

1 The **Bolsheviks** were only a **small group**. They had been outvoted in the All-Russian Council of Soviets on the war issue.

2 From April onwards Lenin's followers went among the **soldiers and people** in Petrograd:
i the **soldiers** had to be shown that an immediate peace with Germany would be for their good;
ii the **people** had to be won over by promises of 'bread' and social reform.

3 June 1917 Brusilov launched another offensive against the Germans. By 2 July he reported failure and the loss of 40000 men. These losses were the last straw. The army retreated in panic.

4 In **Petrograd** the news of the defeat led to widespread **rioting** ('the July Days'). Some members of the Petrograd Soviet wanted to take power. The non-Bolsheviks on the Soviet wanted to wait for elections to be held; Lenin and the Bolsheviks wanted things to get even worse before seizing power.

5 The government used the rioting as an excuse for an attack on the Bolsheviks. In July 1917:
i the **Bolsheviks HQ** was attacked and *Pravda* closed down;
ii **Trotsky** and other leaders were arrested;
iii **Lenin** shaved off his beard and went into hiding.

6 At this point **Kerensky** became Prime Minister. A Menshevik (3.18.8), he was not a revolutionary; his war aims were supported by the middle class.

10.17 The Kornilov Affair

1 Many officers though **Kerensky** too weak a leader.

2 General **Kornilov**, Commander-in-Chief, marched his army against Petrograd, 'to hang the German supporters with Lenin at their head'. Kerensky dismissed him (27 August).

3 On **7 September** Kornilov demanded Kerensky's resignation.

4 Kornilov continued his march to Petrograd.

5 Kerensky appealed to the Bolsheviks for their help.

6 They came on to the streets of Petrograd; some, working on the railway system, switched the trains carrying Kornilov's army into sidings. He never reached Petrograd.

7 Kornilov was arrested without any bloodshed.

8 His plot and its failure put the Bolsheviks in a stronger position.

10.18 Lenin and the overthrow of the Government

1 The Germans supplied Lenin with money to help to overthrow Kerensky–and to end Russia's part in the war.

2 **Lenin** got **Trotsky** to train a small, highly skilled body of **Red Guards** of former officers and soldiers.

3 He also trained **industrial workers** to seize key points in Petrograd when he was ready.

4 Lenin published his campaign of **'Peace by your own feet'**, which called on soldiers to mutiny and **'Land by your own hand'**, which called on peasants to riot.

5 **Kerensky** tried to take action against Lenin. But his troops refused to obey him; sailors on the cruiser, *Aurora*, came out in favour of Lenin and threatened to bombard the capital.

10.19 The October (November) Revolution

1 **25 October** Orders given for the Red Guards to take the telephone exchange and the State Bank.

2 **The Government** met at the Tauride Palace.

3 **25 October, evening** The Bolsheviks demanded the surrender of the government. The *Aurora* fired blanks to frighten ministers and signal the Bolshevik revolution.

4 The government was guarded by a handful of Cossacks, some officer cadets and a Battalion of Women. But the Cossacks deserted, the officers surrendered and although the women were ready to fight, they were persuaded it would be useless.

5 **26–27 October** During the night the Bolsheviks attacked the Palace and arrested the ministers.

6 During that night the 650 delegates of the All-Russian Congress of Soviets came together for their second Congress; 390 of these were Bolsheviks. The Mensheviks (3.18.8) and others condemned the attack on the Provisional Government.

7 **Trotsky,** Commander of the Red Guards, told the Mensheviks **'You may go . . . to the garbage heap of history'**.

10.20 Lenin in power, 1917

1 The **Congress of Soviets** gave power to the 15 People's Commissars–all of whom were Bolsheviks: Lenin was chairman of the Council of People's Commissars.

2 It passed **a decree to seek peace** with Austria and Germany.

3 It proclaimed the **nationalization of all land**, seizing 540 million acres from private landowners and the Church.

4 **Elections,** called by the Provisional Government, were held in the autumn. In these the Bolsheviks won only a quarter of the votes; most support went to the moderate socialists.

5 **The Constituent Assembly** met on **5 January 1918**. It rejected a Bolshevik statement of policy. On **6 January** Lenin's Soviet Executive Committee dissolved the Assembly. Its members went home. Democracy had died.

10.21 The Constitution

1 **January–July 1918** The Congress of Soviets considered Bolshevik proposals for a new form of government.

2 Lenin's opponents accused him of wanting a dictatorship.

3 In **July** a Consitution was agreed:

i it created the **Russian Soviet Federal Socialist Republic**;

ii **supreme power** was given to the **All-Russian Congress of Soviets** whose members were elected in town and rural constituencies;

iii this congress elected an **executive committee** of about 200 members which in turn appointed the **Council of People's Commissars**;

iv this council was dominated by the **Central Politburo of the Bolshevik Party** which had an inner group of **five members**;

v **these five** were dominated by **Lenin**–the dictator who argued that 'the will of a class is at times best realized by a dictator who sometimes can accomplish more by himself'.

10.22 The Treaty of Brest-Litovsk, March 1918

1 **December 1917** Lenin agreed to **an armistice** to end the fighting with the Germans and Austrians.

2 **Trotsky** was sent to negotiate terms for a peace treaty.

3 The Germans refused to accept **Trotsky's terms**.

5 **The German army** advanced further into Russia.

6 **The Bolsheviks** had to accept Germany's terms.

7 **Russia lost:**

i Poland, Finland, Estonia, Latvia and Lithuania and, most importantly, the Ukraine, which became independent;

ii one-third of European Russia, one-third of her ironworks, three-quarters of her coal industry and one-third of her population.

10.23 Lenin's government in action

1 In the early months of 1918 the government issued a number of reforming decrees. **Education** was to be free; everyone was to be covered by a system of **national insurance** which would provide pensions, a health service and assistance for the unemployed.

2 A campaign was launched against **adult illiteracy**.

3 **The calendar** was changed to bring it into line with the rest of the world.

4 **The capital** was shifted from Petrograd to **Moscow**.

5 The **decree on the press** closed down all newspapers except those loyal to the Bolshevik Party and government.

6 **A new secret police force,** named (from its Russian initials) the **Cheka**, was set up. It was this force which organized the Red Terror in which critics were arrested, imprisoned, tortured and killed. The first to be attacked were the Liberals or Cadets (3.17.3); next to suffer were the non-Bolshevik socialists–the Mensheviks and the SRPs (3.17.1). Later Lenin was to use this secret force against the members of his own Party who became critical of his policies. It was the Cheka which murdered the Tsar and his family.

10.24 The Civil War–its origins (*Fig. 10.22A*)

1 The Treaty of **Brest-Litovsk** shocked many Russians.

2 **A Czech legion,** of prisoners of war from the Austrian army, was making its way home from camps in the Far East across Russia. They looted as they went and had to be put down by the Red Guards.

3 In **Siberia**, Admiral **Kolchak**, led a revolt. He wanted the restoration of the Tsar or the return of the Provisional Government.

4 In the **north**, based on Estonia, rebels were led by ex-General **Yudenich**.

5 From the **Crimea** there were revolts led by **Denikin** and later by **Baron Wrangel**.

6 In the **Ukraine** a peasants' army was led by the brilliant **Makhno** who wanted independence for his people.

7 From **Turkestan** came rebels financed by the British.

10.25 The Allies and the Bolsheviks

1 The Allies had sent masses of supplies to the Tsar.

2 After Brest-Litovsk there was a danger that these might fall into German hands.

3 British and French troops were sent to the **Crimea**, to **Murmansk** and to **Archangel** to guard the dumps.

4 **British forces** gave **help to the northern rebels**.

5 The **French** helped the **Poles** and the **rebels from the south** (18.5).

6 **Both Allies** hoped to get a government which would fight the Germans.

10.26 The Reds victorious

1 The Bolshevik government **had many problems** to meet in its first year. There was massive **unemployment** in industry still trying to get back to producing non-war goods. **Food** was even

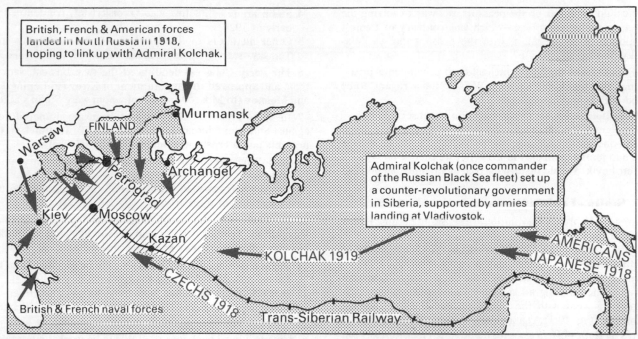

Fig. 10.11A   The Russian Civil War

scarcer than it had been in 1917. And there was the **Civil War** which started in 1918 and went on until 1922.

2 The anti-Bolsheviks contributed to their own defeat:

i some of them wanted to bring back the **Tsar**. This did not appeal to the mass of the people;

ii some wanted to set themselves up as **dictators** and so there were divisions among the rebels;

iii some were getting help from **foreigners**–which offended the national pride of many Russians;

iv some wanted to abolish the earlier **land reforms**.

3 Trotsky proved to be a brilliant organizer and leader. He had the advantage that his forces were fighting in a unified command–unlike the divided commands of the Whites.

10.27 War Communism, 1917–1921

1 The government **nationalized** all the means of **industrial** and **agricultural** production in the territory controlled by the Red Army. So much for 'Land by your own hands'.

2 Workers received **ration cards** so that they could get their wages in kind–in food and coal.

3 This forced the **unemployed** to rob the peasants.

4 The peasants had to hand over all their surplus grain to the Soviet authoritites at prices fixed by the government, ensuring peasant hostility to the government.

5 Men could be forced to work in mines, on roads and canals.

10.28 1921 a year of crisis

1 The Kronstadt rising In 1921 the sailors at the naval base at Kronstadt were angered when Trotsky and the Cheka put down a workers' strike in Petrograd. They revolted and called for a 'third revolution'. Trotsky led the Red Army and the Cheka to put down this rising. Many sailors were massacred.

2 The Great Famine The breakdown in transport and the almost constant fighting throughout the countryside meant that food supplies became continually scarcer. In 1921 things came to a head. Famine and sickness spread across Russia. Millions of people died. It was the American, Herbert Hoover, who organized the **American Relief Administration** to bring in wheat.

3 The New Economic Policy (NEP):

i it was obvious that the **Russian people were not willing to be**

communized. Peasants were not supplying enough food to the towns where there were insufficient goods for them to buy for money received from food sales;

ii in **March 1921** Lenin declared the **end of War Communism** and the onset of a **New Economic Policy**.

(a) Peasants would be allowed to keep part of their grain–for sale whenever they liked. They had to sell (at low prices) part of their output to the government.

(b) People were allowed to set up **small profit-making businesses** which, Lenin hoped, would produce the clothes and other consumer goods which might attract the peasants to sell their food in the hard-pressed towns.

(c) Some hard-working peasants built up profitable farms;

iii many Bolsheviks saw this as a **retreat from Communism**.

10.29 Lenin's death

1 In **July 1918** a member of the SRP, Dora Kaplan, tried to assassinate Lenin. He survived with two bullets lodged in his body–but he never really recovered.

2 In **1922** he had a stroke which left him paralyzed and speechless, although he continued to rule the country.

3 In **1923** he wrote his *Testament* in which he revealed that he was afraid of a quarrel among his followers when he died.

4 On **21 January 1924** he died.

10.30 The apparatus left by Lenin

1 The acceptance by most Bolsheviks of the **dictatorship**.

2 A **controlled Press**.

3 A **secret police** with great power and a grim record.

4 A **people** who saw that they had got rid of one Tsar only to see him replaced by a stronger one.

10.31 Trotsky–Lenin's successor?

1 Lenin thought Trotsky the **most able** of his supporters.

2 Most Bolsheviks admitted **his intellectual superiority**.

3 He had **travelled** widely, **written** many books, led the **Petrograd Soviet** in 1905 (3.24.4) and organized the **Red Army** during the Civil War.

4 But he did many things that raised suspicion:

i he argued (against Lenin) in favour of allowing **free discussion** within the Party about the problems facing Russia. Was he **'too soft'** to lead?

ii he called for a **war on the peasants** as a way of solving the food crisis and rising prices–which was **contrary to Lenin's NEP** policy of co-operation with the peasant masses. Was Trotsky **'too harsh'** to rule?

iii **he condemned the NEP** which allowed private enterprise– although this was Lenin's policy. Was he **'too arrogant'** to be trusted with power?

5 **Many Bolsheviks** also suspected him because:

i he seemed **too clever** for them; they would have liked someone more ordinary;

ii he had **joined them only in 1917**. Before that he had been a Menshevik. Would he turn his coat again if he had power?

10.32 Stalin–Lenin's successor?

1 After the February Revolution, 1917, Stalin became editor of *Pravda*.

2 In **1917** Lenin made him **Chairman of the Commissariat of Nationalities**.

3 During **the Civil War** he organized the defece of **Tsaritsyn** (later called Stalingrad and now Volgograd).

4 Later he went with the **Cheka** to lead the fight against **Kolchak** (Fig. 10.11A) and, later, **Yudenich** (Fig. 10.11A).

5 In **'The Rape of Georgia'**–his home state–he ruthlessly put down a band of rebels.

6 He became **head of Orgburo** which organized the growing Bolshevik Party and most importantly, became **General Secretary of the Central Committee** of the Bolshevik Party. This put him in touch with all the officials throughout the country. He could do small favours for them–and in return they helped to get his friends elected to various Congresses and Committees.

7 **Lenin saw the danger** of Stalin having got all this power in his hands. He thought Stalin **'too rude . . . intolerable . . .'** and in his *Testament* urged his followers to 'think about a **way of removing Stalin . . .'**.

10.33 Trotsky versus Stalin–stage I

1 **Zinoviev** was Party organizer in **Leningrad** and a member of Lenin's inner Cabinet.

2 **Kamenev** ran the Party in **Moscow** and was another of Lenin's inner Cabinet.

3 **Both were opposed to Trotsky,** partly for reasons suggested in 10.31 but also because Trotsky wanted to try to organize **'a world revolution'**. They knew that they had enough problems in Russia.

4 In **May 1924** at a Party Congress **Trotsky** called for a series of Plans aimed at the **more speedy industrialization** of Russia. **Stalin organized the opposition** to this proposal which was defeated. (It is worth noting that in **1929** this became **Stalin's own policy**.)

5 Trotsky wrote *The Lessons of October* in which he showed that **Zinoviev and Kamenov had opposed Lenin's plans** for the revolution in that month.

6 The angry **'bosses'** sided with Stalin and helped to get **Trotsky dismissed** from his post of **Commissar for War** (December 1925). Stalin's friends at the Party Congress approved of this.

10.34 Stalin versus Zinoviev and Kamenev–stage II of the struggle

1 The leaders of the big city parties now tried to use their power to make life easier for their supporters–the **industrial workers**.

2 Under NEP, unemployment was rising, workers went hungry but peasants prospered.

3 The workers wanted more **investment** in industry and government **control of food prices**.

4 **Stalin** argued that this was **'Trotskyism'**, condemned as early as 1924.

5 Other members of the Politburo–**Bukharin, Rykov and Tomsky**–sided with Stalin **against** Zinoviev and Kamenev.

6 **The Party Congress** denounced the two 'bosses', sacked them and approved the appointment of **Kirov** (to Leningrad) and **Molotov** (to Moscow)–both of whom were Stalin's allies.

7 In **1926** Trotsky, Zinoviev and Kamenev joined forces against Stalin and demanded the **end of NEP**, an **attack on the peasants** and a **crash programme of industrialization**.

8 **Stalin's friends** controlled the Congress which jeered at the opposition.

9 **Trotsky** was **expelled** from the Politburo and the Central Committee of the Party.

10 In **1927**, on the tenth anniversary of the October Revolution, **Trotsky** tried to lead a **revolt to overthrow Stalin**. No one followed as they had done in 1905 and 1917.

11 **Stalin** announced that **Trotsky was to be expelled from the Party**; exiled to Alma on the distant Chinese border.

12 In **1929 Stalin banished him** from Russia altogether–by which time Stalin could claim to be the undisputed dictator.

13 By **1929 Zinoviev and Kamenev** had apologized to Stalin and been allowed back into the fold–to be **used at a later date aainst Bukharin and his supporters**, when Stalin adopted Trotsky's policies of industrialization and a war on the peasants. We will study this in Unit 11.

---

11 Russia, 1928–41

11.1 Establishing the Stalin dictatorship

1 **Why possible?** Lenin created a dictatorship (10.22 and 10.30).

2 **Rivals** for power were **eliminated**:

i **Trotsky**, the most able, was first isolated as an 'anti-Leninist' (10.34) before being exiled (10.34);

ii **Zinoviev** and **Kamenev** were first used against Trotsky (10.33) then shown up as 'Trotskyists' (10.34) before they were forced, publicly, to apologize to Stalin (10.34.13);

iii these and other rivals were eliminated in the **purges** (11.2).

3 **The secret police**

i the **Cheka** (10.23.6) was founded by **Lenin** in December 1917. He used it to kill the Tsar and his family at **Ekaterinburg** in July 1918. It was also responsible for killing thousands suspected of being opposed to Lenin and his policies;

ii the Cheka was abolished in 1922. It was replaced by the **GPU**, part of the **NKVD** (the People's Commissariat for Internal Affairs);

iii the **OGPU** broke away from the NKVD in 1923. It was OGPU which was responsible for enforcing the collectivization programme (11.9) when millions of people were killed;

iv in 1934 **OGPU** again merged with the **NKVD** which acted as Stalin's instrument of terror during the purges (11.2).

4 A series of **purges** in which millions were imprisoned without trial and thousands killed, terrorized the population. Stalin faced **little opposition**–and that was crushed by secret police agents supported by a terrified people.

11.2 The great purge

1 1934: Kirov's death

i **1 December 1934** Stalin's ally, **Kirov** (10.34.6), the city boss of **Leningrad**, was murdered;

ii **Yagoda,** head of the NKVD, organized the arrest and imprisonment of **Zinoviev, Kamenev** and **other eminent Party members**–who might have been rivals for Stalin's position;

iii **between 1934 and 1938** millions of people were arrested and imprisoned as possible supporters of Zinoviev and Kamenev;

iv during **1934** the number of Party members fell from 3.5 million to 2.7 million. By the end of **1935** there were fewer than 2 million Party members. Stalin, through Yagoda, had got rid of the remainder;

v in August 1936 **Zinoviev, Kamenev** and **fourteen other prominent Bolsheviks** were brought to trial. They had been with Lenin before 1914, and fought with him in 1917. Now, after years of 'treatment' by the NKVD, they 'confessed' to any charge brought against them;

vi **the sixteen were found guilty and shot.**

2 1937

i in 1936 Stalin killed **some of** those who helped him against Trotsky;

ii in **1937** the NKVD arrested **Radek and sixteen other leaders** who had helped Stalin aainst Kamenev and Zinoviev. Radek was put on trial, sent to a labour camp and, in 1939, shot.

3 1938

i Stalin now turned his attention to others who had once sided with him against Trotsky. **Rykov, Bukharin** and **Tomsky and eighteen other leaders** were brought to trial and shot;

ii **Yagoda,** the head of the NKVD, responsible for millions of arrests and executions, was arrested and executed;

iii his successor, **Beria**, was even more subservient to Stalin and even more ruthless.

4 The purge of the army

In 1937 Stalin arrested Marshal Tukhachevsky and seven other generals, all 'heroes of the Civil War' (10.23–26). Stalin feared they might use their power to end the rightful dictatorship. So he had them executed–after trials in which they 'confessed' to many (often impossible) crimes.

5 By the end of 1938

i almost all the delegates at the **1934 Party Congress** had been executed;

ii almost all the **'old Guard'** of 1914–17 had been executed;

iii in their places Stalin had dependent supporters;

iv eight and a half million people had been arrested; one million had been shot. Seven million were in concentration camps;

v many of these were **industrialists and engineers**. Their arrests helped slow down Russian industrial growth;

vi **the army** lost more officers during the purges than between 1941 and 1945 against the Nazis. Its efficiency suffered as a result.

11.3 Stalin and industrialization–why?

1 At the Treaty of Brest-Litovsk (10.22.7) **Russia lost** a large percentage of its population, industry, coal and iron deposits. If Russia was to grow **strong and richer**, there had to be a programme to industrialize Russia.

2 Western countries, (Britain, France and the USA), had opposed the Bolshevik government in 1917–21 (10.25). Many Bolsheviks feared that they might try to attack Russia to get rid of the new form of government. Russia had to become **militarily strong**–and required industries to produce weapons.

3 Trotsky and others had talked of **'a world revolution'**. Stalin had opposed such ambitious plans. However, he knew that Russia was the **centre of world communism**. Russian (Bolshevik) industrialization would be an **advertisement for Communism**.

4 Unlike Trotsky, Stalin talked of **'socialism in one country'**. If that 'socialism' was to produce results Russian industry would have to be developed to **produce the goods**.

11.4 The first Five Year Plan

1 In his **New Economic Policy** (10.28.3) Lenin had allowed the return to some kinds of private enterprise. The State continued to control the major industries.

2 Trotsky called for 'a crash programme of industrialization' but had been condemned in 1924 (10.33.4).

3 In 1928 **Stalin adopted Trotsky's policies**:

i **a production schedule** was drawn up for all major industries;

ii **targets** had to be achieved in **five years**;

iii before the **end of 1932** most targets had been beaten. Production in coal, iron and electricity generating industries had doubled;

iv huge projects had been completed. Among the more spectacular were the Stalingrad Tractor Works, the Volga-White Sea Canal and the Magnitorsk mettalurgical industry.

11.5 The second Five Year Plan, 1933

1 In 1931 Stalin insisted that **'the tempo must be increased'** if Russia were to catch up with the industrialized west.

2 In **European Russia** there was a consolidation of industries.

3 In **Russia-beyond-the-Urals** there was a huge increase in the number, size and output of factories far from the path of possible invaders from the west.

11.6 Paying for the industrial growth

1 Foreign capital paid for Russia's early industrialization (3.14.6 and 3.16).

2 Western capitalists would not help Communist development.

3 Russia had to pay for her industrialization from her own resources. **Capital investment** went up five times between 1928 and 1931 ('the heroic year'). Much of this investment came from the profits made on collective farms (11.9.3).

4 Most of this went into **heavy industries**.

5 There was little left for investment in **consumer industries**. **Living standards** fell below the level reached under the New Economic Policy.

11.7 Labour and industrialization

1 Young communist **'shock workers'** were sent to give other workers the example of hard, dedicated work.

2 On 25 August 1935 a young worker, **Alexei Stakhanov**, produced fourteen times his usual output of coal. The government encouraged other workers to become 'Stakhanovites'.

3 However, if they did, they received **no more in wages**–they simply had their 'normal target' increased.

4 Workers who protested, those who **failed** to meet their targets and the managers whose factories or mines failed to fulfill their targets, were **arrested** as 'anti-government agents'.

5 The **1938 Decrees** introduced **fines** for such failures and, for workers, **loss of social security benefits**. In **1940** the Decrees were strengthened. Anyone who was twenty minutes late on more than two occasions was to be **sentenced to forced labour**.

11.8 The peasant and Russian industrialization

1 In the unrest of 1917 many peasants took land from their nearest nobleman's estate.

2 Lenin nationalized all land in the name of **war communism** (10.22).

3 The peasants had to hand over all their surplus grain crop to the government. Many hid such surpluses; others even burnt them rather than hand them over to 'the townies'.

4 In **March 1921** Lenin changed the law. Requisition of crops ended. Peasants had to pay their taxes in kind (crops or animals). The rest they could sell.

5 Under this **New Economic Policy** many peasants prospered. Some bought **horses** to pull their ploughs (instead of using their wives and children); some bought **extra land** from the less ambitious. These **kulaks** or prosperous peasants did well out of the revolution.

6 **Trotsky** had said this made a mockery of Bolshevik claims to be Communists. He had wanted a **war on the peasants** (10.31.4). Stalin used this as a weapon against him in 1926.

7 **1928 Bukharin** and other 'right wing' Bolsheviks took up the argument for an **anti-peasant campaign**:

i Russia had to **import machinery** to help industrialization;

ii this could only be paid for by **agricultural exports**;

iii the increasing **labour force had to be fed**;

iv **the peasants** would produce this extra food–and **become richer**;

v **industrialization, therefore, depended on the peasants.**

8 **Stolypin** had argued that a prosperous peasantry would be the best safeguard against revolution (3.31 and 3.32).

9 **Stalin** was forced to **adopt Trotsky's policy** because:

i he needed a continued increase in **agricultural exports** to help his industrialization plans (11.4 and 11.5);

ii there was **no guarantee** that a prosperous peasantry would produce enough–or at the right price;

iii if they did produce and if he did pay what they wanted, then there would rise, in a seemingly Communist country, a **rich and free peasantry**.

11.9 Stalin and the peasants

1 He attacked the **kulaks** as 'enemies of the state' who held the country to ransom. He knew that, if he got rid of them, the other peasants could be easily controlled.

2 In **1929** he announced a plan for the **collectivization** of all farmland–by timetable; 'the lower Volga by the autumn of 1930, the central area and the Ukraine by the autumn of 1931 . . .'.

3 **Collective farms took various forms:**

i **state farms** or sovkhozy. Here workers got wages paid by the government official who ran the farm;

ii **collectives** or kolkhoz. These were more common. On these the land was granted to the peasants of the two or three villages which were united to form the collective;

(a) the **peasants** were allowed private plots near their cottages to grow vegetables and keep chickens and other animals;

(b) **the bulk of the land** was managed by a committee elected by the peasants but chaired by a local Party official;

(c) the workers were divided into **brigades** of between 50 and 100 workpeople. The collective had to produce a certain amount of grain, chickens, pigs and so on each year;

(d) the government took approximately **15 per cent** of the output at about one-eighth of the normal market price and another **5 per cent** at the market price. The government sold this at about **700 per cent profit**. It was this which **provided the money needed for investment in industry** (11.6.3);

(e) another **15 per cent** went to the Machine Tractor Station (11.11.5);

(f) some of the output would be set aside for seed and as reserves against a poor harvest;

(g) the rest, **roughly one quarter of the total output**, was distributed to the workers on the collective according to the number of workdays they had put in on the collective.

4 **The collectives were not always successful:**

i some **workers** put in too much time on their private plots and **slacked** at their collective duties;

ii the **machinery** from the MTS was sometimes **defective** and no one was available to put things right.

11.10 Stalin and the war on the peasants, 1929–33

1 In 1929 many peasants consumed all they produced. There was nothing left for the government to take.

2 Many refused to hand their farms to collective committees.

3 This led to:

i **clashes** between government agents and peasants;

ii a **shortage of food** in the towns. There was bread rationing, food queues, high prices and the danger of the unrest which had led to the February Revolution in 1917.

4 The **kulaks** were to be dispossessed. Government agents were to round up over a million of them and announce the formation of collectives.

5 This announcement led to the wholesale **slaughter of animals** by angry peasants determined to resist the government.

6 The result of this was another **Great Famine**.

7 **Stalin** went ahead with his policy:

i **the army** was sent to help Communist officials get rid of the kulaks. Most of these were deported to the icy wastes of Siberia or the burning deserts of Central Asia;

ii about **13 million kulak families** died.

8 But the committees and less able peasants were unable to run the new, very large farms efficiently. **Crop failure** was common–which added to the famine.

9 When, as happened, **bad weather** also coincided with inefficiency, the result was even worse. At least three million people died of malnutrition during the Great Famine of 1932–33.

11.11 Stalin draws back–in some success

1 The majority of **peasants** survived on food from their private plots.

2 Collectivization was called off when its failure became evident. However, by 1932 some two-thirds of farms had already been collectivized.

3 The policy was resumed later in the 1930s and **by 1939 it was complete**.

4 Collectives became more successful. In 1937 there was a record grain harvest. Millions of peasants learned to drive tractors.

5 **The Motor Tractor Stations (MTS):**

i the first of these was developed to help the peasants around Odessa in 1928–before collectivization;

ii Stalin developed more stations. They got a supply of tractors from industrial plants; drivers and engineers were sent to work them on the collectives;

iii more importantly, lecturers and engineers went to train the collective workers who learnt to use these machines.

11.12 Stalin and the outside world

Units 17, 18 and 23.

12 Peacemaking– Germany and Austria

12.1 Wilson's Fourteen Points (*Fig. 12.1A*)

1 President Wilson issued his Fourteen Points in January 1918.
2 He hoped these would form the basis for peace.
3 The Germans rejected the Points. Ludendorff hoped for a complete victory in 1918 (9.13.2–3).
4 When, in November, the Germans surrendered they hoped that the peace settlement would be based on those Points.

12.2 The four leaders at Versailles, 1919

1 **Wilson** hoped the Allies would accept the Fourteen Points. He pleaded for 'no annexations, no contributions, no punitive damages'. He did not understand the deep enmity between France and Germany.

2 **Clémenceau,** Prime Minister of France, was nicknamed 'The Tiger' because of his determination that France would not be defeated even when the Germans seemed to be winning in March 1918.
He was determined:
 i to punish the Germans as harshly as possible;
 ii to undo the damage done by the 1871 settlement (2.4.4);
 iii that Germany would not be able to start another war.

3 **Lloyd George,** British Prime Minister since 1916, was, at first, in sympathy with Wilson. He realized a harsh treaty would lead to German attempts at 'revenge'. However, the British public wanted to 'hang the Kaiser' and 'make the Germans pay'.

4 **Orlando,** Prime Minister of Italy, wanted:
 i to punish Austria;
 ii to make territorial gains for his own country.

12.3 The 'Three' make Wilson ignore his 'Points'

Look again at Fig. 12.1A and then note the following:
1 **Point 1:** the Allied leaders met in secret.
2 **Point 2:** Britain refused to give up its right to search shipping trading with an enemy during wartime.
3 **Point 3:** tariff barriers were retained–and increased (12.10.2).
4 **Point 4:** there was no real attempt at disarmament (14.10).
5 **Point 5:** Britain and France increased their colonial holdings.
6 **Point 6:** the Allies sent troops to attack the Bolsheviks.
7 **Point 9:** the boundary of Italy was not settled.
8 **Point 13:** post-war Poland contained millions of Germans.
9 **Point 14:** the League of Nations never worked as Wilson had hoped.

12.4 The Conference at Versailles, 1919

1 This was only one post-war peace conference. Others were at:
 i **St Germain**, to arrange a peace with Austria, **Sept. 1919**;
 ii **Neuilly,** to arrange a peace with Bulgaria, **Nov. 1919**;
 iii **Trianon,** to arrange a peace with Hungary, **June 1920**;
 iv **Lausanne,** to arrange a peace with Turkey (13.2–13.7), **July 1923**.
2 There were 70 delegates from 32 victorious countries. They had 60 committees of experts to help them.
3 But the Conference was **dominated by 'The Big Four'** who met secretly and arrived at their decisions.
4 None of the defeated countries was represented at the various peace-making conferences.
5 **Russia,** although an ally in 1914, was not represented. The Allies refused to recognize the Bolshevik government.

Fig. 12.1A Wilson's Fourteen Points

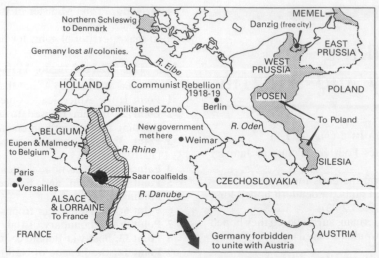

Fig. 12.5A   German losses, 1919

12.5 The Treaty of Versailles, 28th June 1919

1 German losses in Europe (Fig. 12.5A):

i **Alsace and Lorraine** went back to France. Germany lost three-quarters of her iron deposits;

ii **the Saar**, an important coalfield, was to be governed by the League of Nations for fifteen years when France was to have the product of the mines. At the end of that time its inhabitants would vote as to their future (see Unit 23);

iii **West Prussia and Posen**, with four million Germans, were given to Poland, one of the new states created at Versailles;

iv small portions of German territory (and 48 000 German people) were handed to **Czechoslovakia**, another new state;

v **Danzig**, once an important German port, and its 300 000 Germans, was named 'a Free City'; to be governed by the League of Nations;

vi **Memel**, another important port, with 141 000 Germans, was seized to the new country, Lithuania, created by the Treaty (14.8.2);

vii Northern Schleswig (1.10) went to Denmark;

viii **Note** Six and a half million Germans (or one-tenth of the former population) lost their German citizenship and became citizens of other countries.

2 The Rhineland was not all lost. **Eupen** and **Malmédy** were handed to Belgium. The remainder of the Rhineland was named as a **demilitarized zone**. The Allies were to keep armies of occupation there for fifteen years while the Germans were permanently forbidden to have armies or fortifications in this region.

3 German colonies The League of Nations handed these to the Allies to run as Mandates (13.10):

i German East Africa (Tanganyika) went to Britain;

ii the Cameroons went to France;

iii German Samoa went to New Zealand;

iv South West Africa went to South Africa—which refused to carry out the terms of the Mandate to help the local population prepare for independence.

4 German military strength was weakened:

i the air force had to disbanded;

ii the navy had to be surrendered to the Allies;

iii the army was not to exceed 100 000 men—smaller than the Belgian army.

5 Reparations were imposed to pay for the damage caused by the war. This followed the example set by Germany when she imposed such a punishment on France in 1871 (1.12):

i £6 600 million was to be paid in cash (18.4);

ii the merchant navy had to be surrendered to Britain;

iii fixed quantities of coal had to be handed to France;

iv a fixed number of cattle had to be handed to Belgium.

12.6 War Guilt

1 The Germans resented the **'dictated peace'**; they played no part in the negotiations on the terms of the Treaty. They had **either** to accept **OR** reject them and face a continued blockade by the British and the threat of a military attack by France and Britain.

2 But above all the Germans resented **Clause 231** of the Treaty which blamed Germany for the outbreak of the war. Their delegates had to sign a Treaty in which Clause 231 started: 'Germany accepts the responsibilities of Germany . . . for causing all the loss and damage . . . consequence of the war imposed . . . by the aggression of Germany and her allies.'

12.7 To accept or reject?

1 The fall of the Kaiser had led to a **revolution in Berlin**.

2 The first post-war government met at **Weimar**.

3 When the terms of the Treaty were revealed, the government debated them for several days.

4 In the end the Weimar government accepted the Treaty.

12.8 The Hall of Mirrors; French revenge

.1 1871 Bismarck had imposed the harsh Treaty of Frankfurt on France (1.12).

2 Before that Treaty was signed, Bismarck organized the proclamation of the **creation of the German Empire** (1.11). As an insult to defeated France that proclamation took place in the Hall of Mirrors in the former royal palace of Versailles.

3 28 June 1919 The Germans signed the Treaty of Versailles in that **same Hall of Mirrors**. France had her revenge.

12.9 The Treaty of St. Germain—with defeated Austria

1 Austria was separated from **Hungary** (with whom the **Treaty of Trianon** was signed in 1920).

2 She became a small, landlocked country—a pale shadow of the country which had once dominated Europe (see Unit 1).

3 Territory was lost:

i **Yugoslavia** was formed from the old Kingdom of Serbia and from Bosnia and Herzegovina. The Southern Slavs who had lived inside the pre-war boundary of Hungary were handed over to the new state;

ii **Romania** was enlarged by Transylvania (from Hungary) and Bessarabia (from Russia);

iii **Czechoslovakia** was created from the old German kingdom of Bohemia, and from the Northern States of Austria-Hungary;

iv **Poland** gained Galicia from Austria;

v **Italy** was given Trentino, Trieste and part of south Tyrol and Istria.

1 **Austria was to be kept permanently weak,** largely because Italy feared her emergence as a major power. In particular the Treaty forbade the union of Austria with Germany.

12.10 Criticism of the peace settlement

1 There were **too many small states**, unable to defend themselves from attack by any major power.

2 Each state imposed its own **tariff barriers**, contrary to Point 3 of the Fourteen Points. This led to a reduction in international trade, one of the reasons for the post-war depression.

3 Contrary to Point 12, the population of the **new Poland**, was not entirely Polish. The presence of **racial minorities** – Germans, Hungarians and others – in Poland was matched by the presence of similar minorities in **Czechoslovakia** and **Yugoslavia**. This was to cause international unrest in the 1920s and 1930s.

4 **Germany was angered** by the loss of so much territory. It was almost inevitable that she would look for **revenge**.

5 The Allies ignored **Bolshevik Russia** and her legitimate interest in the future of the countries on her border.

6 **The reparations** imposed were too harsh – and were never paid:

i **Keynes,** a leading British economist and an adviser to Lloyd George at Versailles, argued against reparations;

ii if they were to be paid, Germany had to export masses of materials and goods – and so ensure **unemployment** in other industrialized countries;

iii the French insisted on reparations being imposed. When Germany fell behind with her payments, the **French occupied the Ruhr industrial region in 1923**. This only ensured that Germany would fall even further behind in her payments;

iv **MacDonald,** Labour Prime Minister in 1924, helped to organize a plan named after the US minister, Dawes (18.4.6);

v reparations were abandoned in 1932. By that time the Germans had only paid over the money borrowed from America. But in 1932 the reparations problem had helped to create economic problems for the world. It had also helped Hitler to appear as the spokesman for the German hatred for the harsh reparations (see Unit 15).

13 Peacemaking–Turkey

13.1 The importance of this settlement

1 **The end of the old Eastern Question** (4.1–4.4). The defeat of Turkey led to:

i **freedom for the Christians** in the Balkans;

ii a new and successful **challenge to the Sultan's rule**.

2 The emergence of a new, **westernized Turkey**. This was the work, above all, of **Kemal Ataturk** (13.4).

3 The creation of several **Mandated Territories** (see 13.10). This provides us with a chance to examine this system of government.

4 The beginning of the **Palestine problem** (13.13–14). This problem was to become more important in the 1920s and 1930s (22.9). In more recent times it has become better known as the **Arab-Israeli problem** (Unit 37).

5 If you are studying British history, you should note that this settlement played a part in the fall of Lloyd George.

13.2 The Treaty of Sèvres, August 1920

1 **Britain** was anxious to safeguard her **oil interests** in Mesopotamia (now Iraq) and Persia (now Iran) (Fig. 13.9A) and ensure control of **one approach to India**.

2 France wanted to gain influence in the former Turkish Empire. She already had a **Muslim Empire** in North Africa. She hoped to enlarge her empire by gains made in the Middle East.

3 **Italy,** with a small Empire in **North Africa**, hoped to extend it.

4 **The three Allies** tried to obtain **'spheres of influence'** as part of this Treaty.

5 The Treaty never came into force because of the Turkish revolution (13.4).

13.3 The Greeks gain Smyrna, August 1920

1 At Sèvres **Greece** was allowed to retain Smyrna (Fig. 13.9A). A fleet of British, French and American warships guarded a Greek force which landed to take control of this port in mainland Turkey.

2 **Smyrna** was then the scene of a **massacre of Muslims**.

3 This massacre **united the Turks** against:

i the Treaty of **Sèvres**;

ii **the Sultan** who had not been able to prevent it.

4 It was also the signal for the revolution by Kemal.

13.4 Kemal's revolution

1 **1908** Mustapha Kemal had been leader of the **Young Turks** against the corrupt rule of the Sultan (4.12). They had deposed Sultan Abdul Hahmid. Sultan Muhammad V came to the throne.

2 **1915** Mustapha Kemal led the Turks in the **Dardanelles campaign** (9.6). This made him a **popular hero**.

3 **1920** He helped to form a new **Nationalist Party** which pledged itself to the overthrow of the Treaty of Sèvres.

4 He set up a **nationalist government** in **Ankara** in opposition to the Sultan's government in Constantinople.

13.5 Kemal versus the Allies and the Greeks

1 To try to defeat Kemal's revolution, an **Allied force occupied Constantinople** in **March 1920**.

2 **Nationalist leaders and supporters** were arrested and deported.

3 Kemal's government had a great deal of **popular support**. **The majority of Turks** were tired of the corrupt government led by a Sultan who had been unable to avoid defeat by the Allies and the massacre of Smyrna.

4 **France and Italy** realized this. They made agreements in which they **recognized Kemal's government**.

5 **Britain** maintained a pro-Greek attitude.

6 By **September 1922** Kemal's forces had defeated the Greeks and recaptured **Smyrna** and **massacred the Christians** (13.3.2).

13.6 Kemal versus Lloyd George

1 Having driven the Greeks from Smyrna, Kemal decided to invade **Thrace**, and to re-conquer former **European Turkey**.

2 French and Italian troops were withdrawn from **Chanak** where they had been stationed to stop the Turks from entering South Eastern Europe (Fig. 13.9A).

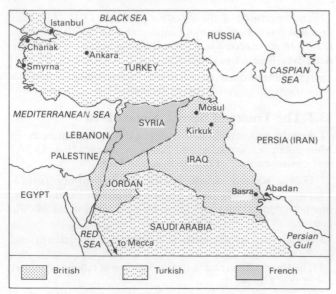

Fig. 13.9A   Dividing up the Turkish Empire, 1923

8 Ataturk In 1934 Mustapha Kemal officially changed his name. He took the name of **Kemal Ataturk** ('the father of the Turks').

13.9 The end of the Turkish Empire

1 The Empire had stretched into South Eastern Europe, North Africa and, as you can see in Fig. 13.9A, into the Arabian Gulf.

2 Britain had a great interest in the **oil fields** in Mosul, Kirkuk and Basra in modern Iraq and at Abadan in Persia.

3 Britain, France and Italy might have liked some parts of this Empire. That is what they, and others, had done in Africa (see Figs. 5.1 and 5.7).

4 This would have run counter to their stated war aims of 'no **annexations**'.

5 During the war, Britain and France had reached agreement on the division of this Empire between themselves. However, this **Sykes-Picot agreement (1916)** never came into operation.

6 At **San Remo in April 1920** the Allied Supreme Council devised a new system of government for colonies of defeated allies.

13.10 The Mandate System

1 There are **two opposing views** of the Mandate System:
i 'A disguise for **colonial annexation . . .**';
ii 'An admission of a **new sense of responsibility** towards backward peoples.'

2 We have seen that the victorious Allies were unwilling to annex the former colonies of the defeated countries (13.9.4).

3 The League of Nations set up a **Mandate Commission** to supervize the work of the Mandated Powers which administered the Mandated Territories on behalf of the League.

4 The Mandated Powers had to **help their territories towards self government** (13.10.1) and to promise not to use them as military bases.

5 The League's **Mandates Commission** received annual reports from the Mandated Powers. It could offer them advice. In fact it had **little power** over the actions of the Powers.

6 This is best seen in the case of **South Africa** which refuses to hand over its mandate for the former **German South West Africa** to the United Nations and treats it as its own territory.

13.11 Britain, Arab nationalism and the War, 1914–18

1 1914 **Turkey** planned to attack Egypt, hoping for support from other countries in the Muslim world.

2 Britain rushed troops from India, Australia and New Zealand.

3 British forces won **victories** at Ismailia and El Kantara.

4 1915 British troops won a victory at Romani which guaranteed the control of the Suez Canal for Britain.

5 1916 The British switched to attack–on Palestine.

6 Allenby won victories at Beersheba, Gaza, Askalon and Jaffa and on 9 December 1917 entered Jerusalem.

7 In **1918** many of Allenby's forces were taken to France.

8 The pro-British **Emir Feisal** supported the British.

9 This support had been won by:
i **T.E. Lawrence** ('Lawrence of Arabia');
ii vague promises that after the war there would be a series of **independent Arab states**, to fill the vacuum that would be created by the final dismemberment of the Turkish Empire.

13.12 Mesopotamia, during and after the war

1 The defence of Mesopotamia was the responsibility of the government of India.

2 1914 **Basra and Kurna** were captured, ensuring British control of the important delta.

3 Only British forces were at Chanak to face Kemal's Turks.

4 Lloyd George appealed to the Dominions (Australia, Canada, New Zealand and South Africa) for help. They refused.

5 The danger of a renewed war was avoided when:
i the British **General Harrington** did not deliver Lloyd George's ultimatum to Kemal telling him to withdraw;
ii **Kemal** did not order his forces to attack the British.

6 11 October 1922 Both sides agreed a **truce**. The Chanak crisis was over. The problem of peacemaking remained.

13.7 The Treaty of Lausanne, 1923

1 This reviewed and changed the terms of the Treaty of Sèvres.

2 Turkey retained part of **Thrace**, including **Adrianople** and the old capital, **Constantinople** (Istanbul).

3 The Straits remained under Turkish sovereignty.

13.8 Kemal reforms Turkey

1 The last of the Sultans, Mohammad VI, was deposed in 1922.

2 The Caliphate (headship of the Islam religion) was then given to a cousin of the Sultan.

3 1924 The Caliphate was abolished. All members of the former royal family were banished from Turkey.

4 Mustapha Kemal, **President of Turkey**, was given almost dictatorial powers in the **new constitution**. He used these powers to try to modernize his country.

5 Religious reforms. Kemal thought that Islam was one of the major reasons for Turkey's decline from power:
i **Sunday** was named the day of rest–and not the Islamic day, Friday;
ii **the fez**, or hat, worn by men when praying, was forbidden;
iii **the chadar**, or veil worn by Muslim women, was abolished;
iv **1928** the Muslim religion ceased to be the official religion of Turkey.

6 Social reforms Kemal wanted to westernize his country:
i the **alphabet** was westernized;
ii **state elementary schools** were established;
iii **women** were encouraged to play an active part in the country's life. In **1922** they were given the **right to vote** in elections for the National Assembly.

7 Political change
i **free elections** were held for a National Assembly in 1922;
ii in **1924** Kemal carried out a **purge** of all the opposition;
iii Turkey became a **one-party state**.

3 The Turks suffered other defeats in 1915. Then **General Townshend** was ordered to attack Baghdad, with insufficient forces.

4 Townshend was defeated at **Kut-el-Amara** (1916). Later General **Maude** took **Kut** (December 1916) and **Baghdad** (March 1917).

5 The British went on to defeat the Turks in Persia and to capture Mosul, the great oil centre (November 1918).

6 **Mesopotamia became a British Mandate** after 1920. The Arabs resented their new rulers and a **serious revolt** broke out in 1920.

7 The British put down the revolt. However, they created the **kingdom of Iraq** under Feisal (13.11.8) who had been driven from Syria by the French.

8 In **1932** Britain recognized the **independence of Iraq** and secured her admission to the League of Nations.

13.13 The politics of Palestine–Arab hopes

1 The first Arab chief to raise the flag of revolt against the Turks was **Hussein, the ruler of the Hejaz**.

2 **The Hejaz**, the coastal strip running down the eastern bank of the Red Sea, was not a wealthy trading or farming state. It was important as it contained the Muslim's sacred city, **Mecca**.

3 Hussein hoped the British would help him win independence from Turkey.

4 **McMahon**, the British representative in Cairo, reached an agreement with Hussein in 1915. This contained a **vague promise of Arab independence** for the traditional Arab lands.

5 One of Hussein's sons was **Feisal**. He went to Versailles in 1919 to claim 'the promised land'. But the hopes of the Hashemite family (Hussein, Feisal and his other brothers) and of Arabs generally grew less as the Powers set up their Mandate System.

6 **The French** offered the crown of a **united Syria** (including Syria and Lebanon) to **Feisal**. But once he had accepted the **French drove him from Damascus**. As we have seen he became ruler of the British Mandate, Iraq (13.12.7).

7 Another of Hussein's sons, **Abdullah**, went to **Amman** in 'British' Palestine (mandated to Britain in 1920) and was proclaimed King by Arab nationalists.

8 1921 The British assigned the area of **Trans-Jordan** (or across the River Jordan) from Palestine for him to rule.

9 **Jordan** remained under British supervision until 1956.

13.14 The politics of Palestine–Jewish hopes

1 By 1914 many thousands of **Jews** from Europe and the USA had gone to live in Palestine, the Biblical home of their people.

2 **The Zionist Movement** had been founded by Theodore Herzl. It demanded the right of Jews to live in Palestine.

3 In 1914 that Movement was led by the British scientist, **Chaim Weizmann**, whose work on explosives was important for Britain.

4 The movement had a great deal of **American support**. By 1917 Britain was anxious to gain the support of the USA. If she could please American Jews they might get Wilson to help Britain.

5 In **1917** the British Foreign Secretary was A. J. Balfour. He wrote to the leader of the British Jews, Rothschild, in what has become known as **'the Balfour Declaration'**. In this he promised that, after the war, Britain would ensure **'a national home for the Jewish people'** in Palestine.

6 As the Mandated Power, Britain let a number of Jews into Palestine.

7 This policy pleased no one:
i the leaders of **world Jewry** resented the limitations on Jewish immigration by the British;

ii the **Palestinian Arabs** resented the influx of Jews.

8 **McMahon** had promised everything to the **Arabs** (13.13.4). Balfour had promised Palestine to the **Jews**. Here lay the seeds for future conflict (Units 22 and 37).

14 The League of Nations

14.1 Its origins–in ideals

1 The League was an attempt to **move away from the old power politics** which had, in the past, led to war.

2 Its supporters hoped that the League would **solve the world's problems peacefully**.

3 It had many weaknesses but was a **brave pioneering effort**.

14.2 Its origins–Wilson's Fourteen Points (*12.1*)

1 We have seen that most of Wilson's Points were ignored or changed in the hard bargaining at Versailles (12.3).

2 His 14th Point (see Fig. 12.1A) was secured.

14.3 The Covenant of the League

1 This was the **constitution** of the League.

2 It had **26 articles** dealing with such things as:
i **arms reduction** and the control of **arms manufacturing**;
ii the duty of the League to **prevent war**;
iii the duty of the member-states to **take any disputes to the League** for a decision. Once a decision had been given there must be no resort to war for three months;
iv if war broke out the League would call on members to apply **economic sanctions**–to stop trading with the aggressor nation;
v if economic sanctions did not end the fighting the League would order **military action** to be taken.

3 This Covenant was included in all the peace treaties signed after the war. This had several results:
i all nations appeared to accept the idea of the League;
ii but the treaties were imposed on the defeated nations. The League appeared, at first, as an **association of the victors**.

14.4 The organization of the League (*Fig. 14.4A*)

1 **The Assembly**
i this was a large body;
ii every nation had the right to send **three delegates** although each nation had only **one vote**;

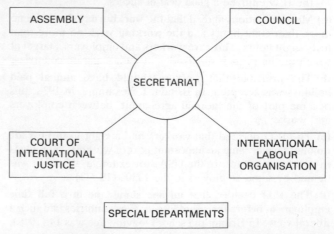

Fig. 14.4A The organization of the League

iii the Assembly **met annually**. It could be summoned to meet at other times for special reasons;

iv **the rights of the world's smaller nations** were recognized– they had the same voting power as the major Powers;

v for a decision to be reached, every member had to vote in its favour. This **decision by unanimity** was a weakness. Any member could block League action. In fact there was a surprising degree of agreement. Most matters were thrashed out in committees and when the final votes were taken those in the minority often preferred to abstain rather than block the will of the majority.

2 The Council

i this smaller body **met at least four times a year** and could be easily called together at times of crisis;

ii **the victorious Allies** (Britain, France, Italy and Japan), **had permanent seats** on the Council. The USA would have had a seat but the Senate refused to ratify the peace treaties (14.6.5.iv–v);

iii **non-permanent members** were chosen from among the smaller member nations. In **1920** there were four non-permanent members. In **1922** this became six, in **1926** it became nine and by **1939** there were eleven non-permanent members chosen, by rotation, from the smaller powers;

iv **decisions** of the Council had to be **unanimous** which led to long arguments and slow progress in times of crisis;

v the Council had **no real power**. It had, for example, **no army** at its disposal. It relied on the goodwill of members;

vi the Council supervised the work of a variety of Commissions (14.5). Some of these were very successful.

3 The Secretariat

i this **international civil service** ran the League;

ii its members were drawn from the peoples of member nations;

iii it had its permanent headquarters at **Geneva**;

iv it was headed by **a Secretary-General**, the first one being an Englishman, Sir Eric Drummond;

v among the **duties** of the Secretariat were:

(a) to implement League decisions;

(b) to provide the factual information needed by the Assembly and Council on issues being discussed;

(c) to keep the records of the various Commissions (14.5).

4 The International Labour Organization (ILO)

i at the League's headquarters, representatives of **governments, employers and workers** met in an annual conference;

ii **one of their aims** was to work for the improvement of working and living conditions throughout the world;

iii they also proposed **new laws** to the various governments;

iv each year the ILO provided information as to how governments were reacting to the decisions already published;

v the ILO enjoyed a **good deal of success**.

(a) Member nations agreed that the **working day** should be no more than eight hours and the **working week** no more than forty-eight hours. This gave workers and employers a target at which to aim in their discussions in their separate countries.

(b) The principle that workers should have **annual paid holidays** was accepted. In Britain, for example, in 1938, this became part of the 'normal agreement' between employers and workers.

(c) The ILO decided that workers had a **right to form trade unions**. This became an important part of workers' campaigns in various countries. In the USA, for example, this right was denied by some employers in the 1930s (19.5.3).

(d) The ILO decided that **no one should be in a full time employment before the age of fifteen**. Few countries had such a liberal view. In Britain the school-leaving-age was 14 (1918).

Only in 1947 was it raised to 15. But the ILO prodded governments into action.

(e) The ILO published information on the **dangers arising from the use of some materials**. It proved that the use of **white lead** in print manufacturing endangered the lives of workers in that industry. Trade unions could then argue with governments and employers to have such substances banned.

5 The Court of International Justice

i this had been set up in the **Hague in 1900** (8.13.6);

ii few nations brought their disputes to the Court. Austria, for example, refused to allow their dispute with Serbia in 1914 to be taken before the Court;

iii in **1922** the **Permanent Court of International Justice** was formally established at the Hague;

iv it had **limited powers**. It could not compel nations to bring disputes before the Court. Nor could it force states to accept its decisions;

v by 1939 its **15 judges** had settled **70 major cases** and had helped **arrange 400 international agreements**.

14.5 The Commissions of the League

1 Smaller committees, or Commissions, were set up to deal with special problems or issues.

2 The Mandates Commission kept an eye on the good government of the Mandated Territories (13.10).

3 The World Health Organization (WHO) campaigned for such things as the attack on preventable diseases.

4 The Drugs Commission drew attention to the danger of certain drugs and to methods of controlling the drugs traffic.

5 The Minorities Commission drew attention to the ill-treatment of various racial minorities and invited states guilty of such ill-treatment to mend their ways.

6 The Commissions for the administration of the **Saar** and of **Danzig** ensured that these territories were properly governed in the name of the League.

7 The Disarmament Commission got the greatest attention in the world's press–and was the one which had the least success (14.10).

14.6 How did the nations judge the League?

1 It had its **first meeting** in Geneva in **1922**.

2 42 nations sent delegates to this meeting.

3 None of the **defeated nations** was represented.

4 Russia was not invited to join; the Western Powers were still unwilling to recognize the Bolshevik government.

5 The United States:

i Wilson was 'the father of the League';

ii in the mid-term elections in 1918, the Republicans won majorities in the House of Representatives and the Senate;

iii Wilson, the Democratic President, was in a weak position because of this Republican opposition;

iv he did not take a Republican with him to Versailles;

v **the Senate** refused to ratify the peace treaties (7.3.3.c). The USA therefore never became a member of the League.

6 France:

i she saw the League as an agency for **enforcing the terms of the Treaty of Versailles**;

ii in particular she wanted it to **guard her security** against the danger of fresh German agression;

iii she hoped it would defend members' interests;

iv when it proved not to be a strong body France turned to other means of safeguarding her interests (18.7–10).

7 Britain:

i she hoped that the League would help solve the world's problems peacefully;

ii but Britain was **not willing to send her forces** to act on behalf of other people's interests;

iii **pacificism** was a feature of British life in the 1920s and 1930s. People's memories of the slaughters of 1914–18 were too fresh for them to be willing to engage in another war.

8 Generally

i nations followed **their own self-interests** rather than the interests of the wider world. This was made clearly evident by the actions of:

(a) **Italy** in 1923 (14.8).

(b) **Japan** in 1931 (17.22).

Both Japan and Italy were permanent members of the League Council. Their disregard for the League was particularly harmful to its claims to be an effective organization.

(c) **Germany,** which joined the League in 1926 but which, under Hitler, walked out when the Disarmament Conference proved to be a failure (14.10). Hitler's subsequent defiance of the League showed it at its weakest.

(d) **Russia,** which joined in **1934**, was expelled in **1939** when she invaded Finland.

ii In conclusion you should note that the power of national sovereignty was greater than the power of internationalism.

14.7 Some early successes

1 Danzig In spite of the rivalry between Poles and Germans, Danzig was established as an International Free City (Fig. 12.5A).

2 Upper Silesia In 1921, plebiscites confirmed the division of this coal-rich area (arranged by the League) between Poland and Germany. Although neither country was really satisfied by the division, they accepted it–and went on to make a trade treaty.

3 The Aaland Islands In 1921 a dispute between Sweden and Finland over the ownership of these islands was settled, peacefully, in favour of Finland.

4 Austria 1922 The Austrian economy was on the point of collapse. The League organized financial help to save Austria.

5 Greece and Bulgaria These were long-term rivals in the Balkans (4.17). In 1925 the Greek invasion of Bulgaria was halted by the League which forced Greece to pay compensation to Bulgaria.

6 These issues involved **only smaller countries**.

14.8 Some early failures

1 Vilna This was a town controlled by Lithuania but which Poland attacked. The League condemned the attack but was forced to allow Poland to hold on to it in **1923**.

2 Memel 1923 Lithuania, which had lost Vilna, invaded Memel and in spite of League protests, held on to it (12.5.1.vi).

Corfu 1923 An Italian on a League Commission was murdered on the Greeco-Albanian border, where Italy wanted to expand. Italy did not take the issue to the League. It bombarded the Greek island of Corfu. The League Council wanted to refer the matter to the Permanent Court of Justice. The Allied Conference of Ambassadors instead allowed Greece to pay an indemnity. The League's most powerful members refused to support it.

14.9 Failing major tests, 1931–39

1 The first major tests of the League concerned Japan's invasion of **Manchuria**. We shall see that the League failed to prevent Japan succeeding in an aggresssion condemned by the League (17.21–22). Japan left the League in 1933.

2 In **the Abyssinian crisis** of 1935 the League again failed to halt the aggressor or help the victim (23.6).

3 Hitler went ahead with his aggressive policy in defiance of the Treaty of Versailles and the League (23.7–13).

14.10 Disarmament Commission and Conference

1 In 1929 the world went through the first stages of the great **depression in trade and industry**. The League had no suggestions to make as to possible solutions to this major crisis.

2 The Covenant (14.3) called for the nations to base their foreign and military policies on collective security (**Article 10 of the Covenant**). It also called, in **Article 14**, for the nations to disarm.

3 The Allies refused to carry out their own decisions. There was no reduction in arms.

4 Originally the League had appointed a **Military Commission** to advise on disarmament. Later this was replaced by a **Temporary Mixed Commission** which had military and civilian members. No agreement was reached on anything.

5 1925 Plans were made for a World Disarmament Conference to meet in 1926. This failed even to agree on the definition of 'armaments' or how they were to be counted.

6 1930 Germany, now a member of the League, asked for a revision of the terms of the Treaty of Versailles; she wanted an **army** as large as the French and a **navy** as large as the British.

7 Britain had some sympathy with the claims; the French refused to accept them.

8 1932 The Disarmament Conference finally met in **London**.

9 The Germans threatened to walk out if they were not given parity with France and Britain (**June 1932**).

10 While the Conference was in session (**1932–34**) Hitler came to power in Germany (January 1933).

11 By the summer of 1933 Hitler had made himself dictator of Germany (15.23). He withdrew from the Conference and resigned from the League.

12 1934 The Conference broke up having reached no agreement.

14.11 Some reasons for the League failure

1 The principle of **nationalism** was stronger than the idea of internationalism; nations were not ready (nor are they today) to put their own national self-interests after international interests. Today this can be seen in such issues as the refusal of the developed world to tackle the issue of underdevelopment (38.4). It can also be seen in the way in which even the newer nations use war as an instrument of policy.

2 Some major powers refused to support the League:

i the USA was never a member;

ii **Germany** left when its interests seemed to be ignored (14.10.11);

iii **Italy** disregarded the principles of the League in the Corfu issue (14.8.3) and proved the League helpless in the Abyssinian crisis (23.6).

3 The League had **no army** at its disposal (14.4.2).

4 If its decisions were to be imposed, particularly against a major power such as Italy, then **Britain and France** would have had to supply the forces required. Neither was willing to do so (14.6.6 and 7). Like the rest of the world they seemed to prefer peace at any price.

5 The diplomacy of the 1920s (Unit 18) and 1930s (Unit 23) was achieved by the Great Powers acting outside the League.

15 Germany, 1919–33

15.1 Unrest, 1918–19

1 **William II** abdicated on 8 November 1918 amid unrest:

i millions **starved** because of the British naval blockade;

ii **revolutionaries** were encouraged by Lenin's success;

(a) a **naval mutiny** broke out in November 1918 (9.13.5.iv);

(b) **socialists** in the Reichstag had demanded the Kaiser's abdication in October–November 1918;

(c) **the government had little support** among the people.

2 **Ebert,** a socialist became **Chancellor**. The unrest grew:

i **soviets** of workers and soldiers were set up on the Russian model. **A Council of Commissars** was created;

ii **a German Republic** was proclaimed by the German Communists who claimed power for the workers' and soldiers' councils.

3 **A Socialist government versus Communist soviets**

i **the mildly socialist government** was opposed to the soviet system. This split the socialist and working class movement;

ii the Kaiser's **civil servants** and officials stayed in office;

iii these were more concerned for the good government of Germany than for a Communist-style revolution.

4 **The Communist revolt**

i the Communists took the name **Spartacist**, after the leader of a slave revolt in ancient Rome;

ii the Spartacists wanted a dictatorship on the Lenin model;

iii their leaders were **Karl Liebknecht** and **Rosa Luxemburg**;

iv on **6 January 1919** ·they led a mob of 100 000 on anti-government demonstrations in **Berlin**; they seized control of the main buildings.

15.2 Crushing the Communists

1 **Weimar** The unrest in Berlin forced the government to flee to Weimar south-west of Leipzig (now in East Germany).

2 **The Free Corps,** a volunteer group of ex-soldiers, was opposed to the socialist government and, above all, to the Communists.

3 The Weimar government asked the Free Corps to help put down the Spartacists.

4 Berlin was retaken; many prisoners, including Liebknecht and Luxemburg, were murdered.

5 This had **three main long-term results**:

i it **encouraged** the Free Corps and other right-wing groups;

ii it led to **bitter enmity** between Communists and Socialists;

iii it made fears of communist revolt seem justified and gave support to the idea that **strong government** was essential, even if that government ignored some civil or political rights.

15.3 The General Election

1 The Germans had a system of **proportional representation**.

2 **The vote** was given to all over twenty-one.

3 The **moderate Social Democrats** emerged as the largest single party.

4 There were many other parties from **Communists** on the extreme left to right-wing Nationalists of the old type.

5 **The Nationalists** with forty-two seats represented the views of the **Prussian Junkers** (1.26.4) and **German industrialists**. They still had the militarist and expansionist views which had led them to support the Kaiser before 1914.

6 **The Communists** wanted a Russian-style revolution.

15.4 A coalition government

1 The system of proportional representation meant that it was almost impossible for a single party to have an overall majority.

2 The Socialists, with the support of some of the smaller parties, formed a coalition.

3 A coalition (or collection) of parties has to try to agree on government policy and actions to be taken. This is very difficult; it tends to lead to governments which actually take very little action–and are 'weak' as a result. (See 15.2.5.(iii))

15.5 The new constitution

1 **The President,** the head of state, elected by **direct election**, had considerable powers:

i he could **dissolve** the Reichstag and order **new elections**;

ii he could use the **army** to put down a revolution;

iii he **chose the Chancellor**, usually choosing the leader of the single largest party in the Reichstag;

iv he **could suspend the constitution** if he thought that unrest required this, and could rule with dictatorial powers (by decree);

v these powers seemd to be a **sensible and stable counterbalance** to the possible weakness of coalition governments (15.4.3). But it put a **great responsibility** on the shoulders of the President who would have to use care in his implementing of his great powers.

2 **The Chancellor** and his Ministers were, in normal times, **answerable to the Reichstag** for their actions. This was a more democratic system than under Bismarck and William II.

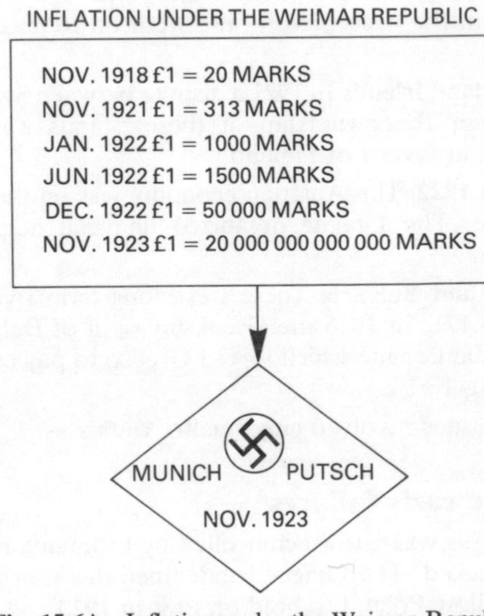

INFLATION UNDER THE WEIMAR REPUBLIC

NOV. 1918 £1 = 20 MARKS
NOV. 1921 £1 = 313 MARKS
JAN. 1922 £1 = 1000 MARKS
JUN. 1922 £1 = 1500 MARKS
DEC. 1922 £1 = 50 000 MARKS
NOV. 1923 £1 = 20 000 000 000 000 MARKS

MUNICH PUTSCH
NOV. 1923

Fig. 15.6A Inflation under the Weimar Republic

3 **The Reichstag** (or Lower House) was elected by the people. It had control over **taxation**–as the Liberals had hoped for in the Prussian Landtag in 1862 (1.7.7).

4 **The Reichsrat** (or Upper House) represented the individual states of Germany. It could not hold up any proposals which had a two-thirds majority in the Reichstag.

5 Because the constitution-making Assembly met in Weimar, the new state became known as the **Weimar Republic**.

6 The first President was the socialist Ebert (15.1.2).

15.6 The initial problems of the Weimar Republic (*Fig. 15.6A*)

1 **The 'stab in the back'** Many Germans claimed that the army had not been beaten by the Allies (9.14.7). They argued that the politicians at home had demanded an end to the war. The army, they said, had been 'stabbed in the back'. This was the view of:

i **ex-soldiers**, many of whom joined one of the numerous societies and gangs which grew up in post-war Germany;

ii **Nationalists** (15.3.5),

2 The 'diktat', or the **Treaty of Versailles**. It had been 'dictated to them' (12.6).

3 The Treaty's terms were very harsh (12.5). The Weimar government was blamed for this.

4 Food shortages continued after the end of the British blockade. Millions of the under-nourished died in the influenza epidemic which swept through Europe in 1919–20.

5 Unemployment was very high.

15.7 The first enemies of the Weimar Republic

1 The **Nationalists**–see 15.3.5;

2 the **officer-class** which opposed **left-wing governments**;

3 **ex-soldiers** who opposed the **Treaty of Versailles**;

4 **Communists** who wanted a **Russian-style revolution** (15.1.4).

15.8 Anti-Weimar risings

1 Communists led uprisings in the **Ruhr** and in **Munich**. These were put down by armed forces on Ebert's orders.

2 In March 1920 the **Free Corps** (15.2.2) tried to seize Berlin. Their leader, **Kapp**, wanted to restore the **Kaiser**. Their rising was defeated by a **general strike** led by socialists and communists.

3 Elections were held during this unsettled atmosphere. The extreme right (**Nationalists**) and the extreme left (**Communists**) gained more seats. This added to the tensions of the time.

15.9 Reparations and the Weimar Republic

1 Reparations were meant to punish Germany.

2 In 1923 the Germans were **unable to pay** their yearly instalment to the French.

3 French and Belgian troops invaded the **Ruhr**.

4 German workers went on strike. This led to a further decline in German **industry**, a rise in **unemployment** and a greater **scarcity of goods in shops**.

5 The scarcity of goods led to **increased prices**.

6 The great inflation of 1923 was caused in part by that scarcity. But it was also caused by the **government's decision to print vast sums of money**. This was intended to reduce the real value of reparations.

7 The effect of this on the mark was devastating (see Fig. 15.6A).

8 The effect of the great inflation was very severe:

i **pensions,** fixed in pre-1923 days, were valueless;

ii **savings,** in uninflated marks, were valueless;

iii **insurance policies** were almost worthless.

9 The middle classes suffered most from the inflation. They were the people who had saved most and taken out most insurance.

15.10 Gustav Stresemann (*1923–29*)

1 In 1923 Stresemann became **Chancellor** and **Foreign Secretary**.

2 He established a **new mark**. This did not help those whose savings had been wiped out. It did however help German industry and trade to recover.

3 In 1924 he persuaded the French to leave the **Ruhr**.

4 In 1924 he negotiated a **reduction in reparations** (18.4.6).

5 In 1925 he got Germany accepted as an equal by other European countries which signed the **Locarno Treaties** (18.8).

6 In 1926 he got Germany admitted as a **member of the League of Nations** when she became a permanent member of the Council (14.6.8c).

7 He persuaded **American banks** to make massive loans to help German industry to recover.

8 Unemployment fell as industry recovered.

9 By 1928 Germany seemed to have recovered:

i **unemployment** was down;

ii **the mark** was a stable currency;

iii **living standards** were rising.

10 Extremist parties became less popular.

15.11 The weakness of Stresemann's 'success'

1 False prosperity Much of the improvement depended on American loans. What if those loans were recalled?

2 Few 'Weimarians' The Germans enjoyed rising living standards and voted the moderate socialists, led by Stresemann, back to power. But few Germans were fervent supporters of the Republic. Nationalists, industrialists, communists and ex-soldiers would still have preferred some other system.

3 The army In spite of the anti-militarist terms of the Treaty of Versailles, the army continued to be a major power in Weimar Germany. The High Command would use that power in its own interests–even if that meant a threat to the Republic. We shall see this more clearly in Unit 15.18.1.

15.12 The 1929 collapse

1 In 1929 reparations were reduced by the **Young Plan** (18.4.8).

2 In October 1929 the **Wall Street Crash** took place. We shall examine the causes and effects of that Crash in Unit 16.15. The immediate effects in Germany were:

i **American banks** re-called loans which propped up German industry and trade;

ii many **German banks** were ruined;

iii **many industries** closed down;

iv **the fall in American demand** for goods led to a fall in German exports which led to other industries closing down;

v **unemployment rose**; by 1931 there were 6 million unemployed in Germany. It looked as if the Republic were going back to the harsh days of 1923 again (15.9).

3 In this atmosphere the extremist parties gained in popularity–one proof that support for the Republican government was very fragile (Table 15.18A).

15.13 Adolf Hitler–early career

1 He was born in **Austria** to middle-class parents.

2 He worked as a **sign painter** in **Vienna** before 1914.

3 In 1914 he joined the army; rose to become a corporal and gained the Iron Cross First Class.

4 In 1918 he was in hospital when the war ended. In his writings he told of his bitterness at the 'stab in the back' (15.6.1), and at the 'dictated peace' with its harsh terms.

5 In 1921 a small group in **Munich** founded the **Nationalist Socialist** (or Nazi) Party.

6 Hitler became President of the Nazis in 1921–22.

7 The Nazis were just one of the many anti-Weimar groups of the period. The **Spartacists** had tried to seize power (15.1.4). So, too had the **Free Corps** led by Kapp (15.8.2).

8 The Nazis also tried to seize power (15.14).

15.14 Munich, 1923

1 By 1923 Hitler had become the undisputed leader of the Nazis:

i he had got the party to adopt the crooked cross (or **swastika**) as its symbol;

ii he became the party's **leading orator**, proclaiming in fiery speeches that Germany's ills (in 1923) were the fault of Jews, Communists, international bankers, foreigners and Weimar socialists;

iii to the **unemployed** he promised work in Nazi Germany;

iv to the **middle classes**, ruined by the great inflation, he promised **stability** and a restoration of **national pride**.

2 He created a 'defence band' which dressed in brown shirts (the **SA**) under an ex-officer, **Captain Roehm**. This broke up left-wing meetings and defended Nazis from similar attacks by communist gangs.

3 These rival gangs threatened law and order.

4 In **1923** the French marched into the Ruhr (15.9.3).

5 **Stresemann** came under Nazi attack because of negotiating over **reparations** (15.10.4) and with the French in the **Ruhr** (15.10.3). Hitler claimed that he would not pay reparations and would drive the French from the Ruhr.

6 On **8 November 1923** after a meeting in the **Beer Hall in Munich** Hitler attempted to seize power:

i he proclaimed himself the **President of Germany**;

ii **Ludendorff**, once the hero of wartime Germany (9.13.2), supported Hitler in this conspiracy.

7 But the commander of Hitler's own forces lost his nerve and went over to the government side.

8 **The Bavarian government** put down the attempted rising, arrested Hitler and, after a trial, sentenced him to five years in jail.

15.15 Mein Kampf (*My Struggle*)

1 In jail, Hitler wrote a book; 'the Nazi bible'.

2 In *Mein Kampf* he set out his ideas on:

i the superiority of the **Aryan race**;

ii his hatred for **Jews** and other non-Aryans;

iii his plans for a **Greater Germany** which he would create by conquering other countries, particularly **Russia**; these conquests would provide extra living space (**'Lebensraum'** for the Germans);

iv **propaganda**, which he said had to be used to win popular support. This he geared to the **level of the least intelligent** and could be as untruthful as was necessary. The **'big lie'** was preferred to the 'little lie' because it would be more effective.

15.16 The fortunes of the Nazis, 1924–29

1 In **1924** the Party had **24 seats in the Reichstag**.

2 In the prosperous 'Stresemann period' the Nazis lost seats. In **1929** they had only **12 seats in the Reichstag.**

3 On his release from jail Hitler declared that he would never again try to seize power. He would work through the Republican constitution even if that meant having to do 'deals' with the hated socialist, communist and Catholic members.

4 He also realized that he would have to get the support of **German industrialists** (to provide money to fund his Party) and of the **Army** (which could prevent him taking power).

15.17 The crumbling of Weimar, 1929–30

1 3 October 1929 Stresemann died.

2 28 October 1929 The start of the Wall Street Crash (15.12.2).

3 **Economic crisis** in Germany – banks closed, unemployment rose.

4 Chancellor **Brüning** proposed:

i **to cut unemployment benefit** (opposed by left-wing members of his coalition government – see 15.4);

ii **to increase taxes** paid by the rich to get the money needed to pay the increasing number of unemployed. This was opposed by the right-wing members of the coalition.

5 Brüning asked the President, Hindenburg, to use his powers and to **rule by decree** (15.5.1.iv).

6 **1930 Election.** The President ordered fresh elections:

i **Hitler**, funded by industrialists who feared communism, recruited (and paid) increasing numbers into his Party;

ii **massive demonstrations** attracted popular support;

iii his party gained a larger number of seats (see Table 15.18A)

Table 15.18A

	Seats in the Reichstag		Unemployment in millions
	Nazis	*Communist*	
May 1924	32	62	0.5
Dec. 1924	14	45	0.5
1928	13	54	2.5
1930	107	77	4.0
July 1932	230	89	6.2
Nov. 1932	196	120	6.0
Mar. 1933	288	81	5.8

15.18 After the 1930 Election

1 **Brüning** remained in power; the army kept him there. General **Schleicher**, head of the army, hoped to be able to use Brüning.

2 **The Communists** gained extra seats (Table 15.18A). They argued that the capitalist system had broken down. Germany could be saved only by a Russian-style government.

3 **The Nationalists**, with **41 seats**, were led by Hugenburg. This party of the extreme right, wanted to see the **undoing of the Treaty of Versailles**. They would give their support to Hitler if needs be (15.21.6).

4 **Brüning** invited Hitler to join a coalition. He refused.

5 **Street violence** increased:

i Nazi storm troopers, led by Roehm, numbered 400 000;

ii communists had their para-military force – 'the Red Banner';

iii clashes became increasingly violent and bloody;

iv millions of ordinary Germans were terrified.

6 **Propaganda** Hitler had recruited **Dr Goebbels** to take charge of Nazi propaganda. In speeches, newspapers, posters and cartoons Goebbels tried to convince the German people to support Hitler.

15.19 The Presidential Election, March 1932

1 In 1932 Hitler stood against the popular but ageing **Hindenburg** in the Presidential election.

2 He polled **11 million votes** as against the **18 million** gained by Hindenburg and **5 million** gained by the Communist, Thaelmann.

3 Hitler used this campaign as a chance to put over his ideas to the whole German people.

4 In **April 1932, Brüning** wanted to use the army to suppress the activities of Hitler's storm troopers.

5 **Hindenburg** refused to let the army get directly involved in 'dirty politics'.

6 Brüning was dismissed and **replaced by von Papen**, leader of the Catholic Centre Party.

15.20 Elections and the politicians, July–November 1932

1 **Von Papen** asked for fresh elections (July 1932), because his government was unstable.

2 **Unemployment** was at its height (Table 15.18A).

3 **The Nazis and Communists** gained seats.

4 Von Papen asked Hitler to join in a coalition. He refused. He wanted total control of the government.

5 **Roehm** and other Nazis asked Hitler to imitate Mussolini (21.10–11) who had won power by the threat of force.

6 Hitler knew that the army could crush such a rising.

7 In **November 1932** von Papen called fresh elections. He hoped to win more seats so that his government could be more secure.

8 **Unemployment** was slowly falling (Table 15.18A).

9 While the **Communists** won even more seats, the **Nazis** lost ground (Table 15.18A) with 196 seats. Had the Nazi movement begun to run out of steam?

15.21 Hitler's path to power, November 1932–January 1933

1 **Terrorism** by the storm troopers was stepped up.

2 **Schleicher,** on behalf of the army, persuaded Hindenburg to sack von Papen. Schleicher became Chancellor.

3 **The Reichstag** refused to support Schleicher.

4 **Hindenburg** refused Schleicher's request to rule by decree (15.5.1.iv).

5 **Von Papen,** anxious to get his own back on Schleicher, advised Hindenburg to **invite Hitler to become Chancellor**.

6 **January 1933** Hitler became Chancellor and head of a government of Nazis and Conservative-Nationalists:

i **Hindenburg,** representative of Prussian militarism, seemed to give his blessings to the Nazis by appointing Hitler;

ii **Nationalists** supported the anti-Treaty government;

iii **Von Papen** hoped that he and the 'old politicians' would be able to control the new, inexperienced Chancellor.

15.22 Establishing the dictatorship, January–March 1933

1 There were **only three Nazis** in the cabinet in January 1933.

2 Hitler called fresh elections, hoping to gain more seats.

3 **The reign of terror, February 1933**

i the Nazis had taken control of a good deal of the German administration–even if not of the Cabinet;

ii **Hermann Goering** was the Nazi Minister of the Interior in Prussia, the largest state. He enrolled thousands of Nazis into the police force which attacked and broke up opposition meetings.

4 **The Reichstag fire** 27 February 1933, the Reichstag building in Berlin was burned down. Hitler accused the **Communists** of planning this as a signal for an uprising.

5 **The attack on the left, March 1933** Thousands of communists and socialists were **arrested**; communist and socialist newspapers were **banned**; **violent attacks** were made on Jewish property.

6 **The election** was held on 5 March 1933 in this atmosphere of crisis and violence. The Nazis gained increased support while support for the Communists fell (Table 15.18A).

15.23 Establishing the dictatorship, March 1933–August 1934

1 With their Conservative-Nationalist allies the Nazis had 341 of the 647 seats in the Reichstag–a **slender majority**.

2 **Terrorism** continued; the **Nazi-controlled police** forced many opposition parties to dissolve themselves. They did not appear in the Reichstag.

3 **The Communist representatives** were expelled from the Reichstag by a vote of the Nazis and their right-wing allies.

4 **Socialist representatives** protested against Nazi tactics.

5 **Mass demonstrations** by Nazi gangs and storm troopers were organized around, and even in, the Reichstag building to frighten representatives into passing an **Enabling Act**.

6 This Act, passed by **441 to 91**, gave Hitler power to **govern for four years** without calling a meeting of the Reichstag.

7 The dictatorship was almost ensured.

15.24 The Fuhrer (or Leader)

1 **Captain Roehm**, commander of the storm troopers, wanted Hitler to follow a radical, socialist policy. This had been the declared policy of the Nationalist Socialists. Hitler knew, in 1933–34, that the industrialists would not approve such a policy.

2 **Roehm,** an ex-army officer, wanted Hitler to incorporate the **SA** (storm troopers) **into the Regular Army** (the Reichswehr). He hoped to gain more power for himself.

3 **The General Staff** despised Roehm and the storm troopers. They would have used their power to overthrow Hitler and the Nazis–as they had overthrown Brüning and von Papen (15.19–21).

4 **Hitler made a deal** with the General Staff:

i he would **get rid of Roehm** and the threat to the power of the General Staff;

ii **the Army would support him** if, on Hindenburg's death, he became President.

5 Roehm and many of his supporters were assassinated on Hitler's orders on **30 June 1934** in what has become known as **'the Night of the Long Knives'**.

6 When, later in 1934, Hindenburg died, Hitler became President **(August 1934)** although he never used that title, preferring to use the term **'Fuhrer'**.

7 This gave him the legitimate control of the Armed Forces as the **Commander-in-Chief**. His power now was complete.

16 The United States of America, 1917–1933

16.1 President Woodrow Wilson (1912–20)

1 Before 1914 Wilson was a **'liberal' President** (7.17).

2 He led the USA **into the war**, 1917 (7.24 and 9.12).

3 He issued his **Fourteen Points**, January 1918 (Fig. 12.1A).

4 At **Versailles** he was under great pressure from Lloyd George and Clémenceau (12.2–3). This prevented him from putting his ideals into practice.

5 The **League of Nations** (Unit 14) was his brainchild.

6 In **1918** there were **mid-term elections** for the House of Representatives and one-third of the Senate (7.3.2). The **Republicans** gained control of both Houses of Congress which voted against US participation in the League (14.6.5).

7 Wilson, a sick man, retired from politics in 1920.

16.2 President Warren Harding (1921–23)

1 Harding, a Republican, won the 1920 Presidential Election.

2 His campaign had been summed up in the slogan **'Back to normalcy'**. By 'normalcy' he meant:

i **no foreign entanglements**; America became 'isolationist';

ii American efforts should concentrate on **internal development**–of industry and commerce–and a **growth in prosperity**.

3 Harding had been Senator for the State of Ohio. As President he took many of his friends with him to Washington.

4 This **'Ohio Gang'** held many important government posts. These businessmen-politicians were as corrupt as many American industrialists in the nineteenth century (7.10 and 7.13–17), e.g.:

i the Head of the Veterans' Bureau stole millions of dollars given to him for the relief of disabled servicemen;

ii the Attorney-General escaped prison on a charge of corruption because he destroyed his bank records before the trial.

16.3 The Teapot Dome Scandal

1 The US navy had oil reserves in fields in the Elk Hills, California and at Teapot Dome, Wyoming.

2 Harding's friend and Minister of the Interior, Albert B. Fall, persuaded another Harding crony, the Secretary of the Navy, to lease those oilfields to the Department of the Interior.

3 He then leased out the fields to oil companies. One company 'boss' paid Fall 200 000 dollars and another paid him 100 000 dollars for these profitable leases.

4 Fall was found out, sentenced to one year's imprisonment, and fined 100 000 dollars.

16.4 The world's richest nation in 1919–20

1 **1914** The USA was a major industrial power (7.9 and 7.12).

2 **1914–18** The US grew even more powerful:
i the Allies bought a great volume of munitions; coal, steel and engineering industries grew rapidly;
ii after 1917 the **US government** spent a great deal of money on arming its own forces;
iii there was a fall in the British and German exports. US industrialists won a **large share in world markets**.

16.5 The 'Red scare' 1918–20

1 The trade union movement was weak in 1914 (7.14).
2 During the war many workers joined unions.

3 Republican politician-industrialists feared that the growing trade union movement might lead to a Bolshevik-style revolution such as had swept the Tsar from power in 1917 (10.11).

4 Politicians and newspaper editors warned Americans against the danger of 'international' trade unionism. In 'isolationist' America, 'internationalism' was a dirty word.

5 **Industrialists** employed gangs of ex-soldiers to break up trade union and/or socialist meetings.

6 **Mitchell Palmer**, Harding's Attorney-General, organized a campaign against foreigners and 'internationalism':
i **police and troops** were ordered to raid magazine offices, public halls, private houses, union headquarters and meetings of any liberal organization;
ii in **1920 6 000 people were arrested**.

7 **Violence bred violence:**
i bombs were placed in **offices** of leading businessmen;
ii many **factories** were destroyed by gang activities;
iii politicians received **bombs** in their mail;
iv **Palmer's own house** was blown up.

8 **Sacco and Vanzetti**
i 15 April 1920, two men were murdered during a wages robbery;
ii police arrested two Italian immigrants, **Sacco and Vanzetti**;
iii they were found guilty on **14 July 1920**;
iv 1920–27; world-wide protests led to many court appeals;
v 1927: the men were executed;
vi it is now generally agreed that the two Italians were innocent and victims of the 'Red scare' campaign.

16.6 President Calvin Coolidge (1923–28)

1 Harding died in **1923**; Vice President Coolidge succeeded.
2 In **1924** Coolidge won the Presidential election.
3 He said: **'The business of America is business'**.
4 He argued that the American prosperity was the result of the freedom which Republican governments gave to industrialists.

16.7 Government policy, 1920–28

1 **Tariffs** were imposed on imported goods:
i **1922**: the Fordney-McCumber Act increased existing tariffs;

ii **1930**: at the start of the Great Depression, the **Hawley-Smoot amendment** further increased tariffs.

2 Industry benefited from the tariffs and from **low taxation**:
(a) **industrialists and businessmen** paid low taxes and had money for industrial and commercial investment;
(b) **consumers** paying low taxes had more money to spend on goods produced by industry.

3 **Anti-Trust legislation**
i before 1914 governments tried to limit the power of large firms (7.13, 7.16 and 7.17);
ii the Republican governments of the 1920s relaxed the laws. Industrialists could do as they wished.

4 **Immigration**
i most Americans were of immigrant stock (7.8.7 and 7.14.1);
ii in post-war America the government tried to limit the flow of immigrants.

1921 The Immigration Act limited the number of immigrants from any one country to three per cent of the number of that nationality living in the USA in 1910.

1924 An amendment to the 1921 Act pushed back the base year to 1890. This allowed the immigration of many from Britain, Ireland and Germany but of few from Italy, Russia and Eastern Europe.

5 **The trade union movement**
i **courts** often declared union activities illegal;
ii **police and troops** were often used to attack the strikers.

6 **Foreign debts**
i US bankers and financiers had lent **10 billion dollars** to the Allies to help them to buy supplies in wartime America;
ii **Britain** had borrowed most of this money but had made even greater loans to her Allies–France, Italy and Russia;
iii if they repaid their loans, Britain would be able to repay the Americans;
iv **repayment would have crippled the debtor countries;**
v Britain asked for all inter-Allied debts to be cancelled;
vi Coolidge refused;
vii to get the money for such repayments, Britain had to sell goods in the USA. But this was made more difficult by the tariff policy (16.7.1).

7 **American loans** were made in the 1920s to Germany to enable her to make her reparations payments and to help her industry to get back on its feet (15.10.7).

8 **Prohibition** During the war there was a growth in the temperance movement and in 1919 Congress passed the **Eighteenth Amendment** to the US Constitution, making illegal the manufacture and sale of alcoholic drink anywhere in the USA. **The Volstead Act, 1919** implemented the 18th Amendment. Wilson tried to veto this legislation but Congress overcame his veto (7.3.3.iii.d).

9 **Women** were given the same political rights as men–by the **Nineteenth Amendment** to the Constitution.

10 **Welfare** Before 1914 the US had started to develop a welfare system:
i **child-labour laws** were passed (7.15.5);
ii **Theodore Roosevelt** wanted a welfare programme (7.16.10);
iii little had been achieved. The Republican politician-industrialists of the **1920s** made no effort to develop such a programme. They refused to increase the **taxes** which would have been needed to pay for such a programme. They preferred a policy of **low taxation** (16.7.2).

16.8 Economic prosperity, 1920–28

1 **Basic industries**
i some (**coal and textiles**) did not grow much;
ii some (**steel**) grew rapidly to provide the material needed by consumer goods industries (see below).

2 Consumer goods industries. Which ones?

(a) Widespread **electricity supply** led to the growth in the demand for many goods—radios, vacuum cleaners and other household gadgets. This led to the growth in the electrical engineering industry and in the industries producing these consumer goods.

(b) The film industry grew rapidly, its 'capital' being Hollywood. The invention of 'the talking pictures' in 1928 led to a further growth in this industry.

(c) Entertainment became a major industry in prosperous America; **cinemas** were built to show films, more **dance halls** were built where crowds of people learned such popular dances as the **Charleston**.

(d) The car industry Henry Ford had introduced **mass production** methods into this industry in 1913. This **assembly-line technique** allowed the production of an increasing number of cars:

1920 there were 9 million cars on US roads;

1930 there were 30 million cars on the roads—and some four million new jobs had been created in the car industry alone. Ford's Model T or **'Tin Lizzie'** was bought by workers in prosperous America.

3 Hire Purchase To help workers to pay the 300 dollars for a car in 1926 (compared with 850 dollars in 1914) business men enlarged, or started, finance companies to lend money to prospective buyers who could then get a car (or other article). Weekly instalments repaid the loan and the interest on it. Such a system helped to:

i **increase the demand for goods**—and so helped industrialists to expand as well as helping to create jobs for many workers;

ii **raise living standards**. Americans bought many things on hire purchase (H.P.)—cars, radios, furniture, as well as holidays away from home.

16.9 Prohibition and crime

1 After January 1920 a 'black market' in alcohol soon developed. Gangs got and sold alcohol, bribed police and judges and fought other similar gangs.

2 'Bootleggers' smuggled drink from Canada, Mexico and Europe.

3 Criminal gangs controlled 'bootlegging'. Armed with machine guns, motor cars helped them to raid other gangs' territories and to attack rivals' vessels and lorries.

4 Irishmen such as **Dion O'Banion** led the first gangs.

5 Italians, usually **Sicilians**, such as **Al Capone**, ran the gangs which first destroyed the Irish gangs and then gained almost complete control of the illegal drink trade and other criminal activities.

6 Capone, based in Chicago, had an income of **60 million dollars a year** from crime. This allowed him to bribe politicians, judges, police and other officials. He was sent to **jail in 1931**—but for the evasion of **income tax**.

16.10 The Ku Klux Klan

1 This secret society was originally formed to terrorize the freed slaves in the Southern States (7.11.7).

2 In the hysterical anti-internationalism of the 1920s the Klan grew rapidly. By 1928 it had 5 million members.

3 It turned to **other targets than the negro**. Jews and Catholics came under attack from the Klan which supported the idea of a White Anglo-Saxon and Protestant people (**WASP**). Socialists and trade unionists were attacked for having links with international organizations.

4 The Klansmen in their long white, hooded cloaks set fire to property, attacked individuals and organized lynching parties in which 'guilty' people were hanged.

5 These activities were another of those outward signs of the violence in isolationist America.

16.11 The stock market boom 1920–28

1 There was a rapid growth in **company profits**.

2 Owners of shares in these companies received, each year, higher dividends—their share in the profits.

3 Their shares became more valuable. If they decided to sell, they could get much more for the share than they had paid.

4 Hire purchase (16.8.3) was used to buy consumer goods.

5 In the 1920s many Americans used a similar system to buy shares in profitable companies:

i the **Wall Street Stock Exchange** allowed a system of 'buying on the margin'; people had to **put down only 10 cents** for each dollar's worth of shares they wished to buy. The rest of the money had to be paid within a few months. People hoped to be able to sell, at a higher price, the shares bought 'on the margin'. They expected enough to make their own final payment *and* a profit;

ii **banks** made it easy for people to borrow money to buy shares. They accepted shares as guarantees for loans. If clients could not repay the loan, their banks could sell the shares.

6 Millions of Americans became **shareholders**.

16.12 The agricultural depression, 1921–28

1 1914–18 American farmers enjoyed a period of prosperity. Foreign imports almost ceased; nations bought American farm produce to make up for the lost output of war-torn countries.

2 American farms became more **productive**:

i **new land** was broken in and farmed;

ii **new machinery** was bought to help to increase output.

3 1920–21 This farming prosperity ended:

i European farmers began to produce again;

ii their output, plus the increased output in America, led **to over-production**;

iii this led to a **drastic fall in farm prices**; prices slumped in **1922** and continued to fall; by **1929** wheat prices were lower than they had been for 400 years.

4 With very much smaller incomes, American farmers bought fewer goods. The future President, Harry S. Truman, owned a drapery store in Kansas City, centre of a prosperous farming industry in wartime. In 1922 Truman found that he could not sell his goods to Kansas farmers—and he went bankrupt.

5 This had a snowball effect; shops bought less from factories, which sacked workmen and announced lower profits.

6 Many farmers had bought their land with a loan from local banks. With lower incomes they could not make the mortgage repayments. Thousands of farmers were thrown off the land by banks which then tried to sell the land to get back the money they had lent.

7 Banks which could not profitably sell the farms they had taken back had to declare falling profits—and banks failed—becoming 'bankrupt'.

16.13 Clouds on the horizon, 1928

1 Many **companies** had lower profits—and lower sales.

2 Many **farmers**, evicted from their farms, were unemployed.

3 America's increasing **wealth was unfairly shared out**. The richest 5 per cent of the population earned one-third of all the money earned in America.

4 The rich spent most of this money on luxuries and on investments in the stock market. They did not buy one-third of all the goods produced by US industry.

5 The rest of the people, with only two-thirds of the American income, could only buy, at best, two-thirds of all that was produced.

6 This led to **under-consumption**; less was bought than was produced. Other people saw this as **over-production**; more was being produced than could be bought.

7 The result was a fall in prices of many goods.

16.14 President Herbert Hoover (1928–1932)

1 Hoover had played an important part in the **American famine relief** sent to Europe after 1918.

2 He was **Secretary of Commerce** under both Harding and Coolidge.

3 Honest and efficient, he was known as **'the Great Engineer'**.

4 Because of the prosperity of America under his Republican predecessors, he won the 1928 Election by a huge majority.

5 He claimed that **'the rugged individualism'** of America was responsible for the growth of prosperity. He claimed that prosperity would increase. There would be 'a chicken in every pot and two cars in every garage'.

29 October 16 million shares 'thrown upon the market for what prices they could get'.

16.16 The effects of the Crash in America

1 Many **large companies** were ruined. Factories and shops closed because employers had no money to pay wages and no hope of selling their goods.

2 Banks which had advanced loans could not recover their money. Many of them ran out of money.

3 Savers could not get their money back from banks–and they, too, were ruined.

4 House buyers who had borrowed to buy their homes could not make the mortgage repayments. Many were evicted.

5 There was a **fall in the output** from factories and other workplaces (Fig. 16, 16A), many of which closed down.

6 Unemployment grew (Fig. 16, 16A). The unemployed with meagre, if any incomes, could buy little if anything. This had a snowballing effect on the demand made for goods from factories–and helps to explain part of the fall in output.

7 Those who had a job were unsure of the future. Would they lose their jobs? Should they hold on to the money they had?

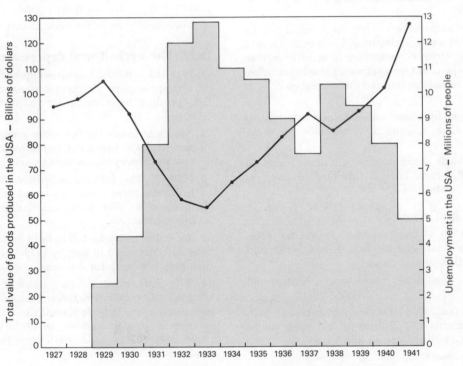

Fig. 16.6A The changing pattern of US industry, 1929–41

16.15 The Wall Street Crash 1929

1 Causes–past:
i **over-production** (16.12.3) and **under-consumption** (16.13.7) led to falling prices, sales and profits and more unemployment;
ii **falling profits** made shares less valuable (16.11).

2 Causes–immediate:
i **banks** had made loans to buyers of shares (16.11.5);
ii **the shares bought** with the loans were taken by the banks as guarantees (or **collateral**);
iii in 1929 banks saw that the value of the shares they held was less than the loans made;
iv many asked clients to repay their loans;
v people then had to sell their shares;
vi with millions trying to sell, share prices fell.

3 October 1929–the Crash
24 October (Thursday) First panic; 13 million shares for sale.
25 October Prices steadied (at a lower level than before).
28 October (Monday) Much heavier selling; prices fall steeply; many people announced heavy losses.

The decline in the number of people willing to make hire purchase agreements (16.8.3) led to a fall in the demand for cars, radios and other consumer goods.

8 Many farmers were evicted when banks tried to get back money loaned to them in more prosperous times. In Iowa, farmers fought off representatives from banks coming to claim their property. They had a slogan 'In Hoover we trusted, now we are busted'.

9 Thousands of **unemployed marched** to Washington to demand government action. They put up ramshackle shelters on the outskirts of Washington; in other cities and towns similar **'Hoovervilles'** were built to shelter the evicted and unemployed.

10 Troops and police tried to clear these camps. Some people thought that America was on the brink of a revolution.

16.17 Hoover and the Depression

1 At first Hoover claimed that 'prosperity is just around the corner'.

2 He refused to spend money on the development of the Tennessee Valley (see Unit 19.4.6).

3 He insisted that private enterprise would solve the problem.

4 But he set up the **Reconstruction Finance Corporation (RFC)**. This government agency lent money to banks, railways and State governments willing to help schemes to provide work.

5 But this body and some tinkering with interest rates did little to improve matters.

16.18 The effects of the Crash in Europe

1 American loans helped European industry to recover (16.7.7).

2 Stresemann had depended on such loans (15.10.7).

3 In the winter of 1929 American banks demanded the immediate repayment of these loans.

4 Austrian, Italian, German and other national banks were forced to try to repay the money, if they could.

5 Many were forced to close down, ruining millions of savers who had put their money into the banks. Thousands of industrialists were also ruined – forced to repay the loans on which they had depended.

6 The rise in American unemployment led to a **fall in the demand** for goods exported by Europe to America. This led to a further rise in European unemployment. Note that the high US tariffs also made exporting to the US very difficult (16.7).

7 The rise of Hitler to power was a major result of the Crash. The relationship between German unemployment and Nazi electoral success is illustrated in Table 15.18A.

16.19 The politicians and the Crash

1 Hitler was one politician who benefited from the Crash.

2 Mussolini claimed credit for policies aimed at bringing down Italian unemployment (21.19).

3 Huey Long, governor and virtual dictator of the State of Louisiana, argued for an American Fascist movement.

4 Franklin Delano Roosevelt

i he was Vice-Presidential candidate for the Democratic Party in the 1920 Election;

ii 1928 he was elected governor of New York State. The State Legislature (7.2.3.ii) was controlled by the Republicans;

iii that Legislature did not pass laws which he proposed in 1928:

(a) to reduce the **length of the working day**;

(b) to provide **compensation for men injured at work**;

(c) to **help the aged and sick**;

(d) to **help farmers** affected by falling prices (16.12).

iv When New York was affected by the Crash he acted quickly:

(a) he claimed that it was the **duty of government** to step in to prevent starvation and hardship;

(b) he set up **committees** of industrialists, trade union leaders, economists and social workers to develop schemes for the unemployed in the State of New York;

(c) he persuaded the Republican legislature to pass a law to allow the spending of **20 million dollars** to help the unemployed.

v In **1930** he ran for re-election as governor. His popularity was reflected in his increased majority;

vi in **1932** he became the Democratic Party candidate in the Presidential Election. In June he promised **'a new deal for the American people'**;

vii he took office in March 1933 claiming that **'the only thing we have to fear is fear itself...'**. We will study his work as President in Unit 19.

17 China and Japan, 1914–49

17.1 A divided China, 1914 (see Unit 6.16–17)

1 The **Manchu dynasty** was overthrown in 1911–12 (6.15).

2 Sun Yat-Sen inspired the revolution of Double Tenth (6.14).

3 He allowed **Yuan Shih-k'ai** to become President, 1912 (6.15).

4 Yuan set himself up as **dictator** (6.16).

5 He had the support of **war lords**, generals who controlled various regions in China.

17.2 China and Japan and the First World War, 1914–18

1 Yuan declared **China to be neutral**.

2 Japan was an ally of Britain since 1902 (6.7.6–7).

3 She **declared war on Germany**:

i Japan seized **Germany's Pacific Islands colonies**;

ii she invaded the German-controlled province of **Shantung** on mainland China, including the port of **Kiao-chow** (6.6.2) promising to return this territory to China.

4 Twenty-One Demands May 1915 (see Unit 6.18.3).

5 Yuan gave way to most demands and started negotiating others.

6 China was controlled by either Japan OR the West.

7 Anti-Japanse activity broke out (6.18.5).

8 Yuan died, August 1916. His successor, Li Yuan-hung restored the 1912 constitution and recalled the 1913 parliament (6.16.2).

9 War lords were too strong for Li; fighting each other, they made life very hard for the Chinese people (6.17).

10 Sun Yat-Sen, accepted as President of China by the Assembly which met in **Canton** (Fig. 17.11A), was in a weak position:

i **war lords** controlled most of China;

ii even **Sun depended** on the support of a war lord;

iii **foreign governments** refused to recognize him as ruler.

17.3 Japan and the Treaty of Versailles, 1919

1 Japan was one of the victorious powers at Versailles.

2 She was given a **mandate** (13.10) over the former German Caroline, Marshall and Mariana Islands.

3 Shantung, including Kiao-chow (Fig. 17.11A), was transferred to Japan.

17.4 China and the Treaty of Versailles

1 China was **angry** at the gains made by Japan.

2 The grant of **Shantung** was against Wilson's principle of 'national self-determination'.

3 Movement of 4 May 1919

i **Peking students** held anti-government demonstration;

ii a **boycott** of Japanese goods was organized;

iii **government forces** arrested many students;

iv the anti-government, anti-Japanese and anti-Versailles **campaign spread**;

v **students and workers** in many towns joined in. The young Mao Tse-tung was one such recruit (17.10.5);

vi the demands by the organizers changed. They asked for:

(a) constitutional government;

(b) western-style **education**;

(c) the suppression of the **war lords**;

(d) an end to **corruption** in official life;

(e) an exclusion of **foreigners** from Chinese trade and industry.

17.5 Sun and the 4 May Movement

1 Sun held only the region around Canton (Fig. 17.11A).
2 He decided to win the support of the **4 May campaigners**.
3 He proposed to make **war on the war lords**.
4 For this he needed an **army**.

17.6 Sun and Bolshevik Russia

1 The **western Allies** supported the **anti-Bolsheviks against Lenin** (10.24–26).
2 They also supported **Japan's anti-Chinese campaign** (17.3).
3 **1920** Lenin gave up Tsarist claims on China.
4 **1921 The Chinese Communist Party** was formed. In 1922 it still had only 200 members.
5 **1922 Sun refused Russian offers of help**. Then his war lord at Canton turned against him. He was saved from assassination by a young supporter, **Chiang Kai-shek**.
6 **1923** Chiang took Sun to **Shanghai** (17.11A) and his businessmen friends. The Russian agent, **Joffe**, met Sun and they agreed:
i Sun would accept the help of the Chinese Communists;
ii Russia would provide various forms of aid (see below).

17.7 Russian aid to Sun

1 **Blucher,** a Russian general, set up a military academy at **Whampoa** near Canton (Fig. 17.11A):
i it **trained young officers** for a Sun-controlled army;
ii **Chiang Kai-shek** was the first commandant;
iii **Chou En-lai,** a Communist, was appointed political educational officer at the academy.
2 **Borodin,** a Russian agent, organized the Kuo Min Tang:
i he helped set up **small cells** in various towns;
ii he showed how to **spread political ideas** among the people;
iii he helped Sun create an army, based on Canton, with Russian money, advisers and equipment.

17.8 A revised Kuo Min Tang (KMT)

1 In **1924** Sun restated the Three Principles (6.13.9).
2 He agreed to set up a **small committee** to make decisions. This, later, led to **party-dictatorship** under Chiang Kai-shek.
3 He allowed Communists to join the KMT. They supported Sun–hoping for complete control later on.
4 **1925** Sun died.

17.9 Chiang Kai-shek's early career (to 1925)

1 Born in **1887**, son of a landowner, he had a private education;
2 **1905** went to Manchu military academy;
3 **1907** sent to Tokyo for further training;
4 **1911** returned to lead the revolution in **Hangchow** (6.14.4–11);
5 **1912** returned from Japan to help Sun (6.16.3) as chief-of-staff.
6 Chiang and Sun travelled to Japan after revolution failed.
7 In **1917** back in Canton (6.19) as Sun's chief adviser.
8 **1918** Chiang quarrelled with Sun's protecting war lord. He went to **Shanghai** (Fig. 17.11A) where he:
i made a **fortune** on the Stock Exchange;
ii made many friends in the **business community**;
iii was popular with the **secret societies and gangs**.
9 **1921** He returned to **Canton** and in 1922 **saved Sun** from assassination (17.6.5).
10 **1923** He was appointed commandant at **Whampoa** (17.7.1).
11 **1925** When Sun died, he became leader of the KMT.

17.10 Mao Tse-tung's early career (to 1925)

1 **1893** born into a poor family, he went to Changsha High School in the capital of **Hunan** (Fig. 17.11A).
2 **1911** He joined **Sun's army** but fought no battles.

3 **1913** He went to Changsha Teachers' Training College where students **opposed Yuan's submission** to foreigners (17.2).
4 **1918** He became assistant librarian, Peking University.
5 **1919** Back in Changsha as a teacher, he **led a students' strike** in support of the **4 May Movement** (17.4.3). He edited a **newspaper** which was suppressed by the local war lord.
6 **1921** He formed the Changsha cell of **Communist Party** and in **July 1921** attended first Party Congress, Shanghai.
7 **1922** He went to **Hunan** (Fig. 17.11A) to organize workers to strike, to fight troops sent against them and to win higher wages for miners and railwaymen.
8 **1924** He joined the KMT (17.6.6).
9 **1925** He was in charge of **propaganda** for the KMT in Canton.

17.11 Chiang's Kuo Min Tang, 1925

1 **Communists** in the KMT were led by Borodin (17.7.2).
2 **Right-wing** businessmen and landlords wanted the expulsion of **western merchants** and a restoration of **order**.
3 **Moderate left-wing members** distrusted the Communists. The **Three Principles** (6.13.9) led them to oppose the right wing. Sun's wife was a member of this group.
4 **Chiang** was distrusted by the **Communists**. He expelled all Communist officers from the army. He favoured the **right-wing group**.

Fig. 17.11A   China in the 1930s

5 **Canton** was Chiang's 'capital'; western governments recognized **the Peking government** controlled by war lords.
6 **Thirtieth May, 1925:**
i an anti-Japanese demonstration in **Shanghai** (Fig. 17.11A);
ii **western police** in the International Settlement arrested some demonstrators;
iii **crowds demonstrated** at the police station;
iv a **British officer** ordered shooting. Ten were killed.
v **The Peking government** reacted feebly. The KMT called it 'imperial agent'.

17.12 The Northern Expedition, 1926

1 Chiang's aims
i to drive the **war lords** from Peking (Fig. 17.11A);
ii **to unite China** under a KMT government in Peking;
iii to drive **the foreigners** from China.

2 His campaign
i he led 100 000 men in attack on **Yangtse valley**;
ii in October 1926 he took **Hankow** (Fig. 17.11A);
iii in March 1927 he took **Shanghai** (Fig. 17.11A);
3 Political agents
i these were under the control of Mao Tse-tung (17.10.9);
ii they educated the peasants against landlords;
iii they educated town workers–against foreign merchants.

17.13 The Shanghai Massacres, 1927

1 **Chiang had succeeded** in the first part of the Expedition.

2 **The Communists** had played a large part in this success. Mao had led the political agents. **Chou En-lai** formed a revolutionary committee in Shanghai.

3 Chiang's **right wing** (17.11.2) resented their success.

4 **He suspected Communists** wanted to 'take over' the KMT.

5 He had **many friends in Shanghai** (17.9.8). With their help:
i he arrested and shot many **Communists**;
ii he expelled his **Russian advisers**;
iii he smashed the **Shanghai Communists organization**.

6 Five thousand were **killed in Shanghai.**

7 More were killed in other towns, including **Mao's wife**.

8 **Chou En-lai,** Chiang's colleague at Whampoa (17.7.1), escaped.

9 **Madame Sun** (17.11.3) thought Chiang had betrayed the revolution.

10 **Her sisters,** married to Chiang and to T.V. Soong, thought that he had done well by setting up a **right-wing dictatorship**.

17.14 The Northern Expedition, 1927–28

1927
1 Chiang marched on to **Peking**, the accepted capital of China.

2 The **war lords** fled to Manchuria (Fig. 17.11A).

3 The KMT army marched through **Shantung** and the port of **Kiao-chow** (Fig. 17.11A) but Chiang ordered it not to fight the Japanese.

1928
1 **Peking** captured;

2 **Nanking** (Fig. 17.11A) named as Chiang's new capital. It was Sun's capital in 1912 (6.14.8).

17.15 Chiang in power, 1928

1 **The Three Principles** were ignored (6.13.9 and 17.8.1):
i there was no elected government, no Parliament;
ii the rights of the peasants were ignored;
iii foreigners were not driven out.

2 He had a **right-wing government** of businessmen and landlords.

3 **Western Powers** made some concessions to Chiang:
i they gave up their control of the **tariff system**;
ii they allowed China to control its **postal system**.

4 They **retained** many powers. There were **International Settlements** in Shanghai and Tientsin (Fig. 17.11A).

5 **Foreign gunboats** patrolled the Yangtse (Fig. 17.11A).

6 **Communists** under Mao held the region around **Canton**.

17.16 Japan–the Tanaka Memorial, 1927

1 Baron Tanaka was Prime Minister of Japan, 1927.

2 His government issued a **policy statement** (Part V.3.1.Q.4).

3 In this 'Memorial' Tanaka outlined polices for:
i the **military conquest** of Eastern Asia;
ii the need to fight and **defeat the USA**, China's friend;
iii the seizure of **Manchuria and Mongolia** (Fig. 17.11A).

17.17 Manchuria, 1928

1 Its ruler was **war lord** Chang Tso-Lin (**'the old Marshal'**).

2 **Japan** controlled its railway lines.

3 1928 Japanese forces **assassinated** 'the old Marshal'.

4 His son, 'Young Marshal', succeeded him.

5 He declared his **loyalty to Chiang Kai-shek**.

17.18 The last war lord

1 **Most war lords** had been defeated, 1927 and 1928.

2 The 'Young Marshal' had accepted **Chiang as ruler of China**.

3 General Feng, **'the Christian General'** was the last war lord.

4 Chiang attacked him: lost 150 000 men but was **victorious**.

17.19 Mao and the Kiangsi Soviet

1 **Chiang** feared Communism more than he hated the Japanese.

2 **The Shanghai Massacre** (17.13) started the war on communists.

3 Mao controlled **Hunan province** (Fig. 17.11A).

4 1928 40 000 of the Red Army killed by Chiang's men.

5 1930 2 000 killed in Communist rising in Changsha.

6 Mao led 10 000 to found a **soviet in Kiangsi** (Fig. 17.11A).

7 He changed the Communist party line:
i the Revolution would not be based on **town workers**;
ii **Chinese peasants** would lead the Revolution;
iii the **Red Army** was made up of peasants;
iv other peasants hid, fed and helped Mao's forces.

8 This was against the principles of the Party (and of Marx) which said that a communist revolution had to follow an industrial revolution and be based on industrial workers.

17.20 Life in Kiangsi

1 **Soviets** were elected and a ruling soviet chosen.

2 **Living conditions** were hard; but officers and men shared equal conditions.

3 **Political agents** educated local peasants against **landlords**.

4 They helped peasants to fight **dishonest merchants**.

5 **Chiang** attacked Kiangsi. Mao had **four principles**:
i 'the enemy attacks, we retreat;
ii the enemy camps, we harass;
iii the enemy tires, we attack;
iv the enemy retreats, we pursue.'

17.21 Chiang versus Mao, 1930–31

1 1930 **Chiang** planned to wipe out the Kiangsi soviet.

2 **Peasants** helped the Red Army.

3 1931 Chiang had lost 23 000 men; Mao still in Kiangsi.

17.22 Japan and Manchuria, 1931

1 Japan controlled **Shantung Province** around Kiao-chow (Fig. 17.11A) and the **Manchurian railways**.

2 She wanted control of **Manchuria** as:
i **a market** for her industries;
ii a source of **raw materials and minerals**;
iii extra living space for her **growing population**;
iv the first stage of the **Tanaka scheme** (17.16).

4 The attack, 1931
i part of the Japanese-controlled **railway was blown up**;
ii **Japanese officers** in Manchuria blamed the Chinese;
iii they attacked **Mukden**, capital of Manchuria (Fig. 17.11A).
iv the 'Young Marshal' was driven south to China;
v Japan put a **three-year-old ex-Manchu** on the throne;
vi the region was re-named **Manchukuo**.

5 **Chiang** appealed to the **League of Nations** when Japan attacked.

6 He did not try to fight the Japanese.

17.23 The League and the Manchurian crisis

1 Japan was a permanent member of the **League Council** (14.4.2).

2 She had signed the **Covenant** (14.3).

3 The League sent a **Commission** under the Englishman, **Lord Lytton**.

4 **The Lytton Commission's report** (1932) condemned Japan.

5 **The League** accepted the report and refused to recognize the re-naming of Manchuria (17.22.4).

6 Japan, in anger, left the League.

7 The League did not taken any further action. **Japan held Manchuria** and it seemed that 'might is right'. This weakened the League.

17.24 Chiang versus Mao, 1932–34

1 Chiang **did not fight the Japanese** when they invaded **Manchuria**.

2 He had fought three campaigns against Mao, **1930–31** (17.21).

3 In a **fourth campaign in 1932** Chiang sent 1 million men and an airforce of 200 planes under two German generals.

4 **Mao** followed his first principle and **retreated** (17.20.5).

5 **Chiang's army** had **encircled the Communists** by October 1934.

6 Mao decided that, rather than accept defeat, he would lead his small band of followers to another, distant part of China.

17.25 The Long March, October 1934–October 1935

1 **15 October 1934** 120 000 men, women and children escaped from the Kiangsi region (Fig. 17.11A).

2 Mao hoped to found a new soviet in the **north west**.

3 Chiang's forces were too strong. **4 000 communists** were killed before the Reds got to the Yangtse River (Fig. 17.11A).

4 Mao then decided to go to north China, where Chiang's rule was at its weakest. This meant a march of **6 000 miles** which lasted for **368 days**.

5 During the march they were attacked by Chiang's forces, by war lords and by bandit gangs.

6 They reached Yenan (Fig. 17.11A) – 20 000 of them.

17.26 Chiang's government, 1930–35

1 **The war lords** had been wiped out or had accepted Chiang's rule.

2 **The Communists** had been driven from Kiangsi to the Japanese-controlled northern region.

3 **His government controlled** most of the vast country.

4 **Western businessmen** came back to the southern ports which enjoyed growing prosperity (Fig. 17.11A).

5 **Shanghai**, 'the Queen of the East', was the wealthiest city and controlled half of China's foreign trade.

6 **New factories** were built – by foreigners and Chinese.

7 An extended railway system, new roads and airlines made **transport easier**. Postal services, telecommunications and other **public services** encouraged western businesses to develop and make **China more industrialized**.

8 **Western firms** had special privileges, 'extra-territorial rights' and angered Chinese remembering Sun's Principles (6.13.9).

9 **Landlords** were Chiang's main supporters (17.11.2). Chiang's government did **little for the peasants** which angered Sun's followers (6.13.9).

10 **The Soong family** Madam Sun (widow of Sun Yat-sen) was critical of Chiang's government from 1927 onwards (17.13.9). One of her sisters had married Chiang, another had married a rich businessman, T V Soong. The Soong family prospered in Chiang's China. The family got many **top jobs in government**; others got **contracts** which allowed the growth of their businesses; **T V Soong** owned banks, factories, airlines and shipping companies. He was a **very westernized Chinese**, out of touch with the ordinary people.

11 He and his brother-in-law Chiang did little for:

i the **6 million peasants** who died in the famines, 1929–32;

ii the 20 000 who died of starvation each year in Shanghai;

iii the regular flooding by China's main rivers which each year devastated the countryside and made millions homeless.

12 Chiang governed with a small inner group of party faithfuls (17.8.2). This ignored the Principle of People's Democracy (6.13.9).

13 Chinese intellectuals grew critical of Chiang's government which favoured the few, ignored the peasants and allowed corruption by the Soongs and others to spread.

17.27 Mao in Yenan

1 In the mountains, Mao set up a new Soviet.

2 **Industry** was developed – partly to manufacture arms.

3 **Peasant farmers** were helped by a fixing of **fair rents**.

4 **The landless** got farms created from formerly unused land.

5 **New farming techniques** helped improve output.

6 Mao and his leading supporters lived, like everyone else, in **homes made in caves**. Everyone worked – in the fields, as political agents in the locality or in the small industries.

7 **Propaganda** was used to win people's support – plays, operas, newspapers, cartoons and posters all being employed.

8 **An army** was trained, because, said Mao: 'Political power grows out of the barrel of a gun'.

17.28 Chiang, the Communists and the Japanese, 1936

1 **The Japanese** had got control of **five northern provinces**.

2 **Chiang** refused to attack them.

3 He sent the **'Young Marshal'** to wipe out Mao in Yenan.

4 **Mao appealed** that 'Chinese ought **not to fight Chinese**'.

5 **November 1936** The 'Young Marshal' signed a truce with Mao and agreed to join him to fight the Japanese.

17.29 The Sian incident, 1936

1 **Chiang flew to Sian** to undo the truce.

2 **12 December** The 'Marshal's' men **arrested Chiang**.

3 **Chou En-lai** was sent by Mao to negotiate. He saved Chiang from assassination by some of the 'Marshal's' men.

4 **Chou and Chiang** agreed to unite to fight the Japanese.

5 **25 December** Chiang released.

6 **January 1937** The war against the Communists was called off.

7 **Feburary 1937** Chiang was proclaimed head of a government of **'The United Front'**. Yenan was called 'the autonomous border'.

17.30 Japan and China

1 At **Versailles**, Japan had gained the **Shangtung Province**.

2 In **1931** Japan had conquered **Manchuria** and extended their control from Shangtung over **five northern provinces**.

3 **Western powers**, including America, saw the Japanese expansion as a **barrier against Russian advance**.

4 The Japanese shared with the western nations many extra-territorial privileges (17.26.8).

5 **Shanghai, 1932** Western nations had a large International Settlement; western police patrolled this area:

i a Japanese was killed during a riot outside the area;

ii the Japanese government sent a naval force to Shanghai;

iii Japanese armed forces moved into Chapei, north of the International Settlement;

iv the Chinese resisted;

v **January 1932** The crowded area of Chapei was bombarded.

6 Chiang did nothing; western countries approved Japan's military defence of western privileges over the Chinese.

17.31 The start of the Chinese-Japanese war, 1937

1 The aims of the **Tanaka group** (17.16) were partly realized by the conquest of **Manchuria** (17.22) and the extra-territorial rights enjoyed in the **five northern provinces**.

2 The Japanese wanted more. They decided to act before the United Front got to work (17.29.7).

3 7 July 1937 Japanese troops were on manoeuvres near Peking.

4 At the **Marco Polo Bridge** (a railway junction near Peking) Japanese troops clashed with Chinese troops.

5 Japanese forces bombarded the city of Wanping, near Peking.

6 They demanded the right to search the city for those who had 'attacked' their forces. The Chinese refused.

7 28 July The Japanese launched a full-scale war by air and land and massacred the 29th Chinese Army guarding Peking.

17.32 The War, 1937–39

1 The Northern War
i Japanese troops landed at **Tientsin** (Fig. 17.11A);
ii there was **little Chinese resistance**;
iii Japan soon controlled most of **northern China** (Fig. 17.32A).

2 Conquering the Yangtse region
i the Yangtse River valley was the **richest region** in China;
ii **Shanghai** was the starting point for an attack on the valley;
iii **August 1937** Japanese naval force and land army attacked Shanghai. Chiang's forces resisted for three months;
iv **3 December 1937** Japanese victory parade through Shanghai;
v their forces conquered most of the Yangtse valley;
vi **12 December 1937** Japanese troops took **Nanking**, the capital of Chiang's China (17.14 and Fig. 17.11A).

3 Chiang's policy
i his forces had resisted in Shanghai–and been beaten;
ii he decided to **'trade space for time'**. He retreated and allowed the Japanese to gain more territory. He hoped that America would, one day, come to his aid.

4 Mao's policy
i the Japanese took the cities and towns; they found it almost impossible to control the countryside;
ii the Communists used **guerilla tactics**, created **'liberated areas'** which Communists ruled. In these areas they collected taxes, reduced rents to gain the support of the peasants;
iii in Japanese-controlled areas they organized guerilla resistance and won the support of patriots who hated the Japanese.

Former French territory   Japanese conquered territory

Fig. 17.32A Japanese conquest of S. East Asia, 1941–43

5 The position in 1939
i **Chiang** had retreated to a new capital, **Chungking** (Fig. 17.11A);
ii the **Japanese** controlled most of the **Chinese coastline**;
iii the **Communists** controlled most of the **north and north-east** and were the leaders of the anti-Japanese movement.

17.33 China, Japan and the Second World War, 1939–45

1 After December 1941 the Chinese-Japanese War became one part of the wider war (Units 25 and 26).

2 The USA became China's ally. General **Stilwell** went to **Chunking** to help organize the Chinese resistance to Japan.

3 He condemned Chiang's forces:
i they **refused** to fight;
ii their men were short of **food**;
iii **wounded men** were allowed to die because of shortages of medicine and doctors;
iv **officers were cruel** to their men;
v he summed things up with 'corruption, neglect, chaotic economy, hoarding, black market, trading with the enemy'.

4 He approved of Mao's forces: 'reduces taxes, rents, interest: raises production and standard of living, people participate in government, practise what they preach'.

17.34 Chiang and Mao, 1945–46

1 Chiang's advantages
i massive aid from the USA;
ii one of the Big Four Allied leaders;
iii he replaced the Japanese occupation forces in the cities and towns in north and east China.

2 Chiang's weaknesses
i **intellectuals** opposed him because of the **dictatorial rule** and its **inefficiences** as reported by Stilwell (17.33.3);
ii **businessmen** suffered from raging **inflation**;
iii **peasants** had been ignored at best and ill-treated generally by Chiang's ill-disciplined forces;
iv **patriots** resented the small part Chiang had played in the anti-Japanese war;
v **his army** was disloyal. Men sold their arms to the Reds and deserted rather than fight.

3 Mao's advantages
i he had won the support of **the peasants** by his land policies;
ii **intellectuals** admired the **honesty** of this government;
iii **businessmen** admired the rule of law which he established;
iv **patriots** admired his persistent resistance to the Japanese.

4 The first clash–Manchuria
i the Communists controlled this area when the Japanese surrendered in **August 1945**;
ii the USA advised Chiang not to re-occupy Manchuria;
iii he decided to do so–and face a war with Mao;
iv **General Marshall** of the USA persuaded Chiang and Mao to work together. On 10 October 1945 ('Double Tenth') they signed an agreement to work together;
v Chiang was really unwilling to consider the spread of Communism with its programme of land reform;
vi Mao was prepared to work in a Coalition Government–but only as a stage towards Communist control of China;
vii **June 1946** Chiang launched a full-scale attack on Communist centres in Central China.

17.35 The Civil War, 1946–49

1 The **Kuo Min Tang** controlled China south of the Yangtse (Fig. 17.11A) and held most of the cities in the north and in Manchuria.

2 The **Communists** controlled the countryside so that contact between KMT forces had to be by air.

3 June 1946–Spring 1947

i Chiang launched a three-pronged attack–towards Shantung, Yenan and Manchuria;

ii he promised that the Reds would be defeated in six months;

iii the Communists retreated from Yenan, made their way to the south and set up a base in the Tapeh mountains;

iv using guerilla tactics, the Communists controlled the route to the north from the Yangtse and threatened the rich Yangtse valley region (Fig. 17.11A).

4 1948

i having gathered and trained a peasant army, Mao went on to the offensive.

ii armed with Russian weapons and American arms sold by corrupt leaders in Chiang's army, Mao drove Chiang's forces into town bases;

iii **by January 1949** the Communists had captured every city north of the Yangtse. Many cities surrendered without fighting. Chiang's men deserted in their thousands. Many of Chiang's generals wanted to negotiate a deal with Mao.

17.36 Communist success

1 In the winter of 1948–49 the Communists won three major battles in **Manchuria**. They then marched to take Peking, 31 January 1949.

2 Other Red forces crossed the **Yangtse** and made their way south (Fig. 17.11A).

3 Red armies drove Chiang's armies into Nanking and Shanghai. In these cities inflation destroyed the savings of the middle class whilst Nationalist executioners were busy killing suspected opponents of Chiang's crumbling régime.

4 Rule by war lords, destroyed by Chiang in 1926 (17.13–14) had reappeared under his leadership. The advance of the Reds was welcomed by most Chinese anxious to have honest, efficient and disciplined government.

5 Shanghai and Nanking were taken in April–May 1949.

6 Chiang's army held out at Canton for a short while before fleeing to Formosa (Taiwan) in December 1949 (Fig. 17.11A).

17.37 The Chinese People's Republic

1 On 1 October 1949 Mao appeared at the Gate of Heavenly Peace of the Imperial Palace in Peking to read his address which inaugurated the People's Republic of China.

2 He promised to raise living standards and to work for world peace. In Unit 33 we will study China under Mao–and after.

18 International Affairs 1919–29

18.1 Influenced by the First World War

1 There was a **widespread desire** to avoid another major war.

2 **France** feared German revenge for her defeat (12.2.2).

3 **Germany** wanted a revision of the Treaty of Versailles (12.5–6).

4 **Reparations** were a major problem.

5 **Britain believed** that the Treaty had been too harsh (12.10.6).

6 **The Covenant** contained anti-war agreements. Nations still looked for ways of enforcing 'collective security'.

18.2 Hopes of the League's supporters

1 It would ensure peace (14.1).

2 All member nations had denounced war as a policy (14.3).

18.3 The League and the real world

1 **To Germans** it appeared as an association of victors (14.3.3), and part of the hated 'dictated peace'.

2 It had **no real power** (14.11).

3 **National self-interest** proved too strong (14.11).

4 **Diplomatic activity** continued outside the League framework.

18.4 German reparations, 1920–29 (*12.10.6*)

1 **France and Belgium** were the most insistent on their payment.

2 **Germany** failed to pay, 1922.

3 **The Ruhr** was occupied by French and Belgian troops, 1923.

4 This helped cause the great inflation in Weimar Germany (15.9).

5 **1924, a new climate**

i **Briand** replaced Poincaré as French Prime Minister. He was more sympathetic to Germany's problems.

ii **Stresemann** (15.10), the new German Foreign Minister, proved to be a good negotiator;

iii **MacDonald,** Labour Prime Minister of Great Britain, wanted to solve the reparations problem;

iv **the USA** gave Germany loans to help industrial recovery.

6 **The Dawes Plan, 1924**

i **Dawes,** an American general, had a new plan for reparations;

ii he proposed that the amount paid would depend on what Germany could afford each year;

iii this was an attempt to balance two objectives:

(a) to ensure that France, in particular, got something out of reparations;

(b) to ensure that Germany's economic recovery was not hindered by over-heavy reparations.

iv **Dawes** proposed that the reparation charges should be met from money paid by the German **customs, railways and industry**;

v the reparations payments would be paid through the **State Bank**;

vi **foreign nations** would have representatives on the Bank's board.

7 **German recovery** was helped by huge **American loans** and by the production of a **new German currency** supported by the Allies.

8 **The Young Plan, 1929**

i **1925–29** there was more agreement among European nations;

(a) **the Locarno Treaties** of 1925 (18.8);

(b) **the Kellogg Pact** of 1928 (18.10).

ii This was the result of personal friendship between Briand, Stresemann and Austen Chamberlain (18.8.1);

iii it led to a further change in the reparations scheme;

iv **Young,** an American financier, knew that Germany was in arrears with her payments since 1921. He devised a new scheme:

(a) it **reduced** the amount of yearly payments;

(b) Germany had to pay **£50 million a year**;

(c) Stresemann accepted the terms;

(d) Hitler and the Nazis campaigned against acceptance;

(e) Stresemann died and the Nazis came to power (15.17);

(f) the plan never came into operation.

9 **Hitler** stopped all reparations payments.

18.5 Russia and Europe, 1919–29

1 **The Allies** had intervened in the Civil War (10.25).

2 **Poland** gained parts of White Russia and of the Ukraine by the **Treaty of Riga, 1921**.

3 Russia was not allowed to join the League. But in 1921 many countries, including Britain, made **trade agreements** with Russia.

4 Russia and Germany were 'outsider' nations.

5 The Treaty of Rapallo, 1922 brought them together:

i they renounced **reparations**;

ii they agreed to resume **diplomatic relations**;

iii they resumed **economic relations**; Germany helped to build Russian industry;

iv Russia allowed Germany to train an **illegal army** and an **illegal airforce** on Russian territory (for illegal, see 12.5.4).

6 Britain, under a Labour government, in **1924**:

i recognized the Bolshevik government;

ii provided loans for Russian economic development;

iii signed a trade treaty with Russia.

18.6 France and Germany, 1919–25

1 Clémenceau had been largely responsible for the harsh terms of the **Treaty of Versailles** (12.2.2).

2 1922 Poincaré became Prime Minister. He had no sympathy with German complaints about the Treaty.

3 1922–23 Poincaré was responsible for the occupation of the Ruhr by French and Belgian troops (18.4.1–5).

4 1924 Briand became Prime Minister. He was more sympathetic to Germany's complaints.

5 Stresemann became Chancellor and Foreign Minister of Weimar Germany in 1923 (15.10):

i he was **critical** of the Treaty;

ii he understood **French fears** of German militarism;

iii he proved willing to **negotiate** with the Allies.

18.7 The Geneva Protocol, 1924

1 The League had had its early failures (14.8).

2 League supporters claimed that **one reason for failure** was the difficulty of defining who was **'an aggressor'**.

3 They drew up the **Geneva Protocol**:

i any country which **refused to accept arbitration** in a dispute was to be labelled the aggressor;

ii every nation in the League would act against an aggressor.

4 The British Dominions were unwilling to accept this–they feared being drawn into a number of European wars.

5 The British government under the Conservative, Baldwin, refused to accept the Protocol in 1925.

6 It never came to anything.

18.8 The Locarno Treaties, 1925

1 These were largely the result of **personal friendship** between:

i **Stresemann** of Germany (15.10) who was concerned about the 'encirclement of Germany by France and the Little Entente' (18.9);

ii **Briand** of France who wanted to have a friendly Germany on the French border;

iii **Austen Chamberlain,** British Foreign Minister, anxious to bring Germany and France closer together.

2 They were signed by Britain, France, Germany, Belgium and Italy.

3 Germany's western frontiers (with France, Belgium and Italy):

i these were accepted as drawn by the Treaty of Versailles;

ii Britain and Italy guaranteed to maintain those frontiers. This pleased France, fearful of German militarism.

4 Germany's eastern frontiers At Locarno the powers accepted treaties signed between Germany and Poland and Germany and Czechoslovakia. But they **did not offer to guarantee** Germany's eastern frontiers. This suggested willingness to see Germany take action to change them–which would have been contrary to the Treaty of Versailles.

5 Germany agreed not to use force against any of her neighbours.

6 The powers agreed to a Conference on Disarmament (14.10).

18.9 France and Germany's eastern neighbours

1 August 1920:

i **Czechoslovakia and Yugoslavia** were 'created' at Versailles from lands taken from Germany and Austria-Hungary (12.9.3);

ii **Romania** was enlarged by the Treaty (12.9.3);

iii in August 1920 the three signed an **Entente***.

2 France made an agreement with this 'Little Entente' agreeing to supply its members with military aid.

3 Poland was another 'new', or rather, re-created country which had gained territory from Germany and Austria as well as Russia.

4 1921 France made an alliance with Poland.

5 1925 These agreements and the alliance were re-affirmed.

6 At **Locarno** (18.8) it was agreed that these treaties should continue.

7 Germany saw this as a French plan to **encircle** her (18.8).

8 France, by seeking such agreements and treaties, showed that she had **little faith in the League**.

18.10 The Kellogg Pact, 1928

1 1927 The League adopted an Assembly resolution to prohibit wars of aggression.

2 Note: you should ask yourself why such a resolution was needed–the Covenant (14.3) already had all the nations agreeing to renounce war. The resolution (1927) was an indication that few people believed in the Covenant. Why, then, should they have had any more faith in their 1927 resolution?

3 1928 Kellogg was the American Secretary of State. He had the support of **Briand** of France (18.3.5) in his search for peace.

4 The Kellogg Pact, 1928

i sixty-five nations signed it including the USA, Russia and Japan;

ii they agreed that for five years (1928–33) they would not go to war except in **self-defence**.

5 Again, the existence of this pact was a sign that the nations disregarded the League, its aims and constitution.

6 A weakness of the Pact was that no one defined 'self-defence'.

18.11 The position at the end of 1929

1 Locarno (18.8) should have made **France** feel secure.

2 Those Treaties had also brought Germany back into diplomatic life. She joined the League in 1926.

3 Reparations had been twice re-negotiated (18.4.6–8) which suggested Franco-German co-operation and a desire for peace.

4 The Kellogg Pact had, once again, had the nations 'outlaw war' which suggested a desire for peace.

5 The Disarmament Conference was under way (14.10) suggesting that nations were willing to 'turn swords into ploughshares'.

6 The Rhineland was evacuated five years ahead of the date fixed at Versailles (12.5.2), showing that France and Germany were willing to live on friendly terms.

7 But there were major weaknesses

i **Briand** hoped that Germany would now be content with the changes made since 1919. In fact **Germany wanted more changes**;

ii **Stresemann** had hoped, in 1929, that France might give even more concessions (on reparations, on German re-armament). In fact, France had made concessions in the 1920s with much ill-will. Briand was not universally popular in France. The French people still distrusted Germany–hence the plans to build the Maginot Line;

iii **Hitler** was not yet in power. But Stresemann had died in 1929; this left a major vacuum in German politics. Hitler was going to fill that vacuum and would have a more forceful policy–towards Versailles, reparations (18.4.9), the Rhineland (23.7), German rearmament (14.10) and the League (14.10).

19 The United States 1932–41

19.1 The 1932 Presidential Election

1 **Hoover,** the President since 1928, was the Republican Party's candidate. In 1928 he had
i **praised the 'rugged individualism'** which, he claimed, had created the prosperity of the 1920s;
ii **promised** 'a chicken in every pot, two cars in every garage'.
2 **The Wall Street Crash, 1929** (16.15), had wrecked the American economy (16.16). Hoover did little until 1932 (16.17). By then:
i **many banks** had gone out of business, millions of people having lost their invested savings;
ii **more banks** were threatened as their clients rushed to take out their savings;
iii **the unemployment level** soared.
3 **Franklin Delano Roosevelt,** Governor of New York State (16.19.4) was the Democratic Party's candidate:
i he came from a **wealthy family**, educated at one of the best schools and universities;
ii he was assistant Secretary for the Navy in **Wilson's government** and Vice-Presidential candidate in 1920 (16.2);
iii he was crippled by **poliomyelitis** which gave him time to study and to develop that strength of character which enabled him to fight his way back into public life;
iv in 1932 he made a 'whistle stop tour' of the States, partly to show himself to the people and assure them that he was fit enough to be President, partly to tell them his policies.

19.2 The 'lame duck' Presidency

1 **The Presidential election** took place (and still does take place) in November of each leap year.
2 The incoming President was not due to take office until the next June.
3 **The outgoing President** was in office but had not real power.
4 Hoover agreed that Roosevelt should take office in March to deal with the many problems facing the country.

19.3 The Hundred Days, 4 March–16 June

1 **The New Deal** Roosevelt had promised this in June 1932
2 In his first hundred days in office, he **persuaded Congress** to pass a great deal of legislation (below).
3 **The Emergency Banking Act.** Roosevelt declared **4th March** to be a bank holiday. This gave time for experts to examine the accounts of the nation's banks. The **Emergency Banking Act** was passed on **9th March**. This forced weak banks out of business. It allowed the government to help stronger banks. In a broadcast, Roosevelt **assured** the people that their money was safe in their banks and **invited** them to put their money (wages, savings, profits) into the banks.

4 **The Banking Act** gave the government more control over banking. It set up the **Federal Deposit Insurance Corporation** which **insured** deposits in banks, **forbade** banks to use clients' money in investment on the Stock Exchange and **gave people more confidence** in the banking system.
5 **The Federal Emergency Relief Administration** (FERA). This agency was given 500 million dollars for:
i **cash relief** for the poor;
ii help to **local authorities** with their poor relief schemes. Roosevelt also used the RFC set up by Hoover (16.17.4).
6 **The Economy Act** reduced the pensions and salaries of state employees, to take into account the **fall in prices** (16.12.3).
7 **Prohibition** (16.9) was swept away and the eighteenth amendment was repealed.
8 **The Civilian Conservation Corps** (CCC) was set up to provide work for the unemployed:
i anyone between the ages of **18 and 25** was allowed to join for **six months** to work on afforestation schemes and other work;
ii they received **30 dollars a month**–and had to send 25 dollars home to **parents and wives**;
iii in 1933 some 300 000 people joined the Corps; by 1940 two million had done so, many rejoining after their first six months;
iv many **found work** after six months; employers welcomed the effort they had made by joining the Corps.
9 **The Civil Works Administration** (CWA) was set up under Harry Hopkins to provide work for unemployed on **public works** schemes, such as the building of roads, schools and other publicly-owned utilities. Four million registered with the CWA in 1933. In 1935 it was replaced by the **Works Progress Administration** (19.5).
10 **The Agricultural Adjustment Administration** (AAA):
i this was set up to **aid farmers**, the first to suffer (16.12);
ii it invited farmers to set up **co-operative marketing schemes**;
iii it gave loans to stop evictions (16.12.6);
iv **advisers** went to help farmers improve soil and methods;
v farmers were asked to **cut production** because of the effects of overproduction on prices (16.12.3). Those who did so were given a **subsidy** which came from **new taxes**:
(a) a tax on **cotton-spinning** subsidized farmers who gave up **cotton production** on their land;
(b) a **flour-milling tax** subsidized those who cut **wheat production**.
11 **The National Industrial Recovery Act** (NIRA) set up:
i the **Public Works Administration** as an extension of the CWA (19.3.9). It provided money for public works schemes undertaken by the government or local authorities;
ii the **National Recovery Administration** (NRA) was formed to draw up rules or 'codes' for industrial relations:
(a) it abolished child-labour, shortened the working week and fixed minimum wages;
(b) employers who accepted the 'code' could display a **'Blue Eagle'** and the government invited people to buy from such firms;
(c) it gave workmen the right to form **trade unions**.

19.4 The Tennessee Valley Authority (TVA) was set up
during the 'Hundred Days'. It deserves to be studied carefully.
1 The Tennessee River runs through **seven states**.
2 The **Valley** was one of the most backward areas in the USA.
3 **Agriculture** in the Valley suffered from:
i **soil erosion** owing to overcropping, winds taking away dusty top soil;
ii **floods** which washed away remaining top soil and ruined many of the poor farmers.
4 **Industry**. There was very little, so there was little alternative employment for the children of the poor farming families.

5 In **1930** Senator **Norris** asked Hoover to set up an Authority to tackle the problems of the Tennessee Valley. It would:

i tackle problems **too big for any single state** to tackle;

ii **build dams** to prevent **flooding** while also providing **hydro-electricity** which would attract **industry**, providing **employment**;

iii set up **factories** to **produce fertilizers** to help farmers to improve their soil.

6 Hoover refused.

7 Roosevelt set up the TVA during his 'Hundred Days':

i it provided **immediate employment** for thousands;

ii it cut across the rights of seven states;

iii it built 16 new **dams** and enlarged five others;

iv it made the river navigable. In **1928** only 48 ton-miles of traffic was carried on the river; in **1941** 161 million ton-miles travelled through the locks;

v it ended the damage previously done by **floods**;

vi it provided **cheap electricity** for farm houses, industries and towns which had never had it before.

19.5 The 'New Deal'–stage 2

1 The rush of legislation and the creation of so many agencies gave evidence of Roosevelt's wish to tackle America's problems.

2 The Works Progress Administration, 1935

i this agency was set up to replace the **CWA** (19.3.9)

ii it paid people to do various public works–e.g., building roads, dams, airports, schools, hospitals and playgrounds;

iii it provided work for artists, actors and writers. The **Federal Theatre Project** sent touring companies to perform plays in major cities;

iv it provided work for **over four million people**, enabled them (as wage earners) to buy goods which created **more employment**;

v it also provided America with schools, hospitals and the like which otherwise might not have been built. The **Hoover Dam** across the Colorado River was one such public work.

3 The Wagner Act, 1935. This replaced that part of the NIRA which had dealt with trade unionism (19.3.11.ii):

i it forced employers to **recognize trade unions** to which their workers belonged;

ii it forced employers to **negotiate** with these unions in matters of dispute and over wages;

iii it forbade employers to interfere with workers' rights to join unions and set up the **National Labour Relations Board** to which workers took their complaints.

4 The Social Security Act, 1935:

i this provided **pensions** for the old and widowed;

ii it provided a **state unemployment insurance scheme**, each local state being free to adopt the scheme as it thought best;

iii this still left America a long way **behind European states** as regards social security.

19.6 The growth of opposition to Roosevelt's policies

1 In 1936 Roosevelt stood in the Presidential elections–and was re-elected for a second term of office.

2 'Revolutionary' was one accusation by his opponents. They knew that for fifteen years there had been no reforming legislation under Harding, Coolidge and Hoover (Unit 16).

3 Hoover attacked four years of the 'New Deal':

i it was an attack on **free institutions**; employers were **forced** to pay minimum wages, recognize trade unions; they were forbidden to employ young children;

ii the NRA, said Hoover, favoured **'Big business'** and harmed 'the little man' with its price fixing and codes;

iii the AAA compelled **farmers** to do as they were told;

iv **planning** (as in the TVA) was said to be Marxist;

v the spending of vast sums of public money or **'priming the pump'** was the idea of the British economist, **Keynes**, whose ideas had been rejected in his own country

4 Some of the schemes had proved to be **unworkable** and had to be amended and improved. This suggested that Roosevelt acted **without enough thought**.

5 Some critics thought that the power of the Federal government had been increased too much.

6 Unemployment had not fallen by very much. The country was still locked into a great depression in 1936 (see Fig. IV.4.3.1A).

19.7 The Supreme Court, 1932–39

1 The Court is **'the Sacred Guardian of the Constitution'** (7.3.4).

2 It hears cases brought by people who think that an Act passed by Congress is invalid under the Constitution.

3 1932 Seven of the nine judges had been appointed in the 1920s by Republican Presidents. Roosevelt could not change things until a judge died or retired; few were willing to retire, although by 1936, the average age of the nine judges was 71 years.

4 1935–36 The Court ruled against Roosevelt:

i the NRA (19.3.11.ii) was declared **invalid**;

ii the AAA (19.3.10) was declared **invalid**;

iii several other lesser measures were also declared **invalid**.

5 This confirmed the opinions of those opponents who thought that Roosevelt's work was 'unconstitutional'.

6 This **angered Roosevelt** and those who thought that what he was doing was to try to get America back to work and so avoid the danger of a revolution (16.16.10).

7 1937 After his sweeping victory in the 1936 election, Roosevelt sent a proposal to Congress asking for laws which would enable him to get a more favourable Supreme Court:

i judges should be encouraged to retire when aged 70;

ii if any judge decided not to retire then, Roosevelt wanted the right to appoint an extra judge although the total number of judges should not exceed 15.

8 Congress refused Members were conscious of the importance of the 'separation of powers' of the President, Congress and the Court. They did not approve of Roosevelt's attempt to 'fiddle' with the composition of the Court.

9 The Court seemed to have learned a lesson. There were no more rulings against Roosevelt's work.

19.8 How successful was Roosevelt?

1 Millions of people had **jobs**, even if only for a short period, because of one or other of his agencies.

2 Labour relations were improved, although many employers resisted the introduction of trade unionism into their firms.

3 Trade unions grew In 1933 only 7 per cent of workers were in a union; by 1938 this had grown to 21 per cent.

4 It has been argued that Roosevelt saved American business or capitalism from more revolutionary policies as favoured by Long and others (16.19.3).

5 But although unemployment fell by 1937 it increased again after that.

6 Very little was done for the most deprived–the black population.

19.9 America and the outside world, 1933–41

1 America was not a member of the **League of Nations** (14.6.5).

2 She played **little part in world affairs** in spite of the Japanese attack on China, Mussolini's attack on Abyssinia (23.6) and Hitler's breaking of the Versailles Treaty (20.6.3 and Unit 23).

3 The Neutrality Act, 1935:
i this **forbade** the sale of **munitions** to warring countries;
ii it **forbade** the lending of **money** to countries involved in war. The USA seemed determined to avoid getting trapped into going to war in defence of its loans as it had done in 1917.

4 The Nazi invasion of Poland saw the outbreak of the Second World War (23.17). Roosevelt broadcast to the American people promising to keep them out of the war.

5 The Neutrality Act was amended to allow the supply of arms to Britain and France.

6 Cash and Carry A Plan was approved which allowed the British and French to buy arms in the USA provided that they paid for them in cash and took them away in their own ships.

7 The sweeping victories gained by Hitler in 1940 (Unit 25) led Roosevelt to ask Congress to approve the spending of millions of dollars on **American rearmament**.

8 The four freedoms In January 1941 Roosevelt, in a broadcast, spoke of the four freedoms for which Britain, now alone, was fighting. These were freedom (i) of **speech**; (ii) of **worship**; (iii) from **want**; (iv) from fear of **other nations**.

9 Lend-Lease Early in 1941 Britain ran out of money to buy arms from the USA. Roosevelt proposed (and Congress passed) a scheme by which the USA would 'lend' the arms to Britain who would 'lease' them for the duration of the war and 'return' them if unused. Roosevelt argued that if they were used, then America had been guarded from the danger of attack by Hitler–and there would be no charge for the arms.

10 The Atlantic Charter In August 1941 Roosevelt met Churchill on board the American warship, *Augusta*, off the coast of Newfoundland. They discussed:
i the **lend-lease** scheme;
ii the possibility of **Japan's** coming in on Germany's side;
iii the possibility of developing an **atomic bomb**; they also issued a statement christened 'the Atlantic Charter':
(a) neither power would try to increase its own power by seizing land from any other country or in any other way;
(b) people throughout the world should be given the **right to choose their own government**; countries conquered by force should be given their independence. This was meant to be an answer to the threat posed by Germany and Japan. But the idea that people should have the right to self-government was seized upon by the colonial countries of the Third World and became an important stage in the growth of the demand for freedom from colonial rule;
(c) after the 'final destruction of Nazi tyranny' the nations of the world should join together to ensure greater prosperity and a lasting peace.

11 American action
i **RAF men** were trained in the USA;
ii **Royal Navy ships** were repaired in US shipyards;
iii from July 1941 **US warships** were ordered to escort British convoys as far as Iceland–which saved many British lives and freed the Royal Navy for other duties elsewhere;
iv **Germany** regarded this as an act of war. In September 1941 a German submarine fired on a US destroyer. In October 1941 a US destroyer was sunk, although officially the USA was not at war.

19.10 For America's part in the Second World War see Units 25 and 26.

20 Hitler's Germany, 1933–39

20.1 Establishing the dictatorship, Jan–March 1933

1 January 1933 Hitler was democratically elected and appointed Chancellor (15.21.6).
2 February 1933 During the run up to fresh elections there were:
i a Nazi **'reign of terror'** (15.22.3);
ii the **anti-left campaign** to weaken the opposition (15.22.5).
3 March 1933 The election gave the Nazis more seats (15.22.6).
4 March 1933 A fresh **anti-left campaign**:
i many opposition **parties dissolved** (15.23.2);
ii **Communists expelled** from the Reichstag (15.23.3).
5 23 March Enabling Act gave him dictatorial powers (15.23.6).

20.2 Winning the army for the dictatorship, June–August 1934

1 Roehm, socialist leader of the SA (20.4.3), wanted:
i **a socialist policy** (15.24.1);
ii **the SA** to be an important part of the Regular Army (15.24.2).
2 Hitler was afraid of:
i **Roehm as an enemy** inside the Nazi Party;
ii the loss of support by **industrialists** (15.24.1);
iii the power of the **Army General Staff** (15.24.3–4).
3 30 June 1934 Hitler got rid of Roehm (15.24.5).
4 August 1934 Hitler succeeded Hindenberg as **President**, but used the title, **Fuhrer**, instead (15.24.6).
5 This made him **Commander-in-Chief** of the Armed Forces all of whose members took an **oath of loyalty** to him (15.24.7).

20.3 Hitler's Chief Ministers

1 Hermann Goering
i he was **Minister of the Interior in Prussia**. This was the largest and most important state in Federal Germany (1.13);
ii he was the first commander of the **Geheime Staatspolizei**, or **Gestapo**, a politically-dominated police force (20.4.5);
iii he organized the **reign of terror** against Hitler's opponents during 1932 and 1933 (15.21–22);
iv following the **Reichstag Fire** (15.22.4) he led the **anti-left campaign** (15.22.5 and 15.23.2–5);
v his men were partly responsible for the assassination of **Roehm and his associates** (15.24.5);
vi **1934** he was in charge of German **industrial development**;
vii **1939–45** he was in command of the **German Air Force**.

2 Joseph Goebbels
i **1922** a **journalist**, he was the Party's best **propagandist**;
ii **1926** he was made Party leader (**Gauleiter**) for **Berlin**;
iii **1927** he founded a Berlin daily paper, *Der Angriff*;
iv **1928** he was elected to the Reichstag (Table 15.18A);
v **1929** he was made chief of **party propaganda**;
vi **1933** he became **Minister of Propaganda and Enlightenment** in Hitler's government (20.1).

3 Heinrich Himmler
i he was an **early member** of the Nazi Party;
ii **1929** Hitler appointed him leader of the **SS** (20.4.4);
iii he succeeded Goering as head of the **Gestapo** (20.4.5);

iv he was responsible for:
(a) the assassinations of **June 1934** (15.24);
(b) **the suppression of opposition** inside Hitler's Germany;
(c) the attacks on the **Jews** (20.8);
(d) the running of the **concentration camps**.

4 Hjalmar Schacht
i **1918** he was partner in a bank at Bremen;
ii **1924** he devised the plan for the restoration of a stable currency by means of issuing a new **Rentenmark** (15.10.2);
iii **1924** he took part in the conference which led to the **Dawes Plan** (18.4) while he was **head of the Reichsbank**;
iv **1933** he was an active supporter of the Nazi Party and of Hitler's accession to power in January 1933;
v **1933–37** he was Hitler's **Economics Minister**:
(a) he devised a scheme to pay for **German re-armament** (20.6.3),
(b) he supported public spending to reduce **unemployment**;
(c) he arranged **trade and currency deals** with countries in Central and Eastern Europe which helped to develop trade and get important imports.

vi **2 January 1939** As President of the Reichsbank he wanted Hitler to reduce spending on armaments so that the budget could be balanced and inflation stopped. **He was sacked**.

20.4   Major Nazi organizations

1 The Nazi Labour Front
i **all workers** were enrolled in this organization;
ii **trade unions** were abolished. The Nazis claimed that they were socialist or communist organizations;
iii **strikes** were forbidden as anti-State activities.

2 The Hitler Youth organization
i this had been formed in the 1920s;
ii through it the Nazis won the support of the young;
iii **boys** 'played' at being soldiers in the 1920s–having uniforms, camps, 'battles' at week-ends. In the 1930s, these former boys were fervent supporters of Hitler's policies;
iv **all other youth organizations** were banned after 1933.

3 The Sturmabteilung (SA)
i Hitler built his own private army, infantry and cavalry, the SA commanded by **Captain Roehm**;
ii the money for this force was provided by industrialists who were afraid of the rise of Communism (15.16.4);
iii the force had **brown shirts** for its uniform;
iv it took part in the **street fighting** in the late 1920s (15.18.5);
v **1930** the two million **stormtroopers** were used to:
(a) **win support** as they marched through the streets;
(b) **disrupt opposition meetings** and so help Hitler to power;
(c) **terrorize the opposition**. January–March 1933, and so help Hitler to establish the dictatorship (15.22).
vi once in power Hitler got rid of Roehm (15.24).

4 The Schutzstaffel (SS)
i Hitler and his powerful ally, Roehm, did not always agree. In 1934 this led to Roehm's assassination (15.24);
ii Hitler organized a **special detachment** to be his own **political executive**;
iii the Schutzstaffel (or **protective squadron**) in their black shirted uniforms was set up in 1928, rival to the SA;
iv it had a **military organization** like the SA but included artillery sections;
v one SS regiment consisted of **Hitler's Life Guards**;
vi like the SA there were **many full time professional members** of the SS. But as with the SA most members served in their **spare time**;
vii there were about 500 000 SS;
viii **1929** Hitler appointed **Himmler** leader of the SS;
ix the SS was the force used in the **Night of the Long Knives** when the leaders of the **SA** were assassinated (15.24).

5 The Geheime Staatspolizei (or Ge-sta-po)
i we have seen that one of Lenin's first acts was to set up a secret police force, the Cheka (10.23);
ii **1933** Hitler set up the **Gestapo** as his secret police force;
iii **Himmler** took control from Goering. The SS (above) and the Gestapo were under one man's control;
iv it was responsible for infiltrating every anti-Nazi organization and by terrorism it stamped out opposition to Hitler;
v it had secret files on every prominent German, including the leading Nazis. Himmler was able to use these to blackmail many people and so gain even more power for himself;
vi it was Himmler's men who led the anti-Jewish campaigns (20.8) and ran the concentration camps.

20.5   Opposition to Hitler's rule

1 Most opposition was crushed
i **the separate Parliaments** of the various States (1.13) were abolished in 1934 by a decree under the Enabling Laws (15.23.5–6);
ii **the Reichsrat**, or second House of the German Parliament, 'disappeared' with the abolition of the separate States;
iii this gave political power to the **Reichstag** which, by the **Enabling Law** gave Hitler dictatorial powers for four years;
iv all political parties, except the Nazi Party, were declared illegal. Those that had not been smashed (15.23.2) simply went out of existence–Nationalists, Catholics, Conservatives;
v **trade unions** were declared illegal (20.4.1).

2 The Catholic Church and Hitler
i Hitler claimed that it was impossible to be a good German and a Christian;
ii **1933** Hitler made a **Concordat** (or agreement) with the Pope which allowed the Catholic Church to run schools and newspapers, and to maintain its churches and cathedrals. Many Catholics saw this as Papal approval for Hitler;
iii the persecution of the Jews (20.8) led to a quarrel with the Catholic Church. In **1937** the Pope issued an Encyclical (or Papal Letter), entitled **Mit Brennender Sorge** (With Burning Anxiety) which condemned Hitler's racialist theories and practices;
iv some Church leaders, such as the Cardinal Archbishop of Munich, preached and wrote against Hitler and the Nazis;
v many priests and the majority of Catholics went along with Hitler's policies because they seemed to be successful.

3 The Protestant (Lutheran) Church and Hitler
i many Lutherans supported Hitler who had given the Germans a new pride and hope;
ii some opposed his anti-Jewish policies;
iii **Pastor Niemoller** led this opposition;
iv he and others were sent to concentration camps.

20.6   Support for Hitler

1 The German middle class
i they remembered the **inflation** and chaos of **1923** (Fig. 15.6A);
ii **1931** they **feared** a repeat of that chaos (15.17.2);
iii they provided leadership for **Roehm's Brownshirts** (20.4.3);
iv they welcomed the **strong, firm government** provided by Hitler.

2 Anti-Communists
i Hitler claimed that he **saved Germany** from Bolshevism (15.22);
ii by signing an **anti-communist pact** with Italy and Japan he claimed that he would **save the world** from Russian Bolshevism;
iii this was welcomed by:
(a) **industrialists** who feared the loss of their property;
(b) the **Church**, afraid of anti-clerical Bolsheviks;
(c) the **middle class** which most feared Bolshevism.

3 Industrialists
i Germany had recovered under **Stresemann** (15.10);
ii **1930** Germany was the world's **second most powerful industrialized nation**;
iii industrialists, such as the 'steel barons' **Thyssen** and **Krupps**, provided much of the **money to finance the Nazi Party**. They also supported the Party in **newspapers** which they owned;
iv they benefited from **German rearmament** after 1933:
(a) half a million men were **conscripted** into the **Werhmacht** (Army);
(b) thousands of **Panzerkamp-wagen** (armoured fighting vehicles) or **tanks** were built;
(c) the **Luftwaffe** (Air Force) bought thousands of aircraft;
(d) the **Germany Navy** was enlarged and hundreds of U-boats built. In **1936** the *Admiral Graf Spee* was launched, a revolutionary kind of fighting **'pocket-battleship'** which could outgun any ship fast enough to catch her and was speedy enough to escape from conventional battleships which would have outgunned her.
v **this rearmament** led to an expansion of the iron and steel, coal and engineering industries;
vi these and other industries also benefited from Hitler's (and Schacht's) development of public works, the building of miles of motorways (or **autobahns**), schools, houses and hospitals.

4 The Army
i the traditional officer-corps helped Hitler's rise to power. **Ludendorff** had taken part in the **1923 putsch** (15.14.6); **Schleicher** had used his influence politically in 1932–33 to help Hitler (15.21.2) and had been assassinated along with Roehm in June 1934;
ii they **welcomed the expansion and rearmament** after 1933;
iii they supported Hitler's demands for a tearing up of the **Treaty of Versailles** and for **equality for Germany** compared with other European nations;
iv they hoped that they would have the **same control in Hitler's Germany** as Army leaders had had when Bismarck controlled Germany after 1870 and when Kaiser William II allowed Schlieffen and the army to determine foreign policy (1.30);
v Hitler was aware of the **opposition** he might get from this **traditional officer class**:
(a) he was **Austrian** by birth; most officers were **Prussian**;
(b) he had only been a **corporal** in 1914–18;
(c) they despised **his Brownshirts** and **terrorist tactics**;
vi he made them take an **oath of loyalty** to him as Head of State in 1934 (20.2.5);
vii they opposed his plans for an expansionary foreign policy (23.9). The success of that policy from 1935 to 1940 made it even less likely that the officer-class would provide opposition to the Fuhrer.

5 The working class
i **employment** was provided for millions after 1933 by:
(a) **conscription** of 500 000 soldiers;
(b) **rearmament,** and industrial expansion;
(c) **public works** such as the building of the autobahns;
(d) **aid to agriculture** to help Germany become economically independent;
(e) **aid to industrial development**. The German car industry produced the 'People's Car' or **Volkswagen**; radio and other industries were also developed.

6 Nationalists from all classes welcomed:
i the evident growing strength of the **Armed Forces**;
ii the regaining of the **Provinces lost** at Versailles (12.5) beginning with the Saar in 1935;
iii **the new confidence** in Germany as the economy boomed.

20.7 Propaganda

1 In *Mein Kampf* (15.15) Hitler made it clear that people's support could be won by clever use of propaganda.

2 By 1922 onwards **Goebbels** was in charge of party propaganda.
3 In his own speeches, Hitler used propaganda against:
i **Jews** (20.8);
ii **Communists** (20.6.2);
iii **Socialists,** such as Stresemann;
iv **foreigners**, who had forced Versailles on Germany.
4 He also **promised**:
i **law and order** in place of 'Bolshevik unrest';
ii **an expanding economy** instead of unemployment;
iii a **'Greater Germany'** instead of one downtrodden by the Treaty of Versailles.
5 Goebbels was another clever orator able to rouse the masses. But as Minister of Propaganda and Enlightenment (20.3.2) he also used:
i **radio**, which was **government-controlled** and put out pro-Hitler propaganda in plays, stories and news bulletins;
ii **the press**, also **government-controlled** and censored. Only items favourable to Hitler were allowed to appear;
iii **marches**, **demonstrations** and **rallies** in which thousands of men sang their songs, chanted their slogans and carried their banners with the sign of the swastika;
iv **sporting events and personalities**. Max Schmelling's victory over the negro, Joe Louis, for the **world heavyweight championship** in 1936 was highlighted as victory for 'the Aryan race'. The **1936 Olympic Games** were held in Berlin and became a means of spreading Nazi propaganda;
v **education:**
(a) **teachers** had to accept Nazi doctrine;
(b) **text-books** were re-written to fit into Hitler's views of history and racial purity;
(c) **children** were recruited into the **Little Fellows** at six, the **Jungvolk** at ten, and the **Hitler Youth** at fourteen. Boys swore loyalty to Hitler as 'the saviour of our country'. Girls, in the **League of German Maidens**, were taught that the mothering of future soldiers was to be their highest aim;
(d) **teachers**, even at Universities, who were lukewarm in their support were sacked. **Books** which the Nazis disliked, were destroyed; in **May 1933** there was a **public burning** of such books in city squares and the grounds of universities.

6 Behind this propaganda there was also the **fear of**:
i the Gestapo;
ii the concentration camps.

20.8 Hitler and the Jews

1 In *Mein Kampf* Hitler 'showed' that the Jews were responsible for the **defeat of 1918** and the economic collapses of 1923.

2 1929–32 The Jews were blamed for the **economic collapse** (15.17). They were the bankers and financiers responsible for the Wall Street Crash and the banking collapses in Germany.

3 *Die Stürmer*, a Nazi newspaper, specialized in anti-Jewish attacks.

4 1 April 1933 Hitler decreed a boycott of all Jewish shops, business houses, lawyers and doctors. Stormtroopers plastered Jewish shops and offices with notices warning the public not to enter; others stood as guards outside such buildings.

5 Spring 1933 Jews were not allowed to enter universities. Later on they were to be banned from certain professions.

6 September 1935 There was a special meeting of the Nazi-packed Reichstag at **Nuremberg**. **The Nuremberg Laws** said:
i Germans of Jewish blood were **deprived of citizenship**;
ii **marriages** between Aryans and Jews were forbidden under pain of death;
iii Jews had to wear a yellow patch (in the form of a star) on their clothes. This marked them off from the rest of people.

7 Concentration camps were built to house Jews and other potential opponents of the Nazis. The first, near Munich, was completed in **April 1933** and housed 5000 prisoners.

8 Many Jews went into exile including:

i theatre and cinema **producers** such as Max Reinhardt;

ii **scientists** such as Einstein;

iii **writers and university teachers.**

9 9–10 November 1938 On 7 November a German Jewish refugee killed a member of the German Embassy in Paris. In reprisal the Nazi government organized a mass attack on German Jews:

i synagogues, businesses and homes were destroyed;

ii during this **Crystal Night** thousands of windows were smashed in Jewish property, and 200 synagogues destroyed;

iii thirty-five Jews were killed in these attacks. 20 000 were arrested for 'resisting the forces'.

10 The Final Solution to the Jewish problem was ordered in 1942 as Hitler decreed the killing of all Jews throughout Europe by mass executions in specially designed gas chambers in the concentration camps. **Six million Jews had died in this way by 1945**.

21 Italy, 1919–39

21.1 A new and divided country

1 Italy had completed its unification only in 1870.

2 **Social problems** in this new country included:

i **widespread poverty** in a country with no coal and little raw material resources as aids to industrialization;

ii **peasant poverty** in the rural south and in the Lombardy Plain, the result of centuries of over-cultivation which had lowered the quality of the crop and made the regions liable to flood damage and erosion;

iii **governments** which paid no attention to these problems.

3 **The religious problem** was the result of:

i the powerful **position of the Catholic Church** in Italy;

ii the **Church's opposition** to the government which had:

(a) taken the **Papal States** in 1860–1;

(b) taken **Rome** in 1870:

iii the **Pope's refusal** to recognize the Italian government while he was **'the prisoner in the Vatican'**.

4 **Socialism** of the Marxist and non-Marxist variety

i among **industrial workers** in the cities of the North such as **Turin and Milan**. These were centres of strikes and discontent;

ii it was **opposed** by important sections of the community:

(a) the **Church**, fearing anti-clericalism;

(b) **landowners** and **industrialists**;

(c) the majority of the professional **middle classes**.

5 **Discredited politicians and a despised democracy**

i the system of **proportional representation** led to the appearance of **many small parties in Parliament**, as in France (2.11.4);

ii these parties ranged from:

(a) **right-wing Conservatives** wanting the King to be more powerful;

(b) **centre parties,** often Catholic-based, anxious for lower taxes;

(c) **moderately left-wing Liberals** supporting increased democracy;

(d) **radical left-wing socialists** willing to work with the King;

(e) **extreme left-wing Communists** waiting for a Bolshevik Revolution;

iii forming a government meant winning support from several of these parties. This led to **weak policies**;

iv the politicians were more interested in the in-and-out of government-forming than in solving the country's problems.

21.2 The War, 1914–18

1 Italy was a member of the **Triple Alliance** (8.7).

2 Its membership **excluded war with Britain** (8.7).

3 **1915** Italy joined the Allies against Germany-Austria.

4 **October 1917** The Italians suffered a major defeat by the Austrians at **Caporetto**.

5 Austrian-German armies took large portions of N.E. Italy.

6 The Allies had to send troops, although already involved in savage fighting on the Western Front (9.11).

7 **October 1918** Austria signed an Armistice while still in occupation of parts of N.E. Italy.

8 **Inflation** was the result of the printing of paper money to pay for the war–munitions, soldiers' pay and the rest.

21.3 The Treaty of Versailles; Prime Minister Orlando (12.2.4)

1 **Hopes** The Italians hoped to gain some or all of

i the province of **Istria**–in former Austro-Hungary–including the ports of **Trieste** and **Fiume**;

ii part of the **Dalmation coast** around **Zara**;

iii **Albania,** created by Austrian power in 1913 (4.18);

iv the province of **Trentino-Tyrol** to the north of Italy.

2 **Actual gains were much smaller**

i a part of Istria, including Trieste but **not Fiume**;

ii **Trentino-Tyrol.**

3 **Losses and new problems**

i **600 000 Italians** had been killed;

ii their gains brought **500 000 Croats and Slovenes** and **250 000 Germans** into Italy, leading to racial problems.

21.4 Discontent, 1919–20

1 **Inflation** (21.2.8) which affected:

i **the middle class,** whose savings were wiped out;

ii **workers** whose wages did not keep pace with rising prices.

2 **Unemployment** which followed from:

i the end of government **orders for munitions**;

ii the **demobilization** of millions of servicemen;

iii **less spending** by the unemployed and the demobilized.

3 **Social unrest** 150 000 ex-soldiers roamed Italy living on charity or banditry.

4 **Inefficient government** 1918–22 There were **five governments** none of which lasted long enough to begin to tackle the problems.

21.5 The discontented organize and act

1 **The Blackshirts** were gangs of ex-servicemen.

2 **The Blueshirts** were nationalists opposed to the Treaty (21.3).

3 **The Greyshirts** were Liberals who wanted efficient government.

4 **The Red Guards** were the Bolsheviks.

5 **Violence** was commonplace:

i workers went on **strike** for higher wages;

ii employers **locked out** workers seeking higher wages;

iii **riots** took place in industrial towns and cities;

iv the police and troops **sided with employers**;

v **rival gangs** attacked each others' meetings.

21.6 Benito Mussolini's early career

1 **1883** Born the son of a **socialist blacksmith**.

2 He went to a **training college for priests** from which he was expelled for stabbing a fellow-pupil.

3 He worked as a schoolmaster and as a journalist.

4 **1912** He was editor of the socialist paper, *L'Avanti* (Forward).

5 **1914** He left the socialist party when it opposed Italy's entry into the war against the Germans and Austrians.

6 He founded a paper, *Il Popolo d'Italia* (The Italian People).

7 **1915** He joined the army but was invalided out, injured while practising with grenades–not by the 'war wounds' he spoke of.

8 **1919** He was critical of the government which failed to deal with Italy's problems (21.4 and 5). He formed the Fascist Party.

21.7 The Fascist Party

1 **Fasces** were the bundle of rods around an axe carried in ancient Rome as a symbol of magistrates' authority.

2 **Fascio** is Italian for a group or a squad. It was used in 1919 to describe various gangs fighting socialists and communists. Many anti-left gangs were supported by wealthier Italians.

3 **1919** Mussolini founded a **Milan Fascio**. It won only 2 per cent of the votes in a Milan constituency.

4 **1921** He founded the **National Fascist Party**. Members wore a **black uniform** and greeted each other with the **Roman salute**.

5 In industrial towns and cities his men attacked gangs of socialists and communists. This gained Mussolini the **support of**:
i the wealthy **landowners and industrialists**;
ii **middle class professional people**–teachers, lawyers and so on.

21.8 Fascism

1 It did not have a worked out political doctrine.
2 Mussolini and other leading Fascists 'invented' ideas and principles as the need arose.
3 Generally it can be said that **Fascism taught that**:
i there was a need for **strong, centralized government**;
ii **the individual had to submit** his interests and will to the interests and decisions of the government;
iii '**Mussolini (Il Duce) is always right**';
iv **Communism** was a threat to be fought;
v Italians could take a **pride in their nation and State**.

21.9 Gabriele D'Annunzio

1 He was a one-eyed poet and orator.
2 **1919** He led an attack on, and captured, **Fiume** (21.3.2).
3 He held it for 15 months before the Italian government helped to drive him out.
4 **He taught Mussolini** the idea of strong action in the name of the Italian people's nationalistic pride.

21.10 The path to power, 1919–22

1 **1919** His **Fascio** won only 2 per cent of the votes in a Milanese constituency (21.7.3).

2 **1919–21** His growing movement (21.7.4) adopted a policy of **violence**. Meetings of socialists and communists were attacked. This won him the **support** of the wealthy, the frightened and the anti-communists.

3 **1921** His Fascist Party (21.7.4) won **35 seats** in the Italian Parliament. He demanded a seat in the government. This was refused, but no government was formed as politicians squabbled for position and power (21.1.5).

4 **1921–22** While Italy had no government, Mussolini's supporters won control of several local councils including **Milan**.

21.11 The March on Rome, 28 October 1922

1 **July–August, 1922** Socialists organized a **General Strike** in protest against government failure to deal with unemployment.

2 **Mussolini's supporters** occupied many **public buildings** in towns in northern and central Italy. They organized **public services** in many of these towns, something which the government ought to have done but was unwilling to do in face of the General Strike.

3 **The Fascists** also **attacked** left-wing organizations and **burnt** the printing press of the *Avanti* newspaper.

4 Early in October, **King Victor Emmanuel III** invited Mussolini to become Prime Minister. He refused, not wishing to appear to be merely another politician of the 'ordinary' kind.

5 **28 October 1922**:
i **30 000 Fascists** 'marched' (by train) from various parts of Italy, threatening to take over the capital, Rome.
ii **Mussolini**, fearing arrest, stayed in **Milan**;
iii **Liberal and left-wing politicians** wanted the King to order the army and police to move against the Fascists;
iv **the King refused** to act. He feared that to arrest Mussolini would suggest that he favoured the socialists and communists;
v **the King** thought that Mussolini was just the '**strong man**' that the divided and violent country needed;
vi again, he invited **Mussolini to form a government**.

21.12 Mussolini's first government, 1921–24

1 There were only **three Fascists** in the Cabinet.
2 This was only a temporary expedient, needed to soothe the right-wing politicians.
3 **All decisions** had to receive Mussolini's approval.
4 He **soon replaced** with Fascists **anyone** opposing his ideas.
5 He founded the **Voluntary Fascist Militia for National Security** which was a private army for his own use.

6 **1923** He proposed that the party which got the largest number of votes in the next election should take two-thirds of the seats in Parliament. His blackshirted army filled the galleries in Parliament. The **Electoral Law** was passed by the frightened members.

7 **1924** During the election there was a great deal of **violence** including **armed fighting**. Fascists got **65 per cent of the vote**.

21.13 The second government, 1924–25

1 **Socialists** demanded an enquiry into the election violence.
2 **Matteotti**, a leading socialist, led the attack on Mussolini:
i he showed that **opposition newspapers** had been attacked, **printing presses** smashed and **newsprint** burned;
ii he named **individuals who had been attacked**;
iii **his campaign** won a good deal of support.

3 Within a week, **Matteotti** was brutally murdered. Mussolini may not have given the order for this murder; but he stood to gain from the removal of his opponent.

4 There was widespread **demand for Mussolini's dismissal**.
5 **The King refused** to sack him.
6 **Opposition members** then left Parliament and held meetings elsewhere. Mussolini then attacked other opponents.

21.14 Fascist 'stability'

1 Mussolini decreed that Italy needed **time to forget** the Matteotti affair.
2 Fascist gangs closed the **offices** of opposition parties, papers and clubs. **Opponents** were attacked, imprisoned and tortured.
3 Remaining **independent papers** were taken over by Fascists.

4 Local government was changed; Fascists replaced existing Mayors.

5 Central government was changed; Mussolini became responsible to the King alone and not to Parliament.

6 The electoral system was changed; lists of possible candidates were drawn up by workers' organizations. From these the Fascist Grand Council (21.15) chose the final list. Electors could accept or reject the list as a whole. In 1929 and 1934 the Fascist list was accepted.

7 University teachers had to take an oath of loyalty to Il Duce.

8 Anti-Fascists were arrested and exiled to the Lipari Islands.

9 Everywhere organized bands of **Fascists terrorized opposition**.

21.15 The Fascist Grand Council

1 Before 1924 membership of the Party had been small.

2 After 1924 a Party card was essential for anyone wanting an official job or an army post.

3 96 Provincial Secretaries appointed by Mussolini ran the Party throughout the country.

4 The Fascist Grand Council consisted of 22 representatives from the various Corporations (21.16).

5 The Council met when Mussolini ordered it to do so.

6 The Secretary-General of the Party had a powerful post. We have seen how Stalin used such a position to win power for himself (10.32).

i **1925** Mussolini appointed a loyal supporter, Farinacci, to the post—and he organized the reign of terror;

ii later, Mussolini dismissed Secretaries—to ensure that none of them stayed long enough to become too powerful.

21.16 The Corporate State

1 13 (later 22) **Corporations** were set up to organize various industries and occupations. There was a Corporation for steel, another for teachers, another for the theatre and so on.

2 Employers and workers were represented on the Corporation which settled pay, working conditions and the running of industry.

3 A Minister of Corporations supervized the Corporations.

4 Members of each Corporation were taught to put the interests of the State before their self-interest (21.8.3).

5 Trade unions were abolished—as unnecessary.

6 Strikes were illegal—disputes were settled by the Corporation.

7 Lock-outs by employers were banned. This appeared to make workers and employers equal; in fact the Corporations were controlled by the wealthy and influential.

8 Mussolini claimed to have **abolished class warfare** by uniting employers, workers and managers in the Corporations.

9 1938 Representatives of the 22 Corporations **replaced Parliament** through the Assembly of Corporations.

21.17 The dictatorship

1 The Corporations controlled economic life.

2 1925, December. Mussolini took away the **King's right** to appoint or dismiss Ministers.

3 1926, January. All **decrees signed by Mussolini** became law.

4 The Fascist Party controlled **local government** (21.15).

5 Propaganda convinced many of Mussolini's success (below).

21.18 Propaganda

1 The Press. Opposition papers were **closed down** (21.14). Many independent papers were controlled by **Fascist editors** (21.14). All papers had to submit everything to a **government censor**.

2 Books had to be approved by the government. Many were banned.

3 Education was strictly controlled:
i **university teachers** had to take an oath of loyalty (21.14);
ii **school teachers** had to be Party members (21.15);
iii **syllabuses** were drawn up by Fascist officials;
iv **text books** were written to fit in with Fascist ideas.

4 Radio was government-controlled.

5 Speeches by Mussolini to organized demonstrations roused great enthusiasm and won him a good deal of popular support.

6 Mussolini was presented as an example to his people of the spirit of Fascism. His **office light** was kept on until late in the evening, to give the impression of hard work. He was often **photographed** in sporting scenes and clothes to present the image of health and vitality.

21.19 Economic 'battles'—and some successes

1 Unemployment was tackled by government spending.
i **The Pontine Marshes** were drained and provided work for thousands. Being near Rome this scheme was an advert for the system;
ii **railways** were electrified, providing more work;
iii **autostrade** (or motorways) were built as were many public buildings—**sports stadiums, railway stations, blocks of flats**;
iv **hydro-electricity schemes** were developed.

2 The Battle of the Lira
i **1925** the lira was over-valued—with large American loans;
ii **1929** the Wall Street Crash led to the recall of those loans;
iii the value of the lira fell. Mussolini decided to force its value back up. One method was the **halving of wages**. This led to a **fall in living standards** and, because people had less to spend, a **rise in unemployment**.

3 The Battle for Grain
i Mussolini wanted to **cut wheat imports**—to help the lira;
ii farmers were **subsidized** to produce more wheat;
iii land suitable for growing **olives and fruit** was ploughed up. **Wheat production rose**; other production fell;
iv the **cost of subsidizing** farmers was very high.

4 The Battle for Births, 1934
i Mussolini wanted a population increase from 40 to 60 million by 1950;
ii large families were encouraged; batchelors heavily taxed;
iii larger families often led to **greater poverty**.

21.20 The Lateran Treaties, 1929

1 The Church had **opposed** the Italian government since 1870 (21.1.3).

2 Mussolini made a **Concordat** (or agreement) with the Church 1929:

i **the Church gained.** Catholicism was recognized as '**the official State religion**'. Bishops and priests received **State salaries**. The Church was free to preach and run schools;

ii **the Vatican**, in Rome, was recognized as an independent State and the government paid for Papal lands lost before 1871 (21.1.3);

iii **Mussolini gained.** The Church **recognized the government**. Bishops and priests were to take an **oath of loyalty**.

3 The propaganda value of these various Treaties was great. Many Italians assumed that the Pope was a Mussolini-supporter. **Foreign governments** saw Fascism as 'respectable'.

21.21 Was he a fraud?

1 There was much **less freedom** than in the past (21.13–18).

2 The rich did better than the less well-off.

3 Living standards fell.

4 His successes were, in reality, very few. Most of his **achievements** (e.g., making the trains run on time) were **superficial** and not long lasting. There were few measures which made radical changes in the nature of Italy's problems. His **achievements** were in the **fields of morale and national pride** rather than in any economic miracle, and in prestige projects rather than in long-term solutions.

21.22 Why was he so popular?

1 **Opposition** was violently crushed and could not express itself.
2 **Propaganda** made him appear a success.
3 **The Church** appeared to support him–and many priests actively did so because of his anti-communism.
4 **Law and order** was imposed and appeared better than the violence which had been common between 1919 and 1925.
5 **The Mafia** was attacked and partly suppressed.
6 **His foreign policy** appeared to be 'glorious'.
7 His **propaganda machine** was successful and convincing.

21.23 Foreign policy

1 **1923** He defied the League over **Corfu** (14.8).
2 **1924** He gained **Fiume** and **Zara** when giving up Italian claims to Dalmatia (21.3.1).
3 **1934** He stopped a German invasion of **Austria** (23.3).
4 **1935** He was a member of the **Stresa Front** (23.4).
5 **1935** He launched an attack on **Abyssinia** (23.6).
6 **1936** He helped Franco in the **Spanish Civil War** (24.11.7).
7 **1939** He invaded **Albania** (23.15.6).

21.24 His fall and death, 1945

1 **May 1940** Mussolini entered the war as France collapsed (25.9.10).
2 **1940–43** Italian troops had varying fortunes in North Africa (Units 25 and 26).
3 **July 1943** The Allies invaded Sicily (26.9).
4 **August 1943** The King dismissed and imprisoned Mussolini.

5 A new government asked for an armistice. Hitler poured troops into Italy. Paratroopers rescued Mussolini and set him up in government again.

6 **April 1945** Mussolini and his mistress were captured by anti-Fascist Italians. Their bodies were hung upside down in a square in **Milan** where Mussolini had begun his march to power (21.7.3).

22 The British Empire, 1908–1939

22.1 The emergence of the Dominions

1 **Independent colonies**
i **Canada** The British North American Act, **1867**;
(a) **united four Provinces** (Quebec, Ontario, New Brunswick and Nova Scotia) in the **Dominion of Canada**;
(b) left each Province its own **local Parliament**;
(c) created a **Union Parliament** for the whole Dominion, with more power than the local Parliaments;
(d) made provision for the **expansion of the Dominion**. British Colombia joined in 1871.
ii **Australia** The Commonwealth of Australia Act, **1900**;
(a) created a **Federation** from six self-governing colonies (New South Wales, Victoria, Western Australia, South Australia, Queensland and Tasmania);

(b) left each colony its own **local Parliament**;
(c) created a **central government**, with an elected Senate and House of Representatives, to deal with defence, commerce, postal systems, railways, immigration and currency.
iii **New Zealand** refused to join the Commonwealth of Australia. In **1907** it was given the status of Dominion.
iv **South Africa The Union of South Africa, 1910**, was created from two self-governing British colonies (Cape of Good Hope and Natal) and two former Boer Republics (Transvaal and the Orange River Colony).

2 **Imperial unity proposals, 1900–14**
i Prime Ministers of the independent colonies met in London in **1887** and **1897** during Queen Victoria's **Jubilees**;
ii **Chamberlain**, Colonial Secretary, 1895–1903, wanted to create an **Imperial 'Zollverein'** (1.3).
iii Australia and New Zealand–the most distant–were most in favour; South Africa and Canada (with racial minorities) were against;
iv Chamberlain's **Tariff Reform** suggestions, including **Imperial Preference**, were rejected in Britain in the **1906 Election**.

3 **Unity and War, 1914·18**
i the dominions were brought into the War by the King's declaration on 4 August 1914. **They had no choice**;
ii **1917** there was an **Imperial War Conference** which tried to agree on closer unity–on defence costs and trade.
(a) they lacked the **will** to agree, fearing also the **costs** which would fall on the colonies (for an Imperial army and navy);
(b) distance and the problem of **communications** would have led to a **British-dominated Empire**. The Dominions opposed this.

4 **Searching for greater independence, 1919–25**
i **Versailles**, 1919 Lloyd George represented the Empire at the Treaty making. Each **Dominion** took part in policy-making discussions. Australia and South Africa received **Mandated Territories** (13.10);
ii **1921** the Prime Ministers' Conferences, London, tried to work out means whereby the Empire could act in common policy;
iii **1922 Chanak** (13.6) the Dominions refused to support Lloyd George's war-like policy;
iv **1923 Lausanne** (13.7) the Dominions did not sign this Treaty;
v **1924 the Empire Exhibition** at Wembley was staged to encourage the mutual buying of 'Empire' goods to help employment:
vi **1925 Locarno** (18.8) the Dominions did not sign these Treaties concerned with European frontier agreements.

5 **Defining Dominion status, 1926–31**
i **1926** A Report by former Prime Minister, **Balfour**, defined the **Dominions** as 'autonomous Communities within the British Empire, equal in status, in no way subordinate one to another in any aspect of their domestic or external affairs, though united by a common allegiance to the Crown and freely associated as members of the British Commonwealth of Nations';
ii this gave the Dominions that **freedom in foreign policy** which they had not had in 1914 (22.1.3) but had acquired by accident in the 1920s (22.1.4);
iii **1931 the Statute of Westminster** was passed by the British Parliament to implement the Balfour Report.

22.2 The demand for Indian independence, 1900–19

1 **1833** The Whig MP, Macaulay, talked of India becoming self-governing 'in some future age'.

2 Western-style **education** had created an Indian **middle class**.

3 There was **little industry** for them to work in. They were **not allowed** into the higher ranks of the Indian Civil Service.

4 1885 The dissatisfied middle class held the **first Indian Congress** in which there were:

i **more Hindus than Muslims**, partly because the **Hindus** were, in general, **richer and more successful** than the Muslims, but also because there were **more Hindus than Muslims throughout India**;

ii **moderates**, who wanted **social reforms** to help the less well-off and changes in law to allow **greater opportunities** for the better educated. They hoped that **peaceful campaigning** would persuade the British to change the law;

iii **extremists**, who thought that an **armed rising** would have to be organized to force the British out of India.

5 1909 John Morley (Secretary of State in the Liberal Government) and Lord **Minto** (Viceroy of India) were responsible for reforms:

i the Imperial **Legislative Council** (or central Council of India) was **enlarged** from 21 to 60 members. 27 of these were elected by Indians; the majority was appointed by the British government;

ii **provincial Councils**. For the first time Indians were to be elected to these Councils;

iii **the franchise** (or right to vote) was based on a property qualification. **The Muslims** were, generally, not as rich as the Hindus. To overcome this problem there was separate representation for Muslims, which pleased the **Muslim League**, formed in 1906.

6 1914–18 During the First World War

i **Indian troops** fought in Europe and the Middle East (13.11);

ii **Indian reformers**, in Congress and the Muslim League, pressed for further reforms, promised for 'after the war';

iii **Extremists** gained control of Congress;

iv **1917 the Russian Revolution** (10.11–12) was seen as an example of how an unpopular government could be overthrown;

v **1918–19** the disappearance of the **Austro-Hungarian Empire** (12.9) showed the Empires could be divided up;

vi **Wilson's Fourteen Points** (Fig. 12.1A) were a strong moral factor in support of Indian nationalism;

vii **1917 Montagu**, the Secretary of State, said that British policy was to involve Indians in the government of their country and to **lead India to self-government within the Empire**:

(a) the British meant **'at some distant future'** such as 500 years;

(b) Indians thought it meant **immediate independence**.

7 1919 The Montagu-Chelmsford Reforms

i the Central **Legislative Assembly**. This was to consist of 106 elected members and only 40 nominated by the British government;

ii **an Upper House**, or Council of State, was created to represent the Princes and large landowners in British India;

iii **a Chamber of Princes** was created for rulers of States not in British India but who had certain matters of common concern with the British Indian government;

iv **provincial Councils** At least 70 per cent of the members of these councils were to be elected;

v **provincial Ministers**, usually British, were responsible to the largely elected Provincial Councils;

vi **the franchise** was greatly extended, but still based on a property qualification. Five million voted for elections to Provincial Councils; one million for the Central Legislative Assembly and about 17,000 for the Council of State;

vii **dyarchy** (dual control) Some powers, concerning such matters as health, education, industry and agriculture, were exercised by **ministers responsible to Provincial Councils**. Others (on law and order, police, terrorism) were reserved to **non-elected executive councils, governors** and, ultimately, to the **Viceroy**;

viii **the Central Executive Council** (a Viceroy's Cabinet) had three Indians out of its six members. The Viceroy still had a deciding vote.

8 Reaction to these reforms

i **The British** thought they had been:

(a) generous in bringing Indians into the system;

(b) sensible, in giving them some control while not giving them complete freedom – which would come 'in the future'.

ii **Indians** thought that the reforms had **not gone far enough**.

22.3 Indian unrest, 1919

1 The Rowlatt Bills allowed judges (usually British) to try cases of terrorism **without juries** and gave Provincial governments (usually British) the power of internment **without trial**.

2 Gandhi (22.4) called on the people to protest by a **hartal** (22.5.2).

3 In the **Punjab** there was widespread rioting, put down by firm action by **Brigadier-General Reginald Dyer**.

4 In the Sikh's holy city, **Amritsar**, four Europeans were murdered. The Provincial Government banned all meetings in the hope that the unrest would die down.

5 18 April 1919 An illegal gathering took place (peacefully) in a square which had only one narrow exit.

6 Brigadier Dyer commanded the troops sent to disperse the gathering. The crowd could not (or would not) disperse. Troops opened fire and 379 people were killed and 1200 wounded.

7 1920 A commission of inquiry condemned Dyer. But in the debate in the House of Commons he received a good deal of support while the House of Lords passed a resolution in his favour.

8 Indians, on the other hand, never forgot Amritsar. Relations between British and Indian were never the same as they had been.

22.4 Mahatma Gandhi, early career

1 1869 born to a wealthy and religious family.

2 1888 To London University and to qualify as a barrister.

3 1891 Practised as a barrister in Bombay.

4 1893 To **South Africa** on business. He stayed:

i he led Asian opposition **against harsh racial laws**;

ii **1899** he organized an Indian Red Cross for the **Boer War**;

iii **1903** he founded a paper, *Indian Opinion*, in Durban;

iv **1906** he led demonstration **against racial laws**;

v **1914** many of the worst racial laws were removed.

5 He was frequently **imprisoned** because of his activities.

6 Many **extremists** in his own side also attacked him because of his **non-violent policies**.

7 1914 He went back to India. When war broke out he went to **London** to organize an Indian ambulance corps.

8 Like many Indians, he hoped that the Indian part in the war would persuade the British to make major concessions.

22.5 Gandhi and Indian politics, 1914–22

1 He was the **religious leader** of the nationalist movement until **1920** when he also became the **political leader**. His political followers called him **Mahatma** which means 'Great Soul' in recognition of the religious nature of his political power. His non-violent policy (22.5.4) was known as **satyagraha** or **soul force**.

2 6 April 1919 He called a **hartal**, a day for Indians:

i **to fast and pray**;

ii **not to do any work**. This would draw British and Indian attention to the demand for independence.

3 In spite of his appeal for non-violence, **many Indians rioted** against the British government (22.3) which, in turn, led to violent behaviour by the government.

4 He supported the **Muslims** in their protest at the treatment of Turkey by the Allies (13.2 and 13.7) and Indian Muslims supported his non-co-operation with the government:

i by **refusing to obey 'unfair' laws**;

ii by **refusing to pay 'unfair' taxes** ('civil disobedience');

iii by **boycotting British imports**. This led to the fostering of home industries, such as **making cloth on small spinning-wheels**. This cut the imports of Lancashire cloth into India.

5 **Violence** was widespread as strikes and riots took place **(1921)** when Gandhi supervized the burning of foreign goods in Bombay.

6 Violence led to **looting** and Gandhi **called off the non-co-operation policy**. He was given almost dictatorial powers by Congress.

7 1922 Although he had called off the policy of non-co-operation and civil disobedience, he was arrested and sentenced to 6 years in jail for 'preaching disaffection'.

22.6 Gandhi and the independence movement, 1924–35

1 **1924** After an operation for appendicitis, he was **released** from jail. He played little part in affairs for three more years.

2 **1927** He was elected **President of Congress**–but refused to accept the post leaving it to his lieutenant, **Motilal Nehru**.

3 **1928 The Simon Commission** visited India to see how the 1919 reforms (22.2.7) were working. Gandhi boycotted the Commission, which had no Indian members, an omission which confirmed the suspicions of Congress. That body had already adopted the recommendation of Jawahalal Nehru, that it should accept nothing less than **complete independence**.

4 **Proposals for a Round Table Conference** The British Labour government proposed a Conference in London to discuss Indian politics. Gandhi asked if this would lead immediately to Dominion status. When the British said this was their 'ultimate' aim, he refused to go to London.

5 **March–April 1930** He made his **march from Ahmedabad to the sea**, where he distilled salt from sea-water. This was to show opposition to the salt tax. In **May 1930** he was sentenced to an indefinite term of imprisonment.

6 **January 1931** He was released from jail, having promised to attend the London Conference. He called off the civil disobedience and boycott campaigns.

7 **1932 The Round Table Conference**. He took Muslims with him when he went to London. The Conference failed to reach any agreement; Indians demanded more progress than Britain wanted to make.

8 **1933** Back in India he called another campaign of **non-co-operation**. During the unrest that followed he was, again, **arrested, jailed and released**. He retired from politics to live in his retreat (**ashram**) at Wardha.

9 He was discouraged by:

i **Hindu-Muslim enmity**. He hoped to lead a united India to independence. Religious bigotry often led to riots by one group against another;

ii **extremists in Congress**, led by younger men such as **Jawahalal Nehru**, who wanted more direct action against the British. Nehru was elected President of Congress in 1936.

22.7 The Government of India Act, 1935

1 This promised **Dominion status** 'in the future'.

2 **Provincial Councils** were given more powers, suggesting the future creation of a **federal system**, such as in the USA (7.2) or Germany (1.13):

i **Provinces** were given **direct aid** through income tax;

ii the system of dyarchy (22.2.7(vii)) was swept away. Local ministries were made responsible to the electors;

iii **the franchise** was extended. Thirty five million people had the vote–on a property qualification;

iv new Provinces were created;

v separate representation for minority religious groups–Hindus and Sikhs–continued with 'reserved seats'.

3 **The weakness** of the proposals were:

i they did not provide **Dominion status**;

ii the **conservative Indian princes** were given one-third of the seats in the Lower House of the Central Legislature and two-fifths of the seats in its Upper House;

iii **dyarchy** was retained by **central government**. Only certain ministers were responsible to the Legislature.

4 The Act proposed the creation of a **Federation of Provinces**:

i this would be **compulsory** for the states in British India;

ii it would be **optional** for the Princely States;

iii this section of the Act would come into operation when **half the Princely States joined**. They never did. Federation never came into effect.

5 Under the Act, the Indian government had no control over Indian foreign policy.

22.8 Progress and failure, 1936–39

1 Although Gandhi had 'retired' he still 'ruled' Congress, whose leaders felt they had to consult him.

2 **1936** The Congress took a full part in the elections.

3 **1936–39 Congress formed the governments** in seven out of eleven provinces. This gave many Indians experience in government–but only at a provincial level.

4 **Muslims** They were in a minority (22.2.4.(i)). They were disappointed by the results of the 1936 elections. Hindu majorities governed provinces in which there were large Muslim minorities.

5 **Muhammad Ali Jinnah** He asked that there should be Hindu-Muslim governments in some provinces. Congress rejected this. This led Jinnah and the Muslim League to develop demands for a **separate state for Muslims**. This was to become Pakistan (34.8).

22.9 Palestine, 1919–39, the seeds of future conflict

1 **Arab hopes, 1918** Arab leaders hoped that a series of independent Arab states would be created out of the Turkish Empire (13.11 and 13.13).

2 **Britain** had proposed the division of much of that Empire with **France** (13.9). The Sykes–Picot agreement came to nothing.

3 **November 1917** Britain issued the **Balfour Declaration**, promising 'a national home for the Jewish people' in Palestine (13.14).

4 **The Mandate** Palestine was mandated to Britain (13.10).

5 In the **1920s** some 10 000 Jews entered Palestine each year.

6 **Arabs** protested, although the British assured them that what had been promised was 'a home for the Jewish people' and not 'a Jewish national state'.

7 **1929 Arabs rioted** and attacked Jewish homes and property.

8 **1933 Jews rioted** because of British restrictions on immigration.

9 **Hitler's** attacks on German Jews (20.8) led to increased numbers trying to enter Palestine. By 1937 there were **400 000 Jews** in Palestine:

i many of them were **better-educated** than most Arabs;

ii they were **supported by money** from world Jewry;

iii this, and their own ability, enabled them to **buy up land, set up businesses and prosper**.

10 **Arab guerillas** attacked Jewish farms, homes and businesses.

11 **1937** A commission, under **Lord Peel**, recommended the **partition of Palestine** into:

i an Arab state;

ii a Jewish state;

iii a British Mandate for Jerusalem and Bethlehem.

12 Partition was **rejected** as an idea by Jews and Arabs. It was also **condemned** by the Mandates Commission (13.10).

13 **1938** Another Commission, under Sir John Woodhead, said that Arabs and Jews were so tangled up that partition was impossible.

14 **1939 A Round Table Conference** was tried–in spite of the failure of the Indian experiment (22.6). This failed too.

15 **May 1939 A White Paper** (or outline of future policy) promised **an end to Jewish immigration** once another 75 000 had been admitted. This meant that the Balfour Declaration was to be abandoned in the face of:

i **Arab hostility** and violence;

ii Britain's belief that she needed the **friendship of Arab states**, with their oil fields and strategic ports.

22.10 Egypt

1 **Before 1914**, Egypt was 'a British sphere of influence' in which a British Consul General really ruled the country (5.16).

2 **1914** Britain kept 250 000 troops in Egypt to guard the **Suez Canal** from Turkish attack.

3 **18 December 1914** Britain declared Egypt to be a **British protectorate**. The Khedive was deposed and his uncle made Sultan.

4 **1919** There was an increase in **Egyptian nationalism** and a demand for complete independence. The leaders of the movement were exiled; rioting followed which was cut down by **Allenby** (9.8), the specially-created High Commissioner.

5 **28 February 1922** Britain recognized **Egypt as an independent sovereign state** but reserved some points for later settlement:

i security of the **Canal**;

ii the **defence** of Egypt from outside attack;

iii the protection of **European interests**, mainly financial;

iv the question of the **Sudan**.

6 **The Sudan** had once been part of Egypt (5.17) but had been separately governed since its reconquest by Kitchener (5.19).

i **19 November 1924** The British High Commissioner of the Sudan, **Sir Lee Stack**, was murdered by Egyptian nationalists;

ii the British insisted on the withdrawal of Egyptians from garrisons in the Sudan;

iii in spite of Egyptian demands for the inclusion of Sudan in a larger Egypt, Britain went ahead with preparations for the emergence of an **independent Sudan**.

7 **1936** an **Anglo-Egyptian Treaty** was signed.

i Egypt recognized Britain's special interest in the **Suez Canal Zone**;

ii **British troops** were to be based in that zone for twenty years.

8 Nationalism continued to develop. It was accompanied by the emergence of a **guerilla movement** which attacked British troops–the symbol of Britain's control of an apparently independent Egypt.

23 International Relations 1934–39

23.1 The uneasy background

1 **The League** was meant to abolish war (14.1 and 14.3).

2 **'Might is right'** was shown in **Corfu** (14.8) and **Manchuria** (17.22–23).

3 **The failure of the League** was due, largely, to its over dependence on Britain and France, neither of whom was willing or able to take a strong line against aggression (14.11.4).

4 **Bolshevism** Many western statesmen thought Russia was the real menace. They were unwilling to fight right-wing aggressors.

5 **Hitler** had left the League (14.10.11)) and started to re-arm (20.6.3).

23.2 The Saar (*Fig. 23.11A*)

1 This was **under French rule**, 1919–24 (Fig. 12.5A). It then came under the rule of a **League Commission** (12.5.1).

2 It was an important **industrial centre**.

3 **January 1935** Under the terms of the 1919 Treaty, there was a **plebiscite**–a vote on a simple issue.

4 Nine out of ten voted for **reunification with Germany**.

5 Following this success, Hitler announced his plans on conscription and rearmament (20.6.3).

23.3 Austria, 1934 (*Fig. 23.11A*)

1 The post-war Treaties forbade Austria's union with Germany.

2 **1932** A right-wing Chancellor, **Dollfuss**, came to power.

3 **March 1933** He suspended parliamentary government and attacked left-wing housing centres and organizations.

4 **July 1934** Dollfuss was assassinated by Austrian Nazis who tried to take over power. They asked for German help.

5 **Schuschnigg**, the new Chancellor, appealed to **Mussolini**, who did not want a strong Germany-Austria on his frontier.

6 Italian troops were rushed to the **Brenner Pass**.

7 **Hitler** called off his plans.

8 **Peace** and the terms of the Treaties had been maintained– but by the threat of force and not by League action.

23.4 The Stresa Front, April 1935

1 **Mussolini** met the Prime Ministers of **Britain** and **France**.

2 They signed an agreement to resist attempts to revise the terms of the Treaty of Versailles.

3 This was obviously aimed against Hitler's Austrian plans.

4 If people had believed in the League such an agreement would not have been needed (see 14.3).

23.5 The Anglo-German naval agreement, June 1935

1 The British Foreign Secretary, Sir Samuel **Hoare**, and Hitler's 'roving Ambassador', **Ribbentrop**, signed this agreement.

2 **The German navy** was to be 35 per cent the size of Britain's.

3 This was **contrary** to the Treaty of **Versailles** (12.5.4) and against the **Stresa agreement**.

4 It angered **Italy** and **France** both of which feared Germany.

5 France signed a **defensive alliance with Russia** to offset the Ten Year Pact signed between Germany and Poland, France's ally (18.9).

6 This naval agreement was the first act of **appeasement**.

23.6 Abyssinia

1 By **1890** Italy had conquered **Eritrea** and part of **Somaliland** on the east coast of Africa.

2 **1896** She tried to unite these regions by conquering part of **Abyssinia**. Defeat at **Adowa** put an end to that plan.

3 **1925** Mussolini proposed Abyssinia for League membership.

4 **1934** There were clashes between Italians and Abyssinians on the border. Mussolini demanded:

i financial compensation;

ii Abyssinian territory.

5 The Emperor of Abyssinia, **Haile Selassie**, appealed to the League.

6 He was advised to **negotiate** with Mussolini.

7 **1935** Italian **troops** moved to Somaliland and Eritrea.

8 **October 1935** Italian **troops invaded Abyssinia**. With modern weapons (**aircraft**) and chemicals (**poison gas**) they defeated the Abyssinians. The League decided:

i Italy was an **aggressor**;

ii **economic sanctions** were to be applied under Article XVI of the Covenant (14.3). **Coal, steel and oil were excluded**;

iii **Austria** and **Germany** ignored this decision. **American** firms also sold **arms** to the Italians.

9 Britain and France allowed Italy free passage through the **Suez Canal** – a sign of **appeasement** of their 'Stresa friend'.

10 **December 1935 Hoare** (23.5.1) and **Laval**, Foreign Minister of France signed a Pact by which:

i **Italy** would get **two-thirds of Abyssinia**, including the coast;

ii landlocked **Ethiopia** (as Abyssinia became known) would have a **corridor to the sea**.

11 There was a public outcry and Hoare resigned. The Plan was dropped and the Italian conquest went on.

12 **May 1936** The conquest was completed. Haile Selassie went into exile. **Italian East Africa** consisted of Somaliland, Eritrea and newly-conquered Abyssinia.

13 **The effects of this victory**

i **the League** had been proved a failure – again;

ii **sanctions**, weakly applied, did not halt the aggressor;

iii **the Stresa Front** was weakened by Anglo-French criticism of Mussolini. In **1937** he withdrew from the **League**;

iv Mussolini was drawn into an alliance with Hitler, who used the crisis to further his own aims (23.7);

v **1935–6** France made an alliance with Russia; they promised to aid one another if attacked.

23.7 The Rhineland (*Fig. 23.11A*)

1 This region had been **de-militarized** in 1919 (12.5.2).

2 This was further agreed in the **Rhineland Pact** signed at **Locarno**, 1925 (18.8).

3 **March 1936** Britain and France (signatories of Locarno) were involved in the Abyssinian crisis.

4 **German troops** marched into the Rhineland. They were outnumbered by better-armed French troops. Hitler gave orders that they were to withdraw if opposed.

5 **Britain and France** were unwilling to stop Hitler:

i the region was described as '**only his own backyard**';

ii neither country was **militarily prepared** for war. Germany spent on arms double the amount spent by Britain and France combined. Her **industrial power** was greater than that of the two possible Allies.

6 **German generals** had opposed Hitler's plan. They feared war.

7 **Hitler's success** illustrated his claim to be '**always right**'.

23.8 The Spanish Civil War, July 1936

In Unit 24 we will see how Hitler and Mussolini used this war to strengthen their friendship and train their forces.

23.9 The Hossbach Memorandum, November 1937

1 **Japan's expansion** was forecast in the **Tanaka Memorial** (17.16).

2 **Hitler's expansionist policy** was summarized in this memorandum prepared by his adjutant, Colonel Hossbach.

3 **November 1937** Hitler called a meeting of military advisers.

4 He told them of **his plans** for expansion (Fig. 23.11A):

i it had to be won 'at the lowest cost';

ii it had to 'solve the German space problem at the latest by 1943–45';

iii 'The first aim had to be to conquer **Czechoslovakia and Austria**'. He told his generals that **Britain** appeared ready to 'give up' both of these countries.

5 His two leading **generals**, Blomberg and von Fritsch, pointed out that we should 'not run the risk of making England and France our enemies'. He **overruled them** as in 1936.

23.10 Hitler's growing confidence, 1937

1 **November 1936** He signed the **Anti-Comintern Pact** with **Japan**.

2 **November 1937** Italy joined the Pact. All three aggressor-nations were now linked in this anti-Russian Pact.

3 **Russia** was weakened by the Stalinist purges (11.2).

4 **German** industrial and military power was growing rapidly.

5 **November 1937 Lord Halifax** (later to be Foreign Secretary) visited Hitler and suggested that Britain would not oppose German moves to occupy **Austria** and the **Sudetenland** (Fig. 23.11A).

23.11 Austria; the Anschluss (*Fig. 23.11A*)

1 **January 1938 Seyss-Inquart** led an Austrian Nazi attempt to seize power. Schuschnigg prevented this.

2 **February 1938** Hitler summoned Schuschnigg to Germany. In a stormy interview he threatened to make war unless Seyss-Inquart was made Minister of the Interior (controlling the police forces in Austria).

3 **Schuschnigg** proposed a **plebiscite** to see if the Austrians wanted to unite with Germany.

4 **Hitler**, fearing a negative vote, rushed troops to the border, threatening an invasion if Schuschnigg did not resign.

5 **Schuschnigg** resigned. **Seyss-Inquart** became Chancellor.

6 **12 March** Seyss-Inquart 'invited' Hitler to occupy Austria and to ward off 'a Communist plot'.

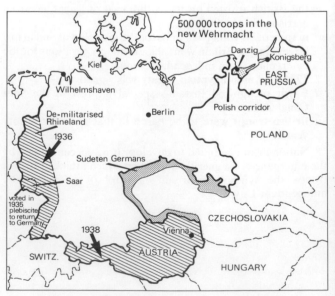

Fig. 23.11A Hitler's expansionist policy, 1933–38

7 **14 March** Austria became a province of a larger Germany.

8 **A plebiscite** showed that 99 in every 100 Austrians favoured this union with successful Germany.

9 **Opposition** was crushed; many were imprisoned, others murdered.

10 **The Jews** came under attack. In June 1938 they were made to strip in public and to crawl around on all fours.

23.12 The Sudetenland (*Fig. 23.11A*)

1 **1919–20** This region was taken from **Austria-Hungary** to help to form the new state, **Czechoslovakia** (12.9.3).

2 It had **3 million Germans**. Its inclusion in Czechoslovakia ignored the notion of 'national self-determination'.

3 It provided the new state with:

i valuable **mineral deposits** and **heavy industry**;

ii the means of producing one-third of her **exports**;

iii manageable and defensible **frontiers**.

4 **1933 Henlein** led Sudeten Nazis who:

i complained of **ill-treatment** by Czechs;

ii demanded **self-government** for the Sudetenland.

5 **1938** Hitler seemed ready to intervene.

6 **Neville Chamberlain**, Prime Minister of Great Britain, thought it possible to arrange things in peaceful discussions. **Eden**, his Foreign Secretary, resigned; Halifax (23.10.5) succeeded.

23.13 Czechoslovakia betrayed, 1938

1 **August 1938** Chamberlain sent **Lord Runciman** to examine the Sudetenland problem, and to persuade **President Benes** of Czechoslovakia to give in to Henlein's demands. Benes agreed to Sudeten self-government (23.12.4). **Hitler was not satisfied**. He described Czechoslovakia as:

i an 'artificial state';

ii 'in alliance with Russia'.

2 **15 September 1938: Berchtesgaden**

Hitler, Chamberlain and Daladier (of France) met. After talks they told Benes that the Czechs would have to make 'sacrifices' by giving up regions where 50 per cent of the population was German.

3 **22 September 1938: Godesberg**

The Czechs refused to the demands made on them. Chamberlain flew to Godesberg to ask Hitler not to invade until he had had another try at persuading the Czechs to give in.

4 **War?**

i in **France** military reservists were called up;

ii in **Czechoslovakia** the army was mobilized;

iii in Britain the Fleet prepared for action; air raid shelters and trenches were built or dug, gas masks issued and anti-aircraft barrage balloons appeared above towns and cities;

iv **Chamberlain**, 'the peacemaker' complained of the stupidity of being involved in 'the quarrel between people in a **faraway country of which we know nothing**'.

5 **29 September 1938: Munich**

Chamberlain flew again, this time to Munich. He met **Daladier** and **Mussolini**. The **Russians** were not invited to the meeting (although they were allies of Czechoslovakia). The **Czechs** were left waiting in a nearby hotel and did not take part in the discussions about their future. The statesmen decided that Germany should take the Sudetenland. A Commission would decide exactly which areas were to be handed over.

6 **Peace?**

30 September Hitler signed a piece of paper expressing his hopes and confidence in 'consultation' as a means of avoiding war. **Chamberlain** flew home. He waved the paper as the sign of **'Peace in our time'**. Few people believed **Churchill** who saw the Munich agreement as a **'disaster** of the first magnitude for Britain and France'.

7 **Czech losses**

i the loss of the Sudetenland meant the loss of:

(a) a good deal of Czech **industry** and source of **raw materials**;

(b) easily defended **boundaries**.

ii **October 1938 Hungary** took advantage of the crisis to take part of Slovakia with its ore deposits and sugar beetfields;

iii **November 1938 Poland** joined in 'the rape of Czechoslovakia' by taking part of **Moravia** with its coal deposits and steelworks.

23.14 After Munich

1 **Beneš** resigned; **Hacha** became President of the smaller state.

2 **Slovakia** and **Ruthenia** demanded independence.

3 **Hacha** produced a federal constitution. **Czechoslovakia** would consist of the states of **Bohemia, Moravia, Slovakia and Ruthenia** each with its own provincial government.

4 **Hitler** took no notice of 'Peace in our time' or Hacha's constitution:

i **13 March 1939** Hitler summoned Hacha to Germany. He made him agree to special rights for any Germans still under Czech rule;

ii without waiting for action, **Hitler ordered the invasion** which brought most of Czechoslovakia under German rule;

iii **Hungary** acted quickly to occupy **Ruthenia**.

5 The Versailles-created state, Czechoslovakia, died.

23.15 Poland (*Fig. 23.11A*)

1 **1925** At Locarno (18.8) **France** signed an alliance with **Poland** as part of her policy of 'encircling' Germany.

2 **1932 Russia and Poland** signed a non-aggression Pact.

3 **1933** this Pact was **confirmed** by a Ten Year Treaty of friendship.

4 **1934 Germany and Poland** signed a Ten Year Treaty of friendship.

5 **April 1939 Britain** gave a guarantee to Poland promising to come to her help if she were attacked.

6 **April 1939 Mussolini** invaded and conquered **Albania**, one of the gains Italy had hoped for in 1919 (21.3).

7 **May 1939** Hitler and Mussolini signed the **Pact of Steel**.

8 **Danzig** (Fig. 23.11A):

i this was made an International City in 1919 (Fig 12.5A) and 12.5.1.v);

ii Poland was given part of Prussia as a **corridor to the sea** (Fig. 23.11A). Hitler wanted to get both Danzig and the corridor which separated East Prussia from the rest of Germany.

23.16 Stalin's rôle

1 **Litvinov**, Russian Foreign Minister, arranged:

i **1932** a non-aggression Pact with Poland;

ii **1935** a defensive treaty with France and Czechoslovakia.

2 Stalin was angered when, at Munich, Russia was not consulted about the future of her Czech ally.

3 **May 1939** Litvinov was sacked.

4 **Molotov**, the new Foreign Minister, and Stalin thought that Munich marked one (if important) stage in the policy of appeasement. This gave the right-wing dictators (Mussolini and Hitler) as well as anti-Communist Japan, whatever they could grab.

5 **July 1939** Molotov held talks with Hitler and with Britain.

6 **Britain** was hesitant in its approaches.

7 **23 August 1939 The Nazi-Soviet Pact** amazed the world:

i it was 'an association of **criminals**' who crushed enemies;

ii it was 'an association of **opposites**'.

8 In this Pact the **Communists and Nazis agreed**:

i **not to fight one another**. Hitler was free to take on Britain and France. He would not have to fight on two fronts as the Kaiser did in 1914 (9.1);

ii to **divide Poland** between their two countries. Russia would regain lands lost in 1917–21 (10.22.7).

23.17 And so to war, 1939

1 **1 September** Germany invaded Poland.

2 **3 September** Britain and France declared war on Germany.

3 **15 September** Russia invaded Poland, met the German troops and the country was divided between the two countries.

4 **Russia** then invaded the Baltic countries lost in 1917– **Estonia, Latvia and Lithuania**.

5 Only **Finland** offered any resistance in a war which began in **November 1939** and ended in Russian victory in **March 1940**.

6 In a futile gesture, the **League expelled Russia**.

24 Spain 1919–39

24.1 Problems, 1919

1 **Economic** In **1898** Spain lost her Empire in **Cuba** and the Philippines (7.21). The loss of these **markets** led to increased **unemployment** and, for those in work, **low wages**.

2 **Agricultural** The majority of Spaniards were **peasants**:

i **rich landowners** had huge estates (**latifundios**), many of which were left unused. Other parts were rented out;

ii **tenant farmers** paid high rents to landowners;

iii there were 2½ million **landless peasants**, some working for **low wages**, many **often unemployed**, all frequently suffering from **starvation**.

3 **Political** The great division between rich landowners and poor peasants was reflected in Spain's political system:

i **the right-wing parties** supported the idea of a strong monarchy. They were supported by the **wealthy**, the **Church**, the **police** and the **army**;

ii **left-wing parties** included:

(a) Socialists who wanted a strong central government to bring in such things as land reform (24.7.2);

(b) **Communists** who wanted a Russian-style **revolution**, the overthrow of the **monarchy** and the **Church**, and the end of the economic power of the **wealthy landowners**:

(c) **anarchists** who were opposed to any form of government;

(d) **syndicalists** who, as in France (2.21), wanted **workers to take control of the industries** in which they worked. Their main support was in industrial centres–the **Basque region** and Catalonia (with its port of Barcelona) (Fig. 24.11A).

24.2 Unrest, 1917–23

1 **1917** Industrial **workers** held a **General Strike** which was crushed by the **army**.

2 **1917–23** As in Italy (21.1.5), the Spanish Parliament (the **Cortes**) contained many small parties. As their leaders jockeyed for power there were frequent changes of government–12 in 6 years. This **political instability** was one reason for little being done to tackle Spain's problems.

24.3 Primo de Rivera, 1923–30

1 He was a **general** in the Spanish army.

2 **The army** had been a **powerful force in Spanish politics** in the 19th century, as in Spanish America today.

3 **1923** The army acted to defend **'the national interests'** against **'parliamentary imperfections'**. General de Rivera was installed to set up an **efficient government**.

4 He had the support of the **right wing** (24.1.3) and the king, Alfonso XIII.

5 **The Church's support** was important in this Catholic country.

6 **A left-wing rebellion** was easily crushed.

7 **The army** and its supporters (nationalist-patriots) approved his decision to fight Moorish rebels in **Spanish Morocco** (Fig. 24.11A). But this was a heavy drain on Spain's scarce resources.

8 **1929** Spain, like other European countries, was affected by the depression following the Wall Street Crash (16.18). **Exports** fell, **unemployment** rose and **living standards** went even lower.

9 **1930** de Rivera quarrelled with King Alfonso XIII and resigned.

24.4 The fall of the monarchy, 1931

1 **The King** had shared in **de Rivera's popularity** which was the result of:

i **financial stability**–until 1929;

ii **increased agricultural output** following on massive irrigation schemes in some 3½ million acres of Spanish soil.

2 **The Depression** ended that popularity while it also **increased** the long-standing **hostility** of;

i **industrial workers** who worked a 9- or 10-hour day and had low wages which made overtime essential;

ii **radical intellectuals** angered by press and postal censorship.

3 When de Rivera resigned, the Opposition became more outspoken.

4 **April 1931** Alfonso XIII abdicated, and left.

24.5 The Second Republic: Part I, 1931–33

1 **Elections** were held for a **new Cortes** which was to write a **new constitution** for Republican Spain.

3 The voters elected a large number of **liberal and radical intellectuals**. These had **little political experience**. They also had **little contact** with ordinary people:

i they were **not sufficiently progressive** to appeal to the socialist and communist extremists;

ii they were **too revolutionary** to gain the support of the industrial and commercial middle class.

3 The Coalition government under **Prime Minister Azaña** included the trade unionist, **Largo Caballero**, as Minister of Labour. His inability to push through industrial and social reforms led him to resign in 1933 when he said, 'the only hope of the masses is social revolution'.

4 **The right-wing** members of the Cortes and their supporters in the country outside were **opposed** to Anzaña's government, Caballero's attempted reforms and the new constitution.

24.6 The new Constitution, December 1931

1 **Women** were given the right to vote. This 'radical' reform provided the right-wing with increased support; women were more under the influence of the Church than were men.

2 **The Church**

i it was to be an **ordinary association** subject to general laws like any other association;

ii **state grants** to the clergy were abolished;

iii convents and monasteries were **dissolved**; their property was **nationalized**;

iv religious orders were **forbidden to teach** in primary and secondary schools.

3 This section of the constitution **angered the right-wing**.

4 The outcry led to **modifications**:

i **religious orders** were allowed to remain–but not the Jesuits;

ii they were still **forbidden to run schools**.

5 This 'step backwards' **angered the left-wing Republicans**.

6 But even after this modification:

i **the right-wing** (landowners, Church, army and police) rallied in defence of the Church against the Republic;

ii **education** suffered from a shortage of schools and teachers. In 1933 over one-third of the children were not in school;

iii the Republic became increasingly reliant on the support of the **industrial working class**–based in the few towns and cities.

24.7 Attempted reforms, 1932–33

1 **Trade unions** pressed for wage increases.

2 **1932 Land reform** was set in motion:

i **wage labourers** were entitled to an 8-hour day. But this did nothing for the millions of unemployed peasants;

ii **tenant farmers** were given the right to appeal against rent increases;

iii **tenants** were to be given a chance to buy their farms by a massive programme of expropriation of the latifundios (24.1.2).

3 This land reform had **very little success**.

i **it was costly**. Owners were to be compensated for their 'lost' land. But Spain did not have the resources to make such payments

ii **It was slow**. Officials in local and central government offices tended to be more conservative than their political 'masters'. They put obstacles in the way of reforming Ministers and delayed expropriation schemes;

4 The promise of 'land for all' had roused **peasants' expectations**. When the government failed to deliver quickly enough, the **peasants squatted** on owners' estates. They had to be driven from their illegal 'squat' by **police and army**. This brought the Radical Republicans into more disfavour–with the peasants.

5 **The Church** owned a great deal of land in Spain. Angry peasants attacked **Church property (May 1931)** because it symbolized all that they thought was wrong with Spain.

6 **The economy** which had slumped in 1929–30, continued to decline. By **1933 exports** were only one-quarter of the 1930 level. This led to **increased unemployment** in industrial Spain.

24.8 The Falange, 1933

1 **January 1933** Hitler came to power in Germany (15.21).

2 About the same time **de Rivera's** son founded the Falange, a Spanish Fascist party.

3 In the troubled Republic it got support from the **right-wing** (24.1.3).

24.9 Elections, 1933

There was a great swing to the right.

1 **Too little** had been done for some voters–peasants, workers, educational reformers (24.6).

2 **Too much** had been done to anger others–Church, landowners and industrialists. They owned many **newspapers** and had the support of **priests** preaching to the Catholic Spanish people.

3 **The extreme left** (symbolized by Caballero) began to believe that democracy could not bring the needed reforms.

4 **Women voters** were conservative.

24.10 Elections 1936 saw a swing to the left.

1 **A popular Front government** (of Radicals, Communists and Socialists) was set up under Azaña.

2 Azaña was **too moderate** for some. He was nicknamed 'the Spanish Kerensky' who would be overthrown by the left-wing Caballero, 'the Spanish Lenin' (see 10.15–20 for Lenin–v–Kerensky in Russia).

3 **1936** The political success of the left led to a wide outbreak of **church-burning** and **priest-killing**. This angered the right wing and alarmed even moderate Republicans.

4 **1936 Peasants seized land** rather than wait for reforms.

5 Many Spaniards shared the view, '**we cannot live with anarchy**'.

24.11 The Civil War, Part I, July 1936–December 1936 (*Fig. 24.11A*)

1 **The Nationalists** was the name taken by the rebels:

i **Franco** was Chief of the General Staff. The government had sent him to the **Canary Islands** because they feared a revolution. In July he flew to **Morocco** to take charge of the rebellion;

ii **the army in Morocco** (24.3.7) was angered by the anarchy on the Spanish mainland;

iii **the army in Spain** played the 'traditional' rôle (24.3.2–3). Its headquarters at **Burgos** (Fig. 24.11A) was the rebel 'capital',

Fig. 24.11A   The Spanish Civil War, 1936–39

iv **the Falange** (24.8) supported the right-wing rebellion;

v **church authorities** sided with Franco's rebellion (24.10.3);

vi **landowners** hoped for an end to land seizure (24.10.4).

2 **The Republicans**, or government forces

i **the Popular Front politicians** (24.10.1) had, after all, been democratically elected in 1936;

ii **industrial workers** supported 'their' government (24.6.6);

iii the Spanish **navy** and **air force** remained loyal.

3 **Advantages–the Nationalists**

i they quickly gained control of the **major wheat-growing areas** and so could feed their troops;

ii they had the better-qualified **military leaders**;

iii they had the important support of the **Church**.

4 **Advantages–the Republicans**

i they had the **industrial centres** which supplied them with **arms** and **munitions**. Nationalists had to import most of theirs;

ii they had the support of **industrial workers** who might have made a strong army. But they were **poorly led**; the easy way in which Cadiz and Seville fell was proof of inefficient command.

5 The League and the Civil War
i **'Liberal' opinion** in democratic countries called for aid to the Republicans;

ii **Eden**, British Foreign Secretary, and **Blum**, Prime Minister in a French Popular Front government, urged **Non-Intervention**. They wanted no aid to be given to either side;

iii **Germany** and **Italy** ignored this plea and aided the rebels;

iv **Russia** ignored the plea and aided the Republicans.

6 Foreign aid to Nationalists
i **Salazar**, dictator of Portugal, sent **20 000 troops** to help the rebels and to help conquer central Spain (Fig. 24.11);

ii **Hitler sent:**
(a) 10 000 soldiers through Vigo (to help Franco in the north) and Cadiz (to help in the south) (Fig. 24.11A);

(b) The Condor Air Legion which was stronger than the Spanish air force (24.11.2). The war provided a chance for Hitler's growing air force (20.6.3.iii.c) to put its training to the test:

iii **Mussolini** sent **50 000 soldiers** through Cadiz and Valencia. These were not well-trained and were often defeated. Italy suffered economically from the cost of this venture.

7 Foreign aid to the Republicans
i **Russia** sent troops, advisers, munitions and food through Barcelona in Catalonia (Fig. 24.11A). These were often the cause of bitter fighting inside the Republican ranks (24.12.3);

ii an **International Brigade of 40 000 volunteers** from many countries went to fight with the Republicans. Many of these were poorly trained.

8 The course of the war, 1936
i by the end of 1936 **Franco's men** had gained control of about **one quarter of Spain** (Fig. 24.11A);

ii **October 1936** Franco was named **Chief of State**.

24.12 The course of the war, 1937

1 Franco's forces in Cadiz and the north made slow progress and were separated from each other by a Republican centre (Fig. 24.11A).

2 Parts of the **Basque country** were taken. The bombing by the Germans of the Basque town of **Guernica** (April 1937) was particularly savage.

3 From **Seville** (Fig. 24.11A) Franco advanced to take the region around **Granada** in the south and, at the same time, advanced north towards **Madrid**.

4 Catalonia, the region based on Barcelona (Fig. 24.11A), was the scene for a bitter struggle between **Stalinists** and **non-Stalinist Communists**. Many Republicans were killed in this 'second civil war'. The Stalinists won; **Caballero** was forced from office and replaced by the Stalinist, **Negrin**.

5 October 1937 Franco was proclaimed as **El Caudillo** (as Hitler was Fuhrer and Mussolini was Il Duce).

24.13 More progress, 1938

1 Franco's men pushed through to the south and the Mediterranean.

2 They by-passed Madrid leaving it under siege.

3 Four columns took part in that siege. Their commander said that he also had the help of **'a fifth column'** of anti-republicans inside Madrid itself.

24.14 The end, March 1939

1 February 1939 Catalonia was conquered by the Nationalists. This was, in a sense, the end of the Republic.

2 28 March 1939 After a year's siege, Madrid fell.

24.15 Reasons for Franco's victory

1 Internally he had the support of **powerful groups**:
i **Army officers** and the **Civil Guard** had the advantages of having been **better-trained** and were **better armed** than the irregular forces of the Republicans;

ii the **aristocracy** and rich **middle class** provided the money to finance his war;

iii **the Church** gave him its moral backing.

2 Foreign aid Aid from Germany, Italy and Portugal (troops, advisers, planes and munitions) outweighed foreign aid to the Republicans in total and in quality.

3 The **neutrality** of Britain and France worked in favour of the Nationalists:
i it put the elected government (Nationalists) and the rebels **on an equal footing**;

ii **it denied the government the aid** it might have expected from other elected governments.

4 The Republican forces were not united:
i Communists and anarchist fought each other;

ii Russian aid was limited; Stalin did not want to get fully involved and he did not really want a Republican (non-Communist) victory.

5 Franco provided the Nationalists with **strong and united leadership**. His rivals were suppressed while his skilful planning of the campaign won him increased support.

6 The League's embargo on arms stopped the Republicans from receiving aid but did not prevent Hitler and Mussolini from sending aid to Franco.

24.16 Some effects of the war

1 Three-quarters of a million people had died.

2 One-quarter of all homes and **one-third** of all animals had been destroyed.

3 £3 billion had been spent, equal to **16 years of the Spanish national income**.

4 Italy and Germany had had 'practice' at war.

5 Democracy had received another defeat.

24.17 Franco in power

1 His government was harshly anti-Communist. Many were imprisoned, executed or exiled.

2 He was harshly repressive to all who fought for the Republic.

3 The Church enjoyed a special place in the nation's life.

4 The Falange was only one part of his Coalition government. Spain did not become as fascist a state as Italy or Germany.

5 The rich and powerful benefited most from his rule – the Church, landowners and industrialists.

6 He allowed a Cortes to be elected in 1942 but it had no power.

7 He did not help Hitler as the Fuhrer had hoped. Gibraltar was not attacked; the Mediterranean was that much safer during the War.

8 1947 He became Chief of State for life with the right to name his successor.

25 The Second World War from 1939 to 1942

25.1 Poland

1 The German Blitzkreig (or lightning war)
i **six Panzer divisions** (heavily armoured but mobile forces) poured into Poland on 1st of September, 1939;

ii the **Luftwaffe** pounded the country from the air and carried **paratroopers** behind enemy defensive lines;

iii **27 September** Warsaw was battered into submission;

iv **3 October** Poland capitulated;

v **Jews** were herded into ghettos. 3 million were to die;

vi **Russia** entered eastern Poland two weeks after the attack from the west. Poland was divided up (23.16).

25.2 The 'Phoney War'

1 **Britain and France** could not save Poland.

2 **German generals** were unwilling to attack France.

3 **France**, secure behind the **Maginot Line**, was **not militarily prepared** to attack Germany and its **Siegfried Line**.

4 **Britain** was even less prepared.

5 Both countries shared **varied hopes**:

i **peace terms** might still be arranged. The 'Munich mentality' dominated most British and French thinking;

ii **a naval blockade** might bring Germany to her knees as in 1917–18 (9.13);

iii **time was needed** to build up British and French forces.

6 Few hostilities took place in the winter of 1939–40 (but see 23.17.5).

25.3 The Naval War, 1939

1 **U-boats** were used to attack:

i merchant and passenger shipping such as the *Athenia* sunk on the day Britain entered the war;

ii the naval base at Scapa Flow, sinking the *Royal Oak*.

2 **German surface raiders**, notably the *Graf Spee* (20.6.3); attacked shipping in the Indian and Atlantic Oceans.

3 The *Graf Spee* was scuttled in Montevideo (20 December 1939) after a running fight with three British cruisers in what became known as the **Battle of the River Plate**.

25.4 'Hotting-Up' the naval war, April 1940

1 Britain and France thought of sending help to Finland (23.17.5).

2 **Norway** lay along the route to Finland.

3 **Swedish steel** came south on this route to Germany.

4 **Churchill**, First Lord of the Admiralty, acted:

i **mines** were laid in Norwegian waters to hinder the Germans;

ii **the German ship** *Altmark* was chased into a Norwegian fiord and boarded by the British ship, *HMS Cossack* (**February 1940**).

5 Britain planned to **invade Norway** to capture its coast.

25.5 The German conquest of Scandinavia, April 1940

1 **Hitler** forestalled British plans.

2 **9 April** Denmark and Norway suffered a **blitzkreig**.

3 **Denmark** surrendered on the same day.

4 **Norway** held out with British help:

i **British** forces landed near Trondheim;

ii **south and central Norway** fell to the Nazis, partly because of a Norwegian 'fifth column' (24.13) under **Quisling**.

5 British help was withdrawn when Nazi forces attacked Holland (25.6) which made German conquest of the rest of Norway easier.

6 **Hitler gained control** of Norwegian iron ore, the entrance to the Baltic and many naval and air bases.

7 **Norway's defeat** was a bad blow for Britain and led to criticism of Chamberlain's government.

8 **7–9 May 1940** After a major debate in Parliament, Chamberlain got only a small majority. He tried to form a Coalition with Labour and Liberal leaders but failed.

9 **10 May Germany invaded Holland and Belgium** (25.6).

10 **10 May Chamberlain resigned; Churchill** became Prime Minister.

25.6 The German conquest of the Low Countries

1 Belgium, Luxemburg and Holland were invaded.

2 **A blitzkreig led to Holland's speedy surrender:**

i **10 May** Rotterdam airfield was captured and the city devastated by low level bombing;

ii **Utrecht** was threatened with the same fate;

iii the government surrendered. The **Queen** and her ministers fled to Britain.

3 **Belgium**

i **German forces** struck through the Ardennes;

ii **paratroopers** dropped behind Belgian forces defending the Albert Canal made Belgian outer defences useless;

iii **panzer divisions** (25.1) drove speedily to cut off troops in the north of Belgium;

iv **20 May** The Germans reached the coast, pushing back British troops defending Belgium.

25.7 France under attack

1 Panzer troops cut across the northern edge of France.

2 **20 May** Abbéville was taken.

3 **24 May** Dunkirk came under attack.

25.8 Dunkirk 24 May–3 June 1940

1 The bulk of the British army was driven back to Dunkirk.

2 200 000 British and 140 000 Allied troops were attacked by German land and air forces.

3 **Hitler** called off a final onslaught

i did he want to allow the **Luftwaffe** a chance to finish off the British? Goering (20.3.1) boasted that it could;

ii did he hope to persuade Britain to **negotiate peace?**

4 **The 'Miracle of Dunkirk'** was the description of the heroic story of hundreds of ships, of all sizes, which sailed to Dunkirk and brought back the besieged men.

5 **The RAF** provided what cover it could. The **Luftwaffe** with its superior forces launched almost countless dive-bombing attacks.

25.9 The fall of France. June 1940

1 For France there was no such miracle.

2 The fall of Belgium made the Maginot Line irrelevant.

3 French troops were scattered and in retreat.

4 People fled from German-occupied areas and Paris.

5 German dive-bombers attacked the crowded roads.

6 **14 June** The Germans took Paris.

7 **General Weygand** advised the government that the Germans could not be stopped. Prime Minister **Reynaud** resigned.

8 **Marshal Pétain** (the hero of Verdun–9.3.7) became head of government. He asked for an armistice.

9 Hitler insisted that the **railway carriage** in which the Germans had signed the armistice on **11 November 1918** be brought from a French museum. At **Compiègne** in 1940 (where the Germans had signed their surrender in 1918) Hitler gave France an armistice. **The shame of 1918** (9.13.6) **had been wiped out**.

10 **Mussolini** had not entered the war in 1939. On June 1940, confident of German victory, he declared war on Britain and France. He attacked France, made a separate armistice and gained a slice of French territory.

25.10 Vichy France

1 Pétain took the title of **Head of the French State**.

2 His government had its headquarters at **Vichy**.

3 **The armistice** gave **Germany** the western coast and northern France. The **Vichy government** agreed to bear the costs of this occupation. **German refugees** in Vichy France were returned to the Nazis. **French prisoners of war** stayed in German hands.

4 **The French fleet** came under Vichy control but most of it was destroyed by British action to keep it out of German hands.

5 **The Vichy government** with its belief in 'authority, law and order' became **fully fascist in 1944**.

6 **Hitler** distrusted Vichy politicians. In **1942** he ordered the occupation of the whole of France.

7 **The Free French** set up an alternative to Vichy collaboration. In 1940 **General de Gaulle** escaped to London and called on Frenchmen to continue the struggle.

25.11 Operation SEALION

1 Germany now dominated Europe.

2 She gained her success in little over 2 months.

3 Hitler expected Britain to make peace.

4 She refused.

5 Operation SEALION was the plan for a seaborne invasion of Britain. 13 divisions were assembled in northern France.

6 The Luftwaffe was sent to destroy the RAF to ensure control of the Channel.

25.12 The Battle of Britain, July–September 1940

1 **Stage 1: 10 July–7 August** Coastal convoys, vital inland targets and some cities were attacked and river estuaries mined. The Germans lost more planes than they had expected.

2 **Stage 1: 8–23 August** Large scale attacks on RAF airfields and on radar stations might have succeeded in knocking out the RAF but Goering switched targets.
Hitler hoped to defeat Britain by cutting off her supply routes before he attacked Russia (25.17).

3 **Stage 3: 24 August–6 September** The Germans bombed factories and military targets defended by the RAF.

4 **Stage 4: 7–30 September** All RAF fighters were based in the south to protect the country against an invasion. Huge raids by day ended after the **Battle of Britain** when Germany lost 60 planes. These raids were called off and the Germans went back to bombing airfields and, at night, London.

5 The RAF lost over a thousand planes and 700 pilots were killed or wounded.

25.13 The 'Blitz', 1940–41

1 **Night-bombing** attacks saw the dropping of:
i high-explosive **bombs**;
ii **incendiaries** which caused widespread fires;
iii parachute **mines** which demolished streets of houses.

2 The civilian population was partially protected by:
i **Anderson shelters** set in the earth and covered with soil;
ii **Morrison shelters** which were indoor steel boxes;
iii **communal shelters**, and underground stations.

3 Heavy **damage** and many **casualties** led to:
i an increased communal spirit;
ii an increase in volunteers for voluntary services.

4 **Coventry** was raided 3 times, starting on 14 November.
Ports were attacked constantly. The attacks on **Merseyside** lasted for 8 nights in May 1941 during which 2000 people died.

5 **Churchill** discovered that ~~the bombing~~ damaged morale but only for a time. But he insisted that the **RAF** should prepare a huge bomber force, under 'Bomber' Harris, to attack German towns.

25.14 The Battle of the Atlantic

1 Hitler called off Operation SEALION.

2 He decided to attack Britain's convoys which brought:
i food and raw materials;
ii foreign war materials.

3 Convoys were organized from the start of the war (9.11.3). Crossing the Atlantic took about 15 days.

4 **U-boats**, in 'wolfpacks', waited until the convoys had little cover from air or surface vessels, then attacked.

5 **Condors** (German heavy bombers) attacked convoys in British waters.

6 **Mines** in British waters were a final obstacle.

7 The battleship *Bismarck* and the cruiser, *Prinz Eugen*:
i came into the Atlantic from the Baltic (May 1941);
ii were attacked by the *Hood* (the 'pride of the navy'). the *Prince of Wales* and the aircraft carrier *Ark Royal*;
iii sank the *Hood*; only three survived of the crew of 1429;
iv drove off the *Prince of Wales*;

v were attacked by Swordfish planes from the *Ark Royal* which crippled the *Bismarck* and left her an easy target for the *Rodney* and the *Duke of York*, battleships which had joined the battle.

8 The *Bismarck* was sunk by torpedoes from the *Dorsetshire* (27 May).

9 The *Prinz Eugen* escaped.

25.15 Winning the Battle of the Atlantic

1 Many ships were lost; in 1941 and 1942, 800 000 tons of shipping was lost each month.

2 **Escort vessels** became better equipped with:
i **asdic and radar** which located the U-boats;
ii **bomb-throwers** armed with more effective depth-charges.

3 Better quality escort vessels appeared in the shape of:
i **faster frigates**;
ii **corvettes** which could ram or otherwise destroy submarines when they came on the surface.

4 **Bomber planes** played their part in 1942 and 1943.

5 In 1943 the number of U-boats being sunk rose sharply from an average of 10 a month (1942) to over 50 a month (1943).

6 At the same time the losses of shipping went down sharply with an average monthly loss of less than 100 000 tons.

25.16 The extension of the war; Italy

1 **June 1940** Italy declared war on the Allies (25.9.10).

2 **October 1940** Mussolini invaded **Greece**.
i **Greece** defeated the Italians and invaded **Albania** (23.15.6).
ii **Mussolini** asked for German help. **Hitler agreed**, seeing a chance to gain influence in the Balkans;
iii **November 1940** Hungary and Romania signed alliances with Germany to provide food and oil;
iv **March 1941** Bulgaria signed an alliance with Germany;
v **April 1941** Germany invaded **Yugoslavia and Greece**. 60 000 British troops were rushed from North Africa to Greece;

vi **May 1941** The British were defeated, **Greece surrendered** and British troops retreated to **Crete**. A German airborne assault captured that island;

vii **The Balkans** were under German control.

3 **Abyssinia** Italian troops invade **British Somaliland**.

4 From **Libya** Italian troops attacked **Egypt**.

25.17 Hitler and Russia; Operation BARBAROSSA
  (Fig. 25.17A)

1 **Why attack Russia?**
i Hitler wanted to **destroy Communism**;
ii he believed that the **Slav people were 'sub-human'**, fit only to work for German industry and Empire;
iii **he needed** to obtain:
(a) **Lebensraum**, living space for Germans (23.9);
(b) **Ukrainian wheat**;
(c) **the oil** from the Caucasus:
iv conquest of Russia would provide a **link with Japan** (25.22);
v with most of Europe and Russia under his control, Hitler would be able to **ignore Britain and the USA**;
vi he would be able to **launch attacks** on **Africa** and the **Middle East** with its oil supplies and the route to **India**.

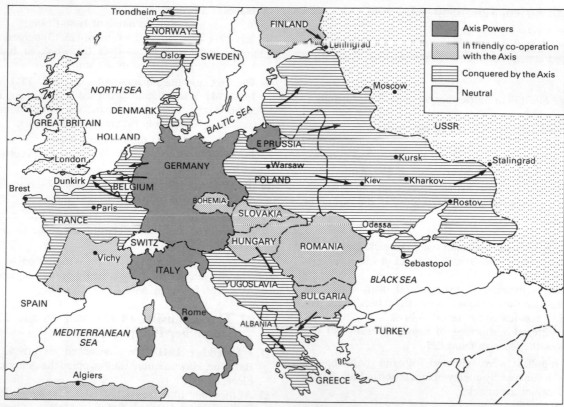

Fig. 25.17A The Axis powers in victory, 1939–42

2 The attack

i the invasion was **delayed** because troops were sent to help Italy in Greece (25.16.2);

ii **22 June 1941** A five-pronged invasion was launched by 153 divisions and 2000 aircraft. Hungary (3 divisions) and Romania (15 divisions) supported the invasion:

(a) **the northern prong** drove for Leningrad);

(b) **a north-central prong** drove towards Moscow;

(c) **the central prong** drove into the Ukraine;

(d) **a south-western prong** drove towards Stalingrad;

(e) **the most southerly prong** made for the Crimea.

3 Speedy success

i **the Luftwaffe** caught the Russian Air Force by surprise and destroyed hundreds of fighters parked on runways;

ii **the Wehrmacht's panzers** rolled in their blitzkreig supported by dive bombers and fighter aircraft;

iii western Russia was speedily overrun; **many Ukrainians** welcomed their release from Bolshevik rule (10.24.6);

iv **July 1941** Smolensk captured. German army into Ukraine;

v **September 1941**:

(a) Germans at the outskirts of **Leningrad** completed the land blockade of this northern 'capital';

(b) in the **Ukraine**, they took **Kiev** having destroyed 5 Russian armies:

vi **October 1941** Widespread German advances:

(a) from **Smolensk** they moved towards **Moscow**. The government was evacuated to **Kuibishev**. At the end of the month there was the **first offensive against Moscow**–which failed;

(b) **from Kiev** further advances were made **into the Ukraine**: After a major battle **Kursk** fell on 3 November;

(c) **in the Crimea, Odessa** (once the centre of revolution–was captured and **Sebastopol** came under siege.

vii **November 1941**;

(a) the sieges of **Leningrad** and **Sebastopol** continued:

(b) a second offensive against Moscow failed;

(c) **Timoshenko** led a counter-offensive which led to the **recapture of Rostov**;

(d) Russia launched a **counter-offensive on the Moscow front**:

viii **December 1941** The Russians' capture of Tikhvin saved Leningrad.

4 A slower progress, to May 1942

i **the Wehrmacht** had been 'invincible' in the summer-autumn of 1941. **The Russian winter** brought progress to a halt:

ii further but slow progress was made in 1942:

(a) **July 1942 Sebastopol surrendered**;

(b) **September 1942 Stalingrad** came under attack. The capture of this city would have opened the **Caucasus** to the Germans:

iii we now know that this was the **limit of German success** and we will see more of this in Unit 26.

25.18 Hitler's mistakes in Russia

1 He delayed the invasion (25.17.2) and lost six weeks of good weather.

2 German attacks took place on **too wide a front**. The German **generals** wanted an all-out drive to **Moscow**. Hitler preferred an attack on the Caucasus with its **oil fields**. The dispersed attack fell between two stools; neither objective was achieved.

3 From November 1941 **'General Winter'** came to the help of the Russians:

i **fuel**, for tanks, aircraft and other motorised vehicles, froze;

ii men had not been supplied with the necessary **clothing**; many died of frostbite;

iii **supplying forces** deep in Russia proved **difficult**.

4 Russian patriotism was roused by the inhuman treatment shown to the population by the conquering invaders:

i Stalin called up memories of Peter the Great and other Tsarist heroes. The Russians were asked to fight **'a Patriotic War'** in defence of **'Holy Russia'**;

ii a **'scorched earth'** policy was followed by the retreating Russians. Everything of value was destroyed–homes, factories, animals, crops in the fields. The Germans were unable to live off the land.

25.19 North Africa, June 1940–May 1942

1 1940

i **September** Italian troops advanced from Libya to Egypt. Britain rushed in reinforcements, South African, Australian and Indian. Tanks were sent from Britain, itself facing threat of invasion;

ii **November** Six Italian battleships were sunk at **Taranto**.

2 1941

i **February Wavell,** commander of the British forces, drove Italian forces from the border of Egypt to **Benghazi**;

ii **March German troops** were sent to support the Italians. The **British navy** won another battle at **Matapan**;

iii **August** In East Africa British troops liberated **British Somaliland** and **Haile Selassie** was restored to the throne of Abyssinia (23.6).

3 1942

i **Rommel**, a brilliant German general nicknamed 'the Desert Fox', drove the British from all of **Libya**, except **Tobruk**;

ii **Auchinleck**, a brilliant British general, with much less equipment than the Germans, drove them back again. He captured **Cyrenaica** and relieved **Tobruk**;

iii **Rommel** suffered a shortage of supplies because of the demands of the **Russian front** (25.17);

iv **British supplies** were affected by the bombing of Mediterranean convoys by enemy planes based in Italy. Malta was under constant air attack.

4 May 1942

i **Rommel** received extra supplies;

ii he launched a massive attack against weakened British forces, drove them from **Libya** and **deep into Egypt**;

iii this threatened the **Suez canal**, the route to **India** and British **oil supplies** from the Middle East;

iv we now know that this was the **limit of Rommel's success**. The Battle of **El Alamein** in July 1942 marked a turning point (26.2).

25.20 The United States and the war, 1939–41

1 Roosevelt had been determined to keep out of the War, 1939.

2 He sold supplies to whoever had gold to buy them (19.9.5).

3 By December 1940, Britain had no more gold.

4 Roosevelt persuaded Congress to pass **Lend-Lease Act** (19.9.9):

(a) this permitted lease or lend of supplies to any government whose defence was thought to be vital to USA;

(b) was applied to supplies for Britain alone, until Russia entered the War when it was extended to Russia.

5 Roosevelt had earlier (January 1941) spoken of **'four freedoms'** (19.9.8).

6 **The Atlantic Charter** was drawn up at a meeting between Roosevelt and Churchill off the coast of Newfoundland (19.9.10).

25.21 Japan and the War, 1939–41

1 Japan was already at war with China (17.30–31).

2 **The Tanaka Memorial** (17.16) had outlined Japanese plans for the 'Co-Prosperity Sphere' southwards.

3 Summer 1940

i the defeat of France left **Indo-China** exposed;

ii the defeat of Holland left **Indonesia** exposed;

iii **Britain's weak position** meant that she was not anxious to take on another enemy. Japan 'persuaded' Britain to close the **Burma Road** and cut off supplies to China.

4 The tripartite Axis, a new treaty between Japan, Germany and Italy, turned the Anti-Comintern Pacts (23.10) into a joint defence pact against any power 'not already engaged in war'.

5 Japanese advance

i troops moved into the **north of Indo-China**;

ii **July 1941** The Vichy government (25.10) agreed to a joint protectorate with Japan over the **whole of Indo-China**. Japanese troops landed in the south.

6 The USA and the Japanese advance, July 1941

i **July 1941** When Japan occupied Indo China, the USA stopped the sale of **oil** to Japan. She had earlier cancelled **trading agreements** between the two nations;

ii **Britain and Holland** took similar steps;

iii **Japan** was dependent on the West for **oil** and certain metals such as **copper**;

iv the USA said that before trade could be restored, Japan had to evacuate Indo-China and China;

v **General Tojo** replaced the civilian Prime Minister of Japan. He believed that Japan should use force to get what it needed;

vi Japanese negotiatiors went to Washington to discuss a settlement while preparations were made for a Japanese attack on American forces in Asia.

25.22 The extension of the war to the Far East, December 1941 (*Fig. 26.6A*)

1 7 December 1941 Japan launched an attack on **Pearl Harbour**, Hawaii where they crippled the American Pacific Fleet.

2 At the same time they attacked American airfields in the **Philippines** and British bases in **Malaya, Singapore** and **Hong Kong**.

3 Reasons for Japan's immediate successes:

i **America was ill-prepared for war**. It took time to mobilize men and resources;

ii **Britain** had made little preparation for war in the East. The **air force** was run down, **land forces** ill-equipped.

4 The extent of Japan's advance, May 1942:

i armies seized Hong Kong, Thailand, Malaya and Singapore, Indonesia and the Philippines, **defeating British, Dutch and US forces**;

ii they invaded New Guinea and **threatened Australia**;

iii they invaded Burma and **threatened India**.

5 The end of the expansion;

i we now know that in May 1942 Japanese advance reached its furthest limit;

ii evidence of that was provided by:

(a) **Coral Sea** where (May 1942) the US won a naval action to the south of New Guinea. American and Australian troops prevented the total conquest of New Guinea itself;

(b) **Midway Island** where the Americans won another victory to the east of Japan (June 1942);

(c) the British 'Forgotten Army' held the frontier between **India and Burma**. The Japanese conquest of Burma was the limit to the extent of their victory in this theatre of war.

25.23 The part to be played by the USA

1 The USA might have come into the war eventually, to help defeat Hitler's Germany.

2 The attack on Pearl Harbour brought her into war against Japan and, because of the Tripartite Pact, against Germany.

3 The USA became the 'arsenal of the free world' because it:

i built new factories and adapted existing ones for producing war materials;

ii developed new, better-built and better-armed ships, planes and tanks in large numbers;

iii sent men to fight in North Africa (26.7), Europe (26.10) as well as against Japan;

iv never faced difficulties of supplies or threats to its own security–unlike the other Allied countries.

26 The Second World War from 1942 to 1945

26.1 May–June 1942 Turning Point in the Pacific

1 **May 1942, The Battle of the Coral Sea**, (*Fig. 26.6A*)
i a Japanese fleet approached Port Moresby, **New Guinea**;
ii it was **defeated** by an American fleet;
iii the immediate **threat to Australia** was removed.
2 **June 1942 The Battle of Midway Island** (*Fig 26.6A*) The Japanese had even heavier losses.
3 In both battles most damage was done by carrier-based aircraft – a new development in warfare.
4 These defeats weakened the Japanese. The Americans could begin their advance (26.6).

26.2 July–October 1942 Turning Point in North Africa

1 Both sides had made dashes across hundreds of miles (25.19).
2 **May 1942** Rommel and the German Afrika Corps drove deep into Egypt.
3 **July 1942** He was checked at the first battle of **El Alamein**, 80 miles from Alexandria.
4 **August 1942** He was defeated at **Alam Halfa**.
5 **23 October 1942 Montgomery** defeated Rommel at the second battle of **El Alamein**.
6 He drove Rommel from **Egypt**, across **Libya** and into **Tunisia**.

26.3 January 1943 Turning Point in Russia

1 **Summer 1942**
i the Germans were within sight of the Caucasus Mountains and **85 per cent of Russia's oil supplies**;
ii **September 1942** Fighting in the streets of **Stalingrad**.
2 **German weaknesses**
i they failed to defeat **Russian guerilla forces**;
ii their **supply lines** were over 3000 miles long;
iii **Hitler's vanity**. He insisted on **'no surrender'** when withdrawal would have saved thousands of lives.
3 **Stalingrad**
i this city was attacked and partly occupied by **240 000 Germans** untrained in street fighting;
ii **Russian forces** surrounded the Germans who suffered:
(a) shortages of **food** and **medical supplies**;
(b) from the savage winter with **30 degrees of frost**.
iii **Hitler** tried to relieve his armies – and failed;
iv because of his order of 'no surrender' **140 000 died**;
v **2 February 1943 Von Paulus**, the German commander, finally surrendered with his **90 000 men**. Hitler called him 'a coward'.

26.4 The Air; Turning Point Number 4

1 Increased output from British factories and from the USA (25.23) led to **Allied air superiority**.
2 **Halifax** and **Lancaster** bombers attacked German towns, cities and industrial regions by night.
3 American **Fortresses** and **Liberators** bombed by day.
4 **Thunderbolts** and **Mustangs** were developed as escort-fighters.

26.5 Turning to attack: Russia 1943–44

1 **Behind the Urals** the Russians made surprising industrial development and produced vast quantities of:

i the **IL-2 Sturmavik ground-attack aircraft** which inflicted heavy casualties on panzers;
ii the **T-34 tanks** with diesel engines, sloping sides and powerful guns.
2 Russia was provided with massive **Allied aid**:
i **8.7 million tons** came through **Vladivostock** and on the Trans-Siberian railway to the Ural industrial area of Magnitogorsk;
ii **4.2 million tons** came via **Persia**, partly Russian-occupied;
iii **4.0 million tons** came via the **Arctic route** in spite of heavy damage inflicted on convoys by U-boats and torpedo bombers.
3 This aid included **10 000 tanks, 18 700 planes. 427 000 trucks** and **1100 locomotives**.
4 **July 1943** At **Kursk** (Fig. 25.17A) **Zhukov** won the largest-ever tank battle and shortly afterwards freed **Orel**.
5 **June 1944** The Germans were driven **over the Russian border**.
6 **December 1944 Romania** and **Bulgaria** were liberated.
7 **January 1945 Hungary** was liberated.
8 **February 1945 Poland** was liberated. But this had followed:
i **1 August 1944 The Warsaw Rising**, as Poles tried to gain their own freedom, independent of Russian aid;
ii **the crushing of the Poles** by the Germans, the Red Army waiting on the Vistula and not interfering. The deaths of so many leading Poles made it easier for Russia after 1945;
iii **the destruction of Warsaw** by German troops.
9 **March 1945** Russian troops entered **eastern Germany**.
10 **April 1945** Russian troops reached **Berlin**.

26.6 Turning to attack in the Pacific (*Fig. 26.6A*)

1 US forces had an **'island hopping'** campaign (Fig. 26.6A) in which they captured certain islands, leaving the Japanese in control of many others.
2 Each attack was **very costly** because of the fanatical defence.
3 The capture of **Tarawa** (Fig. 26.6A) cost **3000 American casualties and 5000 Japanese deaths**.
4 **1944**
i **Slim's 'Forgotten Army'** won the important victory at **Kohimar** which ensured Indian freedom;
ii Australian troops began the clearing of New Guinea;
iii **Guam** and the neighbouring **Mariana Islands** were taken;
iv from the airfields in Guam, Superfortresses flew 1300 miles **to bomb Tokyo**.
5 **Back to the Philippines**
i **General MacArthur**, commander of US forces in the Pacific, had been driven from the Philippines in **1942** but had vowed that he would return at the head of victorious troops;
ii he commanded the troops engaged in 'island-hopping';
iii the US navy won the **Battle of Leyte Gulf** and sank most of the Japanese navy (Fig. 26.6A);
iv in spite of Japanese defence, the Americans captured most of the Philippines in 1944 and **MacArthur entered Manila** in triumph in **February 1945**.
6 **1945**
i **February** Americans captured the island of **Iwo Jima** (Fig. 26.6A) after a month's bitter fighting and **20 000 casualties**;
ii **Okinawa** (Fig. 26.6A) was taken after **40 000 casualties**;
iii Japanese **kamikaze (suicide) pilots' attacks** on the US fleet engaged in the attack on Okinawa;
iv heavy bombing of Japan continued. There remained **2 million Japanese soldiers and 5000 kamikaze pilots** to be defeated.
7 **The end**
i the USA planned **2 invasions of Japan**. Southern Japan was to be taken in **1945** and Honshu in **1946**. The expected casualties would be very high;

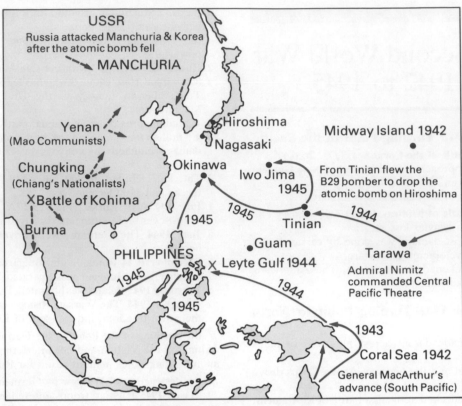

USSR
Russia attacked Manchuria & Korea
after the atomic bomb fell
→ MANCHURIA

Yenan
(Mao Communists)

Chungking
(Chiang's Nationalists)

✗ Battle of Kohima

Burma

Hiroshima

Nagasaki

Okinawa

Iwo Jima
1945

PHILIPPINES

1945

1945

1945

1945

1945

Guam

✗ Leyte Gulf 1944

Tinian

Midway Island 1942

From Tinian flew the
B29 bomber to drop the
atomic bomb on Hiroshima

1944

Tarawa

Admiral Nimitz
commanded Central
Pacific Theatre

1944

1943

Coral Sea 1942

General MacArthur's
advance (South Pacific)

Fig. 26.6A   The defeat of Japan

ii Japan rejected peace proposals made at Potsdam (26.11.9);

iii **6 August 1945** A B-29 dropped **the first atomic bomb** on **Hiroshima**, wiping out vast areas of the city; 80 000 people died;

iv **8 August 1945** Russia attacked Japanese-held **Manchuria** and **Korea**. Stalin knew that his men would not have to fight for very long but Russia would gain influence in the Far East:

v **9 August 1945** The second atomic bomb on **Nagasaki**; 40 000 killed;

vi **15 August 1945** The Japanese surrendered.

26.7 Turning to attack in North Africa

November 1942 Operation TORCH
i this was the Anglo-American attack on North Africa;
ii **Eisenhower's** forces captured **Casablanca**;
iii they drove through **Morocco**, captured **Oran** in **Algeria**;
iv Hitler sent:
(a) orders that there was to be **'no surrender'** (26.3.3.iv.);
(b) **tanks and troops** in six-engined planes;
v **7 May 1943** Montgomery's Eighth Army captured **Tunis**. Rommel was caught in a pincer-movement;
vi **14 May 1943 The Afrika Corps surrendered**.

26.8 August 1942 The Raid on Dieppe

1 Hitler had strengthened his hold over **'Fortress Europe'**.
2 on the northern coast of France the Germans had built the heavily fortified **West Wall** to prevent or hinder invasion.
3 Operation Jubilee was an Allied attack on **Dieppe**.
4 6000 men, mainly Canadians, took part in the raid.
5 3379 Canadians died in the disastrous failure.
6 The Allies learned from the disaster:
i a heavily defended port could not be taken without **too heavy casualties**. This led the Allies to develop their own port, the Mulberry Harbour (26.10.2.iii.b);
ii **defenders** had an easier time than attackers. Their defences would have to be bombed or by-passed;
iii at Dieppe many people had been killed on the beaches. In

an invasion a **strong beachhead** would have to be established, or invading forces would be annihilated.

26.9 The attack on Italy

1 July 1943 From North Africa, the Allies crossed into **Sicily** which was captured in **August**.

2 September 1943 The Allies crossed into **mainland Italy**. At **Salerno** a major battle provided the necessary port.

3 Italy was regarded as the 'soft under-belly of the Axis'.

4 Many Italians changed sides; the **King dismissed Mussolini** and put him in jail.

5 A government under **Marshal Bodoglio** sought an armistice.

6 Hitler rushed troops south to check the Allied advance which began in September.

7 German paratroopers freed Mussolini from jail and set him up with a new Fascist government in the north of Italy.

8 It was **difficult** to conquer Italy:
i its many **mountains and rivers** made invasion difficult;
ii the **Germans** fought fiercely.

9 June 1944 Rome was taken.

10 The north of Italy was not conquered until April 1945.

11 April 1945 Mussolini, captured by Italian resistance fighters, was killed, then hung upside down with his mistress beside him in a square in **Milan**, where his career had begun (21.7).

26.10 The main attack on Fortress Europe, 1944

1 Rommel was commander of the German defences against invasion.

2 Operation OVERLORD was the name of the Allied plan for invasion:
i thousands of **US troops** were trained and stationed in southern England;
ii **Eisenhower** was given command of the invasion;
iii Many **new 'weapons'** were designed to help:
(a) US factories produced thousands of **landing craft**;

(b) British engineers produced an **artificial harbour (Mulberry)** to be towed across the Channel and through which Allied troops could pour into France. **The lesson of Dieppe** had been learned;

(c) a pipe line under the ocean (**PLUTO**) was to take the much-needed oil from Britain to Europe.

3 Diversionary attacks in the **Calais** area persuaded Hitler and Rommel that this was the main target.

4 6 June 1944 130 000 men crossed the Channel:

i they landed on several beaches in **the Normandy area** which was more lightly defended;

ii Rommel still believed that Calais was the main target;

iii the Allies had **command of the seas** so that no vessels came under attack;

iv they also **commanded the skies** – unlike 1940 (25.8);

v the **beaches** were taken; men pushed inland quickly; the ports of **Cherbourg and Calais** were taken, making invasion easier;

vi **1 million men** poured into northern France.

5 The invading forces were helped by **French resistance fighters** who hindered German attempts to stem the advance.

6 August 1944 The Battle of the Falaise Gap broke the German resistance. The way was open for a rapid mobile advance through Western Europe.

7 Air power Allied **fighter-bombers** ruled the skies, attacking German convoys, troop-trains and even solitary German cars.

8 Other weapons There were **bridge-carrying tanks**, a new form of (Bailey) **bridge** which made river-crossing easier, **flare-throwing tanks and flail-tanks** to destroy minefields.

9 25 August Paris was taken. **De Gaulle** (25.10.7) led Free French forces on a triumphal entry.

10 September British paratroopers landed at Arnhem to try to take a bridge across the Rhine. They were not sufficiently protected and **Panzer forces** destroyed them.

11 German weapons At this late stage in the war the Germans produced **V.1 flying bombs** and **V.2 rockets** which fell on Britain until the bases from which they were launched were captured or destroyed.

12 The Ardennes Christmas 1944 Hitler launched a counter-attack in the Ardennes. German troops broke through American lines but were halted before being rolled back in **January 1945.**

13 24 March 1945 Allied forces crossed the **Rhine**.

14 April They linked up with the Red Army (26.5.10)

15 30 April Hitler committed suicide in Berlin.

16 7 May Doenitz, the new head of state, surrendered German forces. the European war was over.

26.11 Wartime Conferences of Allied leaders

1 Churchill met Roosevelt before USA entered the war (25.20.6)

2 Washington, December 1941 They met and agreed:

i **Germany** and not Japan was the **main enemy**. Many Americans wanted to concentrate on defeating Japan (25.22);

ii to set up machinery for **united action** – by industry and by the armed forces.

3 Moscow, August 1942 Churchill explained Anglo-American plans to **Stalin** and got him to agree to the **Operation TORCH** (26.7) and not (as Roosevelt and Stalin wanted) to demand the immediate implementation of operation OVER-LORD (26.10.2).

4 Casablanca, January 1943 Following the success of TORCH (26.7) **Churchill and Roosevelt** met at Casablanca. Here they agreed on:

i **the invasion of Italy** rather than of Northern France;

ii the demand for **unconditional surrender** by the Axis

powers. This would mean that after this war the Germans would not be able to complain of a stab-in-the-back or a dictated peace. (15.6)

5 Quebec, August 1943 Churchill, Roosevelt and Mackenzie-King (Canada) agreed on the strategy for the **defeat of Japan.**

6 Cairo, November 1943 Churchill, Roosevelt and Chiang Kai-shek agreed on the strategy for the **defeat of Japan.**

7 Teheran, November 1943 Churchill, Roosevelt and Stalin agreed:

i that the western Allies would open a **Second Front** in France;

ii that the Russian attack from the east would be **co-ordinated** with that Allied attack from the west;

iii that they would set about forming an **international organization** to replace the League of Nations;

iv that **Russia** would declare **war on Japan** 'at some suitable moment'.

8 Yalta, February 1945 Roosevelt, Churchill and Stalin met in this Crimean town. They agreed:

i on the temporary **division of Germany into four zones** (one of them French) after Germany's surrender;

ii on the punishment of **war criminals**;

iii that Germany would have to pay **reparations**;

iv that **German military power** would have to be paralyzed;

v to organize a conference in San Francisco to launch the **United Nations Organization**;

vi to reaffirm the principles of the **Atlantic Charter** (25.20.6);

vii **to liberate** conquered nations and Axis satellites;

viii to prepare the way in these countries for **free and democratic elections**;

ix that Russia would declare **war on Japan** 'within a few months of the defeat of Germany'.

9 Potsdam, July – August 1945

1 The war in Europe was over (26.10.16); Japan was still fighting.

2 Stalin represented Russia as he had done at other Conferences.

3 Truman replaced Roosevelt who had died in April 1945.

4 Churchill came to the start of the Conference, bringing the Labour leader (and Deputy Prime Minister) Attlee with him.

5 Attlee became Britain's representative after the Labour victory in the General Election, **26 July 1945.**

6 Stalin, Attlee and Truman agreed:

i that the **Oder-Neisse line** should be the new boundary between **Germany and Poland**;

ii to divide Germany into **four zones of occupation**;

iii that Germans living in Poland, Hungary and Czechoslovakia were to be repatriated to Germany to **avoid such minority problems** as the pre-war Sudetenland (12.5.1);

iv to allow a Conference of Foreign Ministers to settle the problems of **a peace treaty**.

10 In later Units we will see how the UNO was set up and worked and how successful, if at all, the Foreign Ministers were.

26.12 Why did Germany lose the war?

1 Germany, like Japan, had an efficient military machine and won easy victories at the start of the war.

2 Overreaching The conquest of most of Europe and a good deal of Russia created the problems of:

i **supplying** the conquering forces over **vast distances** (25.18);

ii providing forces to hold down the **conquered peoples**;

iii the creation of a coalition of hostile powers outraged by **German greed and cruelty**;

iv many **resistance movements**.

3 1940 Hitler failed to destroy:

i the **British army** at Dunkirk;

ii **Britain's determination** to resist. He underestimated the commitment of the British and their **Commonwealth Allies**.

4 1941 He attacked **Russia** hoping for speedy success because:

i he had a contempt for the **'sub-human' Slavs** (25.17);

ii he assumed that **Stalin's purges** had weakened the Russian power;

iii he had seen Russian difficulties in the attack on **Finland** (23.17);

iv he underestimated the **Russian will** to survive and defend 'Holy Russia' (25.18.4).

5 1941 When **Japan** declared war on the USA, Hitler need not have done so. His decision to do so brought the power of the USA to Britain's aid (25.23).

6 The British navy succeeded in winning the Battle of the Atlantic (25.15) which kept supplies coming. By the summer of 1943 the **U-boat campaign** was almost at an end. On the other hand, the British naval blockade affected **supplies to Germany** making her more dependent on supplies from conquered Europe. This made the conquered peoples even more anti-German.

7 Air superiority had been proved, in part, at the Battle of Britain (25.12). By 1942 British and US forces were bombing Germany (26.4). The almost total destruction of towns such as **Hamburg and Dresden** were symbols of that superiority.

8 Scientists in the free world provided Allied leaders with many and varied weapons. **Mulberry and PLUTO** (26.10.2) are examples. **Whittle** invented and developed the world's first **jet aircraft. Barnes Wallis** invented the **'bouncing bomb'** used by the Dambusters to attack the Mohne Dam which provided hydro-electric power to much of German industry.

9 Unconditional surrender Once the Allies had decided on this harsh policy, there was **no chance of a negotiated peace**. Hitler had to fight on in the face of overwhelming odds.

10 Divisions in Germany There had always been a small opposition to Nazi rule (20.5). When, by 1944, it was clear to most people that Germany was going to be defeated, **plots for Hitler's assassination** were developed. The most famous was the attempt of Colonel **Stauffenberg** and the plotters of **20 July 1944** when a bomb was taken into the meeting at Hitler's H.Q. The failure of the plot led to massive arrests and executions. It was, however, a sign of deep division in Germany showing there was **not the same determination** to win as there had been in Britain even in 1940.

27 The United Nations Organization (UNO)

27.1 Its wartime origins

1 January 1941 Roosevelt spoke of **'four freedoms'** (25.20).

2 August 1941 The Atlantic Charter issued by Roosevelt and Churchill declared that:

i basic human freedoms were to be respected;

ii after the war no territory should change hands except with the consent of the inhabitants.

3 January 1942 26 nations involved in the war against Germany agreed at Washington to accept the Atlantic Charter.

4 November 1943 At the Teheran Conference (26.11.7) Allied leaders agreed to set up an international organization.

5 August–November 1944 A conference of delegates from Allied countries at **Dumbarton Oaks**, near Washington, agreed the basic framework for the proposed organization.

6 February 1945 At Yalta (26.11.8) the Charter of the United Nations was agreed.

7 June 1945 At San Francisco representatives of **50 nations** approved the Charter.

8 24 October 1945 The Charter came into effect on what has become known as **United Nations Day.**

27.2 The aims of the founders of UNO were to provide:

1 a replacement for the League of Nations;

2 world peace (Article 1 of Charter);

3 all peoples with equal rights to **self-determination**;

4 cultural, economic as well as political **co-operation**;

5 no interference in the internal affairs of member states, except to enforce measures approved by the Security Council (Article 2);

6 freedom for local collective action against aggression (Article 51). Regional organizations–e.g. NATO and the Warsaw Pact–claim to act under the terms of this Article.

27.3 How UNO differs from the League

1 Russia and the USA were founder members (14.6).

2 Voting in the General Assembly is by simple majority or by a two-thirds majority in certain cases. No member has the veto possessed by members of the League Assembly (14.4.1).

3 The Security Council is in permanent session unlike the League Council (14.4.2).

4 None of the **Peace Treaties** referred to the UNO. In 1919–23 all the Treaties included an article on the League (14.3.3).

5 None of the members has withdrawn permanently. Some members have withdrawn for short periods:

i **in 1950 Russia** withdrew when the other members refused to admit Communist China as a member;

ii **in 1958 France** withdrew in anger at the UNO resolutions about her war with the Algerian rebels;

iii **in 1965 Indonesia** withdrew during her war with Malaysia. But each returned to the UNO. This was different from the experience of the League (14.6.8).

6 The Charter gave the Security Council the right to raise an armed force to be used to resist aggressors and to maintain peace (27.4.2.v). The League had no such power.

7 As countries in **Africa and Asia** gained independence they became members of UNO. The creation of an Afro-Asian group (or **bloc**) created many problems (27.4.1.vi). But it made the UNO **more representative** of world opinion than the League had been.

8 The aims of the UNO were, at one and the same time:

i more **realistic** than the highly idealistic aims of the League–and so were more likely to be achieved;

ii **much wider** than those of the League which had been almost entirely concerned with political objectives.

9 Its **headquarters** are in New York and not in Geneva. The Rockefeller family made a gift to the UNO of the site on which stands the 39-storied building which houses the Secretariat and the smaller building where the Security Council meets.

27.4 The structure of the UNO (*Fig. 27.4A*)

1 The General Assembly

i each member nation has **one vote** in this Assembly, although it may send up to 5 delegates to its meetings;

ii it normally meets in **September** and for a few weeks only;

iii it chooses its own **President** and controls its own *agenda*;

iv it elects the **non-permanent members** to the Security

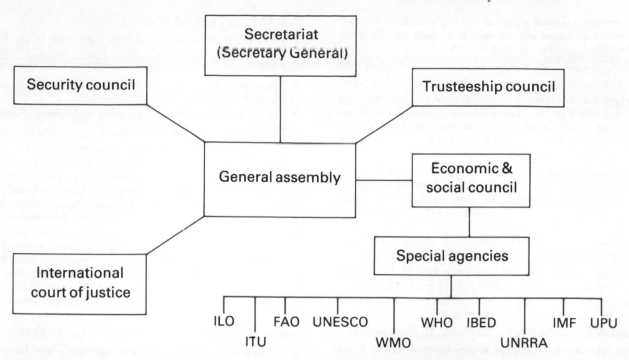

Fig. 27.4A   The organization of the United Nations

Council (27.2), and the members of other Councils and Committees;

v **the number of** members increased from the 50 who met at San Francisco (27.1.7) to **over 150 today**;

vi **the 'new' nations** were mainly from Africa and Asia, but included West Indian countries. They shared many things in common:

(a) **a struggle against colonialism** before independence;

(b) **low standards of living** and a need for aid:

vii they formed the Afro-Asian **'bloc'** and tend to vote together on most issues. Although they depend heavily on aid from and trade with western countries, they have often used their votes **against the interests of the USA** and her western friends. While they claim that they are **'non-aligned'** with either the west or the Russian east, they have tended to **give support to Russia** in their votes in the UNO;

viii **uniting for peace** During the height of the Cold War (28.3) Russia's use of the veto (27.4.2.iv) paralyzed the organization. In other circumstances other permanent members might equally obstruct the work of UNO. The Assembly took things into its own hands in November 1950. By 50 votes to 5 it agreed:

(a) if the Security Council was unable to work because of the veto, then the Assembly could act;

(b) any 7 members (i.e. a majority) **of the Council** or a simple majority **of the Assembly** could call for an emergency debate by the Assembly;

(c) at the same time a **UN Observation Commission** was set up and UNO observers sent immediately to crisis areas:

ix this Resolution turned out to be very important in practice and was used in connection with the crises in **Hungary** (1956), **Suez (1956)** and the **Congo** (1960);

x **voting in the Assembly** is by a simple majority or, in serious cases, by a two-third majority. No country can hold up the Assembly's work by its veto.

2 The Security Council

i This Council is in **permanent session**;

ii it has **five permanent members**; Britain, Russia, the USA, France and China. Until 1971 the **Chinese seat** was occupied by the Nationalist Government in Taiwan (Formosa). Although China was governed by Mao's Communists (17.37), the USA

used its veto to prevent Communist China from being voted into the UN. In 1971–72 there was 'a thaw' in the relations between Communist China and the USA (33.12.14). The USA agreed to allow Communist China to take the Chinese seat in the Security Council;

iii **the non-permanent members of the Council**:
(a) at first there were **six**, elected for a period of **2 years**;
(b) as the number of member-states in the UN grew, the size of the Council was increased. There are **now 10 non-permanent members**;
(c) by general agreement these non-permanent members are chosen to represent various regions and 'blocs'; 2 always come from the **Latin American countries**; 2 from the **West**, 5 from among the **African countries**; 1 from **Eastern Europe**:

iv the permanent members have the right of **veto**. They gave themselves this power as a safeguard against a vote of small nations. **Russia** abused the veto, using it over 100 times before 1950. Since then **every permanent member, except the USA**, has used this power to protect its own interests. This has weakened the power of the Council, but this has been partly overcome by the Assembly's Uniting for Peace decision (27.4.1.viii);

v the Council has a **military staff committee** and has power to raise an **armed force** under UN control. This armed force was used in **Korea** (28.11), the **Congo** (36.5.3), **Palestine** (37.5 and 37.10) and **Cyprus**;

vi the council may also order the imposition of **economic sanctions** against offending nations. This power was used against South Africa (36.21.4) and Rhodesia (36.14.9);

vii the Council controls the election of the Secretary General and the admission of new members;

viii it has power to send **Commissions** to investigate problem areas such as **Kashmir** (34.23.7) and **Indonesia** (35.3.8–10);

ix it has responsibility for organizing plans for **world disarmament**. In fact most talks on disarmament have taken place outside the UN.

3 The Secretariat or 'International Civil Service' draws its 5000 members from every nation. It:

i runs the **headquarters** in New York;

ii implements the **decisions** of the Assembly and Council;

iii brings **problems** before the Council;

iv draws up an **annual report** of the organization's work;

v runs the **technical aid schemes** and funds for the many specialized agencies (27.5.).

4 The Secretary General is appointed by the Assembly on the recommendation of the Council for a period of **five years**:

i **Trygve Lie** of Norway was the first holder of this office. He supported UNO action against Russian aggression in Korea (28.11) and showed himself to be pro-western in other ways. The Russians showed that they would not support a proposal to re-elect him and he resigned in 1952;

ii **Dag Hammarskjöld** of Sweden took up the post in 1952. He helped to make the job of the Secretary General both more important and better-known. He played a major rôle during the Suez crisis of 1956 (37.10) and during the Congo crisis of 1960–61 (36.6.3.). He was killed in a mysterious air crash while engaged on a mission in the Congo, 1961, where he was trying to bring peace to that war-torn country;

iii **U Thant** of Burma succeeded Hammarskjöld. He showed that he was angry and disappointed at the many failures of the UN and it was only with great reluctance that he allowed himself to be re-elected to the post in 1966;

iv **Kurt Waldheim** of Austria succeeded U Thant in 1971.

5 The International Court of Justice is the successor to the League's Permanent Court of Justice (14.4.5). Its 15 judges from various nations meet in the Hague. It has had only limited successes:

i few states accept **its decisions**:

ii In 1965 it decided in favour of South Africa in the dispute over that country's Mandate over South West Africa (27.4.6.iii).

6 The Trusteeship Council consists of the five permanent members of the Council plus six members elected by the General Assembly. It took over the work of the **Mandates Commission** of the League (14.5.2) and is responsible for the **mandated territories** named after the First World War, and for the 11 territories taken from Italy and Japan after 1945. Most of these countries have achieved their independence and now only some **Pacific Islands** and **New Guinea** remain as trusteeship territories administered by Britain, Australia, New Zealand and the USA. The Council has been an improvement on the League's Commission:

i people from the Trusteeship territories have the right of **direct appeal** to the Council. Many hundreds of such appeals were considered by the Council or by the Assembly;

ii the territories are **visited** by inspectors every three years;

iii but the Council **has failed** in respect of South West Africa:

(a) this region, known by Africans as **Namibia**, was administered after 1919 by South Africa (13.10.6);

(b) after 1945 **South Africa refused** to hand it over to the UN;

(c) after 1950 South Africa agreed to **allow UN inspectors** to visit the area but refused to give them adequate information;

(d) **the principle of apartheid** (36.18.4) was extended to the region and in **1960** South Africa **refused to allow UN inspectors** to visit it;

(e) in **1960** Ethiopia and Liberia, representing African countries with an interest in Namibian independence, brought the case of that country's administration to the **International Court**. In **1962** the court decided that it had a right to hear the case. In **1966** it **reversed this decision** so that South Africa retained its hold over Namibia. The development of the revolutionary South West African People's Organization (**SWAPO**) is one result of this failure by the Court and the Trusteeship Council.

7 The Economic and Social Council consists of 18 members appointed by the General Assembly. Its rôle is to supervize the work of the many specialized agencies and their use of the funds voted by the UN (see 27.5).

27.5 The Specialized Agencies

1 These are each organized like the main body of the UN; each has an Assembly, a Council, a Secretariat and a Director-General or Secretary-General.

2 The success of their work depends on the **co-operation** of people from various nations.

3 Each calls on **experts and resources** from every country.

4 The 'alphabet of agencies' includes:

i the **Food and Agricultural Organization (FAO)** with headquarters in Rome. It is mainly concerned with world **food supplies** and **agricultural development** in backward countries. Some of its more important projects have included the combating of **locusts** in South America, the introduction of **school meals** in Greece, the development of **irrigation and improved farming techniques** in South-East Asia and the introduction, in 1961, of an experimental **world food programme** to deal with chronic malnutrition and food emergencies. In **1969** it worked out a new **world plan for Agricultural Development** to benefit 1 billion people by 1985. In **1970** its **World Food Programme** was helping 4½ million people in **75 countries** and there were **385 food-producing projects in 78 countries** being paid for by contributing nations;

ii the **International Bank for Reconstruction and Development (IBRD)** is also called the **World Bank**. It works by:

(a) making loans from its own funds, raised by the sale of stock to member countries and from the issue of bonds in the world's financial centres;

(b) **guaranteeing loans** made by private investors.

Its ability to help in development is limited by:

(c) the need for any project helped to make a **profit**;

(d) the insistence that it **must not compete** with private investment;

(e) its **lack of technical personnel** to oversee the schemes on which its money is being spent.

In spite of these limitations it has provided over **£4 billion** in loans to underdeveloped countries:

iii the **International Development Authority** (IDA) was set up in 1960 to make **loans at low rates of interest** as a supplement to the work of the IBRD;

iv the **International Finance Corporation (IFC)** was set up by the IBRD in **1956** to act as a spur to private investment in under-developed countries;

v the **International Monetary Fund (IMF)** was set up in 1946 to provide the money needed to help countries which had **balance of payments problems**. Member nations put a quota of their own currency into the Fund; they are allowed, when in difficulty, to draw up to four times that amount in gold whenever they have a balance of payments crisis. In **1984** discussions are taking place to increase the amount of money at the Fund's disposal and to allow it to play a more active rôle in the world's financial affairs;

vi the **International Labour Organization (ILO)** is one of the institutions taken over from the League of Nations. As examples of its work, it has produced agreements on such matters as the proper inspection of labour conditions in agriculture, paid holidays, minimum wages, youth employment and training schemes for industrial development. The ILO Assembly meets every year at Geneva with 2 government delegates, 1 employers' delegate and 1 workers' delegate from each member state;

vii the **Educational, Scientific and Cultural Organization (UNESCO)** has its headquarters in Paris. It co-ordinates educational research and promotes international scientific and cultural co-operation. It aims to establish a **minimum world standard of education** including knowledge about agriculture, handicrafts, health, citizenship and world affairs as well as the basic skills of reading, writing and numbers. Through exchange scholarships, international conferences and the exchange of cultural collections, it works to foster international understanding;

viii **International Children's Emergency Fund (UNICEF)** often works in collaboration with some other agency–FAO (27.5.4.i) or WHO (27.5.4.x). It has provided aid for children:

(a) suffering because of **war**, e.g. in Nigeria and Vietnam;

(b) suffering from **epidemics and hunger**;

(c) suffering from **preventible diseases**. It has organized the **vaccination** of 280 million children against **tuberculosis** and the treatment of 32 million against **malaria**;

(d) in deprived countries it has set up over **40 000 health centres** and so helped the work of the WHO.

ix **United Nations Relief and Work Agency (UNRWA)** is the descendant of an earlier **United Nations Relief and Rehabilitation Agency (UNRRA)**. This was set up in 1943 to provide relief in countries liberated from Germany. It existed from 1943 to 1947 and helped in the provision of clothing, food and medical supplies as well as in the rehabilitation of agriculture and industry in Europe. UNRWA has taken the work outside Europe. It has had to cope with the problem of refugees in the **Middle East** following from the Arab-Israeli conflict. It also works with the refugees in **Africa** where civil wars and unrest in Nigeria, Uganda and Kenya have created a major refugee problem;

x the **World Health Organization (WHO)** is another agency trying to reduce human suffering and so increase the sum of human happiness. You should remember that half of the world's children cannot read or write; that three-quarters of the world's people still have little chance of getting to a doctor when ill and even less chance of visiting a dentist. The WHO provided the staff, the centres and the equipment, medicine and drugs which have been used against **cholera epidemics** in Egypt (1949) as well as providing aid for **starving and sick children** (along with the FAO and UNRWA), **attacks on preventible disease** (with UNICEF) and the **spreading of knowledge and medical skills** among people in the under-developed world (with the help of UNICEF and UNESCO);

xi **other agencies** deal with such things as telecommunications, trade, human rights, weather forecasting and civil aviation. These too have played their part in increasing international understanding and co-operation.

27.6 The political activity of the UNO has brought the Organization into most major international problems since 1945.

1 1946 It played a major rôle in getting Soviet troops out of **Persia (Iran)**.

2 1946 It failed to overcome Russian opposition to a UN settlement of the **Greek problem** (28.4).

3 1946–49 It helped to solve the problems following on the demand of Indonesia for independence and Dutch resistance to let go of her colonial possessions. Indonesian independence (1949) owed a good deal to UN influence.

4 1947 It failed to help India and Pakistan to resolve the **Kashmir problem** (34.23).

5 1948 It inherited the **Palestine problem** from Britain (37.3.6vi). Its proposals for the partition of Palestine were rejected by both Arab and Israeli. The UN mediator, **Count Bernadotte**, was assassinated by Jewish terrorists. His successor, **Ralph Bunche**, arranged an armistice in **1949**.

6 1948–49 The UN played no part in the **Berlin Crisis** (28.9).

7 1950 The outbreak of the **Korean War** (28.11) led to the **Uniting for Peace Resolution** (27.4.1.viii) and the despatch of UN forces under US commanders (28.11.14).

8 1956 The Suez Crisis (37.9) saw the UN paralyzed by the vetoes of France and Britain. The Assembly's demand for an end to the fighting was, fortunately for the UN, accompanied by similar demands from Russia and the USA.

9 1956 During the **Hungarian uprising** (30.10.3) the UN condemned Russia's invasion of Hungary–but failed to prevent Russia from continuing with her action.

10 1960–62 The Congo crisis (36.6.3ii) saw the raising of a UN force of 20 000 men trying to bring peace to the country torn by a series of civil wars and the attempted secession by Katanga.

11 1962 The UN supervized the handing over of **Western Irian** (New Guinea) to Indonesia when the Dutch were finally persuaded that colonialism was dead.

12 1963 UN forces kept the peace in **Cyprus**.

13 1965 Another force was sent to **Kashmir** to restore peace between India and Pakistan (34.23.12). The solution to the Kashmiri problem only came when Kosygin of Russia acted as mediator. (34.23.13).

14 1965 UN sanctions were imposed on **Rhodesia** when that 'colony' declared UDI (36.14.9). There is no evidence that sanctions had much effect. There is evidence that many member-states ignored the sanctions' resolutions and continued to trade with the 'criminal' nation.

15 1967 UN forces which had been stationed between **Arab and Israeli forces** were withdrawn at Arab demand. The victory of Israel in the ensuing war and its occupation of more Arab land led to a resolution in 1967 demanding Israeli withdrawal. The continued unrest in the Middle East up to 1983 is a sign of UN inability to enforce its resolutions.

27.7 The failures of the United Nations

1 Causes of

i the unwillingness of the **major powers** to give up their 'rights'. Russia (in Hungary, 1956), Britain and France (in Suez, 1956) and America (in Vietnam) have all been guilty;

ii **the hostility** between East and West weakens the UN, making it incapable of effective action in certain disputes such as the situation in the Middle East where **Israel** is 'a client state' of the USA, and Syria and the PLO are 'clients' of Russia;

iii that hostility led to a weakening of the original resolve that the UN should have an **army** at its disposal. Russia feared that it would be a 'capitalists' army' and so vetoed proposals for such a force. UN forces have to be cobbled together in certain crises–but only when the major powers agree to such a formation. When they do not agree–as in Vietnam and the whole area of Indo-China since 1975–then wars continue.

2 Evidence of

i the USA–USSR confrontation over **Cuba, 1962**. Neither country took its case to the UN. Both seemed prepared to risk a world war. The crisis was settled outside the UN;

ii **Vietnam** Russia and China aided one side and the USA the other in a war in which the UN had no part. Neither did the UN have any part in the peace-making sorties by Henry Kissinger on behalf of US President Richard Nixon (32.24);

iii **disarmament** this was to be one of the main aims of the new organization. In fact world armaments have increased alarmingly since 1945. Such proposals as are made for disarmament are made by the major powers, in bilateral discussions (such as the SALT discussions–32.24).

27.8 Its successes

1 Some **political successes** have been achieved (27.6).

2 Many **social successes** have followed the work of some agencies (27.5).

3 More people are now conscious of the **interdependence** of the countries of the world than was the case before 1939.

4 UNO still exists in spite of its weaknesses and failures.

28 International Relations, 1945–53

28.1 Uneasy allies, 1939–45

1 **Russia** had signed the pact with **Hitler** in 1939 (23.16.7).

2 **Britain** had wanted to help **Finland** against **Russia** (23.17.5).

3 **Stalin** had been suspicious of **Allied failure** to open the **Second Front** in France in 1942 and 1943.

4 **Roosevelt** wanted to see the break up of the **British Empire**.

5 **Roosevelt** made concessions to **Stalin**–and angered **Churchill**.

6 **Stalin** did not enter the war against **Japan** until his spies (including Fuchs) told him that the **Atom bomb** was to be dropped. He knew, then, that the war would soon be over–so he joined in.

28.2 The 'iron curtain' falls

1 **August 1945** Stalin at **Potsdam** (26.11.9).

2 Allied suspicions of Russia's behaviour in **Eastern Europe** (30.2):

i **Poland**; a Russian-dominated government set up. The Polish-government-in exile, which had fought in the West, was imprisoned when it returned to Poland (30.2.1);

ii **Bulgaria, Romania**, and **Albania** were liberated by Russian troops and Russian-dominated governments set up. (38.2.2);

3 **Churchill** drew attention to what was happening;

i **telegram to President Truman, 1945**. 'What is to happen about Russia? **An iron curtain is drawn down upon their Front**. We do not know what is going on behind.';

ii **March 1946 Speech at Fulton, Missouri**. 'From **Stettin** in the Baltic to **Trieste** in the Adriatic, an **iron curtain** has descended across the continent.'

28.3 Why did people talk of the 'Cold War'?

1 **It was not a real (or 'hot') war**. There was no declaration of war between Russia and the USA. When they did fight (in Korea–28.11), they did so under 'assumed' titles.

2 **But it certainly was not a real peace**. The struggle between the two Super-powers was carried on by:

i **propaganda** In their **own countries** they attacked the enemy in articles, cartoons, interviews and speeches. In **neutral countries** they tried to 'win friends and influence people' by the activities of their diplomats and countrymen. **Economic aid** was offered to win friends here; **military aid** was offered to keep a friend in power there;

ii **the build-up of armed forces** Since these had **nuclear weapons** there was fear that a Third World War might break out and destroy mankind.

3 Even when the 'war seemed to lose some of its heat (after 1953) there seemed little chance of peaceful co-existence.

28.4 Greece; the Cold War flares up

1 At Yalta and Potsdam **Greece** was named as a **British sphere of influence**.

2 After the German withdrawal from Greece in 1944, British troops **fought Communist guerillas** to keep a monarchist government in power.

3 **1946 The Communists rose again**, helped by supplies from their Russian-controlled neighbours.

4 **February 1947** Britain decided that she could no longer afford to pay for the defence of Greece. She asked the Americans to help.

28.5 The Truman 'Doctrine'

1 Truman had quickly come to distrust Stalin.

2 He feared that Russia would gain control of Greece.

3 He persuaded Congress to accept an American commitment to 'free' Europe.

4 **March 1947** He spelled out his policy; America would support free peoples:

i **resisting aggression by armed minorities;**

ii **resisting aggression by outside forces**.

5 Congress voted 4 billion dollars to pay for American forces to be sent to **Greece** and **Turkey**.

6 There was to be no 'return to isolationism' as in 1920 (16.2.2).

7 America would not try to 'roll back' communism. It recognized the principle of **co-existence**. It would not allow it to advance further; this was the principle of containment.

28.6 The Marshall Plan

1 **1945–47** America provided essential aid for war-torn Europe through the **United Nations Relief and Rehabilitation Administration (UNRRA)**.

2 This came to an end in 1947. Europe had not completely recovered.

3 **5 June 1947** The US Secretary of State, **George C. Marshall**, announced that the USA would be willing to provide massive aid to help European recovery to go on. European countries should get together to decide how this aid might be spent.

3 **Stalin** announced that no Russian-controlled country would take this aid.

5 **Ernest Bevin**, British Foreign Secretary, persuaded other European countries to form the **Organization for European Economic Co-operation**.

6 Sixteen countries joined the OEEC, with the western part of Germany as an associate member.

7 **April 1948** Congress voted **5.3 billion dollars** for aid to Europe under the Marshall Plan. In fact, by mid-1952 over 13 billion dollars of aid had been given.

8 Food, fuel, machinery, raw material and essential manufactured goods bought with this money helped Europe to get back on its feet.

9 Stalin saw this as an American attempt to dominate Europe.

28.7 Czechoslovakia–a special case

1 This was the **most industrialized state** in Eastern Europe.

2 Between 1919 and 1939 it had been a **liberal democracy**.

3 During the war the **Communists** had played a part in the **resistance (guerilla) movement against the German occupation**.

4 In 1945 **President Beneš** was anxious for Russian help. He agreed to **help the Communist Party to gain increased power**:

i **1945** He agreed to the **banning of the Agrarian Party** as the price to be paid for Communist participation in the government, with **Communist Gottwald as Prime Minister**;

ii he agreed to appoint **Communists to the important Ministries** controlling the **police, communications** (including the radio) and the **armed forces**.

5 **1947** Beneš allowed a **purge of the non-Communist Czech Social Democratic Party** so that a Communist sympathizer became its leader.

6 **Russia rejected the Marshall Plan** (28.6). They insisted that this American offer of aid should be rejected also by their satellites.

7 The Czech government was divided on this issue. There was need of economic and financial aid. But the **Communists** insisted on following the Stalin line. Several ministers resigned and the government became even more strongly Communist-dominated.

8 There were **student demonstrations** against this government, put down by the army and police.

9 1948; the year of decision
i **March 1948** The **elections were postponed** because of Communist fear of popular opposition;

ii **Dr Beneš rejected widespread demands** that the Communists should be dismissed and replaced by 'popular' ministers;

iii **Communist strong-arm gangs** occupied the offices of non-Communist ministers. **Jan Masaryk**, son of the founder of the state in 1919, 'fell from the window of his ministry' and died;

iv **May 1948 Elections were held.** The voters were offered a **single list of candidates** which they could vote for or against;

v there was an overwhelming victory for the **Communist-controlled National Front;**

vi **Beneš**, who had become increasingly opposed to Communist tactics, **resigned. Gottwald became President.** The Communists had 'taken over'.

10 Gottwald ordered a **purge** of the Czech Communist Party. Anyone opposing the Stalinist line was arrested, tried, imprisoned or executed. Among those killed was **Slansky, the Secretary of the Party.**

11 The Catholic Church
i **Archbishop Beran** had been an inmate of a Nazi concentration camp; he led the Church's opposition to the Communists;

ii the government insisted that **all priests should take an oath of loyalty to the state.** Beran rejected this;

iii **1950** most **Church property was confiscated** and monasteries closed;

iv **1951 seven Bishops were arrested and Beran exiled.**

28.8 Germany; the danger of a renewed war

1 At **Yalta** the Big Three (26.11.8) had agreed to divide Germany into **4 zones of occupation;** there was to be a joint administration for the whole country.

2 Berlin was also divided into **4 zones of occupation.**

3 At **Yalta** it was agreed that **Russia** would take **reparations** from Germany to compensate for the over-running and destruction of their country.

4 The four powers co-operated to bring the **leading Nazis to trial at Nuremberg.** Elsewhere, lesser Nazis were brought to trial, often before German judges.

5 1945 Conditions in Germany were very hard. Thousands were **homeless;** there was a shortage of **food and fuel;** the **currency** system collapsed; the stream of **refugees from Poland** made these problems worse.

6 1946 The Americans drew up plans for the reconstruction of Germany; neither the Russians nor French would agree.

7 1946–47 The winter was unusually severe; conditions in Germany became even worse than they had been.

8 1947 The **British and Americans** agreed to unite their 2 zones to help Germany get back to normal.

9 A new currency was introduced to help economic life get started.

10 American and British aid poured into their zones of Germany.

11 France merged her zone with the US and British zones. The Russians refused to co-operate. They also refused to allow western officials into their zone to see how it was being governed.

12 1948 The Marshall Plan was applied to 'western' Germany.

13 1949 West Germany was granted an occupation statute; a German Parliamentary Council drew up a **new constitution.**

14 At the same time the **Russians** proclaimed the foundation of the **German Democratic Republic in their former zone.**

28.9 Berlin: the Cold War flares up

1 February 1948 The Russians announced that the **whole of Berlin** was part of their zone of occupation.

2 June 1949 The London Agreement provided for the formation of a **federal government in Western Germany** (28.8.8).

3 The decision to create a **new currency** (28.8.9) in the western zones led the Russians to claim that this was **against the principles of the Potsdam agreement**–that all 4 powers should co-operate in the government of the whole of Germany.

4 Russia forbade the circulation of the new currency in its zone.

5 This meant that it did not circulate in **Berlin** which is inside the Russian zone.

6 June 1948 Russia closed **all the land links between Berlin and the western zones.**

7 Russia hoped to make it impossible for the western powers to supply and govern their zones of Berlin. The city would then have 'fallen' to the Russians.

8 The Allies replied by a massive airlift. For almost a year, fuel, food and other supplies were flown every day from airports in the western zones **across the Russian zone to the airport in the British zone** in Berlin.

9 May 1949 Russia finally lifted the blockade and Berlin could be supplied by rail, road, river and canal–more easily and more cheaply than by air.

28.10 The North Atlantic Treaty Organization (NATO)

1 March 1947 Britain and France signed the **Treaty of Dunkirk** aimed against a revived Germany.

2 March 1948 The 'Dunkirk Powers' were joined by **Belgium, Holland** and **Luxemburg** (the Benelux countries) in the **Treaty of Brussels** which guaranteed mutual aid against both German and Russian aggression.

3 The Brussels Powers could never have hoped to hold off a Russian attack; they had only 12 divisions of men as compared to the 250 divisions of Russian forces.

4 The blockade of **Berlin** and the Communist take-over in **Czechoslovakia** made **everyone more afraid** of the danger of a Russian attack.

5 April 1949 The 5 Brussels powers allied with the USA, Canada, Norway, Iceland, Denmark, Italy and Portugal in NATO. They were joined later by:
i **Greece and Turkey** (1952);
ii **West Germany** (1955).

6 The USA provides about three-quarters of the cost and the military power of the alliance, and has complete control of the nuclear weapons inside the alliance.

28.11 Korea; the Cold War flares up again
(Fig. 28.11A)

1 Stalin's attempts to extend Russian power was **halted by:**
i **Yugoslavia's break** with the Eastern bloc (30.6.2);
ii the failure of the **Berlin blockade;**
iii the creation of **NATO.**

2 He then turned his attention to the **Far East.** There were Russian backed risings by local Communists in **Malaya** and **Indonesia** in 1948–50. These, too, failed.

3 Korea had been annexed by **Japan in 1910** (6.8.3).

4 1943 At the **Cairo Conference** (26.11.6) it was agreed that **independence** should be restored to **Korea after the war.**

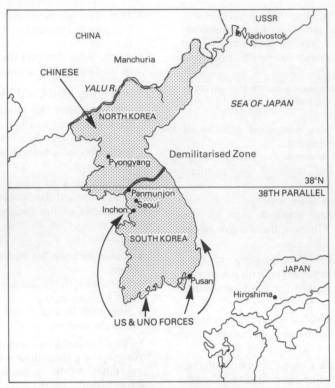

Fig. 28.11A   The Korean War

5 After the surrender of Japan in **August 1945 Korea was occupied by Russian troops (in the north) and US troops (in the south)**.

6 The dividing line between the two zones was the **38th parallel** of latitude.

7 **1948** Russia set up the **Communist Korean People's Republic**.

8 The Americans then set up the **Republic of Korea in the south**.

9 Russia and the USA withdrew their forces.

10 A series of border clashes took place.

11 **1948 The UN** tried to organize **national elections** but failed.

12 **June 1950 North Korean troops** crossed the 38th parallel, over-ran South Korea and pushed her forces back to a small region around the **southern port of Pusan.**

13 **Russia was boycotting the UN** because of its refusal to admit Communist China as a member.

14 America got the **Security Council** to condemn the North Koreans as aggressors and to agree to send a **UN force** to drive them back.

15 This force was mainly American, although soldiers from 15 other nations (including Britain) also took part in the fighting.

16 It was commanded by **General MacArthur** (26.6.5). The UN forces were driven back into the area around Pusan.

17 He organized an **amphibious landing** at the port of **Inchon** behind the North Korean lines and drove the invaders back across the 38th parallel.

18 He then planned to drive them north to the **Yalu River**. China warned the world that if that happened she would join in the war.

19 MacArthur carried out his plan. **The Chinese then entered the war**. UN forces operating far from their supply bases were often defeated and quickly driven south again.

20 MacArthur asked permission to drop the **atomic bomb** on China.

21 America's allies were alarmed at this threat to extend the war which might easily have become the Third World War.

22 President **Truman** was persuaded to **sack MacArthur**.

23 The war continued with heavy casualties on both sides, with neither side able to win a major victory. The 'see-saw' across the 38th parallel saw refugees being driven to the south, peasants having their lands destroyed.

24 **June 1951** Russia proposed at the UN that there should be an **armistice**.

25 Discussions went on–but so did the fighting.

26 **1953** A **truce** was finally agreed and signed at **Panmunjon**. A truce commission was set up to deal with problems between the two Korean states who still have not signed a peace treaty. A demilitarized zone separates the 2 halves of Korea.

27 The effects of the Korean War:

i massive **destruction** in Korea itself;

ii the bitter enmity between the USA and Communist China was intensified. The Cold War thus spread into Asia;

iii anti-Communist feeling in the USA allowed **Senator McCarthy** to gain a great deal of support (32.15);

iv the South East Treaty Organization (SEATO) was set up in 1954 as the Asiatic attempt to imitate NATO and to provide an obstacle to Communist aggression in the Far East.

28.12 1953: an improvement in the atmosphere

1 **March 1953 Stalin died**. He had led Russia since 1924, having taken part in the **Bolshevik revolution of 1917** and the **Civil War**. During that war he had seen **western powers** helping the anti-Bolsheviks (10.25).

2 He had **led Russia against Hitler after 1941,** having seen how the **western powers had appeased Hitler**–even excluding Russia from the **Munich Conference** which decided the fate of Czechoslovakia, Russia's ally (23.13–14).

3 He had taken part in the **Yalta and Potsdam Conferences** and won for Russia a great deal of control over **Eastern Europe** (30.2–3).

4 He had tried to extend that control over **Berlin** (28.8–9) and in **Korea** (28.11).

5 His successor, **Khrushchev**, was a different sort of person.

He did not have the sort of power that Stalin had had inside Russia, nor did he seem to have Stalin's ambitions to extend Russian power abroad. He was prepared to accept the Truman idea of co-existence.

6 One result of this change of leadership in Russia was that there was a 'thaw' in relations between East and West.

29 Russia, 1945–83

29.1 The position in 1945

1 Much of Russia had been devastated. The main food-producing regions had been ruined. There were **food shortages**; food riots had to be put down by the Army and Beria's MVD.

2 **Fear of the West** President Kalinin warned that 'only Hitler's Germany has been defeated', suggesting that the rest of the capitalist West was waiting to destroy Russia.

3 **February 1946** Stalin warned of the dangers from the West. This fear helps to explain his policies in **Eastern Europe** (30.3) where he wanted to create **buffer states**.

4 **Contact with foreigners** Russian soldiers returning from service in the West were 're-educated' so that they 'forgot' the evidence of the higher standards of life in the West. Many were imprisoned, others sent to work in Siberia.

5 **1947 Russia was a closed society** Its people were not allowed contact with the West; few were allowed to travel, few westerners were allowed in. Churchill's 'iron curtain' had come down.

29.2 Industrial recovery

1 **Stalin** returned to the pre-war policy of **building up Russian industry**. His success can be seen in the output figures:

	1945	1953
Coal	149 million tons	320 million tons
Steel	9 million tons	38 million tons
Oil	19 million tons	53 million tons
Electricity	43 billion kw/hrs	133 billion kw/hrs

2 One result of this development was the build-up of **new industrial centres**, many behind the Urals. Sverdlovsk grew from being a village to having 350 000 inhabitants.

3 **Weaknesses of the development**

i **little attention** was paid to **new industries** such as plastics; Russia remained an **old-fashioned industrial country**;

ii in **agriculture** she continued to use heavy tractors which spoiled the soil, ignoring the development (in the west) of new, lighter tractors.

4 **Military spending** continued at a high level. In July 1949 Russia exploded her first atomic bomb.

29.3 Evident problems

1 **Inflation** By 1951 food prices were double what they had been in 1940. Stalin was forced to revalue the rouble in an attempt to check this rise in prices.

2 **The new towns** grew very rapidly; there was always a shortage of housing, families sharing a single room.

3 The high spending on weapons and arms development was one cause of the **constant shortage of consumer goods**.

29.4 The leadership, 1953

1 **5 March 1953** Stalin died.

2 Several people occupied leading positions.

i **Malenkov** was Prime Minister;

ii **Bulganin** was Deputy Prime Minister (1947–55) and represented the power of the Russian army;

iii **Molotov** was the long-serving Foreign Minister;

iv **Khrushchev** was First Secretary of the Communist Party.

3 None of these wanted the powers which Stalin had had.

4 All of them were anxious to pursue policies which would lead to:

i an improvement in **Russian living standards**:

ii **an easing in world tension**.

29.5 Evidence of the change in attitudes

1 **Beria, the head of the MVD, was murdered** in June or July, 1953; none of the 'collective leadership' wanted the secret police to keep its old powers.

2 The official agency, **Intourist**, tried to attract foreign tourists to Russia—although foreigners' journeys inside Russia were carefully controlled.

3 **Malenkov was dismissed** from the post as Prime Minister in 1955. He was not assassinated as might have happened in Stalin's time. In 1958 he was sent to manage a generating station in far-away Kazakhstan.

4 **Bulganin became Prime Minister** With Khruschchev he formed a duumvirate, sharing joint authority although Khrushchev was, in fact, the dominant partner.

5 **1957 The army** became concerned at the growth of Khrushchev's power. An **anti-party campaign** was led by Bulganin. This failed and **Bulganin was demoted** before being expelled from the Central Committee. He then lived in retirement near Moscow.

6 **Khrushchev** became **Prime Minister** in 1958 so that he was the supreme ruler–of party and government.

29.6 Agriculture; Russia's major problem

1 Continuing food shortages proved that **collectivization was not an efficient way of farming**.

2 **Khrushchev** led the campaign for the use of the '**Virgin Lands**' of Siberia;

i **250 000 volunteers** from the Young Communist League (the Komsomol) were recruited to farm in these regions;

ii **120 000 tractors** were sent;

iii **6 million acres** of Siberia and Kazakhstan were ploughed in the first year. By 1955 it was planned that 32 million acres would have been brought under the plough.

3 **Opposition** to the plan was led by **Malenkov** who argued that it would be better for Russia to import food, paying for it by exports of industrial goods.

4 **Khrushchev** argued that in addition to the increased output of wheat there would be increased output of maize. This could be fed to cattle and pigs so providing more meat for the workers.

5 **Success** There were 2 good harvests which seemed to prove Khruschchev right.

6 **Failure** **Soil erosion** led to the creation of dust bowls as the valuable top soil was swept away by the wind.

7 **Food imports** Russia, once the granary of Europe, now had to import grain from **Canada, Australia and, later, the USA**.

8 **Bread rationing** was introduced, indicating a further lowering of living standards for the Russian people.

29.7 A change in foreign policy

1 **Khrushchev supported the policy of co-existence** (28.5.7) which had been first put forward by President Truman in 1947.

2 He argued that Communism **did not need a military victory** over the capitalist west. It would 'crush' the capitalists by its very success as a system.

3 This led to **more contact** between Russian and western politicians and to **more peaceful policies**:

i **Bulganin and Khrushchev visited Britain and other countries**;

ii **Khrushchev**, when in complete power, toured the **USA**;

iii **Summit Conferences** were arranged (29.11) although they rarely led to far reachng changes in policies.

4 1954 Russia took part with the USA and Britain in talks at Geneva which led to the withdrawal of French forces from **Indo-China**. The **'spirit of Geneva'** was the description of the way in which the east and west could work together.

5 1955 The war-time Allies signed a peace treaty with **Austria** and withdrew their forces.

6 However, **suspicion of the west** remained a feature of Russian policy, even under Khrushchev:

i **1955 the Warsaw Pact** was created as a Russian alternative to NATO (28.10), particularly when West Germany was admitted as a member of that Organization. **Albania, Czechoslovakia, East Germany, Hungary, Poland and Romania joined Russia in this Pact**;

ii **1959 Comecon** (the Council for Mutual Economic Assistance) had been created in 1949–the **Russian alternative to the OEEC** (28.6.5). In 1959 it was strengthened as Russia wished to show its hostility to the recently created European Economic Community or Common Market (31.12).

29.8 The Twentieth Party Congress, 1956

1 This was supposed to be a secret meeting of Communist representatives from all over the USSR.

2 There were non-Russian communists from western countries at the Congress–as observers.

3 It was these who brought out the reports of what Khrushchev said in a major and surprising speech. He attacked the memory of Stalin (whom he had served for so long). **He attacked**:

i **Stalin's autocratic rule**;

ii **the purges** of the 1930's;

iii **the mistakes made by Stalin** in the early years of the war;

iv the quarrel with **Tito** (30.6–7).

29.9 The effects of this 'de-Stalinization'

1 Many people imprisoned by Stalin were **released**.

2 The memories of many who had been killed were **rehabilitated**. They were shown not to have been the 'monsters' Stalin had claimed.

3 There were similar policies **throughout Eastern Europe**. We will see in Unit 30 what effects that relaxation had.

4 Some Communists argued that there were **different roads** which might be followed **to the same object–Socialism**.

5 China, under Mao, became **critical of Russia** (29.13).

29.10 Improvements in Khrushchev's Russia

1 There was an increased production of **consumer goods**.

2 The secret police had less power (although they still had some).

3 There was a fall in the number of people sent to **labour camps**–although there were still many who were sent to these 'gulags'.

4 Russia seemed to be beginning to **enjoy** the fruits of the **massive industrialization policies** of the 1930s and 1940s.

5 The launching of the first Sputnik (1957) and of Vostok 1 manned by Yuri Gagarin were signs of technological advance.

29.11 Khrushchev and Germany

1 He was anxious to get the west to recognize **East Germany's independence**. If this were granted, East Germany could stop travel from the west and West Berlin.

2 He also wanted to halt the **flow of refugees** from East Germany. Since 1949 over 2 million had gone, via West Berlin, to the west. This led to a **labour shortage** in East Germany.

3 1958–9 Khrushchev told the Western Allies that they had 6 months in which to leave West Berlin.

4 September 1959 Khrushchev visited **President·Eisenhower** in the US President's 'retreat' at **Camp David**. He withdrew his threat over Berlin.

5 May 1960 A **Summit Conference** was held in **Paris**. Khrushchev had announced his intention to sign a separate peace treaty with East Germany. But the Russians shot down an American 'spy' plane piloted by **Gary Powers**. This led to Khrushchev's walking out of the Summit.

6 June 1961 Khrushchev met **Kennedy in Vienna**. Again he threatened that the west had only 6 months to get out of Berlin.

7 The constant threats to cut Berlin off from the west led to an **increase in the numbers seeking to escape**. Over 1 000 a day were getting out of East Germany.

8 13 August 1961 Two Soviet divisions of tanks were ordered to combat readiness in East Germany. Truckloads of East German Police (the Vopos) lined the boundary between the Soviet and Allied sectors of Berlin.

9 17 August 1961 Workmen began to erect a **wall across Berlin**. The 'Iron curtain' now had physical form.

10 After the building of the Wall

i 60 000 East Berliners lost their jobs in West Berlin;

ii the flood of refugees was halted. People trying to escape to the West now have to take tremendous risks. They still try;

iii there was little chance of further crises in Berlin, although there was the **'Checkpoint Charlie affair'**. In October 1961 10 Soviet tanks turned their guns on 10 US tanks at the crossing point between East and West Berlin. But nothing happened.

29.12 The Cuban affair, 1962

1 1958 Fidel Castro's guerillas overthrew the American-supported government of **Batista**, and attacked American-owned capitalist enterprises, which Castro blamed for the inequalities in Cuban life.

2 The USA refused to recognize the Castro government:

i **it refused to trade with Cuba** from which it had bought most of the sugar crop;

ii it took in, and gave support to, **anti-Castro refugees**.

3 Castro responded by taking over more **American investments** in Cuba.

4 Russia bought the sugar crop and became Castro's major supporter.

5 Russia, Castro and the USA saw the new government as a **model Communist government in the Caribbean**. Castro and Russia hoped, while the US feared, that **other countries in Latin America** might imitate Castro's example and set up Communist governments.

6 April 1961 President Kennedy of the USA allowed a CIA-backed invasion by Cuban exiles. This was a fiasco and both worsened USA hostility and encouraged Castro's supporters in Cuba (32.20.2.iii).

7 October 1962 American 'spy planes' brought back photographs showing that there were **Soviet missiles in Cuba**.

8 President Kennedy announced a **naval blockade** of Cuba until these missiles were removed. He threatened that if a missile were let off, then US forces would retaliate.

9 Khrushchev said the missiles were to **defend Cuba** from the threat of an American-supported invasion by anti-Castro forces. He also claimed that there was no difference between **Russian missiles in Cuba and US missiles in Turkey**.

10 Kennedy said that Castro did not need missiles to defend himself. He argued that the missiles were intended to threaten the USA. The **US air force** and **Polaris nuclear-carrying submarines were put on war footing**.

11 **A Russian convoy** was approaching Cuba (**22–28 October**). Would it challenge the US blockade–and so lead to war? Would it turn back–and indicate a climb-down by Khrushchev?

12 **28 October** Khrushchev announced that the ships would turn back–except for an oil tanker which Kennedy quickly decided could be let through.

13 Khrushchev announced that the **missiles would be removed**.

14 Note that throughout this crisis the USA had forces on its naval base at **Guantanamo** in southern Cuba.

29.13 Khrushchev and China (see also 33.12)

1 **Stalin** had not supported Mao Tse-tung in the 1930s and 1940s. Mao's 'revolution' was based on support from peasants. Marxism taught that the revolution had to be based on industrial workers.

2 **1950** Russia and China co-operated in **Korea** (28.11.18).

3 After 1950 **Russia sent technicians and material** to help in China's industrialization.

4 **Mao had been angered by Khrushchev's attack on Stalin**. It was 'impossible' said Mao, for such a 'monster' to have led the world's first Communist state.

5 **1957** Russia **supplied aid** for Mao's 'Great Leap Forward' (33.10) but then **became angered** when Mao's system of communes did not follow the Russian model.

6 **1957–60** Mao accused the Russians of being **'revisionists'**, of wanting to ignore the teachings of Marxist-Leninism, of being more concerned with developing **consumer industries** than with creating a Communist state. Russia, he argued, was trying to **imitate the west** in its search for material affluence.

7 **1960 The Russians withdrew their aid teams** and sent no more material aid to China.

8 **1964 China exploded her own nuclear bomb**. Mao could now claim to be, at least, equal to Russia. In fact, he claimed to be superior because of the purity of the doctrine which he followed in revolutionary China.

9 **Border disputes** were the result of Russian expansion in the 19th century into the Amur basin and Central Asia. She shared a 4000 mile long frontier with China. Clashes between civilians and armed forces led to a weakening of the relationship between the two Communist 'giants'.

10 As Russia tried to work out peaceful co-existence with the USA, Mao put himself forward as the only real Communist leader.

29.14 Khrushchev's fall, 1964

1 **Political power in Russia** was shared by:
i **the army**, represented by Bulganin until 1957 when he was demoted by Khrushchev;
ii **the Communist Party**, of which Khrushchev was First Secretary.

2 **Khrushchev lost the support** of the leading members of the Party:
i he seemed to be creating for himself that **'cult of personality'** for which he had denounced Stalin;
ii he made **organizational changes** in the Party structure which proved to be **unsound and clumsy**.

3 He lost the support of the hard-liners in the Army and the Party by his Cuban policy (29.12).

4 His **Berlin-German policy** had not led to western recognition of East Germany.

5 During his trips abroad he often behaved in what some saw as **'honest'** others as **'boisterous'** and others as **'foolish'** ways. Some leading Russians thought he was **discrediting** the system.

6 But **his major failures** were:
i his **agricultural policy** in the 'Virgin Lands' (29.6);
ii the continuing **lack of consumer goods**;
iii the clash with **China**.

7 **October 1964** While he was away on holiday there was a meeting of the Party presidium (or governing body). **Khrushchev was dismissed** from both his posts.

8 On returning to Moscow he tried to undo what had happened–but failed. He was succeeded by:
i **President Podgorny**;
ii **Prime Minister Kosygin**;
iii **Party Secretary Brezhnev**.

29.15 Khrushchev's career (a popular examination question)

1 Born 1894 to a peasant family, he worked in the Donetz Basin where he joined the Communist party in 1918.

2 He worked his way up the rungs of the ladder of Party organization.

3 1934 He was second Secretary of the Moscow Party organization; 1935, First Secretary; 1938, First Secretary of the Party in the Ukraine.

4 1934–40 He helped Stalin to carry out the great purges (11.2).

5 1939 He became a member of the Politburo.

6 1941–45 He was a high-ranking political commissar in the armed forces.

7 1945–53 He was the Party's main agricultural expert.

8 1953–54 He ousted Malenkov and became First Secretary of the Party.

9 1955 He was the most prominent member of the collective leadership.

10 1956 His condemnation of Stalin.

11 1957 He rid himself of his rivals, Malenkov, Kaganovich, Molotov and (army leader) Zhukov.

12 1958 He rid himself of Bulganin and became Prime Minister.

13 His 'Virgin Lands' policy (29.6).

14 His relations with foreign powers:
i the USA, including the Summit meetings;
ii Western Europe, including the question of Berlin;
iii China.

15 His fall from power (29.14).

29.16 Agriculture after Khrushchev

1 It was evident that the **Russian system was a failure**. It employed 40 million workers compared to the 4 million in US farming. Yet it could not supply enough for the Russian people.

2 **Kosygin** and **Brezhnev** announced:
i an increase in **wages** for farm workers;
ii **freedom** for collectives to decide on what crops to grow.

3 **1966–71** The changes seemed to work. There was a series of **good harvests**.

4 **1971–72** The harvest was ruined by:
i **a severe frost** which killed off the winter wheat crops;
ii **a drought** which killed off the main crop.

5 Russia was forced **to buy food** from the USA and Canada. This had the following effects:
i it took a good deal of **gold** out of Russia and so made it more difficult for her to buy the **industrial equipment** she needed to continue her modernization plans;
ii **it pushed up world prices**, and was one of the causes of the 'great inflation' with which we have lived since 1973;
iii it made it more likely that there would be **more contacts** between Russian and US officials and so helped détente (29.20).

29.17 Industry after Khrushchev

1 Russian industry was **not up to western standards** as shown by:
i efficiency;
ii productivity per workman.

2 **Kosygin** and **Brezhnev** realized that state-run organizations had to change.

3 **Higher wages** were allowed for workmen who worked harder and produced more. This was the **western-style system of bonus payments**–and the end of 'to each according to his needs'.

4 These higher wages would increase demand for **consumer goods**–and so, it was hoped, would **stimulate industries** producing those goods.

5 To achieve increases in productivity, Russia:
i bought **industrial machinery** from the USA;
ii got Fiat of Italy to re-organize the **Russian car industry**.

6 In May 1973 Brezhnev went to **West Germany** (the 'arch enemy') and asked for **technical aid and capital investment** by the successful Germans.

7 To help increase Russia's wealth Brezhnev and Kosygin proposed the exploitation of the vast gold, copper and oil deposits in Siberia. They found it difficult to recruit Russian workers to go to the inhospitable wastes of Siberia.

8 Note that, in spite of its backwardness, Russia has produced:
i **the Mig 21,** at the time the world's most successful jet fighter;
ii Sputnik 1, the first man-made **satellite** (29.10.5).

29.18 The government and people since Khrushchev

1 **Brezhnev** was the most important of the triumvirate (29.14.8).

2 **Podgorny was ousted** and Brezhnev, Party Secretary, also became President of the USSR.

3 **1975–82** Brezhnev suffered from ill-health but continued to develop that **'cult of personality'** which was favoured by Stalin and Khrushchev.

4 Brezhnev helped his **friends and supporters** into positions of power in the Politburo and dismissed possible rivals.

5 One result of this process was that Russia was governed by a group of **ageing seventy-year olds** who had lost whatever 'fire for revolution' they may ever have had.

6 **Corruption** became fairly commonplace; several senior officials were executed for smuggling, currency offences, dishonest selling or buying on a massive scale.

7 In the relaxed atmosphere of the Khrushchev years, **critics and dissidents** had become more outspoken. Brezhnev's government cracked down on these:
i **writers** such as Daniel, Sinyansky, Pasternak and Solzhenitsyn were punished by exile or imprisonment;
ii critics who passed on **duplicated copies of critical works** were punished severely;
iii **scientists** such as Sakharov, became critical of the government's policies concerning personal freedom. These were imprisoned (often in psychiatric 'clinics');
iv critics drew attention to the way in which the government failed to honour its commitments to **human rights** as outlined in the **1975 Helsinki Agreement** (29.21). Orlov and other such critics set up 'Helsinki' committees to supervize the government's record. These, too, were punished.

8 In old-fashioned Russian tradition, the government attacked the **Jews**, making it difficult, if not impossible, for those who wanted to leave to get to Israel or the west.

29.19 Brezhnev's Russia and the outside world

1 **Eastern Europe** remained united in the Warsaw Pact (29.7.6(i)) but there were two major signs of increased hostility to Russia:
i **Czechoslovakia** had its **'Dubček Spring'** in 1968 (30.11);
ii **Poland** remained, in 1984, an uneasy satellite (30.13–15).

2 **China** was increasingly opposed to Russia. Border clashes along the Manchurian border in 1969 typified this hostility.

3 **India** and **Pakistan** Russia remained more friendly to India than to the western-oriented Pakistan. But Kosygin and Brezhnev played a major rôle in settling the Indo-Pakistan dispute over **Kashmir** in 1965–66 (34.23.13).

4 **Vietnam** received Russian support in its struggle with the USA (35.15.3). When the USA had withdrawn from Vietnam in 1975 Russia supported **Vietnam's attack on Kampuchea** (35.20.3–4).

5 **Africa**
i Russia supported the **Cuban aid to Angola** (36.23.4–8);
ii Russian and Cuban troops were also active in the Eritrean war in the **Horn of Africa** (32.27.4);
iii Russia had always supported **Syria** in her campaign against Israel. In 1983–84 she continued to provide that support, which led to increased US involvement in the Lebanon (37.19).

6 **Afghanistan** had become a republic after a coup in July 1973. General Daoud's republican régime was overthrown by a Russian-supported Revolutionary Council in April 1978. However, this Council was not sufficiently submissive to Russia. On **Christmas Eve, 1979** there was a full-scale invasion by Russian troops. The then President was murdered and a Russian-appointed government installed. There are, in 1984, about 100 000 Russian troops in Afghanistan where they fight a guerilla war against anti-Russian rebels.

7 **Détente** See 29.20
8 **Helsinki** and **Human Rights** See 29.21

29.20 Russia, the USA and détente

1 **Definitions and misunderstandings**
i the **USA** and **Western idea** of détente is that it means:
(a) both East and West share **common interests**;
(b) **confidence** and **understanding** can be increased and improved;
(c) **arms controls** are essential;
(d) **trade agreements** can help build **links** between the two sides:
ii **the Russian idea** of détente is very different:
(a) Russia wants a **relaxation of tension** so that the risk of a global war can be lessened;
(b) in the more peaceful world, the **struggle between capitalist** and **communist systems** could then go on;
(c) **trade, cultural** and **other links** are, for the Russians, of **little real importance**–except where such links serve Russian self-interest. Such links provide Russia with US grain, German technology and an outlet for Russia's surplus of natural gas.

2 **Brezhnev, Nixon and détente, 1968–73**
i **1968** Johnson had signed the **Nuclear Non-Proliferation Treaty** (32.23.7);
ii **1969** in a speech on **Guam Island**, Nixon proclaimed what has become known as the **Nixon Doctrine**. This said that:
(a) the USA would continue to oppose communism;
(b) but the USA hoped that Asian states would learn to defend themselves.
This was much less ambitious than the earlier Truman (28.5) and Eisenhower (32.11) Doctrines;
iii **1971** Nixon supported **China's entry into the UN** (32.24.2 and 33.12.14);
iv **1971–72 Nixon visited China and Russia**, thereby making the contacts which helped détente on its way;
v Brezhnev and Nixon began the preliminary talks on **Strategic Arms Limitations Talks** (SALT)–see 29.20.3.

3 SALT–Mark 1, 1969–72

i both Russia and the USA were concerned at the **cost of the arms race;**

ii both were also aware of the **terribly destructive effects of modern weapons;**

iii both had achieved **Mutual Assured Destruction** (MAD) because the 2 countries each had sufficient weapons to wipe out the other–which would, however, have been given sufficient time to launch its own weapons before itself being destroyed;

iv **November 1969** saw the beginning of talks on limiting defensive anti-ballistic missiles;

v the talks were held at different times in **Vienna, Helsinki** and **Geneva** until some agreement was reached;

vi **May 1972** both countries signed a treaty by which they agreed to make **some reductions in anti-ballistic missile systems**–and to hold further talks (29.20.5).

4 Increased Russian confidence, 1970–80

i **1973–75** the USA finally withdrew from **Vietnam**–a Russian victory as far as the Russians were concerned;

ii from 1970, **Russia** achieved first equality and then **superiority** over the US in terms of **nuclear weapons;**

iii under Johnson, Nixon and Carter, the **USA appeared less willing to take a hard line** towards Russian aggression.

5 Brezhnev and Carter, 1976–80

i **Carter** appeared to be dominated by concern for **Israel** (32.27.7) and **Iran** (32.27.8);

ii he agreed to the continuation of the **second round of SALT negotiations:**

(a) these took place at **Vladivostok** and **Vienna;**

(b) **some agreement** was reached over the numbers and types of missiles possessed by the two Great Powers;

iii but the **US Senate refused to ratify the final Treaty** when it was debated late in 1979;

iv this was followed almost immediately by the **Russian invasion of Afghanistan** (29.19.6);

v **Carter's response** to the invasion was very weak:

(a) he insisted that US athletes should **boycott the Olympic Games, 1980,** which were held in Moscow;

(b) he invited other nations to do the same;

(c) he asked that there should be an **economic boycott** of Russia–while continuing to allow the export of US grain to Russia;

vi by 1980 there was an increasingly **anti-Russian feeling in the US.** This played some part in Carter's defeat in the Presidential Election, 1980 (32.27.8).

29.21 Helsinki and Human Rights

1 Willy Brandt's Ostpolitik

i Brandt became Chancellor of West Germany in 1969, after having been Foreign Minister from 1966;

ii he worked for an **easing of relations with Russia, East Germany** and **Eastern Europe** as a whole;

iii **1972** West Germany signed **Treaties with Poland and Russia** which accepted the existing Polish boundaries–and the loss of former German territory to Poland (30.2.1.viii);

iv he invited other Western countries to try to improve their relationships with the countries of the Eastern bloc.

2 The USA and Russia were, at the same time, having their own various talks (29.20.2–3), which helped Brandt's campaign for closer contacts between East and West.

3 The European Security Conference, 1973–5

i this conference took place in **Helsinki;**

ii the USA, Canada and 33 countries from Europe took part;

iii the talks opened in **July 1973** and the first stages were completed with the **Helsinki Agreement (August 1975):**

(a) this recognized the **frontiers** of eastern Europe, and Soviet dominance of that region;

(b) **West Germany gave up** its claim to be the only German state, so giving official recognition to **East Germany.**

(c) **Russia agreed** to give 21 days notice before holding military manoeuvres near another national border;

(d) **Russia promised** to help reunite **divided families** in Europe, to make life easier for **western journalists** working in the USSR and to encourage **more east-west visits;**

(e) Russia also seemed to agree to allow outside **inspection of her record in human rights.** This encouraged Russian dissidents to compile records of ill-treatment by the government (29.18.7);

(f) Russia agreed to buy US wheat and to export oil to the US. Business backed détente.

4 Belgrade, 1978

i at Helsinki the various powers agreed to meet again in 1978;

ii but this **second Conference was not a success;**

(a) the experience of the previous 3 years showed that there was **no common understanding** between East and West as to the **meaning of human rights** (29.18.7–8);

(b) the US complained at **Russian treatment of dissidents** (29.18.7);

(c) Russia complained that such intervention was a US attempt **to interfere in the domestic affairs of Russia** and her satellites;

(d) nothing was agreed at this Conference, except that a third Conference should be held in 1981;

(e) this series of meetings (or Conferences) ended in **July, 1983 with no further agreements.** While this is depressing, it indicates a more realistic attitude by western powers which appear to have allowed themselves to be too easily hoodwinked by Russia in 1975.

29.22 Mutual and Balanced Force Reduction (MBFR)

1 1973 There was, in general, an **optimistic atmosphere** at this time (29.21.2–4).

2 To take advantage of this hopeful climate a Conference was held at **Vienna in 1973.** Its object was to try to reach an agreement on the **reduction on the number of troops and weapons** held by both east and west in the various countries **in Central Europe.**

3 The Russians, harder-headed than the majority of western representatives, were **unwilling** to agree to any real reduction.

4 The immediate result was, therefore, that there was no agreement–other than to continue to hold similar talks.

5 1981 A fresh series of negotiations opened in **Geneva.**

6 By now the climate of opinion was very different from what it had been in 1973:

i **President Reagan** was in power in the USA. He had already decided to spend an increasing amount of money on national defence;

ii **many European leaders,** including Mrs Thatcher of Britain and Schmidt of West Germany, had realized that, if the American drift to arms' reduction (evident under Nixon and Carter) was ever put into effect, then Europe would be helpless in the face of a Russian attack. This fear made them anxious to ensure that either there were to be genuinely mutual and balanced reductions (to which the Russians wouldn't agree) or that there would be a European system capable of standing up to the Russians;

iii Reagan's hard-line coincided with European fears;

iv he made available, and many European countries willingly accepted, US missiles–**Pershing 2 and Cruise** in particular;

v in spite of the remarkable growth of a European-wide movement such as the British **Campaign for Nuclear Disarmament,** governments in France, Germany, Italy and Britain accepted these weapons. In 1984 the Pershings and Cruise missiles are now installed and ready-armed.

7 In the face of this development the **Russians**:

i **offered a reduction** in their weapons, if the Europeans would agree not to have the new missiles installed;

ii insisted that the new systems would force them **to increase the number of Russian missiles** targeted on western Europe and so increase the risk of war.

8 The Nato powers (28.10) offered a **'zero option'** under which both sides would dismantle all their long-range theatre (i.e. short range and not inter-continental missiles).

7 The Russians rejected this as unrealistic.

8 The result, in **1984 is a stalemate**. The Russians have, however, come back to the negotiating table–from which they had walked away when Pershings and Cruise missiles arrived in Europe.

9 Only the future will tell whether the MBFR talks come to any meaningful conclusion.

30 Eastern Europe, 1945–83

30.1 The questions to be asked

1 How, and over **which countries**, did Russia extend its control?

2 Why did Russia wish to have **this satellite 'empire'**?

3 How, and where, has **anti-Russian feeling** been expressed?

4 How did Russia deal with this 'nationalist' development?

30.2 Which nations were 'taken over', 1945–46?

1 Poland

i **Autumn 1939** Poland's pre-war leaders set up a Free Polish government-in-exile (London). Many Poles got to the west (some via Russia) to fight for the Allies;

ii Polish resistance fighters formed the **Home Army**. Their loyalty was to the government-in-exile in London;

iii **after 1941** Stalin sent agents to help to organize resistance by a Polish Workers' Party loyal to Russia;

iv **Katyn** Before the Russians were driven from Poland **(December 1941)** they massacred 4 000 Polish army officers who might have led post-war opposition to Communism in Poland;

v **1944** the Russian army re-crossed the Polish border;

vi **the nationalist Home Army rose in revolt in Warsaw**. The Red Army waited for the Germans to destroy the nationalists before it defeated the Germans;

vii **a National Council of the Homeland** was set up by Stalin's agents, 1 January 1944. On **31 December 1944** this communist organization decided:

(a) its **National Committee of Liberation** would form the post-war government of Poland;

(b) its chairman (Bierut, educated in Russia and head of the Polish section of the NKVD since 1936) was to be the **new President**;

viii **Yalta, February 1945**. It was agreed that:

(a) the Polish borders would be changed. In the west Poland would be pushed **westwards to the line of the Oder-Neisse rivers**. This gave Poland what had been **German Silesia. In the east**, the Poles would give up some of their **territory to Russia**;

(b) Poland was to have a **'free and independent government'** which would include members of the **Free Polish government-in-exile**:

ix **March 1945 Stalin** invited 16 leaders of the nationalist **Home Army** to visit Moscow–and then put them in **prison**;

x **Stalin refused to honour his Yalta promises**. Poland did not have the 'free and unfettered election' agreed on. A Russian controlled communist government was imposed on Poland.

2 Romania, Bulgaria and Hungary

i These were treated as **defeated countries**, former 'allies' of Hitler's Germany;

ii they were conquered by the **Red Army**, welcomed by local people as **'liberators'** freeing them from rule by the hated Germans;

iii **the Russians set up governments** in each country:

(a) Stalin borrowed a phrase from **Tito** (30.6) and called these governments **People's Democracies**.

(b) Socialists, leaders of Peasants parties and communists formed **coalitions** in Popular Front governments:

iv **some communists** hoped that this gave them a chance to form a **nationalist form of communism. Gomulka of Poland** said 'Our democracy is not similar to the Soviet system';

v **Gomulka and others were wrong**. The Red Army brought:

(a) agents of the **Agitrop Brigade** to spread communist propaganda in the newly liberated countries;

(b) agents of the **NKVD** to recruit local agents for a local secret police;

vi within a short time the **communists abandoned their socialist and Peasants' Party allies**. Some were imprisoned, others kept under house arrest;

vii the Bulgarian Communist leader, **Dimitrov**, showed the intention of the Stalinist agents when he said: 'The Soviet régime and the Popular Democratic Régimes are two forms of one and the same system.' They were **neither Popular** (they had not been elected) **nor Democratic** (they used all the trappings of **Stalinist autocracy** to keep themselves in power).

3 Albania and Yugoslavia In these countries Communist partisans had freed themselves from German occupation with little or no help from the Russians. In both, the communist leaders set up People's Democracy-form governments–but without the burden of Russian agents always behind them.

30.3 Why did Russia want a 'satellite' empire?

1 Western belief Western leaders were angered at the extent of Russian control over Eastern Europe. Churchill's 'iron curtain' references indicate western thinking (28.2.3). They were led to:

i fear further **Russian expansion**–

(a) into **Western Europe**. The crises over **Czechoslovakia** (28.7) and **Berlin** (28.9) proved their points;

(b) into **Asia**. The war in **Korea** (28.11) and Russian-inspired revolutions in **Malaya** (35.5.3) and **Indonesia** (35.3.9) proved the case;

ii think up means of **halting this expansion**. The **'Truman Doctrine'** (28.5) and the formation of **NATO** (28.10) were attempts to halt Russia.

2 Stalin claimed that Russian control of Eastern Europe was essential to Russia's own safety:

i **the Western allies** had aided the **Whites** during the Civil War after 1919 (10.25). The American decision to feed the starving Germans and to **rebuild West Germany** were, to Stalin, proofs of western hopes of launching fresh attacks on the Soviet Union;

ii the Communist-controlled Eastern Europe would provide a **buffer between Russia and this 'expansionist' west**.

3 Russia had been devastated by the war; its economy and agriculture lay in ruins. Stalin intended to use the **resources of**

the satellites to rebuild Russia, so that, in his terms, global communism would be protected.

30.4 Giving form to the Russian control, 1947

1 The west showed its opposition to Russia by:
i the announcement of the **'Truman Doctrine'** (28.5);
ii the declaration of the **Marshall Plan** (28.6).

2 Stalin called all Communist leaders to Warsaw, 1947 to set up the **Communist Information Bureau (Cominform)**.

3 Zhdanov, speaking for Stalin, said that the Truman Doctrine and the Marshall Plan were **twin parts of the American policy** of putting Europe under American control. Cominform would rally not only the Communist states of Eastern Europe; it would also rally the support of communists in western Europe, Vietnam, Indonesia, Egypt and Syria.

4 October 1947 The US Assistant Secretary of State said that the formation of Cominform was 'a deadly serious challenge to the free peoples of Europe and the USA which would have to be met.'

30.5 Extending Communist control, 1947–51

1 Poland
i **1947 The People's Party** (representing the peasants) was **suppressed**. Other political parties were broken up. A National Front of the Workers Party (communist controlled) was the only party allowed to function;

ii **purges**. Some Polish Communists were more Polish than Communist. Stalin's agents expelled **75 000** from the Party;

iii **1948 Gomulka**, Stalin's First Secretary of the Polish Communist Party, had to resign. He was 'too Polish' (30.2.2.iv);

iv **1951 Gomulka** was arrested and imprisoned;

v **the Catholic Church** had the support of about 90 per cent of the Polish people. The uneasy 'peace' between the Church and the government ended in 1951 when the government abolished papal control of the dioceses in the areas taken from Germany (30.2.1.viii). **Cardinal Wyszynski**, head of the Polish church, was **arrested** in September 1953 and not released until October 1956.

2 Hungary
i **1945** A Coalition government was set up and the leader of the Small Farmers' Party became Prime Minister;

ii **1947** All non-Communist members of that government were attacked by Stalin-like purges organized by the Communists. **Imre Nagy**, the then Prime Minister, resigned;

iii **1947** The **elections** gave the Communists a majority of the votes although there was a 35 per cent anti-Communist vote. The Communists put pressure on the non-Communist parties;

iv **1949 In the fresh elections** there was a list of candidates and voters could either support or reject the list. Ninety per cent voted for the Communist-inspired list;

v **The Catholic Church** Russian troops were stationed in Hungary and political trials and purges were frequent. **Cardinal Mindszenty** led the anti-government campaign in defence of Church schools and against the closure of Catholic papers and organizations. He was arrested, tortured, put on trial and imprisoned. The government set up a **National Church**, independent of the Pope and under Communist control.

3 Czechoslovakia came under Communist control in 1948 (28.7).

30.6 Tito, a Communist rebel

1 Tito's career (a popular examination question):
i born 1890, of peasant stock, first worked as a farm labourer;

ii after First World War he became a Communist; frequently visited Moscow;

iii 1928: he was arrested in Zagreb. After release he went to Moscow and attended the Lenin School for two years;

iv 1934: he became a member of the Yugoslav Politburo and in 1937 General Secretary of the Yugoslav Communist Party;

v he dissolved the Party, ordered all members to re-register and ensured that his supporters formed the leadership;

vi during the War he organized resistance to the Nazis. The conquering Germans divided Yugoslavia into:
(a) a nominally independent Croatia which was Catholic and industrialized and contained the major city of Zagreb;
(b) an occupied zone, Slovenia, around the major city of Ljubljana. Here, too, the people were mainly Catholic;
(c) an occupied zone, Serbia, an agricultural area; the majority were either Orthodox Christians or Muslims;

vii Tito recruited his partisans from peoples of all the regions and all the religions. He had to fight not only the Germans but also another resistance movement led by General Mihailovitch. Mihailovitch's movement was entirely Serb and spent a good deal of time fighting Tito's communists – even collaborating with the Germans for that purpose;

viii by 1944 Tito had become the undisputed leader of the anti-German movement, getting aid from the western allies as they advanced through Italy;

ix Stalin wanted a return of the Yugoslav monarchy driven into exile by Hitler. He gave no support to Tito;

x in 1945 Tito headed a Communist government. But he had not been brought to power by Russian 'liberators'. He was independent.

2 Tito's break with Stalin
i In 1945 Tito held elections, abolished the monarchy and set up the Federal People's Republic of Yugoslavia;

ii his constitution was based on the 1936 Stalin constitution. He had his own secret police, purged critics and imprisoned dissidents. In this way he was very much a Communist hard-liner;

iii but he refused to obey Stalin's orders. He would not allow the resources of his country to be used as Stalin wished;

iv 28 June 1948, Stalin ordered the Cominform (30.4.2) to expel Tito because he was not willing to make Yugoslavia 'a Russian colony'.

3 After the break
i Russia ordered the Cominform to break all trade relations with Yugoslavia and she stopped sending economic aid;

ii Tito made trade treaties with western countries and received economic aid from Britain, France and the USA;

iii in 1953 he made a state visit to Britain, the only Communist leader to feel free enough to do so.

30.7 Stalin's attack on 'Titoism'

1 Stalin was afraid that others might follow Tito and find 'a national road to socialism'.

2 He rid himself of most of the very men whom he had appointed to head the governments of his satellites:
i **Dimitrov (Bulgaria)** died in suspicious circumstances in 1949;

ii **Gomulka (Poland)** and **Dej (Romania)** were dismissed from their posts of First Secretaries of their local Parties;

iii **Anna Pauker (Romania), Rajk (Hungary), Slansky** and **Clementis (both Czechoslovakia)** were all executed by the MVD between 1949 and 1952;

iv **Prime Minister Nagy (Hungary)** was on holiday in Switzerland. He resigned by 'phone.

3 All these former leaders were replaced by lesser-known Russian nominees and trusted Stalinists.

30.8 Giving form to Russia's economic control, 1949

1 The Marshall Plan had led to the formation of **OEEC** (28.5.5-6).

2 Stalin set up the Council for Mutual Economic Assistance (**COMECON**).

3 Russia provided technical and industrial **aid** to its satellites to help them to develop their economies.

4 But these economies had to be run to **benefit Russia's own development**, supplying the 'mother country' with the materials which she most needed.

30.9 1953: The first anti-Russian risings

1 March 1953 Stalin and the Stalinist leader of Czechoslovakia died at about the same time.

2 These deaths were the signal for a series of anti-Russian risings in Eastern Europe.

3 East Germany

i the People's Democratic Republic was set up in 1949;

ii a Stalinist, **Ulbricht**, headed the government;

iii Russia took material and machinery worth **£7 billion** to help in its own rebuilding. **East Germany remained much poorer** than West Germany which was helped by Marshall Aid;

iv **wages** were very low while prices rose; each month a flood of refugees fled to the west;

v **May 1953**, the government announced that while wages would remain the same, **every worker had to produce 10 per cent more** than in the previous year;

vi **16 June 1953**, **building workers** went on strike. In the evening a mass of workers marched through the streets of East Berlin demanding 'bread and freedom';

vii **17 June 1953**, over **100 000 people** crowded the streets of East Berlin demanding freedom and improved living standards;

viii **the government's response:**

(a) **military police** were sent to disperse the crowds;

(b) when they failed, **Russian tanks** were brought out. By nightfall the streets were cleared;

ix but during the next 2 days there were anti-Communist demonstrations in over 300 villages and towns. Prisons were attacked and people released;

x but within a few days the power of the Russian-supported **army and police restored order**. East Germany sank back under the rule of its unpopular government.

4 Czechoslovakia Workers in the **Skoda factory** in **Pilsen** rioted and demanded freedom and better living standards. But they were quickly crushed.

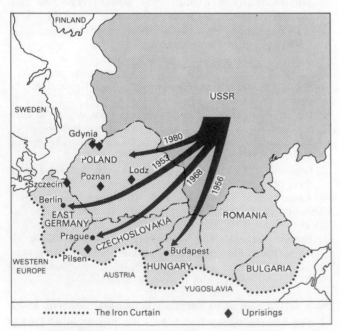

·········· The Iron Curtain   ♦ Uprisings

Fig. 30.9A 'Colonial' revolutions against Russia

30.10 1956: A more serious uprising

1 Khrushchev's condemnation of Stalin (29.8.3) led to 2 serious challenges to Russian control of Eastern Europe.

2 Poland

i **28th June 1956** Car workers at **Posnam** went on strike for better wages and living conditions;

ii this strike, which gathered increasing support, quickly became a **political demonstration**;

iii the crowds in various towns chanted **anti-Russian and anti-Party slogans**;

iv **pitched battles** were fought with police, troops and tanks; 60 people died;

v the Russians were forced to make some **concessions**:

(a) Gomulka was restored as Party Secretary (30.2.iv and 30.7.2);

(b) he was allowed to follow a **more 'liberal' line**:

iv but Gomulka was careful not to break with Russia over foreign policy as laid down by the Warsaw pact (29.7.6).

3 Hungary

i news of the Polish rising led to a similar rising in Hungary. The Hungarians, traditionally anti-Russian, **demanded**:

(a) a **better standard of living**;

(b) an **end to the rule by Rakósi**, the Party Secretary who had tied Hungary to Russia economically and politically;

(c) the **abolition of the secret police** which terrorized the people:

ii **July 1956** The Russians deposed Rakósi, hoping that this would be enough to satisfy the Hungarians;

iii news that **Gomulka** was back in power in Poland led to Hungarian demands that **Imre Nagy** should be appointed Prime Minister;

iv students demonstrated in **Budapest** in favour of **Nagy**. **Party Secretary Gero** agreed to his appointment;

v Nagy announced **negotiations** to get the Russians out of Hungary;

vi **26 October 1956** Russian tanks and troops **left Budapest** where they had killed over 600 people;

vii **new freedoms** were given to press, radio and television; politicians were allowed to form non-Communist parties;

viii **statues of Stalin** were smashed; hundreds of **secret police** were lynched;

ix **Nagy** announced that Hungary was going to **withdraw from the Warsaw Pact** and would become a 'neutralist' state with no allegiance to East or West;

x **the Russians** then sent their troops and tanks back into Budapest to crush the revolution:

(a) **4 November** Budapest was bombed from the **air**;

(b) **artillery and tanks** fired on the rebel-held radio stations, newspaper offices and university;

(c) **20 000 Hungarians** were killed in ten days;

(d) **200 000 Hungarians** fled to Austria:

xi **Nagy** took refuge in the **Yugoslav Embassy** in Budapest. When all resistance was over he and his colleagues surrendered to the government of **János Kádár** who had come back with the Russian tanks;

xii **Kádár promised Nagy his freedom**. But he was kidnapped, taken to Russia and **executed in 1958**. Khrushchev had a Stalinist-like attitude towards some dissidents.

30.11 1968: Czechoslovakia's 'Communism with a human face'

1 In **1953** there was a small rising in **Pilsen** (30.9.4).

2 In **1956**, in the wake of the Twentieth Party Congress, Gottwald's policies were denounced and political prisoners freed.

3 But under the hard-line **President Novotny**, Czechoslovakia continued to be a Stalinist-like state.

4 In **1967 Dubček** became Party Secretary. He took a 'liberal' line towards:

i workers' demands for an increased supply of **consumer goods**;

ii intellectuals' demands for **greater freedom** of expression and an **end to censorship**.

5 January 1968 Novotny was forced to resign. The new President **Svoboda**, co-operated with Dubček to bring in major reforms:

i public meetings were allowed;

ii political parties could be formed;

iii press censorship was abolished;

iv local assemblies in Bohemia and Slovakia were given greater powers;

v political prisoners were released;

vi travel outside the country was allowed;

vii the activities of the secret police were limited.

6 Dubček began negotiating a treaty with West Germany.

7 The Russians then took action:

i **20 August 1968** Russian troops and tanks, supported by forces from **all the Warsaw Pact countries** invaded Czechoslovakia;

ii they entered all the main cities and quickly took control;

iii resistance, particularly in Prague, was strong–but of little value against the tanks and troops.

9 Dubček was arrested and taken to Moscow.

10 President Svoboda refused to negotiate with the Russians without Dubček.

11 Both 'liberals' then negotiated with the Russians who forced the Czechs to give up most of their reforms and to allow Russian troops to stay in Czechoslovakia.

12 Dubček's men were removed from office. In 1970 an anti-Dubček government, **under Husak**, was in power.

30.12 Romania: a special case

1 1941 A pro-Nazi government was in power.

2 1944 Romania was 'liberated' by the Red Army and Communist-dominated government installed in power.

3 Between 1949 and 1952 the Romanian Communist Party was purged by Stalin's agents. **Anna Pauker**, party leader, was executed.

4 The economy was run in Russia's interests until 1956 when Khrushchev abolished a series of trade agreements inside the Warsaw Pact countries. **Romania's leaders** rejected the 'inferior' position which Russia wished Romania to occupy under COMECON's plans. They **would not agree to abandon some industries** which might operate more cheaply elsewhere inside COMECON countries.

4 1963 Romania carried this independent attitude to a **Titoist extreme** by signing a trade treaty with the USA.

5 In the 1970s Russia wanted the Warsaw Pact countries to agree to an extension of that Pact to include countries in the Far East such as Vietnam. This would have involved Eastern European forces in **Russia's quarrel with China**. **Romania led the opposition** to this suggestion.

6 But Romania still follows, internally, an authoritarian, almost Stalin-like policy. It is only in its relations with Russia that she appears to be 'liberal'.

30.13 1970: Poland again

1 In 1970 the Russians could congratulate themselves on the removal of Dubček from power in Czechoslovakia.

2 But in that year Poland became a centre of discontent.

3 Younger people were dissatisfied with the crushing burden of bureaucracy and officialdom.

4 Even the controlled Press demanded more freedom.

5 The economy was in a poor condition:

i state planning led to the production of goods for which there was no demand. There was, on the other hand, a **serious shortage of everyday goods**;

ii **low agricultural production** led to the need to import food from Russia, Canada, the USA and West Germany. Food shortages and rationing were commonplace;

iii **government revenue** did not meet government's costs.

6 December 1970 The government announced **price rises in food, fuel and clothing** ranging from 8 to 60 per cent.

7 This led to **widespread rioting**.

(a) December 15 Rioters set fire to the Party headquarters at **Gdansk**;

(b) rioting spread to other industrial centres;

(c) heavy fighting took place with police and the army.

8 Gomulka was replaced by Gierek.

9 He **cancelled** many of the **recent decisions**:

i **food prices** were frozen for 2 years;

ii **large wage increases** were ordered for the lower-paid;

iii he toured the country inviting discussions of the faults of Polish society.

10 The Church played an active role in these discussions, denouncing methods used by hard-liners to put down discontent. It also demanded democratic freedom of discussion in the press and throughout the country.

30.14 Gierek's government in Poland, 1971–8

1 Younger and more democratic people were given positions in state organizations–many of them not even being Party members.

2 Industry was given more freedom; productivity improved.

3 Western firms were allowed to open factories in Poland while Polish firms borrowed western capital to help their development.

4 1973 Real wages rose by 24 per cent, industrial production by 33 per cent and agricultural production by 19 per cent.

5 1976 The government tried, again, to increase basic prices. This led to widespread resistance and the government was forced to modify its demands.

6 October 1978 Cardinal Wojtyla, Archbishop of Cracow, was elected Pope of the Catholic Church. He took the name of **Pope John Paul II**.

30.15 Poland, Catholic or Communist?

1 In May 1935 Laval of France asked Stalin to allow more freedom for Catholics living in Russia. This, said Laval, would please the Pope. Stalin's reply was: **'The Pope! How many divisions has he got?'**.

2 In various parts of the world the Catholic Church has emerged as a centre of opposition to tyranny.

3 This has been clear in Poland since 1978.

4 The election of Pope John Paul II led to the formation of a number of free trade unions by Polish workers under the general heading of **SOLIDARITY**.

5 It was the SOLIDARITY movement which led the campaigns for freedom, better wages and working conditions in Poland since 1978.

6 This created a **series of problems** for the Polish and Russian governments:

i how far could **democratic freedom** (of press, trade unions and expression) be allowed by a totalitarian system?

ii how far could a Communist government go in allowing the powerful **Catholic Church** to have the freedoms it demanded– to preach, teach in its own schools and universities and to have its own uncensored newspapers?

7 When the demands of some extremists in SOLIDARITY showed that Poles might be led to demand **free elections and freedom to form non-Communist political parties** the Russians intervened. Marshal Jaruzelski was appointed as head of government; martial law imposed; SOLIDARITY leaders arrested or driven into hiding; SOLIDARITY banned.

8 In 1984 the position in Poland was unclear. Former SOLIDARITY head, Lech Walesa is free and allowed to return to his workplace in the Gdansk dockyard. But

SOLIDARITY has not been re-established in spite of Church demands. Only the future will tell what is to happen in Poland. In November 1983, the government announced that, in the New Year (1984) food prices would have to be increased. It was such increases which had led to rioting in 1970 (30.13.6-7) and in 1976 (30.14.6). It is important to note that, in November 1983, the government promised that there would be 'more consultations' before the price rises are finalized in 1984. Some may think that this shows that the government has learnt a lesson from the unrest led by SOLIDARITY; some may think that 'more consultations' will prove to be worth nothing.

30.16 A national 'step-by-step' throughout the period

1 In this complicated Unit, we have followed developments year-by-year. This was necessary, because, as we have seen, developments in one country had their impacts on other countries.

2 However, examiners sometimes ask students to give an account of developments in ONE country throughout the period. For that reason and to help students find their way around the Unit, here is a check list of references which will help follow the changes that took place in the various countries:

  i **Poland**; see 30.2.1; 30.5.1; 30.7.2; 30.10.2; 30.13-15;
  ii **Romania**; see 30.2.2; 30.7.2; 30.12;
  iii **Hungary**; see 30.2.2; 30.5.2; 30.10.3;
  iv **Bulgaria**; see 30.2.2; 30.7.2;
  v **Albania**; see 30.2.3;
  vi **Yugoslavia**; see 30.2.3; 30.6;
  vii **East Germany**; see 29.11.6-10; 30.9;
  viii **Czechoslovakia**; see 28.7; 30.11.

31 Western Europe Since 1945

31.1 The issues to be studied

1 **European unity**
2 **German recovery**

3 The growth of **friendship** between France and Germany which owed much to the work of **Adenauer of Germany** and **de Gaulle of France**.

31.2 Why should European countries come closer together, 1945?

1 In 1939 Europe was the centre of the world's affairs. In 1945 it was a devastated no-man's land between two super powers:
  i there were 25 million people living in refugee camps, or cellars of bombed out buildings;
  ii commerce, industry and transport had been almost destroyed.
2 No country could re-build on its own. Europe had to develop as 'the European family' as Churchill said.
3 Europe had only 2 per cent of the world's land surface. But it had 10 per cent of the world's population which was:
  i the most literate;
  ii the most experienced in trade and industry;
  iii from a common cultural background.

4 The various states could form the richest and most powerful **bloc** in the world. However, without unity Europe would become just a collection of semi-important states squeezed between Russia and the USA.

31.3 A military and defence path towards closer unity

1 **1947** Britain and France signed the **Treaty of Dunkirk**, aimed against the revival of German power.
2 **March 1948** The Dunkirk powers were joined by the Benelux countries in the **Treaty of Brussels** against Germany and Russia.
3 **April 1949** The 5 Brussels powers allied with 7 other nations to form **NATO** (28.10.5). For those seeking to bring about 'a United States of Europe', the formation of NATO was an important step:
  i the alliance had a close **political structure**;
  ii its members put part of their national forces under international commands. Each country gave up part of its sovereignty to a **supra-national (or above nation) authority**.
4 **1952 The European Defence Community**
  i **May 1949** The German Federal Republic was set up (28.8.13);
  ii by **1952** the West Germans were rebuilding their economy. For European statesmen this raised some problems:
  (a) was an increasingly rich Germany to be **excluded** from contributing to the cost of Europe's defence against Russia?
  (b) could Germany be allowed to **re-arm** on part of that contribution towards Europe's defence?
  iii **French fears** of Germany led them to oppose German rearmament;
  iv in **1951** Pléven of France, proposed the formation of a **European army**, including German troops. Britain refused to pool her forces in this international army. Because of the British refusal, the French vetoed their own plan, fearing Germany might become the dominant power in a non-British European army;
  v the **European Defence Community**, which might have provided a major push towards closer unity, did not live up to expectations. Britain, for her own reasons, and France, for her own reasons, were still hesitant about European unity.
5 **1954 The Western European Union** This alliance of Britain, France, West Germany and the Benelux states allowed Germany to become a member of NATO and to control her own conventional weapons. This showed that the various nations could work together; Germany could become part of a 'United Europe'.

31.4 An economic road towards closer unity

1 Until **1947** aid to Europe was provided by UNRRA (28.6.1).
2 In **1947** the **Marshall Plan** was proposed (28.6.3–8).
3 **1948** 16 countries set up the **OEEC** (28.6.5) with West Germany as an associate member. For those seeking 'a United States of Europe' the formation of OEEC was an important step:
  i it had a **permanent administrative staff** and a number of specialist advisory committees to deal with **co-operation** in trade, agricultural, power supplies, fisheries and transport;
  ii it distributed the billions of dollars of aid and helped bring about the **economic rebirth** which could not have been achieved by individual countries working alone.

4 But the OEEC was **limited by national sovereignty**. Each decision by OEEC had to be approved by the individual governments.

31.5 A political path towards closer unity

1 **1945 Britain** was economically and politically, the most

important of the European states. Never conquered, she had, for a time, stood alone against Hitler, provided a home for governments-in-exile and aid to resistance movements.

2 Churchill, even after July 1945, was accepted as the most important European statesman.

3 1946 At Zurich, Churchill called for the re-creation of 'the European family . . . with a structure under which it can dwell . . . a **kind of United States of Europe**.'

4 May 1948 Political leaders from 10 European states met at the Hague and produced a plan for a **European parliament**. Many wanted this to be a true parliament, its members elected directly by the people. But in 1948 Britain, in particular, was unwilling to see the creation of such an important body. What powers might it demand? Would it become a too powerful rival for the national parliaments? Would it lead to the creation of a European Cabinet, a government of Europe?

5 The Council of Europe was the weak result
i members were appointed by **national parliaments**;
ii it met **3 or 4 times a year** at Strasbourg;
iii but it had **no powers** to propose legislation; power remained with the individual parliaments;
iv this made it little more than a **debating society**.

6 Britain, France, the Benelux countries, Norway, Denmark, Sweden, Italy and Eire were the original members of the Council. Later Greece, Turkey, Iceland, Austria, Cyprus and West Germany joined.

31.6 The functionalist road to unity

1 Those who believed in European unity were disappointed with the failure to unite the continent.

2 However they could point to some successful attempts at closer unity:

i **1944** The exiled governments of Belgium, the Netherlands (Holland) and Luxemburg agreed to form a customs union, **Benelux**. This came into being in **1947**. It started by being an agreement on **tariffs**; it went on to develop closer **economic integration** between the three states. In **1960** they set up the **Economic Union** allowing the free movement of people, capital and goods between the three states. People of three countries could live almost as one to get the benefits of economic unity;

ii **1948 OEEC** showed that **economic benefits** brought states together.

3 Leaders from several countries saw that unity might be achieved by joining the nations in an ever-increasing number of specialist organizations. This **functionalist** approach was advocated by **Monnet** of France ('the father of the Common Market'), **Spaak** (Belgium), **Adenauer** (Germany) and **de Gasperi** (Italy).

4 The first successful project took its name from the French Minister who first proposed it—**Robert Schuman**.

31.7 The Schuman Plan, 1950

1 Schuman proposed that **France and Germany** should pool their resources in **coal and steel** under a joint authority independent of the governments of both countries.

2 Other nations could be invited to join.

3 France would benefit. She could allow the development of the great industrial areas of the Ruhr and the Saar, without fearing that they would supply arms against France as they had done in the past.

4 Europe would benefit. The larger coal and steel industries of the 'community' would be more efficient. The larger market would encourage the use of the most up to date methods; larger, more efficient units could be created and the inefficient forced to modernize or to go out of business.

5 Schuman hoped that Britain would join; she was the largest coal producer in Europe and the second largest producer of steel. But **Britain was afraid** of the powers to be given to the

controlling commission (31.8.2). In 1951 a **Labour** government rejected an invitation to the discussions; in 1952 **Conservatives**, under Churchill, the 'great European', refused to join the new community which came into being in July 1952.

31.8 The European Coal and Steel Community (ECSC)

1 France, Italy, West Germany and the Benelux countries were the members of this community.

2 The High Authority was at the head of the Community:
i its **9 experts** were appointed by the 6 governments for a period of 6 years;
ii once appointed they were **not responsible to the governments** as ministers would be. They had to think as 'members of a Community' and not as Germans, Frenchmen.

3 A permanent secretariat administered the Authority's orders.

4 A Court of Justice of 7 international lawyers was set up as a Court of Appeal against decisions of the Authority.

5 A Consultative Assembly was made up of the representatives of the 6 countries at the Council of Europe. This could hand on recommendations to the Authority. It could also dismiss the Authority—by a two-thirds majority.

6 A Consultative Committee of 51 delegates of employers and workers in heavy industry would represent their interests to the High Authority.

31.9 The significance and success of the ECSC

1 The High Authority was a major innovation:
i it had **real international control**. Each member-state of the Community handed over to the Authority its sovereign right to control its coal and steel industries;
ii the Authority had the **right to interfere** in the economic life of the countries involved:

(a) it could **close down** a section of an industry in one state and **spend money** on the development of a section in another. It would be guided not by national but by **Community interests**;

(b) it could rule as illegal the subsidy given to the coal or steel industry of a member government if it gave the industry of the state involved an unfair advantage;

iii the Authority had its **own income** from dues paid to it by the industries involved, not by the governments.

2 Foreign and Economic Ministers from the member-states were forced to consult and work closely with the Authority. **Their Council of Ministers** could not block Authority decisions.

3 Jean Monnet was the Authority's first chairman.

4 The success of the Community was very evident:
i it stimulated **output** in steel;
ii it helped old-fashioned firms to **modernize**;
iii it widened its scope to take into account the **housing** and **social security** for workers in the heavy industries. As men moved freely across national boundaries there had to be supra-national decisions about housing and welfare benefits.

5 Until 1956 the Authority stimulated coal output to meet growing demand. In 1956 coal was hit by competition from cheap oil and natural gas. The Authority lessened the hardship that the fall in coal production caused. It provided **aid to depressed areas** affected by the closure of uneconomic pits.

31.10 Euratom

1 Russia and the USA could afford the high costs of nuclear research. No independent European country could.

2 Only through co-operative action could European countries keep pace with the super powers.

3 Britain was the most advanced European state in this field. But, as with the ECSC, Britain refused to co-operate with Europe.

4 1957 The 6 members of the ECSC set up the **European Atomic Energy Community** (Euratom). This was a High Authority on the ECSC model. It had powers to:
 i hold **stocks** of fissile material;
 ii set up **reactors**;
 iii promote research into the peaceful uses of atomic power.
5 This Authority was advised by:
 i a Council of Ministers;
 ii a scientific and technical committee;
 iii a social and economic committee.

31.11 Konrad Adenauer and the German 'economic miracle'

1 Born in **1876** he became a lawyer in Cologne.

2 He was **Lord Mayor of Cologne, 1917–33**, a member of the Catholic Centre Party, but was dismissed by the Nazis when Hitler came to power (15.21.6).

3 He made little secret of his dislike of the **Nazis**. He was **imprisoned** for short periods in 1933 and 1944 when he was sent to a **concentration camp**.

4 1945 He became **Lord Mayor of Cologne** after Germany's defeat.

5 1946 The Allied Military Government dismissed him.

6 The Christian Democratic Union He was a founder-member of this conservative party and its president, in the British zone, 1946–48.

7 1948–49 He represented North Rhine Westphalia in the parliamentary council of the 3 western zones and was **president** of the council for most of this period.

8 1949 The western Allies created the **Federal Republic** (28.8.13).

9 August 1949 In the elections Adenauer's party won the most seats in the **Bundestag**. He formed a **coalition** with other conservative parties, the main one being the **Christian Social Union**. The CDU-CSU coalition provided a strong and stable government. The opposition was led by the Social Democrats.

10 Adeneur's aims
 i to create a **stable and democratic Germany**, no easy task:
(a) Germany had had very **little experience of democracy**. There was no guarantee that Adenauer would be more successful than the politicians of Weimar had been after 1919;
(b) the majority of adult Germans had **co-operated with the Nazis**; many had been actively working for them. There was no guarantee that they would co-operate with a less exciting form of government:
 ii **to restore Germany economy** so that the people could enjoy a decent standard of living. This was no easy task in war-devastated Germany where the **millions of homeless** were increased by the **flow of refugees** from the east. In 1949 there were some **15 million unemployed** in West Germany. To get these back to work would call for 'a miracle';
 iii **to get Germany accepted** in the concert of powers': this was no easy task with the **memories of the war** still fresh and with the truth about **concentration camps** and the slaughter of **6 million Jews** becoming clearer as time went on;
 iv **to re-unite divided Germany**;
 v **to end the traditional hostility between France and Germany**, a difficult task following the war in which the French has suffered conquest and occupation.

11 Political stability
 i **extremist parties were banned**. A Nazi-style Socialist Reich Party had recruited many ex-Nazis. Adenauer abolished this and similar parties;
 ii **Werner Naumann** recruited ex-soldiers into a **Freikorps**; he was **arrested** and his organization made **illegal**;
 iii **1956 the Communist Party was banned**;
 iv he pushed through an **electoral law**; no party could gain seats in the Bundestag unless it had 5 per cent of the national vote. This prevented the rise of a mass of local parties.

12 Democratic
 i some of Adenauer's actions appeared to be autocratic. Was it 'democratic' to make extremist parties illegal?
 ii but he argued that he had to avoid the mistakes of the Weimar Republic. This democracy had been overthrown because it could not produce a stable government.

13 The German economy and the 'economic miracle'
 i **evidence of success**: Adenauer's government supervised the **rebuilding** of Germany. Work was found for the **unemployed**, for **refugees** from the east. In the 1960s Germany faced a labour shortage. **Foreign workers**, many from Turkey, were drawn to work in prosperous Germany;
 ii **reasons for success:**
(a) allied investments, particularly **Marshall Aid**, provided the stimulus to the rebuilding of West Germany;
(b) wartime destruction created the need for **new building**– industrially and commercially. The West Germans therefore had the most modern and efficient industry;
(c) the Minister for Economic Affairs, Erhard, supervised the 'economic miracle'. **Low interest rates** stimulated investment; **government aid** was provided to ensure industrial, commercial and social **investment** (e.g. schools and universities);
(d) German workers had a tradition for hard work. They helped German recovery by **good labour relations** and willingness to accept **low wage increases** negotiated by their industrial unions;
(e) for several years the Germans spent **little on armaments**. This released resources for industrial investment:
 iii **enjoying the miracle**
By 1963, when Adenauer retired, the **German standard of living** was the highest in Europe. West Germany and Britain have roughly the same population. By 1963 Germany was building twice as many houses as Britain. Germans had higher wages, shorter working hours, higher pensions, better social benefits and longer holidays than British workers.

14 Getting Germany accepted Adenauer ensured German participation in
 i Nato (28.10);
 ii OECC (28.6.5);
 iii ECSC (31.8);
 iv EDC (31.3.4);
 v EURATOM (31.10);
 vi EEC (31.12).
He lost some support, particularly among trade unionists when, in 1957, he insisted on military conscription, the result of German participation in European defence arrangements.

15 To re-unite Germany
 i in 1955 he visited Moscow and arranged for the repatriation of German prisoners still held in the Soviet Union;
 ii as Foreign Minister (as well as Chancellor) until 1955, Adenauer campaigned for the unification of Germany. At the same time he insisted on West German participation in western economic political and military systems (above);
 iii **the Russians** refused to talk of unification while West Germany was, in their eyes, '**the creature of the USA**';
 iv **Adenauer failed** in this part of his policy.

16 To create a Franco-German understanding Germany worked closely with France in the various political, military and economic systems which we have so far examined. But Adenauer tried to build closer relations with France:
 i **March 1950** he called for economic union between France and Germany–before the ECSC had been formed;
 ii **September 1958** he met President de Gaulle;
 iii **1958–62** Adenauer ensured that, at meetings of Ministers of the EEC countries, **Germany normally supported de Gaulle**.

He did not oppose de Gaulle's veto on Britain's application to join the EEC in 1962 (31.15.7);

iv **January 1963** relations between France and Germany reached their high point with the signing of the **treaty of co-operation**. In this treaty the traditional enemies agreed:
(a) on **exchanges** in the field of education and youth so that young people would get to know each other better;
(b) that their **foreign policies** would follow the same line.

17 Growing unpopularity, 1963
i the 'economic miracle' seemed to have **run out of steam**. Europe was suffering an economic recession. Germans blamed their government for the slow economic growth;

ii a new, **younger breed of politicians**, journalists and voters resented Adenauer's autocratic behaviour. They wanted their politicians to be more under popular control;

iii specific incidents such as his attempt to curb the activities of the hostile paper, *Der Spiegel*, raised doubts about his belief in democracy;

iv some resented Germany's being **France's junior partner** in the EEC;

v others were annoyed at his **hostile attitude to Willy Brandt**, the Mayor of West Berlin and a member of the Socialist party. Some thought that Brandt might be able to work out a plan for German re-unification with the Russians.

17 Retirement Adenauer retired in **October 1963**.

31.12 The European Economic Community (EEC)

1 Setting it up, 1955–57
i the success of the ECSC led to demands for ways of improving this economic union;

ii Paul-Henri **Spaak**, Foreign Minister of Belgium, was given the task of working out plans for a wider economic union;

iii meetings were held at **Messina** in Italy and in **1956** the Spaak Committee completed its work;

iv **25 March 1957** The **Treaty of Rome** set up the European Economic Community. The 'Six' Community countries were Belgium, France, Holland, Italy, Luxembourg and West Germany.

2 The immediate aims of the EEC
i it was a **customs union**; by 1967 all **tariff barriers** beween member states would be abolished. There would be a **free movement** of capital, labour and goods inside the Community;

ii there would be a **uniform and low external tariff** on goods coming into the Community;

iii to ensure that there were no hidden tariffs or subsidies the **central authority** would have to interfere in the social and economic policies of the member countries;

iv member states would be handing over more and more sovereignty to a **supra-national organization**. This, claimed some, would lead to **political unity**.

3 The structures of the EEC
i **the European Commission:**
(a) runs the Community day to day;
(b) initially it had 9 members appointed by the governments of the member states but owing them no responsibility;
(c) its first chairman was a German, Walter Hallstein;
(d) it was not as powerful an Authority as that of the ECSC. Its decisions had to be approved by the Council of Ministers and, thus, by the individual governments;
(e) however, its activities were much broader than that of the Authority of the ECSC. In 1967 it was agreed to merge the ECSC and Euratom in the EEC:

ii **the Council of Ministers:**
(a) member states sent their foreign, finance or agricultural ministers depending on the issues being discussed;
(b) the Council had to approve Commission decisions:

iii **the Court of Justice and the Assembly coincided** with those of the ECSC and Euratom and the final merger of all three Communities in 1967 was an indication of the creation of a European Community.

4 The advantages of the EEC
i **a vast new market** had a population of 170 million;
ii **Europe's resources** could be used more efficiently;
iii an **Investment Bank** with a fund of one billion dollars was set up to help the development of the more backward regions of the Community, such as southern Italy and the declining industrial areas like the Ruhr and southern Belgium;
iv a **Common Fund** was set up to help the movement of labour and to provide migrant workers with social security benefits;
v **an Overseas Development Fund** was set up to provide investment in the overseas dependencies of the six member states;
vi the Community provided a **third force in world politics**– dependent on neither Russia nor the USA.

5 The success of the EEC
i **trade** between member states increased rapidly. In 1960–61 it increased by 29 per cent;
ii **trade barriers** were lowered, leading to lower prices;
iii **common prices** were fixed for agricultural products;
iv **living standards** improved;
v **the German mark** became the world's leading currency and it was to Germany that the world's financiers turned for help in periods of crisis in 1968, 1974 and 1978.

6 Difficulties
i **the Common Agricultural Policy** (CAP)–see 31.20;
ii **areas furthest away** from the centre of the Community gained least and became relatively poorer.

31.13 Britain and the EEC, 1955–60

1 Britain had been **invited to the Messina** talks (31.12.1). The 6 members of the ECSC sent senior ministers; Britain only sent a second-grade civil servant. **Britain believed the talks would fail.**

2 Britain welcomed the customs union and the abolition of **tariffs** between member states. She would be willing to join in such a free trade scheme.

3 But she could not join the proposed EEC
i about half of Britain's trade was done with the **Commonwealth countries**. This pattern could not be easily fitted into the tightly knit system proposed for the EEC;

ii membership of the EEC leads to a **loss of sovereignty**, of control of ones own affairs. Britain was opposed to giving up such control.

iii the **Common Agricultural Policy** would lead to a rise in British food prices;

iv Britain already had its **depressed areas**, in Scotland, Northern Ireland, the north-east and Wales. It was feared that these, being furthest away from the centre of the Community, would suffer even more rapid decline;

v Hugh Gaitskell, leader of the **Opposition Labour Party**, declared that to join the EEC would be to reject 'a thousand years of British history'. **Isolationism** was strong in Britain.

31.14 The European Free Trade Association

1 Britain appreciated the benefits of **industrial free trade**.
2 While the Messina talks were going on, she proposed the setting up of a **free trade area** with no internal tariff barriers.
3 She proposed that the **EEC** could be treated as a **single-member state** of such a free trade area.
4 She wanted to **exclude agricultural goods** from the proposed free trade area–because of the cheap food imports she received from New Zealand and Australia.

5 She proposed that there should be **no common external tariff**–so that she could maintain her imperial preference system.

6 There would be **no Commission or High Authority** and no loss of **sovereignty**.

7 **The EEC rejected these attempts** to 'sabotage Europe'.

8 **December 1959** Britain, Norway, Sweden, Denmark, Portugal, Austria and Switzerland formed the **European Free trade Association (EFTA)**.

9 **This was a limited success:**

i **it increased trade** between the members. But its population was much smaller than that of the EEC–and was not as rich.

ii **it was a less natural and less compact unit;**

iii its success, even limited, **depended on Britain** whose trade with EEC countries increased faster than did her trade with EFTA countries.

31.15 Britain tried to join the EEC, 1961–62
(*Fig. 31.15A*)

1 The evident success of the EEC (31.12.5) led many in Britain to wish that Britain would become a member. EEC countries were becoming richer, more quickly, than was Britain. Living standards were higher in Europe.

Joining the club
'He says he wants to join – on his own terms.'

Fig. 31.15A MacMillan tried to change EEC rules

2 In 1961 Prime Minister Macmillan appointed Edward Heath to lead the British negotiating team.

3 He tried to get the EEC countries to agree to Britain's right to safeguard her special interests–Commonwealth trade. He wanted adjustments in the Common Agricultural Policy. He also wanted to make arrangement to cater for the other EFTA countries.

4 While these negotiations were going on Macmillan met President Kennedy and he arranged an Anglo-US arms deal. The USA would provide Britain with Polaris nuclear submarines.

5 General de Gaulle saw this as a sign of Britain's dependence on the USA.

6 De Gaulle feared that Britain might replace France as leader of the EEC and change the organization.

7 He announced a veto on the British application. None of the other EEC states challenged the President's power.

31.16 De Gaulle

1 Born in **1890** he entered the **military academy** of St. Cyr in 1910.

2 At 21 he was commissioned in the 33rd Infantry Regiment. His commanding officer was **Colonel Pétain** (9.3.6).

3 **1914–18** At **Verdun** he was captured by the Germans.

4 After the armistice he went back to St. Cyr as **professor of military history** before being sent to the French staff college where he became aide to Pétain, the commander-in-chief.

5 **1932** He became general secretary of the **Committee of National Defence**. He campaigned for a change in military thinking:

i the next war would be a mechanized war; **tanks** would be more important than old-fashioned infantrymen;

ii that war would be a **war of movement**; there would be no place in it for such massive defences as the Maginot Line.

6 The French ignored his work; Guderian, of Germany, profited from it and became an outstanding tank commander.

7 **1937** De Gaulle was given command of the **507th Regiment of Tanks**, rising to become colonel and commander of the tank brigade of the Fifth Lorraine Army.

8 **15 May 1940** He became brigadier general in command of the 4th Armoured Division.

9 He tried to persuade Reynaud and Weygand to allow him to defend the Marne, the Seine or Paris. But the government had decided to capitulate (25.9.7).

10 **De Gaulle escaped to London**, set up a French National Committee, and assumed the title of leader of all Free Frenchmen.

11 He organized a French Army and Navy in Britain. He failed to seize **Dakar** but brought **Chad and French Equitorial Africa** over to the Allies.

12 He was commander-in-chief of the Fighting French Forces and, after **1943**, **President of the Committeee for National Liberation**.

13 Churchill and Roosevelt did not invite him to any of the war-time conferences (26.11).

14 The Allies allowed him to lead the force into **liberated Paris** where he became **head of the French Provisional Government** in 1944, and chief of the armed forces.

15 The elections of **1945** confirmed him as **president** of the government, **minister of national defence** and head of the armies.

16 **He resigned in 1946** because the politicians could not reach agreement about the future for French industry and economy.

17 **1947** He founded the **Rassemblement du Peuple Français**, a right-wing movement for the regeneration of France rather than an ordinary political party. It believed in strong government, sharing de Gaulle's belief that the President should have very great powers.

18 **He withdrew from the RPF in 1953** and in 1956 it lost most of its seats.

19 **1958** France was in a **political crisis**. Since 1946 there had been 22 short-lived governments, none able to deal with France's problems:

i it had lost its empire in **Indo-China** in 1954;

ii **May 1958** French settlers in **Algeria** rebelled because of the tottering French government's inability to defeat the Muslim rebels who wanted Algerian independence. With the help of the army they set up a Committee of Public Safety in Algiers. They spread the rumour that paratroopers were going to make an airborne assault on Paris to overthrow the government.

20 Many people thought de Gaulle could save the country:

i **the army** thought that he would put down the Algerian Muslims and save it from being shamed as in Indo-China;

ii **the French settlers** thought that he would help the army, put down the Muslims and preserve a French Algeria;

iii **French people** hoped that, while doing his colonial 'trick' he would provide **political stability** at home. They were tired of the too frequent changes in governments.

21 When he came back from retirement de Gaulle became Prime Minister only on condition that he was given a free hand to

i take drastic measures to restore the **French economy**;

ii secure **acceptance of his policies** by referendum.

22 **A new constitution** was promulgated for a Fifth Republic

i **the President**, elected by direct popular elections after 1962, could dissolve the Assembly and rule by decree in times of crisis. This would provide France with the much-needed 'strong government' so desired by the RPF (31.16.17), so lacking since 1946 (31.16.19);

ii the Prime Minister was to be appointed by the President although he had to be responsible to the Assembly;

iii ministers appointed by the President could not be members of the Assembly. This resembled the US system (7.3.3).

23 **A referendum** approved the new constitution. In the elections which followed the Socialists won only 40 seats and the Communists only 10. The new Gaullist Union won 188 seats and had the support of several right-wing groups.

24 **January 1959** De Gaulle became President. He appointed **Michel Debré** as Prime Minister; in **1962** he was succeeded by **M. Pompidou** who became President in succession to de Gaulle in 1969.

25 **His Algerian policy** Once in power de Gaulle began **negotiations** with the Muslim rebels:

i **Colonists** and dissatisfied **army officers** formed the Organisation de L'Armée Secrète (OAS), an extreme right-wing group. Using **terrorist methods** they tried to retain French hold on Algeria, to assassinate de Gaulle (the 'great traitor') and gain influence for their kind;

ii but de Gaulle ignored these attempts at terrorism. He made peace with the Algerian Muslims in 1962 (37.1.6).

26 **His imperial policy**

i in 1958 he offered the states of **French Africa** the choice of independence or of being associated with France in the French Community;

ii the Community gave them self government but France had some control of their foreign policies;

iii France provided aid to former colonies;

iv by 1960 the whole of the French African Empire had chosen independence. France would have no more costly colonial wars.

27 **His foreign policy**

i he distrusted the USA and Britain because of his wartime experiences;

ii he insisted on an **independent French policy**. This led to:

(a) withdrawal from **NATO**;

(b) the creation of a **French nuclear force**;

(c) **opposition to British entry into the EEC**;

(d) **good relations** with Russia, Eastern Europe and China;

(e) refusal to sign the **Test Ban Treaty of 1963**.

28 **His internal policy**

i the government controlled the radio and television. This ensured **control of news items**;

ii De Gaulle held **frequent referendums** (or referenda) to get popular approval for his policies;

iii **he revalued the franc**. The end of the outflow of money to fight colonial wars made France economically stronger;

iv **1963** The French balance of payments problem was finally solved; France began to accumulate **huge reserves of gold**;

v **industrial production** increased;

vi wages and prices were government-controlled, to prevent inflation.

29 **1968** the year of crisis

i Russia's attack on **Czechoslovakia** (30.11.7) showed that there was a good reason to fear **Russian aggression**. De Gaulle's confidence that he could deal with Russia seemed misplaced;

ii **May 1968** **students** rose in rebellion, largely because of the inefficient university system. This snowballed into a general rising;

(a) **workers** took over factories. They had become increasingly dissatisfied with wage control;

(b) **rioters** took over the streets. Some of these were 'out' against government control of the media; others because of de Gaulle's right wing and authoritarian system of government.

iii **De Gaulle showed courage and self-confidence** in view of this widespread hostility:

(a) **he appealed** on television for national unity;

(b) **he promised** workers some social reforms and gained their support against the extreme left-wing students;

(c) **he called** a snap election and destroyed the opposition in the Assembly. He appeared to be stronger than ever.

iv But there was a **third crisis** in the autumn of 1968:

(a) the concessions over wages and social reform had to be paid for. The first result was an adverse **balance of payments** in the autumn of 1968. This led to an **outflow of gold**;

(b) this, in turn, led to a **run on the franc** by foreign speculators. Many French people speculated against their own franc and bought the stable currency, the German mark;

(c) De Gaulle had to ask for massive **international loans** to help him out. It seemed that he would have to **devalue** the franc;

(d) rather than take this humiliating step he **imposed severe restrictions** at home. This created more industrial unrest and led to a further run on the franc.

30 **1969**; the year of defeat and resignation

i he put his proposals to the people and, foolishly, turned the **referendum** into one of confidence in his government;

iii **he lost**. And he resigned.

31 **Gaullism lived on**. In the ensuing election Pompidou, de Gaulle's 'man', won an overwhelming victory for the presidency.

31.17 Britain and the EEC, 1967

1 Labour's Prime Minister, **Harold Wilson**, and the Foreign Secretary, **George Brown**, campaigned throughout Europe to win support for a new application to join the EEC.

2 Once again **de Gaulle vetoed** the application, although Britain was prepared to enter without any of the pre-conditions on which Heath and Macmillan had insisted in 1961–62.

31.18 Britain joins the EEC, 1973

1 **President Pompidou** objected less to Britain's entry.

2 **Heath**, now Prime Minister, made another application for membership.

3 **1 January 1973** Britain, Denmark and Eire joined at the same time. The 'Six' became 'Nine'.

4 **Norway**, another member of the EFTA, held a referendum and the people rejected the idea of membership of the EEC.

5 **Many in Britain demanded a referendum**

i some objected to the **loss of sovereignty**;

ii others feared a **loss of jobs**;

iii others were opposed to the threat of **regulation** of wages, prices, working conditions and the like from **Brussels** which, they claimed, would lead to higher prices and a lowering of prosperity;

iv **trade unions** came out against entry, claiming that the EEC was a producers' club with no benefit to workers.

6 **1975** The new Labour government held a referendum and by a majority of two to one the British people came out in favour of Britain's continued membership of the EEC.

31.19 The EEC 1973–83

1 In spite of the world recession following OPEC's increase in oil prices, the **EEC continued to grow richer**. Britain alone, because of internal policies, did not share fully in that increasing prosperity.

2 **Greece, Spain and Portugal** all became democracies and applied for membership.

3 **Lack of progress** The EEC has not produced the political union for which its founders had hoped:
i **France** continued to 'go it alone' in defence;
ii **Britain**, the only oil-bearing member of the Community, regarded the oil as 'her own' and not Community property;
iii almost all members squabbled over **fishing rights**;
iv Germany, Belgium, France and Britain quarrelled over which of them should shut down which **steel works** as the world demand for steel slumped.

31.20 The Common Agricultural Policy

1 The aim of the policy is to make Europe **self-sufficient** in food as far as is possible.

2 Farmers get a **guaranteed and agreed price** for their products, the price being fixed at an annual review by the Ministers of Agriculture of the member states.

3 The political influence of farmers in **France, Germany and Holland** is very strong. Their ministers have to try to get **as high a price** for their products as they can.

4 This had led to **massive over-production**. There are **'mountains'** of meat, butter and fruit and **'lakes'** of milk and wine held in storage. **The cost of storage** is high, taking about half the total cost of the CAP.

5 **Food importing countries**—and especially **Britain**—resent this system which leads to higher prices and higher taxes.

6 A good deal of the surplus food produced each year is sold off at vastly-reduced prices to Russia and countries in Eastern Europe. While this does not do away with the 'mountains' or 'lakes' it causes resentment in Britain and the countries which pay most into the Agricultural Fund.

31.21 The European Parliament

1 Until 1978 the European Parliament had **little power**:
i **its members** were appointed by the member governments;
ii it had **little control** over the Commission and the Council of Ministers;
iii it was a mere **debating chamber**;
iv not surprisingly, **few eminent politicians** sought to become members of the 'talking shop'.

2 **In 1978** things changed:
i each member state held **elections** for European Members of Parliament (EMP);
ii each member state was allocated a number of seats depending on the size of population. Britain, for example, had 81 constituencies, as had France, Germany and Italy; the smaller countries got fewer seats.

3 In France and Germany—but not in Britain, **leading politicians** became candidates and were elected.

4 In the European Parliament the **EMPs sit in their political groupings**; socialist, conservative, liberal and communist. They do not sit as British, French, German or whatever Members.

5 They have already begun to demand that they should be treated as a **true Parliament**. This would give them **powers over the Commission and the Council of Ministers**. It is too soon to say what success they will have. It may be that this Parliament may see the next step being taken along the road to European integration.

32 The United States, 1945–83

32.1 The effects of the War on the USA

1 After 1941 the USA was the **'arsenal of democracy'**:
i most Russian transport 1944–45 was provided by the USA;
ii **Chiang's armies** were equipped by America (17.34);
iii **Britain** received planes and all sorts of equipment;
iv **16 million US servicemen** fought throughout the world.

2 **US workers** had a vast increase in incomes.

3 **Trade unions** were more important (19.3.11).

4 Black people and other **minorities**, got jobs more easily and became more conscious of the need for social reform.

5 **American bankers** became the world's bankers.

6 **Industry** did not suffer from aerial bombing.

32.2 The Truman administration, 1945–52

1 Truman had run a draper's shop in Kansas City until the low incomes of the US farmers drove him into bankruptcy. He was one of the millions who suffered from the depression in the 1920s.

2 He was 'taken up' by the political boss, Prendergast, who 'ruled' the Democrats in Missouri and got Truman elected as Senator in 1934.

3 In **1944** he was a surprise choice for the **Vice-Presidency**.

4 **April 1945 Roosevelt's sudden death** brought him to the Presidency.

32.3 Domestic problems, 1945

1 **Inflation**, because of too high government wartime spending.

2 Militant and strong **trade unions** seeking higher wages.

3 Nation-wide **strikes** to back up wage demands.

4 The switch **from war to peace**. This went smoothly:
i **12 million servicemen** were demobilized;
ii **industry** got back to making civilian goods;
iii **US farmers** sold their output at home and abroad. They were helped by the US money given to UNRRA (28.6.1).

5 The demand for an **extension of Roosevelt's New Deal**.

6 The growth of **anti-Communism** (32.15).

7 The great gulf in **living standards** between the rich and the very poor—the majority of whom were black.

32.4 The Congressional elections, 1946

1 **September 1945** In his 21 Points Truman promised:
i more **social security**, including a National Health Service;
ii **more jobs**, largely through public works, including low-cost housing for the less well-off;
iii legislation to improve **working conditions**.

2 The elections showed a **swing to the right**:
i **why?** Voters were frightened by **inflation** and the **strikes** which were evidence of labour unrest;
ii **effects**: the **Republicans** gained a majority in Congress.

32.5 Domestic Policy, 1946–48

1 Truman's Bill on **working conditions** was **vetoed** by Congress.

2 Almost all his other **social legislation was thrown out**.

3 The right-wing Congress pushed through the **Taft-Hartley Act, 1947**, to restrict the power of unions:
i Truman vetoed the Bill. His veto was overridden by the combination of anti-unionists in the Congress;
ii the Act provided for:
(a) the abolition of the **closed shop**;

(b) a 60-day **'cooling off' period** before a strike could take place;

(c) power for the President to impose a further **90-day period** if strikes threatened the national interest:

iv it did not prevent the growth of union membership.

32.6 The Presidential Election, 1946

1 Truman was **expected to lose** to Dewey:

i **the 1946 elections** showed a swing against Democrats;

ii **Congress** had thrown out his proposed social reforms;

iii **Dewey** was a popular New York Attorney-General, fighting against crime and communism.

2 Truman went on a **whistle-stop tour** (by rail) meeting millions of ordinary people.

3 The result proved all the polls wrong. **Truman won.**

4 The Democrats also won majorities in Congress.

32.7 Truman's 'Fair Deal'

1 This **extended Roosevelt's New Deal**:

i government financed **public works** to provide jobs;

ii low cost **housing** to help the poorly housed;

iii more **social security legislation** to include an extension of the old age pensions scheme.

2 He proposed to promote **civil rights** for blacks (32.14).

3 But he failed. Southern Democrats allied with Republicans in Congress to reject his proposals.

4 He was also **hampered** by the growth of anti-Communism (32.15).

32.8 Truman's foreign policy, 1945–52

1 He was an **active** President.

2 He avoided the mistakes made by **Wilson** in 1918-20. His delegate at the preliminary meeting of UNO was a leading Republican.

3 He persuaded Congress to vote 3 billion dollars for **UNRRA** (28.6.1) and 5 billion dollars for **other aid**.

4 He had less faith in the **Russians** than Roosevelt.

5 His **Truman Doctrine** (28.5) was the basis of later policy.

6 He was responsible for **Marshall Aid** (28.6).

7 He ensured US membership of **NATO** (28.10).

8 He sent aid, but not men, to help **Chiang against Mao** (17.34.1).

10 He committed the USA to membership of **UNO** and used that membership to fight Communist aggression in **Korea** (28.11).

11 He helped in the rehabilitation of **Japan** (35.2).

32.9 The Presidential Election, 1952

1 **Truman** did not run again.

2 **Eisenhower** was the Republican candidate:

i he was the **wartime hero** and leader;

ii he was commander in chief of **NATO** forces;

iii he had **no party affiliation** but could be made to appeal to almost everyone (anti-Communist; 'strong man'; peacekeeper who would 'bring the boys home from Korea').

3 **Eisenhower** won; the **first Republican President since 1932**.

4 He did not share the isolationist views of some Republicans; he **continued most of Truman's policies**.

5 His **foreign policy** was the work of Secretary of State, **John Foster Dulles**.

32.10 Eisenhower's foreign policy, 1952–59

1 He benefited from the **'thaw'** in the cold war (28.12.6).

2 He sent the **US Seventh Fleet** to deter Communist China from attacking Chiang's forces on Formosa (later Taiwan).

3 He ended the war in **Korea** (28.11.26).

4 **1952–54** The French lost the Empire in **Indo-China**; North Vietnam became Communist-controlled under **Ho Chi Minh** (35.13).

5 **Dulles** developed the **'Domino Theory'**. If one state went communist in S.E. Asia there was a danger of a 'knock-on effect'.

6 **1956** He opposed the Anglo-French **Suez policy** (37.8).

32.11 The Eisenhower Doctrine, 1957

1 This was an updating of the **Truman Doctrine** (28.5).

2 The US would ensure **peace with justice** throughout the world. The difficulty was in the definition of 'justice'.

3 The US was prepared to get **involved anywhere**.

4 **1958** US Marines were sent to **Lebanon** to stop a coup by supporters of Nasser.

5 **1954** Dulles set up **SEATO** as an alliance to halt Communist aggression in South East Asia.

6 **Four billion dollars** was given to aid NATO and SEATO.

7 Dulles developed the principle of **'brinkmanship'**. This meant that Dulles (and the US) would appear to be willing to go to the edge (or brink) of war in defence of a policy, hoping that the threat would lead the Communist enemy to withdraw.

8 This policy failed in **1956** when Russia savaged **Hungary** (30.10.3).

9 Dulles could not stop **Castro's successful revolution in Cuba**.

32.12 Was the foreign policy a success?

1 **US generosity** was said, by enemies, to be a form of 'dollar imperialism' giving the US control of its allies.

2 The growth of independent states in **Africa** (36.1.2) and **Asia** saw the creation of states committed to neither the US nor USSR. Dulles did not understand **Neutralism**; 'those who are not with me are against me'.

3 The US tended to support **right-wing governments** as the best barriers to Communism. **Their failings** were often good advertisements for Communism.

4 **Batista**, in Cuba, **Trujillo** in the Dominican Republic, were typical of the dictators maintained in power by US aid.

5 **Distrust** of the US was **increased** by the work of the **CIA**. In **1954** it helped overthrow a left-wing government in **Guatemala**.

6 The right-wing attitude of Dulles allowed **Russia** to appear as the 'champion of popular opposition to colonialism'.

7 Khrushchev's visit to **Camp David** was of some value (29.11.4) although nothing was decided there or at the **Paris Summit** in 1960 (29.11.5).

32.13 Eisenhower's domestic policy

1 He was a **'moderate'** with no 'Deal' although he left Roosevelt's and Truman's legislation stand.

2 He chose 'eight millionaires and a plumber' for his **Cabinet**. They tried to:

i **reduce government activity** and spending;

ii **reduce taxation**, to leave more for private spending;

iii increase the scope for **private enterprise**.

3 Their policies could be seen working in:

i cuts in spending by the **Tennessee Valley Authority** (19.4);

ii reduction in **company taxation**;

iii handing over to private enterprise of **atomic energy plants**.

4 The USA became **more prosperous** because of the low taxation and *laisser-faire* policies, and because of:

i **less military spending** with the end of the Korean War;

ii **the fall in world prices** in the 1950s.

5 **Eisenhower's success** could be judged by:

i **the total output of goods**–three times that of 1939;

ii **agricultural output**–up by one-third in 1960 compared to 1952;

iii **the number of cars**–one for every 3 people;

iv half US families had **incomes** of over 2000 dollars a year.

6 But in **1960** there were **domestic problems**:

i **inflation**, a world wide phenomenon, was rising;

ii **unemployment** was high; 4½ million or 6 per cent of the workforce was out of work;

iii **taxation** had to increase to pay for the high level of military expenditure. In 1959–60 the government spent more than Truman had spent during the Korean War;

iv vast sums had to be spent to pay **farmers** to take their land out of cultivation as a means of avoiding crop surpluses.

7 Eisenhower had to contend with 2 major problems— McCarthyism (32.15) and the **demand by blacks for civil rights** (32.14).

32.14 Civil rights, 1945–60

1 Since the 1860s there has been **no slavery** in the USA.

2 American blacks were, however, **second-class citizens**:

i in the **southern states**, where black people form a large proportion of the population, **white politicians** passed state laws to prevent them enjoying equal social, educational and political rights;

ii **violent groups**, such as the **Ku-Klux-Klan** (7.11.7) frightened them from taking advantage when these barriers were broken down by federal legislation;

iii blacks had to take the **lowest jobs** and the **worst housing** and use **separate schools**, hotels, transport, public lavatories;

iv in the **northern cities** blacks lived in **slum ghettoes** where they had **poorer education** and **fewer job prospects**.

3 **Truman** tried to end the **segregation in the army** in which there were separate units for black servicemen.

4 1954 The Supreme Court decided that enforced **segregation** of blacks and whites **in state schools** was **illegal**:

i **Eisenhower supported** this all-important decision;

ii **1957** At **Little Rock, Arkansas**, 9 black children tried to enrol in an all-white school. The **state government** encouraged the mob violence which supported its decision not to de-segregate their schools;

iii Eisenhower sent **federal troops** to enforce the law;

iv **other states** still refused to comply with the law. Black parents were afraid to bring their children to white schools.

5 **1955 Blacks in Montgomery, Alabama**, began to protest against segregation in **public buses**. Their refusal to use the public transport system forced the authorities to de-segregate.

6 **Martin Luther King** emerged as the leader of a peaceful but active **Civil Rights Movement**.

7 **1957 The Civil Rights Act** protected the rights of blacks to **vote** in state and national elections.

8 **1960** There was a demand for government **supervision of elections** so blacks were not frustrated by mob violence.

9 **By 1960 blacks**:

i were **more vocal** in their demands;

ii wanted reform to take place **more quickly**;

iii **were moving from the south** to the industrial mid-west and north. Here they would create an **urban problem**.

32.15 McCarthyism

1 The USA had had **anti-Communist hysteria** in the 1920s (16.5).

2 After 1945 the spirit of the **Cold War** increased US suspicions of Russia and of Communists.

3 During Truman's presidency the **Republicans** took up an anti-Communist attitude. They claimed that:

i **Roosevelt had been 'soft to Stalin'**;

ii **Truman failed to halt Russian aggression in Europe**;

iii the **Civil Service was riddled** with Communists;

iv **Mao's victory in China** was aided by US Communists in the State Department.

4 **1949** Truman set up a system of **loyalty checks** for government employees—his response to Republican attacks.

5 **1948** The **Un-American Activities Committee** had been appointed by Congress to investigate the activities of potential Nazi enemies of US democracy. Now it was used against Communists, Socialists and Liberals.

6 The **trial of Alger Hiss, 1949**, added to the anti-Communism:

i Hiss, an official in the State Department, had **advised Roosevelt at Yalta** and had made the arrangements for the **San Francisco meeting of the UNO** (27.1.7);

ii accused of spying for Russia, he was found **guilty of perjury** for having denied that he passed secrets to the Russians.

7 **1950** Congress passed the **Internal Security** Act. This restricted the activities of known Communists and banned the entry into the US of anyone known to have been a member of a Communist organization.

8 **The Korean War** increased the suspicion of communism.

9 **Senator Joseph McCarthy**, junior senator from Wisconsin, saw how to use the Un-American Activities Committee as a way to win popularity and, maybe, higher political office:

i **he bullied witnesses** who appeared before the Committee, accusing them of knowledge of, or part in, some Russian-inspired organization. Many had belonged to anti-Fascist movements in the 1930s or had supported the anti-Franco International Brigade (24.11.7). McCarthy made this appear as un-American;

ii **he smeared, without proof**, organizations, universities, politicians and officials in statements to the Committee;

iii **he claimed, without giving evidence**, that there were known Communists in the State Department. The numbers of such 'traitors' changed with each speech he made;

iv **he won the support of the Churches** by seeming to be the champion of opposition to atheistic Communism.

10 **The 1950 Internal Security Act** was one response to McCarthy's growing power. In **1951** the government decided civil servants could be dismissed if there was '**reasonable doubt**' of loyalty.

11 **Eisenhower's victory in 1952** was due in part to McCarthy and the President **tolerated McCarthy's activities** because he needed Republican support in Congress.

12 **1953** McCarthy became **Chairman of the Senate's Permanent Committee of Investigation**:

i he got the **atomic scientist Robert Oppenheimer** sacked from his government post on flimsy evidence;

ii he organized the **burning of 'subversive books'** by leading US writers;

iii he managed to get an **unofficial censorship** imposed in **literature** and the **film industry**.

13 **1954** A Senate Committee denounced McCarthy's smear attacks on members of the Senate.

14 **1954 He accused Army leaders** of being 'commie-sympathizers'.

15 Fortunately, for democracy, **sanity returned**. TV commentators showed him at work in the Committee and pointed out how undemocratic he was. **The Senate** removed him from his post. He died in **1957**.

16 **McCarthyism did not completely die**. The **John Birch** society carries on similar anti-Communist witch hunts.

32.16 The Presidential Election, 1960

1 The Democratic candidate was **John Fitzgerald Kennedy**:

i his millionaire father, US Ambassador to Britain in the 1930s and 1940s, had opposed US entry into the war;

ii Kennedy was an Irish-American and a Catholic. Many thought that **his religion** could lead to his defeat in 1960.

2 The Republican candidate was **Richard M. Nixon**:

i he had won a Congressional seat in **1946** by a **vicious smear campaign** in California against his rival;

ii he had played a major part in the **uncovering of Hiss** (32.15.6);

iii he had **supported McCarthy's activities**;

iv he had been **Eisenhower's Vice President**.

3 Kennedy won by a narrow majority.

32.17 Kennedy's problems, 1960

1 Domestic economy. The US was suffering from **inflation** and **unemployment** (32.13.6).

2 Urban poverty was largely the result of that unemployment. It was particularly a **black problem**.

3 Blacks and other minorities such as **Puerto Ricans** had a low standard of living and little chance of state aid.

32.18 Kennedy's domestic policy: The New Frontier

1 He had a young, intellectual Cabinet.

2 But he **achieved little**. Some people think that he would have achieved more in a second term, if he had lived. In his presidency:

i **plans for a health service** for the old was rejected by Congress as was a scheme to provide **government money to the state schools**;

ii **he did help blacks** (32.19) but failed to get approval for a **housing bill** aimed at massive slum clearance;

iii **Congress refused** to extend New Deal legislation on social security for the unemployed.

4 In **1962** the **Democrats lost seats** in the Congressional elections. Kennedy's task became even harder.

5 He was assassinated in Dallas on 22 November 1963.

32.19 Kennedy and Civil Rights, 1960–63

1 Southern schools were still mainly **not integrated**.

2 In **5 states not 1 school** was integrated.

3 The Congress of Racial Equality (CORE) was formed by blacks impatient with other long-established black organizations.

4 Kennedy appointed the **first black Federal judge**, the first **black ambassador** and the **first black commander** of a US warship.

5 His brother, **Robert, as Attorney General**, used his legal powers to help **blacks get their voting rights**.

6 1962 A black student, **James Meredith**, tried to enrol at the 'whites only' college at **Oxford, Mississippi**:

i whites rioted; several people were killed;

ii Kennedy sent federal troops and marshals to restore order because the state governor refused to act.

7 In Alabama and other southern states, white police used **brutal methods** against civil rights workers–black and white. Many students were **killed**, more **arrested**. Anyone who attacked them got a sympathetic trial from **all-white juries**.

8 Kennedy's civil rights legislation was held up in Congress by a combination of Republicans and southern Democrats.

9 His death was greeted with applause in many southern states violently opposed to black emancipation.

32.20 Kennedy's foreign policy

1 Lesser points:

i **1961** He set up the **Peace Corps** to allow young volunteers to give assistance to under-developed nations. By 1960 the Corps had 12 000 Americans at work in over 50 countries;

ii **1961** he signed the **Alliance for Progress** with Latin America for economic co-operation and to raise living standards;

iii **1962** he persuaded Congress to make **large tariff cuts** to give encouragement to greater international trade. This led to the 'Kennedy Round' whereby the nation-members of the General Agreement on Tariffs and Trade (GATT) made reductions in many tariffs. Kennedy believed that more trade would be the 'New Frontier' method of lessening world poverty;

iv **1963** he signed the **Nuclear Test Ban Treaty**.

2 Russia

i **1961** He met **Khrushchev in Vienna** but the 2 leaders failed to make any progress on Berlin and nuclear disarmament;

ii **the Berlin Wall** was built after the Vienna meeting (29.11.6–10). In **1963** Kennedy visited the Wall and attacked Russian fear of freedom for the people of the east;

iii **Cuba** In **1961** he approved a **CIA scheme** for an invasion of Cuba by Cuban refugees. This force was wiped out soon after landing in the **Bay of Pigs**;

iv in **1962** there was the **Cuban crisis** (29.12.7–14);

v following that crisis Kennedy and Khrushchev agreed to the opening of a **'hot line'** between the USA and USSR so that leaders might easily be in touch in times of crisis.

3 Europe

i **1961** he attacked the building of the **Berlin Wall** (29.11.10);

ii **1962** he agreed to supply Britain with **Polaris** (31.15.4).

4 Vietnam It was under Kennedy that the USA became totally involved in Vietnam (35.15).

5 Space Kennedy saw Russia's sputnik as an aid to Russian foreign policy. He took the USA into the space age.

32.21 President Lyndon Baines Johnson, 1963–68

1 He was Kennedy's **Vice President** and succeeded him in 1963.

2 He was a more **astute politician** than Kennedy. He used the sympathy which followed Kennedy's killing to push through the social legislation begun by Kennedy.

3 He had always been a **dedicated social reformer**.

4 The Great Society was his hope for the USA:

i he pushed through a good deal of Kennedy's legislation:

(a) money for **rebuilding inner cities** was provided by the **Development Act, 1964**;

(b) federal money was provided for **educational expansion**;

(c) a Social Security Act provided **medical care for the old** ('Medicare');

(d) **minimum wages** were raised and extended to more industries;

(e) a start was made on providing **aid for the unemployed**.

5 1964 Johnson crushed the Republican candidate, **Goldwater**, in the 1964 Presidential Election. This election also helped the Democrats to win more seats in Congress which made Johnson's task easier. But:

i **Southern Democrats and Republicans** still worked against him;

ii **a liberal trade union law** to replace the Taft-Hartley Act (32.5.3) was blocked;

iii Congress passed a **stringent Immigration Act** to make the admission of immigrants more selective.

6 His Presidency saw the **increase of US action in Vietnam** (35.15).

32.22 Johnson and Civil rights

1 Although Johnson was from Texas he had always opposed the southern Democrats.

2 1965 A Civil Rights Act provided black people with:

i **equal rights of admission** to cinemas, theatres and shops;

ii **a guarantee of their right to vote**. This still meant that blacks had to face white mobs when they registered and voted.

3 But basic inequalities remained–in jobs, education and housing.

4 Younger, better educated **blacks turned to extremism**:

i **the Black Muslims** demanded a separate state for US blacks. They taught their followers to respect women, hard work and education;

ii **Black Power movements** decided that even the Muslims would not succeed or would only succeed after a long time. They adopted more violent methods;

iii **1965** the **Watts district of Los Angeles** was almost destroyed by fire during a battle with the police;

iv **1966** similar riots and arson attacks turned **Chicago**, **Newark**, **New Jersey** and **Detroit** into scenes of violent conflict.

5 1968 The **assassination** of the moderate leader, **Martin Luther King**, seemed to many Black Power leaders the best answer that whites could give to calls for moderation.

6 1968 The **assassination** of Robert Kennedy was also seen by blacks as an indirect attack on their equality campaign.

32.23 The effects of the Vietnam War on the USA

1 We will study the causes and course of the War in Unit 35. But we can examine some of the effects of that war now.

2 Inflation grew because of vast spending on armaments.

3 The USA had a severe **balance of payments problem**. The war led to increased spending overseas. Exports did not rise at the same rate.

4 The dollar had been the world's leading currency. The continuing balance of payments problem led to a weakening of the dollar. This was to lead **Nixon to devalue it in 1971-72** (32.25.1).

5 Dissension grew and became widespread:

i **students** became opposed to the war in which they might have to fight. Students rioted in anti-war demonstrations; some were killed by anti-riot police;

ii **1968** saw a world-wide students' movement. In the USA it was marked by a wave of anti-war demonstrations and by students demanding the right to 'participate' in their own education–to write course contents, to decide on the ability of lecturers and to share in College government;

iii **blacks** became more violent. There was a high proportion of black servicemen in Vietnam; on return they would be expected to go back to the unequal state they had left to go to war. Many refused to do so and joined Black Power movements;

iv in the **1968 Olympic Games** US black athletes gave Black Power signs from the victors' rostrum to draw world attention to their frustration and rebellion.

6 The violence was so great that **Johnson** announced that he would **not stand for re-election in 1968** in the hope that a new President would be more acceptable to the people. The Republican Nixon won the election. In 1968 he signed the **Nuclear Non-Proliferation Treaty** to try to limit the spread of nuclear weapons (29.20.2.i).

32.24 Nixon's foreign policy

1 Vietnam After a series of failures and disastrous switches in policy (35.18), he signed a peace treaty in January 1973.

2 China Nixon had made his political mark attacking State Department advisors who, he said in 1949, had helped Mao to victory. In 1971 he helped Communist China to take China's seat at the UNO (33.12.14). His visit to China marked a major stage in détente.

3 Russia The Nixon Doctrine, 1969 (29.20.2.ii), expressed the US commitment to resist Communist aggression. But the reality was different, as we have seen in 32.23.2. As regards Russia:

i he visited **Moscow**, strengthened by the fact that China was now more friendly to the USA than to the USSR (29.20.2.iv);

ii he started off the **Strategic Arms Limitation Talks (SALT)** which came to fruition in **1972** (29.20.3).

32.25 Nixon's domestic policies

These were less successful.

1 1971 The dollar was devalued; the German mark and the Japanese yen were stronger currencies. By 1973 following the vast increases in oil prices (38.9.16-20) the dollar was further weakened.

2 His Council for Urban Affairs tried to tackle the problems of the cities. For much of the period 1968-72 there was less unrest.

3 Unemployment rose to 4 million, in spite of the work-creation involved in arms spending.

4 Inflation continued to rise (32.23.2).

5 Nixon imposed an unpopular **freeze on wages and prices**.

6 Watergate may be, unfortunately, the thing for which Nixon is best remembered:

i in the **1972 Presidential Election** Nixon crushed his Democratic opponent, **George McGovern**;

ii during the campaign some of his supporters broke into the Democratic headquarters in the Watergate Building;

iii in a series of court trials it was shown that Nixon may not have known of the plot to break in. But he played a part in the attempt to pervert justice to get people out of trouble;

iv more and more of his senior officials were tried and sentenced to various fines and/or imprisonment;

v finally he was forced to resign–to avoid the shame of an impeachment and trial;

vi his **Vice President, Agnew**, had already been imprisoned. Gerry Ford became President.

32.26 Carter's inheritance, 1976

1 The Democratic Jimmy Carter defeated the Republican, Ford, in the Presidential Election, 1975. He took office in January 1976.

2 He faced a **series of difficulties**:

i **Congress was suspicious** of the presidency after Nixon. There was a new, bolder attitude towards the White House;

ii **Carter**, formerly governor of Georgia, **had no 'bloc' in Congress**;

iii **the balance of payments crisis** became worse because of the **oil price increases in 1973-74 and 1979** (38.9.17). The dollar became weaker;

iv **inflation** was 4 per cent when he came to power and 10 per cent in 1979.

3 He had **certain aims**:

i **to reduce the budget** and the amount of **government spending**;

ii **to tackle urban poverty**. But he left the solution to the cities. As **city taxes** rose to pay for this, white taxpayers moved out into low-tax country areas. The **urban problem worsened**.

iii **to reduce unemployment**, particularly among blacks. During his presidency **unemployment for whites and blacks rose**.

32.27 Carter's foreign policy

1 He **continued the SALT talks**. In 1972 SALT agreement was signed (29.20.3) and although his proposals for new talks were rejected by Russia in 1977, a fresh round of talks opened later on (29.20.5).

2 Panama In 1978 the Senate approved the Treaty to hand over the Panama Canal to Panama by the year 2000 (7.22).

3 Afghanistan, 1979 The Russians invaded neighbouring **Afghanistan** (29.19.6). Carter took no action, other than announcing a boycott of the Olympic Games to be held in Moscow in 1980.

4 Africa Carter did nothing to prevent the spread of Russian and Cuban influence in Africa. Communist-supporter governments took over in **Angola and Mozambique** as well as in states in the **Horn of Africa**.

5 Dissidents He condemned the persecution of dissidents in Russia, Uruguay, Brazil and South Africa. But he did nothing about the ill-treatment of such dissidents in South Korea, the Philippines and Iran.

6 Mexico had a major oil industry. In the hope of finding a cheap supply, Carter became **more friendly** to Mexico.

7 Carter played a major role in helping **Israel and Egypt** to arrive at a peace settlement. **Sadat, of Egypt**, had gone to Jerusalem where he had addressed the Israeli Parliament (or Knesset); **Begin, the Prime Minister of Israel**, had agreed that the Middle East needed either:

i **an overall peace settlement** which would ensure Arab recognition of Israel and a continuing peace; OR

ii **a peace settlement** between **Israel** and the most powerful Arab country, **Egypt**. At **Camp David**, the Presidential retreat, the 2 leaders were brought together in 1977 and a bilateral settlement was arranged (37.18).

8 The Shah of Iran was driven into exile in **1979** as a result of an Islamic uprising against his western-style and autocratic government. A religious leader, the **Ayatollah Khomeini**, returned to Iran from exile and roused his followers to even greater anti-western fervour. In particular, Khomeini was anti-American; he described the USA as **'the Great Satan'**. One result of this was the seizure by Iranian students of the US **Embassy in Teheran**. Some 50 Americans were held hostage for over a year, while the students tried to bargain for the return of the Shah to stand trial for crimes against the people. Carter tried:

i **economic sanctions** against Iran; these had little effect on the behaviour of a fanatical régime which was even prepared to run down its own powerful oil industry rather than provide fuel for the 'wicked west'.

ii **a military raid** aimed at rescuing the hostages: this failed dismally, making the USA a laughing stock. There is little doubt that Carter's failure in the **1980 Presidential Election** was due as much to this single disaster as to the overall failure of his foreign policy.

32.28 US–Russian détente, 1968–83 *See 29.20*

32.29 US and the Helsinki talks on Human Rights *See 29.21*.

32.30 Reagan's Presidency, 1980–

1 Carter came under increasing attack, 1979–80:

i he took no action against **Russian aggression in Africa** (29.19.5);

ii his policy in **Iran** was an inept failure (32.26.8);

iii his response to the **Russian invasion of Afghanistan** was weak (29.19.6 and 32.17.3).

2 Opinion polls in the USA showed the growth of a demand for a **tougher foreign policy**. There was, for example, a demand for the bombing of Khomeini's Iran.

3 Some, led by **Senator Jackson**, wanted the US to **ban the sale of US grain** to Russia unless the Russians changed their policies–on the treatment of dissidents. However, the government could not afford to offend the US farming lobby. The sales of grain continued. It was argued that:

i not to have sold the grain would have hurt the Russian people–but not the government.

ii if the grain were not sold, the government would have used it as an excuse to rouse the Russian people in an anti-US campaign. Russian nationalism would have become stronger.

4 Ronald Reagan's victory over Carter in the 1980 Presidential Election was due, in large part, to Reagan's willingness to appear to be a tougher person than Carter.

5 The MBFR talks (29.22):

i when these talks seemed to be getting nowhere, Reagan ordered the **deployment of Pershing and Cruise missiles** in Europe;

ii he also ordered an **increase in US spending on defence**.

6 SALT Reagan continued the SALT negotiations. He refused to accept Russian demands for a large reduction of US inter-continental weapons. In spite of several Russian 'walk-outs' the negotiations have not been abandoned.

7 Grenada is a West Indian island and a member of the British Commonwealth. In 1983 there was a coup against a 'moderate' Communist government. Cuban troops and advisers arrived in the island to help the new government. Reagan ordered the invasion of the island, the overthrow of the 'illegal' government and the restoration of some form of democratic government. This was a much harder line than anything that had been attempted since the early days of Vietnam.

8 Lebanon, 1983–4. See 37.19.5.

33 China, 1949–83

33.1 The Chinese People's Republic, 1949

1 1st October 1949 At Peking Mao Tse-tung proclaimed the Chinese People's Republic.

2 Unlike Lenin in 1917

i Mao had fought a **civil war before** gaining power;

ii the new government was **widely accepted** in China and by Russia and her satellites.

3 The Constitutional Congress 14 political parties were at the Congress. Two played a major role and gained places in the government:

i the **Left Kuo Min Tang** which had broken with Chiang Kai-shek;

ii the **Democratic League** of middle-class intellectuals.

33.2 Foreign Policy, 1949–56

1 December 1949 Mao went to Moscow. **Stalin** had provided **little help** to Mao before 1949. **In 1949 he gave**:

i a **military security pact**;

ii **technical and economic aid**.

2 The USA had wanted Mao and Chiang to work together (17.34.4). Once Mao had tied himself to Russia, the **USA broke with China**:

i she **refused to recognize** the Communist government;

ii she **re-equipped Chiang**, now on Formosa (Taiwan);

iii she sent the **Seventh Fleet** to guard the straits between Formosa and the mainland to prevent a Communist invasion;

iv she vetoed Communist China's **membership of the UNO**.

3 The Korean War led to increased hostility (28.11.19) and led to the formation of **SEATO** and **ANZUS** as anti-Chinese organizations.

4 1955 The Chinese, like the Russians, took a **softer line** towards the USA and the west. They also tried to win friends among the uncommitted nations in Africa and Asia:

i **Chou En-lai** led Chinese delegates on foreign tours;

ii they **won friends** such as Nasser, Nehru and Sukarno.

5 This policy operated at the **Afro-Asian Conference, Bandung**, 1955:

i **Russia was not invited** to the Conference;

ii **Nehru tried**, but failed, to get a **united Third World** which would be neutral towards both Russia and the US;

iii **Nasser tried**, but failed, to get the Conference to accept

Egypt as the focal point for the three 'Worlds' of Arab, African and Muslim peoples;

iv **China and India** confirmed their friendship which had been endangered because of the **Indo-Chinese dispute over Tibet**:

(a) India and China share a **2000 mile-long frontier**;

(b) **in Tibet**, Russian, Chinese and Indian influences meet;

(c) **Britain** had invaded Tibet in 1904; China always claimed sovereignty over Tibet which claimed independence;

(d) **1950** China invaded Eastern Tibet;

(e) **1954** India reached an agreement with China, giving up her policy of regarding Tibet as a buffer state (33.16.2);

(f) **Nehru** outlined Indian policy of **co-existence**. China and India agreed to mutual non-aggression.

6 1956 Mao went to Moscow to **advise Khrushchev** on policy in Eastern Europe following the unrest in Hungary (30.10.3).

33.3 Domestic policy, theory and industry, 1949–52

1 Mao wanted **broad agreement** for his policies and the **help** of millions of non-Communist technicians and officials.

2 The **property of leading nationalists** was seized.

3 The **state took control** of banks, gas and electricity supply, railways and heavy industry such as coal and steel.

4 This **nationalization** was done **slowly** and former owners received **compensation**.

5 **Middle-class support** had to be won. Mao tried to ensure that this class (of intellectuals and officials) would be **'purified'** of the corruption practised under Chiang:

i **the Three Anti-Movement** (against corruption, waste and government inefficiency) was launched to re-educate people;

ii **the Five Anti-Movement** was aimed at wiping out bad practices in government and industry. It aimed at abolishing tax evasion, theft of government property, theft of industrial secrets, bribery and fraud.

6 In this unspectacular way **China began to recover**:

i **1949** China produced one-third less than in 1935;

ii in **1952** China produced one-sixth more than in 1935.

33.4 Domestic policy; agriculture, 1949–52

1 China was, largely, a poor agricultural country.

2 Mao had gained his greatest support from the peasants.

3 **June 1950 Land Reform**

i **landowners** had to give their property to the peasants although they, as 'people', were allowed to have their share of the estate. About **1 million landlords were killed** by peasants with bitter memories;

ii **the peasants** were encouraged to form marketing and producers' **co-operatives** to help them become efficient.

33.5 Domestic policy, 1949–52; other changes

1 **Women** were completely emancipated.

2 **Education** was extended to children of every class.

3 **Europeans** lost all their privileges and their investments in China were seized. Only Russian investment escaped.

33.6 Purges, 1949–52

1 As Mao settled into power **he rid himself of some supporters**.

2 Some had joined Mao only in the latter years of the struggle with Chiang. **Some of these were expelled from the party by 1952**.

3 During the **Korean War** there was a **purge** of the faint-hearted who had not wanted to challenge the giant USA.

4 Communists took over **existing youth groups** to gain the young for the government.

5 There were **anti-religious campaigns**. Priests and other ministers were imprisoned or expelled from China.

6 **Propaganda campaigns**, largely through huge wall posters, tried to brainwash the people against foreigners and Christianity and to support Mao and the government.

7 About **1 million people were killed** as 'enemies of the people'.

33.7 The First Five Year Plan, 1953

1 This aimed at **increasing the output by heavy industry**. It was, in some ways, like Stalin's Plans (11.4-5). **But China**:

i started from a **lower industrial base** than Russia;

ii wanted to **move more quickly** than Stalin had.

2 This meant that the **people had to work harder** while getting almost no benefit from their increased output.

3 **Private industry** in these heavy industries was **abolished**.

4 **Slow workers** and the **critics** of the Plan were **purged**.

5 Fig. 33.7A illustrates the **success of this first Plan**.

Production achievements during the first five-year plan 1953-1957

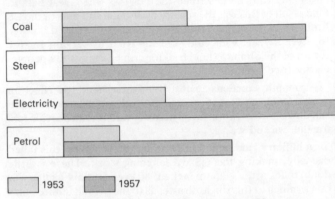

| | 1953 | | 1957 |

Fig. 33.7A China's first Five Year Plan

6 The first Chinese-built **lorries** appeared in 1956; the first **oil-tankers** and **aircraft** in 1957.

7 But even after this 'success' China **only produced 5.3 million tons of steel compared to 20 million tons produced in Britain and 100 million tons in the USA**.

33.8 Collectivization, 1953

1 In 1935 the **grain harvest** was 140 million tons; in 1949 it was only 108 million.

2 An **increased output was essential** to save spending of valuable foreign currency on food imports.

3 But the **peasants did not earn enough** to pay for investment in machinery.

4 So Mao followed the Stalin path of **collectivization** (11.9). This was done in **3 stages**:

i Communist teams (cadres) tried to persuade peasants into **Mutial Aid Teams** of about 10 families. Each retained his own land but all pooled their animals, equipment and labour;

ii this led to a greatly increased output. But this gave rise to a Chinese form of kulak (11.8) or rich peasant, likely to be more of an individualist and less likely to support Communism;

iii so the cadres were sent out again to persuade several Mutual Aid Teams to combine to form a **co-operative**;

(a) **all the land** of the co-operatives would be sown and harvested **in 1 operation**;

(b) **a committee** elected by members of the co-operative would decide on the crop to be grown, the work to be done and where the crop was to be sold;

(c) **profits** would be shared among the co-operative members:

iv again, this led to **increased output**. China's towns and cities were now, for the first time, free of famine;

v cadres encouraged peasants to **form collective farms**:

(a) all private property was abolished;

(b) **peasants were paid** for the work they did on the much larger collective farm:

vi not surprisingly the **peasants resisted this process**:

(a) they had been taught, 1950–52, that they had a **right to own property**;

(b) they had enjoyed the benefits of individual hard work;

(c) they **resisted attempts** to drive them into being wage-earning workers on collectives;

(d) there were **local uprisings** against enthusiastic cadres;

vii the government recognized the danger. **Collectives were broken down** into smaller units:

(a) people worked in **smaller groups**;

(b) they could **organize their own work**, providing it fitted into the party plan for the collective as a whole;

(c) **each peasant was given enough land** for the growing of vegetables and the rearing of a few pigs and hens:

viii **these concessions** were enough to win the support of the peasants. **By 1957 almost all land had been collectivized**;

ix however, even the increased output was barely enough to keep pace with the 2 per cent annual increase in population.

33.9 The Hundred Flowers Campaign, 1957

1 Mao was satisfied with the industrial progress and with the collectivization process.

2 He decided to **allow free discussion** of China's problems.

3 '**Let a hundred flowers bloom and a thousand schools contend**' he said, inviting comment on China's progress.

4 He was **surprised** by the volume of **criticism**.

5 Such criticism had led to crises in Europe (30.10).

6 So he put an end to the freedom and purged the more important of his critics.

33.10 The Great Leap Forward, 1958 (*The Second Five Year Plan*)

1 Mao decided to take a **giant stride** towards the socialist society, making the great changes needed in a few years.

2 **Industry** was to increase output by 30 per cent a year. **Steel output** was to double each year, by:

i **extending traditional steel mills and industries**;

ii '**backyard furnaces**' which ordinary people would set up; every man would become a part-time steel maker.

3 **Agriculture** was to be reformed to produce the food needed by the growing population and to pay for essential imports:

i the 750 000 collectives were reformed into **24 000 communes** each covering about 10 000 acres;

ii **private plots** (33.8.4.vii) were abolished;

iii **the commune** would be not only a farming unit. It was to be something like an **Israeli kibbutz**. It provided common dining rooms, dormitories, nurseries and schools; it provided its own welfare schemes and local government;

iv **the individualism of the peasant was to be wiped out**; the commune would produce a new breed of people.

4 The success and failure of the commune

i **output** 1 million town workers were driven into the countryside to become commune workers. Crops were sown on wider areas. But the **result was disappointing**. The government had hoped for a harvest of 375 million tons; only 250 million tons was produced in 1958. In 1959, 1960 and 1961 a series of floods and droughts made matters worse. In 1962 only 175 million tons were harvested. **The government had to import grain from Canada and Australia**;

ii **attitudes**: peasants **resented** the loss of their private property. They took **less care** of 'communal' tools and machinery than they had of their own property.

5 Industrial failure Most 'backyard steel' was useless.

6 The government steps back

i Mao had not taken into account the **need to prepare the people** for the vast changes proposed by the Great Leap;

ii he had hoped to be able to **do without the technicians and bureaucrats** who were concerned with more efficiency than with the purity of ideological thought. He had hoped to bring the people to accept the need for '**permanent revolution**';

iii **changes**:

(a) **Mao stepped down** from being head of state and **concentrated** his attention on being **Chairman of the Party**;

(b) **Liu Shao-chi became head of state**. With the Prime Minister, **Chou En-lai**, he concentrated on **saving the economy** more than on promoting party ideology;

(c) **the communes were partly broken down**. On 75 000 new communes peasants were given back houses, gardens and plots. The commune retained control of overall planning and of machinery. The day-to-day running of the commune was given to teams which ran individual villages and to brigades which ran groups of villages.

7 Benefits of the Great Leap

i many people had had their **first industrial experience** in the 'backyard furnaces' scheme;

ii millions of Chinese, particularly the young, caught some of **Mao's enthusiasm** for change and permanent revolution.

iii **the commune**, even changed, remained a feature of China.

33.11 The Third Five Year Plan, 1962–67

1 This started from a **broader and deeper base** than existed when Mao launched his first plan in 1952:

i there were **many new industries**–machine tools, motor vehicles, aircraft and electrical equipment;

ii **many industries had grown**–coal, steel, chemicals and cement;

iii there were **many new industrial centres**. In 1952 industry had been concentrated in Manchuria and around the southern ports. By 1962 there were major centres throughout China and a new railway system linked them together.

2 This Plan was hampered by the sudden withdrawal of Russian aid and technicians (33.12.8). But it was **successful**:

i China became the world's **second largest coal producer**;

ii she surpassed Britain in the production of **machine tools**;

iii her **steel industry** matched those of the USA and the USSR.

3 One external sign of her growth was her explosion of **nuclear weapons** (1964) and of a **hydrogen bomb** (1967).

4 Other signs of progress are in the improved standard of living. Within 20 years of taking power the communists had:

i **abolished usury** and the power of money lenders;

ii **ended starvation and famines**;

iii made **government officials more honest**.

5 The individual Chinese is now better fed and clothed, fully employed and enjoys well-developed welfare services.

6 China still remains **largely an agricultural country**, able to identify with other under-developed countries, while also being able to offer them the technical aid they need.

33.12 China and Russia

1 Long-standing hostility

i in the **17th century** Russia occupied the **Amur Valley**;

ii in the **19th century** there were clashes over **Mongolia**;

iii in the **early 20th century** they clashed over mineral-rich **Sinkiang**, bordering on **Kazakhstan**.

2 1945–46 Russia stripped **Manchuria** of its industrial goods.

3 1946–49 Stalin did not aid Mao in his war with Chiang.

4 1949–56 Russia provided **less aid** than she gave to India.

5 Atomic power Russia did not share her secrets with China.

6 Ideological differences, 1956

i after Stalin died, Mao thought of himself as Communism's '**elder statesman**'. The Russians did not agree;

ii **Khrushchev** claimed that an **atomic war** would destroy not only the capitalist west but the Communist world. There would always be **millions of Chinese survivors of such a war**, said Mao.

7 The Great Leap Forward was criticized by Russia as not following the 'Russian path'.

8 By 1960 the dispute had become much fiercer:

i **Mao accused the Russians** of wanting to become more like the west. Khrushchev's visits to the USA and his meetings with Eisenhower and Kennedy were dismissed as attempts to lessen Communist commitment to socialism. **'The ghoulash society'** was Mao's description of Russia as it concentrated on material growth;

ii at the **22nd Party Conference, 1960**, the quarrel became an open one. **Russia withdrew the 1390 technicians** working in China and cut off technical aid, hampering Chinese development.

9 1962 China accused Khrushchev of cowardice in the **Cuban crisis** (29.12).

10 1963 She refused to take part in the negotiations which led to the **Test Ban Treaty**.

11 1964 Khrushchev planned a meeting of all Communist leaders to get them to throw China out of the Communist 'club'. In fact it was Khrushchev who fell from power (29.14).

12 Russia became even more hostile to China during the chaos of the **Cultural Revolution** (33.14).

13 China described Russia as 'a paper tiger' anxious to make peace and détente with the west.

14 1971 It was a major surprise when **China changed her attitude towards the USA** in particular and the west in general:

i it began when China allowed western teams into China to play **table tennis**, a game at which China excelled;

ii 'Ping pong' diplomacy allied with **Nixon's wish for worldwide détente** brought speedy results:

(a) **the USA ended its veto** on China's application to join the UN. **Taiwan was expelled** to make room for Communist China;

(b) **Nixon visited Peking** and started the diplomatic contact between the two countries.

15 1973 Chou En-lai warned the 10th Party Congress to be on their guard against a surprise **attack from the USSR**.

(a) **Border clashes on the Kazakhstan-Sinkiang** border took place in 1968 and 1969;

(b) **Russia** had moved her mobile **missile launchers into Mongolia** to threaten China;

(c) the USSR saw the **aggressive Mao** as an Asian Hitler.

(d) Mao spoke of the **'anti-Chinese atrocities** of the new Czars. . . . Fascist heels trample on the Motherland.'

33.14 The Cultural Revolution 1966–71

1 Reasons for

i **tensions between Mao**, who wanted 'continuing revolution', **and Chou and Liu Shao-chi** who wanted to improve the economy;

ii **Mao's concern as to his successors.** Would they take the Russian line and become too concerned with materialism?

iii **Mao's fear that the west would attack China.** Would the new generation, without experience of the Long March (17.25) and guerilla war, be able to defeat such an attack?

2 The aim

i **to purge the party** of the unreliable;

ii to drive from office and power the 'functionaries'–the **technical experts**, more interested in results than in revolution, and the **party bureaucracy**, the officials more interested in holding onto positions of power and to developing their own careers than in revolution;

iii to get the Chinese people used to the idea of 'continuous revolution'.

3 Its course

i **1967** Mao's main supporter was Defence Minister, **Lin Piao**;

ii he started a **massive propaganda campaign** to ensure that a 'revolutionary' army would guarantee Mao's success.

iii Mao launched a **series of attacks** on writers, historians and intellectuals who disagreed with him. This attack on the country's **cultural leaders** gave the movement its name;

iv Mao undertook his famous **Great Long Swim** in the Yangtze River to prove that, aged 72, he was **still strong enough to lead**;

v he urged the young to **form militant Red Guards**. Millions of young workers and students went on a nation-wide rampage:

(a) **religion** came under attack; temples and statues were smashed;

(b) **government ministers** were attacked and humiliated. Peng Chu, Mayor of Peking, was denounced and forced to resign. **Liu Shao-chi**, Head of State, was expelled from the party he had helped to victory in the 1930s and 1940s. **Teng Hsioa-ping**, the Communist Party General Secretary, was forced to resign;

(c) the Red Guards commandeered **trains**, took over **radio stations**, **arrested** anyone showing 'western tendencies'–by wearing lipstick or expensive clothes or owning some small luxury;

(d) teachers, university professors, journalists and commentators all suffered at the hands of the rampaging mob. Waving the **'Little Red Book'** containing **'The Thoughts of Chairman Mao'** they dominated Chinese life for several years.

4 The effects

i **little, if any, work** was done. Workers were forced to listen to lectures or to take part in demonstrations;

ii some leaders managed to avoid arrest. But Chou had to watch while **nine-tenths of the government was overthrown**;

iii some leaders tried to put an end to the chaos.

5 Civil War, 1971–3

i **Lin Piao**, once named as Mao's successor, tried to get the army to stop the revolution which he had started (33.14.3). Mao discovered this 'treachery'; Lin died in an air crash as he was trying to escape to the west;

ii **Teng Hsioa-ping** argued that Mao could not be the only leader of China. The **leadership ought to be collective**;

iii Teng and others saw that China was **going backwards economically**;

iv **army commanders**, in 7 out of China's 11 military regions, **opposed the Red Guards**;

v **workers** in Wuhan and Shanghai fought pitched battles with the Red Guards; **severe fighting** took place in other cities and communes;

vi finally the **army stepped in** and drove the Red Guards back to the classrooms and workplaces.

6 The end

i Mao was **still Chairman**–until his death in 1976;

ii **Chou, supported by the army**, the **bureaucracy** and **those responsible for running the economy**, emerged as the real leader;

iii **Teng Hsiao-ping** was reinstated in 1973 when he became Deputy Prime Minister to Chou. This was the real sign that the **Cultural Revolution was over**;

iv **not everyone came back**. Liu was not reinstated; the number of officials running the country was reduced from 60 000 to 10 000;

v some 'Maoists' were included in Chou's Politburo–the sign that Chou had to take account of the Revolution.

33.15 The end of Maoism

1 Mao's wife campaigned against Chou's revisionism. But Chou had enough support to resist even this powerful lady.

2 Madam Mao managed to get her ageing husband to drive Teng Hsiao-ping from office when Chou died in January 1976.

3 Mao died in September 1976.

4 This removed his powerful influence which had helped his wife and the 'perpetual revolutionaries'.

5 **Madam Mao and her leading supporters were arrested.**

6 **The army put down pro-Maoist risings** in various provinces. Fighting went on into 1977. Millions were killed.

7 **Teng Hsiao-ping** came back to power. Very quickly he became the real ruler of China. This was the sign that **economic realism** had proved stronger than revolutionary fervour.

8 **Khrushchev waged war on Stalin's memory in 1956.** Teng and his supporters have similarly tried to **abolish the myth of Maoism.**

33.16 China and the outside world

1 **The USA**
i **1946–49** See 33.2.2;
ii **1950** relations worsened during the Korean War (28.11.19);
iii **1971** relations changed abruptly (33.12.14).

2 **India**
i China annexed **Tibet** 1950 (33.2.5.iv);
ii the Dalai Lama, the traditional ruler, was forced to flee after an unsuccessful revolution in 1959;
iii 1965 Tibet became a self-governing region of China;
iv **India was alarmed** at China's Tibetan policy, but remained benevolently 'neutral' to China until 1960;
v **1960** China absorbed the **Burmese province of Wa**, a sign that she had 'imperialist ambitions';
vi **1962** China challenged Indian claims to sovereignty in some parts of the **Himalayas.** The border was ill-defined. China claimed **Ladakh** and other regions which India regarded as hers;
vii **the Indo-Chinese war, 1962**, ended in Chinese success. Indian troops withdrew. China claimed another 15 000 square miles of territory.

3 **Hong Kong**
i China made no attempt to seize the island, ceded by the Manchus in 1842 following the Opium War;
ii nor did she try to take back areas of the mainland (Kowloon and other New Territories) leased by the Manchus to the British in 1898;
iii she also left alone the Portuguese colony of Macao;
iv there were **good economic reasons** for this 'friendly' attitude towards 'western imperialists':
(a) through Hong Kong and Macao, China had access to the **markets of the west**, and to the **financial markets** which she used to get the money needed for her development;
(b) she could have taken them when she wished. This knowledge kept **some countries inclined to be friendly to China**:
v in **1983** the British and Chinese are negotiating the future of Hong Kong and the New Territories–which provide the overcrowded island with living space and, above all, water supplies;
vi Britain hopes that China can be persuaded to recognize Hong Kong as an especially privileged part of China with a special and recognized relationship with the west.

34 The Indian Sub-Continent, 1939–83

34.1 The position in 1939

1 There had been **some progress** towards self-government (22.2–22.7).

2 **The Congress Party** (22.2.4) had become increasingly active.

3 Congress had won majorities in many **provincial assemblies** (22.8.3).

4 **Jinnah**, leader of the **Muslim League**, was anti-Congress:
i he **feared** the creation of a **Hindu India**;
ii he called for a **separate Muslim state**;
iii Congress did not take this threat very seriously.

34.2 India and the War, 1939

1 The Viceroy, Linlithgow, **declared war** on Germany on behalf of India without consulting Congress.

2 **Congress** saw the war as **'a European affair'**. If India was to get involved, Congress demanded **immediate independence**.

3 The British promised **Dominion status** (22.1.5) 'at the end of the war'.

4 **Congress** then **opposed** Indian participation in the war:
i **many leaders** were arrested and imprisoned without trial;
ii **Ghandi, a pacifist**, was arrested for opposing the war effort;
iii in the Provinces, **Congress ministers** resigned in protest.

5 The more **war-like Muslims** supported the war effort:
i Muslims held on to their posts in **provincial governments**;
ii in 1940 the 'loyal' Muslims put forward their policy for a **separate Pakistan**; 'Pakistan or perish' was their slogan.

34.3 The War, 1941

1 **The Japanese** took Burma and got to the **borders of India**.

2 **Gandhi and Congress** argued that the only reason to fear a Japanese invasion of India was because of the British presence.

3 If the British 'quit India', Japan would leave her alone.

4 A minority of Hindus, led by a Congress leader, **Chandra Bose**, went to fight for the Japanese. His **Indian National Army** was made up of some who left India and others recruited from Hindus in Japanese prisoner-of-war camps.

34.4 The Cripps Mission, 1942

1 Britain needed Indian support for the war against Japan.

2 Cripps was a socialist minister in Churchill's coalition.

3 He was sent to consult with Congress and to promise:
i **Dominion status** at the end of the war;
ii **the right to leave the Commonwealth** if they wished;
iii the right to **work out their own constitution**.

4 **Nehru** wanted to accept this offer.

5 **Gandhi** was opposed to it. He proposed a campaign for mass civil disobedience.

6 The **'Quit India' campaign** forced the government to put Congress leaders back in jail, as a threat to Indian security.

34.5 Muslim progress, 1940–45

1 Congress's refusal to co-operate was a mistake:
i it could have had many important posts in government;
ii it would have won the sympathy of the British.

2 It provided **Muslims with unexpected opportunities**:
i in the **Punjab**, a key state, the Muslim League shared the government with British officials;
ii **in Bengal**, a Leaguer was Prime Minister;
iii there were League governments in **Sind and Assam**;
iv **in the North West Frontier Province**, Congress Muslim leaders had been arrested. Leaguers then formed the government.

3 **This growth of Muslim power** showed that Congress did not speak for 'all Indians' as it claimed.

34.6 The Simla Conference, 1945

1 **Wavell**, a new Viceroy, called a Conference of the released **Congress leaders** and the **leaders of the Muslim League**.

2 He put forward, again, the Cripps's proposals (34.4).

3 **Congress claimed** that, since it included some Muslims, it had the **right to nominate Muslim members of a central government**.

4 Leaguers, with their wartime experience (34.5), **denied this**.

5 Hostility between the leaders wrecked the Conference.

34.7 The Pethwick-Lawrence Mission, 1945–46

1 The new Labour government in Britain had promised Indian independence.

2 A Cabinet Mission, headed by Lord Pethwick-Lawrence, and including Cripps (34.4), was sent to try to get agreement.

3 The Mission offered:

i **immediate Dominion status** without any partition of India;

ii **increased powers to provincial governments**–which would help Muslims in states where they were in the majority;

iii the right for **groups of provinces to form a union** within a Federal India. There would have been a Muslim Union of Sind, the North West Frontier Province and the Punjab.

4 The leaders of Hindus and Muslims agreed.

5 But the agreement was wrecked when **Congress** refused to give the **League** the right to appoint all Muslim members of the proposed central government.

6 This was the last chance of achieving a united and independent India for which Gandhi had worked.

34.8 Unrest, 1946–47

1 Wavell, the Viceroy, asked **Nehru to form a government**.

2 **Jinnah**, head of the Muslim League, **joined the government**. But he also declared that Muslims would **no longer follow constitutional methods** to get their separate Pakistan.

3 This encouraged local leaders to use **violent methods** to show their opposition to Congress and the Hindus.

4 **Racial and religious rioting** led to wholesale massacres of Hindus, Sikhs and Muslims.

5 **Provincial governments**, themselves dominated by religious differences, were **unwilling or unable to stop the killings**.

6 **Jinnah** and other Muslim League ministers did all they could to **make it impossible for Nehru's government** to function.

34.9 The Mountbatten Mission, March 1947

1 The Labour Prime Minister, **Attlee**, sent Lord Louis Mountbatten to replace Wavell as Viceroy of India.

2 He was related to King George VI. Attlee hoped that this would gain British support for his policies.

3 He had been Supreme Commander South East Asia in the war against Japan. Attlee hoped this would gain him the support of Indians.

4 Attlee and Mountbatten announced that **Britain would leave India in June 1948**. They hoped to force Indians to agree.

5 Attlee hoped to maintain a united India.

6 Mountbatten quickly realized this was not possible.

7 **June 1947** Mountbatten agreed to the **partition of India**.

8 He fixed an early date for independence, **15 August 1947**.

34.10 The violent birth of two new nations

1 Having decided on the creation of 2 states, Mountbatten set up Commissions to deal with the transfer of power.

2 **The problem of boundaries**, as illustrated in the Punjab:

i the Punjab was to be divided between India and Pakistan;

ii this would divide Sikh from Sikh;

iii Amritsar, the Sikh 'holy place' (22.3), was to be in India cutting off the Sikhs in Pakistan from their 'holy place';

iv **March 1947** While the boundary commission was being set up, Muslims wrecked the Hindu bazaars in Amritsar, burning Hindu homes and murdering the Hindu people;

v the warlike Sikhs, prepared to take action against Muslims on the other side of the proposed boundary;

vi the police, themselves divided racially, did not take action or join in the rioting.

3 Other problems of partition

i **the religious massacres** in the Punjab were only the first. Other, and worse, massacres were to follow;

ii **irrigation schemes** were 'partitioned'. Would Hindus allow 'their water' to flow into the Muslim areas? And vice versa?

iii **the army and navy** contained men of all religions. These All-India forces had to be 'partitioned'. How?

iv **the civil service** was predominantly Hindu but contained people of all religions. This had to be 'partitioned';

v **the railway system** was another All-India system. Would separate governments provide an All-India service?

4 The massacres

i the technical problems (34.10.3) had been foreseen and most of them solved before partition in August 1947;

ii no one had provided for the transfer of millions of people from one new state to another in areas which were religiously divided. Bengal and the Punjab were particularly affected:

(a) 5 million Hindus left West Pakistan for India;

(b) 5 million Muslims left India for West Pakistan;

(c) 1 million Hindus left East Pakistan for India:

iii the scale of killing was horrific:

(a) 500 000 were killed before they left their original homes;

(b) at least 1 million were killed as they made their way by train or walking to their new homes;

(c) it was ironic that the man who tried to stop this religious slaughter–Gandhi–was himself to be assassinated in 1948. It was, perhaps, fortunate that his murderer was a Hindu fanatic who thought that Gandhi had been 'soft on the Muslims'.

6 The princely states

i there were 570 states in India where native princes ruled;

ii in theory, Mountbatten's agreement with Hindus and Muslims allowed these princes to choose their future;

iii most of them were small and had to join one of the new 'giants', depending on their religion;

iv some, notably the Maharajah of Hyderabad, were rich enough to remain independent;

v they felt betrayed when Britain did nothing when India took Hyderabad by force in 1948;

vi Kashmir provided a long-standing problem (34.23).

34.11 The problems facing the new state of India

1 **Mass illiteracy** How would this affect the world's largest democracy?

2 **Starvation** In agricultural India millions lived below an acceptable 'poverty line'; thousands died each week of starvation. How would the independent government cope with this problem, resulting largely from religious problems?

3 **Religion** Hinduism taught India's millions:

i to accept their fate. Would they make efforts to raise living standards?

ii to honour the 'sacred cow'. How would this 'worship' affect attempts at agricultural reform?

4 **Caste** Hindus are divided and sub-divided into hundreds of social castes. Caste determines a person's job, marriage-partner, political loyalty and educational opportunity. Would a government be able to break down these traditional religious divisions?

5 **Economic inequality** was the result of the caste system. Would independent India, under socialist Nehru, be able to alter this inequality?

6 **Women** were regarded as inferior. Would a male-dominated and Hindu-dominated government try to 'modernize' India?

7 **Population** There were 400 million Indians in 1947. The population increased by about 2 per cent a year after that.

8 **Agriculture** There were to be frequent reports of a 'green revolution' by which India had become self-supporting in food. In fact there were regular failures in agriculture. The output in

1964 equalled that of 1961 (but then there were 28 million more mouths to be fed). The output in 1966 was lower than that of 1964.

9 Food imports were essential in most years. But if India was also to import machinery (for her industrialization) she could not afford such food imports.

34.12 Nehru's India

1 It was the world's largest democracy with 170 million voters in 1947.

2 Congress won the first election.

3 **Opposition parties** were created by:

i Communists, eager for a social revolution;

ii the Jan Sanga, representing Hindu traditionalists and opposed to any policies which offended their religious beliefs;

iii other groups, such as that representing the lowest social caste known as Untouchables.

4 Nehru was Prime Minister from 1947 until his death in 1964.

5 In 1950 India became a Republic but remained in the Commonwealth.

6 **Political difficulties:**

i Congress was a much divided Party, split by:

(a) regional differences;

(b) caste;

(c) economic interests. The mill-owning millionaires dominated Congress to the detriment of social reform;

ii there was a great gulf between the rich ruling élite and the majority of Congress supporters;

iii corruption was a fact of Indian life. Even foreign aid was often syphoned off by corrupt officials so that it never achieved what was intended.

34.13 Nehru's foreign policy

1 **Nehru adopted a neutralist stance.** India would favour neither the capitalist west nor the Communist east.

2 He wanted to be an 'honest broker' standing between the two rivals in the Cold War (28.3). He played a major role in bringing the 2 sides together in:

i **Korea** where he helped arrange a truce (28.11.26);

ii **Geneva, 1954**, where he helped end the fighting between France and the Vietnamese (35.13).

3 **India and China:**

i they quarrelled over Tibet, **1950-59** (33.16.2);

ii Nehru tried to get the **1955 Bandung Conference** to accept China as the 'natural' leader of the Third World (38.2.6);

iii **1959-62** there were many border clashes along the ill-defined frontier—particularly in the Himalayan area;

iv **1962** during the Sino-India War India received aid from both Russia and the USA. For this War see 33.16.2.

4 **In 1961** India sent troops into **Goa** to take this Portuguese colony on the Indian mainland. Many people were shocked by this use of force by the 'pacifist' Nehru.

34.14 Economic development

1 To help in her modernization and industrialization India has received a great deal of **aid from both East and West**. This has allowed her to develop economically much faster than would have been the case if she had been forced to stand on her own feet.

2 **Five Year Plans**, the first of which was produced in 1951, have been adopted to try to stimulate industrialization:

i a Planning Commission was set up to produce the Plans and supervize their implementation. Basic industries were nationalized;

ii emphasis was placed on the development of steel, cement and hydro-electricity, essential for industrial progress;

iii by 1961 output of industrial goods had almost doubled. But still only about one per cent of the population worked in industry.

3 Caste Nehru tackled this problem. Discrimination, particularly against the Untouchables, was made an offence.

4 Illiteracy The constitution laid down that free and compulsory education was planned for all children up to the age of 14. This has never been achieved.

5 Agriculture Poor farmers cannot provide the savings needed for investment. Even with foreign aid there has only been small progress. The 25 per cent increase in output achieved by the first Five Year Plan was almost wiped out by the increase in population (see also 34.11.8).

6 Foreign aid This has helped Indian development. But it has been mainly in the form of loans on which interest has to be paid. This is a burden on India's balance of payments.

7 Legal changes In spite of opposition of traditionalists Nehru pushed through:

i the Hindu Marriage Act, 1955, which made monogamy (one wife, one husband) the law and provided for maintenance for Hindu widows and for wives separated from husbands;

ii the Hindu Succession Act, 1956, which gave women equal rights with men to hold and to inherit property.

8 Evidence of success—even limited:

i thousands of villages got an **electricity supply**;

ii millions of **new jobs** were created;

iii **agricultural yields** went up as irrigation schemes and local co-operatives helped some regions to improve.

9 The population problem In 1956 Nehru introduced an intensive programme to encourage birth control. But this had little success:

i the majority of the illiterate peasants did not understand what they were told, and could not 'read the instructions';

ii many religiously orthodox people were offended by the interference with nature—as they saw birth control.

34.15 Lal Shastri, 1964-66

1 Nehru died in May, 1964

2 There was no real struggle for power on the death of India's 'founder', a proof that democracy had taken firm root.

3 Lal Shastri had a long record of service to India:

i he had been imprisoned for 9 years for civil disobedience;

ii he had been a minister under Nehru;

iii he had had particular responsibility for laws against discrimination, part of the social revolution.

4 As Nehru's successor he was opposed by the right-wing (traditionalists) of the Congress. To please them he went to war over Kashmir (34.23).

5 But they resented his attempts at peace in Kashmir (34.23.13).

6 They wanted him to make India a nuclear power.

7 January 1966 Shastri died suddenly.

34.16 Mrs Indira Gandhi, Nehru's daughter

1 **A surprising choice** in a male-dominated country which needed a firm government to cope with its many problems.

2 **A success**

i her government won majorities at elections in 1967 and 1971;

ii between 1967 and 1971 she fought the Syndicate, the party bosses who dominated Congress;

(a) most of them were corrupt and had none of Nehru's idealism;

(b) they assumed they could 'run' Nehru's daughter;

(c) she fought them, splitting Congress. Her left-wing group won majorities in most states in the election of 1971, and she remained as Prime Minister.

3 **Her problems**

i she had to cope with India's **long-standing problems** (34.11);

ii she had also to cope with **new problems**:

(a) **Communists** won power in West Bengal in 1967. Rioting there and in other states forced Mrs Gandhi to bring in decrees allowing direct (presidential) rule 'in times of crisis';

(b) the **Naxalites** were Maoist agitators who imitated the Red Guards (33.14.3.v) and tried to rouse the masses to revolution.

4 Her policies

i economic planning continued on the lines laid down by her father;

ii Hindi was established as a common language to promote national unity;

iii the fourth Economic Development Plan aimed to increase Indian wealth by 6 per cent a year, to provide 19 million jobs and to raise average incomes by 25 per cent;

iv the Plan was a partial success:

(a) it still left the mass of Indians in great poverty;

(b) in 1966 inflation forced the government to devalue the currency in the hope that this would help Indian exporters.

5 Economic set backs

i **1967** there was a **general food shortage**; Bihar state suffered a famine. Thousands died;

ii **1971** the coast of Orissa was struck by a **tidal wave**; thousands died in this one storm alone.

6 Socialism–and approval

i Mrs Gandhi, like her father, was a **socialist**;

ii she **nationalized the banks** and, after the elction of 1971, the **insurance companies**;

iii **education**: she planned to give every Indian child at least 5 years schooling by 1975;

iv in the 1971 Election her party gained 100 more seats and held nearly 350 seats. The Opposition was bitterly divided.

7 Bangladesh

i the flood of refugees from Bengal increased India's problems (34.25.4);

ii so, too, did the war with Pakistan (34.25.7).

8 Population

i Nehru had failed to develop a family planning programme;

ii Mrs Gandhi tried to hurry the programme along:

(a) male vasectomy was advocated and, in some regions, insisted on by government officials;

(b) attempts were made to compel women to accept mechanical methods of birth control:

iii Mrs Gandhi's opponents used this as an excuse to attack her and her government.

34.17 In power, out of power and in power again, 1975–83

1 June 1975 Mrs Gandhi was found guilty of corrupt practices and disqualified from holding electoral office for 6 years.

2 1975–77 She ignored the decision and declared a state of emergency, giving herself power to rule without Parliament.

3 In this period thousands of opponents were imprisoned.

4 March 1977 She was replaced as Prime Minister by Mr Desai.

5 November 1978 She re-entered Parliament as the leading member of the Opposition. She had shown that she had retained a considerable personal and political following.

6 The anti-Gandhi faction of the Congress Party proved to be unable to govern.

7 1979 She became Prime Minister again.

34.18 The problems facing Pakistan, 1947

1 Common problems Pakistan shared with India a number of problems (34.11). She also had her particular ones.

2 An unreal nation

i Pakistan had no historic roots;

ii its 2 separate parts were divided by 1000 miles;

iii the people of the 2 regions were racially and linguistically different.

3 East Pakistan's **jute-growing industry** was cut off from its main outlet, Calcutta, now in Indian Bengal.

4 Political policies–the lack of

i the League had developed no policies, except for the creation of the separate state of Pakistan;

ii Jinnah *was* Pakistan. His death shortly after independence (1948) was a major loss;

iii the assassination (1951) of Pakistan's first Prime Minister, Liaquat Ali Khan, was another disaster;

iv these deaths left lesser men squabbling for power.

34.19 Unrest in the new state

1 1956 Following India's example, Pakistan became a Republic.

2 1957 The army decided to put an end to the political unrest:

i the army commander, **Ayub Khan**, seized absolute power;

ii he promised to clean up the administration before handing power back to 'the politicians'.

3 1960 Ayub was elected President and ruled without Parliament.

4 1965 He was re-elected, defeating Miss Jinnah in the Presidential election.

5 His internal policies

i he had a programme for **economic development** with Five Year Plans for expansion and attacks on corruption and inefficiency;

ii there were **many improvements**:

(a) communications were developed;

(b) house-building expanded;

(c) hydro-electric schemes were built;

(d) there was increased output of jute, carpets and leather goods.

6 Relations with India

i he reached agreement on the **River Indus** (34.22);

ii **Kashmir** remained a problem (34.23).

34.20 The fall of Ayub Khan

1 He won the Presidential election, 1965

2 But he had less support in East than in West Pakistan.

3 He was blamed, unfairly, for the floods and famines which affected East Pakistan.

4 He announced plans for 'basic democracy':

i there would be elections for local councils;

ii there would, later, be elections for councils to send MPs to a central Parliament.

iii Ayub would retain control of the government until Pakistan and its politicians had gained political experience.

5 Many suspected that he intended to hold on to power.

6 Politicians, released from prison, whipped up opposition:

i Ayub was accused of corruption and favouring his family;

ii the religious leaders (mullahs) criticized his lack of religious fervour;

iii Communists argued that he favoured the rich industrialists;

iv landlords complained that he favoured the poor.

7 March 1969 The commander-in-chief, **Yahya Khan**, forced Ayub to resign. He imposed martial law. He promised that 'when the country was ready' he would restore democracy.

34.21 Pakistan's foreign policy

1 Unlike 'neutralist' India, Pakistan favoured the west.

2 1954 She signed a Mutual Assistance Pact with the USA.

3 She joined **SEATO**–against Chinese aggression.

4 She joined other Muslim states (Iraq, Iran and Turkey) in the **Baghdad Pact**–against Russian aggression in the Middle East. Nehru condemned this as a 'step towards war'.

5 Ayub became increasingly friendly to Russia and China;

i **1965** he went to Moscow to get technical aid;

ii with China he settled peacefully frontier disputes over the 200-mile border between Pakistan and China.

34.22 The River Indus

1 The headwaters of the rivers feeding the Indus are in India.
2 India wanted to divert these rivers for irrigation schemes.
3 The Indus is vital to West Pakistan's irrigation schemes.
4 The dispute between the 2 new states was temporarily settled by a truce arranged by the World Bank. This led to a treaty (1960) which allowed for the joint development of the Indus waters:
i new dams would be built in both India and Pakistan;
ii both countries would be guaranteed sufficient water for irrigation development.

34.23 Kashmir

1 **1947** This was a princely state (34.10.6).
2 Its Maharaja was a **Hindu**; his people were mainly **Muslim**.
3 There was a good deal of **communal killing** in 1947.
4 Muslims from the North West Frontier Province invaded.
5 India was asked to send troops to put down this invasion. The Maharaja applied to join his state to Hindu India.
6 Pakistan then invaded the state.
7 The UN arranged a temporary truce. Pakistan was allowed to 'govern' the mountains, India the valleys.
8 The UN proposed to hold a plebiscite.
9 Nehru (a Kashmiri) claimed the state for India. It is worth noting that Nehru refused to accept a plebiscite as a means of settling this dispute–although, in other cases where there was a Hindu majority, he insisted on plebiscites.
10 He held elections there which his friend, Sheik Abdullah, won. But the Sheik declared Kashmir independent–and Nehru imprisoned him.
11 **1964** A meeting was planned between Nehru and Ayub to try to settle the dispute. Nehru died before it could be held.
12 **1965–66** The war broke out again.
13 **January 1966** Prime Minister Kosygin of Russia arranged a meeting between Ayub and Shastri (34.15) at Tashkent.
14 They made another truce. But the Kashmiri problem remains unsolved.

34.24 Yahya Khan's fall

1 **1969** Yahya announced a new Economic Plan and promised elections.
2 **December 1970** Elections were held.
3 The People's Party, led by **Ali Bhutto**, won a majority of seats in West Pakistan.
4 In East Pakistan the **Awami League**, led by **Sheik Mujibur Rahman** won an even greater majority of the seats and an overall majority in the Pakistan Parliament.
5 **The West Pakistanis** refused to accept rule by **Easterners**:
i Bhutto announced that his party would boycott Parliament;
ii Yahya visited the East, hoping to arrange a compromise;
iii Bhutto demanded a government which would satisfy both East and West;
iv the Awami League's electoral policy had been to free East Pakistan from control by the West. Sheik Mujibur would not agree to any compromise; 'the League had won'.

34.25 Bangladesh

1 **March 1971** Yahya outlawed the League and asserted the power of his military government over both regions of Pakistan.
2 Rebels in East Pakistan proclaimed independence for Bangladesh.
3 The military government arrested Sheik Mujibur, but civil war was inevitable.
4 Bengali refugees poured into India from East Pakistan escaping from the savagery of the West Pakistan forces.

5 This put a great strain on India's scarce resources. Eight million refugees had to be fed, housed and otherwise cared for.
6 Frontier incidents were frequent; India and Pakistan started fighting again in Kashmir.
7 December 1971 India and Pakistan went to war. Indian troops, aided by Bangladesh freedom fighters, routed the Pakistanis.
8 End of 1971 Yahya was forced to resign:
i Bhutto became President of West Pakistan;
ii Sheik Mujibur, released from prison, took control of Bangladesh.
9 **The Simla Conference, July 1972**
i **Russia** had supported India during the short war;
ii **China** had given lukewarm support to Pakistan;
iii the **USA** had been very critical of India's action;
iv after the victory, Mrs Gandhi was anxious to reach a settlement;
v **July 1972** an agreement was reached at Simla:
(a) all **troops would be withdrawn** from occupied territory;
(b) 90 000 Pakistani **prisoners-of-war** would be repatriated;
(c) the *status quo* would be maintained in **Kashmir**:
iv but **Bhutto** refused to agree to recognize the existence of the new state, Bangladesh. Because of this refusal, India refused to honour the Simla agreement.

34.26 The post-war Muslim worlds

1 **Pakistan, the former West Pakistan**
i Bhutto tried to frame a new constitution. But his People's Party was not overwhelmingly popular;
ii Pakistanis resented their defeat by India and the loss of East Pakistan, now Bangladesh;
iii China had given little help during the war and Bhutto looked for friends elsewhere;
iv at the same time he announced Pakistan's withdrawal from the Commonwealth which accepted Bangladesh as a new member;
v 1973: things were made worse by vast destruction caused by floods in the Indus valley;
vi Bhutto became increasingly autocratic, corrupt and inefficient;
vii July 1977: **General Muhammed Zia** led an army revolution and overthrew Bhutto. The military government arrested Bhutto who was later executed.
2 **Bangladesh faced major problems**
i the war caused much destruction in a poor country;
ii inflation and food shortages made things worse;
iii there was a good deal of racial tension in this new, small, poor, flood-ridden country:
(a) Moslems hated Hindus;
(b) Bengalis hated Biharis who had fought for Mujib:
iv for the millions of landless peasants there was the ever-present threat of starvation;
v Sheik Mujib and his family were assassinated in August 1975. Assad became President in this restless country.
3 **President General Ziaur Rahman**
i Assad, and several of his successors as President, were assassinated;
ii General **Ziaur Rahman** emerged as President in 1977;
iii he faced several **problems**:
(a) **1978** There was an **influx of Moslem refugees** from Burma, which put a strain on the fragile economy. In time most of these refugees returned to Burma;
(b) **1979** Moslem anger was roused by the **Russian invasion of Afghanistan** and the imposition of an irreligious pro-Soviet government in that country (29.19.6);
(c) many Moslems, including the population of Bangladesh, were affected by the development of a new, more strict, **'fundamental' Moslem faith**. While this 'fundamentalism' is

best seen in **Khomeini's Iran** (32.27.8) it is also evident in **Ghadaffi's Libya** and, more recently, in both **Pakistan** and **Bangladesh**;

iv Ziaur Rahman maintained the traditional **pro-Western** and anti-Soviet attitude which had been followed by Pakistan;

v Bangladesh, and Pakistan, received **help from the Arab oil-producing countries** which helped lessen these countries' problems. However, both of them still face enormous economic difficulties.

35 The Far East 1945–83

35.1 The effects of the War, 1945
1 **Japan** had taken the European colonies (25.22).
2 **Japan's defeat** led to changes in these colonies.
3 The Dutch East Indies became **Indonesia** (35.3).
4 **Malaya** became independent and, enlarged, became **Malaysia** (35.5–6).
5 **French Indo-China** was divided into 3 countries, but only after bitter fighting which, later, involved the USA (35.14–19).
6 Perhaps the most surprising feature of this period in this region has been the rehabilitation of Japan.

35.2 The rehabilitation of Japan
1 **The growth of democracy**
  i General MacArthur led an army of occupation into Japan;
  ii **MacArthur wanted to:**
(a) **break the power of the zaibatsu**, the huge industrial combines whose leaders had often disrupted Japanese political life;
(b) **end the power of the militarists**. Japan was to have no army;
(c) **create a genuine democracy** in the country:
  iii **the constitution of 1947:**
(a) both houses of the **Japanese Parliament** are elected;
(b) **universal suffrage** gives women the vote;
(c) **the government is responsible to Parliament** (as in Britain), and not to the Emperor, as in pre-war Japan;
(d) there is **no official state religion**; religion had been one cause of aggressive nationalism;
(e) **the Emperor Hirohito** remained as ruler but was no longer regarded as a divine being as he had been:
  iv **Political parties** MacArthur encouraged the formation of political parties and legalized the Communist Party.
2 **Economic reform under US occupation**
  i **land reform** 4 million peasants were given their own land. This led to increased agricultural output, the end of starvation and provided greater stability in the countryside;
  ii **trades unions** were encouraged and strikes legalized.
3 **Japan and the Cold War, 1945–53**
  i the US needed a strong Japan as a **barrier to communism**:
(a) **the Communist Party** was made illegal;
(b) **1950** MacArthur set up a **Japanese police force** which soon had its own tanks–and soon grew into an army;
(c) **1951** The USA and Japan signed the **Treaty of San Francisco** which led to the withdrawal of US forces from the mainland. The US held on to **Okinawa** until 1972;

(d) **1960** the USA and Japan signed a **Security Treaty** in which the US guaranteed Japan's defence.
4 **Japanese politics, 1952–83**
  i the 1947 constitution led to **stable governments**;
  ii most governments have been **conservative** in character;
  iii violent battles often took place between the riot police and well-organized **demonstrators**, protesting at times about US influence in Japan, the government's military stance, the danger of Japan becoming a nuclear power and the pollution caused by mass industrialization;
  iv but **election results** continued to show that most voters were satisfied with their government.
5 **Economic expansion, 1948–83**
  i **evidence for**: Japan has, again, become the most industrialized nation in Asia. The Japanese 'economic miracle' is visible in:
(a) **shipbuilding, electronic and motor vehicle industries;**
(b) the continued rise in the **volume of exports**;
(c) the rise in **living standards**;
(d) 1966: Japan's leading part in the planning for an **Asian Development Bank**;
(e) **the International Trade Fair**, EXPO 70, an advertisement for Japan's success:
  ii causes of: the main reasons for Japan's growth are:
(a) modernization and willingness to adopt **modern technology**;
(b) **heavy investment** in modernizatioin and in new industries;
(c) a willingness to **work hard**;
(d) **good industrial relations**: trade unions encourage loyalty to employers who, in turn, look after their workers;
(e) **private competition**, which encourages modernization;
(f) Japan has spent **little on her defence**.
6 **Social problems** follow from industrial expansion:
  i a shortage of building land leads to a **housing shortage** and overcrowding;
  ii **towns** provide problems of sewage and refuse disposal, and pollution of the atmosphere and water supplies;
  iii large firms give high wages and welfare benefits. Most Japanese work for small firms which do not have the capital to adopt such paternalist attitudes. **Low wages are the norm**.
7 **Foreign policy**
  i **China**: trade with China fell after the war. Since Mao's death things have improved. Japan has easier access to the vast Chinese market and helps China's industrial development;
  ii **the USA** maintained close links with Japan, providing her with much of the early investment. Recently the USA has become concerned at the effects of Japanese exports on US employment;
  iii **Europe** also suffered from massive imports of Japanese goods. Negotiations about limiting those imports and increasing imports into Japan have had little success;
  iv **Russia** was not invited to sign the San Francisco Treaty (35.2.3.(c)). She resents the growth of an American-backed economic giant;
  v **peace**: Japan was not involved in either SEATO or Vietnam and so avoided antagonizing China and Russia;
  vi **the UN**: Japan gained admission to the UN in 1956.

35.3 Indonesia
1 In 1939 the 7000 islands of the Dutch East Indies supplied half the world's rubber and pepper.
2 **An Indonesian Nationalist Party**, founded in 1927, had an engineer, **Sukarno**, as one of the leaders.
3 Sukarno spent 13 years in prison; few Indonesians supported him. Most feared rule by the Javanese if the Dutch left.
4 **The War** Japan overran the islands and tried to win support:
  i Nationalist leaders were released from prison;

ii Indonesians could fly their 'national' red and white flag;

iii 1943 Sukarno was given some political power, within the framework provided by the Japanese conquerors;

iv an Indonesian resistance movement was secretly encouraged and helped by Sukarno.

5 The Japanese defeat, August 1945

i the Japanese gave Sukarno's Party an administrative experience denied by the Dutch;

ii towards the end, Japan fixed a date for Indonesian independence, hoping to gain support against the Allies;

iii Japan surrendered on 15 August; Sukarno proclaimed independence on 17 August, before Allied forces arrived.

6 The British and Sukarno, September 1945

i Sukarno had 6 weeks of 'power' before British forces arrived. He formed an army, its weapons taken from the Japanese;

ii in the Republican constitution he named himself as President and Jakarta as the capital;

iii the British wanted only to hand back the colony to Holland. This led to fighting with the nationalists, leading the government to take the Mounbatten line—to get the Dutch to negotiate independence.

7 The Dutch and Sukarno, 1945–47

i a small number of Dutch soldiers and officials returned;

ii Holland hoped to regain full control over its colony. This determination led to clashes with Sukarno's forces;

iii November 1946 Holland agreed to a small change:

(a) Java, Madun and Sumatra were formed into a nationalist-governed republic;

(b) they set up a Federation of the United States of Indonesia, consisting of the Republic, Borneo and the Great East (of the other islands);

iv the Dutch set up separate governments in the small islands of the Great East. These puppet-governments would ensure Dutch control of the Federation;

v they supported an independence movement in West Java which was under Republican control.

8 The Dutch versus the Republic

i Sukarno was angered by Dutch policy (above);

ii the Dutch were angered by his attempts to get the world to recognize his Republic as a separate country;

iii July 1947: the Dutch attacked the Republic. Parts of Java and Sumatra were captured;

iv the Republic appealed to the rest of the world. Australia and newly-independent India helped the Republic's case to the UNO, which showed that UNO recognized the Republic's independence;

v Security Council negotiations led, in January 1948, to an agreement giving Holland the right to rule Indonesia until a plebiscite was held;

vi the Dutch held their own plebiscite, set up separate governments in many islands and set up a Federal government which did not contain anyone from the Republic.

9 Stalin and the Republic, 1948

i September 1948 Stalin ordered a series of world-wide risings;

ii a Communist rising in the Republic was put down by Sukarno's nationalist forces;

iii December 1948 The Dutch then launched their own attack, bombing Jakarta and capturing many Republican leaders.

10 Independence

i the UN called for a cease-fire;

ii the USA cut off all economic aid to Holland;

iii August 1949 A conference was called at the Hague;

iv November 1949 Agreement was reached. The Republic of the United States of Indonesia was to comprise the whole of the former Dutch East Indies;

v 30 December 1949 The Republic came into being as part of a meaningless Netherlands Indonesian Union in which the Republic was equal partner with Holland and the Queen of Holland was the Head of the Union. This Union was dissolved in 1954.

35.4 Indonesia after independence

1 **1954** the Union was dissolved (35.3.7.iii.b).

2 **1957** all Dutch citizens were expelled from Indonesia and their property confiscated.

3 **1962** West Irian, (part of New Guinea) which was retained by the Dutch, was placed under UN administration. 1963 It was handed to Indonesia.

4 Sukarno

i he had confronted the Dutch in West Irian;

ii 1963 he quarrelled with Malaysia which claimed British possessions of Sarawak and Sabah in northern Borneo (35.6.2);

iii Indonesian guerillas fought against Malayan forces in Sarawak and Sabah; parachutists invaded Malaya;

iv Sukarno was condemned by the UN from which he withdrew in 1965. But in 1966 he gave up the anti-Malaysian struggle;

v many Indonesians resented Sukarno's autocratic methods:

(a) the 1950 constitution provided for democratic government;

(b) until 1955 the provisional parliament was appointed, not elected, although political parties were formed;

(c) in the 1955 elections the 4 main parties won roughly the same number of seats. There could be no stable government. Sukarno said that western democracy did not suit Indonesia.

(d) 1956–7 clashes between Javanese and the people of the smaller islands and between right-wing and Communist groups made the shaky government even more unworkable.

(e) 1960 Parliament was dissolved and replaced by a National Front, with a People's Consultative Congress and a Supreme Advisory Council. In fact Sukarno was a dictator:

vi October 1965 a Communist rising was crushed by the army. Sukarno may have organized the rising to allow himself even greater powers—and without Communist opposition;

vii in anti-Communist rioting 87 000 people were killed;

viii January 1966 students rioted when Sukarno included pro-Communists in his government;

ix March 1967 the army overthrew Sukarno and put General Suharto in power.

35.5 Malaya, 1945–65

1 During the war Malayan Chinese formed a guerilla movement.

2 This was under Communist control.

3 In **1948** Stalin ordered a Communist rising.

4 This was not put down until 1960. Few Malays joined the rebels.

5 1957 Malaya became independent. Malay and Chinese leaders co-operated in negotiations leading to independence.

6 The first Prime Minister of Malaya was Tunku Abdul Rahman who remained in power until his death in 1970.

7 1963 Britain handed over her colonies in Borneo. Brunei opted out; Sabah and Sarawak joined the Federation of Malaysia.

35.6 Malaysia, 1963–65

1 Malaysia had a long struggle with Communist guerillas in the north.

2 It also had a war against Indonesia (35.4.4).

3 It was unable to keep **Singapore** in the Federation of Malaysia:

i the population of Singapore was mainly Chinese;

ii Lee Kuan Yew, leader of Singapore, was afraid that the Malays in the Federation would pass anti-Chinese laws;

iii the Malays feared that the thrustful Chinese would dominate the Federation's economy;

iv Singapore wanted free trade, the Federation wanted a tariff system to protect infant industries;

v 1965 Singapore left the Federation and became independent.

35.7 French Indo-China, 1939 (*Fig. 35.7A*)

1 **Cochin-China**, around Saigon, was a French colony.

2 **Annam and Tonkin** (which, with Cochin-China make up modern Vietnam) were only French protectorates.

3 **Cambodia and Laos** were 2 other protectorates.

4 **The 5 states** known as French Indo-China were run for the benefit of France:

i Asiatics were treated as second-class citizens:

(a) they could not form trade unions or political parties;

i education was provided for Asiatics to help them run the French-controlled government and French-owned industry;

iii but the educated minority were allowed only less important jobs, and got lower salaries than Europeans in similar posts.

5 A nationalist movement, the **Vietminh**, had been formed by the leading nationalists. It was particularly strong in the 3 states making up modern Vietnam.

6 **In 1939** its leaders were **Ho Chi Minh** and **Vo Nguyen Giap**.

7 **Ho Chi Minh (1890–1968)**

i he left Vietnam in 1911 to work as a cabin boy;

ii later he worked as a labourer in Paris and as a dishwasher in a London hotel;

iii 1920 he became a Communist: went to Moscow to study. He met Lenin, Stalin and Trotsky;

iv 1930 he founded the Indo-Chinese Communist Party.

8 **Vo Nguyen Giap (1912–   )**

i Giap had been educated in the French system in Indo-China;

ii he qualified as a history teacher and, later, as a lawyer;

iii because of his political activities the French had imprisoned him. His sister had been executed and his wife had died after 2 years in prison.

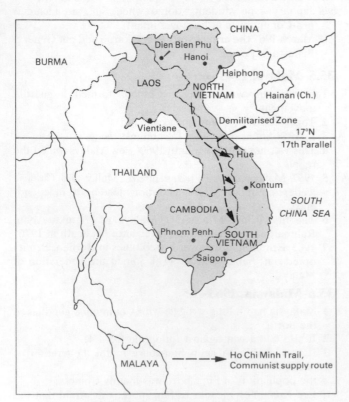

Fig. 35.7A   The war in Vietnam

35.8 Indo-China and the War, 1939–45

1 Ho and Giap led the **guerillas** in night-time campaigns fought in the rice fields, mountains and jungle.

2 Like Mao (17.27.4), the Vietminh gave land to the **peasants** in areas which they controlled and received help from them.

3 The Japanese wartime government united Annam, Tonkin and Cochin China into one region (Vietnam); Cambodia and Laos were governed as 2 separate regions.

4 **Ho's Vietminh** were particularly strong in Vietnam.

5 There was a gap between the Japanese surrender (15 August) and the return of the colonial 'rulers' (3 October).

6 **Ho declared Vietnam independent in August 1945** and united all the nationalist groups in his government.

35.9 The French and the claim to independence, 1945–47

1 The returning French hoped to rule Indo-China as in 1939.

2 **Terrorist raids** on the French suburbs of Saigon persuaded them to negotiate with Ho's 'government'.

3 Ho wanted an independent Vietnam with strong links with France. He wanted a form of **Dominion status** (22.1.5).

4 **March 1946** Negotiations in Indo-China agreed on an **independent North Vietnam** as part of a Federation of Indo-China.

5 **June–September 1946** Ho was in Paris negotiating the details of this agreement with the French government.

6 In Vietnam, Giap's guerillas, extremists and nationalists, denounced Ho for collaborating with the French.

7 The French refused to accept Ho's moderate claims.

35.10 The French try to impose 'independence', 1947–50

1 **1947** The French decided to destroy Ho's 'government'. They got aid from the USA.

2 **The Domino Theory** The USA thought that if one state (eg Vietnam) fell under Communist control, other neighbouring states would also fall to Communism–from *either* internal aggression encouraged by the success of the first 'domino' *or* by external aggression from that newly-independent state.

3 **Bao Dai**

i he had been Emperor of Annam before 1941;

ii until 1947 he was Ho's political adviser;

iii December 1947 France invited him to become President of a new Vietnam. They hoped to win Vietnamese away from Ho.

4 **1948–50** The French wasted time in fruitless negotiation:

i Bao Dai became President and Head of State;

ii he refused to carry out French policy. Like Ho, he was a Vietnamese nationalist;

5 Ho and Giap continued their **guerilla war** against the French.

35.11 The French lose Indo-China, 1950–54

1 Ho's forces were strongest in North Vietnam.

2 The French set out to destroy Ho's power.

3 Their army was stronger and better-armed than Ho's guerillas led by Giap who received some aid from China, now under Mao.

4 The French could capture towns and hold on to them by leaving behind a large force.

5 They failed to conquer the countryside and mountains:

i they built fortified blockhouses to try to prevent Vietminh movement;

ii by night the guerillas passed such posts. They were aided by the peasants in the mountains, the French army and the towns.

6 By 1953 the French had lost 12 000 soldiers, 12 000 members of their Foreign Legion and 14 000 Indo-Chinese soldiers.

7 The war was costing 600 billion francs a year–more than the value of all French investments in Vietnam.

8 Many people wondered whether it was worth fighting.

35.12 Dien Bien Phu, 1953–54

1 Around Saigon the war was one of terrorism and ambush.

2 Further to the west Giap seemed to be planning to invade Laos and to extend the war.

3 General Navarre, the new French commander, decided to trap Giap into a pitched battled which he was confident he would win.

4 November 1953 French paratroopers took Dien Bien Phu, deep inside Vietminh-held territory. Navarre built up the garrison supplied by air from Hanoi.

5 Giap's men captured the surrounding hills.

6 March 1954 The battle of Dien Bien Phu started. Guerilla forces captured French outposts. The French airforce failed to destroy Giap's positions. Giap's men advanced, using captured French material against the beseiged garrison.

7 France asked the USA for more help. The US Secretary of State, John Foster Dulles, talked of dropping 'one or two atom bombs'.

8 The USA agreed to a British proposal for a conference to discuss the Indo-China problem.

9 7 May 1954 Dien Bien Phu fell.

35.13 The Geneva settlement, 1954

1 It was an accident that the Conference opened on 8 May, the day after the fall of Dien Bien Phu.

2 The USA, Russia, Britain and France attended the conference.

3 **The Geneva settlement**

i **France** agreed to withdraw from Indo-China completely;

ii **Cambodia and Laos** became independent;

iii **Vietnam** was divided by the **17th parallel** of latitude into:

(a) a communist-dominated North Vietnam;

(b) a 'free' south under Bao Dai:

iv the agreement provided for **elections** to be held throughout Vietnam in 1956 to choose a government for the whole country;

v **the USA refused to sign this part of the agreement**, fearing that the communists would win the elections.

4 Many of Ho's guerillas were still inside **South Vietnam**. It was these who formed the core of the **Viet Cong** (35.14.5).

35.14 The US and Vietnam: the Eisenhower years, 1952–60

1 **Eisenhower** and his Secretary of State, **Dulles**, had an anti-communist line. The main reasons for this were:

i Eisenhower's experience in NATO during the **Cold War** (28.10);

ii the growth of **McCarthyite anti-Communism** in the USA (32.15);

iii Dulles's belief in the **Domino Theory** (35.10.2);

iv Dulles's rejection of **neutralism** (32.12.2).

2 Until 1954 the **USA was indirectly involved** in Indo-China:

i they had sent **aid** to the French;

ii the USA helped to make the **Geneva agreement**.

3 **October 1955** The USA supported the South Vietnamese plot in which **Bao Dai was overthrown**. As Ho's former adviser (35.10.3) he was 'soft on Communism'.

4 **October 1955** South Vietnam became a Republic, with **Ngo Dinh Diem** as President. His government became increasingly unpopular:

i he did not hold the promised **elections** in South Vietnam;

ii he was a **Catholic**; the majority of Vietnamese were **Buddhists**. They protested at his government's tyranny;

iii he attacked, imprisoned and killed religious fanatics who wanted a Buddhist state, and left-wingers who wanted social reform.

5 **1960** The National Liberation Front was set up by Ho's supporters still in the south (35.13.4) and by other opponents of Diem. The guerilla forces of the NLF became known as the **Viet Cong.**

35.15 The US and Vietnam; the Kennedy years, 1960–63

1 **Laos** was divided between rival factions and the north of the kingdom fell under the control of the Communist **Pathet Lao**.

2 **Cambodia's** Prime Minister, **Prince Sihanouk**, became increasingly critical of US involvement in Indo-China. He hoped to put off a Communist take-over by this anti-US policy.

3 **South Vietnam** was involved in a **civil war** with the 20 000 Viet Cong rebels getting aid from the North and from Russia.

4 Kennedy sent an increasing number of '**advisers**' to help Diem:

i **1962** the number rose from 5000 to 15 000;

ii with them came **military equipment** including helicopters.

5 The unpopularity of the Diem government led Kennedy to agree to a **CIA plot** to overthrow Diem who was assassinated to make way for a military administration.

6 US military aid and the number of military and technical 'advisers' was increased.

7 But the **Viet Cong** had the support of the majority of the peasants. By the time of Kennedy's assassination (November 1963) the Viet Cong controlled about 40 per cent of the countryside. They also terrorized the urban population by bombing campaigns.

35.16 The US and Vietnam; the Johnson years, 1963–68

1 Johnson continued Kennedy's policy and increased the number of advisers.

2 **The Tonkin incident** In August 1964 the war escalated:

i Communist torpedo boats attacked US warships in the Gulf of Tonkin; US carrier planes bombed northern naval bases;

ii in the south the Viet Cong attacked the American base at Bien Hoa near Saigon, destroying many parked Canberra jets;

iii Johnson sent US troops to South Vietnam. By 1967 400 000 troops were involved there;

iv the Viet Cong received an increasing volume of aid from the North. Russian material came from the North to the Viet Cong along the Ho Chi Minh trail through Laos and Cambodia (Fig.35.7A).

3 Much of the war was fought between Viet Cong guerillas and US forces armed with sophisticated weapons.

4 Part of the war consisted of pitched battles between US battalions and battalions of Viet Cong both using modern weapons.

5 The peasants suffered from both sides:

i US forces believed that the peasants supported the guerilla-forces–and destroyed villages;

ii the Viet Cong sometimes gained the support of the peasants by terrorist methods, killing headmen suspected of being sympathetic to the US-supported government.

6 **Bombing the North** As US forces failed to defeat the Viet Cong, Johnson ordered the bombing of North Vietnam.

7 This increased the number of Vietnamese who died in the war. About 3000 a month died in the south, victims of Viet Cong and of US firepower. Thousands more died in the north from the bombing of Hanoi, supply bases and ports.

8 The Hanoi government demanded the end to the bombing. The US demanded an end to the use of the Ho Chi Minh trail.

9 January 1968 The Viet Cong launched devastating attacks in the south. In this **Tet Offensive** they captured, for a short time, 75 per cent of the main towns in the south, including for a time, parts of Saigon.

10 This was in spite of the 750 000 men of the South Vietnamese army, 500 000 US servicemen and 50 000 men from various allied forces aiding the US.

35.17 Johnson calls a halt, 1968

1 There was increasing US criticism of Johnson's policy:
i some 'liberals' opposed the bombing of the North because of its effects on innocent people;

ii some deplored the brutalizing effects of the war on the US forces. Many men became drug users; others attacked their officers; there were reports of massacres of civilians such as the one at My Lai;

iii some were worried at the effects of the war on the US economy. Increased government spending led to inflation and an outflow of dollars, a large deficit on the US balance of payments and a demand from Germany and Japan in particular for a devaluation of the proud dollar;

iv 1968 was the 'year of the students' in France (31.16.29) and elsewhere. US students led anti-war demonstrations;
v there was widespread anger and puzzlement at the failure to beat the Viet Cong.

2 In the autumn of 1968 Johnson ordered an end to the bombing of the North. In return the North agreed to attend preliminary negotiations in Paris with the representatives of South Vietnam, the Viet Cong and the US.

3 Johnson did not stand for re-election in the 1968 Election won by Richard Nixon (32.23.7).

35.18 The US and Vietnam; the Nixon years, 1968–74

1 The talks in Paris made very little progress:
i **President Thieu** of South Vietnam could not agree with the Viet Cong on fair elections for South Vietnam;
ii the US and North Vietnam could not agree on a formula for the **mutual withdrawal from the South**.

2 November 1969 At Guam Nixon announced the end of the Truman Doctrine (28.5). The US would not accept a world-wide responsibility and would withdraw from south-east Asia.

3 Vietnamization Nixon wanted the South Vietnamese to take over their own defence to allow the withdrawal of US forces. By the end of 1970 their number was halved.

4 Increased bombing Nixon could not face the prospect of a Viet Cong victory. He resumed the bombing of the North.

5 Cambodia In 1970 the army had overthrown Prince Sihanouk. His successor, General **Lon Nol**, attacked Communist bases in Cambodia. The Communists fought Lon Nol and seemed about to overthrow him. To save Lon Nol and to hinder the passage of supplies from the North, Nixon ordered the bombing of 'neutral' Cambodia.

6 Laos In March 1971 South Vietnamese troops invaded Laos in an attempt to destroy Communist bases there – and were driven into a disastrous retreat.

7 Withdrawal In 1971 another 100 000 US troops were withdrawn while the bombing of the North was increased.

8 The **Viet Cong** launched a major offensive in March 1972:
i they threatened Thieu's troops near Hue, around Kontum and around Saigon (Fig. 35.7A);
ii the US sent massive supplies to Thieu's troops who, like Chiang's men in 1945–49 (17.34.v) had little stomach for the fight.

iii Nixon increased the bombing of the North and of the Ho Chi Minh trail. The ports of North Vietnam were mined to try to cut off Russian sea-borne aid.

9 Cease fire, January 1973 The USA and North Vietnam agreed on a ceasefire; President Thieu reluctantly agreed:
i areas in the south, controlled by the Viet Cong, came under a Communist Provisional Revolutionary government;
ii **the 17th Parallel** was accepted as the line of demarcation.

10 More US forces were withdrawn, although fighting between North and South continued.

11 The North Vietnamese captured more towns, built new bases and consolidated their power in their one-third of the country.

12 Nixon's involvement in **Watergate**, his resignation and the accession of President Ford weakened US concern for Vietnam.

35.19 The end of the war

1 The North Vietnamese launched a major offensive in 1975 and over-ran a series of **South Vietnamese strongholds**.

2 The coastal towns fell quickly.

3 May 1975 Communist forces took Saigon.

4 1976 The two halves of Vietnam were united in a single Socialist Republic.

5 1977 Vietnam was admitted to **UNO**, after some opposition from the USA.

6 1978 Vietnam joined **COMECON** (29.7.6.ii), its membership sponsored by Soviet Russia but criticized by some east European governments.

35.20 'Indo-China' after the war, 1975–83

1 Russia had provided most of the aid to the North and the Viet Cong. **China** saw a united Vietnam as a Russian puppet in a part of the former Chinese Empire.

2 1978, Chinese forces invaded Vietnam claiming that Vietnamese troops had invaded China. The Chinese were quickly defeated by the Russian-armed Vietnamese. They withdrew and there is an uneasy peace.

3 Cambodia was drawn into the war in 1970 (35.18.5):
i a small Communist party, the **Khmer Rouge**, opposed this involvement;
ii after 1975 the Khmer Rouge defeated the US-supported government of Lon Nol;

iii **Pol Pot** headed a Khmer government which in 1978 slaughtered about 3 million of the 7 million Cambodians, thought to have been loyal to the old régime. In the ensuing chaos another 2 million died from disease and famine, the twin tragedies which marked the re-naming of the country, now called **Kampuchea**;

iv **January 1979** The **Vietnamese**, once the allies of the Khmer invaded the country to help an **ex-Khmer Heng Somrin**, to take power. The Khmers took to the hills and waged a guerilla war in which the Vietnamese invaders were supported by Russia (29.19.4).

4 Vietnam under a Communist government has persecuted those who served the US-supported government. A mass exodus of people trying to escape death in 1978 and 1979 led to the existence of **'the boat people'** seeking refuge overseas.

35.21 A cynical world

1 In the 1960s, and particularly in 1968, there were world-wide demonstrations against the part played by the US in the war.

2 Students led chants of 'Ho, Ho, Ho Chi Minh, the Viet Cong are going to win'.

3 These 'liberals' are surprisingly silent in the face of the cruel effects of the victory they wished for.

36 Africa, South of the Sahara, 1945–83

36.1 The problems of speedy independence

1 1945 South Africa, Egypt, Liberia and Abyssinia were independent.

2 1983 Almost all states in Africa are independent.

3 This speedy change brought **several problems**:

i **democracy**, developed over many centuries in Europe, has, generally, failed in Africa;

ii **expectations**: many African leaders promised too much to their followers in the struggle for independence. The poor states, mainly agricultural, have not been able to satisfy expectations;

iii **tribalism**: most Africans have more loyalty to their tribe than to the nation-state. This had caused much discontent;

iv **corruption**: many leaders saw independence as a chance to enrich themselves and their families;

v interference by **outside countries** and powerful **economic interests** has often made problems worse;

vi **Third World problems** will be examined in Unit 38. Here you should note that African countries suffered from some or all of the following:

(a) harsh **climate**, shortage of **water** and prevalence of **disease**;

(b) overdependence on **one crop** of which the price fluctuates;

(c) **lack of natural resources**;

(d) **lack of economic and social infra-structure** such as roads, skilled workforce and technically qualified people;

(e) **low incomes** which make local investment difficult.

36.2 The Gold Coast becomes Ghana, 1945–57

1 Colonial government under a 1946 constitution:

i a British colonial governor appointed an Executive Council;

ii in the Legislative Council of 31 members, 13 were chosen by the Council of African chiefs, 11 elected democratically and 7 appointed by the governor.

2 Black politics was dominated by the United Gold Coast Convention Party (formed 1941). In 1947 **Kwame Nkrumah** was brought back from studies in the USA to become secretary of this party.

3 1948 Popular rioting against the new constitution.

4 1949 Nkrumah founded the **Convention People's Party** and demanded full independence.

5 1951 A new constitution (under which Nkrumah's party won 34 of the 38 seats in the larger Legislative Council) did not give full independence. During the election campaign **Nkrumah was arrested** for organizing anti-government strikes. Freed after the election he became the **first black Prime Minister (1952)** and led his country to **full independence (1957)**.

36.3 Ghana since 1957

1 March 1957 Nkrumah became President of his re-named country.

2 Industrial development included:

i **developments** in cattle-rearing, forest industries, fishing and improved water supplies to villages;

ii the **Volta River Project**, 1961, which aimed to produce electricity and power for an aluminium smelter built in 1964 and increased irrigation.

3 Social development Nkrumah had promised full employment, free primary education and a national health service. He had a crash programme to build schools and hospitals.

4 Prestige development New government buildings, television station and broadcasting station were built in Accra and a rarely-used motor-way was built linking Accra and Tema.

5 Private investment often took un-African forms such as the building of western-type hotels in Accra.

6 Paying for the development Nkrumah borrowed heavily. Ghana found it difficult to repay her debts even when prices of her main export, cocoa, were high. When prices fell in the 1960s **repayment was impossible**.

7 Unrest because of the government's failure led to an **army plot to overthrow Nkrumah in 1958**. This failed but it led to:

i **1959** a Preventive Detention Act allowing the imprisonment without trial of opponents, including Opposition MPs;

ii the **purging** of Nkrumah's party to get rid of critics;

iii the **deportation** of Muslim leaders;

iv **July 1960** Ghana became a Republic with Nkrumah as President. A plebiscite showed about 90 per cent approval for the change.

8 Nkrumah became even more autocratic

i **the Chief Justice** was sacked for not convicting 3 of Nkrumah's party accused of plotting against him;

ii **the constitution** was changed to give the president power to overturn decisions of the Supreme Court;

iii a referendum agreed with his decision to set up a **one-party state**.

9 Pan-Africanism Nkrumah had ambitious ideas for African development throughout the continent:

i he called the **first conference of independent African** states in Accra in 1958;

ii when the **OAU was set up in Addis Abbaba in 1963** he spoke in favour of the political unification of all Africa.

10 His overthrow, February 1966, was due to increasing discontent with his rule; the economy was in ruins and Ghana could not pay her debts. Politicians opposed to his autocracy combined with the army to overthrow him while he was visiting Peking. He was not allowed to return and died in exile in 1972.

36.4 Uganda

1 In this largely agricultural country the **tribal chiefs**, led by the **Kabaka of Buganda**, had opposed British attempts to give Africans a share in the government of the country. The Kabaka was exiled in Britain between 1953 and 1955.

2 Black politicians had formed many (largely tribal) political parties. In 1960 the 2 largest combined to form the Uganda People's Congress led by **Milton Obote**.

3 1962 Uganda became an independent state, a federation in which Buganda was one state. Milton Obote was the first Prime Minister.

4 1967 Uganda, Tanzania and Kenya formed the **East African Community**, an African form of the EEC (31.12).

5 Tribal rivalries led to many clashes. In **1971 Idi Amin** led an army coup against Obote and replaced him as head of state.

6 Ugandan Asians had a good deal of economic power while most of them refused to give up their British citizenship. Obote had wanted to limit their powers and give Africans chances to get on.

7 1972 Amin announced that all Asians not having Ugandan citizenship had to leave within 90 days. This was condemned by Kenya and Tanzania. Many Commonwealth countries took in the former Ugandan Asians. Many settled in Britain, which, in 1973, passed a **new immigration Act** giving the government power to refuse to accept such 'refugees' even with British passports.

8 1979 The overthrow of Amin:

i **Nyerere of Tanzania** was angered by the tyranny of Idi Amin. This gave **black Africa a poor image** throughout the world:

(a) there was the ill-treatment of the **Asians** (36.4.7);

(b) there was, in 1975, the threatened execution of Mr **Denis Hills**, the British author of an unpublished book which criticized Amin;

(c) in 1976 there was the 'disappearance' of Mrs **Dora Bloch** during the raid on Entebbe by the Israelis (37.17);

(d) in 1977 there was the sudden death of the **Archbishop of Uganda** who had attacked Amin's corrupt and tyrannical rule:

ii **tribal groups** inside Uganda were angered by Amin's rule which favoured the Moslems of northern Uganda (from whom he had originated) at the expense of other tribes and national groups;

iii **border clashes** took place between Ugandan troops and troops from **Tanzania** and **Kenya**. Tanzanian troops finally invaded Uganda to help rebel tribes. Amin was defeated and in April 1979 he fled to Libya.

9 The return of Milton Obote Obote who had been overthrown by Amin in 1971 (36.4.5) returned with the victorious Tanzanian forces. But his government has not brought much peace to Uganda. The small section that had benefited from Amin's rule now found itself under attack. Tribalism remained a powerful and divisive force.

36.5 The Belgian Congo, 1945–60

1 This mineral-rich region contained **150 tribes**.

2 There were **poor communications** inside this very large state.

3 The Belgians had made **no preparations** for independence:

i there were **no elections** until 1957 when only local councils were elected. There were **no African political parties**;

ii there was no African in a leading post in the **Civil Service** and few Africans trained in **administration**;

iii there were **no African army officers**;

iv there were almost **no African graduates and doctors**.

4 **1957–58** Affected by the movement to independence in Ghana and other countries, **Patrice Lumumba**, a Post Office clerk, founded the **Congolese National Movement** seeking early independence.

5 **1959** Large scale unemployment led to **widespread rioting**. The Belgians panicked and in **January 1960** announced that from **June 1960** the country would be independent.

6 **June 1960** President **Kasavubu** named **Lumumba** as Prime Minister of a country whose first Parliament contained 50 parties.

36.6 The Congo becomes Zaire

1 **Immediate problems** facing the country included:

i **tribalism**: tribes in the richer provinces did not want to share their wealth with the poorer regions;

ii **the army** mutinied soon after independence. Many Europeans were attacked and killed;

iii the Belgian government and the mine-owning Union Minière encouraged tribes in mineral-rich areas to seek self-government.

2 **Lumumba** was from the Batatele tribe. hated by the **Kasai** and the people from **Katanga**. He was also hated by the Belgians because he was a socialist who threatened to nationalize their mines:

i **July 1960**, one month after independence, the Kasai and people from Katanga declared their regions to be independent. The Belgians rushed in troops to defend their mines;

ii Lumumba appealed to the **UN** for help.

3 **The UN and the Congo:**

i the UN wanted to maintain the **unity of the Congo**;

ii it formed an **army** from small, 'neutral' countries;

iii but it had **no power to interfere** in the internal affairs of a country. The dispute between Lumumba and Katanga was said to be an internal affair. This led Lumumba to ask for **Russian**

help. An angry Kasavubu then sacked Lumumba who was captured and slain by forces from Katanga.

iv **Moise Tshombe** was declared head of the independent state of **Katanga** and received military and technical aid from Belgium;

v UN Secretary-General **Dag Hammarskjöld** went to the Congo to try to sort out affairs (September 1961). He was killed in a mysterious air crash. UN forces were rushed in to try to end the independence of Katanga (which had made the issue an external and not only an internal affair);

vi after many clashes between UN forces and troops from Katanga led by European mercenaries, the **Katanga rebellion ended early in 1963**.

4 **July 1964** Kasavubu named Tshombe as Prime Minister of the Congo. But there were many **tribal rebellions** against his rule. He used **European mercenaries** to put these down.

5 **A food shortage** made him unpopular in the Congo while his **subservience to European capitalists** made him unpopular throughout Africa. In **October 1965** he was dismissed by Kasavubu.

6 Tshombe went into exile, but was condemned to death in his absence. In 1967 he was imprisoned in Algeria when his aircraft was hi-jacked. He died in 1969.

7 **Mobuto** had been a corporal in the Belgian army who became a general on independence:

i **October 1965** after Tshombe's sacking he overthrew Kasavubu and **became President**;

ii he used the army to put down more **resistance from Katanga**;

iii **1968** he cleared the country of **mercenaries**;

iv he **nationalized** the mines and ended Belgian influence;

v **1970** he was confirmed in office as **President** and in **1971** he re-named the country **Zaire**.

36.7 Kenya

1 Kenya was a major exporter of tea, coffee and sisal but there was **little industrial development** before 1945.

2 Arabs, Asians and a **multiplicity of African tribes** were ruled by a **whites-only government** aiming to please, mainly, the Europeans who had settled in the towns and, particularly, in the Highlands where they ran large farms.

3 **Africans were discontented in 1945:**

i large scale **unemployment** and **low wages** led to **low living standards** for townspeople;

ii the **educated Africans** resented the bar which prevented them holding jobs reserved for Europeans;

iii **many tribes**, but particularly the **Kikuyu**, claimed that Europeans had 'stolen' their land in the past. As nomadic farmers they were used to leaving land 'free' to recover. Europeans had moved on to this unoccupied land.

4 **Kenyatta and the Kikuyu:**

i the Kikuyu were the **largest tribe**. They had their own **Kikuyu Central Association** to run their affairs;

ii in **1929 Jomo Kenyatta** was a delegate to this Association which sent him to London to take part in a commission examining the land question;

iii **1930** Kenyatta returned to Kenya but almost immediately went back to **London to study (1930–32)**. He also studied at **Moscow University (1932–34)** before settling in London. He married an English woman in 1942;

iv **1946** he returned to Kenya as **Principal of the Kikuyu Independent Teachers' Training College**;

v he formed the **Kenyan African Union** (KAU) to replace the Kikuyu Central Association outlawed by the white government.

5 Kenyatta led his people's demand for a share in the government of their country. In **1954 6 Africans** were brought

on to the previously all-white council governing Kenya. But this was too little and too late.

36.8 The Mau Mau terrorists

1 1948 Members of the **banned Kikuyu Association** formed a **secret society** called **Mau Mau**. This became a mass movement in which the Kikuyu were bound together by **terrifying oaths**.

2 1952 Attacks were made to **terrorize** Europeans and thousands of Africans who refused to join Mau Mau.

3 October 1952 Kenyatta and 130 leaders were arrested.

4 The violence increased. Farms were burnt, animals crippled and slain, hundreds of 'loyal' Africans murdered.

5 March 1953 After a massacre of Kikuyu by the Mau Mau, many turned against the society and helped the British to fight it.

36.9 Independent Kenya

1 The war went on until 1960 by which time 10 000 Mau Mau were killed and the government had tried to improve the constitution:

i **1956** each tribe was allowed its **own political party**–but there was to be **no national party**. This was condemned by the OAU, by Africans at the UN and by the Labour Opposition in Britain. But Africans had their first chance to put their representatives into the Legislative Assembly;

ii **1960** Britain produced **another constitution** which denied Africans control of the Legislative Assembly. This was widely condemned–particularly by black Kenyans whose leaders were imprisoned as Mau Mau terrorists.

2 April 1961 The KAU agreed to form a government provided that the government built a home for the still-imprisoned Kenyatta in the Kiambu district where he was exiled.

3 August 1961 Kenyatta was freed; he became, again, the main political leader of the Africans.

4 December 1963 Kenya became an independent republic within the Commonwealth, with **Kenyatta as its first Prime Minister**.

5 In independent Kenya:

i **tribalism** was avoided as Kenyatta chose ministers from more than one tribe;

ii all Kenyan citizens were treated equally. **Many Europeans** stayed on to help run the country;

iii Kenyatta declared the country a **one-party-state**–both to avoid the emergence of tribal parties, and to check the growth of Opposition. He imprisoned one of his former supporters, the Mau Mau leader, Oginga Odinga, for trying to form an Opposition;

iv **Kenyan Asians** who refused to take out Kenyan citizenship were driven from the country in a policy of Africanization. In 1968 60 000 former Kenyan Asians arrived in Britain with their British passports.

36.10 Tanganyika, 1945–61

1 This largest country in Africa is **underpopulated** because of the harsh climate and the ravages of the tsetse fly.

2 It was a **British Mandate** from 1920 to 1947 (13.10) when it came under the UN Trusteeship Council (27.4.6).

3 Successive colonial governors had brought Africans into the **Legislative Council** while always allowing the chiefs to retain some power in the system of indirect rule.

4 Black politics were dominated by the **Tanganyikan African Association** formed in the 1920s. In 1954 this became the Tanganyikan African National Union (TANU) with **Julius Nyerere** as president.

5 Constitutional progress was marked by:

i **1947** the Legislative Council had 15 'official' members and 14 'unofficial' members. All were appointed by the British government. Three of the 'unofficials' were Asian and 4 were African;

ii **1955** a new constitution gave 10 'unofficial' members to each of the 3 racial groups. The government ensured control by its appointment of 31 'official' members;

iii **1957** Tanganyika was given **ministerial responsibility**– government ministers were responsible to parliament;

vi **1958** in the first **elections** under the new constitution TANU won every seat in spite of strong opposition from British supported parties. This success was repeated in 1959 and 1960;

v **1960** Nyerere negotiated **self-government** and in December 1961 Tanganyika became **independent**.

36.11 Tanzania

1 December 1962 Tanganyika became a republic with Nyerere as President.

2 1964 She united with **Zanzibar to form Tanzania**.

3 Problems included the **poverty** of the country with its few **natural resources** and its **'front line'** position in the black struggle with Rhodesia (36.14).

4 Nyerere provided his country with **political stability** without any of the tribal violence common elsewhere.

5 He initiated a **peasant-based form of socialism**, avoiding Russian-like steps towards industrialization. He taught the people that progress would be slow and would have to be earned. He insisted on austerity for himself and his ministers so that there has been none of the family-based corruption common elsewhere.

6 Economic planning has been undertaken by the National Economic Development Corporation which manages most of the economy:

i **nationalization** was widespread;

ii **1964 an economic plan** was drawn up in union with the 2 partners in the East African Community. Industries were to be sited in each country by the Community and not by decisions of the separate governments. The Community Service Organiza- tion controls the currency, customs, postal services, railways and harbours of the 3 states.

7 Nyerere , like Nkrumah, was a **leading member of the OAU**. He called on Africans **to develop, in unity**, the vast resources of their continent with its market of 250 million people.

36.12 The Central African Federation, 1953–63

1 February 1953 Britain set up a Federation of three colonies–**Northern Rhodesia (Zambia), Nyasaland (Malawi)** and **Southern Rhodesia (Zimbabwe)** which had been self- governing since 1923.

2 The Federation was supposed to **achieve independence**.

3 The main problem was racial. Was the Federation to be governed by whites only (as was S. Rhodesia) or by a black majority?

4 Godfrey Huggins of S. Rhodesia was the first Prime Minister of the Federation. He intended that the **whites would rule**.

5 Black Congress Parties were led by **Kenneth Kaunda** (in N. Rhodesia) and by **Hastings Banda** in Nyasaland. Huggins had both **arrested**.

6 Black rioting in 1955 led to 2 British-appointed commis- sions examining the problems of the Federation. Both said that the Federation would fail because of black opposition. The British government refused to send an army to hold it together by force.

7 December 1963 The Federation was dissolved.

36.13 Zambia

1 Zambia (Northern Rhodesia) became **independent** in **July 1964** with **Kaunda** as its first President.

2 It contains **75 different tribes**. In the late 1960s the Vice-President, Kepwepwe, planned to set up a separate Bemba state in the north. Kaunda sacked him.

3 Its main export is copper whose price on world markets swings up and down depending on world demand.

4 1973 Kaunda declared Zambia a **one-party state**, hoping to avoid the rise of tribal factionalism.

5 After 1965 Zambia was another of the **'front line' states** in the struggle with Rhodesia. Kaunda supported the policy of sanctions against Rhodesia, even though this harmed his own trade, dependent as it was on the rail link through Rhodesia to Beira on the coast (36.14.9–11).

6 The Chinese-built Zam-Tan Railway has provided another link to the coast and helps Zambia's trade.

36.14 From Rhodesia to Zimbabwe

1 The break up of the Central African Federation (36.12) left **S Rhodesia** as a self-governing colony where a white minority held total political power.

2 The whites became more right-wing in their views:
i Prime Minister **Todd** was **dismissed** in 1958 for trying to legalize trade unions and to give blacks some greater freedom;
ii his successor, **Whitehead**, lost power when he condemned some forms of **racial discrimination**;
iii 1962 **Winston Field** led the right-wing Rhodesian Front Party to electoral victory.

3 White Rhodesians demanded independence–already given to Zambia and Malawi, their black partners in the Federation.

4 The British Conservative government refused to give power while only 5 per cent of the population had political control:
i Africans had only 15 of the 65 seats in parliament;
ii African political organizations were banned.

5 Field was sacked to make way for **Ian Smith**. Rhodesians hoped he would force Britain to give way. Britain refused to grant independence 'before majority rule'.

6 1964 Wilson's Labour government came to power in Britain. Smith began to talk of making an illegal declaration of independence.

7 11 November 1965 Smith announced the **Unilateral Declaration of Independence** (UDI) and named the country **Rhodesia**.

8 To ensure peace, he imposed **press censorship** and banned African **political meetings**.

9 Britain and the UN imposed **trade sanctions** on the illegally-governed state. Various businesses in Europe and the USA and several states in Africa (South Africa and the Portuguese colonies) provided Rhodesia with access to international markets.

10 To try to stop oil getting in, the **British navy** patrolled the **Beira coast**. Oil got in via South Africa. Meantime, Zambia, which had imported its oil via Beira, suffered until the Chinese built the Zam-Tan Railway (36.13.6).

11 Zambia and **Tanganyika** were 'front line' states in the blacks' fight against Smith. Freedom fighters trained in these states from where they invaded Rhodesia in guerilla attacks.

12 Talks were held between Smith and Wilson of Britain in **1966, 1968** and **1970** without producing agreement.

13 A new Conservative government (**1970**) tried to get a settlement. It sent out the **Pearce Commission** to seek African opinion of the proposed constitution. Black Rhodesians rejected the scheme.

14 Slowly sanctions had an effect. More seriously, the Portuguese gave independence to **Angola** and **Mozambique** (36.23), leaving Rhodesia even more isolated.

15 1975 Smith tried to negotiate a deal with **Nkomo**, the leader of the Matabele section of the guerilla movement. He probably (and rightly) thought that Nkomo would be less demanding and less extreme than Mugabe (36.14.18).

16 1978 Smith announced a new constitution:
i **blacks** were to vote in parliamentary elections and could stand as candidates;
ii if blacks gained a majority **they would hold office**;
iii **the whites would reserve 25 seats** in the small parliament, so having the ability to prevent the passing of important laws, which would have to have a two-thirds majority;
iv **whites would retain control** of the army, police, foreign office and other important posts.

17 Bishop Abel Muzorewa became the first black Prime Minister.

18 Militant blacks led by **Joshua Nkomo** and **Robert Mugabe** (the leader of the Mashona section of the guerilla movement), continued their **guerilla war** on a government in which whites still held control.

19 Talks were held between **Smith, Muzorewa, Nkomo, Mugabe** and **British ministers** to try to find a solution.

20 1979 A new constitution was worked out giving blacks more power. The **guerilla war** was called off. **Robert Mugabe** became the Prime Minister in 1980.

21 He has brought in a number of **socialist reforms**, limiting white power, giving government more control of the economy.

22 He has quarrelled with his former partner, **Nkomo** and **tribal violence** has developed with many Matabele being killed.

23 Many Europeans have moved out of what is rapidly becoming a one-party state.

36.15 Nigeria

1 This large state contained **56 million people** from **150 separate tribes**. It is rich in resources, including oil.

2 Regionalism was a fact of Nigerian life and was enshrined in **early constitutional progress**:
i 1946 A constitution recognized **3 self-ruling regions**:
(a) the northern region was dominated by the **Hausa people**, agricultural by occupation and Muslim by religion;
(b) the western region (including **Lagos**) dominated by the **Yoruba** tribe, many of whom were Christian in religion;
(c) the eastern region was dominated by the **Ibo**, the most Christian and best-educated of the Nigerian tribes.

3 The Yoruba and the **Ibo** tended to dominate the commercial, industrial and official life of the country.

4 Regional politicians who fought for independence:
i **Nmandi Azikiwe** ('Zik') was an American-educated **Ibo** who founded several Nigerian newspapers to preach nationalism;
ii **Awolowo** formed the **Yoruba-dominated Nigerian Youth Movement** as a vehicle for his brand of nationalism;
iii **'Zik'** founded the **National Council of Nigeria and the Cameroons** which from 1944 to 1957 was the dominant party;
iv **The Northern People's Congress (NPC)** party was formed by the **Hausas** to express their kind of nationalism.

5 1951–60 under a new constitution:
i there were **separate Houses of Representatives** for each of the regions. The NPC won 80 of the 92 seats in the Northern House; the Ibo and Yoruba had similar majorities in the Eastern and Western regions;
ii **in the Central House of Representatives:**
(a) 64 seats were reserved for the **north**;
(b) 34 seats were assigned to **each of east and west**:
iii **The Council of Ministers** had 4 members from each region.

6 1960 Nigeria became an independent Federal State.

7 1963 It became a republic with 'Zik' as President and a northerner, Abubakar Tafewa Balewa, as Prime Minister.

36.16 The Civil War

1 1964 There was acknowledged dishonesty at the **elections**; 78 candidates were declared 'unopposed' even though there had been opposition candidates.

2 The Yoruba resented the power of the **Hausa**; Balewa ordered the arrest of **Awolowo**, the Prime Minister of the Western Region.

3 November 1965 In the Western Region elections the **Yoruba** complained of **Ibo manipulation** of the results. Two lists of elected candidates were published – one by the Ibo, one by the Yoruba. Widespread rioting left 2000 dead at the end of 1965.

4 January 1966 The unrest spread. **Prime Minister Balewa, Yoruba leader Akintola** and the **Northern Premier**, the Sardauna of Sokoto, were **all murdered**.

5 The Ibo general, Ironsi, announced that a military government had replaced the civilian government. He promised to divide the country into many provinces, hoping to end the regionalism.

6 The northern Hausa feared the loss of their power. They massacred Ibos living in the north.

7 July 1966 A northerner, General Gowon, led a rising which overthrew Ironsi. Between 10 000 and 30 000 Ibos were murdered in the north in September.

8 May 1967 Colonel Ojukwu, military governor of the Eastern (Ibo) Region announced that the Eastern Region was seceding under the name of **Biafra**.

9 This war lasted until January 1970 when Biafra surrendered.

10 After the war Gowon's government faced **many problems**:

i large scale **unemployment** because of the chaos;

ii increased **tribal hatred** by and for the Ibo who make up one-fifth of the population and are the best educated;

iii the need for a **constitution** which would limit, if it could not end, the regional differences.

11 1975 Gowon's military government was overthrown by a military coup led by Brigadier Murtalla Muhammad, another Northerner. He set himself 2 main tasks:

i to create a **new constitution**, in which there might be less room for the regional divisions to show themselves. Nigeria was, for electoral purposes, divided into 19 states;

ii **to root out the corruption** which had led to some leaders and officials becoming very wealthy and which had been one of the reasons for Nigeria's economic backwardness.

12 1975 Murtalla was assassinated within 6 months. His government continued under the leadership of Lieutenant General Olusegun **Obansanjo** who worked steadily towards the 1979 Elections which re-launched Nigerian politics under a new United States-style constitution.

13 1979 was a landmark in African and Nigerian politics:

i the military leadership **handed back power** to civilian politicians and organized an election;

ii Shehu Shagari, a northern Muslim, became Nigeria's first US-style executive President, after the first elections to be held for 13 years.

14 1983 saw another **General Election** in which, again, Shagari was returned to office. There were, however, doubts as to his ability to hold on to power:

i the 1983 elections had been the occasion of a great deal of **well-publicized corruption and violence**. There were too many Nigerians who were not happy with the outcome of this election;

ii **corruption** had not been attacked; indeed, it **had grown** so that the life-styles of the leading ministers and chief officials had become too much for suffering Nigerians to bear (36.17);

iii the continued **economic problems** (36.17) led to attempts to **cut government spending** and to **cut imports**. These attempts led to:

(a) increased unemployment, particularly among the unskilled who had been attracted to the cities and towns during the 'boom' days from 1973 to 1979 (36.17.2–4);

(b) higher taxes, imposed by the government in efforts to make it more difficult for people to buy imported goods. These higher taxes (on incomes and on goods) have led to a **fall in living standards** for the majority of Nigerians;

(c) even more corruption, as officials and ministers sold the permits and licences needed to do certain work or to import certain commodities. The rich life-style of the corrupt officials was in stark contrast to the much harder lives lived by the majority.

15 In **December 1983** Shagari announced a **fresh budget**. This was intended to **cut living standards** even further, since **taxes** were to be further increased and **government spending** to be cut in another effort to cut the budget deficit which was to be, in 1984, double that which had been forecast – and that would have meant a government overspending of £11.4 billion.

16 Shagari's government was overthrown in what was Nigeria's fifth military coup since independence. Many people had expected the military to stage a coup at the time of the August 1983 elections. In fact they waited until December 1983. Led by **Major-General Buhari** the army has set up a fresh government and has promised, as all governments have promised in Nigeria, to **root out corruption**, to **heal the tribal divisions** and to **restore the Nigerian economy**. Only time will tell how far they have been able to succeed.

36.17 Nigeria's economic progress and decline, 1973–83

1 Nigeria was rich in **oil resources**.

2 OPEC's **sharp rises in oil prices** after 1973 made Nigeria a very rich country.

3 She planned to sell **3 million barrels of oil a day** at 1979 prices of 35 dollars a barrel.

4 Her **economic plans** were based on those figures. She contracted for **major developments** – harbours, roads, urban development, steel, chemical and cement industries and much social development – the provision of schools and hospitals for example.

5 Since **1979** there has been **a fall in world demand for oil** and a rise in oil producing countries. This has led to Nigeria being able to sell only **1½ million barrels a day** at 27 dollars a barrel.

6 Nigeria, in 1983, went through a **serious economic crisis**. She had no financial reserves, a heavy overseas debt and many unfinished projects.

7 This caused **tensions** which, in Nigeria, take the form of **tribal hostility**.

36.18 South Africa

1 The **Union of South Africa** was created in 1910 (5.23) as the British tried to win the friendship of the Boers.

2 The policy of Union governments was always **'whites only government'**:

i **1936 Africans** in the Cape Province were taken off the electoral roll; their position was worse in 1936 than in 1900;

ii **1936** other **non-whites (Asians and Coloureds)** could vote – but only for **white MPs**.

3 1948 The Afrikaaners (Boers) won the election, **Malan** succeeding the 'liberal' Smuts as Prime Minister.

4 Apartheid (the separate development of the Africans) was the official policy of all succeeding **Afrikaaner (or Nationalist) governments**. The black Africans were to have their own Native Reserves, where they could have their own industries and institutions. This was an **unreal policy**:

i **European industry** in African towns needed the blacks to work at various levels – skilled and unskilled, highly qualified and less so;

ii **European homes** needed the labour of black servants.

5 **The Asians and Coloured voters** were removed from the common electoral roll in 1956.

6 **Verwoerd, Prime Minister, 1958-60**, explained apartheid as a policy aiming to allow blacks and whites to live, each in their own 'states' as good neighbours. In practice this meant that Africans living in towns have become **second-class citizens**:

i they have to carry **passes** or identity cards issued only to essential workers but not to their families. Passes have to be shown whenever police ask; anyone not carrying a pass or having an out-of-date pass is **imprisoned** before being **deported** to a Reserve;

ii **Bantu Education Acts** ensured that African children had only a low level of education, fitting them only for poorly-paid jobs;

iii **African housing** was separate from white, and black housing was always liable to be pulled down by white local authorities;

iv **jobs**, particularly those carrying responsibility, were only open to whites.

7 Some Africans had to be allowed to live in towns. But as many as possible were forced to move into the reserves under the **Group Areas Act**.

8 **An Immorality Act** made it a crime for whites to marry or have sexual relations with blacks.

9 **A Suppression of Communism Act** was used to crush African efforts to form political parties or to develop campaigns against apartheid.

10 When Lower Courts failed to condemn blacks, the government created a new and ever-reliable **High Court of Parliament**.

11 **Verwoerd was shot** by a white farmer; he recovered only to be **stabbed to death** in 1966.

12 His successor, **Johannes Vorster**, further developed the policy of apartheid and the creation of **Bantustans** (36.19). He also strictly enforced **petty apartheid**, the laws by which blacks are forbidden to use 'whites only' cafés, public utilities, doors into post offices and hotels, beaches and other leisure facilities.

36.19 Bantustans

1 These were created first by Verwoerd.

2 **Eight regions** were set aside to become self-governing black African states.

3 Although **black Africans make up about four-fifths of the population** of South Africa, the Bantustans were to take only **14 per cent of the land mass** of the Union.

4 The first Bantustan was the **Transkei**. Its Prime Minister was Chief **Matanzima** who soon demanded that the whites leave the Transkei and went on to demand more land for his people.

36.20 Tightening the white grip

1 **1953** It was made a **crime** for African workers **to strike**.

2 **1952 Chief Luthuli**, a moderate, tried to organize a resistance to the segregation laws. He was **deprived of his chieftainship**.

3 A new law permitted **flogging** of anyone breaking existing laws.

4 **March 1960** At **Sharpeville** thousands of Africans gathered to protest peacefully against the **pass laws**: 67 were killed when police fired on the crowd.

36.21 Breaking the grip

1 **1960** South Africa became a **Republic** and had to apply for continued membership of the Commonwealth.

2 **1961** This application was opposed; **Verwoerd withdrew** it and South Africa **left the Commonwealth**.

3 The OAU and the UN constantly condemned apartheid.

4 **1962** The UN imposed a **trade boycott** on South Africa.

Not all countries followed this boycott, preferring to benefit from trade with the rich country which produced most of the world's gold. Sanctions have proved totally ineffective.

5 **1968** The South African government refused to allow the coloured cricketer, **Basil d'Oliveira**, to enter the country as a member of the MCC team. **The tour was cancelled**.

6 **1968-9** Radicals in Britain tried to stop the tour of Britain by the **South African Rugby team**–but failed.

7 **1970** The clashes during the rugby tour led the British government to enforce the cancellation of the **proposed South African cricket tour**. Other Commonwealth countries followed this example; Australia cancelled a tour proposed for 1971.

8 Other international organizations have since taken similar action so that **South Africa is barred** from all international sport.

9 One result of this has been attempts in South Africa to **change the petty apartheid laws** as far as they affect sport. White teams now play coloured and black teams; some black sportsmen have been chosen for national sides; white schools play games against black schools.

10 But this is **not enough** to persuade the world that South Africa is ready to be welcomed back:
  i black sportsmen have **few facilities** and black schoolchildren poorer chances than white;
  ii even if black and white sportsmen are allowed to mix during and immediately after a game, **they are not allowed to have any more contact until the next game**;
  iii the effects of apartheid on sport cannot be removed unless the whole policy is swept away.

36.22 Whites loosen their grip

1 In 1982–83 there were signs that the hardline government, now led by **Botha**, was aware of the need for change.

2 Blacks were allowed to form **trade unions** which could negotiate for wages and conditions and even call strikes.

3 **Asian and Coloured voters** were to be allowed, again, to have a vote. They would be represented by their own separate delegates, although an **all-White Parliament** would continue to control affairs.

4 Some see this as a **step** towards the major change in which blacks would be given their civil and political rights.

36.23 Angola and Mozambique

1 These Portuguese colonies were among the larger states.

2 By the mid-1960s they were, with Rhodesia and South Africa, **symbols of white supremacy** as other states gained their independence.

3 **1964** Portugal signed an agreement for economic co-operation with **South Africa**. She also played a major role in helping **Ian Smith** to resist British attempts to break his illegal régime.

4 **Guerilla movements** by black nationalists developed in Angola in 1961 while the Mozambique Liberation Front **(Frelimo)** was founded to organize the anti-colonial struggle there.

5 Portugal was helped in her anti-terrorist campaigns by **white mercenaries** from Britain, the USA, West Germany and South Africa.

6 The right-wing governments in Portugal refused to enter into negotiations about self-rule.

7 **1974** After the death of the autocratic **Salazar** in Portugal there was a **revolution** which led to the establishment of a democratic system in Portugal.

8 **1975** The new government granted **independence** to both Angola and Mozambique which now became **front line states** in the black struggle against **South Africa** which is the last remaining bastion of white supremacy.

37 North Africa and the Middle East

37.1 Algeria

1 This was the **largest** of the French colonies in N. Africa.

2 For many years **French settlers** had lived in comfort and had done little to help the Muslim Algerians, most of whom lived in poverty.

3 1930s A number of **Algerian nationalist movements** were founded:

i the North African Star was founded by Muslim exiles in Paris and was meant to defend working class interests. By 1936 this had become the **(La) Partie Populaire Algérienne**;

ii Muslim intellectuals, such as **Ferhat Abbas**, campaigned in Algeria for the extension to Muslims of **civil and political rights**;

iii **the Association of Algerian Ulama** set up Algerian **schools** to give Arabic education to the 90 per cent of children ignored by the French colonial school system.

4 1939–45 saw an increase in nationalist activity. Some **welcomed the Germans**, hoping for freedom from French settler rule. **Others** fought in **resistance movements**, hoping to win French sympathy.

5 1945–50 Abbas proposed to **de Gaulle** (31.16.15) that he should allow an **Algerian Republic** to be set up in which French and Arab would be equal. De Gaulle allowed only:

i **equal opportunities** for French and such Arabs as could get on;

ii the formation of an **Algerian Assembly** of 120 representatives elected by Algerian Muslims. This had no real power.

6 1954–62

i France was fighting and losing a war in **Indo-China** (35.11–13);

ii **Muslims** in Pakistan, Arabs in Egypt and blacks in Ghana had or were winning their independence;

iii **1954** The **FLN** (or **National Liberation Front**) was founded by **Ben Bella** to fight a guerilla war against French rule:

(a) this was helped by aid from **Egypt and Russia**;

(b) the French settlers supported the **French army** of 500 000 which was determined not to lose this colony as it had Vietnam:

iv **1955** the **UN** proposed that Algeria should be independent;

v the war continued with **Muslim guerillas** attacking French property in the countryside and towns;

vi **1958** the army feared that the politicians might make a deal with the Muslims. **General Salan** led an **army revolt** which led to the overthrow of the Republic and **de Gaulle's return** to power (31.16.19–20);

vii De Gaulle realized that the French could not win and began **negotiations with the rebel leaders** (31.16.25);

viii French officers and settlers formed the **OAS**, a French terrorist organization aimed at preventing the handover of Algeria (OAS from the French term **Organisation de l'Armée Secrète**;

ix this was ruthlessly **suppressed by de Gaulle**;

x **1962** an agreement was reached which ended the fighting;

xi **Ben Bella**, the first President of the Algerian Republic, was replaced by **Boumedienne** (1965) who described Bella as a despot.

7 The French gave independence to **Morocco and Tunisia** with much less trouble.

37.2 The Arab League

1 Britain had had a great deal of power in the Middle East through its control of Egypt and its Palestinian Mandate.

2 October 1945 Britain helped the formation of the Arab League. **Egypt, Iraq, Syria, the Lebanon and Saudia Arabia** were the first members of the League which was intended to be an obstacle to Russian progress in this region.

3 As other Arab states gained independence they joined and by 1983 the **Sudan, Algeria, Morocco, Tunisia, Libya, Oman, the South Yemen, Kuwait and Bahrein** were member of the League.

4 The **36 million Arabs** shared a common **language and culture**; most of them were **Muslims** and all of them had shared a **hatred of colonial rule**.

5 They also had **similar economic problems**. Even the countries rich in oil had a **mal-distribution of wealth** so that here, and in the non-oil countries, there was a great disparity between the very rich (few) and the very poor (majority).

6 The population of these countries was expanding and there was little chance of them being able to provide decent living standards for their peoples.

7 Above all else these Arab countries were **opposed to Israel**.

37.3 Palestine, 1923–47

1 Palestine became a **British Mandate** after 1923. Wartime promises had led to the growth of **Arab expectations** (13.11-13) and to **Jewish hopes** for a national home (13.14).

2 The **Zionist Movement** had been started by a Viennese Jew, **Theodore Herzl**. At the first Zionist Congress in 1896 he had proposed the idea of a national home for the world's Jews. **The Balfour Declaration** (13.14.5) seemed a British commitment to that idea.

3 1920s 10 000 Jews arrived each year to settle in Palestine. This alarmed the Arabs who saw Jews as representing western imperialism:

i **1922 Winston Churchill** tried to pacify Arabs by saying that the British promised only a national home and not a Jewish state;

ii **1929 Arabs rioted** on a large scale against the 100 000 Jewish settlers who provided themselves with their own security force, the **Hagannah**.

4 The 1930s:

i to pacify the Arabs, Britain imposed **restrictions in 1933** on Jewish immigration. This led to **Jewish riots** against the British;

ii **1933** was the year when **Hitler came to power** (15.21–23) and the demand for entry into Palestine increased. In 1936 some 60 000 Jews were allowed in;

iii by **1937** there were **400 000 Jews** in Palestine; by **1939** some **600 000** facing a hostile 1 000 000 Arabs:

(a) the Jews became more prosperous because of their hard work, technical skills and aid from abroad;

(b) they bought land from Arabs and watched 'the desert bloom':

iv 1937 a major rising by Arabs (**'the Arab Revolt'**) led to the **Peel Commission** which reported that the Mandate could not work and that **Palestine ought to be divided**. The Arabs rejected this suggestion of a Jewish state.

5 1939–45 With the persecution of the Jews by Hitler, many tried to get to Palestine. The British **restricted** the numbers allowed in so that thousands tried to get in illegally.

6 1945–47 There was a world-wide sympathy with the Jews once the news of the **concentration camps** became better known:

i **Bevin**, British Foreign Minister, wishing to please the Arabs, tried to **restrict the numbers** allowed into Palestine;

ii **the Arabs**, angered by the continuous wave of illegal immigrants, **attacked Jewish settlements**. The **Hagannah** defended these;

iii some Jews also organized terrorist gangs, the **Irgun** and the **Stern Gang**, which used the tactics used by partisans fighting against German occupation. Police stations, army posts, government buildings were attacked by bombs and gunmen;

iv the British were giving their Indian Empire its independence. They were also (1947) withdrawing from Greece (28.4) and it is not surprising that they felt unable to maintain their control of Palestine;

v **Truman**, President of the USA, fighting an election campaign (32.6) asked the British to admit more Jews. This would have been a last straw as far as the Arabs were concerned;

vi **Bevin** handed the problem to the **UNO** and on **14 May 1948** Britain withdrew her forces from Palestine;

vii **the Jews** immediately announced the creation of their own state and named it **Israel**;

viii **the UN** suggestion was a **division of Palestine** (giving Israel the portion shaded horizontally in Fig. 37.4A). This was rejected by the Arabs who preferred to try to drive the Jews out.

37.4 The First Arab-Israeli War, 1948

1 The fighting had begun before the British left.

2 **Arab armies** attacked from:

i **Jordan**, which sent the Arab Legion under British General Glubb;

ii **Egypt**, under officers including Neguib and Nasser;

iii **Syria and Saudi Arabia.**

3 The Jews were surrounded and outnumbered.

4 President **Weizmann** and Prime Minister **David Ben Gurion** appealed to the world for help–but little came.

5 UN mediators tried to end the fighting. **Count Bernadotte** was murdered (September 1948) by Jewis terrorists.

6 **The Arabs failed to defeat the Jews:**

i their **leaders** were at odds with one another, each seeking to gain an advantage from the war;

ii their **armies** had **no co-ordinated plans**; the Jews could concentrate on defeating first one and then another;

iii their armies were **badly led**, officers and men fleeing in times of difficulty;

iv **the Jews**, on the other hand, had the **technical skills** of British-trained officers; the **determination** of a people which had no option other than to fight to the bitter end.

7 **February 1949** The War ended. Israel gained more territory than had been alloted to it by the UN proposal of 1948.

8 **Over 1 000 000 Arabs fled from Palestine** to live in refugee camps in Syria, Jordan and Egypt.

37.5 An uneasy peace, 1949–56

1 A UN commission had helped to end the war. **A UN Truce Supervisory Commission** was needed to police the new frontiers.

2 **Jerusalem** was divided between Israel and Jordan.

3 Israel claimed the **Gaza Strip** and only tolerated Egyptian possession of the Strip as a temporary arrangement.

4 There were frequent **Arab terrorist attacks** on Jewish property and **Jewish attacks** on the camps which harboured the terrorists.

5 **Russia** had originally supported Israel in the hope of winning a base in the region. When Israel proved to be 'a client' of the USA, Russia turned to support the Arabs, providing them with arms.

37.6 Nasser's Egypt

1 **Gamal Abdel Nasser** was an army officer who fought against Israel in 1948–49.

2 **July 1952** Nasser was one of the leaders of the coup d'état which overthrew the corrupt **King Farouk**. He was Deputy

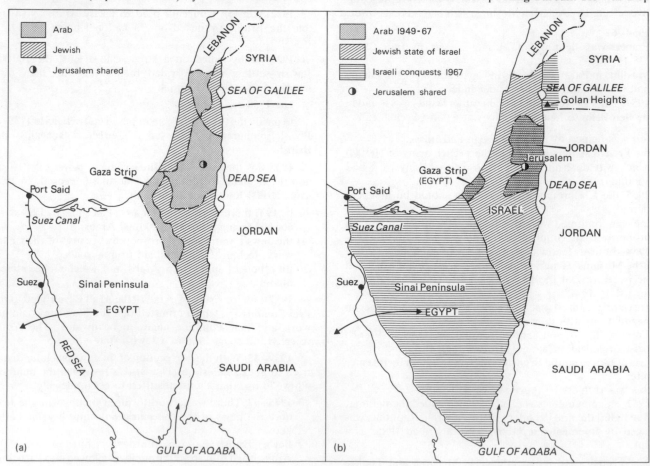

Prime Minister to General Neguib, 1952–54, whom he overthrew and replaced.

3 Nasser saw himself as playing many roles:

i **the Egyptian leader** who would free his country from the last remnants of British control. He negotiated the withdrawal of the 90 000 troops stationed in the Suez Canal area. These left in 1954–55;

ii **the socialist leader** who would provide his people with better living standards. A series of land reforms took land from rich landowners for use by peasants. Social reforms in education, housing and health legislation improved the quality of Egyptian life;

iii **the reforming leader** who, with foreign aid, would build the Aswan High Dam to control the waters of the Nile and provide better irrigation for Egyptian farmers;

iv **the Arab leader** who would unite all the Arab peoples in an Arab Union–and not only against Israel. He formed the United Arab Republic with Syria in 1958 only for it to break up in 1961, to be re-formed (and to include Iraq) in 1963 only for it to break up again.

4 Nasser's ambitions were viewed with alarm by:

i **other Arab leaders**, notably the Kings of Iraq, Jordan and Saudi Arabia. Nasser helped General Kassem to overthrow and murder King Feisal of Iraq (1958) but then faced him as a rival for leadership of the left-wing Arab future;

ii **the USA, Britain and France** which feared both a Nasser-led Arab Union and, more importantly, a Russian-controlled, if Nasser-led, Middle Eastern Union;

iii **France**, fighting her war in Algeria, and angered by Nasser's aid to the Muslim rebels whom he also sheltered when they fled.

37.7 The Baghdad Pact

1 1954 Turkey and Pakistan signed a mutual defence pact.

2 1955 Pro-western King **Feisal of Iraq** also joined that pact.

3 1956 Britain and Persia joined the pact and the USA gave economic aid to its members.

4 1958 Iraq and Jordan formed the anti-Nasser Arab Federation.

5 The western powers hoped that King Hussein of Jordan would now join the Pact. Nasser, fearing this, put pressure on him while also engineering the downfall of Feisal of Iraq. Jordan never joined the Pact.

6 1959 The western powers thought that they had created a powerful bloc, first called the **Baghdad Pact**, then, in 1959, re-named the **Central Treaty Organization (CENTO)**.

37.8 The Suez Crisis, 1956

1 Nasser received aid from the USA and Britain to help to build the **Aswan High Dam**.

2 1955 He asked for more aid to help buy **weapons**. The US refused because Egypt would not be able to afford the repayments for both forms of aid. More importantly, the US feared that Egypt might attack Israel–her 'client state'.

3 Nasser then got the arms from **Russia and Czechoslovakia**.

4 1956 An angry US then **cut the aid** for the Dam and forced Britain to do the same.

5 July 1956 Nasser announced the **nationalization of the Suez Canal Company**, claiming that the revenue from the Canal would pay for the building of the Dam.

6 Eden, Prime Minister of Britain, thought that he had got the support of President **Eisenhower** and US Secretary John Foster **Dulles** for his scheme to overthrow Nasser. Eden saw Nasser as another Hitler or Mussolini who would go from one conquest to another if he were not stopped.

7 The French, part-owners of the Canal Company, were already angered at **Nasser's aid to the Algerian rebels**.

8 The Israelis were angered by **Egyptian-supported terrorist attacks** from the Gaza Strip.

37.9 The Second Arab-Israeli War, 1956

1 Britain and France agreed with Israel for a joint attack on Egypt.

2 October 1956 Israel attacked the **Gaza Strip** and occupied most of the **Sinai Peninsula**.

3 November 1956 Britain and France called on Egypt and Israel to withdraw all forces from the Canal Zone. This would have meant only an Egyptian withdrawal–and from their own territory. Nasser refused.

4 British and French forces attacked. The Egyptian Air Force was destroyed on the ground, troops landed at Alexandria to occupy the Canal Zone.

5 The US and Russia united to condemn the Anglo-French action. The forces were withdrawn but only after:

i **Arab countries** had threatened to cut off oil supplies;

ii **Nasser** had blown up ships to block the Canal;

iii **the British and French** had been made to appear as aggressors and as failures–which led many Afro-Asian states to turn to Russia for leadership.

37.10 An uneasy peace, 1956–67

1 A UN peacekeeping force moved in to **clear the Canal** and to **keep peace** on the old Israel-Egypt border. It also had a post at **Sharm el Sheik** at the entrance to the Gulf of Aqaba which ensured that Israeli ships could sail through to the port of Eliat.

2 Israel still faced **terrorist attacks** from the Gaza Strip.

3 Nasser, having gained a diplomatic victory with the humiliation of Britain and France, became **more popular** in the Arab world. He was also **more anti-Israel** than before.

4 Syria, his partner in the **United Arab Republic**, shelled Israeli settlements from military posts on the **Golan Heights**.

5 1957 The US Seventh Fleet was sent to prop up a pro-western régime in **Lebanon** in the face of Muslim (pro-Nasser) riots.

6 1958 The pro-western **Feisal of Iraq** was assassinated and a left-wing (pro-Russian) government installed.

7 1959 General Kassem took **Iraq out of the Baghdad Pact**.

8 Local nationalists were supported by Egypt in their struggles to get rid of British influence in the **Gulf, Aden and the South Arabian Federation**.

37.11 Growing hostility, 1967

1 Spring 1967 There was an increase in terrorist activity led by the **PLO** (37.13). **Syria** also increased its shelling from the **Golan Heights**.

2 Syria had left the United Arab Republic in 1961 and was now **outbidding Nasser** in the demand for a united Arab attack on Israel.

3 Iraq, under the left-wing Kassem, was claiming to be **more socialist than Egypt** and staking its claim to be the leading Arab state.

4 Saudi Arabia was aiding the anti-Nasser forces in the Yemen and **claiming the leadership** of the less radical Arab states.

5 Nasser felt that he had to take some action to try to regain his former position as the outstanding Arab leader.

6 Jordan, under pressure from the PLO (37.13.4), signed a military pact with Nasser, **4 June 1967**.

37.12 The Third Arab-Israeli War, 1967 (The Six Day War)

1 Moshe Dayan, hero of the 1956 war, was appointed Minister of Defence in Israel. He argued that attack was the best defence.

2 5 June 1967 Israel launched attacks on **all Arab airfields**.

3 Israeli troops drove Egyptian forces across the **Sinai**, advanced to the **Jordan River** against the Jordanians and routed the Syrians on the **Golan Heights**.

4 8 June Hussein of **Jordan capitulated**.

5 11 June 1967 Both **Syria and Egypt surrendered**.

6 Israel refused UN pleas for a return to the old **borders**:

i **Egypt was occupied** as far as the east bank of the Suez Canal;

ii **Syria was partly occupied**, including the Golan Heights;

iii **the West Bank of the Jordan** remained in Israeli hands.

6 Sporadic frontier fighting continued until the UN arranged a cease fire in 1970.

37.13 The Palestinian Liberation Organization

1 This was an organization which contained a number of groups aiming to 'drive Israel into the sea' and to get Palestine back for the Arabs who had fled in 1948–9.

2 Yasser Arafat emerged as its main leader and spokesman, although **more militant groups** followed their own line.

3 1960 Kassem of Iraq formed the Palestinian Army.

4 The PLO was most active in **Jordan** where, in the 1960s, it forced Hussein to abandon his moderate line and to seek an alliance with Nasser (37.11.6).

5 PLO terrorists drew world attention to their case by:

i frequent **raids into Israel**;

ii **hi-jacking aircraft**, many of which were forced to land in Jordan where they were blown up;

iii 1972 PLO terrorists gunned down 100 people at **Lydda Airport, Tel Aviv**;

iv at the **1972 Munich Olympic Games** the Black September Group of PLO terrorists kidnapped Israeli hostages who were killed during a gunfight between German police and the terrorists.

6 The Israelis always took 'an eye for an eye' in revenge attacks on terrorist camps hoping to frighten Arab governments from giving refuge to the PLO.

7 September, 1970 Hussein of Jordan turned on his fellow-Arabs in the PLO when it tried to overthrow him and to run his country. The organization then found most help in Syria.

8 1972 Sadat, Nasser's successor in Egypt, sent Russian advisers home which displeased Syria and created another rift in the Arab world.

37.14 The Fourth Arab-Israeli War, 1973

1 Egypt wanted to get Israel from the **Sinai**; **Syria** wanted to regain the **Golan Heights**.

2 In spite of their different opinions over the PLO and the advantage of Russian aid (37.13.8), they agreed to attack Israel.

3 6 October 1973 was a Jewish Holy Day (**Yom Kippur**):

i **Syria attacked the Golan Heights** and received help from **Jordan, Iraq and Saudi Arabia**;

ii **Egypt** attacked across the **Canal** and broke through the Israeli's defensive Bar-Lev line.

4 The surprising attack was, at first, successful:

i **Russia supplied aid** and technical advice to the Arabs;

ii **the USA was, at first, reluctant** to aid Israel.

5 Once US aid arrived–planes and artillery–Israel drove the Arabs back:

i **the Syrians** were pushed back towards **Damascus**;

ii **the Israeli army** drove through **Sinai** and captured the **west bank of the Canal**, leaving the Egyptian army surrounded east of the Canal and in Port Said.

6 UN mediators and the US Secretary of State, **Kissinger**, arranged a cease fire. UN forces were sent to separate the

Israeli and Egyptian forces although Israel held on to her gains in the **Sinai and on the Golan Heights**.

37.15 The Organization of Petroleum Exporting Countries (OPEC)

1 OPEC was founded in 1961, largely at the initiative of **Venezuela**. Its first aim was to help the oil-owning countries in their negotiations with the multi-national oil companies which, at that time, developed each country's oilfields, paying a relatively small sum to the country concerned.

2 By 1972 the foreign oil companies had lost their control of the industry and were forced to deal with well-educated and able ministers.

3 Saudi Arabia, Kuwait, Libya, Bahrein and Iraq were the leading Arab members of OPEC.

4 Having failed to defeat Israel (and her western allies) by force, the Arabs decided to use OPEC in their fight.

5 1972–73 They pushed up oil prices so that by 1974 they were 4 times as much as they had been in 1972. This resulted in:

i **a flow of money** to the Arab world;

ii quickening **inflation** in the western world;

iii **a slow-down in world trade** as countries tried to solve their balance of payments problems.

6 The Arabs also used their **oil as a weapon**: they threatened to cut off supplies to any country supporting Israel–Holland being the first sufferer.

7 But even in the oil world, the **Arabs were divided**:

i the **'royalists'** such as Saudi Arabia and Kuwait were not as militant as **anti-monarchist** Libya wanted;

ii **Iraq** found itself at war with **Iran** so that it was, itself, short of oil.

37.16 The Lebanon, Stage 1, 1975–6

1 In Lebanon the **Christians and Muslims** had lived in uneasy peace with political power being shared by the 2 groups.

2 1975 Right-wing Christian groups tried to break the power of left-wing Muslim groups. There was bitter fighting in which the capital, Beirut, was devastated.

3 1976 The PLO had supported the Lebanese Muslims–hoping to find a new home for itself after being forced out of Jordan (37.13.7).

4 1976 Syrian and other Arab forces entered Lebanon to try to restore peace–and **Syrians fought the PLO** while Christians looked on.

5 Israel kept a watchful eye on Lebanese affairs (37.19).

37.17 The PLO again, 1976, and Entebbe

1 June 1976 PLO terrorists hi-jacked an Air France plane containing many Jewish passengers and forced it to fly to **Entebbe in Uganda**.

2 Amin (36.4.5) allowed the terrorists to use the old airport as a prison in which they kept Jewish passengers as hostages. They demanded the release of Palestinian guerilras held in Israel and other prisons.

3 The Israelis mounted a rescue operation, flying in an airborne force which rescued nearly all the hostages, killed most of the hi-jackers and the Ugandan guards placed by Amin around the airport.

37.18 Egypt-Israeli peace, 1977

1 October 1977 President **Sadat of Egypt** flew to Jerusalem where he met **Prime Minister Begin of Israel** and addressed the Israeli Parliament (the **Knessett**).

2 Sadat asked that the 2 countries should arrange a peace.

3 Begin made a return visit to Cairo. Sadat was condemned by the Russians, most Arab countries and the PLO for 'betraying the Arab cause'.

4 Sadat could not arrange a total peace; no other Arab state would agree to one. So he made **peace on behalf of Egypt**:

i **Israel** withdrew her forces from the **Sinai** and handed the territory back to Egypt;

ii **Egypt** allowed free access to **Eliat** through the Gulf of Aqaba;

iii **Israel** promised that, in time, she would withdraw from the **Gaza Strip**. Religious fanatics and Israeli nationalists were opposed to this.

37.19 The Lebanon, Stage 2, 1976–84

1 The numerous internal divisions:

i **Christians**: there are at least 12 different (and warring) Christian groups:

(a) one way of looking at these divisions is to consider them from the point of view of **religious belief**. So, there are Greek Orthodox, Russian Orthodox, Roman Catholic and other groups. The most important group are the **Maronites**;

(b) another way is to consider the **family grouping**. Over the years, certain families have become accepted as leaders of some Christian groups. So, there are Christians who support the **Franijeh, Gemayel and Chamoun families**;

(c) it is important to note that these groups have their own **private armies**, have their own **bases** in various parts of towns and cities such as Beirut and in the country as a whole. So, part of East Beirut has become popularly known as **Marounistan**, an area controlled by the Maronites;

(d) these different groups **war with each other** to try to gain more political and territorial power. They make allies of whoever will help them–Muslims, PLO, Israelis and Syrians. But they will as quickly turn against their former ally if this suits them;

ii **Muslims** are also divided into various groups:

(a) the **Shiah Muslims** are those who believe that when the Prophet Muhammed died in 632 his son-in-law, Ali, became the successor. This is the opinion of a minority of Muslims;

(b) the **Sunni Muslims**, who form the majority, believe that the Prophet did not name a successor. They claim that the Muslims as a whole have the right to decide who is to be the leader at any one time;

(c) the **Druzes** are a small group, followers of people who broke away from mainstream Muslimism and who have their own '**secret book**', read only by **chosen leaders** who control the Druze community. They live, mainly, in mountain villages–so that the region is often referred to as 'the Druze Mountains';

(d) some **Muslims are left-wing** in politics and accept the leadership of **Syria**. **Others**, the better-off, **fear a Communist take-over**. The Druzes, hated by both Shia and Sunni groups, have taken on a left wing stance. Led by the **Jumblatt family**, the Druzes have become the most warlike of the anti-Christian groups.

2 Outside influences:

i until 1975, the various groups had lived in an uneasy peace with one another:

(a) political power was shared out (37.16.1);

(b) each of the important groups had its own power base and its own method of raising money. Many of them had their own ports through which they handled the money-making drug traffic;

ii this uneasy peace was broken in 1975 (37.16.2) and the PLO tried to take advantage of the situation in 1976 (37.16.3);

iii the dominant Christian groups accepted help from Muslim and left-wing Syria, which intervened to break the power of the independent Yasser Arafat and the PLO (37.16.4);

iv this led to a long period of bitter civil war. From 1976 to 1982:

(a) Christian groups fought each other to try to gain leadership of the whole Christian community. In 1978 heads of several of the leading Christian families were assassinated by other Christian groups;

(b) the Lebanese government forces, a mixture of Christian and Muslims, fell apart as members tended to drift into the camps of the warring Christians and Muslims;

(c) Israel took advantage of the situation to attack PLO and other bases in South Lebanon, from which Muslims launched raids into Northern Israel;

(d) Israel launched a full-scale invasion in 1976 but was forced to withdraw by US pressure;

(e) 1981 Syria defeated the Christian armies–the armies of those who had, initially, invited Syria to play an active part in Lebanon (37.19.2.iii).

3 The Israeli invasion, 1982:

i **in 1981 Begin** formed a new government. Many of its members were hard-liners, such as **Sharon**, the Minister of Defence;

ii many Israeli leaders wanted to take advantage of the Lebanese war to **wipe out the bases** from which raids were launched into Israel;

iii others seemed to want to **expand Israeli territory** by occupying (permanently, perhaps) South Lebanon;

iv there was a **real fear** among Israelis that a **Syrian-dominated Lebanon** would be a major threat to Israel.

4 The 1982–3 war:

i the Israelis advanced through Lebanon and reached Beirut;

ii they were helped by various Christian forces, anxious to get Syrian forces out of Lebanon;

iii as a result of this war, the **PLO was defeated**–by the Israelis and with the connivance of the Syrians who made little attempt to help Arafat and the PLO;

iv **the PLO forces were driven out of Lebanon**. Some went to Syria; Arafat and others went to Algeria and Jordan. There then took place an **internal struggle inside the PLO**:

(a) Arafat was **condemned** by some who wanted a more warlike attitude towards Israel. Arafat himself seemed to have realized that it would be necessary to negotiate a deal with Israel if the Palestinians were to get any sort of recognition;

(b) in spite of the earlier agreement to withdraw from Lebanon, **Arafat and other PLO forces returned in 1983**. They then had their own **PLO-Civil War** in which Syrians finally defeated Arafat. He was driven away again, and left to find a new home in Egypt:

v **Israeli and Syrian forces** were then engaged in a war for control of Northern Lebanon. Syrian forces were driven back into the northern valley;

vi **Israeli and Druze forces** fought their own war which goes on with Druze forces in control of the northern mountains;

vii under international pressure, **Israel agreed to withdraw** its forces **to South Lebanon**. It also agreed that, **if Syria withdrew** her forces from the North, **Israel would withdraw completely** from Lebanon.

5 The US intervention, 1983–84:

i **Syria** gained increasing control of Lebanese affairs:

(a) she had defeated the **PLO** which had withdrawn;

(b) she had defeated the **Christians** in 1981;

(c) she was supplied with **Russian weapons and advisers**;

(d) in 1983 she had forces which **occupied the North** and maintained the struggle against a weak Christian government under Gemayel:

ii **Reagan** had succeeded in overthrowing a Cuban-led coup in Grenada (32.30.7);

iii he sent 1500 US soldiers, an American Fleet and aircraft **to 'invade' Lebanon**. He claimed that he was acting as the **peacemaker**. As proof of this he had the support of Britain,

France, Italy who sent forces as part of the **multinational peace-keeping force**;

iv in fact, events proved that this was an **anti-Syrian force** which came under attack from Syrian, Druze and Muslim forces;

v this allowed public opinion to label the US and other forces as **'pro-Israeli' forces**;

vi there was a **threat to world peace**:

(a) **Syria** was backed by **Russia**;

(b) if US forces clashed with Syrian forces **would the Russians** stand by and **see their client-state defeated**? Or would they, too, send forces into troubled Lebanon.

6 The uneasier Lebanon, 1984 There seems little hope, in January 1984, that Lebanon will return even to the uneasy peace she enjoyed before 1975 (37.16.1). Israel, Syria and, now, the western powers have forces inside the country. None of these are, at the moment, willing to withdraw. Christians of various groups (37.19.1) and Muslims in their various groups (37.19.1) continue to fight each other.

38 The Third World and some current problems

38.1 What do people mean by the 'Third World'?

1 International relations The term describes countries **not allied to either the capitalist west or the Communist east**. These **non-aligned countries** come, mainly, from Asia and Africa.

2 Political The term describes countries which have **won their independence from some colonial power**. These emergent nations come, again, from Asia and Africa.

3 Economic The term describes countries with a **low standard of living** and which are **trying to become more industrialized** or developed. Such countries have a low average income per head, as can be seen from this table which lists the average income per head of population for selected developed and 'Third World' countries:

Table 38.1A

Country	Population *(millions)*	Per capita income *(US dollars)*	Main exports *(% of whole)*
USA	211	6670	Machinery 27%
West Germany	62	6260	Machinery 29%
United Kingdom	56	3590	Machinery 28%
Zambia	5	520	Copper 95%
Ghana	10	430	Cocoa 64%
Uganda	11	240	
India	595	140	Jute 13%
Bangladesh	76	100	
Somalia	3	90	

4 Geographic Most of these poor countries are south of the Equator (38.2.9).

38.2 Becoming aware of the 'Third World'

1 The Colombo Plan, 1950 was devised by the **Foreign Ministers of the Commonwealth** to help the development of South and South-East Asia (38.7.6.iv).

2 The UN had from the start a **number of agencies** whose main aim was to help to overcome the poverty of Third World countries (38.7.7).

3 Former colonial powers, such as France, took a special interest in the development of their former colonies.

4 Germany, perhaps because of its wish to wipe out memories of Hitler, has been especially generous in its aid to poorer countries.

5 Many private agencies exists in Britain (OXFAM, CAFOD, War on Want and so on) and in other countries to channel aid to poorer countries.

6 1955 At **Bandung** the **Afro-Asian Conference** tried to set up an organization in which Third World countries could unite, aloof from the Cold War.

7 1973 In **Algiers** there was a meeting of leaders of Third World countries, angered by the failure of the developed countries to give sufficient attention to their plight.

8 1976 In **Ceylon**, the leaders met again but, once more, failed to arrive at any real solution to their problem of making the developed world more aware of the increasing gulf between rich and poor countries.

9 Reports by UN agencies, by groups of politicians (such as the Brandt Report) and by the Commonwealth Secretariat ('The North-South dialogue') have shown how little has been done to bridge the gulf between the richer countries (mainly in the northern hemisphere) and the poor (mainly in the south).

38.3 Political unrest makes the problem worse

1 Wars and civil wars have made matters worse for many poor countries. Money, material and men have been used in wars instead of in economic and social development. Examples of countries affected in this way are Uganda, Somalia, Pakistan-Bangladesh, India, Nigeria and Zimbabwe.

2 Tribal conflicts have often led to unrest, rioting and an interference with a country's development. Examples of places affected in this way include **Northern Ireland** (where the Catholic 'tribe' fights the Protestant 'tribe', both using terrorism as a weapon); **Sri Lanka**, where in 1983 the minority Tamils were once again attacked by the majority Sinhalese; **Uganda**, where both the overthrow and later return of Obote were accompanied by horrendous massacres of rival tribes; the **Congo, Nigeria** with its Biafran war; and, in 1984, **Zimbabwe** where the minority Matabele are attacked by the majority Mashona led by Mugabe.

3 Freedom fighters have used terrorist tactics to draw attention to their plight–but have hindered the economic and social development of the country for which they claim to be fighting. Among such 'fighters' are the PLO (37.13), the IRA, the South West African People's Organization (SWAPO) which wants an independent Namibia, and Frelimo (36.23.4).

4 Urban guerillas in developed countries have claimed to be trying to overthrow a western-dominated capitalist system in the hope that some better system may, somehow, be created. Among these are the Baader-Meinhof gang in West Germany, the Red Brigade in Italy, various Black Power groups in the USA where there was also the Simbionese Liberation Army, and the Angry Brigade in Britain.

38.4 The problems of the Third World

1 As can be seen in Table 38.1A, Zambia and Ghana are **heavily reliant on one commodity**. This is typical of under-developed countries. **The price they get for that commodity** varies according to the level of output and the level of world demand. The supply of such items as coffee, sugar, cocoa, wheat and rubber may be very high in a good year and low in a bad year. If world demand is down when supplies are high, prices fall sharply and so does the income of the people and of the country.

2 Table 38.1A also shows the **low incomes** received by the people of some under-developed countries. This may be the result of the poor quality of their work (and equipment or tools); it may be the result of over-production of their principal commodity. But the results of that low income include:

i **lack of money for private investment**. Too few people in under-developed countries earn enough to save; **savings are the source of investment**. Since there are not enough savings, there is also too little local investment in machinery, buildings, equipment and so on;

ii **lack of money for public investment**: the US government can tax its people with their incomes of around 6670 dollars a head (Table 38.1A). With these taxes the government can build schools, roads, harbours, hospitals and all the economic and social infra-structure which helps a developed country to function. Governments in India or Uganda can only collect a **low volume of taxation from their already poor people**. This leads to lack of spending on infra-structure so that the possibility of economic development is even further limited;

iii **lack of spending by consumers**—who have little money. There is little encouragement to merchants and others to build factories because they have little chance of selling their product at home;

iv **a low standard of living**, measured in such things as clothing, food and housing, and reflected in such things as level of education, ability to work and to buy goods.

3 Many under-developed countries suffer from the **climatic problems** explained in 36.1.3.vi.

4 The economic and trading development in **industrialized countries** also make things worse for developing countries:

i **Malaya** used to export natural rubber. The demand for this has gone down with the development of **synthetic rubber**. Other synthetics (rayon, nylon and various plastics) affect world demand for such raw materials as wool, copper, cotton, tin and zinc;

ii **some developing countries** have begun to produce goods which compete with goods produced by industrialized countries. This ought to be welcomed because it will raise incomes, living standards and the social life of the country. **But many industrialized countries** (including Britain) resent such competition and try to prevent imports from developing countries (by tariffs, quotas or bans on such imports).

5 Perhaps the most serious problem for developing countries is the continuous and rapid **growth of their populations**.

38.5 World population since 1945

1 The population of Asia:

i **India**: the population is increasing by 2.6 million every year and there will be 800 million in India by 2000 AD;

ii **Asia generally** now has half the world's population living on only one fifth of the world's land surface. In 1973 there were 2 billion Asians; by 1990 there will be 3 billion;

iii **the main cause of this increase** is not an increase in the number of babies born (**the birth rate**) but the sharp fall in the number of babies and other people dying each year (**the death rate**);

iv **the main causes of the fall in the death rate** include:

(a) the introduction of western **scientific and medical knowledge**. DDT spraying reduced deaths in Ceylon from 22 per thousand to 12 per thousand in 7 years during which period the malarial mosquito was wiped out. Drugs such as penicillin, vaccines for former 'killer' diseases such as diphtheria have allowed people to live whereas formerly they might have died;

(b) improved food production in countries such as India has lessened, although not ended, the numbers dying of starvation each day;

(c) social reforms in such areas as sanitation, education and washing facilities have helped to lower the death rate:

v **among the major effects of this increase in population are:**

(a) the problem of **feeding, housing and employing** the larger number of people;

(b) the economic problem of **paying for the imports** needed to feed and clothe the people;

(c) the slow rise (where there is one) **in the per capita income** because even increased output fails to match the increased population.

2 The populations of developed countries:

i these are the **richest countries** in the world;

ii their populations are **rising only slowly**:

(a) the US population is rising by about 1 per cent a year;

(b) the populations of most European countries, including Britain, are rising by less than one per cent a year:

iii in these countries there has been a **sharp fall in the death rate** and people are living much longer than used to be the case;

iv this ought to have led to increased populations. But while the death rate has fallen, the **birth rate has fallen even more sharply**. The **causes of this fall are**:

(a) the changing roles of women in western society. An increasing number of women wish to follow a career and do not want to have their jobs and careers hindered by child-rearing;

(b) the greater expectations of western men and women. They expect to have an ever rising standard of living. These expectations can often be met only if both husband and wife are working;

(c) a greater knowledge of and willingness to use one of a wide variety of contraceptive methods of birth prevention;

(d) the Abortion Acts which, in an increasing number of countries, allow pregnant women to get rid of their unwanted babies.

3 The populations of African countries:

i the populations of many of these countries is **rising even more sharply than the population of India**;

ii **the causes of these rises are:**

(a) economic development, although often slow, leads to higher living standards. Many people see this as an opportunity to have larger families. Only in western countries do increased living standards lead to a fall in family size;

(b) urban development, a result of economic development, provides both increased job opportunities (and the ability to maintain a family) and housing (in which to shelter that family):

iii the problems following from these rising populations are similar to the problems facing India.

4 Some general observations on the growth in population:

i **food supply:**

(a) in 1966 Mrs Gandhi, Prime Minister of India, asked all her people to eat a little less so that fewer of their fellow Indians would starve to death;

(b) in 1966 the USA government was paying out millions of dollars either to destroy crops or to compensate farmers who agreed to take land out of cultivation. In 1983 the EEC controls vast 'mountains' of unbought wheat, beef and other meat, as well as 'lakes' of unwanted milk and wine;

(c) it might seem simple to transfer the 'unwanted' food of Europe and the surplus crops of the USA to the starving of the Third World. Unfortunately, the economic system is not that simple. The question we have to ask is: Can the poor afford to buy this 'unwanted' or surplus food? Since the answer is 'No', then we have to ask whether the taxpayers in the rich countries would agree to make the payment needed to get the food transferred? Again, regretfully, the answer, for the time being, is 'No'.

ii **birth control:**

(a) western societies have accepted a variety of methods of contraception;

(b) in most countries in the Third World it is still regarded as being socially desirable to have large families;

(c) in these societies, too, there are strong religious objections to birth control;

(d) it is also difficult to educate people in the Third World in methods of family planning because most adults are illiterate and there is a great shortage of doctors and clinics;

(e) in India, Mrs Gandhi and her son, Sanjay, tried to make sterilization compulsory. Widespread objections to this 'dictatorial' behaviour was one reason for Mrs Gandhi's fall from power in 1977;

(f) the gap between the rich west and the poor Third World is growing wider–in spite of international aid and economic development. The main reason for this 'slippage' is the ever-rising population in Third World countries.

38.6 Steps taken to try to solve the problem of world poverty

1 Population control This has been advocated by advisers from the west. It has been accepted as policy by some leaders in Third World countries. But, as Mrs Gandhi discovered, it has not been accepted by the majority of people in these countries.

2 Commodity agreements Third World countries depend on the money earned by their exporting of raw materials or food (Table 38.1A). Brazil depends on coffee exports; Ghana on cocoa exports; Zambia on copper exports:

i the prices of these goods (or commodities) depends largely on the demand from western countries. If the Third World countries increase their output (to try to get their economy moving) while western countries do not increase their demand, the prices of these goods will fall sharply;

ii in many Third World countries these commodities are produced by international companies–largely controlled by western interests;

iii until the 1960s the oil-producing countries gained little benefit from the development of the oil industries in their countries. The formation of OPEC (38.9.12) and the gradual expansion of its control of the world's oil supply, showed how control of a vital commodity could enable poorer countries to get more of the world's wealth;

iv Brazil tried to organize a commodity agreement with the small number of coffee-producing countries. It was hoped that by controlling supply, the world price could be held at a level which would provide the Brazilians with a better income. The agreement had a short term success, largely because a heavy frost wiped out the Brazil coffee crop in 1972–73. Coffee prices rose–but fell sharply when, in the following year, there was a better than average crop;

v other countries have tried to organize commodity agreements covering lead, tin, copper, wool and bauxite. There has been little success to report; the **western countries have been able to limit the effects of such agreements by:**

(a) **using influence to persuade** one or more members of such an agreement to **'break ranks'** and fall in with western needs;

(b) **providing a substitute** for the commodity concerned, e.g. synthetic rubber helped to offset the rubber agreement;

(c) **threatening to use force.** In 1972 the USA tried to seize Chilean copper shipments in protest at the nationalization of that country's copper production. US statesmen such as Henry Kissinger, have suggested that the west might have to use force against a continued Arab control of the world's oil prices and supplies.

3 Increased trade It is clear that if Third World countries are to 'grow' and provide more of their people with a good standard of living, then they will have to be able both to produce and to sell more goods. The world recession which has now lasted since 1973 and has become even deeper since 1979, has led to a fall in world demand for many raw materials. Third World countries have therefore had an even lower income. But there are success stories to report. Among newly-developed and successful countries are Singapore, Korea, Taiwan and the Philippines. These formerly under-developed countries are now among the world's leading trading nations and their peoples have a rising standard of living.

4 Increased development aid 'If you provide a man with a fish, you keep him alive; if you teach him to fish you help him to improve his own life.' A good deal of international aid has been of the 'fish' variety; western countries have helped Third World countries in times of famine or other natural disaster. But there is also a good deal of 'teach him to fish' aid (38.7).

38.7 International development aid

1 Underdeveloped countries need help to develop:

i **their economic infra-structure** Economic development depends, very largely, on a country having such things as:

(a) good power supplies A country needs things such as dams to help to create hydro-electricity, or generating stations to provide fuel-generated electricity;

(b) good transport systems There is little point in increasing agricultural output in country farms if there are no roads to allow the transport of the output to towns and ports;

(c) harbours, to allow the speedy turn-around of ships bringing imports of industrial necessities and taking away exports. In the 1970s the development of Nigeria and Saudi Arabia was hindered by the poor harbour facilities in these countries. Ships had to wait for up to 6 months to be unloaded–which increased costs, led to a good deal of wastage as food rotted and other goods deteriorated;

ii **their social infra-structure** As a country becomes developed it needs a larger and better trained workforce at all levels. This increases the need for **schools, colleges and universities**. In 1976, when it was the world's leading oil producer, Saudi Arabia reported that 75 per cent of its population was illiterate. High figures of adult illiteracy are also reported by other developing countries;

iii **agricultural progress** We have seen that one of the problems facing the Third World countries is that of feeding their populations (38.5). If money has to be spent to import food, then the country will have a balance of payments problem and will be unable to afford the imports of machinery and other goods essential to industrialization. It is important that the developing countries should be helped to increase their food output. This leads to the need for agricultural colleges as well as of machinery and improved strains of seeds;

iv **industrial progress** Industrialization provides a nation's people with better job prospects, higher incomes, better living standards and higher spending by government on social welfare schemes. **To achieve this industrialization** the Third World countries need help to:

(a) buy the essential capital equipment;

(b) construct the necessary factories and works;

(c) manage and operate the new industries.

2 We have seen that they are unable to provide the investment needed from their own resources (38.4).

3 We should also note that, if their industrialization is to succeed, they have to be allowed access to western markets. Too many western countries are unwilling to allow them such access (38.4).

4 Methods of giving development aid:

i **grants may be made by western governments** to governments in Third World countries. These do not have to be repaid and they do not require any interest payments on the amount given;

ii **loans are made by governments, by UN and other agencies, and by banks** to help governments and/or companies in Third World countries to develop. Such loans have to be repaid in time (usually in 10 or 20 years). They also carry an interest charge which is adjusted every 6 months depending on whether western interest rates have risen or fallen in that period. There are **many problems following from giving (and getting) loans**:

(a) a developing country may be persuaded to **take more loans than it can really afford**. In the 1970s western bankers had to try to cope with the huge influx of money from Arab oil-producing countries. They had to pay interest on the money put into their banks by the Arabs; they wanted to get that interest (and a profit) from lending the money out. Many Third World countries agreed to take loans which, in the 1980s, they are unable to repay;

(b) **interest rates can be varied** – usually in an upward direction. Any Third World country which agreed in 1972 to take a loan at a rate of 6 per cent a year found in 1980 that the interest rates had shot up to 15 per cent a year:

iii the Third World country taking the loan assumed that it would be able to pay the interest and repay the capital out of export earnings. In the 1980s many countries have found that their **exports have not matched earlier expectations**. This had led them into increased difficulties as can be seen below.

5 The Nigerian experience, 1970–83:

i oil production in Nigeria expanded rapidly in the period 1970–75. **Output reached 3 million barrels a day;**

ii **oil prices** rocketed from 2 dollars a barrel (1973) to 35 dollars a barrel (1978);

iii **Nigeria's income rose sharply**. She embarked on a massive programme for development. This led to borrowing at rates of interest around 6 per cent a year. There was every expectation that this interest could be paid and the capital repaid out of the expected oil earnings;

iv **in 1983 Nigeria was in deep trouble.** The world demand for oil fell – and **Nigeria sold only 1-1½ million barrels per day. Oil prices have fallen and Nigeria received between only 27–28 dollars per barrel for her oil**. At the same time **interest rates rose and Nigeria had to pay 15 per cent on her large loans**. You will see why this drove her into financial difficulty. Such problems also affect developed countries whose industries may have invested in the country only to find difficulty in getting paid for their goods and investments.

Expectations: 3 million barrels at 35 dollars a barrel = 105m dollars

Reality: 1 million barrels at 28 dollars a barrel = 27m dollars

6 The Commonwealth and aid:

i scholarships and training schemes help to provide **education** for Third World Commonwealth countries;

ii teachers, doctors, engineers and **experts of all kinds** provide varied help;

iii **organizations** operate a variety of schemes of aid:

(a) **the Commonwealth Development Corporation** (CDC);

(b) **the Special Commonwealth African Assistance Plan (SCAAP):**

iv **the Colombo Plan** (38.2.1) was devised by the Foreign Ministers of the Commonwealth in 1950 to help the development of South and South East Asia:

(a) **a Council** organizes training, research, economic development and better health services;

(b) the Plan receives **help from non-Commonwealth countries** such as Japan, and from the UN;

(c) **1958** the ideas behind the Plan were **extended** by the introduction of Commonwealth Assistance Loans;

(d) **1959** in a further development a scheme of **Commonwealth Scholarships** was introduced.

7 The UN and aid:

From the outset the UN has played a major role in providing aid for people in need:

i **1943** the **United Nations Relief and Rehabilitation Administration (UNRRA)** coped with the problem of refugees and emergency relief in the wake of advancing forces;

ii **1943 the Food and Agricultural Organization (FAO)** was set up to study the problem of world food supplies and to encourage the development of agriculture in poorer countries;

iii **1944 the International Monetary Fund** was set up after Anglo-US discussions at Bretton Woods. It gets its funds from contributions by member states and uses those funds to help countries which are in balance of payments difficulties and so helps to promote world trade;

iv **1944 the International Bank for Reconstruction and Development, generally known as the World Bank**, lends money to promote economic development;

v **the Economic and Social Council (ECOSOC)** has set up a number of regional Commissions – for Europe, for Asia and Latin America and for Africa which compile annual Economic Surveys and act as advisers for countries in various regions;

vi **the United Nations Children's Emergency Fund (UNICEF)** has links with ECOSOC and provides aid for a wide variety of schemes aimed at helping children in the Third World. It has organized campaigns against illiteracy and attacks on diseases which particularly affect children;

vii the **World Health Organization (WHO)** and the **UN Educational Scientific and Cultural Organization (UNESCO)** play roles in providing particular forms of aid to developing countries. As such they are part of the overall UN aim of trying to implement one of the pledges made by Roosevelt and Churchill when they signed the Atlantic Charter (19.9.10) in August 1941: 'that all men in all lands may live out their lives in freedom from fear and want'.

38.8 Some of the problems connected with aid

1 Many countries providing aid insist that the recipient country has to **spend the money in the donor country**. This tied aid limits the freedom of the developing country. It also helps the economic well-being of the donor country which may see aid as a means of self-help and not of help to the Third World.

2 The USA and Russia in particular use aid as a **weapon of foreign policy**. Each provides aid only if the recipient government agrees to follow the 'party' line in foreign policy. Thus it is possible to link Korea, Pakistan, Israel and others with the USA and Cuba, North Korea and others with Russia.

3 Too many recipient countries have **wasted a good deal of aid**. Some have spent the money on arms; others have spent it on glamorous projects such as the building of huge sports stadia (Nigeria) and government buildings.

4 A country's development may be helped by the activities of one of the world's **multi-national firms**. The opening of a Ford car plant, an Esso refinery or an ICI chemical plant will provide employment, increase spending power and so help development. But there are many cases of such companies using their economic power to try to control government policy. Latin America has suffered from the activities of US companies; the Middle East suffered, before the formation of OPEC (39.9.12) from the activities of the giant oil companies.

5 Third World countries need aid all the time – but may **need even more aid when the world goes into recession**. It is at such periods that their export prices fall so that their income declines. But it is at precisely such periods that developed nations provide less aid ('we have to help our own people who are unemployed') and try to cut down on imports from Third World countries.

6 The sad fact is that there has been **little switch of resources from the rich countries** (which get richer each year) **to the poorer** (which get richer only slowly if at all).

38.9 Oil and a modern crisis, 1972–83

1 Industrialized countries consumed ever increasing quantities of oil in the 20th century:

i oil was often used to **generate electricity**–it was cheaper than coal;

ii oil drove most of the **modern machinery in factories**;

iii oil, or oil-based products, powered most of the **modern transport systems**–lorries, cars, ships and planes;

iv oil was used to **heat our homes**.

2 Third World countries also used a good deal of oil:

i most poor families **cooked by paraffin stoves**;

ii most poor countries had **no electricity system**. People relied on **oil lamps to light their homes**, shops and offices.

3 Until 1972 oil was a cheap product:

i exploration for oil and exploitation of oil fields was controlled by **large international oil companies**:

(a) most of these were American-owned, e.g. Esso (or, in the USA, Exxon), Texaco, Sonaco;

(b) Britain has been involved in oil exploration from the start. Its interests were safeguarded by the two giant companies, Shell (an Anglo-Dutch company) and the Anglo-Persian Oil Company, later re-named as British Petroleum.

4 These companies paid **small sums to the governments of the countries** in which they exploited oilfields. Before 1945 these countries were:

i **Persia**, now known as Iran;

ii **Iraq**, which as Mesopotamia had been 'created' by Britain (13.9 and 13.12);

iii small sites on the Persian Gulf–e.g. **Kuwait** and **Bahrein**;

iv **Mexico**, which had, however, nationalized its oil industry following a Communist revolution;

v **Venezuela**;

vi various states in the **Dutch East Indies**, now called Indonesia;

vii it is worth noting that the giant oilfields in **Saudi Arabia** had not been properly investigated.

5 1951 The first challenge to the control of the oil companies ('the Seven Sisters' of the industry) was made by the radical Persian (Iranian) politician **Dr Mussadeq**. He nationalized the huge Anglo-Iranian Oil Company and evicted the British from Persia with its huge Abadan oil refineries.

6 The British and Americans responded by increasing oil output from other countries, mainly Kuwait. With only small sales of Persian oil, Mussadeq's government brought Persia to the edge of bankruptcy.

7 1953 Mussadeq was driven from power in a rising organized by the American **Central Intelligence Agency**.

8 1954 The development of Iran's oilfields was taken over by a consortium of British, French, Dutch and US companies. The British had lost their total control.

9 1954–56 Other Arab countries, notably **Saudi Arabia**, did not imitate Mussadeq by trying to expel the oil companies. However, they did **force the companies** to make more generous payments than had been made previously.

10 Oil companies resented being forced to pay what they saw as high prices for oil. To limit any one government's ability to force them to pay such a high price, the companies would threaten to lower production in the 'greedy' country, knowing that they could get what they wanted from another, less 'greedy' country.

11 1962 Venezuela became aware of the fact that her oil deposits would dry up around 1988. She needed an increased income from her existing oilfields to get the money needed to build up an alternative economy which could provide her people with work after 1988.

12 The Organization of Petroleum Exporting Countries (OPEC) was founded when Venezuela persuaded other oil producing countries that they should act together against the oil companies.

13 It took time for the Organization to understand its real power and for Arab countries, in particular, to train ministers able to hold their own in negotiations with the oil companies and with western governments.

14 1973 The **Yom Kippur War** of 1973 (37.14) proved to be a turning point in the history of OPEC:

i the USA and most European countries had supported the Israelis, supplying them with weapons and other aid;

ii Egypt and Syria, financed by the oil producing Arab countries, were heavily defeated;

iii the Arabs decided to use oil as a weapon in their fight against Israel and its western allies.

15 Arab members of OPEC cut their supplies of oil to America and countries which had provided aid to the Israelis (notably Holland).

16 OPEC, guided by Arab interests, announced a doubling (and later a quadrupling) of oil prices.

17 The cuts and the increased prices led to a **series of crises** in the western world in particular, and throughout the rest of the world in general:

i there was a **shortage of oil** in the USA (which imported about 20 per cent of its oil from the Middle East) and in Europe, which depended on the output from the giant Dutch refineries at Rotterdam. Factories had to shut down, industrial output declined; transport became more expensive;

ii **the increased oil prices** led to increases not only in the price of petrol and higher charges for transport. There were also increases in the **price of all oil-based products** from plastics to drugs, from record-sleeves and discs to clothes and motor cars;

iii all industrialized countries had to pay much more for their **oil imports** than had been the case. This increase could not be matched by increased earnings from exports. This created world-wide **balance of payments problems**. Every country tried to put its balance back to rights by cutting other imports. But one country's imports are another country's exports. Cuts in imports by the world's industrialized countries led to falls in exports by other industrialized countries. This created **large-scale unemployment** throughout the world;

iv **the countries of the Third World suffered** in two major ways:

(a) they had to pay more for **their oil imports**. These had already taken a high proportion of their people's incomes. Now, with higher oil prices, spending on oil became an even higher proportion of the spending by poor people. This led to a **fall in living standards**, because people had less money to spend on other things;

(b) **their exports to industrialized countries** fell because of the fall in the total of world trade. The poor countries became even poorer than they had been:

v higher oil prices led to **price increases in almost every industrial product**. This inflation harmed the industrialized countries because it led to a drop in demand for products and so to unemployment. But it harmed the Third World countries even more. They had to pay higher prices for the things they imported. These imports included machinery and other products needed for development. They found that their development aid bought fewer goods than had been expected before 1972. So their development was checked.

18 New sources of oil were hastily developed to try to limit the power of the Arabs. Britain was fortunate in discovering oil in the North Sea. Nigerian oil deposits were also developed as were new fields in Indonesia, Alaska, the Sahara and Ecuador. These new sources were to provide their own problems later on.

19 New sources of energy were also developed. Britain, for example, after years during which its coal industry had been allowed to run down, now developed a new giant coalfield under the sea at Selby in Yorkshire and began the process of opening a new coalfield near Belvoir in Derbyshire. Scientists were asked to investigate the possibility of developing the production of energy from the sun, tide, wind and even sewage.

20 **In 1984** the world is still living with the effects of the increases in oil prices. The **first increases in 1972–73** were followed by a series of increases throughout the 1970s so that by 1979 **oil, which in 1972 had been sold at 2 dollars per barrel, was selling for 35 dollars per barrel**. In particular the world in 1984 has had to try to cope with:

i **inflation or rising prices**. Government attempts to cope with this problem have led to massive unemployment in the western world;

ii **balance of payments problems**. To try to limit, if not end, the deficits on balance of payments, countries have cut their imports–and so increased unemployment in exporting countries.

21 **One unexpected effect of the increased prices was a fall in the demand for oil:**

i as **industry went into recession** there was a drop in demand for oil for industrial purposes;

ii **fewer people flew**–so that some airlines were driven into bankruptcy (Braniff in the USA and Laker in Britain). This drop in demand for air tickets led to a drop in the demand for oil by airlines;

iii **people became more energy-conscious** ('Save it' said the slogan) and used less fuel in cars and at home.

22 At the same time there was an **increased supply of oil from new fields**, largely in Nigeria and Indonesia.

23 This has led, unexpectedly, to a **fall in oil prices since 1979**. Oil now sells at about 27 dollars per barrel. This has upset the economic forecasts of oil-exporting countries.

24 The effects of this are, perhaps, most clearly seen in the case of Nigeria (38.7.5).

25 But the collapse of Nigerian development plans has had effects in countries which had hoped to sell machinery and other goods to expanding Nigeria. **World unemployment has risen following the collapse of such development plans**.

26 The world slump and the consequent drop in the demand for oil has led to a crisis in OPEC itself. Some OPEC countries (Nigeria, Iraq and Venezuela) would like to sell more of their oil. They need the extra income they would hope to get from such increased sales. But that increase, if allowed, would lead to a fall in the demand for oil from other OPEC countries and/or to a further fall in the price of oil. In 1983 OPEC was much more fragile an organization than it appeared to be in its heydays of the 1970s.

39 Abbreviations and a Glossary

ABM Anti-ballistic missile. A ballistic missile is first powered by some explosive or fuel, then depends only on gravity. ABMs are meant to shoot these down.

abdicate (to) To give up some office or power. Nicholas II (10.12.6), Alfonso XIII (24.4.4) and Edward VIII of Britain gave up their thrones.

amnesty The granting of forgiveness, a pardon, usually to political offenders.

anarchy A country without effective government (the aim of Spanish Anarchists (24.15.4.i) or the political and social disorder following from the inability of government to control things.

ANC The African National Congress, a predominantly black organization opposed to the whites-only policies of the South African government (see **apartheid**).

annexation The taking of territory, often without any right.

anti-clericalism A policy opposed to the strong influence of the clergy or the Church in political and social life.

ANZAC The Australian and New Zealand Army Corps (1914–18). ANZAC Day, 25th April, commemorates the landing of the Corps in Gallipoli in 1915.

ANZUS The Australian, New Zealand and United States Pact signed in 1951.

apartheid The South African system for separating the races.

appeasement Reaching agreement by negotiating with and conciliation of a potential aggressor. In the late 1930s it came to be identified with giving way to Hitler.

arbitration The settlement of disputes through the verdict of someone not involved in the dispute.

armistice An agreement to end fighting so that negotiations for a peace treaty can take place.

autarky The plan for economic self-sufficiency in Germany in the 1930s. Nazi Germany wanted to be economically independent.

authoritarian The opposite of 'liberal'. An authoritarian government imposes strict discipline and represses opposition (see **totalitarianism**).

autocracy Rule by one man, a **dictatorship** (see **dictatorship**).

Bolsheviks Those members of the Russian Social Democratic Party who believed that a Marxist Revolution would be brought about only by a small, dedicated organization. They were led by Lenin. The name comes from the Russian word for the MAJORITY which Lenin and his followers had after a debate in 1903.

BOSS The Bureau of State Security, the South African force mainly used to crush anti-apartheid opposition.

bourgeoisie A French word used to describe the middle classes, the capitalist owners of industry.

boycott (to) To unite together to refuse to deal with someone or some nation; to refuse to handle someone's goods.

Bundesrat The Upper House of the German Parliament set up in 1871. It represented the Princes of the federal state (see below. See also **Reichstat**).

caste The term applied to the 2000 divisions of Hindu society in India. There are 4 main divisions: priests, rulers and warriors, traders and farmers, and artisans. Those outside these divisions are called untouchables (see below). **Caste** is hereditary and the members of each caste are equal and united in religion. **Caste** largely determines occupation. It is an exclusive system, with little contact with those outside the caste.

Caudillo The Spanish world for leader; the title taken by Franco.

centre Political parties of the centre are neither extreme socialists (see below) nor extremely conservative (i.e. the right). They have middle-of-the-road policies.

Cheka Lenin's secret police, the name coming from the Russian initials for Extraordinary Commission.

CIA The Central Intelligence Agency (USA).

co-existence A state of international relations in which rivals (such as the USA and USSR) tolerate one another. Neither seeks to bring down the other by force (a 'hot war') although dislike remains. When the dislike becomes very strong the world may have a period of 'cold war'–see below.

Cold war Such a 'war' is fought by various 'peaceful' weapons–such as **propaganda** (see below), **economic**

sanctions (see below), aid (even military) to opponents of the rival régime. The rivals (since 1945 the USA and USSR) have stopped short of military confrontation although they have supported rivals in various 'local' wars as in Vietnam.

colonialism The policy of obtaining and maintaining colonies; opponents of this policy use the word to argue that the colonial (or occupying) power exploits backward or weak people for its own economic benefit.

collectivization The policy of joining together small farms into one large holding. Stalin implemented this policy to destroy the **bourgeois** (see bourgeoisie) kulaks.

COMECON The Council for Mutual Economic Assistance.

COMINFORM The Communist Information Bureau.

Concordat An agreement, usually between the Church and State.

Congress A meeting of delegates. In the USA it is the national legislative body (or Parliament); in India the name was used by Indian politicians campaigning against British colonialism (see above). They were, by using the word, claiming to be the Indian 'Parliament' even though they had no power.

constitution The principles by which a country is governed. In many countries there is a written constitution which expresses these principles in words.

containment The building of alliances in an effort to frighten an enemy and prevent his expansion.

convoy A number of merchant ships sailing together under the escort of warships.

Cortes The Legislative Assembly (or Parliament) of Spain or Portugal.

coup d'état A violent or illegal change of government; the seizure of power by a non-elected group, or by an individual (see **putsch**).

Covenant An agreement setting out the aims and rules (of the League of Nations).

Czech Legion While they were being evacuated from eastern Russia along the Trans-Siberian Railway in 1918, Czech prisoners-of-war overpowered their guards and began a private march to Moscow. They were halted by Trotsky's Red Army outside Kazan. The plight of this Legion was the official reason for the various foreign interventions in the Russian Civil War.

Dail The Lower House of the Irish Parliament.

democracy (from **demos**, the Greek word for **the people**) Rule by the people; a system of government which allows the mass of the people (the electorate) to have some control over their rulers; a system which tolerates minority views.

DMZ A demilitarized zone as in the Rhineland after 1919 (12.5.2) and in Korea after 1953 (28.11.26) and such as was proposed by various people for Central Europe in the 1960s.

depression A fall or reduction in the amount of industrial and trading activity such as followed (i) the First World War, (ii) the Wall Street Crash, 1929 and (iii) the rise in oil prices after 1973.

desegregation The ending of **segregation** (see below).

détente The easing of strained relations between rival States. It is a part of the policy of **co-existence** (see above).

dictatorship Rule by one man who has usually gained power by a **coup d'état** (see above) and who suppresses **democracy** (see above) in his **totalitarian** State (see **totalitarianism**).

diktat The imposition of severe terms by a victor on a defeated nation. Often used of the Treaty of Versailles – by Germans.

Distressed areas Those areas of Britain which suffered severe unemployment during the **depression** (see above) during the inter-war period.

dole The amount of money paid weekly by the State to unemployed workers.

Dominion A term used to describe the first self-governing (and therefore independent) parts of the British Empire – Australia, Canada, New Zealand and South Africa. **Dominion status** was defined in 1926 and in the Statute of Westminster, 1931. Dominions were free from British control but retained a connection with the British Throne.

Duma Originally this described the Russian elected town councils. It was more commonly used in the 19th century by liberals as the title of their proposed Russian Council of State – or Parliament.

EEC The European Economic Community, or Common Market.

EFTA The European Free Trade Association.

emancipation The setting free of people – from slavery (in the USA) or serfdom (in Russia) or from legal disabilities (such as women suffered).

Enosis The proposed political union between Cyprus and Greece.

Entente A friendly understanding between people in which they settle their past differences. The **Entente Cordiale** between Britain and France, 1904, was followed by an Anglo-Russian Entente in 1907.

EOKA The initials of the Greek words meaning Revolutionary Organization for Cypriot Struggle. The organization was founded in 1955 and had a campaign of anti-British sabotage and terrorism in the hope that this would force the British to agree to **enosis** (see above).

FAO The Food and Agricultural Organization (of The United Nations).

federal This is used to describe the system of government in which several States form a unity (or union) but remain independent in internal affairs. It is also used to describe the policy of supporting a central government as opposed to those who favour government by separate States or Provinces. Australia, Canada, Germany and the USA have federal systems of government.

FLN The initials of the French words for the National Liberation Front (of Algeria).

franchise The right to vote (see **suffrage**).

Fuhrer The German word for leader, taken by Hitler in 1934.

GDR The German Federal Republic (East Germany).

GPU The Russian initials for the State Political Department, once the name for the Russian secret police, later the **OGPU** (see below).

guerilla A fighter engaged in irregular warfare, usually as a member of an organization resisting the government. **Guerilla** warfare describes the methods used by resistance movements who use hit-and-run tactics and sabotage. **Urban guerillas** refers to groups operating in towns. **Guerilla** is a Spanish word and was first used to describe fighters resisting Napoleon's rule in Spain.

humanitarian Someone campaigning for some humane purpose or welfare.

ICBM Intercontinental ballistic missiles (see **ABM** above).

immigrants People who come to live, as permanent residents, in a foreign country.

imperialism The extension of the power of one country over other (usually backward) countries. **Dollar imperialism** is a term used by critics to describe the process by which the US government and US firms gain control of the economy of a country. **Russian imperialism** is used to describe the extension of Russian control of Eastern Europe and, more recently, Afghanistan.

indemnity Usually used to describe a sum of money, a sort of fine, forced out of one country by another after a war (see **reparations**).

Independence The freedom granted to former colonies when the colonial power gives up control. **Independence movements** are organizations campaigning for independence. They often use **guerilla** tactics (see above) when the **colonialist** power (see above) refuses to accept their demands (see **FLN**).

infallibility Strictly this means to be unable to err (or make a mistake). **Papal infallibility** is one aspect of the power of a Pope when speaking *ex cathedra* as defined in 1870 by the Vatican Council (see **Vatican**).

inflation A general increase of prices and a fall in the purchasing value of money. It usually results from an increase in the quantity of currency, as in Germany in 1923. It may also be the result of increased raw material prices, as with oil after 1973.

integration The merging together of peoples of different races into one society; the **integration in US schools** refers to the attempts to abolish **segregated schools** (see below) so that black and white children attended the same school.

investment The spending of money on stocks and shares; the spending of money by individuals or governments on various projects. Such spending creates employment, but may lead to **inflation** (see above).

IRA The Irish Republican Army which used **guerilla tactics** (see **guerilla**) in its fight for Irish **independence** (see above) from Britain. Since 1922 it has campaigned for the incorporation of Ulster into a United Ireland.

isolationism The policy of staying out of involvement in the affairs of other countries. It is particularly used to refer to US foreign policy after 1920.

Izvestia One of the two official Soviet newspapers. It means 'news'. See also **Pravda**.

Jesuits Members of a **religious order** (see below) in the Catholic Church founded by St Ignatius of Loyola in 1534. Often very influential with Catholic rulers and politicians, it was usually the first to be attacked by **anti-clericals** (see **anti-clericalism**).

Junkers The exclusive Prussian aristocracy.

KGB The Russian 'secret branch' as the secret police was known after Stalin's death. (See **MVD** below.)

Lebensraum (living space) Territory which Germans (particularly the Nazis) claimed was necessary for natural development. Such territory was often rich in natural resources.

Mafia Criminal gangs originating in Sicily which were hostile to government and police. Italian **immigrants** (see **immigrants**) into the USA organized crime through Mafia families.

Mandates Areas of the German and Turkish colonial Empires which were placed under the control of Powers named by the League of Nations so that they could be prepared for **independence** (see **Independence**).

manifesto The publicly stated policy (usually in writing) of an organization, usually of a political party.

MBFR Mutual and Balanced Force Reduction.

mediate (to) To intervene, or form the connecting link, between two rival groups in the hope of bringing them to agreement (see **arbitration**).

Mig The Russian air design team of Mikoyan and Gurevich.

ministerial responsibility The responsibility of government ministers to parliament where ministers have to answer for their actions. In many countries this is regarded as an essential part of **democracy** (see **democracy**). It does not exist in an **autocracy** (see **autocracy** or **dictatorship**).

MIRV Multiple Independently-targeted Re-entry Vehicle, a ballistic missile.

MVD The initials of the Russian secret police when it changed from being the **NKVD** and before it became the **KGB**.

NASA National Aeronautics and Space Administration (USA).

nation The people of a country under one government.

nationalism Patriotic feeling; pride in one's own country. It may take the form of a campaign for independence (see above) in a colonial country. It may lead to a campaign to make one's nation united and strong. It may lead to a desire to make one's country supreme over others.

nationalization The taking over of the ownership of private property, e.g. the nationalization of the coal industry made it the property of the nation instead of the property of private mine owners.

NATO The North Atlantic Treaty Organization.

NEP The New Economic Policy developed by Lenin and ended by Stalin.

NKVD The name of the Russian secret police during its most notorious period under Stalin's direction (see **MVD** above).

NLF The National Liberation Front, a title used by **nationalists** fighting a **guerilla** war (see **guerilla**) in (i) Aden and (ii) Vietnam.

OEEC The Organization for European Economic Co-operation.

OGPU The Central State Political Department, the name of the Russian secret police which succeeded the **Cheka** (see **Cheka**).

OPEC The Organization of Petroleum Exporting Countries.

pacifism The belief that all war is wrong. Pacifists refuse to take an active part in fighting during a war.

Pact An agreement or treaty.

Pan-Slavism A belief that the whole (*pan* = Greek for all) Slavonik peoples should work together; they shared a common (orthodox) religion and common enemies (Austria and Turkey).

partisan A word used in the Second World War to describe anti-German **guerillas** (see **guerilla**), particularly in Yugoslavia, Italy and France.

panzer German armoured troops.

plebiscite A vote of all the people in a given area on a particular issue. In 1935 the people of the Saar voted in a plebiscite to be re-united with Germany.

PLO The Palestine Liberation Organization which engages in **guerilla** war (see above) against Israel.

pogrom The organized massacre of a minority group, especially of Jews in Russia (from the Russian word for **destroy**).

police state A state in which a secret police supervizes the people's activities.

Politburo The small group of leaders who control Soviet policy-making. It takes charge of the Communist Party of the Soviet Union when its Central Committee is not in session.

Pravda Another official Soviet newspaper. It means '*Truth*'. (See **Izvestia** '*News*'). Russians joke that they get plenty of Izvestia but not much Pravda in their newspapers.

proletariat Wage-earners who have no property and depend on their daily labour for their subsistence. Marxists use it to describe the working masses who, they say, are kept down by the **bourgeoisie** (see **bourgeoisie**).

propaganda A word used by critics of attempts to spread a certain doctrine or belief; the means of spreading a belief. It comes from the Latin *propagare* (meaning to multiply plants by layering).

prohibition This usually refers to the attempt to ban the manufacture and sale of alcoholic drink in the USA between 1920 and 1933.

protection A system of tariffs (see p.158) to protect home industries against foreign imports. It is the opposite of free trade.

protectorate A country which is controlled and/or developed by a stronger country. Some **Mandated** territories (see **Mandates**) became known as Protectorates.

puppet (state) A country which claims to be independent but which is actually controlled by a greater power (see **satellite**).

purge (to) To get rid of 'undesirable' people in the army or state; particularly applied to Stalin's policy in the 1930s.

putsch From the Swiss word for 'blow'. A German attempt at a **coup d'état** (see p.156); particularly applied to Hitler's attempt to seize power in 1923.

race People of common descent, perhaps of a distinctive ethnic group. People of different races may be found in one **nation** (see **nation**) as in the USA and South Africa.

radical From the Latin word for **root**. Someone who campaigns for major reforms and changes.

reactionary Someone opposed to change who may, even, want to 'turn back the clock' and undo past reforms.

referendum A vote on a single issue (see **plebiscite**).

Reichstat The Upper House of the German Parliament in the Weimar Republic. It replaced the **Bundesrat** (see **Bundesrat**) and represented the states in the Federal state.

Reichstag The Lower (or popularly-elected) House of the German Parliament.

religious order A society of men or women who have bound themselves by vows (of poverty, chastity and obedience) to live together and to serve God in a special way. Many are particularly concerned with education and were enemies of the **anti-clericals** (see **anti-clericalism**; see also **Jesuits**).

reparations Compensation for injury or damages imposed by the victorious country and paid by the conquered. They were similar to an **indemnity** (see **indemnity**) but were a compensation rather than a fine.

Republic A state without a monarchy, that has a president as the head of state.

revisionism (i) The demand for change of some treaty such as the Treaty of Versailles. (ii) More recently it has been used about Communists who seek to 'revise' Marx's teachings. It is most often used by those who think that a violent revolution is essential as an attack on revisionists who think that Communism can be achieved by peaceful means. Mao Tse-tung denounced Khrushchev as a revisionist; China is now ruled by such revisionists.

SALT The Strategic Arms Limitation Talks.

SAM Surface to Air Missiles.

sanctions Penalties or methods used to put pressure on nations committing what others condemn as illegal actions. **Economic sanctions** involve restrictions on trade. **Military sanctions** involve entering into war.

satellite (i) A country, seemingly independent, but in reality controlled by a greater power (see **puppet**). (ii) One of the artificial bodies sent into orbit around the earth or other planet.

SD A Social Democrat.

secession A separation or breaking away of one part of a union (of states or races). The Southern States wanted to break away from the Federal United States; Biafra wanted to break away from Nigeria.

segregation A separation, usually imposed, of different groups of people. (See **apartheid**, **desegregation** and **integration**.)

Senate The Upper House of the US Congress.

socialism A political and social theory which argues that the community as a whole should own and control the means of production (see **nationalization**), distribution and exchange. In its extreme form it is Marxist.

soviet A council or committee elected in a district of Russia. In 1905 and 1917 soviets were formed by revolutionaries. (See **USSR**.)

SR Social Revolutionary.

suffrage The right to vote (see **franchise**).

SWAPO The South West African People's Organization which campaigns for the **independence** (see **independence**) of the **Mandated** territory which was formerly German South West Africa.

tariffs Taxes on imports. (See **protection**.)

totalitarianism A system of government which does not allow a rival to the ruling party. Nazi Germany and Soviet Russia are examples of totalitarian régimes.

tribalism Loyalty to the tribe rather than to the **nation** (see **nation**), a feature of some independent African states.

TVA The Tennessee Valley Authority (USA).

U-2 The Lockheed spy-plane (USA).

UDI A Unilateral Declaration of Independence by a country claiming **independence** (see **independence**) without the permission of the colonial power (e.g. Rhodesia, 1965).

ultimatum A final proposal or statement of terms, the rejection of which by the opposition (party or nation) leads to a break in friendly relations and may lead to war.

USSR The Union of Soviet Socialist Republics. (See **soviet**, **socialist** and **republic**.)

UNICEF The United Nations International Children's Emergency Fund.

UNO The United Nations Organization.

UNRRA United Nations Relief and Rehabilitation Administration.

untouchables Those who are outside the Indian caste system (see **caste**). They do the most menial jobs and are the most underprivileged.

V1; V2 From the initial of the German *Vergeltungswaffen*; reprisal weapons. V1 was a flying bomb (or 'doodle bug'); V2 was a supersonic rocket.

VSO Voluntary Service Overseas.

Vatican (i) The Pope's palace and official residence in Rome; (ii) Vatican City is an independent state created by the Lateran Treaty, 1929. (iii) Vatican Council of the world's Catholic hierarchy held in (a) 1870 (see **infallibility**) and (b) 1962–65.

veto The right to reject a law or a proposal. Such a power is possessed by rulers, presidents, some Upper Houses of Parliament and by the permanent members of the Security Council of the **UNO** (see above). Every member of the League of Nations had such a veto.

Watergate This complex of buildings contained the headquarters of the Democratic Party during the Presidential election in 1971. Republican burglars broke in and the subsequent scandals surrounding this break-in led to the resignation and imprisonment of the Vice-President, Spiro Agnew, and the resignation of the President, Richard Nixon.

WHO The World Health Organization.

welfare state A state with comprehensive social services and social security systems in health and education and against sickness, unemployment and old age.

ZAPU The Zimbabwe African People's Union which led to the **guerilla war** (see **guerilla**) by African **nationalists** (see **nationalism**) trying to overthrow the whites-only government which had declared **UDI** (see **UDI**).

Zionist A supporter of the colonization of Palestine by the Jews. The World Zionist Organization was founded in 1897.

Part III
Unit self-tests:
questions and answers

Unit 1 Self-Test Questions:

1 Choose the right options from Lists **B** and **C** to accompany the dates in List **A**. One has been done for you as an example.

List A	List B	List C
1 1870	*11* The Enabling Law	*21* Tirpitz
2 1871	*12* Suspension of May Laws	*22* Caprivi
3 1872	*13* Death of two Kaisers	*23* Togoland
4 1878	*14* The fall of Bismarck	*24* Versailles
5 1879	*15* The Vatican Council	*25* Hamburg
6 1884	*16* Opening of the Kiel Canal	*26* William II
7 1888	*17* Creation of the German Empire	*27* Pius IX
8 1890	*18* The Naval Bill	*28* Falk
9 1895	*19* Start of the Kulturkampf	*29* William I
10 1897	*20* The Colonial Conference, Berlin	*30* Leo XIII

Example A*1*, B*15*, C*27*,

2 Which political party grew because of the Kulturkampf?
3 Who founded the German Socialist Party?
4 Which Danish Duchy was included in united Germany?
5 Name the two territories taken from France in 1871.
6 Which Treaty ended the Franco-Prussian War?
7 Which house of the German Parliament was elected by the popular vote?
8 Who was the founder of the German Navy?
9 Who was Chancellor of Germany in 1914
10 Choose the correct Option to answer question 10

After 1878 in Germany, Bismarck was successful in gaining the political support of the:

(A) Catholics against Junkers (D) Socialists against Junkers
(B) Catholics against Socialists (E) Socialists against Liberals
(C) Liberals against Junkers

Unit 2 Self-Test Questions:

1 Which battle signalled the end of the Second Empire?
2 Which French politician first proclaimed a Republic?
3 Where did the first Assembly meet after the defeat of 1871?
4 Name the two territories lost to Germany in 1871.
5 Who was head of the government which put down the Commune?
6 Name the Napoleonic Marshal who became president of France.
7 Who were the three Monarchist claimants to the throne of France after 1871?
8 Give the names of the TWO houses of the French Parliament.
9 Who was the first President who could be called a convinced Republican?
10 Name ONE colony gained by the Republicans in EACH of the following: *i* North Africa, *ii* Asia.
11 Name the 'general on a black horse' who seemed to threaten the stability of the Republic.
12 Which French engineer built the Suez Canal?
13 Name the leader of the French socialists in 1914.
14 Choose the correct Option to complete the following sentence:

In France, those who supported Dreyfus and argued that he had been unjustly treated, were probably also:

(A) imperialists (C) militarists (E) monarchists
(B) anti-clericals (D) anti-semitics

Unit 3 Self-Test Questions:

1 Against each of the names listed below select the correct letter in the key. One has been done for you as an example.

Name	Key
1 Alexander II	**A** Reactionary Procurator of Holy Synod
2 Alexander III	**B** Terrorists who tried to kill Alexander II
3 de Witte	**C** District Councils
4 Duma	**D** Advised the Tsar to declare war, 1904
5 Cadets	**E** Hoped for a peasants' rising

Name	Key
6 Narodniki	**F** A reforming Minister, 1907–11
7 Nicholas II	**G** Name of Russian Liberal Party
8 Nihilists	**H** Organized a workers' soviet, 1905
9 Plehve	**I** An assembly called in 1906
10 Pobedonostsev	**J** The last of the Tsars
11 Stolypin	**K** Minister of Finance, 1892–1900
12 Trotsky	**L** The 'Liberator' Tsar
13 Zemstvos	**M** Became Tsar on his father's assassination

Example 1 (**L**)

2 What do the following initials stand for? *i* SDLP *ii* SRP
3 Which Marxists wanted: *i* a small, active party, *ii* a mass movement?
4 What was the Iskra (the Spark)?
5 Which Treaty ended the Russia-Japanese War?
6 Which Tsar issued a Manifesto promising constitutional government?
7 When was that Manifesto issued?
8 Name the Russian priest who led a protest march in 1905.
9 Choose the correct option in answer to the following: In domestic affairs, Alexander II copied western ideas when he agreed to introduce

(A) massive vodka duties
(B) professional and immovable judges
(C) railway and steel nationalization
(D) responsible and elected Ministers
(E) social insurance schemes

Unit 4 Self-Test Questions:

1 Which people first rose in rebellion against Turkey in 1875?
2 Name the three independent states which helped them in 1876.
3 What was the religious link between Russia and the rebels?
4 What did EACH of the following hope to gain from the Congress of Berlin, 1878? *i* Austria *ii* Russia *iii* Britain.
5 Name the Turkish Sultan in 1877–78.
6 Name the most important battle in the Russo-Turkish War?
7 Name the Turkish capital in 1878.
8 Which British statesman was alarmed at the Russian advance?
9 Which movement linked Russia with the rebels?
10 Name the Treaties which ended *i* the First Balkan League War, *ii* the Second Balkan League War.
11 Name the new state created by the Balkan League Wars.
12 Which Balkan state was most dissatisfied by this new creation?
13 Which Balkan state was involved in the Second but not the First Balkan War 1912–13?
14 Which Balkan state lost most following the Second Balkan War?

For Questions 15–16 choose correct options.

15 An important result of the Balkan Wars (1912–13) was to
  (A) confine Turkey's presence in Europe to eastern Thrace
  (B) give Austria hope of controlling Macedonia
  (C) leave Russia to remilitarize the Black Sea
  (D) make Bulgaria the dominant power in the Balkans
  (E) satisfy Serbia's desire for a port on the Adriatic
16 Which of the following claimed leadership of the Slav races in 1914? (A) Bosnia (B) Herzogovina (C) Montenegro (D) Romania (E) Serbia

Unit 5 Self-Test Questions:

1 Against each of the names listed below select the correct letter in the key. The first has been done for you as an example.

Name	Key
1 Adowa (**I**)	**A** wanted a larger German Empire
2 Bismarck	**B** profited from illegal slavery in the Congo

Name	Key	
3 Cetawayo	**C**	acquired Bechuanaland for Britain
4 Chamberlain	**D**	led the Boer Republics against the British
5 Fashoda	**E**	led an ill-fated attack on the Boers
6 Jameson	**F**	an expansionist Colonial Secretary
7 Khedive	**G**	called a Colonial Conference, 1884–5
8 Kruger	**H**	led the Zulus against the British
9 Leopold II	**I**	the scene of an Italian defeat, 1896
10 Matabele	**J**	the scene of an Anglo-French confrontation, 1898
11 Rhodes	**K**	the title of the ruler of Egypt
12 Transvaal	**L**	marked the border between Portuguese and British colonies in East Africa
13 William II	**M**	a southern African people
14 Zambesi	**N**	a Boer Republic

2 Which parts of the Turkish Empire were seized by *i* France in 1881; *ii* Italy in 1911–12?

Questions 3–8 are concerned with Egypt and the Sudan.

3 Name the Egyptian nationalist leader in 1881–2.
4 At which battle was he defeated in 1882?
5 Name the British Official sent to reorganize Egyptian affairs.
6 Name the Arab who led the anti-Egyptian revolt in the Sudan in 1893.
7 *i* When and *ii* where was General Gordon killed?
8 Which British army commander avenged Gordon's death?

Unit 6 Self-Test Questions:

1 With which countries was Japan at war in *i* 1894 *ii* 1904?
2 With which country did Japan make an alliance in 1902?
3 What was the name of the Chinese Royal family in 1902?
4 Name the Chinese leader who helped form the Kuo Min Tang before 1914.
5 Name the unsuccessful revolution in China in 1900.
6 What was the meaning of **Double Tenth?**

Fig. III.6.1

7 Examine the map of the Far East in 1905 (Fig. III.6.1) and then name:

i island A	*v* colony E	*ix* island J
ii railway B	*vi* province F	*x* colony K
iii port C	*vii* colony G	
iv peninsular D	*viii* battle H	

(*Question 7 formed part of a question in JMB 1980 O Level*)

Unit 7 Self-Test Questions:

1 Name the TWO Houses which make up the US Congress.
2 What do Americans mean by 'the Administration'?
3 With which industry do you most associate each of the following: *i* Rockefeller, *ii* Carnegie, *iii* Morgan?
4 Who appoints the judges to the Supreme Court?
5 For how long are the judges appointed?
6 From whom did the US buy the Louisiana Purchase in 1803?
7 In which region was gold discovered in 1848–49?
8 Which animal formed the basis of the Red Indian economy?
9 By what name did Americans describe the monopolies formed by Rockefeller and other capitalists?
10 What was the main purpose of the Interstate Commerce Commission?
11 Which President first attacked the power of the monopolies?
12 What do the initials KKK stand for?
13 Which President gave his name to the Teddy-bear?
14 Which President was assassinated in 1901?
15 Which US President declared war on Spain in 1899?
16 Which Pacific Island was the main centre of that War?
17 In which island did the Americans build their naval base of Pearl Harbour?
18 Which city became the centre for the American meat trade?

Unit 8 Self-Test Questions:

1 Name the following:
i The British Prime Minister in 1914.
ii The town in North Africa to which **the Panther** was sent.
iii The two countries which signed the Entente Cordiale, 1904.
iv The people with whom Britain was at war, 1899–1902.
v The Balkan country which received an Austrian ultimatum, July 1914.
vi The British Foreign secretary, 1914.
vii Two North African territories in which Britain and France were in dispute in 1900.
2 'We want eight and we won't wait'.
i What did the makers of that slogan **want**?
ii In which country was the slogan popular between 1906 and 1914?
iii Which country's policy had led to the demand for **eight**?
Questions 3–9 are based on this extract from a Treaty signed by Bismarck. Choose the correct Options for answers to questions 3–5

'Germany and Russia have resolved to confirm the agreement established between them in view of the expiration in June 1887 of the secret Treaty signed in 1881 and renewed in 1884 by Germany, Russia and Austria-Hungary.'

3 The Treaty from which this extract is taken was known as
(**A**) Dreikaiser-bund
(**B**) Dual Alliance
(**C**) Reinsurance Treaty
(**D**) Treaty of Berlin
(**E**) Triple Alliance

4 The Treaty said that both countries would remain neutral if either was at war with a third power except in the case of Russia attacking

(**A**) Austria or Germany attacking France
(**B**) Japan or Germany attacking Italy
(**C**) Poland or Germany attacking Britain
(**D**) Romania or Germany attacking Denmark
(**E**) Turkey or Germany attacking Belgium

5 In the Treaty, Germany agreed to help Russia to set up a regular and legal government in
(**A**) Albania
(**B**) Bulgaria
(**C**) Greece
(**D**) Hungary
(**E**) Montenegro
6 When did that Treaty lapse?
7 Who was to blame for that lapse?
8 Which of the two countries, Germany and Russia, then made a major switch in foreign relations?
9 How was this switch shown?

Unit 9 Self-Test Questions:

1 Name the following:
i the British commander on the Somme 1916–17.
ii The French commander on the Marne in 1914.
iii The French commander who led the defence of Verdun 1916.
iv The German admiral at the Battle of Jutland 1916.
v The Englishman who organized the Arab revolt.
vi The President who brought the USA into the war in 1917.
vii The British commander in the Gallipoli campaign.
viii The Supreme Allied Commander, Western Front 1918.
ix The nation which was defeated at Tannenberg.

x The port occupied by Allied forces to ensure supplies to Serbia.

xi the British liner, carrying American passengers, sunk in 1915.

2 Name the following battles:

1 It halted the German advance on Paris 1914.

2 It saw the first use of massed tanks in battle.

3 It made a hero of a future French President.

4 In which British forces defeated those led by von Spee.

Unit 10 Self-Test Questions:

1 Against each of the names listed below select the correct letter in the key. One is done for you as an example

NAME		KEY	
1	Archangel	**(A)**	Led government routed by Lenin.
2	Brest-Litovsk	**(B)**	'Evil Monk' with influence over Tsar.
3	Denikin	**(C)**	Red Army Leader in the Civil War.
4	Kerensky	**(D)**	Port where British soldiers stationed.
5	Kiev	**(E)**	Led an anti-Bolshevik 'coup' in 1917.
6	Kolchak	**(F)**	Scene of German defeat of Russians.
7	Kornilov	**(G)**	Scene of Treaty which ended Russian part in war.
8	Kronstadt	**(H)**	Leader of Siberian 'Whites' in Civil War.
9	Rasputin	**(I)**	Leader of southern 'Whites' in Civil War.
10	Romanov	**(J)**	Family name of Russian royal Family.
11	Tannenberg	**(K)**	Naval base where sailors revolted against Lenin.
12	Trotsky	**(L)**	Centre of Ukranian revolt against Lenin.

Example *1* **(D)**

Unit 11 Self-Test Questions:

Choose the correct option in answer to the following questions.

1 Five Year plans for the industrialization of Russia were introduced by:

(A) Kerensky **(B)** Trotsky **(C)** Stalin **(D)** Kamenev **(E)** Rykov

2 During the Russian Civil War the Red Armies were led by:

(A) Beria **(B)** Kamenev **(C)** Lenin **(D)** Trotsky **(E)** Stalin

3 Lenin's New Economic Policy.

(A) allowed only private trading and industry

(B) established a mixture of private and nationalized industry

(C) forbade any private trading and industry

(D) proved to be a failure

(E) was intended to help win the Civil War.

4 Lenin was forced to abandon War Communism because;

i industrial production had collapsed.

ii it was not in line with Communist ideas.

iii the peasants resented the Red Army's seizure of their crops.

iv there was widespread famine.

v Trotsky was opposed to it.

(A) *i ii* and *iii*; **(B)** *iii iv* and *v*; **(C)** *i ii* and *v* **(D)** *i iii* and *iv*; **(E)** *ii iii* and *v*

5 The kulaks were:

(A) pace-setting industrial workers.

(B) members of the Russian secret police.

(C) prosperous peasants.

(D) Stalin's inner cabinet.

(E) fighters in the Civil War.

Unit 12 Self-Test Questions: (Fig. III.12.1)

Examine the map of Germany and her neighbours in 1919 and then answer the following questions:

1 Name shaded Territory A. *(1 mark)*

2 State the provisions made in the Treaty of Versailles regarding Territory A. *(2 marks)*

3 Name the provinces in Area B *(2 marks)*

4 State the provisions made in the Treaty of Versailles regarding the provinces in Area B. *(1 mark)*

5 State the provision made in the Treaty of Versailles concerning shaded Territory C. *(1 mark)*

6 Name State D *(1 mark)*

7 Name the state of which most of State D had been part before 1918 *(1 mark)*

8 Name State E. *(1 mark)*

9 State the provisions made in the Treaty of Versailles concerning the future of State E. *(1 mark)*

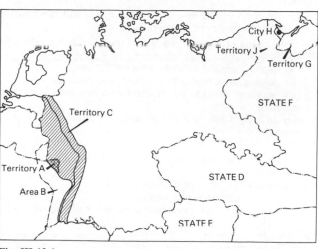

Fig. III.12.1

10 Name State F. *(1 mark)*

11 Name three states between which State F had been divided before 1918. *(3 marks)*

12 Name Territory G. *(1 mark)*

13 Name the state which ruled Territory G after 1919. *(1 mark)*

14 Name City H. *(1 mark)*

15 State the provisions of the Treaty of Versailles concerning City H. *(1 mark)*

16 What purpose was Territory J intended to serve? *(1 mark)*

(AEB 1977, O Level)

Unit 13 Self-Test Questions:

1 What name did Kemal take in 1934?

2 By what name was Kemal known in 1920?

3 With which movement was Kemal associated in 1908?

4 Where did Kemal frustrate the Allies in 1915?

5 Which city was the capital of Turkey?

6 In which city did Kemal start his revolution?

7 Give TWO ways in which Kemal tried to improve the position of women.

8 Give TWO ways in which Kemal tried to westernize Turkey.

9 What name is given to the kind of power that Britain had over Palestine after 1920?

10 Name THREE regions in the former Turkish Empire in 1914 which came under British control after 1920.

11 Name TWO regions in the former Turkish Empire which came under French control after 1920.

12 Who were the authors of the Anglo-French agreement on the division of the Turkish Empire?

13 Name the British Foreign Secretary who, in 1917, promised to create a Jewish home in Palestine.

14 'A disguise for colonial annexations of the traditional sort'. 'An admission of a new sense of responsibility towards backwards peoples'. These opposing views were both expressed about the system devised at the 1919 Peace Conference for dealing among other places, with:

(A) Algeria and Morocco **(B)** Dalmatia and Macedonia

(C) Eritrea and Somaliland **(D)** Latvia and Lithuania

(E) Palestine and Syria

Unit 14 Self-Test Questions:

1 Which statesman was keenest to see a League of Nations formed?

2 In which document did he first state the case for a League?

3 In which city did the League have its headquarters?

4 Name the TWO most important ruling bodies of the League.

5 What was the name of the League's Court of Law?

6 What do the initials ILO stand for?

7 What name was given to the system of government devised for the former colonies of the defeated Powers?

8 Which of the major Powers *i* never joined the League; *ii* joined in 1926 but left in 1933; *iii* was expelled in 1939?

9 Name the issues over which the nations named in answers to question **8** *ii* and **8** *iii* left the League.

10 Supply the missing word in the following statement:

'The League could impose . . . sanctions against any member-state which went to war'.

11 In which crisis and against which country did the League order the imposition of sanctions?

12 The League of Nations reacted to the Manchurian Dispute by:
(A) persuading the USA to join the League.
(B) asking the Chinese to evacuate the province.
(C) sending the Lytton Commission to investigate the problem .
(D) inviting Chinese Communists to administer the province.
(E) requesting Japan to withdraw from the League.

13 Which of the following activities of the League were successful?
i checking the spread of disease.
ii conducting impartial plebiscites.
iii lending money to prevent economic collapse in some countries.
iv re-settling refugees.
v returning prisoners of war.

(A) *iv* and *v*   (C) *ii iv* and *v*   (E) All
(B) *ii* and *iv*   (D) *i ii iii* and *v*

Unit 15 Self-Test Questions:

Questions 1–13 are based on the following quotations from Hitler's writings and speeches.

(a) 'The stab in the back . . .'; "the 'Diktat'"; 'the Aryan race';
(b) 'All propaganda must be popular and . . . adjusted to the most limited intelligence.'
(c) 'When our political meeetings first started. I made it a point to organize a suitable defence squad . . .'
(d) 'When I resume active work . . . instead of working to achieve power by an armed coup, we will have to hold our noses and enter the Reichstag against Catholics and Marxist members . . .'

1 What group in particular, complained of 'the stab in the back'?
2 What did Germans understand by the 'Diktat'?
3 Who, according to Hitler, made up 'the Aryan race'?
4 In which German city did Hitler start his 'political meetings'?
5 What was the popular name for Hitler's 'defence squad'?
6 Name the leader of that 'defence squad' who was assassinated in June 1934.
7 What was the title of the book in which Hitler outlined his policies?
8 Where did he write this book?
9 Where and when had Hitler attempted 'an armed coup'?
10 Name the German general who had supported his coup.
11 What was the Reichstag?
12 Name the leader of the 'Catholics' in 1932.
13 Which political party represented the Marxists?
14 Who was Foreign Secretary of Germany from 1923 to 1929?
15 What did he accomplish for *i* reparations; *ii* the Ruhr; *iii* Germany and the League of Nations?
16 What Treaty was signed in 1925 between Germany, France and other countries?
17 What was the most important single cause of the rise in unemployment in Germany after 1929?
18 Which two political parties gained support between 1929 and 1932?
19 Who was President of Germany in 1932?

Unit 16 Self-Test Questions:

Questions 1–7 are based on the diagram which appeared in YREB 1980 CSE Level. The questions are adapted from the questions set by that Board in that year, and from questions on this topic set by other Boards.

1 Which of the following terms best describes 'mass production', private enterprise; assembly line; limited liability; soviet power?
2 Which car manufacturer was most responsible for introducing this system of production?
3 Name the famous car he produced during the boom years.
4 What do the letters HP stand for?
5 With which of the following industries do you most closely associate the 'demand for consumer goods'; textiles; coal; electricity; gas?

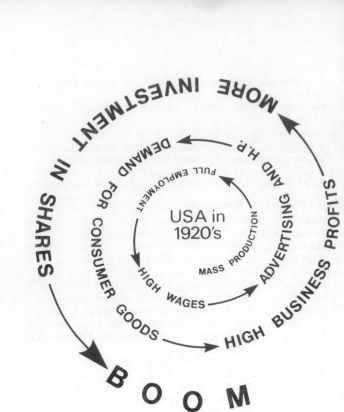

Fig. III.16.1

6 Which of the following industries did not share in the 'boom'; film; steel; agriculture; electrical goods?
7 In what year did the 'boom' come to an end?

Questions 8–12 are based on the list of American cities. Washington; Chicago; Detroit; New York; Los Angeles

8 Which might be described as 'the capital of the car industry'?
9 In which city did Al Capone have most power?
10 Which city was nearest to the centre of the film industry?
11 In which city would you find Wall Street?
12 which city is the political capital of the USA?

Unit 17 Self-Test Questions:

The following questions are based on the map, Fig. III.17.1 from Oxford 1980 'O' Level.

1 Name country A.
2 With which country was Japan allied in 1902?
3 Name port X.
4 From which country did Japan take this port?
5 In which year did the seizure take place?
6 Name region C.
7 In which year did Japan annex that region?
8 Name region D.

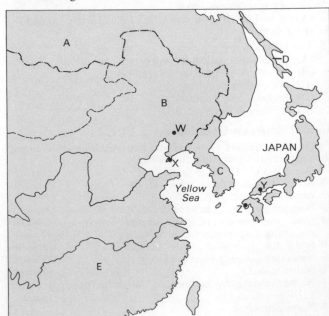

Fig. III.17.1

9 In which year did Japan gain that region?
10 Name area B.
11 Name the capital marked W.
12 In which year did Japan invade area B?
13 What new name did Japan give to the region B?
14 Name the leader of the League Commission sent to report on the Japanese attack on region B.
15 In which year did that Commission report?
16 What was Japan's response to the League's action?
17 Give the years in which Japan
 i reached a naval agreement with the USA:
 ii launched a full scale attack on mainland China:
 iii attacked Pearl Harbour.
18 With which two European countries did Japan sign an agreement in 1936?
19 Name *i* city Y and *ii* city Z.
20 Name country E.
21 In which year did country E become a Republic?
22 Who led and inspired that Republican revolution?
23 Who tried to set himself up as dictator of E between 1912 and 1916?
24 Which country made 'Twenty-One Demands' on country E in 1915?
25 What was the name of the leading political party in country E in 1920?
26 What were the 'Three Principles' on which that party was based?
27 Who led that ruling party in 1927?
28 In which city and in what year did the leader of the ruling party order an attack on the Communists.

Unit 18 Self-Test questions:

1 In which document did Wilson propose 'a general association of nations . . . under specific covenants'?
2 What is a 'covenant'?
3 In what year was the 'association' founded?
4 The Washington Conference was held in 1921–22.
 i Name the FOUR countries which took part.
 ii What terms were agreed about naval armaments?
5 In what year were the Locarno Treaties signed?
6 Name the German Foreign Minister at Locarno.
7 Which FOUR countries, other than Germany were involved in the Locarno Treaties?
8 Why did France welcome the Locarno Treaties?
9 What was the main agreement in the Kellog-Briand Pact?
10 In which year was that Pact signed?
11 In which years did Germany *i* and enter and *ii* leave the League?
12 'The High Contracting Parties guarantee the maintenance of the status quo resulting from the frontiers between Germany and Belgium and between Germany and France as fixed by the Treaty of Peace signed at Versailles on June 28 1919'.
(A) Washington Agreement **(D)** Dawes Plan 1924
1922 **(E)** Locarno Pact 1925
(B) Treaty of Rapallo 1922
(C) Treaty of Lausanne 1923

(London 1980 O Level).

Unit 19 Self-Test Questions:

Questions 1–12 are based on the cartoon (Fig. III.19.1) and adapted from AEB 1981, O-Level and Of. 1981, O-Level.
1 Name the character carrying the bin.
2 Name the character walking away.
3 With which party are the slogans in the bin associated?
4 What did the initials GOP stand for?
5 Who had referred to 'Rugged Individualism'?
6 Which TWO of the following would *i* have agreed with the principle of 'Rugged Individualism, *ii* have disagreed?
 (A) Coolidge; **(B)** Keynes; **(C)** Marx; **(D)** Harding
7 In which year was the cartoon published?
8 What was the significance of 'Chicken Pot'?
9 Which other slogan shown in the bin had been used in association with 'Chicken Pot'?
10 What event had shown as false the slogan 'Prosperity is around the corner'?
11 What term was applied to the policy which replaced the policies being thrown out in the bin?

Fig. III.19.1

12 Was the cartoonist in favour of the bin-throwing?
13 What did the following sets of initials stand for:
 i CCC; *ii* NRA; *iii* AAA?
14 Name the British economist whose ideas were adapted by the man throwing away the bin.
15 Which of the following statements about the Tennessee Valley Authority is NOT correct?
(A) It was created in 1933 as part of the government's programme to get the country out of the depression.
(B) It was an unnecessary interference in the internal affairs of the States of the Valley.
(C) It built great hydro-electric power stations to provide cheap electricity to farmers and industry.
(D) It re-planned the whole economic life of the valley in a way that individual states by themselves could not do.
(E) It brought new employment and prosperity to the whole Tennessee Valley.
 (Question 15 from WY & LREB 1981, CSE Level).

Unit 20 Self-Test Questions:

Read the following extract and answer the questions below.
 'I once took over a state faced by ruin thanks to its ___ in the promises of the rest of the world and to the bad ___ of democratic government . . . I have conquered ___ *in Germany* re-established order and enormously incre___ the production and at the same time tried to further the edu___ and culture of our people.

 I have succeeded in finding useful work once more for ___ whole of *seven million unemployed* . . . Not only have ___ united the German people politically but I have also rearm___ them, I have also endeavoured to destroy sheet by sheet tha___ treaty which in its 448 articles contains the vilest oppression which peoples and human beings have ever been expected to put up with. I have brought back to the Reich, provinces *stolen from us in 1919.* I have led back to their native country millions of Germans who were torn away from us and were in misery . . .

 You, Mr. Roosevelt, have a much easier task in comparison. You came to power to the head of one of the largest and wealthiest states in the world.'
 Extract from a speech to the German Reichstag
April 28th 1939.

1 Who made this speech?
2 What was **the German Reichstag?**
3 Why was there no opposition to the speaker in that Reichstag?
4 Which year was the speaker referring to in line 1?
5 What had caused **chaos in Germany** in that year?
6 Which of the speaker's Ministers was particularly in charge of **education and culture**?
7 What was the name of the **bad régime of democratic government**?

8 Suggest TWO ways in which the **7 million unemployed** were found work.
9 Name the treaty mentioned in the passage.
10 Name ONE of the **provinces stolen from us in 1919** which had been brought back to the Reich.
11 What position did **Mr. Roosevelt** hold?
12 In which year had he come to power?
13 What main task faced Mr. Roosevelt when **he came to power**?
14 What name was given to Roosevelt's policies?
(Questions adapted from YREB 1972, CSE Level).

Unit 21 Self-Test Questions:

Choose the correct option in answer to each of the following.

1 One reason for Italian discontent after the First World War was that
(A) they were on the losing side
(B) their King was a dictator
(C) their German Allies had let them down.
(D) they received less land than they had expected.
(E) Italy was not Socialist.

2 Mussolini gained power in 1922 because
(A) the army did not oppose him
(B) the King was out of Italy
(C) the Fascists organized a successful general strike
(D) Fascists controlled the police and civil service
(E) he won the election 1922

3 Mussolini's paper was called
(A) Il Duce
(B) Pravda
(C) The Fascist News
(D) Il Popolo d'Italia
(E) Eskra

4 Mussolini attacked Corfu to
(A) capture Trieste
(B) invade Albania
(C) help the League of Nations
(D) teach the Yugoslavs a lesson
(E) impress the Italian people

5 When Mussolini attacked Abyssinia the League of Nations
(A) asked countries to supply Abyssinia with guns
(B) banned the sale of oil to Italy
(C) imposed economic sanctions on Italy

6 Mussolini
i banned non-fascist organizations
ii encouraged strikes
iii controlled the press
iv forced schools to use Fascist text books
v developed Italy's hydro-electric resources
(A) i iii iv iv
(B) i ii iii
(C) ii iv v
(D) i iii v
(E) ii iii iv v

7 Musssolini believed that:
i everyone should obey the state
ii a military government was best
iii discipline was important
iv opposition should be encouraged to criticize government
v government violence was justified.
(A) i ii iii
(B) iii iv v
(C) i iii v
(D) i iv v
(E) ii iii iv

8 Which of the following is a statement of FACT?
Fascism is a system which:
(A) denies minority rights
(B) favours strong government
(C) opposes ideas of human liberty
(D) prevents economic progress
(E) attacks the working class

Unit 22 Self-Test Questions:

1 This question is concerned with the history of India
i Who proposed reforms of the Indian government in 1909?
ii When did Montagu make his famous declaration?
iii Why was 1935 important in the history of India?
iv What is the religion of the majority in India?
v Which religious group was represented by Jinnah?
vi For which religious group was Amritsar 'a holy city'?
vii What name was given to the system of Dual Control, 1919?
viii What tax did Gandhi attack in his 'march to the sea'?
2 Which crisis in the 1920s highlighted Dominion Independence?
3 Which Treaties did the Dominions NOT sign in i 1923, ii 1925?
4 Which Act of Parliament implemented the Balfour Report 1926?

5 What was the main difference between the entry of the Dominions into the War in (i) 1914 and (ii) 1939?

Choose the correct option in answer to the questions 6–7

6 In his campaign for independence Gandhi urged people to:
(A) attack British property
(B) increase imports
(C) stop making clothes
(D) refuse to pay certain taxes
(E) kill British soldiers

7 'It became a parliamentary Monarchy in 1922 but British troops remained in one area'
This refers to:
(A) Burma
(B) Egypt
(C) Eire
(D) Malaya
(E) South Africa

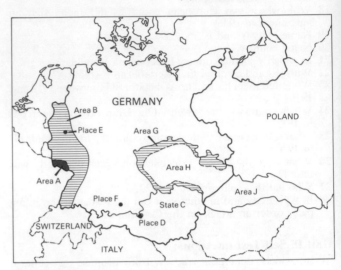

Fig. III.23.1A

Unit 23 Self-Test Questions:

Study the map (Fig. III.23.1A) and then answer the following questions (adapted from AEB 1978 and 1980 O Level).

1 Name the small, shaded area A.
2 When, and by what process, did it come under Hitler's rule?
3 Name the large, shaded area B.
4 What action did Hitler take regarding area B in March 1936?
5 Which TWO countries might have stopped that action?
6 Name state C.
7 Hitler wanted an 'Anschluss' with state C. What did he mean?
8 Name the Chancellor of State C in i 1933; ii 1938.
9 Who prevented Hitler's attempt at 'Anschluss' in 1934?
10 When did Hitler gain control of state C?
11 Name places D, E and F where important meetings were held in 1938.
12 Which major European power was not at any of those meetings?
13 Name shaded Area G.
14 Name the state of which Area G had been part in 1914.
15 What language was spoken by the majority in Area G?
16 Of which state was it part in 1938?
17 Name the president of Areas G, H and J from 1935 to 1938.
18 Name THREE European countries which signed an agreement giving Area G to Germany.
19 Name Area J which was occupied by Germany in March 1939.
20 Name Area H which became a German Protectorate, March 1939.

Unit 24 Self-Test Questions:

1 Name the following;
i the last King of Spain before the Civil War.
ii the German Air Legion helping the rebels.
iii the Spanish Fascist political party.
iv the non-Russian volunteers fighting in Spain.
v TWO dictators, other than Hitler, helping the rebels.
2 Which town was i the rebel headquarters; ii bombed by the Germans in April 1937.
3 Read the list and say which supported i the Republicans and ii the rebels.

(A) Socialists; (B) The Church Authorities; (C) Liberals; (D) Anarchists; (E) Landowners; (F) The Basques; (G) most army officers.

For questions 4–5 choose the correct option as your answer

4 Popular Front movements wanted joint action between:
(A) communists and fascists
(B) fascists and pacifists
(C) pacifists and nationalists
(D) nationalists and socialists
(E) socialists and communists

5 In the 1930s fascist and communist régimes gave people
(A) a free press but no religious liberty
(B) racial purity but no religious liberty
(C) political choice but a censored press
(D) religious freedom but no right to vote
(E) the right to vote but no political choice

(*Questions 4–5 adapted from London 1982 and 1983 O Level.*)

Unit 25 Self-Test Questions:

1 What name was given to the German method of very rapid attack?
2 Which country was the first to be attacked by this method?
3 What was the name of the French line of fortifications along the Franco-German border?
4 What name was given to the period of war, October 1939–April 1940?
5 Which country was attacked by Russia in November 1939?
6 In which French town was a government set up supporting the Germans?
7 Name the leader of that government.
8 Read the following passage. From the list below choose the correct word or date.

Germany invades Russia

Operation . . . *1* began in June . . . *2* . . . and as usual the *3* . . . tanks were completely successful. The . . . *4* divisions swarmed all over . . . *5* . . . and by September had captured . . . *6* . . . and were besieging . . . *7* . . . Moscow itself was not many miles to the East.
The 'enemy in the East' had been struck down, crowed an exultant . . . *8* . . . But this mastermind who believed in the invincibility of the . . . *9* . . . had omitted to provide it with adequate . . . *10* . . . equipment and November saw the onset of bitter weather.

(A) 1941	(F) Leningrad	(M) Panzers
(B) Berlin	(G) Western Russia	(N) Fuhrer
(C) Luftwaffe	(H) 1943	(P) Winter
(D) Blitzkrieg	(J) Kiev	(Q) Barbarossa
(E) Emperor	(K) Wehrmacht	
	(L) Defeat	

(*Question 8 from ALSEB 1977, CSE Level*).

Unit 26 Self-Test Questions:

1 What, in wartime, did the following code names stand for;
i Barbarossa; *ii* Mulberry; *iii* Overlord; *iv* Pluto; *v* Sealion; *vi* Torch?

2 Against each of the SIX battles (A)–(F) put the appropriate letters from (G)–(N) to indicate the enemies involved.
(A) Matapan; (B) Midway; (C) Stalingrad; (D) El Alamein; (E) Arnhem; (F) Okinawa;
(G) America; (H) Britain; (J) France; (K) Germany; (L) Italy; (M) Japan; (N) Russia.

Questions 3–6 are based on this ultimatum:

'To the commander of the Sixth Army: The Sixth German Army, the units of the Fourth Armoured Corps and the troops attached to them as reinforcements have been completely surrounded. We propose to you the following terms of surrender . . .'

3 This ultimatum was delivered at
(A) Leningrad; (B) Moscow; (C) Smolensk; (D) Stalingrad; (E) Warsaw.

4 The Commander to whom it was addressed was:
(A) Zhukov; (B) Timoshenko; (C) Rommel; (D) von Paulus; (E) von Kluck.

5 Three months before this surrender a major victory was won at:

(A) Arnhem; (B) Kohimar; (C) Monte Cassino; (D) Caen (E) El Alamein

6 The surrender was condemned by.
(A) Stalin; (B) Churchill; (C) Roosevelt; (D) Hitler; (E) Attlee;

Unit 27 Self-Test Questions:

Read the extract below and answer the questions which follow.
' . . . The Big Three at Yalta in February 1945 all recognized the need for a revised international organization to replace the ill-fated League of Nations and an outline scheme was approved. In June 1945 the representatives of fifty states met to found the United Nations.

Like the League, the UN has an Assembly in which each member country had one vote. The job of peace keeping was assigned to the Security Council. . . . Closely connected are the International Court of Justice and the Trusteeship Council. A number of subsidiary agencies are grouped together under the Economic and Social Council . . .

In 1948 the General Assembly approved by a large majority the issue of the Declaration of Human Rights, the first international Bill of Rights in human history. Since 1945 the United Nations has sought to resist aggression and preserve order by the use of armed forces internationally provided under its own command . . . But it has been perhaps through its subsidiary agencies that the UN has made its greatest contribution towards bringing into existence a true world community . . .'

1 Who were the 'Big Three' statesmen who met at Yalta (Line 1)?
2 *i* Where and *ii* when had they met before this?
3 Which of the 'Big Three' was missing from *i* the first session of the Potsdam Conference in July 1945; *ii* the second session of that Conference, August 1945.
4 Explain the absences noted in *i* and *ii* above.
5 Where did the 'League of Nations' (Line 3) have its headquarters?
6 Where are the headquarters of the 'United Nations' (Line 5)?
7 Who donated the land on which the UN buildings stand?
8 Where did 'the representatives of fifty states' meet in June 1945 (Line 4)?
9 Why has the membership of the UN increased greatly since 1945?
10 What power did each member of the League Assembly have which is not possessed by the members of the UN Assembly?
11 What power does each of the permanent members of the Security Council possess to safeguard its own interests?
12 *i* In what year and *ii* because of what crisis was the Uniting for Peace resolution passed by the UN Assembly?
13 Which two major nations were members of the UN in 1945 who were not members of the League in 1920?
14 Name THREE Secretary Generals of the UN.
15 Where did the UN order the 'use of armed forces' (Lines 16–17); *i* 1950–52; *ii* 1956; *iii* 1960–61; *iv* 1963–64?
(*Adapted from JMB 1981, O Level.*)

Unit 28 Self-Test Questions:

Study the map (Fig. III.28.1) and then answer the questions

1 Name the TWO Summit Conferences held in 1945 at which the Occupation Zones were discussed and confirmed.
2 Name the only Allied leader who was at both Conferences.
3 Name the occupying power in *i* zone A; *ii* zone B; *iii* zone C; *iv* zone D?
4 What name was adopted by the state formed out of zones B, C and D in May 1949.
5 What name was adopted by the state formed out of zone A?
6 Name line E, drawn mainly along two rivers, which marked the German-Polish boundary.
7 Where was Churchill speaking when he spoke of 'an iron curtain' descending across Europe?
8 Name city F which Churchill chose as the northern end of that curtain.
9 Name city G at the southern end of that curtain.
10 Name TWO states, other than Poland, on the eastern side of the curtain.
11 Name state K, an uneasy member of the eastern bloc.
12 What did the initials UNRRA stand for?
13 Which country contributed most to UNRRA?
14 Which Plan, developed in 1947, replaced UNRRA?

Fig. III.28.1

15 Who was President of the USA in 1947?
16 Over which country did that President make a major stand in 1947?
17 Name city H and say how it was governed in 1945–49.
18 Why was it a centre of crisis between March 1948 and May 1949?
19 What organization was formed in April 1949 as a result of that crisis?
20 Name FOUR countries which joined that organization in 1949.
21 Name the organization formed by Russia in 1955 in opposition to the organization named in answer to question 19.
22 What action did Russia take in city H in 1961 which gave substance to Churchill's talk of 'an iron curtain'?

(*Map and questions adapted from AEB and Oxford O Level, and many CSE Boards.*)

Unit 29 Self-Test Questions:

1 In January 1961, the USA broke off diplomatic relations with Cuba because:
(A) the democratic administration of Batista had been overthrown
(B) Castro's troops had been sent to Africa
(C) American investments had been taken over
(D) Russian rockets had been installed around Havana
(E) The invasion of the Bay of Pigs had been repulsed

2 NATO CENTO, AND SEATO were organizatons which ALL had the common objective of:
(A) checking Russia's advance into western Europe
(B) providing aid to developing countries
(C) defending British and French colonial possessions
(D) restricting the expansion of world communism
(E) restraining Chinese ambitions in southern Asia.

3 An important, though temporary, agreement between the USA and the USSR took place in:
(A) 1947 over the civil war in Greece
(B) 1954 over the withdrawal of French forces from Indo-China
(C) 1956 over the Anglo-French invasion of Egypt
(D) 1961 over the establishment of the Organization of American States
(E) 1971 over the election of Allende's government in Chile

4 The Marshall Plan and the Truman Doctrine were 'twin pillars of a single policy' meant to lead to the
(A) frustration of communism
(B) liberation of Czechoslovakia
(C) protection of Berlin
(D) re-unification of Germany
(E) termination of unemployment

5 Which of the following best defines **revisionism** as used in the 1970s by the Chinese to describe the Soviet Union?
(A) Departure from the doctrines of Marxist-Lenism
(B) Indifference to the welfare of industrial workers
(C) Insistence on the dictatorship of the proletariat

(D) Resort to the veto in the UN Security Council
(E) Support for the liberation movement in colonial countries

6 In the 1970s the Chinese followed a policy which they had denounced in the 1960s when it had been pursued by Russia. It was:
(A) commitment to nuclear disarmament
(B) diminishing hostility to the USA
(C) growing friendship with the Third World
(D) increasing antagonism towards the Commonwealth
(E) support for world revolution

Unit 30 Self-Test Questions:

Study the map (Fig. III.30.1) and then answer the following questions:
1 Name state A.
2 Name state B. In which year did the Communists take control of that country?
3 Who became Prime Minister of state B in 1968?
4 Name state C. Who became Prime Minister of that country in 1970 only to resign in 1971?
5 Name state D.
6 Name state E. In which year did the Russians crush a rising in that country?

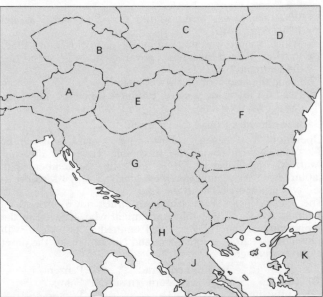

Fig. III.30.1

7 Name state F. In which year did that country sign a 'most favoured nation' trade treaty with the USA in defiance of Russia?
8 Name state G. Who ruled that state in 1945?
9 Name state H.
10 Name *i* state J and *ii* state K.
11 Which western Ally provided the military help to resist the communists in state J in 1946–47?
12 Which country took on that rôle in 1947?
13 Name the political organization set up to ensure that Russia's allies depended on her.
14 Which state was expelled from that organization in 1948?
15 When was that organization dissolved?
16 Name the organization set up in 1949 to ensure Russian control of the economies of the satellite states.
17 Name the Church leaders attacked by the Communists after 1945 in *i* state B; *ii* state C; *iii* state E.
18 Identify by letter and name the country in which the Solidarity trade union movement developed.
19 In which of the following years was there *not* a workers' rising against Communist governments in Eastern Europe; 1950; 1953; 1956; 1968; 1971?

(*Map and questions adapted from Oxford 1980, O Level.*)

Unit 31 Self-Test Questions:

Study the map (Fig. III.31.1) and then answer the questions below.
1 Give the **name** and the **number of each of the original six members of the EEC.**

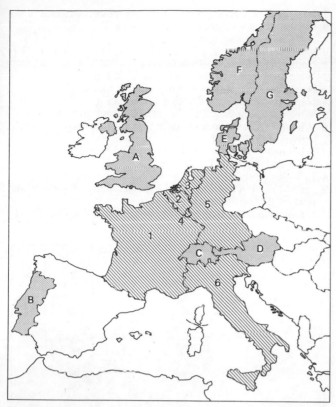

Fig. III.31.1

2 To which organization did the **lettered** countries belong in the 1960s?

3 Indicate by **names** and **letters** the five lettered countries which did NOT join the EEC in 1973.

4 Which British Prime Minister tried to get Britain into the EEC in 1961–2?

5 Who vetoed Britain's application in 1962?

6 Who was Chancellor of Germany in the 1950s?

7 Who was the German Economic Minister most responsible for West Germany's 'economic miracle'?

8 Indicate by **number** and **name** the countries in Benelux.

9 In which year did Britain join the EEC. Who was the Prime Minister at that time?

10 What happened about Britain's membership in 1975? Who was Prime Minister at that time?

(*Questions based on map and questions (adapted) from London 1981, O Level.*)

Unit 32 Self-Test Questions:

1 At the outbreak of the Korean War the British government
(A) condemned US aggression
(B) supported Russian attempts to mediate
(C) committed troops to fight
(D) urged invasion of China
(E) vetoed UN intervention

2 After years of US opposition the 1970s saw the reunification under communist rule of
(A) Cyprus
(B) Korea
(C) Nigeria
(D) Pakistan
(E) Vietnam

3 Between 1969 and 1972 the USA and USSR made an agreement known as SALT on:
(A) the construction of submarines
(B) intercontinental ballistic missiles
(C) the 'open skies' proposal
(D) multiple rôle aircraft
(E) the exploration of space

4 In the late 1970s the USA fostered good relations with
(A) Argentina because of beef
(B) Canada because of wheat
(C) Cuba because of sugar
(D) Mexico because of oil
(E) Peru because of tin

5 In 1945 both the USA and USSR carried out promises to:
(A) finance the Marshall Plan
(B) cancel war debts
(C) create a Jewish state
(D) share atomic secrets
(E) join the United Nations

6 Towards which of these was the USA LEAST friendly in 1972?
(A) Argentina
(B) Brazil
(C) Chile
(D) Haiti
(E) Venezuela

7 In 1946 the US urged Britain to:
(A) admit more Jews to Palestine.
(B) transfer Palestine to France
(C) bring Palestine into the Empire
(D) surrender Palestine to Jordan
(E) expel all Arabs from Palestine

8 If invading armies were to cross the 38th Parallel war would break out in
(A) Afghanistan
(B) Israel
(C) Korea
(D) Malaysia
(E) Vietnam

9 In the 1960s US policy drove
(A) Canada into the arms of France
(B) Cuba into the arms of Russia
(C) Greece into the arms of Turkey
(D) Israel into the arms of Britain
(E) Japan into the arms of China

10 A good example of détente was
(A) Carter's concern on energy
(B) Brezhnev's policy in Czechoslovakia
(C) Heath's Common Market policy
(D) Nixon's visit to China
(E) Schmidt's attacks on terrorism

11 The US showed her dislike for Cuba by
(A) admitting more immigrants
(B) cutting sugar imports
(C) increasing trade in copper
(D) cutting her armaments
(E) cutting tariffs on coffee

Unit 33 Self-Test Questions:

Examine the map (Fig. III.33.1) and answer questions 1–15

1 Name State A.

2 In which year did Chinese and US troops clash there?

3 By what name is island B known now?

4 Who ruled it in 1950?

5 What US force prevented Communist China from taking that island?

6 What decision taken in 1971 altered the relationship between Island B, China and the major powers?

7 Name Area D.

8 With which major power has China clashed there?

9 Name State E.

10 Which colonial power controlled it in the 1950s?

11 How was China involved there at the time?

12 Identify areas *i* Y and *ii* Z

13 Which European states have interests there?

14 Why might a continuing European interest in Z be an advantage to China?

15 What is the significance of the year 1998 with regard to Z?

(*Questions and map adapted from Oxford 1981, O Level.*)

Unit 34 Self-Test Questions:

Look at the map Fig. III.33.1 then answer the questions below.

1 Name Province F which has been disputed by India and Pakistan since 1947.

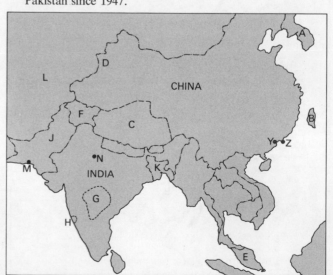

Fig. III.33.1

2 Why was that Province of particular interest to India's Prime Minister 1947?
3 Who arranged a truce in the fighting over the Province in *i* 1949; *ii* 1966?
4 Where was that second truce (1966) arranged?
5 Name Province G whose ruler refused to join India in 1947?
6 When was that Province forced to join India?
7 Name Area C occupied by Chinese forces in 1950.
8 Who was the traditional ruler of Area C?
9 When did that ruler flee from Area C?
10 What decision did China make about Area C in 1965?
11 Name Province H occupied by Indian troops in 1961.
12 Which European power had colonized Province H until 1961?
13 Which TWO areas made up Pakistan in 1947?
14 Who was *i* the first head of state in Pakistan; *ii* Pakistan's first Prime Minister
15 Which area is known as Bangladesh?
16 When did that state come into being?
17 Name; *i* Country L; *ii* City M; *iii* City N.
18 What is the religion of the majority of people in *i* India; *ii* Pakistan?
19 Which Indian leader of the independence movement was assassinated in 1948?

20 *i* Who was India's first Prime Minister? *ii* Name his daughter who also became Prime Minsiter of India. *iii* When did she first fall from power?

(*Map and questions adapted from various papers at O and CSE Level.*)

Unit 35 Self Test Questions:

Study the map of Indo-China (1954–1974) (Fig. III.35.1) and then answer the questions.

1 Name *i* Country A and *ii* country B.
2 What is the boundary line E by which they were partitioned?
3 In which year did that partitioning take place?
4 Name *i* Country C and *ii* Country D.
5 At which conference did these countries gain independence?
6 Which European power had controlled A,B,C and D in 1945?

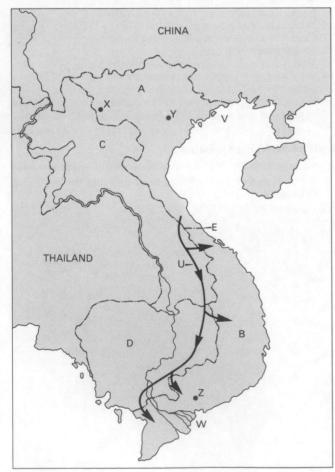

Fig. III.35.1

7 Identify X where a major battle took place in 1954.
8 Identify the two capital cities *i* Y and *ii* Z.
9 Name the river system W.
10 What is the main crop grown in the delta area around W?
11 Name the Gulf region marked V.
12 What took place in the Gulf area V in 1964?
13 Name the US President at the time of that incident.
14 Name route U marked with a thick line.
15 Why was it important to the independence movement?
16 Why did the existence of route U lead to an increase in US activity in 1970–71?
17 What name was given to the offensive launched from country A on country B in 1968?
18 In which year did the US forces leave country B?
19 Name *i* the US President and *ii* his Secretary of State at the time of that withdrawal.

(*Map and questions adapted from many papers at O and CSE Levels.*)

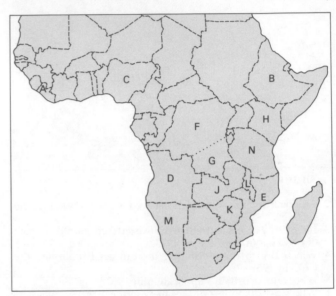

Fig. III.36.1

Unit 36 Self-Test Questions:

Study the map of Africa (Fig. III.36.1) and then answer the questions below.

1 *i* Identify state F. *ii* Which European power had colonized this state? *iii* In which year did it become independent?
2 *i* Identify region G which tried to secede from state F. *ii* Name the head of state in region G who was assassinated.
3 *i* Identify state H. *ii* When did it become independent? *iii* Who was its first President?
4 Identify state M giving the name for this state used by: *i* South Africa; *ii* African nationalists.
5 *i* When did South Africa leave the British Commonwealth and become a Republic? *ii* What was the issue which led to South Africa's exclusion from the Commonwealth?
6 Give the modern name for the Gold Coast. *ii* When did it become independent? *iii* Name its first African Head of State.
7 Which two African states were independent in 1900?
8 *i* Which were the two Portugese colonies? *ii* When did they become independent?
9 *i* In which state did Idi Amin take power? *ii* Name his successor.
10 Which three states made up the Central African Federation? In your answer give the names by which they were known in 1950 and their modern names.
11 In which state did Ian Smith declare UDI? *ii* In which year?
12 Which state was a British Mandate between 1919 and 1964?
13 With which states do you associate the following; *i* Azikwe; *ii* Nyerere; *iii* Kaunda; *iv* Mugabe; *v* Mobutu?
14 In which states were the rebels known as *i* Mau Mau; *ii* Biafrans?

(*Map and questions adapted from a number of papers at O and CSE Level.*)

Unit 37 Self-Test Questions:

1 From the list below choose the words which complete the following passage. There are more words than you need to fill the gaps in the passage.

On the day the British left, the Jews said that their new State of . . . *1*, was born. The Arabs invaded the new State and were beaten. Only Jordan's . . . *2* . . . fought well. 600,000 Arab refugees left for the refugee camps to become the basis for the modern anti-Jewish force, the . . . *3* . . . led by . . . *4* . . . In 1956 Egypt under . . . *5* . . . nationalized the . . . *6* . . . Even with . . . *7* . . . help he was defeated by the Jews in 1956 and 1967. His successor attacked the Jews in 1973 on their Holy Day of . . . *8* . . . Since then the Jews and Egyptians have worked for a peaceful solution of their problems after a meeting at . . . *9* . . . arranged by *10*.

(A) Camp David	**(G)** President Sadat	**(N)** Arab Legion
(B) Aswan Dam	**(H)** Colonel Nasser	**(O)** Palestine
(C) Palestine	**(J)** Pentecost	Liberation
(D) Stern Gang	**(K)** Yom Kippur	Organization
(E) Yasser Arafat	**(L)** Russia's	**(P)** America's
(F) Foreign Legion	**(M)** Israel	**(Q)** Geneva
		(R) Suez Canal
		(S) President Carter

(*EMREB 1981, CSE Level.*)

2 Name the following;
i Israel's first Prime Minister.
ii The woman who became Prime Minister of Israel.
iii The country which sided with Britain and Israel in 1956.
iv The British Prime Minister during the Suez Crisis 1956.
v Nasser's successor as President of Egypt.
vi The Israeli Prime Minister who negotiated peace with Egypt.

Choose the correct Option in answer to each of questions 3 and 4.

3 At the end of the Second World War, the US government put pressure on the British government to:
(A) admit more Jews into Palestine
(B) transfer the Palestinian mandate to France
(C) absorb Palestine into the Empire
(D) surrender the Palestinian mandate to Jordan
(E) expel all Arabs from Palestine.

4 Efforts to bring peace between Egypt and Israel in the years 1948–83 involved at different times all of the following EXCEPT
(A) the demand that Arab states recognize Israel's right to exist
(B) expulsion of Israel from the UN
(C) recommendation that Palestine be partitioned
(D) policing of Israel's boundaries by UN troops
(E) demand that Israeli troops withdraw to former frontiers

(*Questions 3 and 4 from London 1982, O Level*).

Unit 38 Self-Test Questions:

1 For what do the following sets of initials stand?
i PLO: *ii* IRA; *iii* UNRRA; *iv* FAO: *v* SWAPO; *vi* IMF.

2 Study this outline of a Five-year Plan for Tanzania announced by its President in 1964. Then answer the questions below.

Total expenditure was estimated at £246 000 000 of which one-half would have to be raised overseas–£102 000 000 being allotted to the Central Government, £10 000 000 to local authorities, £18 000 000 to the East African Common Services Organization, and £116 000 000 to the private sector of the economy.

The Plan aimed at raising the annual average income per head from £19.6 to £40.1 by 1980, and the average life expectation from between 35 and 40 to 50 years. With a view to making Tanzania practically self-supporting in manpower in all economic fields, the Plan envisaged the training of 3 200 doctors, scientists, engineers, and graduate teachers, nearly 10 000 engineering and laboratory technicians and non-graduate teachers, and 16 000 office and skilled workers, as well as the recruitment of 450 expatriate civil servants and 1 200 teachers.

i Which two states joined together to form Tanzania?
ii Name the President who announced this Plan.
iii Which of the 1964 figures best show why Tanzania had to borrow from overseas one-half of the money needed?
iv Which 1964 figure reflects the effects of a low income?

v How much money did Tanzania plan to raise overseas?
vi If all this money were borrowed, how much interest would Tanzania have to pay each year if the rate of interest was **(A)** 5%; **(B)** 10%; **(C)** 15%?
vii Did interest rates **(A)** rise or **(B)** fall between 1964 and 1980?
viii How did Tanzania hope to get the money needed to pay that total interest each year?
ix How did the increase in oil prices after 1973 affect Tanzania's **(A)** spending on imports; **(B)** earnings from exports?
x What is meant by **expatriate?**

3 Read this extract from the resolutions adopted at the first conference of OPEC. Then answer the questions which follow. 'The members of OPEC pledge themselves to secure a steady income for the producing countries, an efficient, economic and regular supply of oil to consuming countries and a fair return on their capital to those investing in the industry.'

i What do the initials OPEC stand for?
ii In which year did OPEC hold this first conference?
iii Name ONE country in EACH of the following which is a member of OPEC: **(A)** Africa; **(B)** South America: **(C)** The Middle East.
iv What, in the oil industry, was meant by 'the Seven Sisters'
v Name the Iranian Prime Minister who nationalized the Iranian oil industry in 1951.
vi Which country suffered most from that nationalization?
vii What event of 1973 caused OPEC to increase its prices sharply?
viii Which of the following countries uses the most oil: **(A)** India; **(B)** China; **(C)** USA; **(D)** Japan; **(E)** West Germany?
ix Why did oil-importing countries suffer from deficits in their balances of payments between 1973 and 1979?
x How, by trying to cure those deficits, did these countries help to create world-wide unemployment?

Choose the correct option in answer to questions 4–9

(4) Which of the following is NOT true of the IMF and the International Bank?
(A) They were set up at Bretton Woods in 1944
(B) They enable easy exchange of currencies
(C) They arrange loans to keep currencies steady
(D) They give loans to help with important projects
(E) They try to distribute the world's wealth more equally

(5) The Bandung Conference of 1955 may best be described as
(A) an American-Asian Conference of capitalist states.
(B) a conference of international relief agencies.
(C) a European-Asian conference of the Commonwealth.
(D) a summit conference of the world's super-powers.
(E) an Afro-Asian conference of countries of the Third World.

Questions 6–9 are based on these trade figures for 1974

Country	Commodity
Zambia	. . . X . . . (making up 98% of total exports
Sao Tome	Cocoa (making up 90% of total exports)
Mauritius	Sugar (making up 88% of total exports)
Guinea-Bissau	Groundnuts (making up 66% of total exports)
Ghana	. . . Y . . . (making up 55% of total exports)

6 'X' in the second column of this table represents:**(A)** copper; **(B)** cotton; **(C)** oil; **(D)** rubber; **(E)** sugar.
7 'Y' in the second column of this table represents:
(A) copper; **(B)** oil; **(C)** cocoa; **(D)** rubber; **(E)** sugar.
8 These figures show that the years of colonialism left these countries:
(A) dependent on US loans
(B) commercially prosperous
(C) overspecialized in their economies
(D) politically unstable
(E) dependent on European markets.

9 Since these figures were published in 1974, these countries have:

(A) benefited from increased prices for their products
(B) suffered because of falling demand for their goods
(C) benefited from increased import prices
(D) suffered from falling import prices
(E) benefited from the world boom

Answers

Unit 1 Answers:

1 (A)*2*, (B)*17*, (C)*24*; (A)*3*, (B)*19*, (C)*28*; (A)*4*, (B)*11*, (C)*29*, (A)*5*, (B)*12*, (C)*30*,
(A)*6*, (B)*20*, (C)*23*, (A)*7*, (B)*13*, (C)*26*; (A)*8*, (B)*14*, (C)*22*; (A)*9*, (B)*16*, (C)*25*;
(A)*10*, (B)*18*, (C)*21*;

2 The Centre Party (Or Catholic Party	**6** Frankfurt
3 Lasalle	**7** The Reichstag
4 Schleswig	**8** von Tirpitz
5 Alsace and Lorraine	**9** Bethmann-Hollweg
	10 (B)

Unit 2 Answers:

1 Sedan	**4** Alsace and Eastern Lorraine
2 Gambetta	
3 Bordeaux	**5** Thiers
	6 MacMahon

7 *i* the Bourbon Count de Chambord; *ii* the Orléanist Count of Paris; *ii* the Napoleonic Prince Imperial.
8 The Senate and the Chamber
9 Grévy

10 *i* Tunisia *ii* Annan or Tonkin
11 Boulanger
12 Ferdinand de Lesseps
13 Jean Jaurés
14 Option (B)

Unit 3 Answers:

1 2(M); 3(K); 4(I); 5(G); 6(E); 7(J); 8(B); 9(D); 10(A); 11(F); 12(H); 13(C).
2 *i* Social Democratic Labour Party; *ii* Social Revolutionary Party.

3 *i* the Bolsheviks; *ii* the Mensheviks	**6** Nicholas II
	7 October 1905
4 A Marxist newspaper	**8** Father Gapon
5 Portsmouth, USA	**9** Option (B)

Unit 4 Answers:

1 The Serbs living in Bosnia.
2 *i* The Serbians *ii* Bulgarians *iii* Montenegrins.
3 They were all members of the Orthodox Church.

4 *i* expansion into Bosnia and Herzogovina *ii* The break up of Turkey and the expansion of the Slav nations *iii* to preserve Turkey and stop Russia getting her way.

5 Abdul Hamid	**11** Albania
6 Plevna	**12** Serbia
7 Constantinople	**13** Romania
8 Disraeli	**14** Bulgaria
9 Pan Slavism	**15** Option (A)
10 *i* London *ii* Bucharest	**16** Option (E)

Unit 5 Answers:

1 2(G); 3(H); 4(F); 5(J); 6(E); 7(K); 8(D); 9(B); 10(M); 11(C); 12(N); 13(A); 14(L).

2 *i* Tunis; *ii* Tripoli	**6** The Mahdi
3 Arabi Pasha	**7** *i* 1885; *ii* Khartoum
4 Tel-el-Kebir	**8** Kitchener
5 Evelyn Baring (Lord Cromer)	

Unit 6 Answers:

1 *i* China; *ii* Russia	**4** Sun Yat-sen
2 Great Britain	**5** The Boxer
3 The Manchus	**6** 10th October 1911

7 *i* Sakhalin *ii* the Trans-Siberian *iii* Port Arthur *iv* Liao Tung *v* Wei-hai-Wei *vi* Korea *vii* Kiao-chow *viii* Tshushima *ix* Formosa *x* Hong Kong

Unit 7 Answers:

1 *i* the Senate *ii* House of Representatives
2 The President and his Ministers of Cabinet
3 *i* Oil *ii* Steel *iii* Banking

4 The President	**12** Ku Klux Klan
5 For life	**13** Theodore (Teddy) Roosevelt
6 Napoleon I	
7 California	**14** McKinley
8 The buffalo	**15** McKinley
9 Trusts	**16** Cuba
10 To regulate the trusts	**17** Hawaii
11 Cleveland	**18** Chicago

Unit 8 Answers:

1 *i* Asquith; *ii* Agadir; *iii* Britain and France; *iv* the Boers; *v* Serbia; *vi* Grey; *vii* Egypt and Morocco.
2 *i* Battleships of the **dreadnought** class; *ii* Britain; *iii* Germany's.

3 Option (C)	**7** William II, Kaiser of Germany
4 Option (A)	
5 Option (B)	**8** Russia
6 1890	**9** She entered into an alliance with France, 1894

Unit 9 Answers:

1 *1* Haig; *2* Joffre; *3* Pétain; *4* Scheer; *5* Lawrence; *6* Wilson *7* Hamilton; *8* Foch *9* Russia; *10* Salonika; *11 Lusitania*.
2 *1* Marne; *2* Cambrai; *3* Verdun; *4* Falkland Islands

Unit 10 Answers:

1 2(G); 3(I); 4(A); 5(L); 6(H); 7(E); 8(K); 9(B); 10(J); 11(F); 12(C).

Unit 11 Answers:

1(C); 2(D); 3(B); 4(D); 5(C).

Unit 12 Answers:

1 The Saar coalfields.
2 The coalfields came under French control for five years. The region was governed, after 1919, by the League of Nations.
3 Alsace and Lorraine.
4 These were returned to France from whom Germany had taken them in 1871.

5 The Rhineland was named as a demilatarized zone. Germany was not to have any armed forces or fortifications in this territory.

6 Czechoslovakia　**7** Austria-Hungary　**8** Austria
9 Austria was not to be allowed to unite with Germany.
10 Poland　**11** Germany, Russia and Austria-Hungary
12 East Prussia　**13** Germany　**14** Danzig
15 Danzig was named a 'Free City' governed by the League of Nations.
16 Territory J was West Prussia which was handed to Poland to provide it with a 'corridor to the sea'.

Unit 13 Answers:

1 Ataturk−the Father of the Turks	**4** At the Dardanelles
	5 Constantinople (Istanbul)
2 Mustapha Kemal	**6** Ankara
3 The Young Turks	

7 *i* Women no longer had to wear the traditional veil over their faces; *ii* in 1922 women got the right to vote.

8 *i* The alphabet was westernized; *ii* Sunday was made the day of rest instead of the Islamic Friday; *iii* Western-style elementary education was started.

9 The Mandate System
10 *i* Palestine; *ii* Jordan; *iii* Iraq.
11 *i* Syria; *ii* Lebanon.
12 Sir Mark Sykes, for Britain, and Georges Picot, for France.
13 A. J. Balfour　**14** Option (E)

Unit 14 Answers:

1 President Woodrow Wilson　**2** His Fourteen Points
3 Geneva　**4** The Assembly and the Council

5 The Court of International Justice
6 The International Labour Organization   **7** A Mandate
8 *i* The USA; *ii* Germany; *iii* Russia.
9 *i* The failure of the Disarmament Conference; *ii* the invasion of Finland.
10 'Economic' sanctions.
11 In the Abyssinian crisis and against Italy.
12 Option **(C)**   **13** Option **(E)**

Unit 15 Answers:

1 The army—which claimed that politicans had betrayed it in 1918.
2 The Treaty of Versailles   **3** The Germans; the Anglo-Saxons
4 Munich   **5** Stormtroopers or Brownshirts   **6** Roehm
7 *Mein Kampf*   **8** In jail   **9** In Munich in 1923
10 Ludendorff   **11** The Lower House of the German Parliament
12 von Papen   **13** The Communist Party   **14** Stresemann
15 *i* reparations were eased by the Dawes Plan and the Young Plan; *ii* he persuaded the French to withdraw their troops from the Ruhr occupied in 1923; *iii* Germany became a member of the League in 1926 and was elected a permanent member of the Council.
16 The Locarno Treaties   **18** The Wall Street Crash
18 The Nazis and Communists **19** Field Marshall Hindenburg

Unit 16 Answers:

1 Assembly line	5 Electricity	9 Chicago
2 Henry Ford	6 Agriculture	10 Los Angeles
3 The Ford Model 'T'	7 1929	11 New York
4 Hire purchase	8 Detroit	12 Washington

Unit 17 Answers:

1 Russia	16 Japan resigned from the League
2 Great Britain	17 *i* 1921; *ii* 1937; *iii* 1941.
3 Port Arthur	
4 Russia	18 Germany and Italy
5 1905	19 *i* Hiroshima *ii* Nagasaki
6 Korea	20 China
7 1910	21 1912
8 Sakhalin	22 Sun Yat—Sen
9 At the Treaty of Portsmouth, 1905	23 Yuan shi–K'ai
	24 Japan
10 Manchuria	25 The Kuo Min Tang
11 Mukden	26 *i* Nationalism; *ii* Popular Sovereignty; *iii* People's Livelihood.
12 1931	
13 Manchukuo	
14 Lord Lytton	27 Chiang Kai-shek
15 1932	28 Shanghai; 1927

Unit 18 Answers:

1 In his Fourteen Points of January 1918
2 An agreement OR a constitution   **3** 1919
4 *i* The USA, Britain, France and Japan *ii* That the British, American and Japanese navies would maintain their size in the ratio of 5:5:3 respectively.
5 1925   **6** Stresemann   **7** Britain, France, Belgium and Italy.
8 They guaranteed the French frontier with Germany.
9 The nations renounced war as a method of settling disputes.
10 1928   **11** *i* 1926; *ii* 1933. **12** Option **(E)**

Unit 19 Answers:

1 Franklin Delano Roosevelt   **2** Herbert Hoover
3 The Republican Party
4 The Grand Old Party (referring to the Republicans)
5 Herbert Hoover, when President.
6 *i* agreed—Coolidge and Harding;
ii disagreed—Keynes and Marx.   **7** 1933
8 Hoover had promised that there would be a 'chicken in every pot'.
9 He had also promised 'two cars in every garage'.
10 The Wall Street Crash, October 1929   **11** The New Deal
12 In favour—Roosevelt is shown as a sympathetic character.
13 *i* The Civilian Construction Corps;
ii The National Recovery Act;
iii The Agricultural Adjustment Act.
14 John Maynard Keynes   **15** Option **(B)**.

Unit 20 Answers:

1 Hitler
2 The Lower House of the German Parliament
3 Communists had been expelled in 1933; socialists and others terrorised into either staying away or into supporting Hitler.
4 1933
5 The Wall Street Crash
6 Goebbels as Minister for Propaganda
7 The Weimar Republic
8 Re-armament: building autobahns; other public works.
9 The Versailles Treaty.
10 The Saar; the Rhineland; Sudetenland.
11 President of the USA   **12** 1933   **13** Unemployment
14 The New Deal

Unit 21 Answers:

1(D); 2(A), 3(D); 4(E); 5(C); 6(A); 7(C); 8(B).

Unit 22 Answers:

1 *i* Morley and Minto *ii* 1917 *iii* Because of the Government of India Act *iv* The Hindus *v* The Muslims *vi* The Sikhs *vii* Dyarchy *viii* The salt tax
2 Chanak
3 *i* 1923 Lausanne; *ii* 1925 Locarno
4 The Statue of Westminster.
5 *i* 1914; they were brought in by the King's Declaration of War; *ii* 1939; each separately decided to side with Britain.
6 **(D)**   **7(B)**

Unit 23 Answers:

1 The Saar
2 In 1935. Its inhabitants voted in a plebiscite to return to Germany.
3 The Rhineland.
4 He sent troops in (1936) and re-fortified it.
5 France and Britain.   **6** Austria
7 A union between Germany and Austria.
8 *i* Dolfuss; *ii* Schuschnigg.
9 Mussolini   **10** 1938
11 D-Berchetsgaden (15th September 1938); E-Godsberg (22nd September 1938); F-Munich (29th September, 1938)
12 Russia
13 The Sudetenland. **14** Austria-Hungary. **15** German
16 Czechoslovakia. **17** Beneš. **18** Britain, France, Italy (and Germany). **19** Slovakia. **20** Bohemia.

Unit 24 Answers:

1 *i* Alfonso XIII; *ii* The Condor Legion
iii The Falange; *iv* The International Brigade;
v Salazar (Portugal), Mussolini.
2 *i* Burgos; *ii* Guernica
3 *i* (A), (C), (D), (F); *ii* (B), (E), (G);
4 **(E)**   **5 (E)**

Unit 25 Answers:

1 Blitzkreig.   **2** Poland.   **3** The Maginot Line.
4 The Phoney War   **5** Finland   **6** Vichy   **7** Marshal Pétain
8 *1*(Q); 2(A); *3*(D); *4*(M); *5*(G); *6*(J); *7*(F); *8*(N); *9*(K); *10*(P).

Unit 26 Answers:

i Hitler's invasion of Russia.
ii The artificial harbour used in the invasion of Europe.
iii The Allied invasion of Normandy
iv The P(ipe) L(ine) U(nder) The O(cean) from Britain to France.
v Hitler's planned invasion of Britain.
vi The American invasion of Algeria.
2 (A/HL): (B/GM): (C/KN): (D/HK): (E/HK): (F/GM).   **3(D); 4(D); 5(E); 6(D);**

Unit 27 Answers:

1 Churchill, Roosevelt and Stalin.
2 Teheran; November 1943
3 *i* Roosevelt; *ii* Churchill
4 *i* Roosevelt had died and been replaced by Truman.
ii Churchill had been defeated in the 1945 General Election and had been replaced by Attlee.

5 Geneva.   **6** New York.   **7** The Rockefeller Foundation.
8 San Francisco
9 As former colonies gained independence they applied for and obtained membership of the UN.
10 The veto.   **11** The veto.   **12** 1950; the Korean Crisis.
13 Russia and the USA.
14 Trygve Lie; Dag Hammarskjöld; U Thant; Kurt Waldheim.
15 *i* Korea; *ii* Suez; *iii* the Congo; *iv* Cyprus.

Unit 28 Answers:

1 Yalta and Potsdam   **2** Stalin
3 *i* Russia; *ii* Britain; *iii* America; *iv* France.
4 The German Federal Republic   **5** The German Democratic Republic.   **6** The Oder-Neisse line   **7** Fulton in Missouri, USA
8 Stettin   **9** Trieste   **10** Bulgaria, Hungary, Romania, Albania, Greece, Yugoslavia.
11 Yugoslavia.
12 The United Nations Relief and Rehabilitation Administration.
13 The USA   **14** The Marshall Plan   **15** Truman
16 Greece
17 Berlin. It was divided into four occupying zones.
18 Russia closed the road, rail and river approaches from the western zones so that the western zones of Berlin could not be supplied in the normal way.
19 NATO.
20 France and Britain (the Dunkirk powers), the Benelux Countries (Belgium, Holland and Luxemburg), Norway, Iceland, Denmark, Italy, Portugal, Canada and the USA. Greece and Turkey joined in 1952, West Germany joined in 1955. France has since left NATO.
21 The Warsaw Pact.   **22** The building of the Berlin Wall.

Unit 29 Answers:
1(C); 2(D); 3(B); 4(A); 5(A); 6(B).

Unit 30 Answers:

1 Austria	**6** Hungary; 1956	**12** The USA
2 Czechoslovakia; 1948	**7** Romania; 1963	**13** Cominform
3 Dubček	**8** Yugoslavia; Tito	**14** Yugoslavia
4 Poland; Gomulka	**9** Albania	**15** 1956
5 Russia	**10** *i* Greece	**16** Comecon
	ii Turkey	
	11 Great Britain	

17 *i* Archbishop Beran; *ii* Cardinal Wyszynski; *iii* Cardinal Mindszenty
18 State C; Poland   **19** 1950

Unit 31 Answers:

1 1, France; 2, Belgium; 3, Holland; 4, Luxemburg; 5, West Germany; 6, Italy.
2 EFTA; the European Free Trade Area.
3 C, Switzerland; D, Austria; B, Portugal; F, Norway; G, Sweden.
4 Harold Macmillan
5 President de Gaulle
6 Konrad Adenauer   **7** Dr. Erhardt
8 2, Belgium; 3. Netherland (or Holland); 4, Luxemburg.
9 1973. Edward Heath.
10 Britain had a referendum concerning membership. Harold Wilson.

Unit 32 Answers:
1(C); 2(E); 3(B); 4(D); 5(E); 6(C); 7(A); 8(C); 9(B); 10(D); 11(B).

Unit 33 Answers:

1 Korea.   **2** 1950   **3** Taiwan   **4** Chiang Kai-shek   **5** The Seventh Fleet   **6** The USA supported China'a admission into the UN in place of Chiang Kai-shek's 'China'
7 Sinkiang   **8** Russia   **9** Malaysia (or Malaya only, in 1950)
10 Britain
11 China supported the rising by the Malayan Communist Party
12 *i* Y = Macao; *ii* Z = Hong Kong and Kowloon
13 Portugal (in Macao) and Britain (in Hong Kong)
14 Hong Kong provides China with access to western markets, technology and capital.

15 The 'New Territories' of Kowloon were ceded to Britain by China in 1898 under a lease of 99 years. In 1998 these areas revert to China. Without them (and their water supplies) Hong Kong would become almost uninhabitable.

Unit 34 Answers:

1 Kashmir   **2** Nehru was born of Kashmiri Brahmin stock.
3 *i* The UN: *ii* Prime Minister Kosygin of Russia.
4 Tashkent   **5** Hyderabad   **6** 1948   **7** Tibet
8 The Dalai Llama   **9** 1959
10 Tibet became a self-governing region of China.
11 Goa   **12** Portugal   **13** Areas J and K   **14** *i* Jinnah; *ii* Liaquat Ali Khan.   **15** Area K   **16** 1971
17 *i* L = Russia; *ii* M = Karachi; *iii* N = Delhi
18 *i* Hinduism; *ii* Islam or Mohammedanism   **19** Gandhi
20 *i* Pandit Nehru *ii* Mrs Indira Gandhi *iii* 1977

Unit 35 Answers:

1 *i* North Vietnam; *ii* South Vietnam
2 The 17th parallel of latitude

3 1954	**8** *i* Hanoi; *ii* Saigon
4 *i* Laos; *ii* Cambodia	**9** The Mekong Delta
5 Geneva, 1954	**10** Rice
6 France	**11** Tonkin
7 Dien Bien Phu	

12 Torpedo boats attacked a US warship
13 Lyndon Johnson   **14** The Ho Chi Minh Trail
15 The North Vietnamese sent aid and supplies to the Viet Cong in South Vietnam
16 The US ordered the bombing of that route which passed through neutral countries.
17 The Tet Offensive   **18** 1973   **19** *i* Nixon; *ii* Henry Kissinger

Unit 36 Answers:

1 *i* Zaire; *ii* Belgium; *iii* 1960.
2 *i* Katanga; *ii* Tshombe.
3 *i* Kenya; *ii* 1963; *iii* Kenyatta;
4 *i* South West Africa; *ii* Namibia.
5 *i* 1961; *ii* its policy of apartheid.
6 *i* Ghana; *ii* 1957; *iii* Nkrumah.
7 A-Liberia; B-Abyssinia.
8 *i* D-Angola; E-Mozambique. *ii* 1975.
9 *i* Uganda; *ii* Milton Obote.
10 J-Northern Rhodesia, now Zambia: K-Southern Rhodesia, now Zimbabwe; L-Nyasaland, now Malawi.
11 *i* K-Southern Rhodesia; *ii* 1965.
12 N-then Tanganyika now (enlarged) Tanzania.
13 *i* C-Nigeria; *ii* N-Tanzania; *iii* J-Zambia; *iv* K-Zimbabwe; *v* F-Zaire.
14 *i* H-Kenya; *ii* C-Nigeria.

Unit 37 Answers:

1 *1*(M); 2(N); 3(O); 4(E); 5(H); 6(R); 7(L); 8(K); 9(A); 10(S);
2 *i* Ben Gurion; *ii* Golda Meir; *iii* France; *iv* Eden; *v* Sadat; *vi* Begin.   **3** (A)   **4** (B)

Unit 38 Answers:

1 *i* The Palestine Liberation Organization
    ii The Irish Republican Army
    iii The United Nations Relief and Rehabilitation Administration
    iv The Food and Agricultural Organization
    v The South West African People's Organization
    vi The International Monetary Fund
2 *i* Tanganyika and Zanzibar
    ii Julius Nyerere
    iii £19.6, the average income per head
    iv 35 and 40, the average life expectation
    v £123 million
    vi (A) £6.15 million; (B) £12.30 million; (C) £18.45 million.
    vii They rose as a result of the effects of the increase in oil prices on the economies of industrialised countries.
    viii She hoped to earn more from exports than she spent on imports.

ix (A) spending went up – to pay for oil and because of the increased prices of essential manufactured goods; (B) export prices either fell, or rose more slowly, than did import prices, because of the fall in demand for Tanzania's products.

x Someone from outside the country; in this context it probably means 'white', 'English' or, perhaps, 'European'.

3 *i* The Organization of Petroleum Exporting Countries
   ii 1960
   iii (A) Nigeria, Libya, Algeria; (B) Venezuela, Mexico; (C) Saudi Arabia, Kuwait, Bahrein, Iraq
   iv The major oil companies which once controlled the industry
   v Mossadeq; *vi* Britain; *vii* The Yom Kippur War
   viii The USA
   ix They had to spend more on oil than they had done before.
   x They cut their imports of non-oil products and so cut the level of each others exports.

4 (E)   5 (E)   6 (A)   7 (C)   8 (C)   9 (B)

Part IV
An analysis of question style and examination hints

1 What are the examiners looking for?

1 The aims of the study of History

Most Examination Boards explain, in their syllabuses, what aims have been set for history students. These may be summarized as follows:

1 to assist candidates in their understanding of themselves and their place in the world;
2 to develop sound critical judgement on human affairs;
3 to stimulate a lasting interest in History and provide an introduction for the further study of the subject;
4 to allow candidates to study a topic in depth which will provide an introduction to methods of research (for some Boards only).

2 The objectives of the examination

The examination is intended to test the candidate's ability to:
1 recall relevant facts;
2 read evidence and draw conclusions from it;
3 extract relevant material from more than one source;
4 appreciate the views held by people in other places and at other times;
5 understand historical extracts, maps and diagrams;
6 select and arrange relevant information and to give it appropriate expression logically, clearly and imaginatively;
7 appreciate relationships between cause and effect.

3 Examiners are not out to trick you

Each examination paper is set by a team of examiners who want to give candidates a fair chance to show their ability. This can only be done by asking straightforward questions. An analysis of the questions should help you to understand the variety of questions which may be asked and how they should be answered. It is not the fault of examiners if candidates do not always understand the question or fail to answer the question which has been asked.

4 Marking the paper

1 Examiners give marks for correct information given. You can make it easier for them to do this if you set out your work neatly. Essay-type answers should be written in organized paragraphs which will help examiners to see more easily the points you are making – and which deserve marks.
2 Examiners do not take marks away for mistakes. They will simply ignore them. Wrong answers and mistakes do, however, reduce your chance of getting full marks while they will also have taken part of your scarce time.
3 Each answer is marked on its own merit. If you give a completely wrong answer for a whole question the examiner will still give you the marks you deserve for the rest of the paper.

5 Examining the examiners

Some people think that the marks you are given depends on which examiner marks your paper. This is not so because various steps are taken to make sure that marking by different examiners is standardized.

1 Before marking begins, meetings are held to agree a common marking policy. This is made easier by some Boards which allocate marks for particular parts of questions and show this on the papers. But even Boards which do not make the allocation so publicly, insist that their examiners leave their meetings with a clear idea of how to distribute marks for various parts of questions.
2 Each examiner has to send in samples of his marking at regular intervals during the marking. This allows his supervisor

to check that he is following the agreed allocation of marks. The supervisor sees papers marked by a number of examiners so that he can compare one with another. This enables him to tell one examiner that he is marking too easily or another that he is being too strict. In this way there is a common standard among examiners.

3 The introduction of fixed-response questions including multiple-choice questions, has made standardization easier. So, too, has the use of computers which enable Chief Examiners to check on the work of supervisors and examiners.

2 Fixed-response questions

There is an increasing use of such questions because they are easy to mark and because they demand a wide spread of knowledge from candidates. Even if your Board does not use such questions, you will find that you would benefit from answering the examples set here and in Part V, Sections 1.1-3; this would make good revision.

These questions appear easy to answer, particularly where, as will be seen, possible answers are given. In fact this is far from the case. The questions have been specially designed by teams of experts and they have been tested in schools before being used in the examination. You will find that many Boards set a limited time in which these questions have to be answered, which puts additional pressure on the candidates. There are different types of fixed-response questions. Your teacher will tell you which sort your Board uses. They are:

1 Multiple-Choice Questions

In such questions an incomplete statement or question (**the stem**) is given together with five, or sometimes four, possible answers (or **responses**). You have to choose the one response that correctly fits the stem. The wrong answers are called **distractors**. Examples of these questions can be found in Self-Test Units 1-4, 8, 11, 14, 18, 21-2, 24-6. A wider selection appears in Part V.1.1.

Multiple choice questions may be used to test:

1 simple recall or fact, e.g.:
The USSR's membership of the League of Nations lasted from
(a) 1920 until 1939   (d) 1934 until 1939
(b) 1926 until 1933   (e) 1938 until 1945
(c) 1929 until 1945
The correct answer is (d) (Unit 14.6.8).

2 relationships, e.g.:
Disarmament and economic sanctions were, respectively, the issues leading to the withdrawal from the League of Nations of
(a) Germany and Italy   (d) Russia and Germany
(b) Japan and Germany   (e) Germany and Russia
(c) Italy and Japan
In this question candidates are asked to show that they understand the two different reasons for the withdrawal from the League of two countries. The correct answer is (a) (Units 14, 20, 21 and 23).

3 understanding, e.g.:
The immediate aim is the formation of the proletariat into a class, the overthrow of the bourgeois supremacy and the conquest of political power. What political ideology may best be said to have this aim?
(a) anarchism   (d) marxism
(b) capitalism   (e) populism
(c) fascism
The correct answer is (d).

4 recall, understanding and relationships, e.g.:
Austrian Germans could have claimed in the 1920s that they were not given the right to self-determination, as they were
(a) forbidden to join the League of Nations
(b) denied any access to the Adriatic Sea
(c) forbidden to trade with their neighbours
(d) denied any control over Hungarian affairs.
(e) forbidden to unit with the Weimar Republic.

The correct answer is (e). Some candidates may see this as a simple **recall** because they have learned it as a fact. But even the learning of that fact was itself an exercise in understanding the meaning of **self-determination** and of the terms of the Treaties drawn up after the First World War.

5 more complex relationships, e.g.:
In the period 1946–49 Mao Tse-tung was able to force the Nationalists from the Chinese mainland because he
 i won control of the countryside
 ii was supplied with weapons by America
 iii used effective guerilla tactics
 iv used propaganda to good purpose
 v promised land to all the peasants.
(a) *i   ii*   (d) *i   iii   v*
(b) *iii   iv   v*   (e) *i   iii   iv   v*
(c) *ii   iii   iv*

You will see that the examiners (WYLREB, 1981, CSE Level) have given most of the reasons for the Communist victory in China. The points they have given could well be used as guide-lines for a traditional essay-type question (Section IV.4.9). You can get part way towards the answer by noting that the Americans did not help Mao Tse-tung; this allows you to eliminate *ii* and so to eliminate Options (a) and (c). You ought to know that Mao won the countryside–*i*, which does not appear in Option (b). You should also know that propaganda against Chiang was always an important 'weapon' for Mao–*iv*. Since *iv* does not appear in Option (d) you are then left, by elimination, with Option (e) as the correct answer. Many of you will have got that answer without the elimination steps.

Example 5 is taken from a paper set by the WY and LREB which asks candidates to answer 60 such questions in 75 minutes, a reminder of the pressure on candidates taking papers containing such questions. Examples 1-4 are taken from papers set by London at O Level where candidates have to answer 60 questions in one hour. When tackling such papers you should not waste time on a question which you find difficult to answer; go on with the other questions and hope that you will have time to to come back to attempt the questions you have left unanswered.

2 Sentence completion with responses and distractors
This is a form of multiple-choice question used by some CSE Boards, e.g.:
Read the following passage. Choose the words from part ii which follow the passage and write in the missing parts of the passage.
i In a famous speech, _____ spoke of an _____ having divided Europe from the Arctic to the Mediterranean Sea. To the east of it Russia organized countries like _____ into a military alliance called the _____, in answer to the Western Alliance's _____. Short of outright war, the two super-powers had opposed each other in _____. There the _____ blocked land communications. The _____ saved it from starvation and unemployment by organizing an _____. This was part of the _____.

ii		
Spain	Americans	North Atlantic
Fortified Wall	Smuggling	Treaty Organization
Churchill	Poland	Berlin
Roosevelt	Airlift	Russians
Moscow	Iron Curtain	Cold War
Warsaw Pact	Russo-German	China
Treaty of	Pact	Germans
Dunkirk	'Phoney War'	

(See Unit 28)   (*EMREB, 1980, CSE Level*)
You will find other examples of this type of question in Section V.1.3.

3 Linking People, Places and Events, e.g.:
Against each of TEN of the people listed below, the the appropriate letter as indicated in the following key. The first one is done for you; do not include this in your ten.
(A) President of Ghana 1957
(B) Leader of the Free French who later became President of France
(C) An American Civil Rights leader who was assassinated in 1968
(D) The President of Uganda.
(E) German foreign minister in the 1920s
(F) Secretary General of the United Nations
(G) Emperor of Japan in 1945
(H) French general who became commander-in-chief of the allied armies in 1917

(I) President of Czechoslovakia in 1938
(J) French representative at Versailles in 1919
(K) British Prime Minister during World War Two
(L) President of Germany in 1932
(M) The Biafran leader in 1967
(N) The founder of Czechoslovakia in 1919
(O) Became the President of the USA after Watergate
(P) The Chinese leader overthrown by Communists in 1949

1 Idi Amin	**(D)**	9 Hirohito _____	
2 Churchill _____		10 Clémenceau _____	
3 Gerald Ford _____		11 Chiang Kai-shek _____	
4 Hindenburg _____		12 Martin Luther	
5 Colonel Ojukwu _____		King _____	
6 General de Gaulle _____		13 Beneš _____	
7 Stresemann _____		14 Foch _____	
8 Kwame Nkrumah _____		15 Kurt Waldheim _____	
		16 Thomas Masaryk _____	

(*ALSEB, 1978, CSE Level*)

You will see that such questions allow examiners to cover a great deal of historical material in a seemingly simple question. Candidates who have studied the material in the units in Part II should have little difficulty with such questions. There are examples of this type of question in Part V.1.4. Even if your Board does not use this type of question you will still find it a useful revision-exercise to tackle them.

3 Free-response questions

These are called *free-response* because the examiners do not provide you with possible answers. You have to provide the answers without any guidance. There are many kinds of such questions.

1 Questions requiring a short answer often of only one or two words e.g.:
i Who was the Tsar of Russia from 1894 to 1917? (Unit 3)
ii Of which Caribbean island was Batista dictator from 1933 to 1958? (Unit 32)
iii Who was the first Prime Minister of Ghana? (Unit 36)
These are three of 40 similar questions in Section 1 of a paper set by the SEREB for CSE candidates in 1981. Candidates had to answer 20 such questions in 'about ten minutes'. Many CSE Boards set this type of question. Together with a friend you could devise your own list of such simple questions for mutual testing. Take only ONE question from each of the sections of the syllabus so that you have 40 or so questions on a list.

2 Short answer questions on one theme e.g.:
Name FOUR of the following: (See Unit 15)
i The President of Germany 1925–1934
ii The German industrial area occupied by French troops in 1923
iii The leader of a revolt against the German Republic
iv The German Foreign Minister from 1923 to 1929
v The American plan to aid Germany in 1924
vi The new German unit of currency set up in 1924
     (*Part of a question set by EMREB, 1980, CSE Level.*)
You could, with the help of a friend, construct similar tests on any of the topics in Part II. These would be useful revision exercises.

3 Sentence completion e.g.:
i _____ was the ruler of Spain between 1939 and 1975. (Unit 24)
ii In 1939 the Russian armies invaded _____. (Unit 18)
iii In 1961 Berlin was divided by a _____ built by the Russians.
(Units 28 & 30)
     (*Part of a question set by WJEC, 1982, CSE Level.*)
You will see that this is another form of the one word answers as explained in IV.3.1.

4 Questions examining relationships e.g.:
Choose FIVE of the following and next to each one chosen write the name of the political party with which each is most commonly associated. Choose your answers from the list of parties given below. You can use any one answer more than once if you wish.

Democrat;	*Republican;*	*National Socialist;*
Christian Democrat;	*Communist;*	*Conservative;*
Liberal;	*Kuo Min Tang;*	

(a) T. Roosevelt _____
(b) B. Disraeli _____
(c) Sun Yat-sen _____
(d) H. Hoover _____
(e) H. Goering _____
(f) Chou En-lai _____
(g) K. Adenauer _____
(h) E. Heath _____
(i) J. Carter _____
                    (*ALSEB, 1980, CSE level.*)
This type of question has become popular with examiners in recent years. As with the questions in IV 2.2.3 these questions allow examiners to cover a great deal of material in a single question. They also allow examination of candidates' knowledge of historical terms as well as their relationship to people and/or events.

5 Short notes on unrelated topics e.g.:
This is a popular form of question among both O-Level and CSE Level examiners, e.g.:
1 *Write on any four of the following:*
(a) Boulanger; **(b)** Keir Hardie; **(c)** Kerensky;
(d) Ludendorff; **(e)** Kemal Ataturk; **(f)** Mahatma Gandhi;
(g) Tito; **(h)** Charles de Gaulle; **(j)** Fidel Castro.

2 *Write short paragraphs (5-6 lines) on four of the following to show that you understand their meanings and historical importance.*
(a) Treaty of Frankfurt 1871; **(b)** Franco/Russian Alliance 1894; **(c)** Treaty of Shimonoseki 1895; **(d)** Russo-Japanese War 1904–05; **(e)** Ku Klux Klan; **(f)** Washington Conference 1921–22; **(g)** The Long March 1934; **(h)** The Phoney War 1939–40   (*ALSEB, 1980, CSE Level.*)

Answer to such questions should:
1 be continuous prose–in spite of the reference to notes in some of the questions;
2 provide the examiner with enough material to give you the maximum mark available. To achieve this you should make sure you have:
   i put the person, place or event in its historical context;
   ii explained what the person did, what happened at the place concerned or what the Treaty said;
   iii explained the historical importance of the person, place or event.

Answers to such questions should avoid the two most common faults, which are:
1 making them too long. You do not have time to waste on providing more than is required for the marks awarded;
2 making them too brief. A one or two line answer will not provide the examiner with enough material.

6 Questions on commonly used terms e.g.:
Choose FIVE of the following terms, then
(a) *Explain what you understand by the term chosen.*
(b) *Give ONE example to show what you mean*
Make sure that you put the correct number next to your answer
i an ultimatum *ii* a convoy *iii* abdicate *iv* putsch *v* a satellite state *vi* inflation *vii* a Super Power *viii* a coup d'état *ix* universal suffrage *x* democracy
                    (*ALSEB, 1980, CSE Level.*)
Some Boards ask for the definition of **one** (e.g. self-determination; **and** follow it with a second part; e.g. *Explain the meaning of the term* **self-determination**. *Illustrate how this principle was put into effect by the terms of the peace treaties of 1919–20.* (*WJECm 1983, O Level.*) In Unit 39 of Part II you will find terms and abbreviations which have been used in O Level and CSE Level papers in the past six years.

7 Brief essays on TWO unrelated topics, e.g.:
Write short essays on TWO of the following, explaining their historical importance:
The war at sea, 1914–18; the Gallipoli campaign, 1915; the home front, 1914–18; Japan's invasion of Manchuria, 1931; the Spanish Civil War, 1936–39.
                    (*SEB Ord. Grade, 1981*)

These questions look like the short notes discussed in 5 above. Indeed the topics of these two-essay questions may well be used in the short notes questions. But you must appreciate that the examiners have allocated **ten marks** for each of these brief essays. You will have to provide them with enough relevant material if you wish to earn those marks. As in the short notes answers you should provide:

1 the historical context and
2 the historical importance of each case.

But unlike the answers to the short notes questions, you should develop your answer more fully.

8 Directed essays

These were first introduced by CSE Boards. They have become increasingly common in papers set by O-Level Boards. They vary in type to include:

1 people and a related theme e.g.:
*Examine the importance of **three** of the following in the history of the Indian sub-continent **since** 1947;* Jawahalal Nehru; Mrs Indira Gandhi; Morarji Desai; Ayub Khan; Ali Bhutto; Sheikh Mujibur Rahman. (Unit 34)
(*London 1982, O Level.*)
Outline the main features of the Arab–Israeli dispute. You may use the following headings as a guide.
(a) Palestine 1945–48; the creation of Israel.
(b) The First Arab-Israeli War 1948.
(c) The Suez Crisis 1956.
(d) The Six-Day War 1967.
(e) The Yom Kippur War 1973.
(*YREB, 1982, CSE Level.*)

2 a related theme, e.g.:
(a) *Explain how each of the following helped Hitler and the Nazi party to win support between 1918 and 1933:*
 i the Treaty of Versailles 1919;
 ii the Great Inflation 1923;
 iii the depression of 1929;
(b) *Explain how Hitler came to establish a dictatorship after the elections of March 1933.* (Unit 15)
(*SEB, 1981, Ord. Grade.*)
Write an account of the Spanish Civil War, 1936–39. You should include in your answer:
(a) Problems which existed for many years before 1936;
(b) The events which started the war;
(c) Foreign attitudes and intervention in the war;
(d) Who was successful and why;
(e) Results of the war for Europe. (Unit 24)
(*ALSEB, 1982, CSE Level.*)

3 the work of an individual, e.g.:
What were Hitler's aims in foreign policy? Explain how he tried to achieve these aims between 1933 and 1939 by referring to his policies towards: the Saar; the Rhineland; Austria; Czechoslovakia; Poland and Russia. (Units 20 and 23)
(*ALSEB, 1980, CLSE Level.*)

9 The traditional long essay

This type of question is still common in O-Level papers and in a small number of CSE papers. They are the most difficult questions to answer because, often unaided by sub-divisions or headings, the candidate has to decide:

1 the content;
2 the depth of treatment;
3 the length required.

Before beginning to answer such questions, you should:

1 Jot down the **key words** relating to each answer. Do not, immediately, worry about the order in which you jot things down. It is most important to get down words which will provide you with paragraph headings (as are provided in guided-essay questions).

2 Do this **for each question** which requires this kind of planning. You will often find that as you are jotting down something about your second or third question it will remind you of something you should have put down in the plan for your first question. If, having made the plan for the first answer, you had then written that answer, you would only have realized that you wanted to say something more **after** you had planned your second or third answer. Examiners do not like it

when candidates put in asterisks with requests to 'Please turn to the end of the paper for further information on this question'. This shows that you have not thought your work out carefully. You can avoid that mistake by **planning all your answers** before beginning to write any out in full.

3 Go back over your jumble of headings and **put them into order**. Read the question again to make sure that you are covering all the points mentioned in the question and that you are not going to commit either or **two common faults**. These are:
i To leave out something which is obviously asked for. Examiners are always being surprised by candidates who have failed to see that in the question they are asked for **(a)**, **(b)** and **(c)** but who ended up by only answering **(a)** and **(b)**.
ii To answer a **question which was not asked** so that you waste time writing irrelevant material. This happens when candidates do not notice such things as:
(a) the **dates** in a question. A question asks: 'Why did Hitler come to power in 1933?' does not need an answer including accounts of his domestic and foreign policies **after** 1933.
(b) the **subdivisions** in a guided-essay question.
(c) the **wording**. '*An account of . . . .*' is a very different question from '*Account for . . . .*'

4 All this should take you about 15 to 20 minutes. Some Boards provide reading time before the start of an examination. But even if your Board is not this generous, do not think that the 15 to 20 minutes has been wasted. By planning your answers you will be better able to tackle the task of writing them. However, do not spend more than 20 minutes in planning. Examiners sometimes see scripts and answer books where the plans are as long as the answers and where some answers have not even been completed because too much time was spent on planning.

An example of planning an answer

Describe and account for the main changes in Japan since 1945.
(*WJEC, 1983 O Level.*)
The key words ought to occur to you if you have studied Unit 35 in Part II. These are (not in any order):

Introduction: the pre-war industrial development, linked with aggressive militarism, lack of democracy and warlike foreign policy.

Main changes

1 democratic constitution (and end of 'divinity' of Emperor); popularly elected parliament; encouragement of political parties and trade unions. Mainly due to MacArthur's determination to change things and Japanese acceptance of their defeat.

2 land reform giving land to 4 million peasants: creates stability.

3 conservative governments; left-wing weak; radical protests sometimes end in riots, e.g. against US influence in 1960s.

4 economic expansion–Japan now third greatest trading power; dominates many industries. **Due to** initial US spending during occupation and after 1950, to make Japan a bulwark against Mao; Japanese wish to regain prestige after defeat, will to work, to accept new technology; low defence budget (money available for investment); industrial relations–people accept low wages in paternalistic firms where strikes are rare.

5 social changes–high standards but overcrowding and pollution in large towns; many traditions lost.

6 foreign relations; uneasy relations with Russian and China now being improved; the west hostile to Japanese trading success.

Conclusion: In search for new markets how will Japan get on with the pragmatic leaders in post-Mao China: How will Japan overcome its lack of oil? Will the western countries take action to halt the flow of Japanese imports? But an economic miracle has taken place within a democratically-run country.

Essays and the unit headings in Part II

One of the reasons for setting out the material in each unit in Part II is to help candidates learn the key words which they need to make the essay-plans. If you have studied the different units you ought to be able to make out plans for each essay in your examination paper.

4 Stimulus-based questions

Almost all Boards (both for O Level and for CSE Level) now set questions based on some sort of stimulus material. This may take one of a variety of forms as will be seen below. Some Boards may have a complete section of paper based on such material. Candidates taking the Alternative Syllabus of the SEB should note that their Paper 1 (worth 40%) consists entirely of this form of question as does Section B of their Paper 2 (worth 20%). Check with your teacher or the syllabus to see what types of material are used by your Board and how much of this material your particular Board uses in its examinations.

Stimulus questions are often divided into a number of sub-questions. The first few of these are usually simple and may require only a single word answer. The later questions may require extended answers. Some of the sub-questions will test mere factual recall while others may test understanding, judgement, evaluation, interpretation and ability to judge bias.

Examining Boards often show on the paper the mark-allocation for the sub-questions. You should use this as a guide to the length of the answers to the various sub-questions. In tackling these stimulus-based questions you should always:

1 take **time to study** the material carefully and in detail;

2 read the questions thoroughly and make sure that your answers are relevant. If the questions ask for **evidence** from the material provided, make sure that you offer this in your answer.

3 **mark your answers clearly**; e.g. a(i), b(iv) and so on;

4 for the sub-questions which require long answers ensure that your answers are relevant and that they are written in **continuous prose**.

1 Written extract (for other examples see Part V.3.1)

1 *Study these extracts from the Charter of the United Nations and then answer questions (a) to (d) which follow* (The maximum mark for each sub-question is indicated in brackets.)

> **Article 1**: The purposes of the United Nations are: To maintain international peace and security, and to that end to take effective collective measures for the prevention and removal of threats to the peace.
> To develop friendly relations among nations based on respect for the principle of equal rights and self-determinations of peoples.
> To achieve international co-operation in solving international problems of an economic, social, cultural or humanitarian character . . .
> **Article 7**: There are established as the principal organs of the United Nations: a General Assembly, a Security Council, an Economic and Social Council, a Trusteeship Council, an International Court of Justice and a Secretariat.

(a)

i State the function of each of the **principal organs** or the United Nations as mentioned in Article 7 and

ii show how the power exercised by the first two of these **principle organs** has changed during the years since the creation of the United Nations. *(6+2)*

(b)

i What is the meaning of the phrase **effective collective measures** as used in Article 1?

ii With reference to events in Korea, describe how such measures were used by the United Nations in fulfilment of the purposes outlined in the first paragraph of Article 1. *(1+3)*

(c)

i What is the meaning of the phrase **equal rights and self-determination of peoples** as used in Article 1?

ii With reference to events during the 1970s in *either* Middle East *or* Cyprus, show to what extent the United Nations has attempted to support this principle. *(1+)*

(d)

Examine the work of the United Nations to achieve its aims in **international co-operation**, as outlined in the third paragraph of Article 1. *(4)*

(Unit 27) *(London, 1982, O Level.)*

Guidance on answering

(a) there are six **principal organs** listed in Article 7. Marks will be awarded in *i* for a brief description of the function of each (i.e. 6 marks) and *ii* for a note on the increased power of the General Assembly (under the Uniting for peace resolution) as against the power of the Council where the permanent members may use their veto.

(b) Effective collective measures may take various forms. *i* **Economic measures** may be used – as against the illegal regime in Rhodesia after UDI. *ii* Military action may be used in the sending of **peace-keeping forces** as used in Cyprus, the Middle East and the Congo. *iii* The sending of **an Army** ordered to fight – as in Korea.

In answer to **(b)** *ii* you should note the absence of the Russian delegate from the Security Council when the USA proposed sending a UN army to drive back the invasion by North Korea.

A sentence on MacArthur's leadership and another on the course of the war would gain the 3 marks allocated.

(c) The phrase refers to the UN aim of helping people to achieve *i* a democractic form of government made up of *ii* people of their own nation. The UN has tried to achieve those aims:

i In the Middle East by **(a)** recognizing the independence of Israel in 1948; *ii* sending peace-keeping forces aimed at preventing the domination of the area by either Arab or Israeli forces; *iii* trying to end, in 1983, the occupation of Lebanon by Syrian forces in the north and Israeli forces in the south.

(d) This calls for a paragraph on the work of some of UN's agencies: **economic** (IMF and World Bank); **social** (UNESCO) and **humanitarian** (UNICEF and UNCTAAD proposals for aid to the third world).

If you have studied the relevant unit in Part II you should be able to answer these sub-questions.

2 *Read the following two extracts which describe events in Russia in 1917 and then answer the questions which follow.*

i In the days of the great struggle against the foreign enemies, who for nearly three years have tried to enslave our fatherland, the Lord God has been pleased to send down on Russia a new heavy burden. Internal popular disturbances threaten to have a disastrous effect on the future conduct of the war . . . in agreement with the **Imperial Duma**, we have thought it well to renounce the throne of the Russian Empire.

(Abdication of Czar Nicholas II in March 1917)

ii **The Provisional Government** is absolutely powerless. . . . The **Kornilov method** is the only way by which the bourgeoisie can control. But it is force which they lack. . . . **The Army is with us** . . . only by **the victory of proletarian dictatorship** can the revolution be achieved. . . . **The Soviets** are the most perfect representatives of the people. . . .

(Trotsky quoted in *Ten Days that shook the World*)

(a) Why had this 'great struggle against the foreign enemies' been such a failure for the Russians?

(b) What had been the causes of 'internal popular disturbances' not just at this time, but earlier in the reign of Nicholas II?

(c) Use the words in bold type to describe events in Russia from the abdication of the Czar to the November Revolution.

(d) Account for the eventual success of the Bolsheviks in 1917.

(Unit 10) *(EAEB, 1977, CSE Level.)*

Guidance on answering

(a) This requires an answer to the question: 'Why did Russia do badly in the First World War?' In the relevant unit in Part 2 you will find the answer, the key words to which are: the failure of industry to deliver enough munitions; the failure of the transport system to cope with domestic and wartime demands; the influence of the Tsarina and the weakness of the Tsar; the heavy losses at the front which, coupled with news of unrest at home led to mutiny and desertion.

(b) Again you will find the answer to this sub-question in the Unit 10 in Part II. The key words to the answer are: peasant unrest because of shortage of land and government control of grain supplies and prices; industrial unrest because of poor living and working conditions; political unrest because of the activities of the various political parties – the Cadets (and their demand for parliamentary government); the SRP (with their policy of terrorism), the SDLP (with its plans for a revolution); the **betrayal** of the 1905 Revolution by Nicholas II.

(c) The Imperial Duma was the Russian Parliament which assumed power when the Tsar abdicated. It set up:

The Provisional Government which under, first Prince Lvov and later Kerensky, wanted to continue the war. It proposed democratic elections for a Constituent Assembly and the postponing of consideration of Russia's real problems until the war has been won. It never took strong enough action against the Bolsheviks who under Lenin and Trotsky worked for its overthrow.

Kornilov was a leading general who planned to march on the capital, overthrow the Provisional Government and establish a new autocracy. The Provisional Government had to ask the Bolsheviks for help against this threat which showed the weakness of the Government and gave the Bolsheviks more credit than they deserved.

The army had become increasingly mutinous as had the navy. Lenin promised to bring peace and advised soldiers to seek 'Peace by your own legs'–i.e. to desert from the army.

The proletariat was the industrial working class: its **dictatorship** is the Bolshevik description of the government to be set up by the Bolsheviks.

The Soviets were councils of workers and other groups set up first during the 1905 Revolution and set up again in 1917. These were popularly elected–and came under Bolshevik control only after November 1917.

2 Questions based on a map

This is a common form of stimulus-based questions. In Self-Test Units 7, 12, 17, 23, 28, 30, 31, 33-5 you can see how Boards have used maps as the basis for short (often one word) answers. Boards also use maps as the basis for questions which resemble guided essays (see IV.3.8). In the example below you can see how a Board used a map as the basis for a variety of types of questions.

(a) *Examine the map of Russia, 1914–1921 and then name the following:*
  i Country A   *iv* City D   *vi* Railway F
  ii Town B   *v* River E   *vii* area G
  iii Battle C
(b) Why were the following important during this period
  i Kronstadt; *ii* Ekaterinburg; *iii* Brest-Litovsk?
(c) Describe the main events which took place in Petrograd in October 1917.
(d) Trace the course of the civil war and explain why the Bolsheviks were successful.

(Unit 10)   (*JMB, 1982, O Level.*)

3 Questions based on statistics or graphs.

Note that if you have a **clear ruler** you will be able to look along the lines more easily.

Study the graphs on the USA 1929–1941 (Fig. IV.3.1A) and then answer the questions below.

 1 Name the event of October 1929 which was the main cause of the depression in America.   (*1*)
 2 What was the total value of goods produced in the USA in 1933?   (*1*)
 3 Who became President of the USA in 1933?   (*1*)
 4 What percentage of America's 'working population' was unemployed when he came to power?
 5 Describe the policies used by this President to reduce unemployment and increase production.   (*10*)
 6 Use the graphs to explain how successful these policies were in solving the problems of unemployment and falling production. Which problem was solved more successfully? Why did you choose that one?   (*5*)
 7 Give ONE reason for the rapid increase in production after 1940.   (*1*)
(Unit 19)   (*ALSEB, 1980, CSE Level.*)

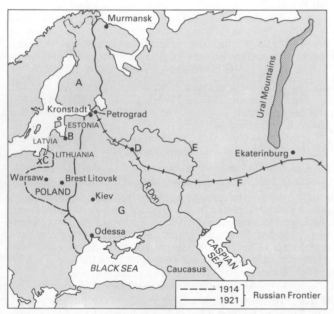

Fig. IV.2.1A   Russia, 1914–21

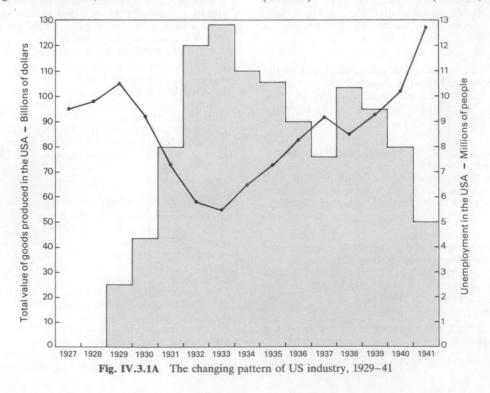

Fig. IV.3.1A   The changing pattern of US industry, 1929–41

Fig. IV.4.4.1A Bravo, Belgium!

4 Questions based on cartoons

Examiners often use cartoons as the stimulus for questions on foreign affairs, as you can see from the two examples given here and from the examples given in Part V.3.4. An analysis of the papers set by all the Boards shows that examiners from diffcrent Boards use the same cartoons. Some will use the cartoon as the basis for single-word answers. Others will use them as the basis for what is, really, a guided-essay question—as in the first example below.

 1 *Look at Fig. IV.4.4.1A and answer the question below.*
(a) Why is Belgium represented as a small boy? (2)
(b) What demand is Germany making on Belgium, and why?
(3)
(c) Explain fully how an assassination at Sarajevo set in motion a train of events which led directly to this demand.
(9)
(d) How did Great Britain react to Germany's demand, and why? (4)
(Unit 8)   (*EAEB, 1980, CSE Level.*)

Suggestions for the answer
(a) Belgium was a small country compared to Germany. The artist is making a propaganda point to rouse British sympathy for 'gallant little Belgium',
(b) In Units 8 and 9 in Part II you will have studied the Schlieffen Plan which required that German troops should pass through Belgium on their way to northern France and to the encirclement of Paris.
(c) The marks allocated to this sub-question indicate that the answer has to be fairly long—maybe three or four paragaphs. You will find the material on which to base your answer in Unit 8 of Part II. Briefly what you have to do is to show how Austria's demands on Serbia were supported by Germany; how and why Russia mobilized when Austria declared war on Serbia; why Germany, allied to Austria, declared war on Russia—and on France; why this led to the need to invade Belgium.
(d) Britain had not declared war as had the other major powers because she had no formal alliance requiring her to do so. But she was bound to oppose Germany's advance into Belgium for reasons explained in Unit 9 of Part II. These reasons included the 1839 Treaty by which the major powers has guaranteed the permanent neutrality of Belgium. Britain

entered the war because of what the German Chancellor dismissed as 'a scrap of paper'.
 2 The cartoon shown here (Fig IV.4.4.2a) was used by the Oxford O-Level examiners in 1981 and by the London O-Level examiners in 1982. It is interesting to compare the different questions set by different examiners (see Units 29 and 30).
Examine the Punch cartoon. Answer all the following questions: (*Oxford, 1981, O Level*)
 1 (a) Explain fully the significance of:
  i the empty stand labelled 'Yugoslavia'
  ii the reaction of the bear on the stand labelled 'Hungary'
(b) Suggest the most likely date of the cartoon.
 2 Identify the politician shown in the cartoon.
 3 (a) Name the military agreement which existed between the country which this politician led and most of the countries indicated in the cartoon.
(b) In what year had this agreement been made?
(c) Name **two** countries, not shown in the cartoon, which were included in this agreement.
 4 Apart from the language and the source, give **two** ways in which the cartoon can be identified as a pro-western view of this agreement.
 5 Apart from the military agreement, name **two** other institutions which existed during the period 1945–56 to promote unity amongst the communist states of Eastern Europe.
 6 **In not more than 300 words**, outline and explain the major developments in Eastern Europe between 1949 and 1956, **either** (a) from the point of view of the politician shown in the cartoon **or** (b) from the point of view of a pro-western commentator.
*Study the accompanying satirical cartoon of 1956 and then answer questions (a) to (f) below. (**The maximum mark for each sub-question is indicated in brackets.**)*
            (*London, 1982, O Level*)
(a) Which Soviet leader is depicted in this cartoon as being the **animal trainer**? (*1*)
(b) Explain the message that the scene in the cartoon is meant to convey. (*1*)
(c)
 i Why is the stool in the foreground of the cartoon shown as empty? (*2*)

Fig. IV.4.4.2A The animal trainer

ii Show how an important predecessor of 'the trainer' had attempted to deal with this particular 'animal'. *(4)*

(d)

i Which of the 'animals was giving the trainer the most serious trouble at the time the cartoon was published?

ii Describe his handling of this 'animal' during the crises of that year. *(1+4)*

(e)

i Which of the 'animals' was to give his 'trainer' the most trouble in 1968?

ii Describe this trainer's handling of the 'animal' during that year. *(1+4)*

Suggestions for the answers

You will see that some of the questions in the two papers are the same (e.g. Oxford 2 and London (a)). If you have studied Unit 30 in Part II you will also realize that Hungary is the answer to London **(d)** *i* and that the answer to London **(d)** *ii* will be similar to the answer to Oxford question 1 **(a)** *ii*. Notice that in London question (b) and Oxford question 4 you are asked to interpret the evidence before you.

Now for suggestions as to the answer–to Oxford questions.

1 (a)

i Tito had been expelled from the Cominterm by Stalin.

ii In 1956, the year of the cartoon, Hungary was in revolt against Russian control

2 Khrushchev is the animal trainer. It was his denunciation of his 'important predecessor' (London question **(c)** *ii*) Stalin which had sparked off general unrest in Eastern Europe.

3 (a) The Warsaw Pact **(b)** 1955 **(c)** Rumania and East Germany.

4 *i* It suggests that Khrushchev on behalf of Russia held down the states of Eastern Europe by force (the whip and uniform). Russia was depicted as an old-fashioned imperialist power.

ii The bars of the cage indicate another 'control', another way of showing that Iron Curtain of which Churchill had spoken. Note too the unrest of Poland and Hungary– indications of the 'animals' unwillingness to accept Russian domination.

5 *i* Cominform which was dissolved in 1956; *ii* Comecon.

6 On suggestions for answering this question see below Part IV.5.

5 Imaginative essays

This kind of essay is becoming increasingly popular with O-Level and CSE-Level examiners. Sometimes the question appears after another set of questions based on an extract–and the imaginative essay is linked with the subject in the extract. Sometimes as in the Oxford question which you have just read (Part IV.4.4.1 question 1) the imaginative essay question is based on a cartoon on which other questions have been set. But in many Boards the question stands without any preceding stimulus material, e.g.:

1 EITHER

A Imagine you were a War Correspondent at Gallipoli during the Dardenelles Campaign. As the Campaign nears its end, write a despatch for your newspaper which should include some or all of the following: the reasons for the Campaign, the attacks by the Navy and Army, the conditions of the men fighting, the reasons for the lack of success and what you think will be the results of failure. (Unit 9)

OR

B Choose TWO of the following and write them as though you were the person living at the time:

i a pre-war Suffragette defending her militant campaign;

ii an airman describing the part he played in the war (Unit 9)

iii a German's general's reaction to the Treaty of Versailles (Unit 12)   *(SEB Ord. Grade, Alt,. 1980.)*

2 Imagine that you are **EITHER** (a) Lenin arriving in Russia during April, 1918 and write a speech in which you explain to your followers why the present government must be overthrown;

OR (b) Kerensky during September and prepare a speech justifying your policies and explaining why the Bolsheviks should be resisted.

(Unit 10)   *(Oxford, 1980, O Level.)*

3 Imagine that you were a Jew living in Germany between the two World Wars. Explain the reasons for the Nazis rise to power and how Hitler's policies affected you. (Units 15 and 20)

4 Imagine that you are a journalist and have been asked to write about events under the following newspapers headlines. Choose TWO of them and write short accounts of the matters to which they refer.

(a) Blackshirts march on Rome

(b) American Stock-Market collapse

(c) Who set fire to the Reichstag?

(d) The Recovery of Turkey 1923–38

(e) Dunkirk–Victory or defeat?

(f) The Battle of Britain

(g) Hitler invades Russia

Hints and suggestions for answering these questions

1 Play the game By this the examiners mean that candidates have to play the part assigned to them by the question. If asked to write a letter, the answer should appear in the form of a letter with an address, date (making sure it is historically correct) and correct salutation (are your writing to an editor, a friend, a nobleman or servant?).

2 Be historically correct

i Use the **correct** dates for events.

ii Name the **right people** when writing your answer.

iii Name the **right materials** where relevant. There were no Spitfires in the First World War (question 1B above).

iv If writing for or to a newspaper, use the name of one suitable for the time–remembering that Rupert Murdoch only came to the newspaper scene in the very recent past.

3 Involve yourself personally in your account when this is possible. In question 1A and 1B you should really be the reporter (1A) or the suffragette, airman or general (1B). You should use such phrases as 'from where I stood . . .', 'from my point of view . . .'.

4 Use the question Sometimes, as in question 1A and as in the Oxford question 4.2.i above the examiners give you some guide lines. It is a good idea to make sure that you devote a paragraph to each of the points offered as guides and that you cover **every point**–and more if you are able.

5 The length of the answer The examiners point out that they expect long answers to these questions. You should treat them as a traditional essay or a directed-essay question. Plan your answer carefully (see IV.8.9) to make sure that you have enough material on which to base the answer. Notice that if there are **parts to the question** (as in question 1B and question 4) that the examiners expect the answers to each of the parts to be of roughly the same length. You should lose marks if, for example, you wrote a page on one part and only two or three lines on another.

6 Making a plan If you have studied the material in the various units in Part II you should have enough material on which to base an answer. Let us take question 2(a) as an example.

i How would Lenin have addressed his followers? 'Friends? Comrades? Fellow Russians?'

ii On what grounds would he have attacked the Provisional Government's failure to deal with the land problem (what was it?; who was interested in it?). How would Lenin deal with this problem?–'Land by your own hands', advocating attacks on landowners.

iii Insistence on continuing the war. Why did Kerensky and others want to do this? Should the workers fight 'the capitalists' war? How would Lenin deal with this?–'Peace by your own feet'–a call for desertion and mutiny.

iv Who had appointed the Provisional Government? Was it as 'democratic' as the workers' soviets? Lenin's cry 'All power to the soviets'.

v What would he call on his followers to do? Prepare for an attack on the Government? Get armed? Join Trotsky's Red Guards?

vi What names would he have used–of places, people and events?

Part V
Examination Questions

1 Fixed-response questions

1.1 Multiple Choice

Guidance on answering this type of question is given in Part IV.2.1 and examples of this type were given in Self-Test Units 1-4, 11, 14, 18, 21, 22, 24 and 26. In this section there are 50 questions, about the length of an examination paper which a Board would expect candidates to answer in **one hour**.

1 Which of the following methods did Bismarck use to try to deal with the growth of socialism in Germany?

1 He imposed a strict censorship of the socialist press.
2 He introduced measures such as sickness and old-age insurance.
3 He came to terms with the Catholic Centre party.
4 He won over the Social Democrats by appointing them as ministers.

(a) *1* only   (c) *2* and *4* only   (e) *2, 3* and *4* only
(b) *1* and *3* only   (d) *1, 2* and *3* only

2 One important reason for the failure of the Paris Commune was that it

(a) accepted the authority of the Bordeaux Assembly
(b) aroused republican opposition in the capital
(c) decided to continue the war against Germany
(d) lacked popular support in the provinces
(e) sought the disbandment of the National Guard

3 The chief reason which lay behind the early ending of the first Russian national Duma was the

(a) corruption and incompetence of Stolypin
(b) failure of the Bolsheviks to offer it genuine support
(c) humiliating outcome of the war with Japan
(d) refusal of the Tsar to grant it real power
(e) deposition and murder of Nicholas II

4 The outcome of the Second Balkan War produced feelings in Bulgaria and Serbia respectively of

(a) complacency and anxiety   (d) resentment and jubilation
(b) disappointment and frustration   (e) satisfaction and dismay
(c) elation and disillusion

5 The aim of British governments in trying to keep a firm hold on ALL FOUR of Cape Colony, Cyprus, Egypt and Zanzibar in the 1800s was to

(a) guard against the collapse of Turkey   (d) exploit mineral resources
(b) accommodate surplus population   (e) prevent French expansion in northern Africa
(c) protect the sea routes to India

6 The Treaty of Portsmouth was concluded in 1905 to end the

(a) Boer War   (d) Russo-Japanese War
(b) First Balkan War   (e) Second Balkan War
(c) Chinese-Japanese War

7 Which of the following is a statement of FACT rather than of opinion about the reasons for the outbreak of war in 1914?

(a) Austria issued an ultimatum to Serbia and rejected the Serbian reply
(b) Britain was bound by treaty commitments to the French
(c) France was confident that conflict would result in the recovery of Alsace-Lorraine
(d) Germany was determined to invade Belgium and occupy the Belgium ports
(e) Russia could on preserve her monarchy by winning a great national victory

8 Germany's main aim in 1914 in trying to implement the Schlieffen Plan, was to

(a) avoid the danger of a prolonged war on two fronts
(b) prevent the landing of a British army
(c) secure Italian support
(d) reach the line of the River Marne
(e) reduce the risk of enemy naval intervention

9 Which of the following statements about Lenin are true?

1 He contributed to the rift between the Bolsheviks and Mensheviks
2 He played a leading part in the revolution which caused the Tsar to abdicate
3 He established a system of one-party government in Russia
4 He refused to allow any form of private enterprise in his New Economic Policy
5 He undertook the ruthless collectivization of Russian agriculture.

(a) *1* and *3*;   (b) *1* and *4*;   (c) *2* and *3*   (d) *2* and *5*; (e) *4* and *5*

10 By the terms of the Paris peace settlement of 1919, the whole of the Rhineland region was to be

(a) incorporated into the French Republic   (d) permanently de-militarized
(b) permanently de-industrialized   (e) administered by the League of Nations
(c) granted independence

11 Iraq, Palestine, Syria and Transjordan have it in common that they were all

(a) controlled by France in 1914   (d) overrun by the Axis Forces in 1940
(b) mandated by the League in 1920   (e) dominated by Russia in 1945
(c) annexed by Kemal in 1922

12 The Weimar Republic has been called 'a perfect democracy'. Which of the following was NOT provided for in its constitution?

(a) voting by all adults   (c) proportional representation
(b) direct election to the Chancellorship   (d) direct election to the Presidency
(e) voting by secret ballot

13 During the 1920s American farmers were generally not very prosperous because

(a) cheap foreign produce was flooding into America
(b) few farmers could afford to use tractors for farming
(c) over-production had led to a fall in prices
(d) the American people were eating too much wheat and beef
(e) the government was buying up surplus production

14 On the 'Night of the Long Knives' (30th June 1934)

(a) Hitler attempted a 'putsch' at Munich
(b) the leaders of the SA (Brownshirts) were murdered
(c) the Reichstag was destroyed by fire
(d) there was a massive destruction of Jewish property

15 In the period 1946–49 Mao Tse-tung was able to force the nationalists from the Chinese mainland because he

i won control of the countryside
ii was supplied with weapons by America
iii used effective guerilla tactics
iv used propaganda to good purpose
v promised land to all the peasants

(a) *i* and *ii*; (b) *iii*, *iv* and *v*; (c) *ii*, *iii* and *iv*; (d) *i*, *iii* and *v*; (e) *i*, *iii*, *iv* and *v*

16 The League of Nations was handicapped from its very start by its association with the

(a) British Empire, which caused hostility among statesmen of the Dominions
(b) First World War, which caused hostility among those opposed to the War
(c) lesser powers, which caused hostility among the great powers
(d) Paris Peace Settlement, which caused hostility among those dissatisfied with the Peace
(e) United States, which caused hostility among the leaders of Europe

17 The New Deal in the United States was introduced by
(a) Calvin Coolidge: (b) Franklin D Roosevelt:
(c) Warren Harding: (d) Woodrow Wilson.

18 'It gave France a third unfriendly fascist power on its borders.' 'It' was
(a) Franco's victory in Spain
(b) The Anschluss
(c) The reoccupation of the Saar
(d) Belgium's entry into the Ruhr
(e) The March on Rome

19 French and Italian troops were withdrawn but the British Government ordered its troops to stand firm to prevent
(a) Franco invading Portugal   (b) Japan seizing Shanghai
(c) Hitler entering the Rhineland
(d) The Red Army taking Archangel
(e) Kemal crossing the Dardanelles

20 Fear of having a possible left-wing state for a neighbour prompted
(a) Britain to abandon the Washington Conference
(b) France to occupy the Ruhr
(c) Germany to remilitarize the Rhineland
(d) Italy to join the Stresa Front
(e) Portugal to ignore the Non-Intervention Agreement

21 In the 1930s Eritrea, Ethiopia and part of Somaliland were united as
(a) British East Africa
(b) the Casablanca Powers
(c) the East African Community
(d) the Monrovia Powers
(e) Italian East Africa

22 When the Germans invaded their country in 1941 the Russians
(a) appealed to the League of Nations
(b) asked Italy to help them
(c) retreated and destroyed everything of value
(d) surrendered
(e) used lightning attacks

23 The main purpose of BOTH the Casablanca and Teheran conferences held in 1943 was to
(a) agree the strategy for defeating Germany
(b) discuss the proposed frontiers of the post-war world
(c) draft the articles of the United Nations Charter
(d) examine the conflicting ideologies of the east-west Alliance
(e) organize the campaign for liberating China

24 The Allies were able to launch their D-Day landings in France only after they had
(a) broken the Siegfried Line
(b) won the Battle of the Ardennes
(c) secured control of Belgium
(d) won the Battle of the Atlantic
(e) defeated the French Resistance

25 A crisis in which the United Nations intervened was that in
(a) Vietnam   (c) Czechoslovakia   (e) Berlin
(b) Budapest (Hungary)   (d) Korea

26 The United Nations Organization is pledged by its Charter to 'wage war' on:
(a) the exploitation of resources
(b) capitalism and the profit motive
(c) colonialism in Africa
(d) poverty and want
(e) the spread of communism

Questions 27 to 29 are based on this conversation of 1949
Speaker 1 We might well have seen a new socialist and democratic Europe if your country had not intervened with troops and bribes.
Speaker 2 We had to intervene to prevent your country stamping out democratic freedom. As it is, you now control half the countries of Europe.
Speaker 1 But we have jut given way over Berlin. So unlike you, we are prepared to make concessions.

27 The countries of **Speaker 1** and **Speaker 2** were respectively
(a) the USA and Britain
(b) Britain and the USA
(c) the USSR and the USA
(d) Britain and the USSR
(e) the USSR and Britain

28 **Speaker 1's** mention of **Bribes** was a reference to
(a) Lease-Lend
(b) economic sanctions
(c) an International Monetary Fund
(d) war reparations
(e) Marshall Aid

29 **The Berlin concession referred to by Speaker 1** was the
(a) adoption of a uniform German currency
(b) building of an effective boundary wall
(c) freeing of prisoners from Spandau
(d) relaxation of transport restrictions
(e) unification of the four Allied zones

30 Under the rule of Nikita Khrushchev there was in Russia
(a) a decline in military spending
(b) a drop in the total output of heavy industry
(c) a fall in the standard of living of the Russian people
(d) an increased emphasis on producing consumer goods
(e) a reduction in contacts with the West

31 Since 1945 the Russians have had to use troops to crush freedom movements in
  i Bulgaria   *iii* East Germany   *v* Romania
  ii Czechoslovakia *iv* Hungary
(a) All   (c) *ii iv v*   (e) *i iii v*
(b) *i ii iii*   (d) *ii iii iv*

32 Beneš; Nagy; Dubček. These three were ALL important in eastern Europe after 1945 for their
(a) support for the arming of the Warsaw Pact
(b) opposition to the dominance of Russia
(c) support for the Roman Catholic Church
(d) opposition to the policies of Yugoslavia
(e) support for the establishment of the German Democratic Republic

33 In the period 1945–54 which country best proved, in its continued resistance to Russian domination, that 'Communists do not automatically shed their patriotism'?
(a) Bulgaria   (c) Yugoslavia   (e) Romania
(b) Czechoslovakia   (d) Poland

34 The Schuman Plan implemented in 1952 was primarily concerned with
(a) German reunification
(b) distribution of US aid
(c) coal and steel production
(d) membership of UNO
(e) nuclear disarmament

35 The retirement of de Gaulle in 1969 provided
(a) Algeria with the opportunity to achieve the aims of the FLN
(b) Britain with the opportunity to renew its membership application to the EEC
(c) France with the excuse to abandon its military obligations to NATO
(d) Italy with the opportunity to sever its association with EFTA
(e) West Germany with the excuse to improve relations with COMECON

36 **Dollar Imperialism** had been seen in operation in the twentieth century in the case of
(a) big US investments in Latin America
(b) repeated tariff reductions in USA
(c) continuing US exploitation of Alaskan gold mines
(d) successive current devaluations in the USA
(e) US participation in Western Europe

37 'In 1950 Communist Chinca took control of the government of a neighbouring state which earlier in the century has been a Chinese possession and which languished under an archaic governmental system"
Which state does this describe?
(a) Amur   (c) Hong Kong   (e) Tibet
(b) Formosa   (d) Mongolia

38 The 'Cultural Revolution' was designed to
(a) encourage more criticism of the writings of Chairman Mao
(b) foster closer relations with Russia
(c) improve trading contacts with the West
(d) revive the 'true' spirit of communism in the Chinese people
(e) strengthen the army's grip on the universities

39 In 1966 the Soviet Union invited the Prime Minister of India and the President of Pakistan to meet at Tashkent to discuss the

(a) continuing conflict over Kashmir
(b) future provisions of Russian aid
(c) status of Burma
(d) recent expulsion of Portuguese colonists
(e) deteriorating situation in Afghanistan

40 Japan's foreign policy in the 1950s 1960s and 1970s can best be described as one which
(a) avoided binding commitments
(b) favoured imperialist expansion
(c) provoked international tensions
(d) renounced economic competition
(e) sought communist alliances

41 The idea that the overthrow of any non-communist state in South East Asia would be the prelude to the successive overthrow of others and thus increase the power of international communism, was often referred to in the 1960s as
(a) the Domino theory   (c) gradualism   (e) the Kennedy doctrine
(b) defeatism   (d) revisionism

42 'Kasavubu first dismissed Lumumba and then dismissed Tshombe. He was himself deposed shortly afterwards. In the meantime, UN forces had intervened in the Country'. These events took place in
(a) the Congo   (c) Nigeria   (e) the Gambia
(b) Malawi   (d) Uganda

43 Rapid steps towards the independence of Mozambique and Angola in the mid-1970s were the immediate consequence of a
(a) constitutional proposal by Britain
(b) diplomatic intervention by China
(c) military withdrawal by South Africa
(d) political upheaval in Portugal
(e) terrorist campaign in Rhodesia

44 The Six-Day War, 1967 began when
(a) America withdrew its aid for the building of the Aswan Dam
(b) France invaded the Suez Canal zone
(c) Egypt crossed into the Sinai Desert
(d) Israel bombed Egyptian airfields
(e) Syria attacked the Golan Heights

45 Civil War and chaos existed in the Congo in 1960 because
(a) nobody had been trained to run the country after independence
(b) some of the people were Moslems, others Christians
(c) the Indian minority tried to seize power
(d) the white people were oppressing the coloured people
(e) there was a bad harvest and widespread famine

46 To what does the expression **The Third World** refer?
(a) Africa, Asia and Latin America
(b) The Arab states of the Middle East
(c) The British Commonwealth and Empire
(d) The USA and north America
(e) Russia, China and the Communist Powers

47 In Europe the most frequent causes of death in the 1970s were
(a) heart disease and cancer   (d) poliomyelitis and malaria
(b) heart disease and malaria   (e) poliomyelitis and cancer
(c) cancer and typhoid

48 The purpose of the International Monetary Fund is to promote
(a) industrial employment by making automation unnecessary
(b) merchant banking by providing easy credit
(c) nationalized industries by subsidizing unprofitable ventures
(d) relief work, by encouraging medical research
(e) world commerce, by making currency available

49 The Colombo Plan (1950) was a plan devised by Commonwealth foreign ministers to
(a) reconcile India and Pakistan in Kashmir
(b) develop the economy of south and south-east Asia
(c) establish free tade in the Indian sub-continent
(d) improve relations between America and China
(e) unite Sierra Leone and Uganda in a federation

50 During the Six-Day War (1967) Israel gained
i both banks of the Suez Canal   *iv* the Golan Heights
ii the whole of Jerusalem   *v* the West Bank of the Jordan
iii Sinai
(a) *i ii iii*   (d) *i iv v*
(b) *ii iii iv v*   (e) *i iii iv*
(c) *ii iii v*

Source of questions
SEREB, CSE Level–questions 6, 14 and 17
EMREB, CSE Level–questions 25 and 26
WY AND LREB, CSE Level–questions 1, 15, 22, 30, 31, 38, 44, 45 and 50
The remaining questions are from *London, O-Level papers 1981–83*

Answers to Multiple Choice Questions V.1.1

1 (d); 2 (d); 3 (d); 4 (b); 5 (c); 6 (d); 7 (a); 8 (a);
9 (a); 10 (d); 11 (b); 12 (b); 13 (c); 14 (b); 15 (e);
16 (d); 17 (b); 18 (a); 19 (e); 20 (e); 21 (e); 22 (c);
23 (a); 24 (d); 25 (d); 26 (d); 27 (c); 28 (e); 29 (d);
30 (d); 31 (d); 32 (b); 33 (c); 34 (c); 35 (b); 36 (a);
37 (e); 38 (d); 39 (a); 40 (a); 41 (a); 42 (a); 43 (d);
44 (d); 45 (a); 46 (a); 47 (a); 48 (e); 49 (b); 50 (b).

1.2 Questions requiring a single word, phrase or sentence as answer

1 Name the French aviator who flew the English Channel in 1909.
2 Name the port in Morocco to which a German gunboat was sent in 1911.
3 In which town was Archduke Ferdinand assassinated in 1914?
4 What was the name of the German military plan to defeat France before Russia could fully mobilize?
5 To control which Strait was the Gallipoli Campaign fought?
6 Name the British liner carrying American passengers sunk by a German submarine in February 1915.
7 In which city did the event known as 'Bloody Sunday' take place in 1905?
8 Give the name of the monk or 'holy man' who dominated the Russian Royal family until his murder in 1916.
9 Which Yugoslavian city did the Italian adventurer Gabriele D'Annuzio occupy in 1919?
10 In 1923 which part of Germany was occupied by French and Belgian troops?
11 Which 1925 treaty guaranteed Belgium's frontiers?
12 Which British statesman returned from Munich in 1938 claiming he had gained 'Peace in our Time'?
13 Name the Act under which the United States agreed to supply Britain with armament in 1941.
14 'Never in the field of human conflict was so much owed to so few.' To which battle in World War II did this refer?
15 What is the meaning of the phrase 'the final solution' to the Jewish question in Germany?
16 Which major world power was admitted to the United Nations in 1971?
17 Who was the Indian Nationalist leader assassinated in 1948?
18 Under which leader in 1956 did the Egyptian government nationalize the Suez Canal?
19 What was the name of the United State' plan to provide economic aid to Europe after World War II?
20 Where is 'Checkpoint Charlie'?

(*SWEB, 1973, CSE Level*)

1.2 Answers

1 Blériot; 2 Agadir; 3 Sarajevo; 4 the Schlieffen Plan;
5 the Dardanelles; 6 the *Lusitania*; 7 St Petersburg;
8 Rasputin; 9 Fiume; 10 the Ruhr; 11 Locarno;
12 Neville Chamberlain; 13 Lend-Lease; 14 the Battle of Britain;
15 the extermination of the Jewish race;
16 China; 17 Gandhi;
18 Nasser; 19 Marshall Plan (or Aid); 20 Berlin.

1.3 Sentence completion. (See also IV.2.2.)

Complete the account (below) by choosing the words to fill the blank spaces. You have been given a list of words from which you can make your choice.

Stalin, his real name was **1**_____, came from Goril in the Caucasian mountains. After the death of Lenin in 1924, he became increasingly powerful and forced his rival, **2**_____ ____ to leave Russian and seek refuge abroad. In Russia, Stalin adopted a range of policies in an effort to achieve **3**'_____'.

First, he planned to develop Russian industry rapidly in a number of stages called **4**_____. The first of these plans was started in **5**_____. Stalin also adopted a new policy for agriculture. By a programme of **6**_____, he brought all farmland under state-ownership. Some wealthy peasants, **7**_____, opposed the scheme.

Many were killed or sent to labour camps.

During the 1930s, the Russian dictator plotted to remove his rivals in a series of **8**_____. This was triggered off when **9**_____, one of Stalin's closest advisers, was assassinated. In a wave of terror, many old and trusted Bolsheviks were arrested and executed or allowed to suffer at the hands of the dreaded secret police, the **10**_____.

(a) Five Year Plans	(l) Grigori Zinoviev
(b) 1931	(m) New Deal
(c) plebiscites	(n) Trotsky
(d) collectivization	(o) kulaks
(e) Leonid Beria	(p) Serge Kirov
(f) Cominform	(q) NKVD
(g) purges	(r) Josef Djugashvili
(h) Vladimir Ulyanov	(s) 1928
(j) Gestapo	(t) Fascists
(k) 'Socialism in one Country'	(u) Siberia

(SREB, 1981, CSE Level)

1.3 Answers

1 (r); 2 (n); 3 (k); 4 (a); 5 (s); 6 (d);
7 (o); 8 (g); 9 (p); 10 (q);

1.4 (see also Part IV.2.3 and Self-Test units 1, 3 and 10)

Against each of the people listed below, put the appropriate letter as indicated in the following key. The first one is done for you.

(a) Used the title 'Il Duce'
(b) Prime Minister of Great Britain 1939
(c) British General in World War I
(d) The leader of Indian passive resistance movement
(e) Secretary of UN killed in an air crash in the Congo
(f) Founder of the Red Army
(g) The American president with the 'New Deal'
(h) Was forced by Russians to resign as leader of Czechoslovakian government
(i) The Russian post-World War II politician famous for his 'brinkmanship'
(j) The head of the Vichy Government 1940–45
(k) Japanese emperor at the time of World War II
(l) American president who resigned after Watergate
(m) Flew to England in 1940, from Germany to try and arrange British surrender
(n) Became Britain's Labour Prime Minister in 1945
(o) Was Hitler's Minister of Propaganda

1 Leon Trotsky	(f)	9 Alexander Dubček	_____
2 Rudolph Hess	_____	10 Nikita Khrushchev	_____
3 Hirohito	_____	11 Benito Mussolini	_____
4 Marshall Pétain	_____	12 Mahatma Ghandi	_____
5 Richard Nixon	_____	13 Douglas Haig	_____
6 Clement Attlee	_____	14 Franklin Roosevelt	_____
7 Neville Chamberlain	_____	15 Dag Hammsarskjöld	_____
8 Joseph Goebbels	_____		

(ALSEB, 1977, CSE Level)

1.4 Answers

1 (f); 2 (m); 3 (k); 4 (j); 5 (l); 6 (n); 7 (b) 8 (o);
9 (h); 10 (i); 11 (a); 12 (d); 13 (c); 14 (g); 15 (e).

2 Free-response questions

2.1 Typical questions O Level and Scottish Ordinary Grade

1 Describe Bismarck's relations with **(a)** the Catholic Church, **(b)** the Liberals, **(c)** the Socialists **and (d)** the minority races of the German Empire.   *(AEB, 1980, O Level.)*

2 Outline the events in France in the period 1870–75 which led to the establishment of the Third French Republic. Why was it a republican form of government that was established?   *(Cambridge, 1980, O Level.)*

3 Show how each of the following helped to create tension and instability in France between 1870 and 1906:
the Commune, 1871; the Constitution 1875; the Boulanger Affair; the Panama Scandal; the Dreyfus Affair.   *(JMB, 1980, O Level.)*

4 Why were there revolutions in Russian in 1905 and 1917?   *(JMB, 1979, O Level.)*

5 What attempts at reform were made by the Tsarist government in Russia between 1906 and 1914? Why did these reforms not satisfy the opponents of the Tsarist regime?   *(Cambridge, 1980, O Level.)*

6 **(a)** Explain why both Britain and Russia were interested in the decline of the Turkish Empire in the nineteenth century. **(b)** Describe the events in the Turkish Empire between 1875 and 1878 which led to the Congress of Berlin.

(c) Imagine you were a reporter covering the Congress of Berlin for your paper. Write a report describing Disraeli's achievements and indicate, from the agreements made at the Congress, whether you think Disraeli brought back 'Peace with Honour'.   *(SEB Trad., 1981, Ord. Grade.)*

7 Describe Austria's policy in the Balkans between 1878 and 1914. Why did she come into conflict with Serbia?   *(Cambridge, 1980, O Level.)*

8 Describe and explain the problems of China between 1911 and 1941.   *(AEB, 1977, O Level.)*

9 What did the Japanese gain and lose by warfare between 1895 and 1945?   *(JMB, 1979, O Level.)*

10 'Unsuccessful both at home and abroad.' How far do you agree with the verdict on Woodrow Wilson?   *(JMB, 1981, O Level.)*

11 Give an account of Bismarck's relations with other European powers between 1870 and his resignation in 1890.   *(AEB, 1980, O Level.)*

12 Explain the contribution of each of the following to the outbreak of the First World War:
(a) the system of alliances in Europe;
(b) naval and colonial rivalry;
(c) the crises of Algeciras and Agadir;
(d) Balkan tensions 1908–13;
(e) the Sarajevo assassination.   *(JMB, 1981, O Level.)*

13 Describe Germany's plans for winning the war before the end of 1914 and their results in practice between August and December 1914. Why did the plans not work?   *(Cambridge, 1981, O Level.)*

14 Give an account of TWO of the following:
(a) the terms of the Treaty of Brest-Litovsk; **(b)** the part played by Trotsky in the Civil War, 1918–21; **(c)** the struggle between Trotsky and Stalin to succeed Lenin.
In each of your choices show the effect upon the course of the Russian Revolution.   *(Cambridge, 1980, O Level)*

15 What were Lenin's aims after the October Revolution? How far has he achieved them by the time of his death?   *(JMB, 1980, O Level.)*

16 Why were there revolutions in Russia in 1917?   *(O & C, 1977, O Level.)*

17 Give an account of Russian relations with the rest of Europe from the Treaty of Brest-Litovsk (March 1918) to the Conference of Yalta (February 1945). How do you account for the greatly increased importance of Russia in European affairs by 1945?   *(London, 1979, O Level.)*

18 Describe Stalin's policies after 1928 for **(a)** industrialization, **(b)** agriculture, and **(c)** for dealing with political opposition. Why did he consider these policies essential for Soviet Russia?   *(Cambridge, 1981, O Level.)*

19 How were **(a)** Austria, **(b)** Hungary and **(c)** Turkey affected by the Peace Treaties after the First World War?   *(JMB, 1980, O Level.)*

20 List the terms of the Treaties which concluded the First World War. Give *four* criticisms of the terms.
(*AEB, 1981, O Level.*)

21 Describe the career and achievements of Kemal Ataturk.
(*AEB, 1980, O Level.*)

22 What led to the establishment of the League of Nations after World War I and how was it organized? Why did it have such limited success in the period 1919–39?
(*Cambridge, 1981, O Level.*)

23 What were the main difficulties experienced by the Weimar Republic in the period 1919–1931? Why was it unable to survive the events of 1932–33?
(*Cambridge, 1981, O Level.*)

24 Describe and account for the rise to power of the Nazi Party in Germany between 1919 and 1934.
(*Oxford, 1981, O Level.*)

25 (a) Explain how each of the following helped Hitler and the Nazi party to win support between 1918 and 1933:
 i the Treaty of Versailles 1919;
 ii the Great Inflation 1923;
 iii the depression of 1929;   12
(b) Explain how Hitler came to establish a dictatorship after the elections of March 1933.   8
(*SEB Trad., 1981, Ord. Grade.*)   20

26 What were the main economic and social developments of the 1929s in the USA? Account for the Wall Street Crash of 1929.
(*Cambridge, 1980, O Level.*)

27 What were the principal causes and affects of the Great Depression?
(*O & C, 1977, O Level.*)

28 Describe and explain the problems of China between 1911 and 1941.   (*AEB, 1977, O Level.*)

29 'Chiang Kai-shek's enemies were the warlords, the Japanese and the communists.' How effectively had Chiang Kai-shek dealt with each of these enemies by 1949?
(*London, 1980, O Level.*)

30 Describe **(a)** the reasons for, **(b)** the terms of and **(c)** the significance of EACH of the following:
 i the treaty of Rapallo 1922;   (6 marks)
 ii the Locarno Treaties 1925;   (7 marks)
 iii the Kellog-Briand Pact 1928.   (7 marks)
(*AEB, 1981, O Level.*)

31 What measures were introduced by President Franklin D Roosevelt to solve the economic problems of the USA? How successful were his policies?
(*Cambridge, 1981, & Oxford, 1980, O Level.*)

32 Describe Hitler's rule in Germany between 1933 and 1939.
(*AEB, 1977, O Level.*)

33 Why did Mussolini come to power in 1922? How successfully did he deal with Italy's domestic problems?
(*O & C, 1979, O Level.*)

34 What successes and what failures did Mussolini have in his foreign policies?   (*AEB, 1980, O Level.*)

35 Describe the main changes which took place in the relationships between Britain and her overseas territories between 1919 and 1939.   (*AEB, 1981, O Level.*)

36 Write an account of the career of Mahatma Gandhi. What was his contribution to the achievements of Indian independence?   (*Cambridge, 1980, O Level.*)

37 How and why did Italy's relations with Britain, France and Germany change between 1933 and 1940?
(*AEB, 1980, O Level.*)

38 Describe German foreign policy between 1935 and 1939 and account for its success.   (*JMB, 1980, O Level.*)

39 Outline the events which led to the Civil War in Spain. Why was General Franco victorious in this war?
(*Cambridge, 1980, O Level.*)

40 Describe and explain the German victories in the Second World War until late in 1942.   (*O & C, 1980, O Level.*)

41 Why did Germany lose the Second World War (1939–45)?
(*JMB, 1981, O Level.*)

42 Describe the organizations of the United Nations. What part did the United Nations play EITHER in Korea between 1947 and 1953 OR in Cyprus between 1964 and 1974.
(*AEB, 1978, O Level.*)

43 Describe the policies of the Western powers towards Germany in the period from the Yalta Conference, February 1945 to the establishment of the German Federal Republic, May 1945. Explain the hostility of the USSR towards these policies in this period.   (*Cambridge, 1980, O Level.*)

44 Explain what is meant by 'the cold war' and trace its development from the Potsdam Conference ot the end of 1955.
(*AEB, 1981, O Level.*)

45 Why did war break out in Korea in 1950? Describe the main events of the war and outline the results.
(*WJEC, 1983, O Level.*)

46 Describe the political career of ONE of the following: **(a)** de Gaulle; **(b)** Khrushchev; **(c)** Nixon.
(*JMB, 1980, O Level.*)

47 Describe the methods used by the Soviet Union to establish her influence over Eastern Europe in the years 1945–50. Why and in what countries, were attempts made after 1950 to reduce this?   (*Cambridge, 1981, O Level.*)

48 Describe the stages by which the countries of Western Europe have moved towards greater unity since 1945.
(*Oxford, 1980, O Level.*)

49 Explain the importance in the European Community of:
(a) the Commission;   **(b)** the European Court;
(c) the Common Agricultural Policy.
Why did successive British governments criticize the Common Agricultural Policy during the 1970s?
(*Cambridge, 1983, O Level.*)

50 Describe the political and economic recovery of West Germany between 1949 and 1963. Why was West Germany able to achieve such a rapid economic recovery?
(*Cambridge, 1983, O Level.*)

51 What have been the main internal problems of the USA since 1945?   (*JMB, 1980, O Level.*)

52 Describe the domestic and foreign policies of President Lyndon Johnson, 1976–78. (*Oxford, 1980, O Level.*) Similar questions, but on the policies of other Presidents, appear regularly.

53 What were Mao Tse-tung's achievements EITHER **(a)** before 1949 OR **(b)** from 1949 until his death?
(*JMB, 1981, O Level.*)

54 What were the main problems facing Pakistan between 1947 and 1970? Describe the events which led to the creation of Bangladesh.   (*WJEC, 1983, O Level.*)

55 Describe **(a)** the increasing involvement of the USA in the Vietnamese War under the Presidencies of Eisenhower, Kennedy, and Johnson;
(b) the closing stages of the Vietnamese struggle under Nixon.
(*AEB, 1979, O Level.*)

56 What were the main problems facing the emerging African nations? Choose any ONE nation which has achieved independence since 1957 and show how far it had succeeded in overcoming its problems by 1970.   (*AEB, 1980, O Level.*)

57 Either **(a)** How and why did independence in the Congo and Nigeria bring about civil war in these countries? What were the results of these struggles?
Or **(b)** Describe the importance of **three** of the following in the history of Africa since 1945; *i* Jomo Kenyatta; *ii* Dr. Nkrumah; *iii* Julius Nyerere; *iv* Ian Smith; *v* Dr. Verwoerd.
(*AEB, 1981, O Level.*)

58 Choose **four** of the following and write a paragraph on each, pointing out its importance in the history of the Middle East; **(a)** the Abadan Crisis 1951; **(b)** the Suez Crisis 1956; **(c)** the United Arab Republic 1958; **(d)** the Yemen Civil War 1962; **(e)** the 'Six Day War' 1967; **(f)** the 'Yom Kippur War' 1973.   (*AEB, 1981, O Level.*)

59 Why and how have relations between Jews and Arabs resulted in conflict since 1945?   (*JMB, 1981, O Level.*)

60 With references to the years since 1919, examine the development of **either** popular music **or** cinema, showing how the development which you choose illustrates the meaning of the term mass culture.   (*London, 1982, O Level.*)

61 Describe the main developments in passenger transport since the First World War. What benefits and problems have they created?   (*Oxford, 1980, O Level.*)

62 Trace the main stages in the development of space exploration.   (*Oxford, 1982, O Level.*)

63 What did you understand by the term **the third world**? By reference to precise examples, show how the development of countries of the third world since 1945 has been (**a**) hindered by foreign powers and (**b**) helped by foreign assistance.
(*London, 1982, O Level.*)

64 How have the size and distribution of the world's population changed since 1919? Explain the reasons for these changes.   (*Cambridge, 1983, O Level*)

65 Either What was the Brandt Report? Why is it important? **Or** Explain the increasing economic and political importance of oil in the last twenty years.   (*WJEC, 1983, O Level.*)

66 What is the meaning of détente? In what ways did it influence the relations of the world powers in the 1970s? What were the results?   (*WJEC, 1982, O Level.*)

67 Explain the importance of any three medical advances made throughout the world during the years since 1919. How do you account for the fact that, in spite of increased availability of medical aid, some parts of the world have still been afflicted by serious epidemics in recent years?
(*London, 1983, O Level.*)

68 Discuss the importance in this period of **two** of the following: Nationalist guerilla movements; the pollution of the environment; the nuclear arms race; food supplies in the Third World; the population explosion; rising oil prices.
(*O & C, 1982, O Level.*)

2.2 Typical Questions CSE level

1 Describe the rule of Bismarck after the unification of Germany.   (3 marks)
What policies did he follow in maintaining Germany's international position?   (8 marks)
What was his attitude in Germany towards
Socialism   (3 marks)
Catholics   (3 marks)
Social Reform?   (3 marks)
OR
What were the main threats to the Third Republic in France? Use the following the help you:
Revenge against Germany. Popularity of Monarachy or Dictatorship. The Church. Scandals and crisis in French politics. Political instability.
(*SREB, 1980, CSE Level.*)

2 Answer the following questions based on the background to the Russian Revolution of 1917.
(**a**) *i* Why was there so much discontent in Russia during the period 1900–1917.   (6)
ii What were the 'soviets'?   (2)
(**b**) *i* Describe the events that took place in January 1905 on Red (Bloody) Sunday in St. Petersburg.   (3)
ii What reforms did the Czar promise and how far were they carried out?   (6)
(**c**) How did Russia's performance in World War I seriously undermine the position of the Czar?   (3)
(*NWREB, 1979, CSE Level.*)

3 Read the following passage:
'After 1900, the reputation of Nicholas II's government suffered disastrously. The period saw the most terrible military and naval defeats, the court fell under the evil influence of Rasputin; conditions of life in Russia grew steadily worse. Russia was ripe for revolution by 1917. Lenin was in exile waiting for the right moment. Germans provided that moment.'
i Describe briefly the military and naval disasters referred to in the above passage.   (8)
ii Write a paragraph about Rasputin.   (3)
iii In what way had conditions of life in Russia grown worse since 1900?   (3)
iv Who was Lenin?   (3)
v What is meant by the last two sentences of the extract?   (3)
    (20)
(*WMEB, 1980, CSE Level.*)

4 *i* Write a brief paragraph about the Treaty of Berlin 1878, pointing out its importance.   (4)
ii Why was the Turkish Empire so weak in the period from 1870 to 1914?   (4)
iii Describe how the Balkan kingdom of Serbia gained from this weakness in this period.   (4)
iv What happened to the Balkan provinces of Bosnia and Herzegovina in 1908?   (2)
v Why were the Serbians very upset about this?   (2)
vi Why did these provinces become very important in 1914?   (4)
    (20)
(*WMEB, 1979, CSE Level.*)

5 (**a**) What is meants by 'the scramble for Africa'?   (1)
(**b**) Name TWO African territories gained by 1914 by each of the following European countries: *i* Great Britain; *ii* Germany; *iii* France; *iv* Portugal.   (8)
(**c**) What strategic and economic benefit could European countries gain by possessing areas of Africa?   (6)
(**d**) Describe what happened at Fashoda in 1898.   (5)
(*ALSEB, 1980, CSE Level.*)

6 *i* Explain why China was in such a weak and defenceless state in the first part of the 20th Century by writing short paragraphs about:
(**a**) Chinese backwardness in technical matters;   (2)
(**b**) Weak government and the War Lords;   (2)
(**c**) Overpopulation and poor farming methods;   (2)
(**d**) Western influence in keeping China divided;   (2)
    + (2)
ii Describe the main efforts made by the Chinese to free themselves of Western influence by writing short paragraphs about:
(**a**) The Boxer Rebellion;   (2)
(**b**) Dr. Sun Yat-Sen and the Kuo Min Tang;   (2)
(**c**) The Revolution of 1911;   (2)
(**d**) The Civil War 1916–1926.   (2)
    + (2)
    (20)
(*WMEB, 1978, CSE Level.*)

7 (**a**) What were the main features of the American System of Government in 1870?
You should include in your answer: the powers of the president, the Congress and the Supreme Court and how they were chosen.   (10)
(**b**) Explain the following problems which faced the United States and say how far they had been solved by 1914.
i the Southern States;
ii the opening of the West.   (10)
(*ALSEB, 1981, CSE Level*)

8 Choose FOUR of the following and for each one chosen:
(**a**) Describe what it was.
(**b**) Explain the part it played in starting the First World War.
i The Dual Alliance 1879; *ii* Alsace and Lorraine; *iii* the Berlin-Baghdad Railway; *iv* The Naval Arms Race; *v* The Bosnian Crisis 1908–1909; *vi* The Agadir Crisis 1911; *vii* The Balkan Wars 1912–1914; *viii* The invasion of Belgium 1914.
    (4×5)
(*ALSEB, 1980, CSE Level.*)

9 The assassination of the Archduke Francis Ferdinand at Sarajevo on June 28th 1914 led to the outbreak of the general European war.
(**a**) Why was the Archduke assassinated?   (5)
(**b**) Write an account of the assassination.   (5)
(**c**) Describe the events which followed from his assassination which led to most of the countries of Europe being involved in the fighting by August 4th 1914.   (10)
    (20)
(*ALSEB, 1979, CSE Level.*)

10 Use the following guide to describe the work of (**a**) the British army **and** (**b**) the British navy in the Great War 1914–1918.
i The Western Front; the first battle of Ypres; trench warfare; the battle of the Somme 1916; the battles of 1917; Germany's defeat in 1918.

ii the blockade of Germany; the defeat of the submarines; actions against the German fleet.

(*ALSEB, 1977, CSE Level.*)

11 Your answers to the following questions may be in single words, phrases or paragraphs.

(a) Why did Austria declare war on Serbia?

(b) Who invented the German plan to avoid war on two fronts?

(c) Briefly explain the basic features of this plan.

(d) Why did Britain declare war on Germany on August 4th 1914

(e) Describe the nature of the fighting on the Western Front after the failure of the plan.

(*EAEB, 1979, CSE Level.*)

12 This question refers to Russia between 1917 and 1939.

(a) *i* State TWO effects of the Civil War.

  ii Explain the New Economic Policy.

  iii What was a collective farm? (7)

(b) Describe

  i Trotsky's quarrel with Stalin.

  ii Russian industrial developments 1928–39.

(c) Explain

  i How Russia was helped by Germany in the 1920s.
  (5)

  ii Why Russia was hostile to Germany after 1933.
  (5)

(d) Give THREE ways in which Russia tried to protect herself against Germany between 1933 and 1939 by military means and agreements. (3)

(*ALSEB, 1977, CSE Level.*)

13 Assess Lenin's success in consolidating the Bolsheviks' seizure of power in the 'November Revolution' in Russia in the following aspects.

(a) The establishment of the Communist dictatorship.

(b) Peace with Germany.   (d) War Communism.

(c) The Civil War.   (e) The NEP

(*EAEB, 1978, CSE Level.*)

14 This question is about Russia under Stalin.

(a) Explain how Stalin was able to defeat Trotsky in the battle for leadership after Lenin's death.

(b) Explain why and with what results Stalin collectivized agriculture.

(c) Explain clearly how Stalin improved Russia's industrial strength between 1928 and 1941.

(d) What were the PURGES of the 1930s? Why were they carried out and with what results?

(*LREB, 1980, CSE Level.*)

15 (a) Name the FOUR leaders who were the peacemakers at Versailles in 1919. (4)

(b) What did they decide about each of the following?

i Reparations; *ii* Disarmament; *iii* Germany's frontiers; *iv* Austria-Hungary. (16)

(*ALSEB, 1980, CSE Level.*)

16 Explain how FIVE of the following are connected with the peace settlement made with Germany 1919.

(a) Alsace-Lorraine; (b) Demilitarization;

(c) Polish Corridor; (d) Diktat; (e) War-Guilt;

(f) Reparations (g) Fourteen Points.

(*EMREB, 1979, CSE Level.*)

17 (a) When and why was the League of Nations founded?

(b) Briefly describe the functions of the ASSEMBLY, The COUNCIL, the SECRETARIAT and the COURT OF INTERNATIONAL JUSTICE of the League of Nations.

(c) What were the chief weaknesses of the League?

(*LREB, 1980, CSE Level.*)

18 Write an account of the aims, organization and achievements of the League of Nations before 1930. Explain clearly the reasons for its failure after this date, emphasising the importance of the Manchurian Crisis 1931 and the Abyssinian Crisis 1935–6.

(*YREB, 1972, CSE Level.*)

19 Explain (a) the reasons for Hitler's rise to power in Germany and (10)

  (b) his domestic policy 1933–39. (10)

(*ALSEB, 1977, CSE Level.*)

20 Write an account of the Weimar Republic in Germany. The following guide lines will help you. What was the Weimar Republic?–Stresemann's aims and difficulties over the Versailles Treaty–Stresemann's attitude to England, France and the League of Nations rearmament–reasons for the rise of Hitler–the Great Depression.

(*ALSEB, 1981, CSE Level.*)

21 Using the following outline, write an account of Hitler's career to 1934:

Early life to 1918; Nazi party and the Munich Beer Hall Putsch (1923); *Mein Kampf*: the Depressioin and the growth of the Nazi party (1929–1932); Hitler becoming Chancellor in 1933: how he had secured himself in power by the time of Hindenburg's death (1934).

(*NREB, 1979, CSE Level.*)

22 'In 1929 the economy of the entire world outside of Russia was stricken by a period of depression more dramatic and widespread in its consequences than any similar crsis in the nineteenth century.'

(a) Use the following headings to explain the causes of the 'World Economic Depression'.

  i Overproduction of raw materials in the 1920s.

  ii Decreased world trade.

  iii The 'Wall Street Crash'.

  iv Europe's dependence on American finance.

(b) What were the 'dramatic and widespread consequences' of this crisis in Europe?

(*EAEB, 1978, CSE Level.*)

23 Write paragraphs about FOUR of the following aspects of American life in the period from 1919 to 1939:

The FBI	The New Deal
Prohibition	The Tennessee Valley
Immigration Act of 1921	Authority
The Wall Street Crash 1929	Hollywood

(*WMREB, 1978, CSE Level.*)

24 Write an account of the careers of Chiang Kai-shek and Mao Tse-tung between 1919 and 1939. The following information should help you.

Foundation of the Communist Party 1921

Death of Sun Yat-Sen 1925

Fall of Peking to the Kuo Min Tang 1928

The Long March

(*ALSEB, 1979, CSE Level.*)

25 Japanese expansion between the wars

(a) What was discussed and decided at the Washington Naval Conference 1922 and what were the consequences for Japan?

(b) Explain why Japan invaded Manchuria in 1931.

(c) What action did the League of Nations take when the Japanese invaded Manchuria, and what was Japan's reaction?

(d) Why did Japan invade China in 1937 and what were the effects of this invasion on *i* the Civil War in China; *ii* American policy towards Japan?

(*LREB, 1980, CSE Level.*)

26 (a) What were reparations? Why were they imposed on Germany after the First World War?

(b) Why did she fail to pay reparations in 1922?

(c) As a result of Germany's failure to pay, what action did France and Belgium take in 1923?

(d) What was the Dawes Plan (1924) and how did it affect Germany's ability to pay?

(*LREB, 1978, CSE Level.*)

27 (a) Show how Franklin D. Roosevelt's New Deal between 1933 and 1939 aimed at bringing immediate economic relief to the unemployed, and reforms to industry, agriculture, finance, waterpower, labour and housing.

(b) From which section of the community did President Roosevelt receive opposition to the New Deal and what were their arguments against it?

(*EAEB, 1976, CSE Level.*)

28 Hitler became Chancellor of Germany in January 1933.

i Describe the policy which he followed from 1933 to 1939 to crush all opposition and build up the idea of himself as the supreme dictator of Germany. (14)

ii At the same time he managed to make Germany moderately prosperous. How did he do this? (6)
(20)

(*WMREB, 1981, CSE Level.*)

29 (a) Why was there dissatisfaction in Italy after the First World War?
(b) How did Mussolini come to power in 1922?
(c) Explain how Mussolini established a Fascist State in Italy.
(d) Give TWO reasons why Mussolini embarked on an aggressive foreign policy.
(e) Describe ONE of those foreign involvements in detail.
(*LREB, 1980, CSE Level.*)

30 Using the following headings to describe the main developments in Britain's relations with India before 1939.
(a) The Morley-Minto Reforms 1909
(b) The Montagu Declaration 1917
(c) Mahatma Gandhi
(d) The Round Table Conference 1930
(e) The Government of India Act 1935
(*EAEB, 1976, CSE Level.*)

31 What were Hitler's aims in foreign policy? Explain how he tried to achieve these aims between 1933 and 1939, by referring to his policies towards the Saar; the Rhineland; Austria; Czechoslovakia; Poland and Russia.
(*ALSEB, 1980, CSE Level.*)

32 'In opposition to the left-wing and anti-clerical policy of the Spanish Republican Government, General Franco attempted a *coup d'état*. Britain and France tried to maintain a policy of non-intervention from outside but this was flagrantly broken. The horror and destruction of this war dragged on for three years.'
(a) What was the 'left-wing and anti-clerical policy' (Line 1)?
(b) From which sections in Spanish society did each side draw its support?
(c) How and by whom was the 'non-intervention' policy so flagrantly broken?
(d) Why were Franco and the Nationalists eventually victorious?
(e) What was the importance of the Spanish Civil War in the wider context of Europe?
(*EAEB, 1977, CSE Level.*)

33 'France, the United Kingdom, and the Dominions declared war in 1939. Other countries, including the United States and the Soviet Union, joined them later, but not until they had been attacked by the Axis Powers or their allies.'
(a) Why did France, Great Britain and the Dominions declare war on Germany in 1939?
(b) Name a country (apart from the Soviet Union) which was attacked by Germany in 1939. Why did Hitler attack that country, and what was the result?
(c) When and why did Hitler attack the Soviet Union, and why was he successful in the first few months of the attack?
(d) What caused America to enter the war?
(*MREB, 1977, CSE Level.*)

34 'Germany lost the Second World War in the 'Water of the Atlantic; in the Deserts of North Africa; in the Snows of Russia and on the Beaches of Normandy.' Take each of these areas and provide facts and details which would support the statement. (*ALSEB, 1977, CSE Level.*)

35 (a) *i* What was the main objective of the United Nations Organization as indicated in Article One of the Charter? (1)
ii Describe briefly the organization and purpose of FOUR of the following bodies within the United Nations:
General Assembly; Security Council; Economic and Social Council; Trusteeship Council; International Court of Justice; Secretariat. (4×3)
(b) Describe the part played by the United Nations in TWO of the following: Greece (1946–7); Palestine (1945–56); Cyprus (1964). (*NWREB, 1981, CSE Level.*)

36 Answer the following questions based on the development of Europe after 1945.
(a) *i* Briefly describe the problems that faced liberated Europe after 1945. (5)
ii What was the 'Iron Curtain' so described by Churchill in 1946? (4)
iii Name TWO of Russia's satellites in Eastern Europe. (2)
(b) *i* By what methods did the Russians hope to seize Berlin in 1948? (5)
ii Why were they unsuccessful? (3)

iii Name the military alliance formed in 1949 to prevent communist aggression in Europe. (1)
(*NWREB, 1980, CSE Level.*)

37 'From Stettin in the Baltic to Trieste in the Adriatic an iron curtain has descended across the Continent.' (Churchill at Fulton in 1946.)
What exactly did Churchill mean by 'an iron curtain'? (2)
Describe some of the events that occurred during the years at the height of the 'cold war' in Europe. (8)
When was NATO set up and what was the purpose of this organization?
What is meant by 'peaceful co-existence'? To what extent has there been a thaw in the relations between East and West and how would you describe the situation today? (4)
(*SREB, 1980, CSE Level.*)

38 Answer the following question on the spread of communism in the Far East since 1945.
(a) *i* Which country declared itself a People's Republic on September 21st 1949? (1)
ii To which island off mainland China did the Chinese Nationalists retreat in 1949? (1)
iii Name TWO countries (excluding Russia) on the borders of China which had become communist before 1956. (2)
(b) *i* Describe as fully as you can how China and the USA became involved in the Korean War 1950–54. (9)
ii Name the treaty organization created on September 8th 1954 to prevent further communist aggression in the Far East. (1)
iii Name TWO signatories of that treaty. (2)
(c) Why was the USA unable to prevent South Vietnam becoming communist? (4)
(*NWREB, 1979, CSE Level.*)

39 *i* What were the main aims of Russian policy under Khrushchev and his successors towards the Western Powers? (5)
ii With what success did they achieve these aims? (5)
iii Describe Russian relations with China since 1960. (5)
iv Explain why these two countries have become very suspicious of each other. (5)
(20)
(*WMEB, 1978, CSE Level.*)

40 Answer the following questions on the policies and achievements of Nikita Khrushchev.
(a) *i* Whom did Khrushchev succeed in February 1955? (1)
ii Name the new Russian Prime Minister with whom Khrushchev worked. (1)
(b) *i* At what meeting in February 1956 did Khrushchev launch his famous attack on Stalin? (2)
ii Describe as fully as you can the criticisms that Khrushchev made against Stalin at that meeting. (5)
iii What did Khrushchev mean by 'peaceful co-existence with the West'? (3)
iv Describe the steps by which the Seven Year Plan begun in 1958 was to improve the lives of ordinary Russian men and women. (4)
(c) What reasons did the opponents of Khrushchev give for his dismissal in 1964? (4)
(*NWREB, 1980, CSE Level.*)

41 In 1948, Albania and Yugoslavia were probably the only two Communist states in Europe where the majority of the people supported the Communist Party.
(a) If the above statement is true, why did Poland, Hungary, Bulgaria, Romania and Czechoslovakia all have Communist governments by 1948? (2)
(b) How and why did the Eastern part of Germany become a Communist state in 1949? (5)
(c) How and why was Yugoslavia different from other Communist states in Europe? (5)
(d) Describe the causes, events and results of the Czechoslovakian Rising of 1968 and the problems which began in Poland in 1979. (8)
(*ALSEB, 1982, CSE Level.*)

42 Why and how was the European Economic Community formed? How does it work and what problems has it faced in recent times?
(*SEREB, 1981, CSE Level.*)

43 Why was the post-war period of the 1940s and 1950s especially favourable to anti-communist feeling in the USA? Describe the career of Senator Joseph McCarthy between 1950 and 1954. Why did he finally arouse the opposition of the President and the condemnation of the Senate?

(*LREB, 1978, CSE Level.*)

44 Write an account of the development of the People's Republic of China since 1949. Mention as many as you can of the following: How China is governed; agricultural and industrial policy; the Great Leap Forward; the Cultural Revolution; Nuclear weapons; China's relations with Russia and the rest of the World; any other points which you think are relevant.

(*ALSEB, 1980, CSE Level.*)

45 Choose FOUR of the following leaders and explain the Part they played in achieving independence in India or Pakistan or in the subsequent history of their country.
(a) Mahatma Gandhi; (b) Muhammad Jinnah; (c) Nehru; (d) Lord Mountbatten; (e) Ayub Khan; (f) Mrs Indira Gandhi.

(*ALSEB, 1978, CSE Level.*)

46 (a) *i* Describe briefly the methods by which Gandhi hoped to win independence for India. (5)
ii What was the main fear of the Moslem League about an independent and united India? What policy did the League suggest as a solution? (3)
iii Why was there fighting in Kashmir in 1948 and 1965 and how were ceasefire agreements brought about?

(4)

(b) *i* What policy, up to 1962, did India strictly adopt towards the West and the Soviet Union? (1)
ii Why was India forced to seek military aid from the USA in 1962? (2)
(c) *i* Why was the newly created state of Pakistan particularly difficult to govern? (4)
ii Which former past of Pakistan now forms the new independent state of Bangladesh? (1)

(*NWREB, 1979, CSE Level.*)

47 Use the following headings to explain the situation in Vietnam since 1945. (a) French attempts to regain control; (b) Geneva Conference; (c) Causes of American intervention; (d) The Vietnam War; (e) The establishment of a reunited Vietnam.

(*EAEB, 1977, CSE Level.*)

48 In 1945, only four independent states existed in Africa but by 1966 most of the continent had freed itself from colonial rule.
(a) Name TWO independent states of Africa in 1945. (2)
(b) Explain the meaning of colonial rule. (2)
(c) Describe the way in which TWO African countries achieved and maintained independence in the period after 1945.

(2×8)

(*ALSEB, 1979, CSE Level.*)

49 The Middle East
Read the following passage carefully
1 'The most decisive stroke in the Six Day War of 1967 occurred at its very outset. Beginning at 0745 hours on 5th June, Israel's fighter-bombers . . . paralyzed the . . . air force, destroying most of its aircraft on the ground. . . . In his Voice of Israel broadcast Colonel Wallach emphasized "the prime importance of the Israeli air force's actions in destroying the hostile air forces and gaining air superiority over the battlefields. . . . The Israeli Defence Force had grasped the importance of armour already in the Sinai campaign of 1956. Since then this corps has been strengthened and improved. Its excellent technical level enabled it to carry out a diversified (wide) range of combat missions: break through fortified enemy localities; encircling movement over terrain normally considered uncrossable by armour; combat of armour against armour . . .".'

Part A
i Which country's air force was attacked by the Israelis on 5th June 1967? (line 3)
Why was destruction of this air force 'or prime importance' (line 6) to the Israelis?
ii 'The Israeli Defence Force had grasped the importance of armour already, in the Sinai campaign of 1956' (lines 9 &

10). Name one western country Israel helped in that war. What had been the cause of the 1956 war?
iii Name two things for which Colonel Wallach said Israeli tanks could be used (lines 12-14).
iv Name two areas from Arab countries by Israel in the 1967 war.
v Why was the 'Yom Kippur' War so called?
vi Which Middle East Country had a civil war in 1976?
Part B
In a paragraph (10-12 lines) describe the conflict between Arabs and Jews in Palestine from 1900 to 1948.

(*SEREB, 1978, CSE Level.*)

50
i Why is the Arab world of such vital importance to the West? (2)
ii Why did the Arabs object very strongly to the setting up of a Jewish state in 1948? (2)
iii Who were the Palestinians? What did they do to hit back at the Israelis? (4)
iv Describe very briefly the three wars between Jews and Arabs from 1956 to 1973. (2×3)
v What territories did the Israelis gain as a consequence of these wars? (3)
vi Which of these areas are they particularly anxious to retain? Show how this had made the making of a peace treaty very difficult. (3)

(*WMREB, 1980, CSE Level.*)

51 Write an account of man's conquest of air and space **either** (a) before 1945 **or** (b) since 1945.

(*WJEC, 1980, CSE Level.*)

52 Read the following passage carefully and answer the questions which follow it.
'The **annual** increases in world population is estimated to be more than 80 millions–a figure which is about 42% greater than the total population of the United Kingdom. In the developed regions the rate of increase is moderate, but in the developing areas the population is soaring. By AD 2000 the peoples of the less-developed areas will have doubled their numbers, and already the population explosion is affecting human beings adversely in many parts of the world.'
(a) What do you understand by a developed region? (3)
(b) Name ONE country in which the population is increasing at a moderate rate. (1)
(c) Name TWO countries in which the population is soaring.

(2)

(b) What is the relationship between a country's birth rate and its standard of living? (3)
(e) Explain the adverse effects the population explosion is already having in many parts of the world and say what can be done to remedy these effects. (9)

(*EAEB, 1981, CSE Level.*)

53 What do we mean by the 'Third World'? (4 marks)
Explain your answer by dealing with two countries in the Third World. (2×8 marks)

(*SREB, 1981, CSE Level.*)

54 Choose TWO of the following problems facing the contemporary world and for each one chosen:
(a) explain what the problems are;
(b) describe the attempts that have been made to overcome the problem.
Refer to as many areas of the world as possible.
(c) Say how successful these attempts have been.
i world resources; *iii* terrorism;
ii race; *iv* the spread of nuclear weapons.

(*ALSEB, 1982, CSE Level.*)

2.3 Write short notes on
In Part IV.3.5 you will find guidance as to the way in which this type of question should be answered. You should also look again at Part IV.3.7-8 because the items chosen for the 'short notes' type of question are also used by examiners as material for guided-essay type questions.

1 Write briefly about any TWO of the following:
(a) The Russian Revolution (1917); (b) the Emperor Haile Selassie; (c) the European Economic Community; (d) the Suez Crisis (1956). (*NI, 1980, O Level.*)

2 Write short notes on **four** of the following: the first battle of the Marne; the Spartakists; Amritsar; the New Economic Policy; Rapallo, Laval; the Reichstag Fire; Guernica; Admiral Darlan; the Katyn Massacre.

(*O & C, 1982, O Level.*)

3 Write on **four** of the following: Alexander II of Russia; the Balkan Wars 1912–13; the Sarajevo assassination; the League of Nations; Stalin's domestic policies; the United Nations Organization.

(*JMB, 1979, O Level.*)

4 (on one theme) Describe and explain the importance of the following in the Second World War; the 'phoney War'; the evacuation at Dunkirk; the North African Campaigns; the Second Front.

(*JMB, 1980, O Level.*)

5 Write short paragraphs (5-6 lines) on FOUR of the following to show that you understand their meanings and historical importance.
Make sure that you put the correct letter next to your answer,

(a) Congress of Berlin 1879	**(h)** Battle of El Alamein
(b) Reinsurance Treaty 1887	1942
(c) Revolution in China 1911	**(i)** Greek Civil War
(d) The Fourteen Points 1918	1945–49
(e) Treaty of Sèvres 1919 and	**(j)** The Berlin Wall
Treaty of Lausanne 1923	**(k)** The Great Leap
(f) Mussolini's Corporate	Forward
State	**(l)** The IRA
(g) National Industrial	
Recovery Act 1933	

(*ALSEB, 1981, CSE Level.*)

6 Write **one** sentence **only** about any **ten** of the following (10×1):
(a) Leon Trotsky; **(b)** Ramsay MacDonald; **(c)** the Ku Klux Klan; **(d)** the Statute of Westminster 1931; **(e)** the Special Areas Act 1934; **(f)** the Munich Agreement of 1938; **(g)** Vichy; **(h)** Iwo Jima; **(j)** PLUTO; **(k)** NATO; **(l)** Formosa; **(m)** UNESCO; **(n)** the Warsaw Pact; **(o)** Kwame Nkrumah.

(*WJEC, 1980, CSE Level.*)

7 (on one theme) Choose THREE of the following which are all connected with the First World War, 1914–18.
Write about each one you have chosen and explain its importance in the war.

The German Invasion of	The Dardanelles Campaign
France	The Battle of Jutland
Trench Warfare	The War in the Air
The Blockade of German	
Ports	

(*LREB, 1982, CSE Level.*)

3 Stimulus-based questions (see Part IV.4.1 for guidance)

3.1 Written extract (See Part IV.4.1 for guidance)

Some boards use written extracts as the basis for Objective Tests. You will find examples of such Tests in Self-Test Units 8, 20 and 27.
Most boards use an extract as the basis for a variety of questions e.g.:

1 Bloody Sunday 1905
Sire–We working men and inhabitants of St. Petersburg, our/wives, and our children and our helpless old parents, come to You, Sire, to seek for truth, justice and protection. We have been made beggars; we are oppressed; we are near to death. The moment has come when death would be better than the prolongation of our interminable sufferings. We have stopped work and have told our masters that we shall not work again until they comply with our demands. We ask but little; to reduce the working day to eight hours, to provide a minimum wage of a rouble a day, and to abolish overtime. Officials have brought the country to complete ruin and involved it in a shameful war. We working men have no voice in the way the enormous amounts raised from us are spent. These things, Sire, have brought us to the walls of Your palace. We are seeking here our last salvation. Do not refuse to help Your people. Give orders that elections to a Constituent Assembly be carried out under conditions of universal, equal and secret suffrage. If You will not give these orders and will not

answers our prayers, we shall die here on this Square before Your palace.

Petition to the Tsar 22nd January 1905
(a) 'We have been made beggars, we are oppressed' (line 4). Briefly describe the conditions of the Russian urban working class at this time. (3)
(b) Write an account of the 'shameful war' (line 12) in which Russia was involved. (6)
(c) What is meant by a 'Constituent Assembly' (line 17)? Did the Tsar make any concessions in this matter? (3)
(d) What was the outcome of the attempt to present this petition? (2)
(e) Outline the events of 1905 in Russia after 'Bloody Sunday'. (6)

(*O & C, 1980, O Level.*)

2 (a) Article 231 The Treaty of Versailles
The Allied and Associated Governments affirm and Germany accepts the responsibility of Germany and her allies for causing all the loss and damage to which the Allied and Associated Governments and their nationals have been subjected as a consequence of the war imposed upon them by the aggression of Germany and her allies.

(b) From the *Publication of the Reparations Commission*, (London 1923)
On 26th December, 1922, after careful examination of the German defence, the Commission took the following decision:
It was unanimously decided that Germany had not executed in their entirety the orders passed under Annex IV, Part VIII of the Treaty of Versailles, for deliveries of timber to France during 1922.
1 What do you understand by reparations? Explain the link between Article 231 and reparations.
2 Name TWO of Germany's wartime allies covered by Article 231.
3 Which country pressed most strongly for the imposition of reparations and why? Name the British economist who criticized reparations in 'The Economic Consequences of the Peace'?
4 What action was taken by France and Belgium in response to the statement contained in Extract 2? What was the main economic consequence of their response?
5 In what ways did the Germans respond to this action?
6 What was the significance of the Dawes Commission?

(*Oxford, 1980, O Level.*)

3 Lenin on his comrades
Comrade Stalin, having become General Secretary, has concentrated an enormous power in his hands; and I am not sure, that he always knows how to use that power with sufficient caution. On the other hand, Comrade Trotsky . . . is distinguished not only by his exceptional abilities–personally he is, to be sure, the most able man in the present Central Committee–but also by his too far-reaching self-confidence and a disposition to be too much attracted by the purely administrative side of affairs.

These qualities of the two most able leaders of the present Central Committee might, quite innocently, lead to a split; if our party does not take measures to prevent it, a split might arise unexpectedly. I will not characterize the other members of the Central Committee as to their personal qualities. I will only remind you that the October episode of Zinoviev and Kamenev was not, of course, accidental but that it ought as little be used against them personally as the non-Bolshevism of Trotsky.

Stalin is too rude, and this fault, entirely supportable in relations amongst us Communists, becomes insupportable in the office of General Secretary. Therefore, I propose to the comrades to find a way to remove Stalin from that position and to appoint to it another man who in all respects differs from Stalin only in superiority, namely more patient, more loyal, more polite and more attentive to comrades, less capricious etc. . . .

Lenin's Testament
(a) What part did Stalin play in the affairs of Russia between 1915 and 1924? How had he concentrated an enormous power in his hands as General Secretary? (*line 2*). (3)

(b) What were Trotsky's 'exceptional abilities'? (*line 5*). Describe his role in the Revolution in 1917 and the subsequent civil war. (6)

(c) Explain the main issues which divided Trotsky and Stalin. Show how the 'split' (*line 13*) developed after Lenin's death. What happened to Trotsky? (7)

(d) Who were Zinoviev and Kamenev? (*line 16*) (2)

(e) Account for the failure to 'remove Stalin' (*line 22*) (2)

(*O & C, 1978, O Level.*)

4 Study this extract from the **Tanaka Memorial,** a document which was widely accepted as a policy statement prepared by the Japanese premier, Baron Tanaka, in 1927, and then answer questions **(a)** to **(e)** which follow. (**The maximum mark for each sub-question is indicated in brackets**)

Line 1 For her self-protection as well as others, Japan cannot remove the difficulties in Eastern Asia unless she adopts a policy of blood and iron. However, in implementing this policy we must face the United
Line 5 States, which has been turned against us by China's policy of fighting poison with poison. If we want to crush China in the future, we must first crush the United States. To conquer China we must first overwhelm Manchuria and Mongolia. To conquer the
Line 10 world we must first conquer China. If we are successful in conquering China, the remainder of the Asiatic nations and the South Sea countries will fear and surrender to us. Only then will the world admit that Eastern Asia is ours and will not dare
Line 15 to challenge our rights.
The method of gaining actual rights in Manchuria and Mongolia is to use the area as a base and, while pretending trade and commerce, penetrate the rest of China. With these countries secured, we shall seize
Line 20 the resources of all the country. And with China's resources at our disposal we shall conquer India, the Archipelago, Asia, Minor, Central Asia and even Europe.

(a) Identify and explain two of Japan's **difficulties in Eastern Asia** (*line 2*) at this time.

(b) Describe the stages by which Japan succeeded in its efforts to **overwhelm Manchuria** (*line 9*) and subsequently made progress to **conquer China** (*line 10*). (3)

(c) In what ways did Japanese foreign policy at this time inevitably cause Japan to **face the United States** (*line 4-5*)? What steps were taken later to **crush the United States** (*line 8-9*)? (4)

(d) Name **three** of the **Asiatic nations and the South Sea countries** (*line 12*) that surrendered to Japan in the early 1940s. (4)

(e) What led to the ultimate collapse of the Japanese conquests and of the ambitions put forward in this extract? (5)

(*London, 1979, O Level.*)

5 During a crisis in our country's history, which had its roots in unemployment, the New Deal was born. The administration of Franklin Roosevelt was the first in our Country's history to acknowledge the responsibility of the Federal Government for the solution of the problem. It recognized that freedom and constitutional democracy could not stand for long side by side with bread lines of willing workers. It recognized also that the key to the solution of the problem lay in increasing the purchasing power of the people, thereby making the demand for goods more nearly equal to the potential supply.

The New Deal never developed an effective or lasting answer to the central problem with which it sought to deal. The methods used sought to deal with a fundamental maladjustment by means of temporary or emergency agencies of government to which Congress was asked to give wide discretionary power. The New Deal did not solve the unemployment problem; it only managed to relieve it. And the measures of relief opened the way to those abuses of ill-defined governmental power which provided the principal basis for the flood of propaganda against the entire progressive program of the Roosevelt Administration.

(*Jerry Voorhis, Confessions of a Congressman*)

(a) Explain the 'crisis in our country's history, which had its roots in unemployment' (*lines 1-2*). (5)

(b) What policies did Roosevelt adopt to increase 'the purchasing power of the people' (*line 9*)? (4)

(c) Give examples of the 'temporary and emergency agencies of government to which Congress was asked to give wide discretionary power' (*line 15*). Explain their purpose and functions. (5)

(d) Comment upon the criticisms made of the New Deal that it 'never developed an effective or lasting answer to the central problem with which it sought to deal' (*line 12*) and 'did not solve the unemployment problem' (*line 17*).

(*O & C, 1981, O Level.*)

6 The Suez Crisis 1956
Examine carefully the extract below from the British Prime Minister's speech in the House of Commons on 31st October 1956 and then answer the following questions.

'Yesterday morning, the United States representative tabled at UNO a resolution which was in effect a condemnation of Israel as the aggressor in the events of the last few days. We felt that we could not associate ourselves
5 with this and we said so. . . . The Egyptian Government have made clear over and over again, with increased emphasis since the seizure of the Canal, their intentions to destroy Israel. . . . In these circumstances is there any Member of this House who can consider Egypt as an
10 innocent country whom it is right to exonerate at the Security Council by condemning Israel as an aggressor? . . . As to our own request, to both sides, to cease fire and withdraw, Israel accepted that request last night and declared her willingness to take practical steps to carry it
15 out. The Egyptian Government rejected it. . . .

I must remind the House that we have recently been to the United Nations and we went with proposals for the future of the Canal . . . but they were vetoed by the Soviet Government. Can we be expected to await the develop-
20 ment of similar procedures in the situation of much greater urgency that confronts us now in and about the Canal? The action we had to take was bound to be rapid. . . .

In entering the Suez Canal area we are only protecting a vital international waterway. . . .
25 Now I wish to say something about our relations with the United States in the matter . . . it is, of course, an obvious truth that safety of transit through the Canal, though clearly of concern to the United States, is for them not a matter of survival as it is to us. . . . I also informed
30 the United States Government of our reasons for concern and our anxieties as to whether the Security Council was the method to deal with the increasing dangers that faced us . . . that experience showed that this procedure was unlikely to be either rapid or effective.'

(a) Explain why and how the British Government came to own such a large number of shares in the Suez Canal.

(b) Why and how had Egypt taken control of the Canal in 1956?

(c) 'Israel . . . the aggressor' The Egyptian Government . . .intention to destroy Israel' (*lines 3-8*). Explain the hostilities between Israel and Egypt.

(d) What conditions accompanied the British 'request to cease fire' (*line 12*) which made the Egyptian government reject it?

(e) What was the Security Council? Explain the statement that 'proposals for the future of the Canal . . . were vetoed by the Soviet Government' (*line 17*).

(f) Who was the British Prime Minister who made the speech? What did he mean by the phrase 'entering the Suez Canal area. . . .' (*line 23*)?

(g) Explain the attitude of the USA towards British intervention in the Suez Canal Area.

(*JMB, 1982, O Level.*)

7 'For some years before 1914 Europe had been drifting towards war and had become divided into two heavily armed camps. The three main areas of disagreement were **(1)** French and German suspicion over armaments and territory. **(2)** German and British rivalry over colonies and the navy and **(3)** the clashing ambitions of Austria-Hungary and Russia in the Balkans. On several occasions in the previous decade war had seemed imminent but the catastrophe had been averted. The condition of Europe in 1914 has been likened to a

powder-magazine; it needed only a spark to cause an explosion. This spark was provided by the Sarajevo Incident.'
(a) Name the 'two heavily armed camps'. What was Britain's relationship with one of these groups?
(b) Give details of each of the 'three main areas of disgreement' between the powers as outlined above.
(c) Select TWO of the occasions between 1904–1914 when 'war had seemed imminent'. Explain the circumstances and state how war had been averted.
(d) What was the Sarajevo Incident? Trace the stages from this to the involvement of the Powers in war in 1914.

(*EAEB, 1977, CSE Level.*)

3.2 Map based questions

(See Part IV.4.2 for guidance and for references to the use of maps as the basis for Objective Tests–used in this book in various Self-Test Units.)

1 Examine the map of North Africa 1905–1914 (Fig. V.3.2.1A) and then answer the following questions.
(a) Name

> *i* town A *ii* island B acquired by Italy in 1912 *iii* colony C *iv* colony D *v* naval base E *vi* sea F *vii* battle G *viii* battle H *ix* colony J *x* colony K

(b) Which European power established a protectorate over Tunisia in 1881?
(c) Why and how did Britain acquire an interest in the Suez Canal?
(d) How did Britain deal with the Sudan between 1884 and 1898?
(e) What happened at Fashoda in 1898 and how did it effect international relations?

(*JMB, 1981, O Level.*)

2 Study the map of the Western Front in World War I (Fig. V.3.2.2A) and answer the questions which follow.
(a) Name
i the army which held the front, north of River B, against the Germans.
ii the army which held the front, south of River B against the Germans.
iii the battle fought at River B in 1916.
iv City A, site of fierce battles throughout the war.
v Fortress D.
vi The German defensive line C.
(b) How are the following connected with World War I?
i 'that contemptible force'.
ii the 'Tiger'.
iii 'They shall not pass'.
iv 'With our backs to the wall each one of us must fight on to the end.'

(*EMREB, 1979, CSE Level.*)

3 The shaded area is the Hapsburg Empire as it was in 1914. The map (V.3.2.3A) shows how this Empire was divided up in 1919.
1 Which letter marks *i* Austria; *ii* Hungary?
2 Name country F which was created by the peace settlement of 1919. Name TWO of the nationalities living in this multi-national state.
3 Name country B which was another 'new' country. Name TWO of the nationalities living in this multi-national state.
4 Name country G and say why it was enlarged while Bulgaria was not.
5 Name country A and name the economically important area which it gained from the former Hapsburg Empire.
6 Name country E. Why was it given area H?
7 Name area J. Which two countries claimed this area? Name port X and the man who seized that port in 1919.
8 Name TWO new states which had large Polish, Hungarian and German minorities.
9 Why was the policy of national 'self-determination' impossible to apply to the countries in the former Hapsburg Empire?

(Adapted from many papers, including *Oxford, 1981, O Level & NWREB, 1979, CSE Level.*)

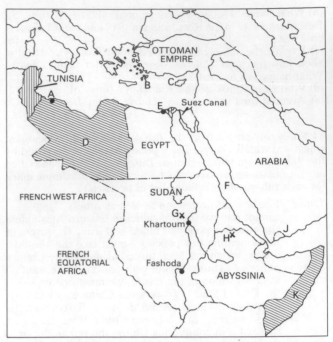

Fig. V.3.2.1A   North East Africa, 1875–1914

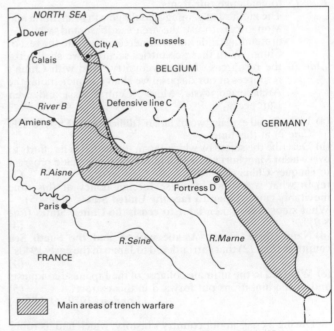

Fig. V.3.2.2A   The Western Front, 1914–18

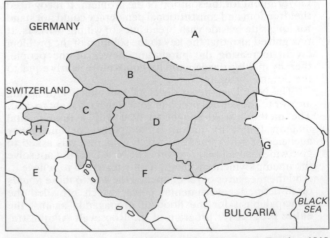

Fig. V.3.2.3A   The break up of the Austro-Hungarian Empire, 1919

Fig. V.3.2.4A Hitler's expansionism

4 Look at the map (Fig. V.3.2.4A) which shows German expansion in the period from 1936 to 1939.
i Write a commentary on each of the occupations given in the key, explaining what led up to them and what their consequences were. (18)
ii In some of these occupations, a policy of 'appeasement' was attempted. What does this mean? (2)

(20)

(WMREB, 1979, CSE Level.)

5 Study the map (Fig. V.3.2.5A) and then answer the questions which follow.
1 Which power controlled Korea before 1945?
2 Along which line was Korea partitioned in 1945?
3 Which power 'controlled' North Korea from 1945 to 1948?
4 What justified this decision?
5 Which power 'controlled' South Korea?
6 Name *i* capital city A; *ii* capital city B; *iii* country C.
7 Name *i* country D; *ii* its head of state after 2nd September 1949; *iii* the rival whom he had just defeated.
8 What was the immediate cause of the Korean War, 1950?
9 What, in particular, **allowed** the Security Council to vote to send troops to help South Korea?
10 Who initially commanded the UN forces in Korea?
11 Name city H.
12 Why was that city so important in September 1950?
13 Name port G. What took place there in September 1950?
14 Who was President of the USA in 1950?
15 Why did he dismiss the head of the UN forces?
16 Name river F.
17 Which country sent troops to help North Korea in 1950?
18 Name one country from each of the following, apart from the USA, who participated in the UN action in Korea: *i* North America; *ii* South America; *iii* NATO; *iv* the Commonwealth; *v* Africa.
19 Name J where an armistice was signed.
20 In what year was that armistice signed?
21 What event in Russia helped the search for that armistice?
22 Who was President of the USA when the armistice was signed?

(Adapted from *Oxford, 1981, O Level*, and *NWREB, 1980, CSE Level.*)

3.3 Questions based on statistics

1 Answer the following questions based on Russia's economic development during this period.
(a) *i* Describe the main features of the New Economic Policy introduced by Lenin in 1921.
ii Why were the Five Year Plans introduced by Stalin in 1928?
(b) Study the figures below on Russian industrial production and answer the following questions.

Russian Industrial production 1900–1938 (m = Million)

	1913	1928	1932	1938
Coal	29 m. tons	35 m. tons	64 m. tons	132 m. tons
Iron & Steel	8 m. tons	7½ m. tons	12 m. tons	32 m. tons
Electric power	1000 m. Watts	2000 m. Watts	5000 m Watts	11 000 m. Watts
Tractors		1000	50 000	176 000
Oil	9 m. tons	12 m. tons	22 m. tons	32 m. tons

i How much coal and oil did Russia produce immediately before the outbreak of World War I? (2)
ii By how many thousands had tractor production increased during the period of the first Five Year Plan? (1)
iii How were Russian workers encouraged to meet the targets of the Five Year Plans? (3)

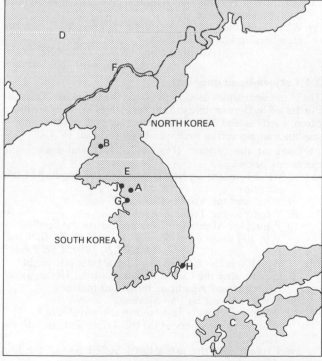

Fig. V.3.2.5A The Korean War, 1950–53

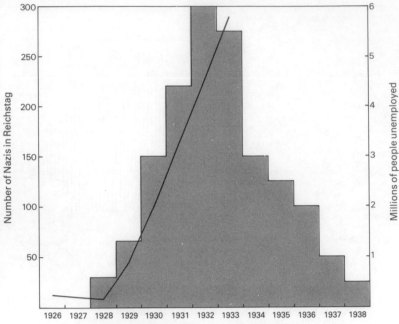

Fig. V.3.3.1A   The rise of the Nazi Party

iv What punishments might be given to those workers who did not meet the targets of the Five Year Plans?   (3)
v Why was the Third Five Year Plan abandoned in 1941?
(*NWREB, 1979, CSE Level.*)

2 Look at the graphs on Germany between the wars (Fig. V.3.3.1A) and answer the questions which follow.
i What was the Reichstag?
ii In which year between 1926 and 1933 was the number of Nazis in the Reichstag at its lowest?
iii In which year did unemployment in Germany reach its peak?
iv How many people were unemployed in that peak year?
v Give ONE important reason why unemployment rose so sharply after 1929.
vi Account for the rise in the number of Nazis in the Reichstag after 1929.
vii Name ONE other party which increased its numbers in the Reichstag during this period.
viii Name ONE Member of the Nazi party, other than Hitler.
ix Give THREE promises Hitler made to the German people which helped him to gain power.
x Give TWO reasons why Hitler's policies helped reduce unemployment after 1933.
xi Why does the graph not show figures for Reichstag membership after 1933?
(Adapted from *YREB, 1979, CSE Level,*
and *ALSEB, 1981, CSE Level.*)

3.4 Cartoon-based questions

These are sometimes used as the basis for Objective Tests (as illustrated by the example in Self-Test Unit 19). They are more often used as the basis for more general questions. For guidance in answering such questions see Part IV.4.4.

1 Look at the cartoon (Fig. V.3.4.1A) and answer the questions below.
(a) *i* What is meant by 'the bonfire' in the heading of this cartoon?
ii What was the Triple Alliance?
iii What was the Triple Entente?
iv Why does Alsace-Lorraine appear on the bonfire?
v Why did some Great Powers quarrel in the Balkans?
(*EMREB, 1980, CSE Level.*)
(b) *i* Which was the fatal match that set the pile alight?
ii Explain why the cartoon shows Bosnia, Herzegovina, Algeciras and Agadir as burnt-out matches.
iii What is meant by Pan-Slavism?
iv Which states were involved in the naval race?
v Who were members of (a) the Triple Entente; (b) the Triple Alliance?
vi Explain why the artist has labelled one of the logs Alsace-Lorraine.
(*EAEB, 1978, CSE Level.*)

2 Look at the cartoon (Fig. V.3.4.2A) and then answer the questions below.
(a) *i* The cartoon was drawn on the occasion of the last of the peace-time Christmases between the wars. What was the year of the cartoon?
ii Which of the young children of the family, named on the bedhead was in the process of disappearing into 'Santa's' sack at this time?
iii Which 'child' named in the bedhead never disappeared into 'Santa's' sack at all?   (3)
(b) In the case of (a) *i* give an account of the events leading to:
i the loss of a portion of this state's territories in the preceding autumn, and

Fig. V.3.4.1A   Bonfire Europe, 1914

Fig. V.3.4.2A Europe can look forward to a Christmas of peace

"EUROPE CAN LOOK FORWARD TO A CHRISTMAS OF PEACE"—HITLER

ii the total disappearance of the state the following spring.

(6)

(c) Describe how the 'child' who was 'Santa's' next victim came to be seized by him before the Christmas following this cartoon.

(5)

(d) Select TWO of the states named on the bedhead which were still independent on the outbreak of war, and explain how they passed into 'Santa's' control.

(*London, 1981, O Level.*)

3 Examine the cartoon (Fig. V.3.4.3A) and then answer the following questions.

i State the month and year this cartoon was published. (2)

ii Name the character depicted on the left. (1)

iii Name the character depicted on the right. (1)

iv Name the country represented by the body on the ground.

(1)

v Explain the object of the cartoonist in putting insulting language into the mouths of the characters, while they are apparently on amicable terms. (5)

iv Describe the relations between the two characters portrayed in the cartoon from 1933 to the date of its publication.

(10)

(*AEB, 1977, O Level.*)

4 Imaginative essays

For guidance on how to answer this type of question (which is becoming increasingly common at both O Level and CSE Level) see Part IV.5.

1 Read the extract below and answer the questions which follow.

'At first it looked as if the murder at Sarajevo was not going to lead to war after all. For when Serbia received the cruel and unjust ultimatum from Austria she gave way on almost every point. In fact she might have given way altogether, if she had not been promised help by Russia. Russia, of course, had plenty of good reasons and excuses for risking war to help Serbia. She declared that Austria-Hungary's bullying of the Serbs was an insult to the whole Slav people, and that it was time that Austrians and the Germans were taught a lesson. Besides the Russians had a great fear. They were afraid that once Serbia had been swallowed up, the Germans would push through the Balkans to Turkey and seize the Dardanelles.'

(a) Name the TWO people murdered at Sarajevo.

ii Which country sent the 'ultimatum' (*line 3*) to Serbia?

(b) According to the passage,

i why did Serbia not give way on all points of the ultimatum?

Fig. V.3.4.3A The scum of the earth

ii why did Russia have 'plenty' of good reasons and excuses for risking war to help Serbia'? (*line 6*)

(c) Imagine yourself **either** a German **or** British soldier in August 1914. Write a letter to a friend explaining the policies, alliances, and events that have led to war; also describe your feelings now that war has just begun.

(*NWREB, 1981, CSE Level.*)

2 Choose TWO of the following and write letters to a newspaper on them as though you were a person living at the time:

i how Britain should react to the Sarajevo Assassinations and the Austrian ultimatum to Serbia;

ii why America should declare war on Germany;

iii how and why Germany should be made to pay for the war at the Versailles Conference.

(*SEB, Ord. Grade. Alt., 1981.*)

3 Imagine you were a Bolshevik in Russia in 1917. Write a speech urging the people to revolution. Explain clearly in your speech the faults of the Tsar's government, the conduct of the war and the conditions of the peasants and the factory workers. Point out the ways in which your party would change things when they gained power.

(*ALSEB, 1980, CSE Level.*)

4 Imagine you are a Russian peasant who is writing a brief history of Russia from 1900–1924. Outline the major events in Russian history during this time, and relate how these events changed your way of life, and standard of living.

(*NI, 1982, CSE Level.*)

5 Either:

Imagine that you are a supporter of the Weimar Republic leaving school in 1920. Explain the fortunes of the Nazi Party in Germany between 1923 and 1933 as you might have seen them.

Or

Imagine you lived in a large American city like Detroit or Chicago in the 1920s. Describe your life at the time, explaining clearly the importance of the following:

Life at work on the assembly line;

Social life–fashion, jazz, entertainment;

Prohibition and its effects;

Organized crime.   (*ALSEB, 1979, CSE Level.*)

6 Write the election speech at the end of Roosevelt's first term in which you EITHER

(a) support OR **(b)** condemn the policies he has been pursuing.

(*Oxford, 1981, O Level.*)

7 Read the following part of a speech made in the House of Commons in March 1936 and then answer the questions below.

'The violation . . . is serious because of the menace to which it exposes Holland, Belgium, and France. I listened with apprehension to what the Secretary of State said about **the Germans declining even to refrain from entrenching themselves during the period of negotiations**. When there is a line of fortifications, as I suppose there will be in a very short time, it will produce reactions on the European situation. It will be a barrier across Germany's front door which will leave her free to **sally out eastwards and southwards by the other doors**,'

(a) *i* Name the statesman who made this speech.   (1)

ii What international crisis is under debate and in what year did that crisis take place?   (2)

(b) *i* What does the speaker mean by 'the Germans declining even to refrain from entrenching themselves during the period of negotiations' (*line 4-5*)?   (2)

ii Against which countries did Germany 'sally out eastwards and southwards by the other doors' (*line 9*)?   (3)

iii Why did Great Britain take no military action against Germany to halt the latter's aggression?   (3)

(c) Imagine yourself in 1939 a supporter of the policy of appeasement. Write a letter to a friend giving your reasons for support of that policy, and then show how the events of 1938–39 have led you to doubt the wisdom of appeasement.   (9)

(*NWREB, 1980, CSE Level.*)

8 On the relationships between the Great Powers in Berlin after the Second World War:

EITHER **(a)** Give an account of the events of 1948–9 in Germany as it might be written by a pro-western historian

condemning the Russian attempt to block the approaches to Berlin from the west OR **(b)** write the account of the crisis of 1948–9 as it might be experienced by a person living in west Berlin.

(*Adapted from Oxford, 1981, O Level.*)

5 Questions based on terms, words and abbreviations

5.1 Introduction

1 Examiners at both O Level and CSE Level base whole questions or parts of questions on this sort of material. You will find examples of such whole questions in Part IV.3.6; part-questions based on this material can be found throughout the range of questions in this book.

2 It will pay you **to understand** (without trying to learn by heart) the definitions found in Unit 39 of Part II. You should also know what the various sets of initials in that unit stand for.

5.2 O-Level questions

1 Select **four** of the following terms, explaining what is meant by each, and then write a paragraph on an example of each, within the period, 1914–1939.

(a) anarchy;   **(b)** war of attrition;   **(c)** depression;
(d) inflation;   **(e)** nationalism;   **(f)** reactionary.

(*AEB, 1977, O Level.*)

2 Explain what is meant by **five** of the following terms. In each case support your definition by giving an example. Write briefly about each example.

(a) coup d'état;   **(b)** manifesto;   **(c)** emancipation;
(d) laissez-faire;   **(e)** autocrat;   **(f)** charter;
(g) concordat;   **(h)** radical;   **(i)** boycott.

(*JMB, 1981, O Level.*)

3 Explain the meaning of any **five** of the following terms, illustrating each answer with an example from the period between 1870 and the present day.

(a) pan-slavism;   **(b)** concordat;   **(c)** socialism;
(d) armistice;   **(e)** mandate;   **(f)** ultimatum;
(g) colonialism;   **(h)** police state;   **(i)** isolationism;
(j) détente.

(*JMB, 1980, O Level.*)

5.3 CSE Level Questions

1 Choose FIVE of the following terms, then, in the space provided below:

(a) Explain what you understand by the term chosen.

(b) Give ONE example to show what you mean. Make sure that you put the correct number next to your answer.

i pan-slavism	*vi* concentration camp
ii ersatz foods	*vii* Domino theory
iii a Mandate	*viii* Neutral country
iv economic sanctions	*ix* arbitration
v Concordat	*x* tariffs.

(*ALSEB, 1981, CSE Level.*)

2 Choose FOUR of the following terms, then, in the space provided below:

(a) Explain what you understand by the term chosen.   (2)

(b) Give ONE example to show what you mean.   (1)

Make sure that you put the correct number next to your answer.

i republic	*v* Third World country
ii entente	*vi* conscription
iii 'speakeasies'	*vii* plebiscite
iv witch-hunt	*viii* exiled

(*ALSEB, 1982, CSE Level.*)

Index